Lecture Notes in Information Systems and Organisation

Volume 76

Lecture Notes in Information Systems and Organization—LNISO—is a series of scientific books that explore the current scenario of information systems, in particular IS and organization. The focus on the relationship between IT, IS and organization is the common thread of this collection, which aspires to provide scholars across the world with a point of reference and comparison in the study and research of information systems and organization. LNISO is the publication forum for the community of scholars investigating behavioral and design aspects of IS and organization. The series offers an integrated publication platform for high-quality conferences, symposia and workshops in this field. Materials are published upon a strictly controlled double blind peer review evaluation made by selected reviewers.

LNISO is abstracted/indexed in Scopus

Daniel Beverungen · Christiane Lehrer ·
Matthias Trier
Editors

Transforming the Digitally Sustainable Enterprise

Proceedings of the 18th International Conference on Wirtschaftsinformatik, Paderborn, Germany, 2023, Vol. 3

Springer

Editors
Daniel Beverungen
Department of Information Systems
Paderborn University
Paderborn, Nordrhein-Westfalen, Germany

Christiane Lehrer
Department of Digitalization
Copenhagen Business School
Frederiksberg, Denmark

Matthias Trier
Department of Information Systems
Paderborn University
Paderborn, Nordrhein-Westfalen, Germany

ISSN 2195-4968 ISSN 2195-4976 (electronic)
Lecture Notes in Information Systems and Organisation
ISBN 978-3-031-80124-2 ISBN 978-3-031-80125-9 (eBook)
https://doi.org/10.1007/978-3-031-80125-9

This Springer imprint is published by the registered company Springer Nature Switzerland AG
The registered company address is: Gewerbestrasse 11, 6330 Cham, Switzerland

Organization

Conference Chairs

Prof. Dr. Daniel Beverungen, Paderborn University, Germany
Prof. Dr. Dennis Kundisch, Paderborn University, Germany
Prof. Dr. Milad Mirbabaie, Paderborn University, Germany
Prof. Dr. Oliver Müller, Paderborn University, Germany
Prof. Dr. Guido Schryen, Paderborn University, Germany
Prof. Dr. Simon Thanh-Nam Trang, Paderborn University, Germany
Prof. Dr. Matthias Trier, Paderborn University, Germany

Program Committee Chairs

Prof. Dr. Daniel Beverungen, Paderborn University, Germany
Prof. Dr. Christiane Lehrer, Copenhagen Business School, Denmark
Prof. Dr. Matthias Trier, Paderborn University, Germany

Doctoral Consortium Chairs

Prof. Dr. Martin Matzner, Friedrich-Alexander-Universität Erlangen-Nuremberg, Germany
Prof. Dr. Guido Schryen, Paderborn University, Germany
Dr. Miriam Stumpe, Paderborn University, Germany
Dr. Sandra Zilker, Friedrich-Alexander-Universität Erlangen-Nuremberg, Germany

Local Arrangement Chair

Prof. Dr. Dennis Kundisch, Paderborn University, Germany

Sustainability Chair

Prof. Dr. Simon Thanh-Nam Trang, Paderborn University, Germany

Website and Social Media Chair

Prof. Dr. Milad Mirbabaie, Paderborn University, Germany

presentations, we invited the authors to present their research in three different presentation formats, comprising thought-provoking paper sessions, pitch paper sessions, and classic paper sessions. We take the positive feedback as evidence that the new formats spiced up the presentations, while attracting a greater audience and promoting more inspiring discussions. Second, regarding diversity, the Wi23 was the first WI conference to establish diversity in all track chair teams in terms of gender and age. As a program committee, we approached eleven women and nine men to serve as heads for our 20 tracks and asked them to assemble their track chair teams in line with two guidelines: Each track should include men and women, as well as involve at least one young scientist as track chairs. Third, perhaps most notably, we moved the conference from winter to September to avoid the pandemic's repercussions to interfere with the conference once again.

We want to thank all authors, track chairs, associate editors, reviewers, and committee members for devoting their valuable time to organizing and hosting the Wi23. Particular thanks are also due to the entire organizing team from Paderborn University, who worked with all their hearts and souls to welcome our community to Paderborn for a conference that is inspiring, fun, and an asset for developing strong professional and personal relationships.

Finally, we sincerely thank the sponsors who generously supported our conference. Their commitment made it possible to provide a conference experience that we found unique. Special thanks apply to our gold sponsors DATEV eG and the Software Innovation Campus Paderborn (SICP), our silver sponsors 29FORWARD, Arvato, Finanz Informatik, Heinz Nixdorf Stiftung Westfalen, UNITY, Weidmüller, and our bronze sponsors myConsult, Springer, and SpringerGabler. KONTOR N and Störtebecker Braumanufaktur helped us to make the conference reception a truly memorable event.

As the program committee of the Wi23 conference, we wish you an insightful read of the proceedings. May the research published at this conference stimulate fresh thinking, inspire you to develop new ideas, and build an appreciation for the normative principles that digital transformation can offer as guidance for the further progress of digital transformation. We are convinced that in a world that is transforming at incredible speed, it is on us to envision and build the type of society we desire.

Paderborn, Germany
Frederiksberg, Denmark
Paderborn, Germany
September 2024

Daniel Beverungen
Christiane Lehrer
Matthias Trier

Contents

Smart Cities and Digital Government

Digital Education and Learning

About the Editors

Daniel Beverungen is Professor of Information Systems and Enterprise Systems at Paderborn University, Germany. His research interests include service research, business process management, and the design of innovative information systems.

Christiane Lehrer is Associate Professor at the Department of Digitalization at Copenhagen Business School, Denmark. Her research interests include data-driven innovation, user behavior, and sustainable information systems.

Matthias Trier is Professor of Information Systems and Social Computing at Paderborn University, Germany, and Visiting Professor at Copenhagen Business School, Denmark. His research interests include digital social user behavior such as the appropriation of social media and collaboration platforms in companies' digital participation, the influence of electronic discourse, cooperation in virtual reality, and event-driven dynamic network analysis.

Business Models, Digital Transformation and Entrepreneurship

Antecedents of Non-ownership Business Model Offerings in the Mechanical Engineering Industry—A Set Theoretic Approach

Philipp Scharfe

Abstract The emergence of Industrial Internet of Things (IIoT) technologies drives the offering of non-ownership business models (NOBMs) in the mechanical engineering industry. In a NOBM mechanical engineering firms as machine providers maintain machine ownership and sell their customers only the machine use and/or performance. While literature has already discussed the influence of multiple individual contextual antecedents on the decision of mechanical engineering firms whether to offer NOBMs, little is known about the interplay of these antecedents. By drawing on 16 interview-based cases and fuzzy-set Qualitative Comparative Analysis (fsQCA), we applied a configurational perspective and identified each two configurations of four key contextual antecedents (high digital service capabilities, high machine standardization, high share of large customers, and high market competition) that lead to presence or absence of NOBM offerings by mechanical engineering firms. Moreover, we used our case insights to discuss the interplay of these antecedents within the identified configurations.

Keywords Non-Ownership Business Models (NOBMs) · Contextual antecedents · Mechanical engineering industry · Manufacturing industry · Fuzzy-set Qualitative Comparative Analysis (fsQCA)

1 Introduction

The emergence of Industrial Internet of Things (IIoT) technologies drives the introduction of new business offerings in the mechanical engineering industry. One of these new offerings are part of so-called non-ownership business models (NOBMs). In NOBMs, mechanical engineering firms as machine providers still design and produce the machines. However, they maintain ownership and do not sell them

P. Scharfe (✉)
Business Information Systems, esp. Business Engineering, Technical University of Dresden, Dresden, Germany
e-mail: philipp.scharfe@tu-dresden.de

D. Beverungen et al. (eds.), *Transforming the Digitally Sustainable Enterprise*, Lecture Notes in Information Systems and Organisation 76,
https://doi.org/10.1007/978-3-031-80125-9_1

to their customers anymore. Instead, they sell machine use and/or performance (Adrodegari et al. 2015, 2018; Ehret and Wirtz 2010, 2017; Selviaridis and Wynstra 2015). A prominent NOBM example from the mechanical engineering industry is the 'Sigma Air Utility' model from the compressor manufacturer Kaeser. In this model, customers no longer buy the compressors. Instead, they only pay for the compressed air they consume. Kaeser remains the owner of the compressors and builds and operates the compressors on behalf of the customers (Bock et al. 2019). In NOBMs, the machine customer benefits from the machine provider taking over the risks and burdens associated with the acquisition and operation of the machine. Therefore, the machine customer can avoid high investments in expensive machines (capital commitment). Moreover, since the provider takes over burdens related to the operation of increasingly complex machines (especially maintenance), the machine customer can fully focus on its core business. On the other side, taking over these burdens (especially the typically profitable service and maintenance business) allows the machine provider to realize new revenue and profit opportunities (Bock et al. 2023; Hypko et al. 2010a, b; Schnaars et al. 2022).

However, despite these benefits and opportunities for the machine customer and provider, this business model has yet to be widely applied in practice. For example, a recent study shows that only 14% of German mechanical engineering firms offer non-ownership services (Relayr 2022). A key reason that machine providers still hesitate to offer NOBMs are the financial and operational risks associated with this business model for them. For example, since the machine providers are paid during the machine usage time, they risk losing money if the customer is unable or unwilling to pay (Böhm et al. 2016; Hypko et al. 2010a; Wiengarten et al. 2013). Based on literature, we identified four key contextual antecedents (the levels of digital service capabilities, market competition, machine standardization, and type of customer base) that affect the risk level of the machine provider and thus influence whether they opt to offer a NOBM (e.g., Bock et al. 2019; Guajardo et al. 2012). These contextual antecedents can lead in different manifestations (e.g., presence or absence of high machine standardization) to the offering of NOBMs (Schnaars et al. 2022). Moreover, these antecedents interact with each other. For example, a high market competition level may lead to NOBM offering despite a customer base that increases the risk for the machine provider (Hou and Neely 2018; Selviaridis and Wynstra 2015). This implies that it is not enough to focus on these contextual antecedents individually, as existing literature does (e.g., Hou and Neely 2018; Schnaars et al. 2022), but on their combination and the resulting configurations. Therefore, we want to answer the following research question: *What configurations of contextual antecedents lead to presence or absence of NOBM offerings by mechanical engineering firms?* To answer this research question, we first conducted 16 primary interview-based case studies with firms that fulfill certain prerequisites for the offering of NOBMs (e.g., customer's demand for this business model) and decided for or against NOBM offering. Second, we applied configurational theory by using fuzzy-set qualitative comparative analysis (fsQCA) to identify multiple combinations of the four mentioned contextual antecedents, also referred to as conditions, that lead to presence or absence of NOBM offerings. We contribute to a more nuanced understanding of the NOBM offering decision (Ragin 2009). Moreover, these configurations can support practitioners in their assessment whether to offer a NOBM or not.

This paper is organized as follows. The second section introduces NOBMs and relevant contextual antecedents. In the following two sections, we describe our methodology and the results. In the fifth section, we discuss the contributions and limitations.

2 Research Background

2.1 Non-ownership Business Models

As in many other domains, the transformation to so-called 'service-oriented' business models is also a key phenomenon in mechanical engineering. In this regard, Adrodegari et al. (2015) distinguish between ownership-oriented and service-oriented business models. In ownership-oriented business models, product ownership is still transferred to the customer, and related add-on services are offered. In contrast, in service-oriented business models the provider maintains the ownership of the product and only the function of the product is sold as a service. NOBMs belong to the latter type (Adrodegari et al. 2015; Adrodegari and Saccani 2017; Neely 2008; Sjödin et al. 2020).

Generally, a business model can be defined as a "rationale of how an organization creates, delivers, and captures value" (Osterwalder and Pigneur 2010, p. 14). Al-Debei and Avison (2010) formulated four central dimensions to describe the design of a business model: (1) The value proposition describes the core value offering and the targeted customer segment(s). In a NOBM, as central offering, the customer can use the machine as product for a certain period of time. This usage includes associated services, such as financing, maintenance, installation, dismantling, training, and/or consulting (Adrodegari et al. 2015; Gebauer et al. 2017). After this period, the customer can extend the usage, buy the machine, or return it to the provider. (2) The value architecture describes the configurations of core resources and capabilities needed for the offering. In a NOBM the machine provider (or a finance partner) maintains machine ownership. Moreover, to provide the mentioned associated services, the machine providers need key capabilities, such as IIoT technology for machine supervision or a related service infrastructure (Wittkowski et al. 2013). (3) The value network concerns the position of the company in the value network and the relationships with various stakeholders. These stakeholders include NOBM financial partners (to finance the upfront investment, support the payment scheme design, and provide insurance) and technology partners (to provide the necessary technical infrastructure) (Hypko et al. 2010a; Ng et al. 2013). (4) The value financing pertains to the cost, revenue, and pricing structure. Regarding the pricing scheme, literature distinguishes between three key schemes for NOBMs: pay-on-access (fixed, regular fee; e.g., classic rent or lease), pay-per-output (e.g., pay-per-produced unit or usage time), and pay-per outcome (payment depends on results set in the contract; e.g., cost savings or service level achievements) (Adrodegari et al. 2015).

2.2 Contextual Antecedents for NOBM Offering

Scholars discussed a plethora of contextual antecedents, or conditions, that lead to presence or absence of NOBM offerings by mechanical engineering firms (e.g., Bock et al. 2019; Schnaars et al. 2022). These antecedents can be classified into three main groups. The first group (i.e., market demand, expected financial value added for the provider, a sufficient service network, and sufficient equity or dept for machine pre-financing) comprises necessary antecedents (i.e., they have to be fulfilled) that a firm offers a NOBM (Hypko et al. 2010a; Schnaars et al. 2022). The second group (i.e., high digital service capabilities, a high share of large customers, high market competition, and high machine standardization) includes four conditions that may not be necessary but sufficient for offering a NOBM (i.e., they can be absent or present). Their necessity or sufficiency depends on the combination with the other factors (Schnaars et al. 2022; Selviaridis and Wynstra 2015; Wittkowski et al. 2013). The third group (e.g., well-monitorable usage environment of the machine) includes factors that a mechanical engineering company uses to determine whether to offer a NOBM to an individual customer. For this, of course, the mechanical engineering company must generally offer a NOBM (Schnaars et al. 2022). In this study, we focus on the four antecedents of the second group, since we are interested on their combinations and their interplay.

As the first condition, high *market competition* in machine sales and the associated service business can lead to the offer of NOBMs. If the machine provider is not paid by the customer in advance but over the contract period of the machine, not the customer but the machine provider is responsible for the upfront machine financing. This can be an additional sales argument in a competitive environment (Bock et al. 2019; Wittkowski et al. 2013). In addition, customers may purchase the machines from one provider but maintain them themselves or contract another (often cheaper) vendor to do the maintenance. In the case of a NOBM, however, the machine provider takes over the maintenance, often also provides the spare parts, and can secure the corresponding service revenues (Bock et al. 2019). With this antecedent we want to investigate how high competition as one possible important driver for the NOBM offering decision is interacting with the other conditions (Schnaars et al. 2022).

As second condition, a high level of *machine standardization* supports the offer of NOBMs because these machines can be offered to another customer without major additional cost and effort after the NOBM contract ending or in case of customer bankruptcy. In addition, standard machines reduce the transaction costs for the machine provider, as no customer individual services and investments (in training or equipment) need to be offered (Schnaars et al. 2022; Toffel 2008). In contrast, other literature argues that more customized machines are more suitable for NOBMs because then machine provider's payment can depend at least in part on the fit of the machine to the individual customer needs. This allows the provider to gain another selling point with the customer and thus an advantage in case of high market competition (Guajardo et al. 2012; Hypko et al. 2010a).

A third condition are high *digital service capabilities*. These refer to advanced machine sensing, data transmission, and analytics capabilities by the potential machine provider. These capabilities are relevant for the planning and implementation of NOBM service offerings. For example, remote access can improve fast troubleshooting, or predictive maintenance can prevent machine downtime. This is particularly important for NOBMs, as the provider's payment is often, at least to some extent, based on usage and performance parameters (Glas and Kleemann 2017; Selviaridis and Norrman 2014). Moreover, these capabilities are relevant for the protection of fraud by the customer. Since the machine provider carries the risk of machine failures, it is necessary to determine if such failures are the customer's (e.g., through misusage) or the machine provider's (e.g., through insufficient maintenance) fault (Grubic 2014; Schnaars et al. 2022). Therefore, in case of other risk increasing contextual antecedents (e.g., a large base of small customers where the provider is unsure about machine usage) high digital service capabilities can reduce the machine providers risk and support the decision to offer a NOBM (Jovanovic et al. 2016; Selviaridis and Wynstra 2015).

As fourth condition, a high *share of large customers* may lead to the offering of NOBMs since typically large firms are more financially stable and have a lower risk of bankruptcy and therefore reduce the uncertainty for the machine provider (Cathcart et al. 2020). Moreover, literature argues that there is even a higher demand by large firms since small firms are often owner-managed and these owners often do not want to share property (Smith and Wakeman 1985; Wittkowski et al. 2013). On the other hand, literature argues that non-ownership is a substitute for high investment (Wittkowski et al. 2013). Since smaller firms usually lack capital for high investments, they have a corresponding demand for NOBMs. With a high share of small customers and the corresponding demand, this can lead to the offering of NOBMs by machine providers (Smith and Wakeman 1985; Wittkowski et al. 2013). Figure 1 shows our research model. A Venn diagram should denote our configurational perspective. The left side shows the interacting antecedents leading to the outcome (right side).

3 Research Method

Data collection: For our data collection, we relied primary on semi-structured interviews with mechanical engineering firms. We found the participating companies over a search on the German Mechanical Engineering Federation member list, a podcast series (Klemkow 2023), and our own network. We tried to include companies with different sizes (ranging from small to large) and from different mechanical engineering sectors. Moreover, before we started the interviews with the case companies, we conducted one more interview with a consultant to gain a deeper practical insight into NOBMs and to improve our interview guideline. The resulting dataset includes

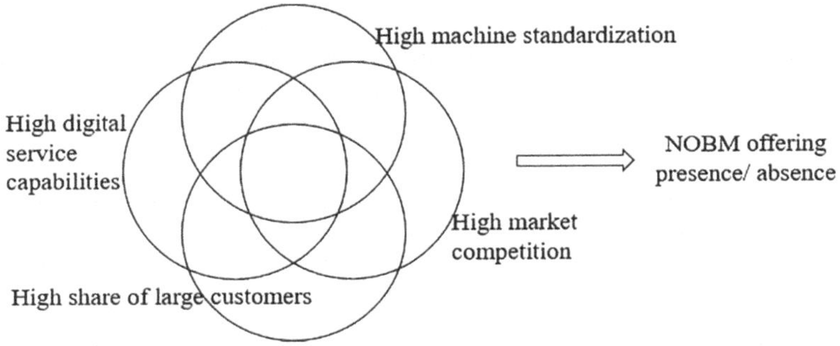

Fig. 1 Research model

16 cases of European mechanical engineering companies (or company segments) that fulfill according to the interview partners the antecedents of the first group (i.e., sufficient demand, sufficient capital for pre-financing, etc.) and then decided for or against the offering of a NOBM for this company (or company segment). NOBMs are offered in 11 of the 16 cases. The machines in one case are relatively homogeneous. From our 16 cases, 12 cases represent each one company. The other four cases belong to two companies (cases Delta/ Ny and Theta/ Xi belong each to one company). We could identify each two cases for these two companies because these companies offer two different machine types (each representing one company segment). Overall, we included 14 mechanical engineering companies in this study. On the one hand, with 12 of these 14 companies, we conducted one semi-structured interview (duration between 30 and 75 min). On the other hand, for the two remaining companies (cases Iota and Kappa), we found extensive interviews with a company representative in a podcast series (Klemkow 2023). Table 1 presents an overview of the cases and the position of the interview partners.

Fuzzy-Set Qualitative Comparative Analysis: To analyze the combination of contextual conditions leading to the introduction of a NOBM, we used fsQCA. This configurational method supports the analysis "how configurations of conditions lead to outcomes and, thereby, richly explain the dynamics of complex digital phenomena" (Mattke et al. 2022, p. 208). Configurations are defined as "a specific combination of [conditions] that produces a given outcome of interest" (Ragin 2009, p. xix). In other words, fsQCA investigates the "interplay between multiple conditions that influence an outcome" (Mattke et al. 2022, p. 209). In fsQCA, cases are designated into sets depending on their characteristics. A case can have non-membership (fully out) or full-membership (fully in) in a condition. Partial membership scores are possible, too. Correspondingly, fuzzy-set values (ranging from 0 for non-membership to 1 for full membership on a continuous range) are the basis for the analysis (Fiss 2011; Pappas and Woodside 2021). The fsQCA approach investigates how membership in conditions lead to membership in an outcome. Moreover, fsQCA is particularly useful for a small sample size of 12–50 cases with rich data (Park et al. 2020). Literature also suggests collecting at least as many cases as theoretically possible

Table 1 Case study overview and calibration table

Case	ME sector	PO	SZ	IT	CO	ST	CU	NO
Alpha	Healthcare	BD	S	0.66	0.33	0.33	0.66	0.66
Beta	Materials handling	BD	S	0	1	0.66	1	0.66
Gamma	Materials handling	SE	L	1	1	1	0.33	1
Delta[1]	Food processing	SE	M	0.66	1	1	0	1
Epsilon	Machine tools	SA	M	1	0.66	1	0.66	1
Zeta	Machine tools	FI	S	0.33	0.66	0.66	0.33	0.66
Eta	Power transmission	SA	L	0.33	1	0	1	0.66
Theta[2]	Metallurgy	SA	L	1	1	0.66	1	0.66
Iota*	Metallurgy	SA	S	0.33	1	0.66	0.33	1
Kappa*	Food processing	SA	S	0.33	1	1	0.66	0.66
Lamba	Machine tools	FI	M	1	0.66	1	0.66	1
My	Healthcare	SE	L	0.33	1	1	0.33	0.33
Ny[1]	Food processing	SE	M	0.66	0.66	0.33	0.66	0
Xi[2]	Metallurgy	SA	L	1	0.66	0	1	0
Omikron	(Micro) Electronics	MA	S	0.33	0	0.66	1	0
Pi	(Micro) Electronics	MA	S	0.66	0	0.33	1	0

[1/2]Cases belong to the same company; [*]Data collection via podcast and not via semi-structured interview; ME: mechanical engineering; PO: department of interview partner; BD: business development; SE: service; SA: sales; FI: finance; MA: firm management; SZ: Company size; S: small firms: < 1000 employees; M: medium-sized firms: 1000–10,000 employees; L: large firms: > = 10,000 employees; IT: high digital service capabilities; CO: high market competition; ST: high machine standardization; CU: high share of large customers; NO: NOBM offering

configurations (with 2^n configurations and n = number of conditions) (Schneider and Wagemann 2012). Based on this background, our fsQCA presents with 16 cases a sufficient number for four conditions.

For our fsQCA approach, we performed four main steps: (1) articulating the research topic and building the research model, (2) calibrating the data, (3) deriving configurations by analyzing the truth table, and (4) discussing the configurations (Brosig et al. 2022; Park et al. 2020). More precisely, we followed the example of similar QCA studies with a qualitative interview-based data collection and a small sample size (less than 20 cases) (Soto Setzke et al. 2021, 2020). In the first step, we defined the outcome and selected the four core conditions which resulted in the proposed research model (see Fig. 1). We combined an inductive and deductive approach by relying on the identified literature and the case- and interview-based insights to identify the four conditions. We first conducted an open coding, followed by an axial coding. In the second step, we did the data calibration. In this step, the conditions and the outcome are transformed into fuzzy sets on a scale from zero to one (Pappas and Woodside 2021). For the final assignment of fuzzy-set values to each condition/the outcome and case, see Table 1. In order to do so, we needed to create a calibration scheme that quantifies how much (i.e., to what degree) a case belongs to a specific set (Ragin 2009). Therefore, we first defined the ideal states (fully in = 1/ fully out = 0) as anchor points. Regarding the level of detail, we decided for a four-value scale (in addition to 1/0 for fully in/out; more in than out = 0.66/ more out than in = 0.33). Such a scale has proven practical in similar studies (cf. Soto Setzke et al. 2021). The final scales with the set-scores (see Table 2) were derived either theory-based (e.g., for the condition of high digital service capabilities, we used Schnaars et al. 2022) or, if not available, based on in-depth cross-case and in-case comparisons (Brosig et al. 2022). For the NOBM offering scale, for example, we used the threshold value of 5%, as this value, according to our findings from the interviews, delimits companies with a NOBM that has just started (NOBM share < 5%) or is already more established (≥5%).

In the third step of our approach, we first analyzed the necessary conditions and then built the configurations with the truth table analysis. To do so, we used the fsQCA software program. In using the fsQCA software, we follow the instructions of Pappas and Woodside (2021).We used a frequency threshold of only one, as this is recommended for such a small sample size (Ragin 2009). Moreover, we chose a raw

Table 2 Calibration scheme

Condition	0 (Fully out)	0.33 (More out than in)	0.66 (More in than out)	1 (Fully in)
High digital service capabilities	No remote internet connection of provider to machine	Connection of provider to machine and descriptive analysis/ monitoring	Connection of provider to machine and predictive analysis	Connection of provider to machine and prescriptive analysis
High market competition	Low competition in machine sales and services	Low competition in machine sales and high in service	High competition in machine sales and limited in service	High competition in machine sales and service
High machine standardization	Completely customized to individual customer needs	Customer individual machine based on standard components	Standardized machine with small customer adjustments	Fully standardized machine
High share of large customers	Machine customers are mainly small (annual revenue < = 40 Mio. €)	Machine customers are small and large; majority small	Machine customers are small and large; majority large	Machine customers are mainly large firms
NOBM offering	No NOBM offered and not planned	No NOBM offered but planned	NOBM share < 5%[a]	NOBM share > = 5%[a]

[a]Indicates how many of the annual machine deliveries are in a NOBM; the rest are sold traditionally

consistency threshold of 0.85, which is higher than the generally accepted threshold of 0.75 (Schneider and Wagemann 2012). The raw consistency "indicates the proportion of configurations that show the outcome" (Mattke et al. 2022, p. 220). PRI consistency represents an alternative consistency measure and "is used to avoid simultaneously subset relations of configurations in both the outcome and the absence of the outcome (i.e., negation)" (Pappas and Woodside 2021, p. 10). For the PRI consistency, we chose a widely recommended cut-off value of 0.65 (Schneider and Wagemann 2012). After we reduced the truth table by using the frequency, raw consistency, and PRI consistency thresholds, we received configurations of conditions that lead to the outcomes of interest (Pappas and Woodside 2021). In the fourth step, we discussed the configurations.

4 Results

Table 3 presents the identified configurations of conditions that lead to the NOBM offering presence or absence. For both outcomes, each two configurations were identified. We followed the established QCA convention and marked the presence of a condition with a black circle and the absence of a condition with a crossed-out circle. If there are blank spaces, the condition can be either present or absent. Moreover, in fsQCA, there are core and peripheral conditions for explaining the outcome. We only identified core conditions. The identified solutions have a consistency of 0.91 and 0.87. That is well above the commonly accepted level of 0.8 (Ragin 2008). In addition, the coverage values of both solutions (0.74 and 0.64) allow explaining a considerable share of both outcomes. In the analysis of necessary conditions, we received for the condition high market competition with the outcome NOBM offering a consistency value of 0.891. For the condition high share of large customers with the outcome of no NOBM offering, we also received a consistency value of 0.897. Although these two values do not exceed the generally accepted threshold for a necessary condition of 0.9, this value is relatively close to the threshold. These conditions can thus be considered as necessary ones. Two configurations are leading to the offering of NOBMs. In the first configuration (O1) a combination of high market competition, high machine standardization, and high digital service capabilities leads to NOBM offering. This solution is indifferent regarding a high share of large customers. The second configuration (O2) states that the absence of high digital service capabilities, presence of high market competition, and a high share of large customers leads to NOBM offering. High machine standardization can be present or absent. For not offering NOBMs also two configurations exist. In configuration N1, the presence of high digital service capabilities and a high share of large customers, in combination with the absence of high machine standardization leads to not offering a NOBM. This solution is indifferent regarding high market competition. The last configuration (N2) states that in case of the absence of high digital service capabilities and high market competition, in combination with a high share of large customers and a high machine standardization, mechanical engineering firms decide against the NOBM offering.

Table 3 Solution chart for NOBM offering

Conditions/ Outcomes	Offering		Not offering	
	O1	O2	N1	N2
High digital service capabilities	●	⊗	●	⊗
High market competition	●	●		⊗
High machine standardization	●		⊗	●
High share of large customers		●	●	●
Raw coverage	0.57	0.36	0.59	0.3
Unique coverage	0.4	0.18	0.35	0.05
Raw consistency	0.94	0.83	0.86	1
Solution coverage	0.74		0.64	
Solution consistency	0.91		0.87	

Black circles: presence of a condition; Crossed-out circles: absence of a condition; Empty cell: condition either present or absent; Identified only core and no peripheral conditions; Frequency cut-off: 1; Raw consistency cut off: 0.85; PRI consistency cut-off: 0.65

For both outcomes, the respective first configuration (O1/N1) is more relevant due to the higher coverage values.

5 Discussion

5.1 Observations and Patterns Across Configurations

As noted above our results show two distinct configurations of contextual antecedents each for the offering and non-offering of NOBMs. Since we identified multiple configurations that lead to the same outcome, we can demonstrate that the decision of mechanical engineering firms whether to offer a NOBM or not does not depend on the influence of individual factors, but is more complex; that is the combination of different contextual antecedents is relevant for explaining this decision (Ragin 2009).

Machine providers in the *first configuration* of contextual antecedents (O1; e.g., cases Gamma or Delta) described that "the hardware, i.e., the [machine] itself, is becoming increasingly commoditized. And even in the premium segment, the [machines from different providers] do not differ much from each other" (Gamma). This situation, which refers to high machine standardization, leads to increased market competition, another key characteristic of this first configuration. The interview partners in cases Gamma and Delta further describes that they reacted to this increased competition in two different and connected ways. First, they developed advanced digital services (e.g., predictive maintenance or production and machine usage optimization solutions). By doing so, these machine providers want to provide another quality-based unique selling point beyond the machine hardware. The second way of reacting to this high competition is the offering of a NOBM, whereas the high digital service capabilities act as an important enabler. For example, these capabilities allow them advanced maintenance as part of the service bundle. Driven by high competition and the ability to monitor the machines through digital service capabilities, these machine providers offer these machines to all customer bases (presence or absence of a high share of large customers).

Based on the in-depth analysis of the cases that have the characteristics of the *second configuration* (O2), we split this configuration into two sub-configurations (O2.1 and O2.2). These two sub-configurations have the same characteristics as shown in Table 3 (absence of high digital service capabilities, presence of high market competition and high share of large customers), but for O2.1 the condition of high machine standardization is present. In O2.2 this condition is absent. Examples for the first sub-configuration (O2.1) are the cases Beta or Kappa. They also face the challenge of high market competition resulting from the 'commodity' of their standard machines. These rather smaller firms responded as in the first configuration by offering a NOBM and developing the necessary 'basic' monitoring capabilities. However, they did not reach high digital service capabilities yet (i.e., no predictive or prescriptive services). Moreover, since these machine providers work mostly with large customers with long-term relationships, their risk of customer bankruptcy or fraud is limited. For the second sub-configuration (O2.2), we found only one case (Eta). Eta also reacted to the high competition by adapting the machine components to the individual customer processes to achieve customer targets (e.g., increased overall equipment effectiveness; OEE). This connection was already described in literature (Guajardo et al. 2012). As an additional selling point, Eta offers a NOBM where payment is based (at least partially) on this target achievement (e.g., if the OEE is higher than with the old machine components, Eta earns more). Moreover, this NOBM can be offered because Eta has machine monitoring capabilities and a stable base of large customers they trust (financially and operationally). This is very important because Eta makes significant initial investments in the design of customized machine components.

Two examples for the *third configuration* (N1) are the cases Ny and Xi. Their core NOBM offering inhibitor was the limited standardization of the machines. The interview partners described that even in the case of a trustworthy and financially stable base of large customers, it was too risky for them to offer their machines in a NOBM arrangement because they cannot sell these machines on the used machine market or give them to another customer without significant retrofit effort. Moreover, Ny emphasized that if they wanted to offer this customer individual machines in a pay-per-output or pay-per-outcome arrangement, they lack the necessary experience for the payment scheme calculation since every machine project is new. Since in contrast to N1 in O2.2 customized machine (components) are offered in a NOBM, we compared the corresponding case examples (Ni or Xi for N1 and Eta for O2.2). We identified one main difference. In contrast to the other cases, the machine components in Eta have a lifetime not significantly exceeding the contract duration. Therefore, there is a limited risk for Eta of being unable to sell the machine on the used machine market.

In the cases belonging to the last and *fourth configuration* (N2; e.g., Omikron or Pi) the key NOBM offering inhibitor was the limited market competition, regardless of the other conditions (especially despite high machine standardization as a risk reducing antecedent for the machine provider). The interview partners in these cases described that the reason for this limited competition is typically the development (and patenting) of a specific hardware component, enabling them to differentiate from the competition. Generally, most machine providers preferred traditional sales over a NOBM because the former entails the lowest (financial and operational) risk. Based on our results, we consider the conditions of high market competition and high machine standardization as the two most relevant ones for the decision of the machine providers on whether to offer a NOBM or not. While high market competition is already highlighted in the literature as a key driver for the NOBM offering decision (e.g., Schnaars et al. 2022), the high importance of machine standardization is not emphasized in existing literature (Böhm et al. 2016; Schnaars et al. 2022).

Moreover, in the configurations O1 and O2.1, some of our interviewees (e.g., Gamma or Epsilon) mentioned as another offering driver the '*high profitability*' if the NOBM is in the form of a short-term standard machine rental (duration a few months up to two years), where the customer has an instant need for a machine. This high profitability is based on a comparison with traditional sales and longer-term oriented NOBM offerings. For example, the interview partner at Epsilon described that one of their "customers needed additional machines on short notice because a customer's automotive production line was scheduled to run for two more years." The interview partners explained that since the machine users have specific needs and delivery commitments, they are also willing to pay more for the machine, resulting in higher profitability for the provider. However, in such a business, the machine provider has to keep a pool or fleet of standard machines ready to be offered at short notice, which favors larger providers. Moreover, the machine providers need a high utilization rate of their rental machines. Overall, high profitability as another driver for NOBM offerings was only emphasized to a limited extend in literature (Böhm et al. 2016; Schnaars et al. 2022).

5.2 Contributions, Limitations, and Future Research

In this paper, we investigated which configurations of contextual antecedents or conditions lead to the presence or absence of NOBM offerings by mechanical engineering firms. To reach this research objective, we relied on 16 interview-based cases and fsQCA as a set-theoretic approach.

Theoretical contributions: Our paper contributes to a more nuanced understanding of contextual antecedents' influence on mechanical engineering firms' NOBM offering decisions in two connected ways. First, we identify each two configurations of antecedents that lead to the presence or absence of NOBM offerings. This configurational perspective is new since other literature (e.g., Hypko et al. 2010b; Schnaars et al. 2022) identified multiple antecedents but have yet to investigate their interplay. With our study, we show that this offering decision does not only depend on individual antecedents. Instead, the interaction of these antecedents also plays an important role. Second, we not only identify the four mentioned configurations of antecedents, but also describe the interactions between these antecedents based on our in-depth case insights in detail. For example, for the first configuration (O1), we describe the interplay between the antecedents of high digital service capabilities, high machine standardization, and high market competition. With our study, we respond on recent calls for research on drivers and barriers for the NOBM offering in the mechanical engineering industry (Hypko et al. 2010b; Schnaars et al. 2022).

As the case companies change key elements of their business model by introducing a NOBM, our study also contributes to research on antecedents for business model innovation (Foss and Saebi 2017). In a methodological context, we show that the steps of Soto Setzke et al. (2020, 2021) are well-suited to calibrate interview-based (qualitative) data into fuzzy-sets. We access this approach as appropriate for research cases where it is difficult to acquire large sample sets.

Practical implications: Practitioners (such as business development managers of mechanical engineering firms or consultants) can compare the configurations and case descriptions with their situation and use them as a decision support tool whether to offer a NOBM or not.

Limitations and future research opportunities: As with any research, our study has several limitations. First, our sample with 16 cases is still relatively small. This limits the generalizability of our results. Nonetheless, we intended to explore the contextual antecedents and their interplay using in-depth qualitative interview-based data. Future research can investigate our results by relying on larger data sets (e.g., by conducting a survey). Second, researchers may have concerns of the findings since we calibrated data from interviews into fuzzy-sets. However, we tried to follow established guidelines from the literature and described our calibration scheme in detail (Brosig et al. 2022). Third, although our configurations have relatively high coverage and consistency values, we might have omitted some relevant contextual antecedents as conditions that would allow even more detailed insights. Moreover, future research could investigate how the configurations of contextual antecedents (e.g., level of market competition or machine standardization) influence the actual design of the NOBM (e.g., if the machine providers offer an access-based, a pay-per-output or pay-per-outcome payment scheme or on what partners they rely on). Since most companies have just started to implement NOBMs, research should investigate the success factors of these business models in a few years when companies have long-term experience with this business model.

In *conclusion*, we hope that our configurations and related insights will help mechanical engineering firms in their decision on whether to offer a NOBM or not, as well as foster future research in that field.

References

Adrodegari, F., Alghisi, A., Ardolino, M. & Saccani, N. (2015), From Ownership to Service-oriented Business Models: A Survey in Capital Goods Companies and a PSS Typology, *in:* 'Proceedings of the 7th Industrial Product-Service Systems Conference - PSS, industry transformation for sustainability and business', CIRP, pp. 245–250.

Adrodegari, F., Bacchetti, A., Saccani, N., Arnaiz, A., & Meiren, T. (2018), 'The transition towards service-oriented business models: A European survey on capital goods manufacturers', *International Journal of Engineering Business Management* **10**, 1–10.

Adrodegari, F. & Saccani, N. (2017), 'Business models for the service transformation of industrial firms', *The Service Industries Journal* **37**(1), 57–83.

Al-Debei, M.M. & Avison, D. (2010), 'Developing a unified framework of the business model concept', *European Journal of Information Systems* **19**, 359–376.

Bock, M., Wiener, M., Gronau, R. & Martin, A., (2019), Industry 4.0 Enabling Smart Air: Digital Transformation at KAESER COMPRESSORS, *in*: 'Digitalization Cases, Management for Professionals', Springer International Publishing, pp. 101–117.

Bock, M., Wiener, M. & Saunders, C. (2023), 'Non-Ownership Business Models in the Manufacturing Industry: Uncertainty-Exploiting versus Uncertainty-Mitigating Designs and the Role of Context Factors', *Electronic Markets*, **33**(1), 1–18.

Böhm, E., Backhaus, C., Eggert, A. & Cummins, T. (2016), 'Understanding outcome-based contracts: benefits and risks from the buyers' and sellers' perspective', *Journal of Strategic Contracting and Negotiation* **2**(1-2), 128–149.

Brosig, C., Bley, K., Strahringer, S. & Westner, M. (2022). The Missing Piece – Calibration of Qualitative Data for Qualitative Comparative Analyses in IS Research, *in*: 'Proceedings of the Thirtieth European Conference on Information Systems', AIS.

Cathcart, L., Dufour, A., Rossi, L. & Varotto, S. (2020), 'The differential impact of leverage on the default risk of small and large firms', *Journal of Corporate Finance* **60**, 101541.

Ehret, M. & Wirtz, J., (2017), 'Unlocking value from machines: business models and the industrial internet of things', *Journal of Marketing Management* **33**(1-2), 111–130.

Ehret, M. & Wirtz, J. (2010), 'Division of Labor between Firms: Business Services, Non-Ownership-Value and the Rise of the Service Economy', *Service Science* **2**(3), 136–145.

Fiss, P.C. (2011), 'Building Better Causal Theories: A Fuzzy Set Approach to Typologies in Organization Research', *Academy of Management Journal* **54**(2) 54, 393–420.

Foss, N.J. & Saebi, T. (2017), 'Fifteen Years of Research on Business Model Innovation: How Far Have We Come, and Where Should We Go?', *Journal of Management* **43**(1), 200–227.

Gebauer, H., Haldimann, M. & Saul, C.J. (2017), 'Competing in business-to-business sectors through pay-per-use services', Journal of Service Management **28**(5), 914–935.

Glas, A.H., Kleemann, F.C. (2017), 'Performance-based contracting: contextual factors and the degree of buyer supplier integration', *Journal of Business & Industrial Marketing* **32**(5), 677–692.

Grubic, T. (2014), 'Servitization and remote monitoring technology: A literature review and research agenda', *Journal of Manufacturing Technology Management* **25**(1), 100–124.

Guajardo, J.A., Cohen, M.A., Kim, S.-H. & Netessine, S. (2012), 'Impact of Performance-Based Contracting on Product Reliability: An Empirical Analysis', *Management Science* **58**(5), 961–979.

Hou, J. & Neely, A. (2018), 'Investigating risks of outcome-based service contracts from a provider's perspective', *International Journal of Production Research* **56**(6), 2103–2115.

Hypko, P., Tilebein, M. & Gleich, R. (2010a), 'Clarifying the concept of performance-based contracting in manufacturing industries: A research synthesis', *Journal of Service Management* **21**(5), 625–655.

Hypko, P., Tilebein, M. & Gleich, R. (2010b), 'Benefits and uncertainties of performance-based contracting in manufacturing industries: An agency theory perspective', *Journal of Service Management* **21**(2), 460–489.

Jovanovic, M., Engwall, M. & Jerbrant, A. (2016), 'Matching Service Offerings and Product Operations: A Key to Servitization Success: Existing conditions, such as product characteristics or market attributes, may determine the success of a move toward servitization', *Research-Technology Management* **59**(3), 29–36.

Klemkow, J. (2023), https://subscribedindustry.podigee.io/. Accesses: 02.02.2023

Mattke, J., Maier, C., Weitzel, T., Gerow, J.E., Thatcher & J.B. (2022), 'Qualitative comparative analysis (QCA) in information systems research: status quo, guidelines, and future directions', *Communications of the Association for Information Systems* **50**, 208–240.

Neely, A. (2008), 'Exploring the financial consequences of the servitization of manufacturing', *Operations Management Research* **1**, 103–118.

Ng, I.C.L., Ding, D.X. & Yip, N., (2013), 'Outcome-based contracts as new business model: The role of partnership and value-driven relational assets', *Industrial Marketing Management* **42**(5), 730–743.

Osterwalder, A. & Pigneur, Y. (2010), *Business model generation: A handbook for visionaries, game changers, and challengers*. John Wiley.

Pappas, I.O. & Woodside, A.G. (2021), 'Fuzzy-set Qualitative Comparative Analysis (fsQCA): Guidelines for research practice in Information Systems and marketing', *International Journal of Information Management* **58**, 102310.

Park, Y., Fiss, P.C. & El Sawy, O.A. (2020), 'Theorizing the Multiplicity of Digital Phenomena: The Ecology of Configurations, Causal Recipes, and Guidelines for Applying QCA', *Management Information Systems Quarterly* **44**(4), 1493–1520.

Ragin, C.C. (2009), Qualitative comparative analysis using fuzzy sets (fsQCA), *in* 'Configurational Comparative Methods: Qualitative Comparative Analysis (QCA) and Related Techniques', Sage Publications, Thousand Oaks, pp. 87–122.

Ragin, C.C. (2008), *Redesigning Social Inquiry Fuzzy Sets and Beyond*. University of Chicago Press.

Relayr (2022), https://relayr.io/de/relayr-studie-entscheider-der-deutschen-industrie-setzen-auf-equipment-as-a-service-als-zukunftsmodell-fuer-den-maschinenbau/. Accessed: 03.02.2023.

Schnaars, N., Galipoğlu, E., Haasis, H.-D. & Kotzab, H. (2022), Performance-based Contracting im Maschinen- und Anlagenbau, in: 'Smart Services, Forum Dienstleistungsmanagement', Springer Fachmedien Wiesbaden, pp. 277–304.

Schneider, C.Q. & Wagemann, C. (2012), *Set-Theoretic Methods for the Social Sciences: A Guide to Qualitative Comparative Analysis*. Cambridge University Press.

Selviaridis, K. & Norrman, A. (2014), 'Performance-based contracting in service supply chains: a service provider risk perspective', *Supply Chain Management: An International Journal* **19**(2), 153–172.

Selviaridis, K. & Wynstra, F. (2015), 'Performance-based contracting: a literature review and future research directions', *International Journal of Production Research* **53**(12), 3505–3540.

Sjödin, D., Parida, V., Jovanovic, M. & Visnjic, I. (2020), 'Value Creation and Value Capture Alignment in Business Model Innovation: A Process View on Outcome-Based Business Models', *Journal of Product Innovation Management* **37**(2), 158–183.

Smith, C.W. & Wakeman, L.M. (1985), 'Determinants of Corporate Leasing Policy', *The Journal of Finance* **40**(3), 895–908.

Soto Setzke, D., Opderbeck, L., Böhm, M. & Krcmar, H. (2020). Pathways to Successful Business Model Innovation in the Context of Digital Transformation, *in*: Proceedings of the Twenty-Fourth Pacific Asia Conference on Information Systems', AIS.

Soto Setzke, D., Riasanow, T., Böhm, M. & Krcmar, H. (2021), 'Pathways to Digital Service Innovation: The Role of Digital Transformation Strategies in Established Organizations', *Information Systems Frontiers*, forthcoming.

Toffel, M.W. (2008). Harvard Business School Technology & Operations Mgt. Unit Research Paper No. 08–063, https://papers.ssrn.com/sol3/papers.cfm?abstract_id=1090237. Accessed: 23.12.2022

Wiengarten, F., Pagell, M. & Fynes, B. (2013), 'The importance of contextual factors in the success of outsourcing contracts in the supply chain environment: the role of risk and complementary practices', *Supply Chain Management: An International Journal* **18**(6), 630–643.

Wittkowski, K., Moeller, S. & Wirtz, J. (2013), 'Firms' Intentions to Use Nonownership Services', *Journal of Service Research* **16**(2), 171–185.

Conflicting Identities During Digital Transformation Efforts of an Incumbent Automotive Firm

Anna Keilbach, Andreas Hein, and Helmut Krcmar

Abstract Most manufacturing firms that undergo digital transformation fail to seize the expected benefits. A key reason is that those firms fail to extend their identity of operational excellence with a digital service provider identity, leading to tensions at the interface—the product. Although research has addressed individual aspects of organizational identity, how organizational identity evolves in incumbent firms remains to be understood. In a case study with a leading automotive manufacturer, we show how two conflicting identities lead to paradoxical tensions and how separating them through a spinoff shifts these tensions. This study provides initial results on conflicting organizational identities during digital transformation.

Keywords Digital transformation · Organizational identity · Paradoxical tensions

1 Introduction

Incumbent firms must implement digital technologies into their products and processes to meet customer expectations and keep pace with competitors (Tilson et al. 2010; Yoo et al. 2010). However, to seize digital technology for competitive advantage, firms must adapt their organizational identity (OI) as digital technologies intertwine with established routines, procedures, and beliefs of critical constituents (Tripsas 2009; Wessel et al. 2021). Especially incumbent manufacturers face a unique

A. Keilbach (✉) · A. Hein · H. Krcmar
Department of Information Systems, Technical University of Munich, Munich, Germany
e-mail: anna.keilbach@tum.de

A. Hein
e-mail: andreas.hein@tum.de

H. Krcmar
e-mail: helmut.krcmar@tum.de

D. Beverungen et al. (eds.), *Transforming the Digitally Sustainable Enterprise*, Lecture Notes in Information Systems and Organisation 76,
https://doi.org/10.1007/978-3-031-80125-9_2

challenge during digital transformation (DT) as they must integrate two identities (Svahn et al. 2017): First, the identity of operational excellence to create complex physical products of high quality and, second, the identity of being a service provider that can enhance this product through digital services.

However, integrating both identities of manufacturing excellence and digital service offerings is challenging and can lead to paradoxical tensions (Soh et al. 2019; Svahn et al. 2017; Wessel et al. 2021). Car manufacturers, for example, follow long product development cycles and freeze design before production (Svahn et al. 2017), leading to tensions with agile software development practices. This tension illustrates that having both OIs in parallel can lead to a state of bipolarity. To avoid DT-related OI tensions, firms established spinoffs that separate OIs into two organizations. Thus, the operational excellence manufacturer and the service provider do not have to respond directly to each other but can communicate through the interfaces of their respective firms (Santos and Eisenhardt 2005).

Extant research has investigated two aspects of OI: OI formation—the development of a new organization, and OI change—the transition from one OI giving away to another OI. Scholars such as Gioia et al. (2013) have studied these aspects on a micro- and macro-level. However, DT differs from IT-enabled organizational transformation as it requires firms to develop a new OI (Wessel et al. 2021) by *keeping their old* (i.e., *product manufacturer*) *and infusing it with a new* (i.e., *service provider*). The different identities can lead to tensions between existing hierarchical structures and new structures required for DT (Dremel et al. 2017; Haskamp et al. 2022; Svahn et al. 2017). An identity shift can also lead to organizational resistance and inertia, ultimately failing DT initiatives (Haskamp et al. 2021; Tripsas 2009; Vial 2019).

While the literature on OI and DT is separated, little research has focused on the intersection between these concepts, as recent calls for future research illustrate (e.g., Gioia et al. 2013; Riasanow et al. 2019; Wessel et al. 2021). Theory about how OI evolves during DT and how OI can cause paradoxical tensions leading to inertia is sparse. Thus, there needs to be more conceptual clarity on how organizations manage conflicting OIs in the process of DT, e.g., the discrepancy between existing and emerging OI (Gurbaxani and Dunkle 2019; Keller et al. 2022). Therefore, the research question of this paper is: *How does the OI evolve in incumbent firms during DT?*

To approach the research question, we followed an in-depth case study (Yin 2018) by interviewing 45 employees concerned by DT of an incumbent automotive firm and its corporate spinoff, which was established during our data collection from 2019 to 2023. The automotive firm faces severe challenges on different organizational levels while undergoing DT efforts, thus, providing an appropriate case to examine how the DT and introduction of a digitized product (i.e., an autonomous driving car) led to a state of bipolarity reflected in the tensions of two conflicting OIs.

This study is the first effort to shed light on the difficulties incumbent manufacturing firms face when attempting to extend their operational excellence identity by being a service provider during DT. We identified that paradoxical tensions occur due to the conflicting OIs, thus providing scholars with a better understanding and practitioners with guidance. We derived different types of paradoxical tensions rooted in

OI through multiple rounds of coding Field (Gioia et al. 2012) and employing OI as a theoretical lens. Moreover, we provide new insights into the DT phenomenon and paradoxical tensions. Last, our derived implications inform future research on this topic.

2 Theoretical Foundation

DT has sparked the interest of academics and practitioners over the last two decades (Kraus et al. 2021; Vial 2019) by considering the data-driven impacts of technologies for strategic change (Warner and Wäger 2019). Despite being closely related to IT-enabled organizational transformation (ITOT), as both are technology-related phenomena, DT differs from ITOT: In ITOT, digital technology *supports* the value proposition and *reinforces the existing OI*, whereas in DT, digital technology *redefines* the value proposition and *lead to a new OI* (Wessel et al. 2021). Due to the digital technology-induced changes' scale, scope, and speed, DT can be viewed as an evolutionary extension of ITOT (Vial 2019).

Further, DT puts forth digitized products that embed digital technologies in physical products and require extensive data collection while being designed, manufactured, and used (Porter and Heppelmann 2014). Digitized products support value co-creation with customers and other stakeholders (e.g., through continuous feedback possibilities) and provide insights into data (e.g., data collection on usage) that can serve as input for new service offerings (Sandkuhl et al. 2019). The redefined value proposition triggers organizations to develop digital capabilities during DT. At the same time, incumbent manufacturers face challenges to software and digital service adaptation as this was previously outside their area of expertise.

The concept of OI originates from Albert and Whetten (1985) but remains relevant in light of recent developments demanding organizational change (Gioia et al. 2013). OI is characterized as central, distinctive, and enduring and reflects organizational members' perspective of *"who we are as an organization"* (Albert and Whetten 1985; Gioia et al. 2013). Thus, OI is a *"self-reflective"* internal notion where multiple identities or interpretations may exist in different organizational units (Gioia et al. 2013). Additionally, OI is culturally profoundly rooted in the organization (Schultz 1992), helping its members to give meaning to their collective history, practices, and experiences and creating awareness for outsiders (Ravasi and Schultz 2006). Gioia et al. (2013) point out that organizational members might perceive their OI as stable even though it is changing: *"The labels are stable, but their meanings are malleable"* (p. 126).

Historically, it had been thought that organizations need a stable OI to function (Albert and Whetten 1985). Later, identity instability was theorized to be beneficial in allowing organizations to adapt to changing environments (Gioia et al. 2000). Although having positive effects, identity changes often result in tensions between members with different views of the organization. In addition, the more deeply rooted the OI, the more resistance can be expected from organizational members (Gioia et al. 2000).

Organizations that undergo DT typically experience identity conflicts, *"a concept involving multiple organizational identities vying for preeminence or privilege"* (Corley and Gioia 2004, p. 201). Previous research suggests that firms must relinquish the old identity to embrace the new one (Elsbach and Bhattacharya 2001), which is impossible when still producing physical products that integrate digital services. To bypass these tensions, *"keeping the existing and emerging OI separate from one another"* (Keller et al. 2022, p. 43) through developing a spinoff might be an option. In this way, the operational excellence identity and the digital service identity can interact indirectly through the interfaces of their respective firms. However, whether an OI separation through a spinoff works or is just a problem shift remains to be understood. Further, research lacks how OI evolves in incumbent firms during DT and how those firms can deal with conflicting identities keeping their old OI (i.e., operational excellence) and infusing it with a new (i.e., service provider).

3 Methodology

Our study is motivated by a theoretical and phenomenon-focused problematization (Monteiro et al. 2022) of evolving OI that sheds light on conflicting identities and paradoxical tensions during DT. Thus, we conducted a case study (Yin 2018) in one of the world's leading premium automobile manufacturers (hereafter AutoCorp) with a long history and profound expertise in automotive manufacturing processes. Since 2010, AutoCorp adopted more and more digital technology to advance its product from electromechanical to autonomous vehicles. Therefore, AutoCorp first worked increasingly with software suppliers and then hired software engineers that have been spun off through the foundation of its corporate software firm (hereafter SoftwareCorp) in 2019. However, AutoCorp's DT efforts are not moving fast enough due to several sources of internal resistance, pointing to a fruitful phenomenon to study OI. Shaped by OI conflicts and internal tensions during DT, the case offers access to this significant phenomenon (Eisenhardt and Graebner 2007).

3.1 Sampling

Between 2019 and 2023, we collected primary data through interviews and secondary data through on-site observations, meeting discussions, company presentations, archival data, and news articles at AutoCorp and SoftwareCorp. We conducted 45 interviews with employees that faced changes during the DT in different departments and hierarchical levels (Eisenhardt and Graebner 2007). Additionally, our inclusion criteria were employees with points of contact to the vehicle and varying histories

Table 1 Interviewees

Number	Interviewees	Roles
12	Project manager	UX/UI; strategy and innovation; standardization; innovation; digital assistant; HR transformation; autonomous driving; cross-sectional coordination; digitization of workflows
1	Technical engineer	Processes
2	Scrum master	Pre-development
4	Software developer	Simulation; pre-development
5	Product owner	Process management; processes & methods
2	Principal	Corporate strategy
6	Change facilitation manger	Change management; communication
2	Development engineer	Autonomous driving
3	Strategic coordinator	Autonomous driving; agile coach
8	Systems engineer	Systems engineering; processes, methods

at the company. Some interviewees were employed by SoftwareCorp and previously worked at AutoCorp, which gave us a unique perspective. Once we got in touch with interviewees that met the sampling criteria, we arranged the time and venue of the interview (Table 1).

3.2 Data Collection

We performed data collection and analysis following a rigorous procedure. A semi-structured guideline (respectively for the interviews before and after the spinoff foundation) provided an overall outline and improved reliability (Yin 2018). After five initial interviews, we adjusted the interview protocol to account for new insights. During the interviews, we asked interviewees to share their understanding of OI and their experiences with the DT's impact on different OI dimensions. Interviews typically had a duration of 45 min and were audio-recorded. We stopped when we reached saturation, i.e., the improvements brought by additional interviews were considered marginal (Strauss and Corbin 1990). Following those established methods helped us to increase the equivalency, credibility, and dependability of the results, which can be considered alternative terms to reliability and validity proposed in quantitative studies (Sinkovics et al. 2008).

3.3 Data Analysis

After transcribing all audio files, we analyzed the data in MAXQDA by following the process of open, axial, and selective coding (Glaser et al. 1968). Throughout this data analysis process, we investigated the evolving OI to explain inertia in DT processes. We started with an inductive approach by openly coding 1st-order concepts (Gioia et al. 2012) that constitute concepts close to the interview data. Next, we applied a deductive approach by using the dimensions of OI as our theoretical lens since our objective was to identify the tensions of OI in the context of DT. Therefore, we operationalized OI based on established dimensions: key values, capabilities, practices, routines, structure, strategy, and culture (Gioia et al. 2013; Van Rekom and van Riel 2000). Next, we conducted axial coding by seeking similarities and differences in the 1st-order concepts deriving a more manageable number of similar concepts labeled as 2nd-order themes (Gioia et al. 2012) describing the OI challenges and tensions during DT. Last, we employed selective coding to distill the 2nd-order themes into 2nd-order aggregate dimensions that describe reasons for inertia in DT during two phases (before and after the spinoff creation).

4 Results

The results are structured according to two temporal phases: Phase 1 describes the evolution of OI within AutoCorp when the firm initiated the integration of digital technology within its vehicles. Phase 2 encompasses the foundation of the spinoff, which is responsible for AutoCorp's software development. We investigated OI tensions within AutoCorp, SoftCorp, and between the firms in this phase.

4.1 Phase 1: Initiation of the Digital Transformation Journey, Including the Integration of Digital Technology into the Vehicle

Since 2010, AutoCorp has involved more and more digital technology in their vehicles, such as connectivity to music, Bluetooth interfaces, and an integrated navigation system with wireless internet access. To offer these digital functions and services, AutoCorp commissioned software development companies. However, integrating the delivered software packages as a black box proved difficult in the complex vehicle system, so software developers were hired in-house by AutoCorp. As explained in the following, this led to different tensions between the manufacturers and software engineers.

Tensions due to the history and established organizational structure. Traditionally, AutoCorp focuses on electromechanical vehicles instead of digitalization. For example, employees still refer to themselves as 'sheet metal benders' and, thus, *"never required a strong IT (mindset)"* (Software Developer 4). The function-oriented organizational structure of business units (management, technical development, finance, human resources, production, sales & marketing, and procurement & IT) and the mass production approach are still prominent. However, the embedded software connects physical components requiring new *organizational structures* and *practices*. Thus, functional silos must be broken up to allow cross-functional collaboration (Project Manager 2, Scrum Master 1, Principal 1). This starkly contrasts with AutoCorp's historical-grown identity following a strict hierarchical structure with clear responsibilities. Due to the clash of the conflicting mindsets, the new identity has grown in isolation within the firm leading to direct tensions between manufacturers and software engineers.

Tensions due to different practices. While the senior management endorsed software development within AutoCorp, the new departments' practices had to comply with the corporate *legacy practices*. That is long product development cycles and freezing design before production. As a result, software developers could not take full advantage of short, agile cycles. One reason is that most AutoCorp employees still embraced an engineering mindset that clashed with the digital world making it difficult for the incumbent car manufacturer to undergo DT (Agile Coach, IT Project Coordinator, PMT Manager 1, PMT Manager 2, Product Portfolio Manager, Quality Manager). Another challenge is the ambiguity between the values lived and communicated. AutoCorp's management encourages its workforce to engage in new complex technologies. However, its actions rarely reflect courageous behavior, e.g., risks are seldom taken to allocate a budget for future digitally savvy projects (e.g., Project Manager 6, Project Manager 7).

4.2 Phase 2: Expansion of Software Capabilities and Foundation of a Spinoff

AutoCorp continued to invest in integrating software features and developing automated driving functions to keep up with the competition and meet customer demands. In doing so, AutoCorp experienced severe difficulties managing the digitized vehicle as an overall functioning system. Despite needing more digital competencies, the conflict between the 'old' product manufacturer and the 'new' service provider identity represented a barrier to the firm's DT. Hence, in 2010, the parent company of AutoCorp decided to establish the corporate spinoff SoftCorp supporting all brands under the parent company with software developed in-house and the establishment of a uniform software platform. As a reaction to the previous direct OI conflicts, the identity of being a service provider was spun off into the newly formed SoftCorp as a central software unit. This was reflected in the distinction between the product components (hardware and software) and the organizational activities (mechanical engineering and software development) (e.g., Project Manager 2, Project Manager 6, Product Manager 2). Thus, the conflicting OIs became increasingly isolated and separated.

Tensions due to history within AutoCorp. Within AutoCorp, tensions exist between the current state of pure manufacturing excellence and the target state of digital transformation. While some of the employees interviewed expressed the urgency of DT on an organizational and product level to ensure further competitiveness, the definition of 'who we are as an organization' is still rooted in motorsport events. The internal combustion engine is ingrained in employees' minds and their understanding of the company. It is an emotional aspect of a proud *history* and excitement (e.g., Technical Engineer 1, Project Manager 6, Project Manager 7). This bond is also evident in day-to-day business, as some interviewees indicated that each employee recognizes their contribution to DT in their everyday tasks (Technical Engineer 1, Project Manager 4). Thus, AutoCorp must align its identity rooted in the history of excellent electromechanical vehicles with DT. Among others, thoughts are, *"Are we a hardware manufacturer while somebody else develops software? Are we building a hardware-software construct within an intelligent accord or a vehicle in a hardware-software union?"* (Project Manager 2). These considerations and changes take time to be entirely accepted by employees at all levels, especially integrating the identity as a service provider into the existing identity as a manufacturing company (Project Manager 2, Project Manager 4, Principal 2).

Tensions due to AutoCorp's legacy within SoftCorp. Although the spinoff SoftCorp was newly founded, many legacy assets of the automotive Group were incorporated into the new software company. On the one side, the spinoff enabled a breakout of existing structures and established practices to evolve new ones suitable for software development. Conversely, a large percentage of SoftCorp's employees came from other Group manufacturing brands. Thus, *values and practices* manifesting a manufacturing orientation were brought along from these previous employees and influenced the identity-forming of SoftCorp. However, the 'DNA' and legacy of AutoCorp and its Group's brands contradict SoftCorp's mission and vision (Project Manager 2, Project Manager 4, Change Facilitation Manager 3), preventing it from reaching its full potential. Finally, SoftCorp employment contracts that allow former AutoCorp employees to return to their former employer hindered full engagement, anchoring, and *identification* with the company (Project Manager 2, Technical Engineer 1, Software Developer 2, Principal 1, Change Facilitation Manager 1).

Tensions due to novelty between AutoCorp and SoftCorp. Due to the novelty of SoftCorp being responsible for a unified software platform and automotive cloud, several tensions occurred between AutoCorp and SoftCorp. First, the Group's brands do not yet have *confidence* in SoftCorp. One reason is that SoftCorp does not yet have a long track record; its projects are only in development status and progressing slowly. In addition, failures and mistakes by one company lead to a decline in confidence in the capabilities of the other companies and as a basis for blaming each other rather than collaborating to solve problems jointly (e.g., Product Manager 1, Project Manager 7). Second, the collaboration between AutoCorp and SoftCorp is further complicated because SoftCorp's *position* has not been regulated within the Group. For example, SoftCorp's expectations, authorities, and activities are unclearly articulated and communicated (e.g., Project Manager 2, Principal 2). While some employees view the spinoff as a software supplier to the automotive industry, others consider it an individual brand on par with Group's brands, such as AutoCorp. Third, the Group's objective of creating digitally enabled vehicles enhanced through digital services is complicated by the spinoff's organizational and product separation (physical car vs. immaterial software and services). Consequently, employees lose sight of the automotive Group's common objective and vision thinking only in their functional division (Software Developer 2, Principal 2, Product Manager 1). Among others, software-related activities are viewed as not in line with AutoCorp's core principles, making it challenging to produce, e.g., autonomous driving vehicles. These obstacles stem from the different business interests of AutoCorp as a traditional, incumbent manufacturer and SoftCorp as a software company and digital services provider, which are difficult to align.

5 Discussion

We sought to answer the research question of how the OI evolves in incumbent firms during DT to understand why DT initiatives can lead to inertia. To do so, we first identified the changing OI dimensions and then the paradoxical tensions between the old and new OI. Our in-depth study between 2019 and 2023 enabled us to investigate OI changes and conflicts during DT over time. Our study yielded positive and negative effects before the spinoff creation, when software engineers were united in a division within the manufacturing firm, and after the spinoff creation, when software engineers got divided into two separate organizations. Based on our results, we derived two implications (Fig. 1).

First, DT disrupts the existing OI as integrating the identity of being a service provider requires changes in OI dimensions and new ones. The *direct OI conflicts* led to organizational tensions as two diverse ways of working (long product development vs. agile software development) clashed. For example, digitized products, such as autonomous vehicles, offer new possibilities; thus, product understanding needs to be changed. Additionally, new capabilities and knowledge became necessary to develop

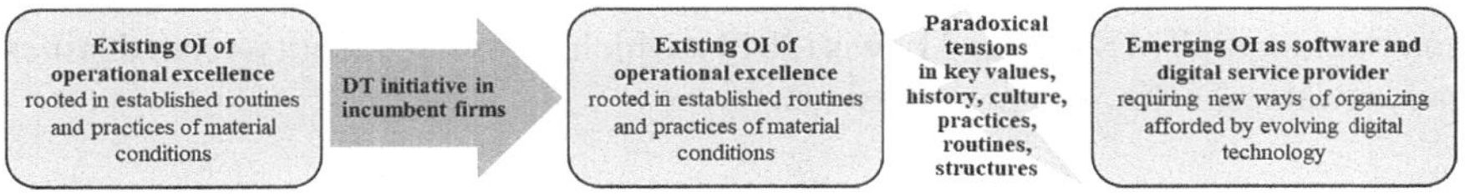

Fig. 1 Theoretical framework of OI during DT within incumbent firms

digitized products. However, in cases of urgent troubleshooting, having product- and software-focused employees in one organization leads to faster problem-solving due to direct collaboration. As a takeaway, product-orientated employees need clarification about their contribution towards DT. Otherwise, it might hinder the integration of a digitized service provider identity. Therefore, education and clarity of everyone's contribution to the firm's DT vision are crucial.

Second, through the spinoff, no new identity can be formed. The manufacturing firm can focus on engineering innovations (e.g., BEVs), while the spinoff is responsible for software and service innovations. Thus, this pathway avoids direct identity conflicts as there are, i.e., fewer direct communication. In turn, this leads to *indirect identity conflicts* in the form of organizational tensions that manifest in the product vision: aiming for a well-engineered vehicle with technical innovations (e.g., electric engine) for mobility versus aiming to achieve an experience space for diverse occasions using vehicles. The problem shift due to the spinoff thus complicates the joint product development, which requires collaboration and mutual agreement at one point. Hence, expectations, hand-over formats, and processes must be clarified between the firms to better benefit from the spinoff pathway.

Comparing these two states, we see that the spinoff did not lead to developing a new OI that combines being a manufacturer and providing digital services. Instead, it led to isolating both OIs in different firms, which increased identity-related boundaries (Santos and Eisenhardt 2005). Albeit removing the state of bipolarity and subsequent paradoxical tensions within one firm, we have first evidence in the second phase that AutoCorp centers back to its old identity, rendering the first promising DT approaches of phase 1 obsolete.

These insights yield promising contributions to the literature on OI (e.g., Albert and Whetten 1985; Corley and Gioia 2004), DT (e.g., Vial 2019; Wessel et al. 2021), and paradoxical tensions (e.g., Smith and Lewis 2011; Soh et al. 2019; Viljoen et al. 2022). The first contribution pertains to OI in the context of DT, exploring the evolving OI and the state of bipolarity. We followed Wessel et al.'s (2021) call that DT is more complex and should be distinguished from ITOT as it is characterized by the emergence of a new OI by providing insights on how conflicting OIs evolve and may be addressed.

Second, the identified paradoxical tensions due to keeping the old OI (i.e., product manufacturer) and infusing it with a new OI (i.e., service provider) can explain why DT initiatives lead to inertia and remain unsuccessful. We were interested in investigating the interrelations of DT and OI and the underpinning reasons for failed DT initiatives. While previous research on paradox theory noted a range of competing tensions in DT, our study links paradoxical tensions to OI and supports explanations of its occurrence. Additionally, we provide an extension to the paradox theory category "belonging" of Smith and Lewis (2011), which considers identity-related issues such as values, roles, and memberships.

Third, the awareness and reasons for tensions during DT of incumbent firms will inform future research and provide clarity to practitioners. We emphasize that incumbent firms must not only consider product transformations but also strategically consider their OI transformation, such as finding ways to balance the identity of operational excellence with being a service provider. Our study encourages managers to prepare for, accept and reflect on these OI tensions during DT.

While we conducted many interviews, we acknowledge that our data derives from an automotive firm and its corporate spinoff. Our main limitation is how much our findings are generalizable beyond our case. Thus, we recommend future research in other incumbent firms facing DT initiatives to investigate how OI evolves and whether these cases also experiencing paradoxical tensions. Further, we need to find out if separating conflicting OIs through a spinoff is an approach that can effectively reduce OI tensions. As the spinoff as executive action to handle identity bipolarity has relevance, comparative cases that allow theorizing, e.g., contextual factors that can explain why the spinoff strategy works or does not work, would yield valuable results. In addition, digitized products offer a platform for cooperation with different stakeholders. Hence, new organizational forms (e.g., forming ecosystems or strategic alliances, partnering with or acquiring startups, creating subsidiary firms) occur with varying impacts of OI and might lead to a state of OI multi polarity. Thus, future research on OI challenges during DT is fruitful to investigate.

6 Conclusion

We found that the case firm continues to be strongly product and manufacturing-oriented while avoiding the infusion of the identity of being a service provider. This has been expressed by spinning off all recently hired software-oriented employees by founding an independent firm. Our findings show that OI is the cause of resistance to change on various levels (e.g., employees' decision-making and behavior of employees and structure) and, thus, the source of organizational tensions leading to organizational inertia during DT. Therefore, the required changes based on the digitized products remain unsuccessful, especially in critical parts of the organization where the former OI is still strong (i.e., the production). Further, our paper provides the first evidence of OI bipolarity due to DT and how this can lead to organizational and product tensions. We point out that the cause of organizational tensions is friction between the identity of operational excellence and the identity of being a digital service that manifests on different organizational levels.

References

Albert, S., & Whetten, D. A. (1985), Organizational identity. In L. Cummings & B. Staw (Eds.), *Research in organizational behaviour* (Vol. 7, pp. 263–295).

Corley, K. G., & Gioia, D. A. (2004), Identity ambiguity and change in the wake of a corporate spin-off. *Administrative Science Quarterly, 49*(2), 173-208.

Dremel, C., Wulf, J., Herterich, M. M., Waizmann, J.-C., & Brenner, W. (2017), How AUDI AG established big data analytics in its digital transformation. *MIS Quarterly Executive, 16*(2), 81–100.

Eisenhardt, K. M., & Graebner, M. E. (2007), Theory building from cases: Opportunities and challenges. *Academy of Management Journal, 50*(1), 25-32.

Elsbach, K. D., & Bhattacharya, C. (2001), Defining who you are by what you're not: Organizational disidentification and the National Rifle Association. *Organization Science, 12*(4), 393-413.

Gioia, D. A., Corley, K. G., & Hamilton, A. L. (2012), Seeking qualitative rigor in inductive research: Notes on the Gioia methodology. *Organizational Research Methods, 16*(1), 15–31. https://doi.org/10.1177/1094428112452151

Gioia, D. A., Patvardhan, S. D., Hamilton, A. L., & Corley, K. G. (2013), Organizational identity formation and change. *Academy of Management Annals, 7*(1), 123-193.

Gioia, D. A., Schultz, M., & Corley, K. G. (2000), Organizational identity, image, and adaptive instability. *Academy of Management Review, 25*(1), 63-81.

Glaser, B., Strauss, A., & Strutzel, E. (1968), The discovery of Grounded Theory; Strategies for qualitative research. *Nursing research, 17*(4), 364. https://doi.org/10.1097/00006199-196807000-00014

Gurbaxani, V., & Dunkle, D. (2019), Gearing up for successful digital transformation. *MIS Quarterly Executive, 18*(3).

Haskamp, T., Dremel, C., Berente, N., Yoo, Y., & Uebernickel, F. (2022), Punctuated Multi-Layered Liminality in Digital Transformation: The Case of an Automotive Platform. 43rd International Conference on Information Systems, Copenhagen.

Haskamp, T., Marx, C., Dremel, C., & Uebernickel, F. (2021), Understanding inertia in digital transformation: A literature review and multilevel research framework. Proceedings of the 42nd International Conference on Information Systems, Austin, Texas.

Keller, R., Ollig, P., & Rövekamp, P. (2022), Pathways to developing digital capabilities within entrepreneurial initiatives in pre-digital organizations. *Business & Information Systems Engineering, 64*(1), 33-46.

Kraus, S., Jones, P., Kailer, N., Weinmann, A., Chaparro-Banegas, N., & Roig-Tierno, N. (2021), Digital transformation: An overview of the current state of the art of research. *SAGE Open, 11*(3), 1-15.

Monteiro, E., Constantinides, P., Scott, S., Shaikh, M., & Burton-Jones, A. (2022), Qualitative research methods in information systems: a call for phenomenon-focused problematization. *MIS Quarterly: Management Information Systems.*

Porter, M. E., & Heppelmann, J. E. (2014), How smart, connected products are transforming competition. *Harvard Business Review, 92*(11), 64–88.

Ravasi, D., & Schultz, M. (2006), Responding to organizational identity threats: Exploring the role of organizational culture. *Academy of Management Journal, 49*(3), 433-458.

Riasanow, T., Soto Setzke, D., Böhm, M., & Krcmar, H. (2019), Clarifying the notion of digital transformation: A transdisciplinary review of literature. *Journal of Competences, Strategy & Management, 10*(1), 5–31.

Sandkuhl, K., Wißotzki, M., Schmidt, R., & Zimmermann, A. (2019), On the effect of digitalization of products and services on enterprise architectures. 28th International Conference on Information Systems Development, Toulon, France.

Santos, F. M., & Eisenhardt, K. M. (2005), Organizational boundaries and theories of organization. *Organization Science, 16*(5), 491-508.

Schultz, M. (1992), Postmodem Pictures of Culture: A Postmodem Reflection on the "Modem Notion" of Corporate Culture. *International Studies of Management & Organization, 22*(2), 15-35.
Sinkovics, R. R., Penz, E., & Ghauri, P. N. (2008), Enhancing the trustworthiness of qualitative research in international business. *Management international review, 48*(6), 689-714.
Smith, W. K., & Lewis, M. W. (2011), Toward a theory of paradox: A dynamic equilibrium model of organizing. *Academy of Management Review, 36*(2), 381–403. https://doi.org/10.5465/amr.2009.0223
Soh, C., Yeow, A., Goh, Q., & Hansen, R. (2019, Dec), Digital transformation: Of paradoxical tensions and managerial responses. Proceedings of the 40th International Conference on Information Systems, Munich, Germany.
Strauss, A., & Corbin, J. M. (1990), *Basics of qualitative research: Grounded theory procedures and techniques*. Sage Publications, Inc.
Svahn, F., Mathiassen, L., & Lindgren, R. (2017), Embracing digital innovation in incumbent firms: How VOLVO cars managed competing concerns. *MIS quarterly, 41*(1), 239–253. https://doi.org/10.25300/misq/2017/41.1.12
Tilson, D., Lyytinen, K., & Sørensen, C. (2010), Research commentary — digital infrastructures: The missing IS research agenda. *Information Systems Research, 21*(4), 748–759.
Tripsas, M. (2009), Technology, identity, and inertia through the lens of "The Digital Photography Company". *Organization Science, 20*(2), 441-460.
Van Rekom, J., & van Riel, C. B. M. (2000), Operational measures of organizational identity: A review of existing methods. *Corporate Reputation Review, 3*, 334-350.
Vial, G. (2019), Understanding digital transformation: A review and a research agenda. *Journal of Strategic Information Systems, 28*(2), 118–144. https://doi.org/10.1016/j.jsis.2019.01.003
Viljoen, A., Hein, A., Przybilla, L., Soto Setzke, D., & Krcmar, H. (2022), Striving for Global Optima in Digital Transformation: A Paradox Theory Approach. 43rd International Conference on Information Systems, Copenhagen.
Warner, K. S., & Wäger, M. (2019), Building dynamic capabilities for digital transformation: An ongoing process of strategic renewal. *Long range planning, 52*(3), 326-349.
Wessel, L., Baiyere, A., Ologeanu-Taddei, R., Cha, J., & Blegind-Jensen, T. (2021), Unpacking the difference between digital transformation and IT-enabled organizational transformation. *Journal of the Association for Information Systems, 22*(1), 102-129.
Yin, R. K. (2018), *Case study research and applications: Design and methods* (6 ed.). Sage publications.
Yoo, Y., Henfridsson, O., & Lyytinen, K. (2010), Research commentary—The new organizing logic of digital innovation: An agenda for Information Systems Research. *Information Systems Research, 21*(4), 724–735. https://doi.org/10.1287/isre.1100.0322

Understanding Business Process Evolution in Digital Ventures

Tobias Wuttke, Thomas Haskamp, Michael Perscheid, and Falk Uebernickel

Abstract Business processes are at each company's core and must be adapted permanently to react to changing markets, substantial growth, or legal regulations. Especially digital ventures have the potential to evolve fast, and consequently, their business processes need to change at the same speed. Two streams of literature have looked into this. Traditional business process management sees business processes, once implemented, as relatively stable. In contrast, digital entrepreneurship literature highlights the inherent flexibility of digital ventures. Based on a multiple case study of five digital ventures, we analyze how entrepreneurs deal with this tension when business processes evolve. Building on entrepreneurial bricolage, we propose two types of resource recombination that we find, namely, usage of existing private resources and re-configuring of resources already being used within the venture. These insights contribute to extending our understanding of the evolution of business processes.

Keywords Digital ventures · Digital entrepreneurship · Business process management · Business process evolution

T. Wuttke (✉) · M. Perscheid · F. Uebernickel
Hasso Plattner Institute, University of Potsdam, Potsdam, Germany
e-mail: tobias.wuttke@hpi.de

M. Perscheid
e-mail: michael.perscheid@hpi.de

F. Uebernickel
e-mail: falk.uebernickel@hpi.de

T. Haskamp
European Research Center for Information Systems, University of Münster, Muenster, Germany
e-mail: thomas.haskamp@ercis.uni-muenster.de

D. Beverungen et al. (eds.), *Transforming the Digitally Sustainable Enterprise*, Lecture Notes in Information Systems and Organisation 76,
https://doi.org/10.1007/978-3-031-80125-9_3

1 Introduction

Digital ventures are professionally funded and young firms that work on digital market offerings (Lehmann et al. 2022). They are characterized by their ability to expand their user base at an outstanding pace by drawing on and adding digital infrastructure (Huang et al. 2017). Examples such as Amazon and Google were able to grow to a scale that took industrial companies decades to reach (Huang et al. 2017). However, the rapid scaling of digital ventures presents unique organizational challenges, such as managing rapidly growing revenue and headcount, that incumbents do not face (Lehmann and Recker 2022; Tumbas et al. 2015). To meet their new organizational challenges, digital ventures are forced to formalize and evolve business processes from the ground up (Lehmann and Recker 2022). Traditional business process management (BPM) is based on the careful modeling of business processes (Baiyere et al. 2020). With that, it aims to improve processes' efficiency and quality in a relatively stable environment (Recker et al. 2009). However, this stability contrasts with the flexibility that potentially poses the competitive advantage of digital ventures (von Briel et al. 2017). This means digital ventures are caught between structure (BPM perspective) and flexibility (digital entrepreneurship perspective). While both perspectives advance our knowledge of how business processes and digital venturing unfold, current research only began to explain the dynamics behind the evolution of business processes in digital ventures (Tumbas et al. 2017b). Moreover, this knowledge would assist entrepreneurs in making informed decisions regarding creating their business processes and aligning them to their rapidly evolving requirements. This advances our understanding of balancing structure and flexibility in business processes to facilitate entrepreneurial growth instead of hindering it. Thus, we define our research question as follows: *How are digital ventures developing their business processes by relying on digital technology in their early phases?* We build on a case study with multiple digital ventures from a startup accelerator to address this question. Our study shows different practices of how early-stage digital ventures improvise to create business processes on top of low-specificity digital technologies.

2 Related Work—Business Processes in Digital Entrepreneurship

We investigate business processes in the context of *digital entrepreneurship*, which Davidson and Vaast (2010) define as pursuing new venture opportunities presented by new media and internet technologies. Concerning the current understanding of business process evolution in digital ventures, Tumbas et al. (2017a) find that "born digital" ventures depend heavily on digital technologies during periods of rapid growth. In another study, Tumbas et al. (2017b) report on the importance of digital technologies for various purposes, including establishing knowledge flows, allowing for transparency, reducing redundancies, and formalizing business processes. Furthermore, von Briel et al. (2017) explore how digital technologies enable new venture creation processes and introduce the concept of specificity, which measures a digital technology's adaptability and malleability. They suggest that highly specific digital technologies increase the potential for compression and conservation mechanisms, which reduce time and resource requirements but decrease the potential for combination and generation mechanisms, which create new artifacts, such as devices, functionalities, and business models.

For our understanding of the phenomenon of business process evolution, we draw on a definition from the BPM literature, which understands business processes as "as a set of activities performed in coordination in an organizational and technical environment. These activities jointly realize a business goal" (Weske 2012, p. 5). Their management—*BPM*—oversees "how work is performed in an organization to ensure consistent outcomes and to take advantage of improvement opportunities" (Dumas et al. 2013, p. 1). Notably, Baiyere et al. (2020) analyze how the logics of BPM change when a venture enters a digital transformation. They identify the careful modeling of business processes (process logic), the design of process-aligned IT infrastructure (infrastructural logic), and procedural actors (agential logic) as dominant for traditional BPM.

One specific lens to understand business process evolution in digital ventures is *entrepreneurial bricolage*. Baker and Nelson (2005) describe the concept as "making do by applying combinations of the resources at hand to new problems and opportunities" (Baker and Nelson 2005 p. 333). Its idea stems from the field of visual arts and describes the creation of works of art from a collection of different resources available to the artist. Lévi-Strauss (1967) took the term bricolage and applied it to the intellectual realm. In the spirit of improvisation, the bricoleur gathers resources that can be used in a later scenario. Even though the bricoleur does not know how, the collected resources will eventually affect the final solution (Matthews 2021). LeLoarne and Maalaoui (2015) applied the bricolage lens to analyze how high-tech entrepreneurs model their business processes, finding that they rely on a trial-and-error approach. Similarly, Karanasios et al. (2022) applied the bricolage lens to the digital transformation of micro-enterprises with significant resource constraints, concluding that these enterprises utilize techniques such as re-purposing, appropriating, and improvising to make the most of their limited resources. Baiyere et al. (2020) also found this improvisational spirit in the context of business process enactment in incumbent firms. The authors find that employees at companies undergoing digital transformation are implementing processes by improvising with already available tools, such as Microsoft Excel.

3 Research Approach—Multiple Case Study

Since the evolution of business processes in digital ventures is a recent phenomenon that should be investigated in its real-world context, we rely upon a multiple case study to investigate the evolution of business processes (Yin 2009). Our cases are

Table 1 Companies participating in the study

Type of product/service	Founding year	Interviewee (and ID)
SaaS and hardware solution for machine error monitoring	2010	CEO (I01), developer (I02)
SaaS app for dementia prevention	2021	CTO (I03)
SaaS solution for product management	2021	CEO (I04)
SaaS solution to book workplaces in hybrid teams	2019	CTO (I05), admin (I06)
SaaS solution to connect music producers and loop creators	2019	Team lead (I07)

startups from an accelerator in their seed phase following a Software-as-a-Service (SaaS)-based subscription business model. Our embedded unit of analysis includes the changing hiring, sales, and product development processes of the startups in which digital technologies presumably play a crucial role. Table 1 gives an overview of the participating ventures.

This study's primary data collection method is qualitative interviews (Schultze and Avital 2011). We triangulate the interview data with public information and startup internal materials such as slide decks (Yin 2011). To analyze our data, we rely on the Gioia methodology (Gioia et al. 2013), which means that we coded the transcribed interviews over multiple rounds in which themes emerged inductively.

4 Preliminary Findings

This section presents the preliminary findings of our study on the evolution of business processes—hiring, sales, and product development—in digital ventures.

Regarding the *hiring process*, the digital ventures within our sample relied on different process variations based on the work division of the founding team. For business related roles, the CEO usually conducted one or two interviews (I01, I02, I04), while for technical roles, the CTO conducted multiple interview rounds, including coding challenges (I01, I02, I03, I05). Digital tools like Zoom, Microsoft Teams, and Notion facilitated the hiring process, while all ventures used LinkedIn to search for candidates. Only one venture used Personio for its HR processes (I05, I06). One software developer mentioned receiving payslips via WhatsApp (I02).

The *sales processes* of digital ventures are tailored to their target audience. For businesses-to-business sales (I01, I02, I04, I05), a basic sales funnel is in place, typically supported by a customer relationship management system (I04, I05) or Notion (I01, I02). For business-to-customer sales (I07), Notion is used to streamline sales processes. However, I03 is an exception, as its venture builds an app designed for patients, while its sales target insurance funds. Video conferencing tools such as Zoom or Teams are commonly used for customer calls. In one interview (I04), a respondent mentioned using their sister's university Zoom account, which provides a premium account for free.

The *product development processes* of the ventures in our study were predominantly based on agile software development. All ventures used GitHub for source code version control and relied on Kanban boards to track progress. Some ventures (I03, I04, I07) utilized Notion, while others (I01) used the product management app Shortcut. One venture (I01, I02) implemented a unique communication strategy using WhatsApp to streamline the development process, specifically for merging pull requests on GitHub.

To unpack the business process evolution, we leveraged the concept of entrepreneurial bricolage, which revealed two types of business process bricolage with digital technologies: *usage of private resources* and *re-configuring existing resources within the venture*. The first type of business process bricolage we identified was visible in two of our cases. Table 2 gives an overview.

Interview I02, for instance, provides an example of the *usage of private resources* in the HR process. A software developer working in a startup told us that he receives his payslips via WhatsApp messages: "And apart from that, I somehow get my payslip sent via WhatsApp every month" (I02). The founders needed a simple way to communicate with their employees, so they chose to use a private messaging app that was widely available and accepted. When hiring the first employee, they needed to send out payslips (making do) and find a solution by re-purposing their existing resources. They could use the app they already had in place (re-combination of resources) to send out the payslips conveniently and effectively. This approach allowed them to make the most of what they had rather than invest in new tools or processes.

Table 2 Usage of private resources for business process execution

Context	Quote
Use of private messaging app WhatsApp to send payslip to employees as part of HR processes	"And apart from that, I somehow get my payslip sent via WhatsApp every month. (Laughs)" (I02)
Use of private short messaging app WhatsApp to inform developers about the progress of their developments in GitHub (venture's source code version control system) as part of the product development process	"Cooperation [is] sometimes a bit difficult, because people are not there full time and logically don't always have an exact plan of what's going on. That's why we introduced at least the other day that [the founder] always writes in our WhatsApp group when any pull requests have been merged, so that we at least have a rough overview of what's going on somehow at the moment." (I02)
Use of the CEO's sibling's Zoom account to save costs	"I'm using my sister's Zoom account. She still studies and gets the premium account for free." (I04)

The second type is *re-configuring existing resources within the venture.* Table 3 lists our findings.

An example of this approach is a venture using the collaborative note-taking app Notion since its inception (I03). As the company expanded and hired more employees, it faced the challenge of teaching new employees how to use its content management system (CMS) to upload content for display in its app (making do). This became too time-consuming for the CTO. Since they face resource constraints, he decided to leverage their existing Notion workspace and created a page with a short video tutorial explaining how to manage content using the CMS to address this issue (re-combining existing resources for a new purpose): "[...] people have often asked me, hey, how do I do this now [...]. And before I sit down with people every time for a meeting and explain to them for three quarters of an hour how it works, I thought, you can just make a video explanation of how you do it. And then you have automated it a bit. It's actually working quite well so far, [...] it's a bit of an education tool" (I03). This solution allowed the company to make the most of its existing resources and re-purpose them for new use rather than investing in new tools or training programs.

Table 3 Re-configuring existing resources within the venture

Context	Quote
Use of Microsoft Teams (team communications app) to track working hours as part of the payroll process	"And Microsoft teams we still use sometimes, for the stand-ups, and we have this, yeah, timesheet-like thing in there, so you kind of record how much you work." (I02)
Use of Notion (note-taking app) to create and host educational content for employees as part of the product development process	"[...] because people have often asked me, hey, how do I do this now, I don't know how to do it. And before I sit down with people every time for a meeting and explain to them for three quarters of an hour how it works, I thought, you can just make a video explanation of how you do it. And then you have automated it a bit. It's actually working quite well so far, [...] a bit of an education tool." (I03)
For all new business processes: If a new process needs to be added, Notion and existing Notion templates are used and adapted to support it	"Notion is our operating system." (I07), "Notion has templates that we adapt to our needs." (I07), "Notion's functions are not narrow, like Word or PowerPoint, but rather broad." (I07)
Use of Notion (note-taking app) to guide employee onboarding as part of the HR process	"The entire [company] intranet is hosted on Notion. [...] When you start here, all the steps are described. But also the individual teams, Tech, Customer Success, Business, Commercial, for example, all have their sides plus input. FAQs, for example, are also on Notion for the individual teams." (I06)

5 Discussion and Outlook

Our findings indicate that digital ventures use bricolage to create business processes using digital technologies. This involves (1) *usage of existing private resources* or (2) *re-configuring existing resources within the venture.*

Regarding (1), we can confirm the findings of Karanasios et al. (2022), stating that entrepreneurs are using private resources such as micro-loans to afford business purposes. Regarding (2), however, we noticed that digital ventures seem to use digital technologies with low specificity to arrange business processes (von Briel et al., 2017). Entrepreneurs in our sample utilized versatile tools such as Teams and Notion for various purposes. While Teams is primarily intended for video calls and text messaging, it is also used to track employees' working hours (I02). Notion, a note-taking app, on the other hand, serves as a Kanban board for product development and as a tool for onboarding employees during hiring (I03). Following the argumentation of von Briel et al. (2017), such tools should have a low potential for enabling compression and conservation mechanisms, which might affect their potential to improve organizational efficiency. However, low-specificity digital technologies have a high potential to enable generation and combination mechanisms, making them appropriate resources for the bricolage of business processes. Hence, according to von Briel et al. (2017), early-stage ventures rank efficiency below flexibility when choosing low-specificity tools. Building on this, we conclude that low-specificity technologies are enablers of business process bricolage in early-stage ventures: *The lower the specificity of digital technology, the higher its potential to be used in business processes bricolage in early-stage digital ventures.* This proposition is particularly interesting given that the literature on BPM emphasizes how technology provides a structure for organizing business processes, as exemplified by IT infrastructure alignment (Baiyere et al. 2020). However, in many cases, implementing new digital tools may require actors to adhere to a pre-determined process imposed on them through the use of new technology. In contrast, early-stage digital ventures appear to operate differently. Thanks to the low specificity of digital technology and its editability (Yoo et al. 2010), digital entrepreneurs can leverage digital tools to design and re-organize their business processes in a flexible and improvisational manner. This approach enables them to manage the tension between structure and flexibility. By embracing bricolage, digital ventures construct loosely-structured business processes (BPM perspective) by experimenting with editable technologies to maintain flexibility (digital entrepreneurship perspective). In this finding, we see a clear link to the concept of organizational ambidexterity (March 1991), as digital ventures take initial steps towards structured processes (exploitation) while leaving room for experimentation and improvisation (exploration). Future research could leverage the process-technologyfit framework by Ahmad and Van Looy (2022) to investigate the alignment between technology and business processes in digital ventures at various developmental stages. This study would provide insights into the changing preferences of digital ventures for low-specificity tools as they grow and mature.

Our preliminary findings initially explore how digital ventures apply bricolage to manage their business processes. We examine three key business processes in digital ventures: hiring, sales, and product development. We have chosen these processes because they are essential for the entrepreneurial growth of digital ventures: a digital offering needs to be developed and sold by employees who need to be hired. Therefore, our results are limited to these processes, while others may be present in early-stage digital ventures. In the next phase, we plan to collect additional data from the cases, including digital trace data generated by digital ventures. As our early findings are based on initial observations of our digital venture cases, they are meant to stimulate discussion rather than being considered definitive or broadly applicable results.

References

Ahmad, T., Van Looy, A., 2022. About a Process-Technology Fit for Process Improvements in an Ambidextrous Environment, in: Marrella, A., Weber, B. (Eds.), Business Process Management Workshops, Lecture Notes in Business Information Processing. Springer International Publishing, Cham, pp. 166–178. https://doi.org/10.1007/978-3-030-94343-1_13

Baiyere, A., Salmela, H., Tapanainen, T., 2020. Digital transformation and the new logics of business process management. European Journal of Information Systems. https://doi.org/10.1080/0960085X.2020.1718007

Baker, T., Nelson, R.E., 2005. Creating Something from Nothing: Resource Construction through Entrepreneurial Bricolage. Administrative Science Quarterly 50, 329–366. https://doi.org/10.2189/asqu.2005.50.3.329

Davidson, E., Vaast, E., 2010. Digital Entrepreneurship and Its Sociomaterial Enactment, in: 2010 43rd Hawaii International Conference on System Sciences. Presented at the 2010 43rd Hawaii International Conference on System Sciences, IEEE, Honolulu, Hawaii, USA, pp. 1–10. https://doi.org/10.1109/HICSS.2010.150

Dumas, M., La Rosa, M., Mendling, J., Reijers, H.A., 2013. Fundamentals of Business Process Management. Springer Berlin Heidelberg, Berlin, Heidelberg. https://doi.org/10.1007/978-3-642-33143-5

Gioia, D.A., Corley, K.G., Hamilton, A.L., 2013. Seeking Qualitative Rigor in Inductive Research: Notes on the Gioia Methodology. Organizational Research Methods 16, 15–31.

Huang, J., Henfridsson, O., Liu, M.J., Newell, S., 2017. Growing on Steroids: Rapidly Scaling the User Base of Digital Ventures Through Digital Innovaton. MIS Quarterly 41, 301–314.

Karanasios, S., Senyo, P.K., Effah, J., Zorina, A., 2022. Digital Bricolage: Creating a Digital Transformation from Nothing. ICIS 2022 Proceedings.

Lehmann, J., Recker, J., 2022. Offerings That are "Ever-in-the-Making": How Digital Ventures Continuously Develop Their Products After Launch. Bus Inf Syst Eng 64, 69–89. https://doi.org/10.1007/s12599-021-00730-y

Lehmann, J., Recker, J., Yoo, Y., Rosenkranz, C., 2022. Designing Digital Market Offerings: How Digital Ventures Navigate the Tension Between Generative Digital Technology and the Current Environment. Management Information Systems Quarterly 46, 1453–1482.

LeLoarne, S., Maalaoui, A., 2015. How high-tech entrepreneurs bricole the evolution of business process management for their activities. Business Process Management Journal 21, 152–171. https://doi.org/10.1108/BPMJ-03-2014-0024

Lévi-Strauss, C., 1967. The savage mind. University of Chicago Press.

March, J.G., 1991. Exploration and Exploitation in Organizational Learning. Organization Science 2, 71–87. https://doi.org/10.1287/orsc.2.1.71

Matthews, M., 2021. The Case for Information Bricolage in IS Research: A Theoretical Proposal. PACIS 2021 Proceedings.

Recker, J., Rosemann, M., Indulska, M., Green, P., 2009. Business Process Modeling- A Comparative Analysis. Journal of the Association for Information Systems 10. https://doi.org/10.17705/1jais.00193

Schultze, U., Avital, M., 2011. Designing interviews to generate rich data for information systems research. Information and Organization 21, 1–16. https://doi.org/10.1016/j.infoandorg.2010.11.001

Tumbas, S., Berente, N., vom Brocke, J., 2017a. Born digital: Growth trajectories of entrepreneurial organizations spanning institutional fields., in: ICIS 2017 Proceedings.

Tumbas, S., Berente, N., vom Brocke, J., 2017b. Digital Capabilities for Buffering Tensions of Structure, Space, and Time during Entrepreneurial Growth, in: ICIS 2017 Proceedings.

Tumbas, S., Seidel, S., Berente, N., 2015. The 'Digital Façade' of Rapidly Growing Entrepreneurial Organizations. ICIS 2015 Proceedings.

von Briel, F., Davidsson, P., Recker, J., 2017. Digital technologies as external enablers of new venture creation in the IT hardware sector. Entrepreneurship Theory and Practice 42, 47–69. https://doi.org/10.1177/1042258717732779

Weske, M., 2012. Business process management - concepts, languages, architectures, 2nd edition. Springer.

Yin, R.K., 2011. Applications of case study research. SAGE Publications.

Yin, R.K., 2009. Case study research: Design and methods. SAGE Publications.

Yoo, Y., Henfridsson, O., Lyytinen, K., 2010. Research Commentary — The New Organizing Logic of Digital Innovation: An Agenda for Information Systems Research. Information Systems Research 21, 724–735. https://doi.org/10.1287/isre.1100.0322

Digital Markets, Platforms and Data Spaces

Exploring Platform Types and Related Concepts in Service Research—A Systematic Scoping Literature Review

Philipp Hansmeier

Abstract Service exchange is considered as an integral component of digital platforms. Academic research differentiates between technical, economic, and social platforms, yet scholars face a multitude of diverse platform sub-types being inconsistently utilized. To address that issue and to provide a lexical platform definition overview, this study conducts a systematic scoping literature review on platform types and related concepts in the service domain. The systematic analysis of 49 high-quality service journal articles reveals that numerous digital platform sub-types exist in service research with overlapping definitions. Moreover, several relationship marketing constructs are investigated as central related concepts. This article is the first to explore divergent platform term definitions in the service domain and thus contributes a complementary service science lens on digital platforms alongside IS research.

Keywords Digital platform · Platform types · Service lens · Literature review

1 Introduction

Digital platforms frequently enable service provision and consumption. With a globally rising availability of smart devices (Ostrom et al. 2015), a broad spectrum of citizens is continuously accessing cyber-physical ecosystems on a daily basis (Wortmann and Flüchter 2015; Zhang et al. 2012). In these digital ecosystems appear several platform types predominantly building on service exchange (Bartelheimer et al. 2022; Taylor 2018). For instance, not only the message delivery process through social media platforms is a frequently consumed service, but also booking flexible ridesharing services by means of commercial platforms has become omnipresent (Cachon et al. 2017). Thus, digital platforms are deeply embedded in service contexts (Bartelheimer et al. 2022). Apart from these ordinary examples exist

P. Hansmeier (✉)
Department of Management Information Systems, Paderborn University, Paderborn, Germany
e-mail: philipp.hansmeier@upb.de

D. Beverungen et al. (eds.), *Transforming the Digitally Sustainable Enterprise*, Lecture Notes in Information Systems and Organisation 76,
https://doi.org/10.1007/978-3-031-80125-9_4

several other platform types within service contexts. Whereas established literature predominantly considers digital platforms from technical (de Reuver et al. 2018), economic (Cennamo and Santalo 2013), and social (Perren and Konzinets 2018) perspectives, this rather broad segmentation contains a heterogenous pool of platform sub-types (Bartelheimer et al. 2022). Due to definition inconsistencies of the platform sub-types in service research such as mobile, multi-sided, or service platforms (Hagiu and Wright 2015; Lusch and Nambisan 2015; Manner et al. 2013), it remains unclear what platform types and related concepts take on central relevance in service research. This ambiguity concerns not only scholars but also practitioners seeking suitable platforms for customer interactions. Therefore, research is urgently required to respond to that issue. *RQ: which digital platform types and related concepts are distinguished in service research?*

To address the proposed research question, this study is the first to conduct a systematic, scoping literature review on digital platforms in the service sector. It thus contributes to service science by providing a platform definition overview and highlighting research streams and gaps through a service lens. Beyond that, this contribution adds a foundation for subsequent research may targeting the harmonization of platform definitions. Moreover, the results can serve practitioners to better understand digital platforms and to discover the platform type most suited to engage with their customers. The following sections provide insights into the state of research, method, results, and discussion. Finally, conclusions, limitations, and future research avenues are outlined.

2 Background

Since 2010, scientific interest in digital platforms has considerably risen, leading to a broad range of platform types and related concepts being regularly, but without critical distinction, utilized in research and practice. Digital platforms are "a mediating entity operating in two- or multi-sided markets, which uses the internet to enable direct interactions between two or more distinct but interdependent groups of users to generate value" (Beverungen et al. 2020, p. 513). In this respect, contemporary platform research examines a variety of platform types and related concepts which can be understood from technological, economic, or social perspectives (Bartelheimer et al. 2022).

Starting with the first perspective, Tian et al. (2019, p. 1) define a technological platform as "an extensible technological foundation which allows complement providers to interact with users." In contrast, another study (Gawer 2014) regards technological platforms not solely from the purely technical standpoint. Instead, Gawer (2014, p. 1240) also takes economic elements into account: "(1) federate and coordinate constitutive agents who can innovate and compete; (2) create value by generating and harnessing economies of scope in supply or/ and in demand; and (3) entail a modular technological infrastructure composed of a core and periphery."

By this stage, a first example of how platform type definitions can deviate becomes visible.

The second perspective encompasses economic platform types, being all manifested by "the exchange of concrete economic resources in a quid pro quo fashion" between the present platform partners (Loi et al. 2009, p. 403). For instance, there are e-commerce, service, and peer-to-peer platforms. Relying on Huang et al. (2011, pp. 2171–72), an "e-commerce platform provides users with a variety of business component […] to complete the online transaction process […] with a series of support services." Apart from e-commerce platforms, scholars show interest in service platforms. Service platforms are "value proposition(s) consisting of a modular structure that invites to and facilitates value co-creation […] in a continuous service process" (Löfberg and Åkesson 2018, p. 768). Lastly, in the context of peer-to-peer sharing platforms, Wirtz et al. (2019, p. 458) define these as "two- or more-sided […] platforms through which people collaboratively provide and consume capacity-constrained assets and resources."

Switching to the last perspective, social platforms—recognized as "an environment that provides social entities and interactivity […] through digital applications" (Mitchell-Wong et al. 2008, p. 361)—are a major part of platform research. Interestingly, this social platform definition by Mitchell-Wong et al. (2008) is strongly overlapping with Kaplan and Haenlein's (2010, p. 60) definition of social media platforms as they define this platform type as "a platform to facilitate information exchange between users." Finally, another social media platform definition overlaps with the previous platform definitions: "website, or varying interfaces and software combinations through which user-generated content, interaction […] are communicated" (Wade et al. 2020, p. 1306).

Taken together, this state of research indicates how inconsistent literature on several platform definitions, being linked to diverse related concepts, deviates from each other.

3 Research Method

Responding to both the gap and research question, this article draws on the method of a systematic literature review. Systematic literature reviews aim to generate comprehensive insights into a particular discipline by systematically summarizing and reviewing established wisdom (Brandhorst 1982; Hulland and Houston 2020). For this purpose, a scoping review approach—critically analyzing and evaluating studies in terms of topics and contents—after Paré et al. (2015) is applied. Concretely, Levy and Ellis's (2006) input-processing-output model is utilized. This literature review includes highly ranked, service-oriented journal articles, adhering to the VHB JOURQUAL 3 ranking system (Hennig-Thurau and Sattler 2015; Plomp 1990) within the time period from 2010 to mid 2023 as the number of platform-related articles in academic literature has been continuously increasing since then (Bartelheimer

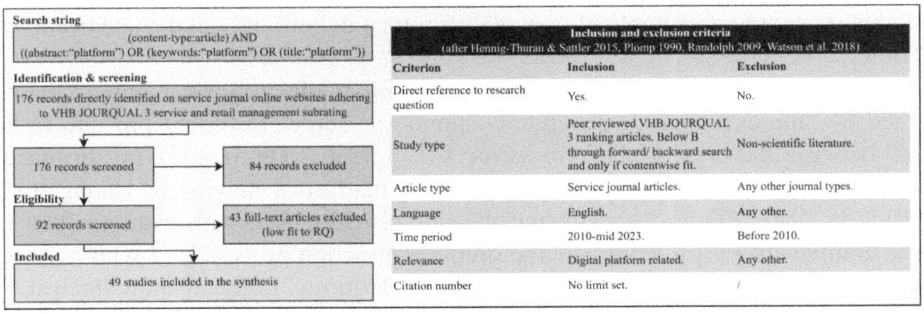

Fig. 1 Search strategies and procedures

et al. 2022). Furthermore, Fig. 1 informs about the search procedures after Moher et al. (2009) and inclusion criteria.

After the identification of 49 articles in total, all platform types, related concepts, and their definitions are gathered and added if missing. To create the classification scheme, a qualitative content analysis (Mayring 2000) of the platform type and related concept definitions is performed to find contentwise and thematic overlaps (see chapter 4.1). As in the case of the discovered platform types, no suitable concepts for a deductive classification exist; explorative-inductive procedures, respectively, the category formation are required (Mayring 2000). In contrast, the related concepts are assigned to deductive categories by matching them with established literature (Mayring 2000). In alignment with the platform type and related concept definitions, coding rules are defined (Mayring 2000) to aggregate the mentioned platform types and related concepts into seven categories. In terms of the classification scheme development, every platform type and related concept being contentwise core element of the study, is considered. Quality criteria after Hulland and Houston (2020) are ensured while adhering to the VHB JOURQUAL 3 service and retail management subrating (Hennig-Thurau and Sattler 2015).

4 Results

4.1 Organizational Framework for Classification of Research Contributions

After the classification, there are seven superordinate categories: three platform type-specific and four related concept-specific categories. The first category—general internet of things (IoT) platform (types)—is defined as "the middleware and the infrastructure that enables the end-users to interact with smart objects" (Mineraud et al. 2016, p. 5). All platform types being assigned to this category predominantly share technological functions of connecting platform parties. In contrast, the second category, labeled entertainment platforms, contains platform types that aim to enhance "enjoyment of life by offering interactive play-based multimedia applications which precisely target social needs" (Senger et al. 2012, p. 704). Then, the economic exchange platforms category merges platforms that rely on exchanging economic goods (Loi et al. 2009). Shedding light on the four related concept-specific categories, the category named customer-focused relational concepts covers popular relationship marketing constructs (Palmatier et al. 2006). However, the classification of the final three categories follows Beverungen et al.'s (2020) theory identifying the platform participant roles of customer, seller, and (infrastructure) provider. Accordingly, the customer-seller platform interactions category incorporates concepts requiring direct interaction between customers and sellers (Beverungen et al. 2020). Conversely, the seller-specific platform interactions category only implies concepts with active seller activity (Beverungen et al. 2020). Ultimately, the platform provider infrastructure antecedents category focuses on platform provider-specific concepts to enable participants' interactions (Beverungen et al. 2020).

4.2 Results of Literature Search Process and Classification of Articles

Next, the relevant N = 49 articles are mapped according to the proposed organizational framework (Tables 1 and 2). After that, the discussion outlines the listed contributions and platform types sorted by the four identified related concept categories.

5 Discussion

5.1 Contributions to Customer-Focused Relational Concepts Category

The first category and research stream labeled customer-focused relational concepts covers contributions investigating popular relationship marketing constructs (Palmatier et al. 2006) in the context of digital platforms to varying degrees.

As first insight, service research in the context of platforms and customer-focused relational concepts predominantly targets the topic of *customer participation (commitment, engagement, and involvement)*, being defined as "customer behaviors (that) go beyond transactions and may be specifically defined as a customer's behavioral manifestations that have a brand or firm focus, (even) beyond purchase" (van Doorn et al. 2010, p. 254). For instance, Benoit et al. (2016) regard member's ability, role clarity, and enjoyment as antecedents determining consumer participation on online and social media platforms. Thereby, an online platform, being the most

Table 1 Platform types in service research (inductive classification)

Authors	General IoT platform (types)				Entertainment platforms		
	Digital platform	Mobile platform	Online platform	Platform (unspecified)	Live-streaming platform	On-demand platform	Social media platform
Algharabat et al. (2018)							X
Algharabat et al. (2020)							X
Andreassen et al. (2018)							
Bai et al. (2019)						X	
Ballantyne and Nilsson (2017)							X
Baum et al. (2018)							X
Benoit et al. (2016)			X				X
Bernstein et al. (2020)							
Cachon et al. (2017)							
Cao et al. (2013)							
Carlson et al. (2018)							X
Chen et al. (2018)			X				
Cho and Menor (2010)			X				
Ciuchita et al. (2022)	X						
Fehrer et al. (2018)							
Filieri et al. (2022)							X
Giertz et al. (2022)					X		

(continued)

Table 1 (continued)

Authors	General IoT platform (types)				Entertainment platforms		
	Digital platform	Mobile platform	Online platform	Platform (unspecified)	Live-streaming platform	On-demand platform	Social media platform
Gong et al. (2023)							
Griffith et al. (2018)			X				
Guillemot and Privat (2019)			X				
Guyader (2018)			X				
Ha et al. (2022)			X				
Harwood and Garry (2015)							X
Hazée et al. (2020)	X						
He et al. (2023)			X				
Heinonen and Medberg (2018)			X				
Hogreve et al. (2019)			X				X
Hollebeek et al. (2020)				X			
Klaus and Zaichkowsky (2020)							
Konzinets (2022)							
Lee et al. (2018)							
Li et al. (2023)							
Lin et al. (2019)			X				X
Liu et al. (2023)							

(continued)

Table 1 (continued)

Authors	General IoT platform (types)				Entertainment platforms		
	Digital platform	Mobile platform	Online platform	Platform (unspecified)	Live-streaming platform	On-demand platform	Social media platform
Markfort et al. (2022)				X			
Martínez-de-Albéniz et al. (2022)							
Mathwick and Mosteller (2017)							
Mody et al. (2020)							
Munzel and Kunz (2014)			X				
Rios et al. (2022)			X				
Siddiq and Taylor (2022)							
Smedlund (2012)							
Taylor (2018)						X	
Thakur (2018)		X					
Uhrich et al. (2023)			X				
Wang et al. (2015)		X					
Warren and Hanson (2023)							
Wei et al. (2018)							X
Wirtz et al. (2019)							
∑	2	2	14	2	1	2	11

(continued)

Table 1 (continued)

Authors	Economic exchange platforms										
	Bot-driven platform	Engagement platform	E-commerce platform	Multi-sided platform	Networking platform	Online shopping platform	Peer-to-peer platform	Review platform	Ridesharing/ ridehailing platform	Service platform	(Two-) sided platform
Algharabat et al. (2018)											
Algharabat et al. (2020)											
Andreassen et al. (2018)			X								
Bai et al. (2019)											
Ballantyne and Nilsson (2017)											
Baum et al. (2018)					X						
Benoit et al. (2016)											
Bernstein et al. (2020)											X
Cachon et al. (2017)							X			X	
Cao et al. (2013)										X	
Carlson et al. (2018)		X									
Chen et al. (2018)											
Cho and Menor (2010)											
Ciuchita et al. (2022)											
Fehrer et al. (2018)				X							

(continued)

Table 1 (continued)

Authors	Economic exchange platforms										
	Bot-driven platform	Engagement platform	E-commerce platform	Multi-sided platform	Networking platform	Online shopping platform	Peer-to-peer platform	Review platform	Ridesharing/ ridehailing platform	Service platform	(Two-) sided platform
Filieri et al. (2022)											
Giertz et al. (2022)											
Gong et al. (2023)									X		
Griffith et al. (2018)											
Guillemot and Privat (2019)											
Guyader (2018)							X				X
Ha et al. (2022)											
Harwood and Garry (2015)		X									
Hazée et al. (2020)											
He et al. (2023)											
Heinonen and Medberg (2018)											
Hogreve et al. (2019)											
Hollebeek et al. (2020)											

(continued)

Table 1 (continued)

Authors	Economic exchange platforms										
	Bot-driven platform	Engagement platform	E-commerce platform	Multi-sided platform	Networking platform	Online shopping platform	Peer-to-peer platform	Review platform	Ridesharing/ ridehailing platform	Service platform	(Two-) sided platform
Klaus and Zaichkowsky (2020)	X									X	
Konzinets (2022)										X	
Lee et al. (2018)						X					X
Li et al. (2023)			X								
Lin et al. (2019)							X				
Liu et al. (2023)										X	
Markfort et al. (2022)											
Martínez-de-Albéniz et al. (2022)											X
Mathwick and Mosteller (2017)								X			
Mody et al. (2020)					X						
Munzel and Kunz (2014)								X			
Rios et al. (2022)											
Siddiq and Taylor (2022)									X		
Smedlund (2012)										X	

(continued)

Table 1 (continued)

Authors	Economic exchange platforms										
	Bot-driven platform	Engagement platform	E-commerce platform	Multi-sided platform	Networking platform	Online shopping platform	Peer-to-peer platform	Review platform	Ridesharing/ ridehailing platform	Service platform	(Two-) sided platform
Taylor (2018)											
Thakur (2018)				X							
Uhrich et al. (2023)											
Wang et al. (2015)											
Warren and Hanson (2023)										X	
Wei et al. (2018)		X									
Wirtz et al. (2019)							X				
∑	1	3	2	2	2	1	4	2	2	7	4

Table 2 Platform-related concepts in service research (deductive classification)

Authors	Customer-focused relational concepts							
	Customer lifecycle	Customer participation	Customer experience	Affectivity	E-WOM	Loyalty	Satisfaction	Trust
Algharabat et al. (2018)		X			X			
Algharabat et al. (2020)		X				X		
Andreassen et al. (2018)						X		
Bai et al. (2019)								
Ballantyne and Nilsson (2017)								
Baum et al. (2018)					X			
Benoit et al. (2016)		X						
Bernstein et al. (2020)								
Cachon et al. (2017)								
Cao et al. (2013)						X		
Carlson et al. (2018)	X	X						
Chen et al. (2018)		X						
Cho and Menor (2010)								
Ciuchita et al. (2022)					X			
Fehrer et al. (2018)								
Filieri et al. (2022)				X				
Giertz et al. (2022)		X						

(continued)

Table 2 (continued)

Authors	Customer-focused relational concepts							
	Customer lifecycle	Customer participation	Customer experience	Affectivity	E-WOM	Loyalty	Satisfaction	Trust
Gong et al. (2023)								
Griffith et al. (2018)				X	X		X	
Guillemot and Privat (2019)								
Guyader (2018)								
Ha et al. (2022)								
Harwood and Garry (2015)		X						
Hazée et al. (2020)								
He et al. (2023)								
Heinonen and Medberg (2018)					X			
Hogreve et al. (2019)	X				X			
Hollebeek et al. (2020)		X						
Klaus and Zaichkowsky (2020)			X					
Konzinets (2022)		X						
Lee et al. (2018)								
Li et al. (2023)								X
Lin et al. (2019)		X						
Liu et al. (2023)								

(continued)

Table 2 (continued)

Authors	Customer-focused relational concepts							
	Customer lifecycle	Customer participation	Customer experience	Affectivity	E-WOM	Loyalty	Satisfaction	Trust
Markfort et al. (2022)								
Martínez-de-Albéniz et al. (2022)								
Mathwick and Mosteller (2017)		X						
Mody et al. (2020)								
Munzel and Kunz (2014)					X			
Rios et al. (2022)								
Siddiq and Taylor (2022)								
Smedlund (2012)								
Taylor (2018)		X						
Thakur (2018)		X					X	X
Uhrich et al. (2023)								
Wang et al. (2015)	X							
Warren and Hanson (2023)								
Wei et al. (2018)								
Wirtz et al. (2019)								X
$\sum$	3	13	1	2	7	3	2	3

(continued)

Table 2 (continued)

Authors	Customer-seller platform interactions						
	AI-bot	Pricing	Retailing	Reviewing	Sharing	Social withdrawal	Value co-creation
Algharabat et al. (2018)							
Algharabat et al. (2020)							
Andreassen et al. (2018)							
Bai et al. (2019)		X					
Ballantyne and Nilsson (2017)							X
Baum et al. (2018)			X				
Benoit et al. (2016)							X
Bernstein et al. (2020)					X		
Cachon et al. (2017)		X			X		
Cao et al. (2013)							
Carlson et al. (2018)							X
Chen et al. (2018)							
Cho and Menor (2010)							
Ciuchita et al. (2022)							
Fehrer et al. (2018)							X
Filieri et al. (2022)							
Giertz et al. (2022)							
Gong et al. (2023)					X		
Griffith et al. (2018)							
Guillemot and Privat (2019)							X

(continued)

Table 2 (continued)

Authors	Customer-seller platform interactions						
	AI-bot	Pricing	Retailing	Reviewing	Sharing	Social withdrawal	Value co-creation
Guyader (2018)					X		
Ha et al. (2022)			X				
Harwood and Garry (2015)							
Hazée et al. (2020)					X		
He et al. (2023)							
Heinonen and Medberg (2018)							X
Hogreve et al. (2019)							
Hollebeek et al. (2020)							
Klaus and Zaichkowsky (2020)	X						
Konzinets (2022)							
Lee et al. (2018)							
Li et al. (2023)							
Lin et al. (2019)							
Liu et al. (2023)		X					
Markfort et al. (2022)							
Martínez-de-Albéniz et al. (2022)		X					
Mathwick and Mosteller (2017)							
Mody et al. (2020)							
Munzel and Kunz (2014)				X			

(continued)

Table 2 (continued)

Authors	Customer-seller platform interactions						
	AI-bot	Pricing	Retailing	Reviewing	Sharing	Social withdrawal	Value co-creation
Rios et al. (2022)					X		
Siddiq and Taylor (2022)					X		
Smedlund (2012)							X
Taylor (2018)		X					
Thakur (2018)				X			
Uhrich et al. (2023)							X
Wang et al. (2015)							
Warren and Hanson (2023)		X					
Wei et al. (2018)						X	
Wirtz et al. (2019)					X		
∑	1	6	2	2	8	1	8

Authors	Seller-specific platform actions		Platform provider infrastructure antecedents					
	Service management	Service quality	Digital servicescape	Multi-sided marketplaces	Network effects	Peer-to-peer markets	Platform business model	Service ecosystem
Algharabat et al. (2018)								
Algharabat et al. (2020)								
Andreassen et al. (2018)				X				
Bai et al. (2019)								
Ballantyne and Nilsson (2017)			X					X
Baum et al. (2018)								
Benoit et al. (2016)								

(continued)

Table 2 (continued)

Authors	Seller-specific platform actions		Platform provider infrastructure antecedents					
	Service management	Service quality	Digital servicescape	Multi-sided marketplaces	Network effects	Peer-to-peer markets	Platform business model	Service ecosystem
Bernstein et al. (2020)								
Cachon et al. (2017)						X		
Cao et al. (2013)					X			
Carlson et al. (2018)								
Chen et al. (2018)					X			
Cho and Menor (2010)		X						
Ciuchita et al. (2022)								
Fehrer et al. (2018)						X	X	
Filieri et al. (2022)								
Giertz et al. (2022)								
Gong et al. (2023)								
Griffith et al. (2018)								
Guillemot and Privat (2019)								
Guyader (2018)						X		
Ha et al. (2022)								
Harwood and Garry (2015)								

(continued)

Table 2 (continued)

Authors	Seller-specific platform actions		Platform provider infrastructure antecedents					
	Service management	Service quality	Digital servicescape	Multi-sided marketplaces	Network effects	Peer-to-peer markets	Platform business model	Service ecosystem
Hazée et al. (2020)								
He et al. (2023)							X	
Heinonen and Medberg (2018)								
Hogreve et al. (2019)	X							
Hollebeek et al. (2020)								
Klaus and Zaichkowsky (2020)								
Konzinets (2022)								
Lee et al. (2018)							X	
Li et al. (2023)								
Lin et al. (2019)						X		
Liu et al. (2023)		X						
Markfort et al. (2022)							X	
Martínez-de-Albéniz et al. (2022)								
Mathwick and Mosteller (2017)								
Mody et al. (2020)						X	X	

(continued)

Table 2 (continued)

Authors	Seller-specific platform actions		Platform provider infrastructure antecedents					
	Service management	Service quality	Digital servicescape	Multi-sided marketplaces	Network effects	Peer-to-peer markets	Platform business model	Service ecosystem
Munzel and Kunz (2014)								
Rios et al. (2022)								
Siddiq and Taylor (2022)								
Smedlund (2012)							X	
Taylor (2018)								
Thakur (2018)								
Uhrich et al. (2023)								
Wang et al. (2015)								
Warren and Hanson (2023)								
Wei et al. (2018)								
Wirtz et al. (2019)					X			
$\sum$	1	2	1	1	3	5	6	1

researched platform type of the general IoT platform category, is defined as "a digital service that facilitates interactions between two or more distinct but interdependent sets of users (whether firms or individuals) who interact through service via the Internet" (OECD 2019, p. 20). Contrary to that, Harwood and Garry (2015) assume gamification positively affects customer enjoyment leading to increased engagement, trust, and loyalty on engagement and social media platforms. In this regard, engagement platforms (as part of the economic exchange platforms) are "physical or virtual touchpoints designed to provide structural support for exchange and integration of resources, and thereby co-creation of value between actors in a service ecosystem" (Breidbach et al. 2014, p. 596). Lastly, new service research topics cover algorithmic branding to increase consumer engagement (Konzinets 2022) and commitment in the context of live-streaming platforms (Giertz et al. 2022). Here, a live-streaming platform is known as "an environment for novel engagement behaviors and monetization structures" (Giertz et al. 2022, p. 33).

However, the two concepts of *e-WOM*—positive or negative customer (online) statements about company assets (Hennig-Thurau et al. 2004)—and customer *loyalty*—consistent consumer commitment or repetitive repurchases of preferred same-brand goods (Oliver 1997)—are frequently inspected too. Examples include two investigations by Algharabat et al. (2018, 2020) observing significant influences of consumer involvement, customer brand engagement, and participation on *e-WOM* and client *loyalty* on social media platforms. Interestingly, the term social media platform, known as "a platform to facilitate information exchange between users" (Kaplan and Haenlein 2010, p. 60), is widely examined in the entertainment platforms category. Drawing on the often-mentioned concept of *customer lifecycle (behavioral intentions, adoption, usage, and repurchase)*, Hogreve et al. (2019) observe broad service recovery transparency to enhance *e-WOM* and purchase intentions, once again, on social media platforms. Recently, research on *e-WOM* lives up again by using netnography (Heinonen and Medberg 2018) and elaborating an user-created communication affordances framework for digital platforms (Ciuchita et al. 2022). So, service research often explores *e-WOM*.

Turning to the less researched themes in the customer-focused relational concepts category, customer *satisfaction, trust,* and *affectivity* during the *customer experience* play a major role. *Satisfaction* as affective customer response to consumed company assets (Giese and Cote 2000) and *trust* as client's overall perception of the provider's honesty, ability, and willingness to help (Keh and Xie 2009), highly depending on the degree of information asymmetry between the interacting parties (Li et al. 2023), receive attention in Thakur's (2018) study. Thakur's (2018) findings indicate brand engagement to positively mediate the effect of customer *satisfaction* and retailer *trust* on online review intentions within mobile and multi-sided platforms (general IoT platforms and economic exchange platforms categories). With regard to these platform types, Manner et al. (2013, p. 1375) claim "mobile platforms to enable third parties to extend and enhance functionalities of products and services by mediating these to consumers." Alongside the rather technical definition of mobile platforms (Manner et al. 2013), a multi-sided platform "enables direct interaction between two or more distinct sided (while) each side is affiliated with the platform" (Hagiu and

Wright 2015, p. 5). Comparing mobile and multi-sided platforms (Hagiu and Wright 2015; Manner et al. 2013), a distinction gets blurry as both platform definitions entail enabling interactions.

Lastly, the concept of actor *affectivity* (*emotions, emotional bonding, and attachment)* during the *customer experience* is likely to be under-researched as there are only two studies on that topic in the specific contexts of ridesharing (Griffith et al. 2018) and robot encounters (Filieri et al. 2022). In line with that, it remains fundamentally unclear how *customer experience* in virtual environments and especially on digital platforms, can be conceptualized. Moreover, research is confronted with the unanswered question which emotions and emotional triggers occur at distinct touchpoints during the whole customer journey in virtual spheres. To sum up, the first research stream compromises established customer relational concepts (Palmatier et al. 2006) on the popular digital platform types, such as online and social media platforms, but lacks knowledge regarding mobile platforms and related concepts like *customer experience* and emotions.

5.2 Contributions to Customer-Seller Platform Interactions Category

Moving to the next category (customer-seller platform interactions), this research stream sheds light on direct customer-seller interactions (Beverungen et al. 2020). To begin, the data illustrates that *pricing, sharing, and value co-creation* are immensely investigated, while the topics of *artificial intelligence robot (AI-bot), retailing, reviewing, and social withdrawal* are rarely linked to platforms in service research.

Service literature concerning the widely explored related concept of *pricing* being a joint decision-making process about the value of goods (Arsanjani 1977) encompasses on-demand, two-sided, and service platforms. For example, Bai et al. (2019) and Martínez-de-Albéniz et al. (2022) theoretically study the challenge of selecting optimal (dynamic) prices to maximize platform profits under conditions like perishable, seasonal goods, time- and price-sensitive customers on on-demand and sided platforms. Here, the rather little inspected on-demand platform (in the entertainment platforms category) is specified as "platform that connects waiting-time-sensitive customers with independent service providers" (Taylor 2018, p. 704). Nevertheless, wisdom is lacking in cases of declining demand or growing competition. This gap is addressed by Bernstein et al. (2020), describing that even in case of enhanced competition on a two-sided platform (entity of economic exchange platforms category) like Uber or Lyft, prices increase with growing demand in the sharing economy. In contrary, other contexts, such as healthcare, show that greater competition can result in lower prices and higher service quality (Liu et al. 2023). Besides the traditional *pricing*, digital tipping on service and sided platforms currently receives greater attention (Warren and Hanson 2023). In this respect, a two-sided platform is "one in which 1) two sets of agents interact through a [...] platform, and 2) the decisions of each set of agents affect the outcomes of the other(s)" (Rysman 2009, p. 125). Interestingly, Cachon et al. (2017) label Uber and Lyft in the sharing context as a service instead of two-sided platform. While surprising at first glance, this case indicates how businesses can unite elements of more than one platform type. Also, the definitions reveal the closeness of both platforms as Lusch and Nambisan (2015, p. 162) define a service platform as "a modular structure that [...] facilitates the interaction of actors and resources" (Lusch and Nambisan 2015, p. 162).

Recapturing the *sharing* concept, Guyader (2018) and Belk (2014) affirm that *sharing* economy practices, including ridesharing on online platforms, cannot be classified as true *sharing* because these practices are market-mediated and rather refer to the idea of renting (pseudo-*sharing*). Moreover, ridesharing is investigated concerning vehicle purchase decisions (Gong et al. 2023) and potential competition by autonomous driving vehicles (Siddiq and Taylor 2022) on ridesharing/ ride-hailing platforms. These economic platforms "match drivers and riders to trips, using dynamic prices to balance supply and demand" (Ma et al. 2020, p. 53). In this respect, service research investigates not only functional and psychological barriers to neglecting *sharing* (Hazée et al. 2020) but also the subject of matching on online dating platforms (Rios et al. 2022) too.

The final intensely debated issue in the customer-seller platform interactions stream is the concept of *value co-creation*. Generally, *value co-creation* is characterized by a joint co-construction between customers and firms to generate mutual value (Prahalad and Ramaswamy 2004). Recently, Fehrer et al. (2018) present a conceptual approach comparing Vargo and Lusch's (2016) service-dominant logic (SDL) and the platform business model logic (PBML) value co-creation. Compared to the SDL, which is grounded on actor's resource integration and service exchange, the platform business model logic highlights the additional characteristics of non-hierarchical collaboration while the platform actors benefit from a symbiotic service exchange on a multi-sided platform (Fehrer et al. 2018). In another study, Guillemot and Privat (2019) discover co-creation and collaborative consumption on online platforms from a non-commercial perspective accentuating the importance of social values, relationship-building, mutual value, individual and collective well-being. Enlarging this notion, Uhrich et al. (2023) spot hedonic, social, symbolic, utilitarian value in customer-to-customer interactions.

Turning the attention to the less researched concepts in the customer-seller platform interactions category, *social withdrawal* (avoiding social interaction) as counterpart of actor co-creation is found on social media and engagement platforms (Wei et al. 2018). Wei et al. (2018) notice enhanced *social withdrawal* if participants receive information about other users in advance in virtual, crowded areas but also due to psychological stress. However, research does not holistically capture triggers for *social withdrawal*.

Additionally, strategic *retailing* appears to be little researched yet. To start, Ha et al. (2022) investigate choice problems regarding online retailing channels on online platforms. Apart from that field, Baum et al. (2018) quantitatively support significant influences of both product testers and the community sense on the customer's attitude toward promoted goods and purchasing intentions in the context of social media and networking platforms. Staying in this field, Klaus and Zaichkowsky (2020) investigate artificial intelligence voice robots on service and bot-driven platforms. In total, Klaus and Zaichkowsky (2020) clarify that a bot-driven platform features an *artificial intelligence robot (AI-bot)* as primary service provider to enhance convenience, offer a more effortless and less time-consuming experience by autonomously anticipating human needs. Beyond these benefits, relationship-building mechanisms between humans and *AI-bots* (as friends or life coaches) are unexplored (Klaus and Zaichkowsky 2020). Thus, researchers are encouraged to respond to the questions what roles artificial intelligence can hold in virtual environments and which central use cases are reasonable.

The last rather unresearched subject deals with customer *reviewing* motives. Indeed, there are four *reviewing* motives identified by Munzel and Kunz (2014): (1) positive experiences and supporting other consumers, (2) negative experiences and warning other consumers, (3) establishing social bonds, (4) hoping for personal benefits. These motives are linked to online and review platforms (Mathwick and Mosteller 2017). Concluding these observations, *pricing, sharing, and value co-creation* are strongly researched, whereas *social withdrawal, strategic retailing*, and *AI-bots* are not.

5.3 Contributions to Seller-Specific Platform Interactions Category

The subsequent research stream exclusively involves seller-specific platform interactions and responsibilities with the two related concepts of *service management (communication, service failure, service recovery)* and *electronic service (e-service) quality*.

Hogreve et al. (2019) consider *service management* in terms of service failure and the upcoming recovery attempts on online and social media platforms. Principally, service failures are performances not reaching customer expectations and the subsequent service recovery represents organizational reparation attempts (Hess et al. 2003).

The second relevant related concept of this category is *(e-)service quality*, known as efficiency and effectivity degree of a system facilitating retailing and delivery processes (Parasuraman et al. 2005). In the beginning, Cho and Menor (2010) conceptualize four e-service encounters for online platforms covering informational, self-directive, intervenient, and intensive service encounters. After Cho and Menor (2010) represent podcasting or file-sharing websites informational encounters, whereas user-guidance happens in self-directive encounters. Intervenient and intensive encounters share the same concepts of collaboration and joint contribution, but intensive encounters explicitly expand this idea by satisfying personal needs with customization (Cho and Menor 2010).

Overall, *service management* and *(e-)service quality* seem to be greatly researched by popular marketing studies (e.g., see Hart et al. 1990; McCollough et al. 2000; Parasuraman et al. 1994, 2005) but due to rapidly progressing technical innovation in the last few years, *e-service quality* need an update for the contexts of mobile apps and digital platform environments.

5.4 Contributions to Platform Provider Infrastructure Antecedents Category

The last category—platform provider infrastructure antecedents—builds on the IS research stream of technology-based infrastructures and ecosystems (Barrett et al. 2015).

Initiating with the strongly explored concepts, *network effects* rely on formal and informal relationship-building (Wolff and Moser 2008). Sticking to the formal *network effects*, Fehrer et al. (2018) conceptualize three business network types, including firm-centered, solution and open networks in the context of multi-sided platforms. Whereas firm-centered networks are limited to internal members, the open solution networks also allow everyone to participate for resource integration (Fehrer et al. 2018). Unlike Fehrer et al. (2018), Wirtz et al. (2019, p. 458) concentrate in their conceptual study on direct (same-side) and indirect (cross-side) *network effects* on peer-to-peer platforms. The term direct network effect is applied when the utility of a distinct service for one group (e.g., social media users) increases with more same-group users (e.g., family and friends) joining the platform (Wirtz et al. 2019). Opposed to the direct effects, the value generated by indirect *network effects* only grows if a group having other abilities (not being available before) joins (Chen et al. 2018; Wirtz et al. 2019).

Moving to another widely investigated concept, service research is highly interested in *peer-to-peer markets,* described as "a decentralized structure where all peers cooperate with what they have available" (Sousa et al. 2019, p. 3). By comparing the peer-to-peer platform (Wirtz et al. 2019) and *peer-to-peer market* (Sousa et al. 2019) definitions, it is evident that platform type and related concept overlap. Since peer-to-peer engagement is little research yet (Lin et al. 2019), it seems promising for future work.

Finally, the concept of *platform business models* is missing, which draws on digital platforms to link suppliers and demanders (Appelfeller and Feldmann 2018). On this matter, Fehrer et al. (2018) differentiate between three *platform business model* properties: multi-sided platform/ market to enable interactions, platform ecosystem as technology system to run applications, and platform ecosystem as platform-based markets with network of partnerships. In contrast, Wirtz et al. (2019) take a different perspective detecting pipeline and *platform business models.* In this regard, Markfort et al. (2022) elaborate on three business model innovation patterns: skimming (aligning existing value creation practices with a new platform), revenue generation (through service improvements by platform integration), and orchestration (collaboration between several platform ecosystem partners) (Markfort et al. 2022). Parallel to that, research outlines three revenue sources of *platform business models*: pay-per-click advertising, pay-per-impression display advertising, and membership fees (Lee et al. 2018). Nonetheless, the current off-platform trend—meeting on the platform but transacting off-platform to avoid commissions—complicates the revenue generation for platforms (He et al. 2023).

However, the concepts of *multi-sided marketplaces, digital servicescape* and virtual *service ecosystems* have been less extensively researched. Referring to the *multi-sided marketplaces,* Andreassen et al. (2018) argue triadic business models with two or more groups resemble *multi-sided marketplaces.* Aside from that, Ballantyne and Nilsson (2017) address *digital servicescape* and virtual *service ecosystems* in the area of social media platforms. In comparison with the traditional concept (Booms and Bitner 1981), the digital servicescape has technology-mediated communication, virtual avatars and is less tangible (Ballantyne and Nilsson 2017). Nevertheless, Ballantyne and Nilsson (2017) encourage further investigation of how the *digital servicescape* affects the *customer experience.* Besides that, research is scarce on how to conceptualize and design a *digital servicescape* in virtual environments. Simultaneously, research is invited to investigate how the term digital (service) ecosystem can be defined and conceptualized.

6 Conclusion, Limitations, and Future Research

This article contributes a systematic literature review by investigating meaningful platform types and related concepts in service research. By critical linkage and evidence-based classification of articles, three platform types and four related concept categories become apparent as key insights. In case of platform types, there are the categories general IoT platforms, entertainment platforms and economic exchange platforms, each covering a varying number of platform types. Interestingly, these platform types have been unequally investigated as online (entity of general IoT platforms) and social media platforms (part of entertainment platforms) are mostly addressed by service researchers. Similar observations concern the related concepts as customer participation (entity of the customer-focused relational concept category), value co-creation and sharing (part of customer-seller platform interaction category) and platform business model (entity of platform provider infrastructure antecedents category), which are regularly mentioned. In turn, the category of seller-specific platform interactions receives little attention. To conclude, the findings reveal a growing relevance of platforms in the service sector and allow academics as well as practitioners to distinguish several platform types from a definitional perspective. Practitioners benefit even further by facing a pool of platform types that may encompass suitable platforms to engage with their customers. Nonetheless, some platform type definitions in service research still overlap. From this, we learn that further research, including a mutually agreed collection of platform definitions (e.g.,

Table 3 Avenues for future research

Platform definition separation	• How can research form an accepted understanding of platform type definitions? • What are key criteria to distinguish the overlapping platform types/ definitions?
Customer-focused relational concepts	• How can customer experience be conceptualized in virtual environments and esp. on digital platforms? • How can the customer experience be conceptualized in analog and digital spheres, including the transition phase? • Which emotions occur at distinct touchpoints during the whole customer journey in virtual environments? • What factors trigger emotions of platform participants in virtual contexts?
Customer-seller platform interactions	• Which use cases for artificial intelligence exist in virtual environments and on digital platforms? • What roles can artificial intelligence hold in virtual environments? • Which factors cause social withdrawal in cyber-physical environments?
Seller-specific platform interactions	• Which analog and digital factors affect the perceived service quality in virtual environments and esp. on digital platforms?
Platform provider infrastructure antecedents	• How can the servicescape be conceptualized and designed in virtual environments? • How can a digital (service) ecosystem term be conceptualized and defined?

through a Delphi study and beyond service research), is needed. In fact, this literature review faces two limitations. It compromises only the VHB JOURQUAL 3 service and retail management subrating from 2015, which may need an update in certain cases after nearly a decade. And a time period from 2010 until mid 2023 may exclude platform types and related concepts from previous years. Apart from that, Table 3 lists eminent research questions on identified gaps that needs urgent clarification.

References

Algharabat, R., Rana, N. P., Dwivedi, Y. K., Alawan, A., & Qasem, Z. (2018). "The Effect of Telepresence, Social Presence and Involvement on Consumer Brand Engagement: An Empirical Study of Non-Profit Organizations," *Journal of Retailing and Consumer Services* 40, 139–149.

Algharabat, R., Rana, N. P., Dwivedi, Y. K., Alawan, A. A., Baabdullah, A. M., & Gupta, A. (2020). "Investigating the Antecedents of Customer Brand Engagement and Consumer-Based Brand Equity in Social Media," *Journal of Retailing and Consumer Services* 53, 1–31.

Andreassen, T. W., Lervik-Olsen, L., Snyder, H., van Riel, A. C. R., Sweeney, J. C., & van Vaerenbergh, Y. (2018). "Business Model Innovation and Value-Creation: The Triadic Way," *Journal of Service Management* 29 (5), 883–905.

Appelfeller, W., & Feldmann, C. (2018). *Die Digitale Transformation des Unternehmens. Systematischer Leitfaden mit Zehn Elementen zur Strukturierung und Reifegradmessung*. Springer Gabler: Berlin.

Arsanjani, M. H. (1977). "International Control Over the Pricing of Resources: A Configurative Approach," *Yale Journal of International Law* 3, 251-338.

Bai, J., So, K. C., Tang, C. S., Chen, X., & Wang, H. (2019). "Coordinating Supply and Demand on an On-Demand Service Platform with Impatient Customers," *Manufacturing and Service Operations Management* 21 (3), 556–570.

Ballantyne, D., & Nilsson, E. (2017). "All that Is Solid Melts into Air. The Servicescape in Digital Service Space," *Journal of Services Marketing* 31 (3), 226–235.

Barrett, M., Davidson, E., Prabhu, J., & Vargo, S. L. 2015. "Service Innovation in the Digital Age: Key Contributions and Future Directions," *MIS Quarterly* 39 (1), 135-154.

Bartelheimer, C., zur Heiden, P., Lüttenberg, H., & Beverungen, D. (2022). "Systematizing the Lexicon of Platforms in Information Systems: A Data-Driven Study," *Electronic Markets* 32, 375-396.

Baum, D., Spann, M., Füller, J., & Thürridl, C. (2018). "The Impact of Social Media Campaigns on the Success of New Product Introductions," *Journal of Retailing and Consumer Services* 50, 1-9.

Belk, R. (2014). "Sharing Versus Pseudo-Sharing in Web 2.0," *Anthropologist* 18 (1), 7-23.

Benoit, S., Bilstein, N., Hogreve, J., & Sichtmann, C. (2016). "Explaining Social Exchanges in Information-Based Online Communities," *Journal of Service Management* 27 (4), 460-480.

Bernstein, F., DeCroix, G. A., & Keskin, N. (2020). "Competition between Two-Sided Platforms Under Demand and Supply Congestion Effects," *Manufacturing & Service Operations Management* 23 (5), 1043–1061.

Beverungen, D., Kundisch, D., & Wünderlich, N. V. (2020). "Transforming into a Platform Provider: Strategic Options for Industrial Smart Service Providers," *Journal of Service Management* 32 (4), 507-532.

Booms, B. H., & Bitner, M. J. (1981). "Marketing Services by Managing the Environment," *The Cornell H.R.A. Quarterly* (May 1982), 35–40.

Brandhorst, T. (1982). *Cataloging. ERIC Processing Manuel, Section V*. National Institution of Education: Washington, DC.

Breidbach, C. F., Brodie, R. J., & Hollebeek, L. (2014). "Beyond Virtuality: From Engagement Platforms to Engagement Ecosystems", *Managing Service Quality*, 24 (6), 592-611.

Cachon, G. P., Daniels, K. M., & Lobel, R. (2017). "The Role of Surge Pricing on a Service Platform with Self-Scheduling Capacity," *Manufacturing & Service Management* 19 (3), 368-384.

Cao, H., Jiang, J., Oh, L.-B., Li, H., Lia, X., & Chen, Z. (2013). "A Maslow's Hierarchy of Needs Analysis of Social Networking Services Continuance," *Journal of Service Management* 24 (2), 170-190.

Carlson, J., Rahman, M., Voola, R., & De Vries, N. (2018). "Customer Engagement Behaviours in Social Media: Capturing Innovation Opportunities," *Journal of Services Marketing* 32 (1), 83–94.

Cennamo, C., & Santalo, J. (2013). "Platform Competition: Strategic Trade-Offs in Platform Markets," *Strategic Management Journal* 34, 1331-1350.

Chen, Y.-J., Dai, T., Korpeoglu, C. G., Körpeoğlu, E., Sahin, O., Tang, C. S., & Xiao, S. (2018). "Innovative Online Platforms: Research Opportunities," *Manufacturing & Service Operations Management* 22 (3), 430-445.

Cho, Y. K., & Menor, L. J. (2010). "Toward a Provider-Based View on the Design and Delivery of Quality E-Service Encounters," *Journal of Service Research* 13 (1), 83-95.

Ciuchita, R., Medberg, G., Penttinen, V., Lutz, C. & Heinonen, K. (2022). "Affordances Advancing User-Created Communication (UCC) in Service: Interactivity, Visibility, and Anonymity," *Journal of Service Management* 33 (4/5), 688-704.
De Reuver, M., Sørensen, C., & Basole, R. C. (2018). "The Digital Platform: A Research Agenda," *Journal of Information Technology* 33, 124-135.
Fehrer, J. A., Woratschek, H., & Brodie, R. J. (2018). "A Systematic Logic for Platform Business Model," *Journal of Service Management* 29 (4), 546-568.
Filieri, R., Lin, Z., Li, Y., Lu, X., & Yang, X. (2022). "Customer Emotions in Service Robot Encounters: A Hybrid Machine-Human Intelligence Approach," *Journal of Service Research* 25 (4), 614-629.
Gawer, A. (2014). "Bridging Differing Perspectives on Technological Platforms: Toward an Integrative Framework," *Research Policy* 43, 1239-1249.
Giertz, J. N., Weiger, W. H., Törhönen, M., & Hamari, J. (2022). "Content versus Community Focus in Live Streaming Services: How to Drive Engagement in Synchronous Social Media," *Journal of Service Management* 33 (1), 33-58.
Giese, J. L., & Cote, J. A. (2000). "Defining Consumer Satisfaction," *Academy of Marketing Science Review* 1, 1-24.
Gong, J., Greenwood, B. N., & Song, Y. (S.). (2023). "An Empirical Investigation of Ridesharing and New Vehicle Purchase," *Manufacturing & Service Operations Management* 25(3), 884-902.
Griffith, D. A., van Esch, P., & Trittenbach, M. (2018). "Investigating the Mediating Effect of Uber's Sexual Harassment Case on Its Brand: Does It Matter?" *Journal of Retailing and Consumer Services* 43, 111-118.
Guillemot, S., & Privat, H. (2019). "The Role of Technology in Collaborative Consumer Communities," *Journal of Services Marketing* 33 (7), 837-850.
Guyader, H. (2018). "No One Rides for Free!: Three Styles of Collaborative Consumption," *Journal of Services Marketing* 32 (6), 692-714.
Ha, A. Y., Tong, S., & Wang, Y. (2022). "Channel Structures of Online Retail Platforms," *Manufacturing & Service Operations Management* 24 (3), 1547-1561.
Hagiu, A., & Wright, J. (2015). "Multi-Sided Platforms," *International Journal of Industrial Organization* 43, 162-174.
Hart, C. W., Heskett, J. L., & Sasser, W. E. (1990). "The Profitable Art of Service Recovery," *Harvard Business Review* 68 (4), 148–156.
Harwood, T., & Garry, T. (2015). "An Investigation into Gamification as Customer Engagement Experience Environment," *Journal of Services Marketing* 29 (6/7), 533-546.
Hazée, S., Zwienenberg, T., van Vaerenbergh, Y., Faseur, T., Vandenberghe, A., & Keutgens, O. (2020). "Why Customers and Peer Service Providers Do Not Participate in Collaborative Consumption," *Journal of Service Management* 31 (3), 397-419.
He, E. J., Savin, S., Goh, J., & Teo, C.-P. (2023). "Off-Platform Threats in On-Demand Services," *Manufacturing & Service Operations Management* 25 (2), 775-791.
Heinonen, K., & Medberg, G. (2018). "Netnography as a Tool for Understanding Customers: Implications for Service Research and Practice," *Journal of Services Marketing* 32 (6), 657-679.
Hennig-Thurau, T., Gwinner, K. P., Walsh, G., & Gremler, D. D. (2004). "Electronic Word-of-Mouth via Consumer-Opinion Platforms: What Motivates Consumers to Articulate Themselves on the Internet?" *Journal of Interactive Marketing*, 18 (1), 38-52.
Hennig-Thurau, T., & Sattler, H. (2015). "Teilrating Dienstleistungs- und Handelsmanagement," *VHB-JOURQUAL* 3, 1.
Hess, R. L., Ganesan, S., & Klein, N. M. (2003). "Service Failure and Recovery: The Impact of Relationship Factors on Customer Satisfaction," *Journal of the Academy of Marketing Science* 31 (2), 127–145.
Hogreve, J., Bilstein, N., & Hoerner, K. (2019). "Service Recovery on Stage: Effects of Social Media Recovery on Virtually Present Others," *Journal of Service Research* 22 (4), 421-439.
Hollebeek, L., Smith, D., Kasabov, E., Hammedi, W., Warlow, A., & Clark, M. (2020). "Customer Brand Engagement during Service Lockdown," *Journal of Services Marketing* 35 (2), 201-209.

Huang, M., Zhao, Y., & Zhu, L. (2011). "Research for E-Commerce Platform Security Framework Based on SOA," *4th International Conference on Biomedical Engineering and Informatics*, 2171–2174.
Hulland, J., & Houston, M. B. (2020). "Why Systematic Review Papers and Meta-Analyses Matter: An Introduction to the Special Issue on Generalizations in Marketing," *Journal of the Academy of Marketing Science* 48, 351–359.
Kaplan, A. M., & Haenlein, M. (2010). "Users of the World, Unite! The Challenges and Opportunities of Social Media," *Business Horizons* 53 (1), 59-68.
Keh, H. T., & Xie, Y. (2009). "Corporate Reputation and Customer Behavioral Intentions: The Roles of Trust, Identification and Commitment," *Industrial Marketing Management* 38, 732-742.
Klaus, P., & Zaichkowsky, J. L. (2020). "AI Voice Bots: A Services Marketing Research Agenda," *Journal of Services Marketing* 34 (3), 389-398.
Konzinets, R. V. (2022). "Algorithmic Branding through Platform Assemblages: Core Conceptions and Research Directions for a New Era of Marketing and Service Management," *Journal of Service Management* 33 (3), 437-452.
Lee, J.-Y., Fang, E., Kim, J. J., Li, X., & Palmatier, R. W. (2018). "The Effect of Online Shopping Platform Strategies on Search, Display, and Membership Revenues," *Journal of Retailing* 94 (3), 247-264.
Levy, Y., & Ellis, T. J. (2006). "A Systems Approach to Conduct an Effective Review in Support of Information Systems Research," *Informing Science Journal* 9, 181-212.
Li, L., Fang, X., & Lim, Y. F. (2023). "Asymmetric Information of Product Authenticity on C2C E-Commerce Platforms: How Can Inspection Services Help?," *Manufacturing & Service Operations Management* 25 (2), 631-647.
Lin, M., Miao, L., Wei, W., & Moon, H. (2019). "Peer Engagement Behaviors: Conceptualization and Research Directions," *Journal of Service Research* 22 (4), 388-403.
Liu, Y., Wang, X., Gilbert, S., & Lai, G. (2023). "On the Participation, Competition and Welfare at Customer-Intensive Discretionary Service Platforms," *Manufacturing & Service Operations Management* 25 (1), 218-234.
Löfberg, N., & Åkesson, M. (2018). "Creating a Service Platform: How to Co-Create Value in a Remote Service Context," *Journal of Business & Industrial Marketing* 33 (6), 768-780.
Loi, R., Mao, Y., & Ngo, H.-Y. (2009). "Linking Leader-Member Exchange and Employee Work Outcomes: The Mediating Role of Organizational Social and Economic Exchange," *Management and Organization Review* 5 (3), 401-422.
Lusch, R. F., & Nambisan, S. (2015). "Service Innovation: A Service-Dominant Logic Perspective," *MIS Quarterly*, 39 (1), 155-176.
Ma, H., Fang, F., & Parkes, D. (2020). "Spatio-Temporal Pricing for Ridesharing Platforms," *ACM SIGecom Exchanges* 18 (2), 53-57.
Manner, J., Nienaber, D., Schermann, M., & Krcmar, H. (2013). "Six Principles for Governing Mobile Platforms," *Wirtschaftsinformatik Proceedings 2013* 86, 1375-1389.
Markfort, L., Arzt, A., Kögler, P., Jung, S., Gebauer, H., Haugk, S., Leyh, C., & Wortmann, F. (2022). "Patterns of Business Model Innovation for Advancing IoT Platforms," *Journal of Service Management* 33 (1), 70-96.
Martínez-de-Albéniz, V., Pinto, C., & Amorim, P. (2022). "Driving Supply to Marketplaces: Optimal Platform Pricing When Suppliers Share Inventory," *Manufacturing & Service Operations Management* 24 (4), 2367-2386.
Mathwick, C., & Mosteller, J. (2017). "Online Reviewer Engagement: A Typology Based on Reviewer Motivations," *Journal of Service Research* 20 (2), 204–218.
Mayring, P. (2000). "Qualitative Content Analysis," *FQS* 1(2), 1-10.
McCollough, M. A., Berry, L. L., & Yadav, M. S. (2000). "An Empirical Investigation of Customer Satisfaction after Service Failure and Recovery," *Journal of Service Research* 3 (2), 121-137.
Mineraud, J., Mazhelis, O., Su, X., & Tarkoma, S. (2016). "A Gap Analysis of Internet-of-Things Platforms," *Computer Communications* 89–90 (1), 5–16.

Mitchell-Wong, J., Goh, S. K., Chhetri, M. B., Kowalczyk, R., & Vo, B. Q. (2008). "Framework for Open, Distributed and Self-Managed Social Platforms, in: Camarinha-Mahos, L. M. & Picard, W. (eds.) *Pervasive Collaborative Networks*. Springer: New York, 361-368.

Mody, M., Wirtz, J., So, K. K. F., Chun, H. H. E., & Liu, S. Q. (2020). "Two-Directional Convergence of Platform and Pipeline Business Models," *Journal of Service Management* 31 (4), 693–721.

Moher, D., Liberati, A., Tetzlaff, J. & Altman, D. G. (2009). "Preferred Reporting Items for Systematic Reviews and Meta-Analyses: The PRISMA Statement," *Annals of Internal Medicine* 151 (4), 264-269.

Munzel, A., & Kunz, W. H. (2014). "Creators, Multipliers, and Lurkers: Who Contributes and Who Benefits at Online Review Sites," *Journal of Service Management* 25 (1), 49–74.

OECD. (2019). *An Introduction to Online Platforms and Their Role in the Digital Transformation*. OECD Publishing: Paris.

Oliver, R. L. (1997). *Satisfaction: A Behavioral Perspective on the Consumer.* Irwin/McGraw-Hill: New York.

Ostrom, A. L., Parasuraman, A., Bowen, D. E., Patrício, L., & Voss, C. A. (2015). "Service Research Priorities in a Rapidly Changing Context," *Journal of Service Research* 18 (2), 127-159.

Palmatier, R. W., Dant, R. J., Grewal, D., & Evans, K. R. (2006). "Factors Influencing the Effectiveness of Relationship Marketing: A Meta-Analysis," *Journal of Marketing* 70, 136–153.

Parasuraman, A., Zeithaml, V. A., & Berry, L. L. (1994). "Alternative Scales for Measuring Service Quality: A Comparative Assessment Based on Psychometric and Diagnostic Criteria," *Journal of Retailing* 70 (3), 201-230.

Parasuraman, A., Zeithaml, V. A., & Malhotra, A. (2005). "E-S-Qual – A Multiple-Item Scale for Assessing Electronic Service Quality," *Journal of Service Research* 7 (3), 213-233.

Paré, G., Trudel, M.-C., Jaana, M., & Kitsiou, S. (2015). "Synthesizing Information Systems Knowledge: A Typology of Literature Reviews," *Information & Management* 52, 183-199.

Perren, R., & Kozinets, R. V. (2018). "Lateral Exchange Markets: How Social Platforms Operate in a Networked Economy," *Journal of Marketing* 82, 20-36.

Plomp, R. (1990). "The Significance of the Number of Highly Cited Papers as an Indicator of Scientific Prolificacy," *Scientometrics* 19 (3/4), 185-197.

Prahalad, C. K., & Ramaswamy, V. (2004). "Co-Creation Experiences: The Next Practice in Value Creation," *Journal of Interactive Marketing* 18 (3), 5-14.

Randolph, J. (2009). "A Guide to Writing the Dissertation Literature Review," *Practical Assessment, Research, and Evaluations* 14 (13), 1-13.

Rios, I., Saban, D., & Zheng, F. (2022). "Improving Match Rates in Dating Markets through Assortment Optimization," *Manufacturing & Service Operations Management* (in press), 1–58.

Rysman, M. (2009). "The Economics of Two-Sided Markets," *Journal of Economic Perspectives* 23 (3), 125-143.

Senger, J., Wälisch, T., John, M., Wang, H., Belbachir, A. N., Kohn, B., & Smurawski, A. (2012). "Serious Gaming: Enhancing the Quality of Life among the Elderly through Play with the Multimedia Platform SilverGame", in: Wichert, R. & Eberhardt, B. (eds.). *Ambient Assisted Living. Advanced Technologies and Social Change.* Springer: Berlin Heidelberg, 317–331.

Siddiq, A. & Taylor, T. A. (2022). "Ride-Hailing Platforms: Competition and Autonomous Vehicles," *Manufacturing & Service Operations Management* 24 (3), 1511-1528.

Smedlund, A. (2012). "Value Cocreation in Service Platform Business Models," *Service Science* 4 (1), 78-88.

Sousa, T., Soares, T., Pinson, P., Moret, F., Baroche, T., & Sorin, E. (2019). "Peer-to-Peer and Community-Based Markets: A Comprehensive Review," *Renewable and Sustainable Energy Reviews* 104, 367-378.

Taylor, T. A. (2018). "On-Demand Service Platform," *Manufacturing & Service Operations Management* 20 (4), 704-720.

Thakur, R. (2018). "Customer Engagement and Online Reviews," *Journal of Retailing and Consumer Services* 41, 48-59.

Tian, J., Zhao, X., & Xue, L. (2019). "Technological Compatibility between Platforms and Multi-Homing of Third-Party Developers," *ICIS 2019 Proceedings*, 1–9.
Uhrich, S., Grohs, R., & Koenigstorfer, J. (2023). "Customer-to-Customer Interactions in the Sport Fan Context: Typology, Framework (C2CIF) and Directions for Future Research," *Journal of Service Management* (in press), 1–18.
Van Doorn, J., Lemon, K. N., Mittal, V., Nass, S., Pick, D., Pirner, P., & Verhoef, P. C. (2010). "Customer Engagement Behavior: Theoretical Foundations and Research Directions," *Journal of Service Research* 13 (3), 253-266.
Vargo, S. L., & Lusch, R. F. (2016). "Institutions and Axioms: An Extension and Update of Service-Dominant Logic," *Journal of the Academy of Marketing Science* 44, 5-23.
Wade, J. T., Roth, P. L., Thatcher, J. B., & Dinger, M. (2020). "Social Media and Selection: Political Issue similarity, Liking, and the Moderating Effect of Social Media Platform," *MIS Quarterly* 44 (3), 1301-1357.
Wang, R. J.-H., Malthouse, E. C., & Krishnamurthi, L. (2015). "On the Go: Mobile Shopping Affects Customer Purchase Behavior," *Journal of Retailing* 91 (2), 217-234.
Warren, N. B. & Hanson, S. (2023). "Tipping, Disrupted: The Multi-Stakeholder Digital Tipped Service Journey," *Journal of Service Research* (in press), 1–16.
Watson, R., Wilson, H. N., Smart, P., & Macdonald, E. K. (2018). "Harnessing Difference: A Capability-Based Framework for Stakeholder Engagement in Environmental Innovation," *Journal of Product Innovations Management* 35 (2), 254-279.
Wei, S. M., Ang, T., & Anaza, N. A. (2018). "The Power of Information on Customers' Social Withdrawal and Citizenship Behavior in a Crowded Service Environment," *Journal of Service Management* 30 (4), 23-47.
Wirtz, J., So, K. K. F., Mody, M. A., Liu, S. Q., & Chun, H. E. H. (2019). "Platforms in the Peer-to-Peer Sharing Economy," *Journal of Service Management* 30 (4), 452-483.
Wolff, H.-G., & Moser, K. (2008). "Effects of Networking on Career Success: A Longitudinal Study," *Journal of Applied Psychology* 94 (1), 196-206.
Wortmann, F., & Flüchter, F. (2015). "Internet of Things. Technology and Value Added," *Business & Information Systems Engineering* 57 (3), 221-224.
Zhang, H., Lu, Y., Shi, X., Tang, Z., & Zhao, Z. (2012). "Mood and Social Presence on Consumer Purchase Behaviour in C2C E-Commerce in Chinese Culture," *Electronic Markets* 22, 143-154.

Trust Me, I'm an Intermediary! Exploring Data Intermediation Services

Julia Christina Schweihoff, Ilka Jussen, and Frederik Möller

Abstract Data ecosystems receive considerable attention in academia and practice, as indicated by a steadily growing body of research and large-scale (industry-driven) research projects. They can leverage so-called data intermediaries, which are mediating parties that facilitate data sharing between a data provider and a data consumer. Research has uncovered many types of data intermediaries, such as data marketplaces or data trusts. However, what is missing is a 'big picture' of data intermediaries and the functions they fulfill. We tackle this issue by extracting data intermediation services decoupled from specific instances to give a comprehensive overview of how they work. To achieve this, we report on a systematic literature review, contributing data intermediation services.

Keywords Data sharing · Data ecosystems · Data intermediaries

1 Introduction

Ensuring flourishing inter-organizational data sharing requires consensus about what the process entails. For this purpose, the European Commission proposed the *European Strategy for Data*, with the Data Act (DA) as one of its core elements (European Commission 2022a). Among other things, the DA defines the nature of fair digital

J. C. Schweihoff (✉) · I. Jussen · F. Möller
Industrial Information Management, TU Dortmund University, Dortmund, Germany
e-mail: Julia.Schweihoff@tu-dortmund.de

I. Jussen
e-mail: Ilka.Jussen@tu-dortmund.de

F. Möller
e-mail: Frederik.Moeller@tu-dortmund.de; Frederik.Moeller@isst.fraunhofer.de

F. Möller
Information Systems and Data-Driven Enterprise, TU Braunschweig, Braunschweig, Germany

Fraunhofer ISST, Dortmund, Germany

D. Beverungen et al. (eds.), *Transforming the Digitally Sustainable Enterprise*, Lecture Notes in Information Systems and Organisation 76,
https://doi.org/10.1007/978-3-031-80125-9_5

environments to spur data-driven innovation and enable novel data-driven services (European Commission 2022b). Notably, the overarching goal seems to be to build data-sharing ecosystems (i.e., data ecosystems) in which organizations share data in a legally compliant manner to create value (Capgemini Research Institute 2021). Sharing data is usually associated with a plethora of untapped potential, which, if used adequately, can assist in creating a brighter future and tackling global challenges, such as *sustainable tourism* (World Economic Forum 2021). Data sharing contributes to developing new services for end consumers and intensifying inter-organizational cooperation and value creation. To this end, major initiatives, such as the *Catena-X Automotive Network* (Catena-X 2023), aim to generate a secure and sovereign data ecosystem across their supply chains in the German automotive industry. Novel applications include compliance with the Supply Chain Act, which mandates accountability for supply chain partners (e.g., suppliers), for instance, to prevent child labor (Federal Ministry for Economic Cooperation and Development 2023). Other goals include making processes along the value chain more transparent and traceable to reduce resource consumption and support circular economy design (Handelsblatt 2023). However, various barriers prevent effective data sharing between organizations, which are usually associated with a lack of reciprocal trust and transparency (Opriel et al. 2021; Fassnacht et al. 2023). One way to enhance trust in data ecosystems is to install a so-called *data intermediary* that "*facilitates the use of data for other actors*" (Oliveira et al. 2019). These data intermediaries (e.g., data marketplaces or data trusts) can be shaped differently based on the setting they are implemented and the specific needs of the data ecosystems (Oliveira et al. 2019; Richter and Slowinski 2019). The importance of intermediation services is emphasized in the Data Governance Act (DGA): *"intermediation services between data holders [...] and potential data users, including making available the technical or other means to enable such services; those services may include bilateral or multilateral exchanges of data or the creation of platforms or databases enabling the exchange or joint exploitation of data, as well as the establishment of a specific infrastructure for the interconnection of data holders and data users [...]" (European* Commission, 2020*)*. Given the background of the DA and the DGA and, at the same time, the current push of politics, economy, and research to generate data ecosystems, we propose a classification of data intermediary services in the context of data sharing. Because of the above, we pursue the following research question: *How to classify data intermediary services (data intermediation services) in the context of data sharing?*

To answer this research question, we structure the paper as follows. First, we present the theoretical background focusing on data sharing and the importance of intermediaries. Then Sect. 3 explains our research design with a detailed description of our literature review. In Sect. 4, we present our findings from the literature review regarding the services of data intermediaries. Finally, Sect. 5 concludes our paper with an overview of the contributions and limitations of our research as well as an outlook on further research opportunities.

2 Data Sharing Through Data Intermediaries

Sharing data is more than a technical process since it represents a socio-technical transaction between a *data provider* and a *data consumer* that needs to consider an array of decisions (Jussen et al. 2023). One of these decisions is identifying a suitable data ecosystem governance structure, which includes variants, such as peer-to-peer or the implementation of a *data intermediary* (Wernick et al. 2020). Oliveira et al. (2019) define intermediary-based data ecosystems as those that depend "*on the presence of data intermediaries in order to generate value from data*" and that it "*is a role that facilitates the use of data for other actors.*" Janssen and Singh (2022) define the data intermediary as "*a mediator between those who wish to make their data available, and those who seek to leverage that data. The intermediary works to govern the data in specific ways and provides some degree of confidence regarding how the data will be used*". Resulting, these illustrative definitions imply that the intermediary is 'in the middle', between a *data provider* and a *data consumer*. Data intermediaries can have a variety of purposes, such as *ensuring data quality* (e.g., Oliveira and Lóscio 2018) or *organizing data-sharing transactions* (e.g., Agahari et al. 2021). However, the nature and specifics of data intermediaries remain blurry (Wernick et al. 2020) and highly contextual (Oliveira et al. 2019; Janssen and Singh 2022).

Figure 1 shows visualizations of data intermediaries. We derived these visualizations in part from the literature and brought them to a comparable level of detail using existing illustrations from the papers. One major common feature of the visualizations of the different authors is that the intermediary always fulfills some role between at least two other actors. Kioses et al. (2007) illustrate intermediaries for data exchange between buyers and suppliers in the example of invoices. Otto et al. (2019) also considered a real-world case in their paper, the *International Data Space*. In their visualization, the intermediary is placed between different actors. Intermediaries can take on various sub-roles in their role as "*trusted entities*", such as *broker service provider*, *clearing house, identity provider*, *app store*, and *vocabulary provider* (Otto et al. 2019).[1] Intermediaries can also appear in the form of *data marketplaces* or *platforms* (Cirullies and Schwede 2021; Marotta et al. 2022; Sterk et al. 2022). These platforms can be „*created and maintained by one or more intermediaries*" (Eisenmann et al. 2011).

3 Research Design

To answer the research question outlined above, we explore the literature to extract knowledge about *data intermediation services* in the context of data sharing. Subsequently, our research strategy is a *concept-centric systematic literature review* (Webster and Watson 2002; vom Brocke et al. 2015). We take a *descriptive approach*

[1] For more detailed explanations of the individual roles, we refer to Otto et al. (2019).

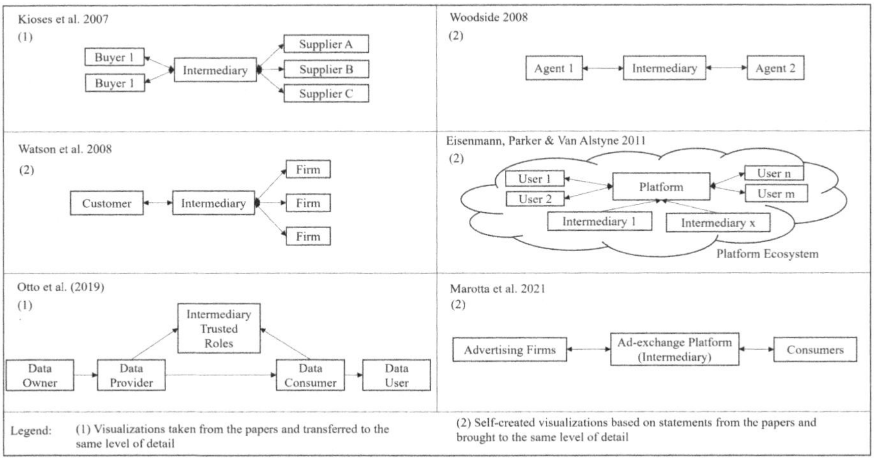

Fig. 1 Illustrative conceptualizations of data intermediaries

as described by Paré et al. (2015), which aims to show what the understanding of *data intermediation services* is in the literature and follow the procedure suggested by Templier and Paré (2015) for conducting a literature review (indicated in bold below).

First (1), we defined a set of keywords that we identified as likely to yield relevant literature on data intermediaries. Resulting, we used combinations of "*intermediary*", omitting the prefix *data* to be as comprehensive as possible. From our experience, we found that "*trustee*", "*trusted third-party*", and "*marketplace*" as likely synonyms that could potentially enrich the literature sample. We entangled these keywords with "*data sharing*" or "*data exchange*" accommodating the prevailing blurriness between these concepts (e.g., Jussen et al. 2023). The following example by Koul et al. (2018) illustrates the diversity of terms in this field, further substantiating our search strategy: "*The* ***data sharing*** *process is managed by a* ***data marketplace****, a* ***trusted third-party*** *handling the market participants' request and managing the agreements between them*[2]" (**formulating the problem**).

Second (2), we identified relevant databases that contain peer-reviewed literature published in conference proceedings and journals (Levy and Ellis 2006). To cover conference proceedings, predominantly in the Information Systems (IS) research field, we searched the database of the *AIS*, which hosts high-quality conferences, such as *ECIS* or *ICIS*. We extended the IS focus by searching in *Scopus*, *IEEE Xplore*, and *Web of Science*, which indexed various journals, such as *Electronic Markets* or *BISE* (**searching the literature**).

Third (3), we defined filter mechanisms to focus on those papers that report on data intermediary services or functionalities. Subsequently, to be included, papers must deal with a type of data intermediary, even though the exact wording is not

[2] Highlighting of relevant terms by the authors (bold).

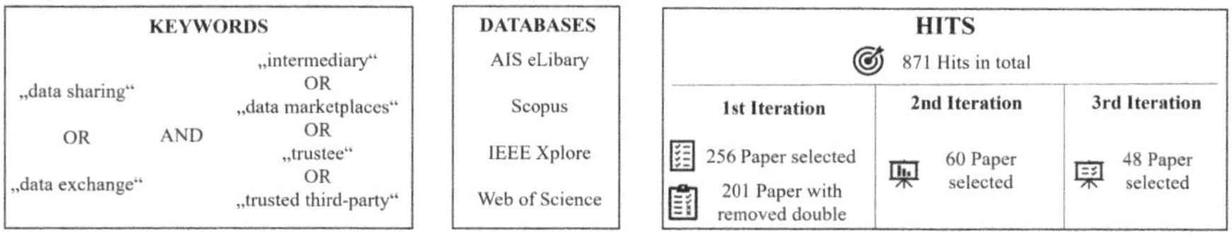

Fig. 2 Keywords, databases, filtering process, and hits

a precondition for inclusion (**screening for inclusion** and **assessing quality**). For example, Abbas et al. (2021) investigate business data sharing through data marketplaces, which we classify as a data intermediary, not by name, but by the concept, and subsequently included it in the literature sample. We started with a body of literature containing 871 hits across databases, which we reduced (e.g., removing doubles, thematic analysis, accessibility, and language) in three iterations to 48 for in-depth analysis (see Fig. 2 for details).[3]

Fourth (4), two authors analyzed the literature using a concept-centric approach to extracting information about data intermediation services (**extracting data**). During the *1st iteration*, we reviewed the *abstracts* and *titles* of the papers and only included German or English papers focusing on "*Data Intermediaries*" within a B2B context. In the *2nd iteration*, we analyzed the papers more closely and excluded papers dealing with the issue of data sharing but not data intermediaries. For example, some papers reported on using the blockchain for data sharing. However, we found it to be a substitute for an intermediary (e.g., Albrecht et al. 2018). The *3rd and final iteration* examined the selected papers for specific aspects mentioned in connection with data intermediation services. Finally, the number of selected papers was 48. Since our search showed theoretical satisfaction after the 3rd iteration, we decided against a further forward/backward search (e.g., Webster and Watson 2002).

Table 1 shows illustrative literature statements and the corresponding codes. Initially, we started by extracting intuitive elements of the papers, such as visual representations (see Fig. 1). To analyze the literature statements systematically, we employed Gioia diagrams (examples for this are Leemann and Kanbach 2022; Osterrieder et al. 2020) (**analyzing and synthesizing data**). These types of diagrams are part of grounded theorizing and are 'traditionally' used to analyze, for example, transcribed interviews and generate concepts and theory from them (Gioia et al. 2013). However, we found the procedure highly systematic and helpful for analyzing the literature statements we extracted, which is why we adapted it to our systematic literature review (see Fig. 3) and used it to outline a clear thread between literature statements and a class of services.

[3] List of all analyzed papers is available on request.

Table 1 Examples of our literature coding

Example literature statement	Coding
"*Due to legal issues, negotiation data must be monitored by a trusted third party (TTP). This allows for independent third-party monitoring of the business transactions (…)*" (Woodside 2008)	Monitoring of legal, data and business transactions by a trusted third party
„*A Trusted Third Party (TTP), a non-profit organisation, pseudonimises the data to minimise the risk of reidentification. Access and recombination of the data is provided through this service.*" (van den Broek and van Veenstra 2015)	Pseudonymization of the data Control data access
"*Some data marketplaces offer an enterprise data marketplace as an additional service. An enterprise data marketplace functions as a private data marketplace that enables organizations to share data (…).*" (van de Ven et al. 2021)	Provide a data infrastructure (e.g., in the form of a data marketplace)

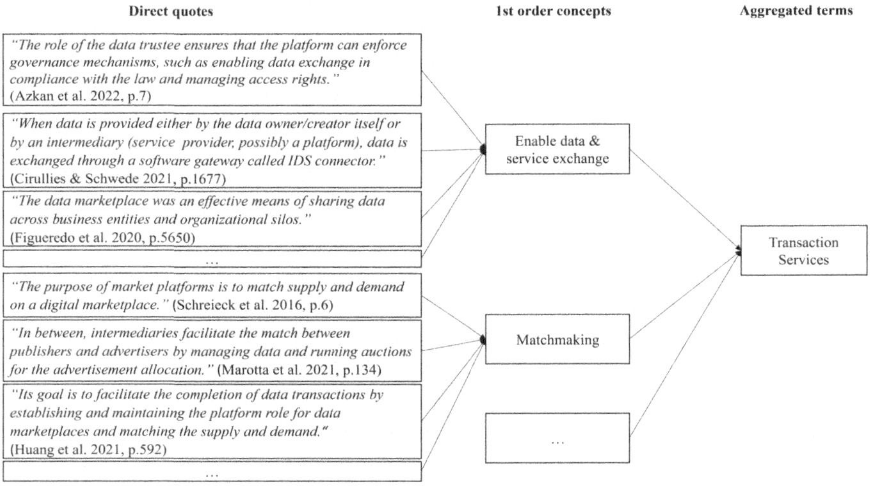

Fig. 3 Illustrative visualization of the Gioia diagram (based on Gioia et al. 2013)

4 Findings: Data Intermediaries in Data Ecosystems

In the following, we provide a fivefold classification of data intermediation services. This classification is a product of iterative content aggregation, in which we ordered the services we extracted based on their thematic alignment. The resulting field of aggregated terms is the service categories we found prevalent in data intermediaries.

Table 2 Data intermediation service types

Service type	Definition	Distribution	Examples
Transactions service	Transaction services focus on enabling the general data-sharing process	18 papers	E015 (2023) Sovity (2023)
Governance service	Governance services aim to regulate the legal aspects of data sharing	10 papers	CDQ (2023)
Sovereignty service	Sovereignty services ensure compliance with policies and data ownership	17 papers	Sovity (2023) GXFS.eu (2023) Snowflake (2023)
Technology service	Technology services provide a data infrastructure for sharing and storing data	26 papers	GXFS.eu(2023) Dawex (2023)
Data service	This service focuses exclusively on the resource of data	13 papers	CDQ (2023) Catena-X(2023)

At this point in our research, we did not look for mutually exclusive categories, but for the '*big picture*'. Resulting, it is to be expected that these categories overlap conceptually (Table 2).

Below, we will explain each service class in more detail and enrich them through practice examples. Please note each service is highlighted in bold, reflecting the 1st order of concepts from the literature analysis (see Fig. 3). The services we find are non-exclusive, and there may be some overlap.

4.1 *Transaction Services*

Transaction services enable data ecosystems by matching data providers and consumers or supporting activities in the data-sharing process. One primary service of data intermediaries is **to enable data and service exchange**. As visualized in Fig. 1, the intermediary takes the position between data providers and data consumers and *enables* the general *exchange of data and services*. Perscheid et al. (2020) define the role of the intermediary as "*coordinate users*" and "*enable the exchange of products and services*" to promote collaboration. In addition to facilitating the general exchange of data and services, this also includes bringing together data providers and data consumers so that data exchange can occur in the first place. Bringing the actors together is also classically referred to as **matchmaking**. For example, data marketplaces connect data providers and data consumers in their role as an intermediary. Agahari et al. (2021) define this service as "*a matchmaking service between data providers and data buyers, rather than a facilitator of data exchange between the two parties*." This may involve matching demand and supply, but also data providers and data buyers, or different markets (Schreieck et al. 2016; Demchenko and Gommans 2019; Agahari et al. 2021; Huang et al. 2021). Intermediaries gather information

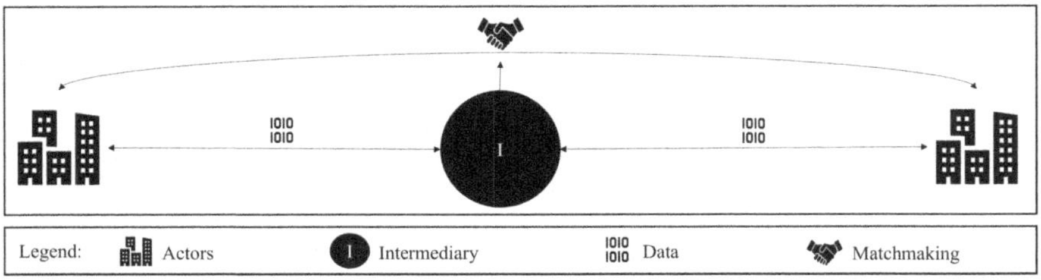

Fig. 4 Visualization of transaction services

over time, enhancing matchmaking capabilities (Marotta et al. 2022). An example is E015 (2023), an Italian API-Ecosystem and data marketplace that enables application developers to tap into APIs.

There is a broad range of reasons why data sharing fails between organizations. One is the participants' lack of know-how on how to design and implement the data-sharing process (Gelhaar et al. 2021), requiring them to receive **support in facilitating data sharing**. Bastiaansen et al. (2019) see the responsibility of the intermediary to provide "*adequate service options for the data sharing supporting processes that match the data provider's business policies.*" Companies such as Sovity (2023) tackle this issue by providing support services around data sharing (e.g., data space connectors).

Some see the responsibilities of data intermediaries to **resolve conflicts.** Conflict resolution is a pivotal service to enable long-term and sustainable data sharing. Woodside (2008) describes this service as "*independent third-party monitoring of the business transactions, and for resolution of conflicts between parties*". The ability of the intermediary enhances and requires its trustworthiness (Bastiaansen et al. 2019, 2020). Figure 4 visualizes the basic logic of transaction services. The various actors are in contact with the intermediary, which takes its conceptual place 'in the middle,' enabling and supporting data exchange.

4.2 Governance Services

Second, we found services relating to organizing **governance** in the ecosystems. These services provide legal agreements on an ecosystem level and observe their compliance. First, the governance services include the **definition of legal agreements**. Azkan et al. (2022) highlight that " *the role of the data trustee ensures that the platform can enforce governance mechanisms, such as enabling data exchange in compliance with the law and managing access rights.*" Thus, there are different ways in which these governance specifications can be designed. For example, it can be a data management and governance framework (Demchenko and Gommans 2019), but also market rules (Huang et al. 2021) or a contract that includes data usage/sharing agreements (Noorian et al. 2014; Bastiaansen et al. 2019, 2020). In these cases,

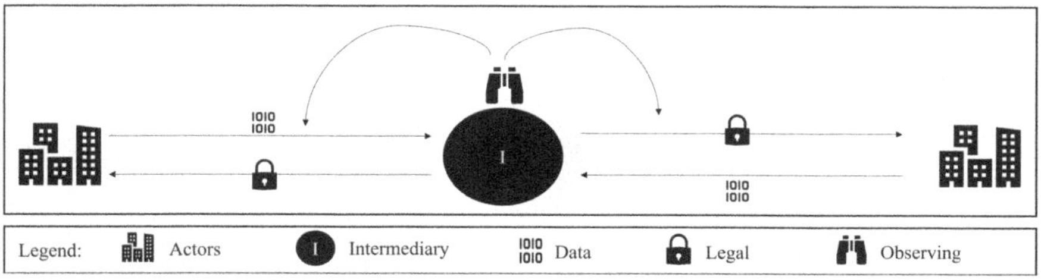

Fig. 5 Visualization of governance services

it is up to the intermediary to protect the data of the actors (Watson et al. 2008). This aspect leads to the second service in the governance services area: **observing and auditing legal compliance**. Woodside (2008) sees a trusted entity's activity as "*monitors the interaction for auditing and legal purposes.*" For example, it aims to prevent manipulation and ensure transparency (Demchenko and Gommans 2019; Agahari and Reuver 2022). This service is also closely related to conflict resolution. Conflicts can be counteracted by monitoring compliance with legal requirements (Woodside 2008). An example of governance services is provided by CDQ (2023), providing data quality rules.

In addition to monitoring legal compliance, intermediaries can **monitor interactions** between actors (Woodside 2008). This can be ensured, for example, through role interaction protocols (Kurtz et al. 2019). Figure 5 visualizes the governance service. The actors have each entered legal agreements with the intermediary and now share their data monitored by the data intermediary.

4.3 Sovereignty Services

Data sovereignty services ensure compliance with policies (e.g., access or usage control) that uphold the self-determination of data ownership by the data provider (e.g., Zrenner et al. 2019). For data intermediaries, we propose four data sovereignty services. A key aspect of this service is **to ensure data sovereignty**. Bastiaansen et al. (2019) see the role of the intermediary in supporting data sovereignty and Bastiaansen et al. (2020) highlight that "*restricting proliferation of the metadata to their 'home' intermediary roles that a data provider or data consumer has subscribed to, will prevent such loss of control and will therefore increase the level of data sovereignty.*" It becomes clear that the service of providing data sovereignty to an intermediary is decisive for "*enabling data exchange and integrating/involving data markets into B2B relations*" (Demchenko and Gommans 2019). One example for providing data sovereignty as a service is Sovity (2023). Their approach focus on "*open-source software, establishes a self-determinded control of data usage, to gain full value out of data*" (Sovity 2023). A core service regarding the implementation of data sovereignty is **anonymizing and pseudonymizing data**. This should minimize

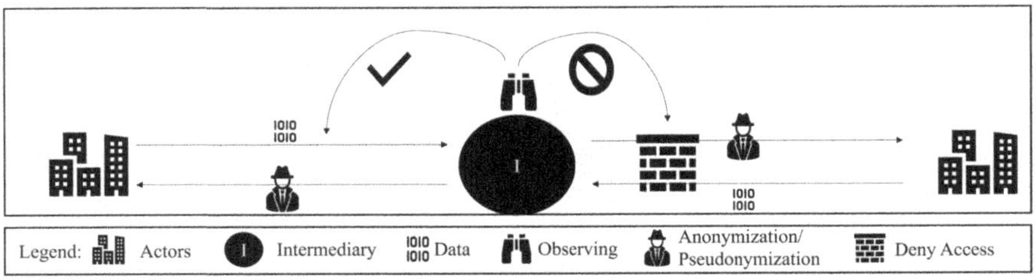

Fig. 6 Visualization of sovereignty services

the risk of reidentification (van den Broek and van Veenstra 2015). Susha et al. (2017) refer to this service as " *"mediated revealing" (*i.e. *aggregating and anonymizing datasets before transfer to the user)*" creating a win–win situation for both the data provider and data user. In addition to anonymization and pseudonymization, **certification** is a key component of the sovereignty services. According to Bastiaansen et al. (2019), this strengthens the trust function. For example, certification can be implemented by using a decryption key (Sonehara et al. 2011). GXFS.eu (2023) is an example of a certification service. The core content of its activity represents the creation of a federated system in which data can be shared. Access to this system is regulated by an authentication & authorization service. This is intended to enable a "*trusted, decentralized and self-sovereign manner*" without the need for a "*central source of authority*" (GXFS.eu 2023).

The last identified service in the data sovereignty services framework is **data access control**. In this case, the intermediary has *"control over how data and service flows between platform participants*" (Kurtz et al. 2019). This can happen for a wide variety of reasons. For example, the intermediary may have "*an incentive to strategically and selectively reveal certain consumer data but not others, regulation of data exchanges may actually increase consumers' welfare and/or firms' payoffs*" (Marotta et al. 2022). A side effect of this control is to strengthen the privacy of individual actors and is intended to prevent data manipulation (Roa et al. 2017; Agahari and Reuver 2022). For instance, Snowflake (2023) provides a platform for secure data sharing, including controlled data access. Figure 6 visualizes the sovereignty service. It shows the data exchange between two actors via an intermediary. The intermediary ensures data sovereignty as well as anonymization and pseudonymization. Access to the data is also controlled. Two scenarios are shown in the figure. On the left, the actor is granted access, while on the right, access is denied.

4.4 Technology Services

One service range deals with providing **technology**, such as infrastructure, or ensuring standardization in data sharing. As already mentioned, a decisive obstacle to data sharing is the lack of know-how regarding the implementation of data sharing

(Gelhaar et al. 2021). In addition to implementation at the organizational level, this point often also relates to the technical level, such as the data infrastructure or a standardized sharing process. **Standardization** is vital in data sharing because it enables data exchange by creating interoperability among stakeholders (Bastiaansen et al. 2019). For example, Bastiaansen et al. (2020) state that "*from a usercentric perspective, the focus of standardization must be on accessibility of the functionality provided by the intermediary organizations providing services on the legal concepts of data sharing agreements and usage contracts*". The aforementioned GXFS.eu (2023) project offers certification services as well as standardization. Besides implementing standardization, the intermediary can **provide the data infrastructure**. According to Agahari et al. (2021), the goal of this service is "*to ease the burden for data providers and consumers*". This service can be implemented in the form of software, but also hardware, other data-related services (e.g., cloud services), the provision of a platform (Öksüz 2014; Fuerstenau and Auschra 2016; Schreieck et al. 2016; Demchenko and Gommans 2019; Kurtz et al. 2019; Schmidt 2022; Woroch and Strobel 2022). For example, the data infrastructure service can provide data storage (Watson et al. 2008; Kurtz et al. 2019; Azkan et al. 2022; Bergman et al. 2022). The provision of infrastructure via an intermediary "*will allow for trustworthy and transparent trading and exchange of user data among applications*" (Noorian et al. 2014). An example of this service is the company Dawex (2023). They provide a data platform through which companies can build their data marketplace to share data with their customers, partners, or within the company.

Figure 7 visualizes the technology service. The intermediary assumes the central role by providing a platform, for example, a data marketplace, through which the various players can share their data. This platform can include other services, such as taking care of governance and sovereignty issues so that the platform's actors can rely on standardized processes and not face the obstacle of implementing the technical implementation of data sharing.

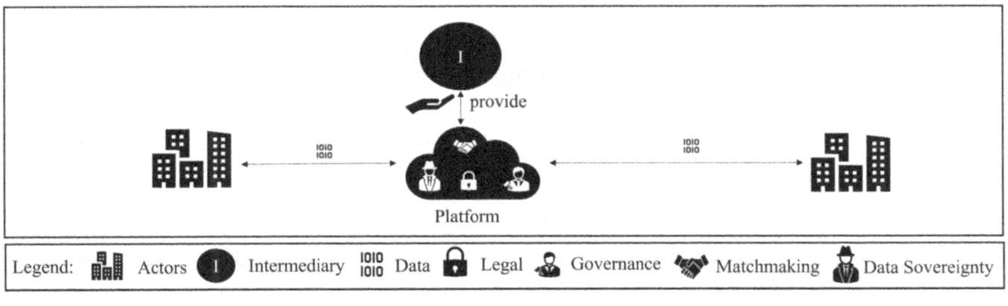

Fig. 7 Visualization of technology services

4.5 Data Services

Data Services are the final service dimension we identified in our analysis. This service focuses exclusively on the resource of data. On the one hand, there is a focus on aggregating the necessary data and ensuring that this data has specific quality characteristics.

A key aspect of data sharing is the **quality** as well as the **integrity** of the data (Winter and Davidson 2017). Agahari et al. (2021) highlight that "*data marketplaces offer complementary applications and services such as data visualizations, data valuation, and data analytics*". The importance of ensuring data quality is also highlighted by (Demchenko and Gommans 2019) that "*data traded as economic goods must possess/demonstrate such properties as measurable quality, identifiability, veracity, non-rivalry/re-usability, privacy, compliance and comply with the FAIR principles*". Ensuring data quality can play a critical role in conflict resolution (Bastiaansen et al. 2019) and motivate participants to participate in data sharing (Huang et al. 2021). One example from the field is CDQ (2023), which offers companies a platform, security standards, and data quality assurance. This is guaranteed by the fact that the data platform "*provides access to 70+ trustworthy open and premium data sources and offers easy data mapping and system integration*". One goal of intermediaries (e.g., in the form of a data marketplace) is to make data "*more accessible to potential users*" (Figueredo et al. 2020). This **data aggregation** service goes hand in hand with quality assurance since the choice or provision of data (sources) to the consumer also determines the possible quality of the data (Winter and Davidson 2017). Catena-X (2023) offers an example of such a service to aggregate data in the automotive industry and make it accessible to participants in the ecosystem. Figure 8 visualizes that the intermediary enables data exchange between different actors. By checking the data provided by the actors, the data intermediary ensures the required data quality. In doing so, the intermediary can draw on data provided by the actors and publicly available data, aggregate them and make them available.

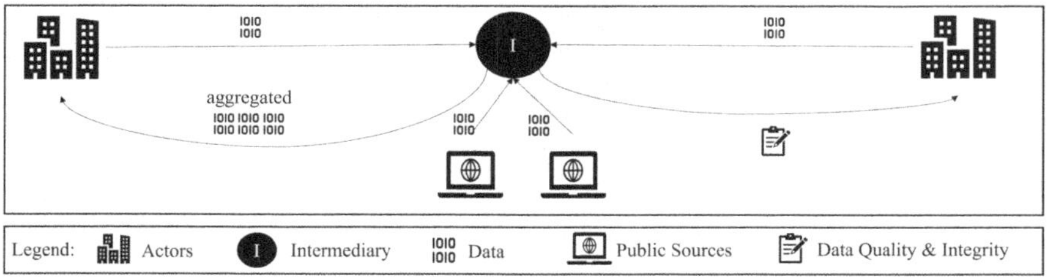

Fig. 8 Visualization of data services

5 Contributions, Limitations, and Outlook

The paper has multiple **contributions**. Primarily, we give an overview of services a data intermediary can fulfill. We see this as highly useful against the background of the DA and DGA and mandating the installment of neutral data intermediaries. While there is research reporting on several data intermediaries, taking a big-picture approach and extracting services holistically is a novel contribution. For **research**, this overview can help others to go into more detail about specific services and complement our findings. Indeed, the findings can act as a link between different streams of literature investigating demarcated types of intermediaries, such as *data marketplaces* (e.g., Abbas et al. 2021), *data trusts* (e.g., Stachon et al. 2023) or roles in *data space* (e.g., Otto et al. 2019; Otto and Jarke 2019). In particular, we took a broader approach, decoupling the services from specific instances. Consequently, they can be used flexibly and as a repertoire of services and functionalities tailored to specific scenario requirements. Additionally, this approach can inspire researchers dealing with a particular data intermediary (e.g., data trust) to consider novel services not from that domain and potentially integrate them. For **practice**, we see a relevant issue with the DGA and DA that potentially requires practitioners to accommodate data intermediaries to offer specific services in a specific way. While, at this point, our research does not compare the service spectrum with requirements from legislation, this could be a potential next step for practitioners aiming to implement data intermediaries or data ecosystems in general.

The paper has several **limitations**. Currently, the research builds on a systematic literature review, which we complemented by finding single practice examples (see above). This means that we can have missed articles, that the keywords we chose excluded potentially relevant literature, and that we analyzed the literature based on our interpretation and experience. Given that data intermediaries are relevant in practice (e.g., Advaneo GmbH 2023), and European Legislation (e.g., European Commission 2020) facilitates their implementation, we expect a growing body of research and projects to emerge in the near future. Subsequently, we provide a snapshot of current research and expect it to be needing updates frequently.

There are multiple ways forward for **new research**. Primarily, we see methodological complementation as particularly interesting. For example, by integrating more data sources (e.g., interviews), the field of data intermediaries can be explored more in-depth and broader. In particular, conducting an interview study with data intermediary users and operators should be highly valuable to explore relevant issues that are hard to conceptualize from the literature, such as the *neutrality* of intermediation services. Data intermediary research requires interdisciplinary research since the DGA and DA might mandate specific functions, and incorporating neutrality can touch on data intermediary business models. Resulting, what comes into play is the role of data intermediaries investigated from an IS research perspective, legal, and business. This entails researching business models for data intermediaries since they are prerequisites for long-term competitive sustainability. The categories as they are now are non-mutually exclusive and have overlapping characteristics. Exploring whether there are characteristics (e.g., conflict resolution) that should be exclusive to one category is the next step in our research.

Acknowledgements This research and development project is funded by the German Federal Ministry of Education and Research (BMBF) within the Incentives and Economics of Data Sharing Funding Action (IEDS004). The author is responsible for the content of this publication.

References

Abbas, A.E., Agahari, W., van de Ven, M., Zuiderwijk, A. & Reuver, M. de (2021) Business Data Sharing through Data Marketplaces: A Systematic Literature Review. *Journal of Theoretical and Applied Electronic Commerce Research*, 16(7), 3321–3339. Available from: https://doi.org/10.3390/jtaer16070180.

Advaneo GmbH (2023) *Advaneo Data Marketplace*. Available from: https://www.advaneo-datamarketplace.de/database/en/ [Accessed 9 March 2023].

Agahari, W., Dolci, R. & Reuver, M. de (2021) Business Model Implications of privacy-preserving technologies in data marketplaces: The case of multi-party computation. In: *Proceedings of the 29th European Conference on Information Systems*, A Virtual AIS Conference.

Agahari, W. & Reuver, M. de (2022) Rethinking consumers' data sharing decisions with the emergence of multi-party computation: an experimental design for evaluation. In: *Proceedings of the 30th European Conference on Information Systems*, Timisoara: Romania.

Albrecht, S., Reichert, S., Schmid, J., Strüker, J., Neumann, D. & Fridgen, G. (2018) Dynamics of Blockchain Implementation – A Case Study from the Energy Sector. In: *Proceedings of the 51st Hawaii International Conference on System Sciences*, Hawaii: USA.

Azkan, C., Möller, F., Ebel, M., Iqbal, T., Otto, B. & Pöppelbuss, J. (2022) Hunting the Treasure: Modeling Data Ecosystem Participant Value. In: *Proceedings of the 43rd International Conference on Information Systems*, Kopenhagen: Denmark.

Bastiaansen, H., Dalmolen, S., Kollenstart, M. & Punter, M. (2019) Infrastructural Sovereignty over Agreement and Transaction Data ('Metadata') in an Open Network-Model for Multilateral Sharing of Sensitive Data. In: *Proceedings of the 40th International Conference on Information Systems*, Munich: Germany.

Bastiaansen, H., Dalmolen, S., Kollenstart, M. & van Engers, T.M. (2020) User-Centric Network-Model for Data Control with Interoperable Legal Data Sharing Artefacts. In: *Proceedings of the 24th Pacific Asia Conference on Information Systems*, Dubai: UAE.

Bergman, R., Abbas, A.E., Jung, S., Werker, C. & Reuver, M. de (2022) Business model archetypes for data marketplaces in the automotive industry: Contrasting business models of data marketplaces with varying ownership and orientation structures. *Electronic Markets*, 32(2), 747–765.

Capgemini Research Institute (2021) *Data Sharing Masters: How smart organizations use data ecosystems to gain an unbeatable competitive edge*. Available from: https://www.capgemini.com/de-de/insights/research/data-sharing-masters/ [Accessed 22 February 2023].

Catena-X (2023) *Catena-X*. Available from: https://catena-x.net/en/ [Accessed 25 January 2023].

CDQ (2023) *CDQ*. Available from: https://www.cdq.com/ [Accessed 25 January 2023].

Cirullies, J. & Schwede, C. (2021) On-demand Shared Digital Twins – An Information Architectural Model to Create Transparency in Collaborative Supply Networks. In: *Proceedings of the 54th Hawaii International Conference on System Sciences*, Hawaii: USA.

Dawex (2023) *Data Exchange Platform*. Available from: https://www.dawex.com/de/ [Accessed 7 March 2023].

Demchenko, Y. & Gommans, L. (2019) Open Data Market Architecture and Functional Components. In: *Proceedings of the 17th International Conference on High Performance Computing & Simulation*. Dublin:Ireland.

E015 (2023) *E015 digital ecosystem: regione lombardia*. Available from: https://www.e015.regione.lombardia.it/ [Accessed 7 March 2023].

Eisenmann, T., Parker, G. & van Alstyne, M. (2011) Platform envelopment. *Strategic Management Journal*, 32(12), 1270–1285. Available from: https://doi.org/10.1002/smj.935.

European Commission (2020) *REGULATION OF THE EUROPEAN PARLIAMENT AND OF THE COUNCIL: on European data governance (Data Governance Act)*. Available from: https://eur-lex.europa.eu/legal-content/EN/TXT/PDF/?uri=CELEX:52020PC0767&from=DE [Accessed 23 March 2022].

European Commission (2022a) *A European Strategy for data*. Available from: https://digital-strategy.ec.europa.eu/en/policies/strategy-data [Accessed 22 February 2023].

European Commission (2022b) *Data Act: Commission proposes measures for a fair and innovative data economy*. Available from: https://ec.europa.eu/commission/presscorner/detail/en/ip_22_1113 [Accessed 11 November 2022].

Fassnacht, M., Benz, C., Heinz, D., Leimstoll, J. & Satzger, G. (2023) Barriers to Data Sharing among Private Sector Organizations. In: *Proceedings of the 56th Hawaii International Conference on System Sciences*, Hawaii: USA.

Federal Ministry for Economic Cooperation and Development (2023) *More fairness in global supply chains – Germany leads the way*. Available from: https://www.bmz.de/en/issues/supply-chains [Accessed 9 March 2023].

Figueredo, K., Seed, D. & Wang, C. (2020) A Scalable, Standards-Based Approach for IoT Data Sharing and Ecosystem Monetization. *IEEE Internet of Things Journal*, 9(8), 5645–5652.

Fuerstenau, D. & Auschra, C. (2016) Open Digital Platforms in Health Care: Implementation and Scaling Strategies. In: *Thirty Seventh International Conference on Information Systems*, Dublin: Ireland.

Gelhaar, J., Gürpinar, T., Henke, M. & Otto, B. (2021) Towards a taxonomy of incentive mechanisms for data sharing in data ecosystems. In: *Proceedings of the 25th Pacific Asia Conference on Information Systems*, Dubai: UAE.

Gioia, D.A., Corley, K.G. & Hamilton, A.L. (2013) Seeking Qualitative Rigor in Inductive Research. *Organizational Research Methods*, 16(1), 15–31. Available from: https://doi.org/10.1177/1094428112452151.

GXFS.eu (2023) *Gaia-X Federation Services GXFS*. Available from: https://www.gxfs.eu/de/ [Accessed 7 March 2023].

Handelsblatt (2023) *Dax-Konzerne und Mittelständler schaffen Cloud-Plattform für Autoindustrie*. Available from: https://www.handelsblatt.com/unternehmen/industrie/catena-x-dax-konzerne-und-mittelstaendler-schaffen-cloud-plattform-fuer-autoindustrie/28954264.html [Accessed 22 February 2023].

Huang, L., Dou, Y., Liu, Y., Wang, J., Chen, G. & Zhang, X. et al. (2021) Toward a research framework to conceptualize data as a factor of production: The data marketplace perspective. *Fundamental Research*, 1(5), 586–594. Available from: https://doi.org/10.1016/j.fmre.2021.08.006.

Janssen, H. & Singh, J. (2022) Data intermediary. *Internet Policy Review*, 11(1). Available from: https://doi.org/10.14763/2022.1.1644.

Jussen, I., Schweihoff, J., Dahms, V., Möller, F. & Otto, B. (2023) Data Sharing Fundamentals: Definition and Characteristics. In: *Proceedings of the 56th Hawaii International Conference on System Sciences*, Hawaii: USA.

Kioses, E., Pramatari, K., Doukidis, G. & Bardaki, C. (2007) Measuring the Business Value of Electronic Supply Chain Collaboration: The Case of Electronic Invoicing. In: *Proceedings of the 20th Bled eConference*, Bled: Solvenia.

Koul, N.A., Sabrina, A. & Morin, J. (2018) Agreements Framework for Data Market Ecosystem. In: *Proceedings of the 13th Pre-ICIS Workshop on Information Security and Privacy*, San Francisco: USA.

Kurtz, C., Wittner, F., Semmann, M., Schulz, W. & Böhmann, T. (2019) The Unlikely Siblings in the GDPR Family: A Techno-Legal Analysis of Major Platforms in the Diffusion of Personal Data in Service Ecosystems. In: *Proceedings of the 52nd Hawaii International Conference on System Sciences*, Hawaii: USA.

Leemann, N. & Kanbach, D.K. (2022) Toward a taxonomy of dynamic capabilities – a systematic literature review. *Management Research Review*, 45(4), 486–501. Available from: https://doi.org/10.1108/MRR-01-2021-0066.

Levy, Y. & Ellis, T. (2006) A Systems Approach to Conduct an Effective Literature Review in Support of Information Systems Research. *International Journal of an Emerging Transdiscipline*, 9, 181–212. Available from: https://doi.org/10.28945/479.

Marotta, V., Wu, Y., Zhang, K. & Acquisti, A. (2022) The Welfare Impact of Targeted Advertising Technologies. *Information Systems Research*, 33(1), 131–151.

Noorian, Z., Iyilade, J., Mohkami, M. & Vassileva, J. (2014) Trust Mechanism for Enforcing Compliance to Secondary Data Use Contracts. In: *IEEE 13th International Conference on Trust, Security and Privacy in Computing and Communications*, Exeter: United Kingdom.

Öksüz, A. (2014) Turning Dark into White Clouds – A Framework on Trust Building in Cloud Providers via Websites. In: *Proceedings of the 20th Americas Conference on Information Systems*, Savannah: USA.

Oliveira, M.I.S., Barros Lima, G.d.F. & Farias Lóscio, B. (2019) Investigations into Data Ecosystems: a systematic mapping study. *Knowledge and Information Systems*, 61(2), 589–630. Available from: https://doi.org/10.1007/s10115-018-1323-6.

Oliveira, M.I.S. & Lóscio, B.F. (2018) What is a data ecosystem? In: *Proceedings of the 19th Annual International Conference on Digital Government Research: Governance in the Data Age (dg.o '18)*, New York: USA.

Opriel, S., Möller, F., Burkhardt, U. & Otto, B. (2021) Requirements for Usage Control based Exchange of Sensitive Data in Automotive Supply Chains. In: *Proceedings of the 54th Hawaii International Conference on System Sciences, Proceedings of the Annual Hawaii International Conference on System Sciences*, Hawaii: USA.

Osterrieder, P., Budde, L. & Friedli, T. (2020) The smart factory as a key construct of industry 4.0: A systematic literature review. *International Journal of Production Economics*, 221, 107476. Available from: https://doi.org/10.1016/j.ijpe.2019.08.011.

Otto, B. & Jarke, M. (2019) Designing a multi-sided data platform: findings from the International Data Spaces case. *Electronic Markets*, 29(4), 561–580. Available from: https://doi.org/10.1007/s12525-019-00362-x.

Otto, B., Steinbuß, S., Teuscher, A. & Lohmann, S. (2019) *Reference Architecture Model: Version 3.0*. Available from: https://www.fraunhofer.de/content/dam/zv/en/fields-of-research/industrial-data-space/IDS-Reference-Architecture-Model.pdf [Accessed 11 September 2021].

Paré, G., Trudel, M.-C., Jaana, M. & Kitsiou, S. (2015) Synthesizing information systems knowledge: A typology of literature reviews. *Information & Management*, 52(2), 183–199. Available from: https://doi.org/10.1016/j.im.2014.08.008.

Perscheid, G., Ostern, N.K. & Moormann, J. (2020) Determining Platform Governance: Framework for Classifying Governance Types. In: *Proceedings of the 41st International Conference on Information Systems*, Hyderabad: India.

Richter, H. & Slowinski, P.R. (2019) The Data Sharing Economy: On the Emergence of New Intermediaries. *IIC - International Review of Intellectual Property and Competition Law*, 50, 4–29. Available from: https://doi.org/10.1007/s40319-018-00777-7.

Roa, J., Villarreal, P. & Fantinato, M. (2017) Institutional Violence Complaints in Argentina: A Privacy Study. In: *Proceedings of the 50th Hawaii International Conference on System Sciences*, Hawaii: USA.

Schmidt, M.-C. (2022) Determination of Relational Success? On the Interrelation of Digital Industrial Platforms and Buyer-Supplier Relationships. In: *Proceedings of the 26th Pacific Asia Conference on Information Systems, Annual Pacific Asia Conference on Information Systems*, July, 5–9, Taipei-Sydney.

Schreieck, M., Wiesche, M. & Krcmar, H. (2016) DESIGN AND GOVERNANCE OF PLATFORM ECOSYSTEMS - KEY CONCEPTS AND ISSUES FOR FUTURE RESEARCH. In: *Proceedings of the 24th European Conference on Information Systems*, Istanbul: Turkey.

Snowflake (2023) *Snowflake: Customer Stories: Snowflake Data Cloud*. Available from: https://www.snowflake.com/en/why-snowflake/customers/ [Accessed 25 January 2023].

Sonehara, N., Echizen, I. & Wohlgemuth, S. (2011) Isolation in Cloud Computing and Privacy-Enhancing Technologies. *Business & Information Systems Engineering*, 3, 155–162. Available from: https://doi.org/10.1007/s12599-011-0160-x.

Sovity (2023) *sovity - Data Sovereignty as a Service*. Available from: https://sovity.de/de/start/ [Accessed 7 March 2023].

Stachon, M., Möller, F., Guggenberger, T. & Tomcyzk, M. (2023) Understanding Data Trusts. In: *Proceedings of the 31st European Conference 2023*, Kristiansand: Norway.

Sterk, F., Peukert, C., Hunke, F. & and Weinhardt, C. (2022) Understanding Car Data Monetization: A Taxonomy of Data-Driven Business Models in the Connected Car Domain. In: *Proceedings of the 17th International Conference on Wirtschaftsinformatik*, Nürnberg: Germany.

Susha, I., Janssen, M. & Verhulst, S. (2017) Data Collaboratives as a New Frontier of Cross-Sector Partnerships in the Age of Open Data: Taxonomy Development. In: *Proceedings of the 50th Hawaii International Conference on System Sciences*, Hawaii: USA.

Templier, M. & Paré, G. (2015) A Framework for Guiding and Evaluating Literature Reviews. *Communications of the Association for Information Systems*, 37, 112–137. Available from: https://doi.org/10.17705/1CAIS.03706.

van de Ven, M., Abbas, A.E., Kwee, Z. & Reuver, M. de (2021) Creating a Taxonomy of Business Models for Data Marketplaces. In: *Proceedings of the 34th BLED eConference*, Online Conference.

van den Broek, T. & van Veenstra, A.F. (2015) Modes of Governance in Inter-Organizational Data Collaborations. In: *Proceedings of the 23rd European Conference on Information Systems*, Münster: Germany.

vom Brocke, J., Simons, A., Riemer, K., Niehaves, B., Plattfaut, R. & Cleven, A. (2015) Standing on the Shoulders of Giants: Challenges and Recommendations of Literature Search in Information systems research. *Communications of the Association for Information Systems*, 37(9), 205–224.

Watson, R.T., Piccoli, G., Brohman, M.K. & Parasuraman, A. (2008) Customer-Managed Interactions: A New Paradigm for Firm-Customer Relationships. *MIS Quarterly Executive*, 4(2), 319–327.

Webster, J. & Watson, R.T. (2002) Analyzing the Past to Prepare for the Future: Writing a Literature Review. *MIS Quarterly*, 26(2), xiii–xxiii. Available from: http://dl.acm.org/citation.cfm?id=2017160.2017162.

Wernick, A., Olk, C. & Grafenstein, M. von (2020) Defining Data Intermediaries - A Clearer View through the Lens of Intellectual Property Governance. *Technology and Regulation*, 65–81. Available from: https://doi.org/10.26116/techreg.2020.007.

Winter, J.S. & Davidson, E. (2017) Investigating Values in Personal Health Data Governance Models. In: *Proceedings of the 23rd Americas Conference on Information Systems, Annual Americas Conference on Information Systems*, Boston: USA.

Woodside, J.M. (2008) Dynamic Healthcare Connectivity and Collaboration with Multi-Agent Systems. In: *Proceedings of the Fourteenth Americas Conference on Information Systems*, Toronto: Canada.

World Economic Forum (2021) *6 ways data sharing can shape a better future*. Available from: https://www.weforum.org/agenda/2021/04/six-ways-data-sharing-can-shape-a-better-future/ [Accessed 13 February 2023].

Woroch, R. & Strobel, G. (2022) Show me the Money: How to monetize data in data-driven business models? In: *Proceedings of the 17th International Conference on Wirtschaftsinformatik*, Nürnberg: Germany.

Zrenner, J., Möller, F., Jung, C., Eitel, A. & Otto, B. (2019) Usage control architecture options for data sovereignty in business ecosystems. *Journal of Enterprise Information Management*, 32(3), 477–495. Available from: https://doi.org/10.1108/JEIM-03-2018-0058.

Governance of Decentralized Platform Ecosystems

Vincent Heimburg, Hanna Alakbarov, and Manuel Wiesche

Abstract Platform governance is critical for the success of digital platform ecosystems (DPEs). However, we know little about the governance of decentralized DPEs. Studies on centralized DPEs find that platform owners decide about, implement, and adapt the governance practices over the lifecycle of a platform ecosystem. It remains unclear what the growing body of literature on decentralized platform ecosystems reveals about their governance. To close this gap, we conducted a structured literature review of Information Systems literature. In 54 studies, we find five key dimensions of governance of decentralized DPEs. We contribute to literature by contrasting the governance practices, mechanisms, and processes of centralized DPEs and decentralized DPEs. We highlight three main differences: Ex-ante definition rather than an evolution of governance, distributed and overlapping roles (platform founders, platform enhancers, platform validators), and collective decision-making by fractional platform owners.

Keywords Digital platforms · Decentral · Blockchain · Distributed · Decentralized autonomous organizations

1 Introduction

The rise of digital platform ecosystems (DPEs) has revolutionized economic transactions for organizations and individuals. Platform governance is critical to the success of DPEs (Schreieck et al. 2022). Thus, it is an important topic in Information Systems

---

V. Heimburg (✉) · H. Alakbarov · M. Wiesche
Chair of Digital Transformation, TU Dortmund University, Dortmund, Germany
e-mail: vincent.heimburg@tu-dortmund.de

H. Alakbarov
e-mail: hanna.alakbarov@tu-dortmund.de

M. Wiesche
e-mail: manuel.wiesche@tu-dortmund.de

D. Beverungen et al. (eds.), *Transforming the Digitally Sustainable Enterprise*, Lecture Notes in Information Systems and Organisation 76,
https://doi.org/10.1007/978-3-031-80125-9_6

(IS) research and beyond (Chen et al. 2022; Halckenhaeusser et al. 2020). Platform governance refers to the task of aligning and steering goals, strategies, and behavior of the autonomous participants in DPEs (Chen et al. 2022).

IS research finds that governance of centralized DPEs is an ongoing process shaped by a single platform owner. The platform owner organization defines, adapts, and enforces the platform governance practices over the lifecycle of the platform (Tan et al. 2015; Schreieck et al. 2022). This makes a platform owner more powerful than the other participants in the DPE. Namely, platform complementors and end-users depend upon the decisions of the platform owner (Chen et al. 2022). Lately, the fairness and distribution of power in DPEs are factors in question regarding platform regulation and platform self-regulation (Cusumano et al. 2021; Cutolo and Kenney 2021).

Decentralized DPEs are increasingly subject to research. Researchers especially study the potential and use of blockchain technology in inter-organizational relationships (Chong et al. 2019). To this end, some IS research refers to decentralized autonomous organizations (DAOs) (Ziegler and Welpe 2022). However, some studies consider decentralized DPEs without blockchain technology. Examples of such platforms include Wikipedia, which some elected volunteers govern, and Stack Overflow, which is cooperatively governed by a core group of decision-makers (Kretschmer et al. 2022). Some scholars see decentralized DPEs as a solution for some of the problems of centralized platforms. For example, the potentials are to reduce coordination costs or to improve the distribution of power (Chong et al. 2019; Chen et al. 2021).

As centralized DPEs, decentralized DPEs require governance mechanisms. Yet, the mechanisms differ, for example, due to the decentralization of decision rights in the DPE (O'Mahony and Karp 2022). In addition, the absence of a central authority affects the governance dynamics. The distribution of authority might change the state of knowledge on the coordination of platform participants (Hsieh and Vergne 2023). Thus, it remains unclear what current research knows about the governance of decentralized DPEs.

This incites us to study the governance of decentralized DPEs in more detail and motivates our research question: *What are governance mechanisms for decentralized digital platform ecosystems?*

To answer the question, we conducted a structured literature review in high-impact journals and conference proceedings. The search yielded 309 sources, in which we analyzed findings on the governance of decentralized DPEs. In total, we selected 54 publications that help to understand the idiosyncrasies of governance of decentralized DPEs.

The outcome of integrating the relevant findings is five key dimensions of governance of decentralized DPEs that contain different categories. We discover the distributed and overlapping roles, that a fundamental facet of the governance of decentralized DPEs is the necessity to define the governance mechanisms ex ante, and that the governance is relatively inflexible. We also discover some implications of collective decision-making in decentralized DPEs.

2 Background

2.1 Digital Platform Ecosystems

We define a digital platform ecosystem (DPE) as a sociotechnical system comprising of a central platform owner (alternatively platform provider) that implements governance mechanisms to facilitate value-creating interactions between the platform owner and autonomous complementors on the supply side and end-users on the demand side. Thus, a DPE always consists of a platform owner as an intermediary and participants on different market sides (Hein et al. 2020). End-users can be consumers, but also organizations, e.g., on business-to-business platforms (Hein et al. 2019).

In contrast, a mere (digital) ecosystem is a network of organizations that collaborate, which creates synergies. It does not necessarily have a central platform owner as an intermediary or multiple market sides (de Reuver et al. 2018).

Digital platform ecosystems can be centralized or decentralized. In centralized DPEs, a single organization serves as the platform owner. In decentralized DPEs, the role of the platform owner distributes across multiple organizations. Decentralized DPEs can base on an underlying blockchain, while also non-blockchain decentralized DPEs exist (Chen et al. 2021; O'Mahony and Karp 2022).

2.2 Governance of Centralized Digital Platform Ecosystems

Platform governance is about aligning and steering the goals, strategies, and behavior of the autonomous participants in digital platform ecosystems (DPEs) and enforcing the governance (Chen et al. 2022). Research on centralized DPEs highlights four key dimensions of platform governance: roles, rules, incentives, and boundary resources (Schreieck et al. 2016; Chen et al. 2022). Figure 1 illustrates these dimensions of governance mechanisms in centralized DPEs.

The allocation of roles is a key element of understanding the governance of centralized DPEs. A single platform owner organization maintains the privilege of governing and orchestrating the DPE. Thus, it decides on the platform's rules, incentives, and boundary resources. In turn, complementors and end-users participate in the DPE under the given rules and incentives and complementors use the boundary resources (Chen et al. 2022).

Concerning rules, the platform owner defines access conditions and decision rights in the DPE. This includes questions of balancing platform openness and control, which are popular in IS platform research (Benlian et al. 2015; Ondrus et al. 2015; Schreieck et al. 2022).

A platform owner also governs the DPE by defining the monetary and non-monetary reward structures on the platform. This helps to start, maintain, and steer the participation of complementors and end-users in the DPE (Chen et al. 2022).

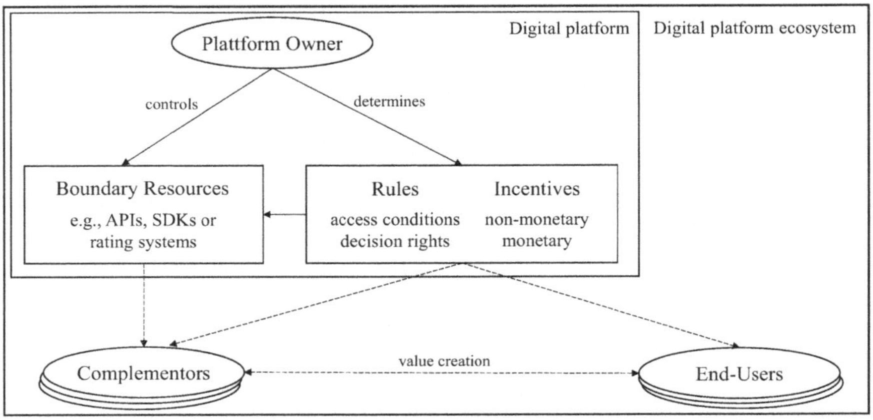

Fig. 1 Dimensions of the governance of centralized digital platform ecosystems (DPEs)

The fourth dimension of platform governance mechanisms is boundary resources, which relate to the rules and incentives. With the goal of materializing specific rules and incentives, the platform owner controls the boundary resources complementors may use (Ofe and Sandberg 2023). The boundary resources provide rules for the interactions by providing (technical) guardrails to platform participation and increase platform participation by supporting the development of products or services (Krijestorac et al. 2020; Ghazawneh and Henfridsson 2013). Examples of boundary resources include application programming interfaces (APIs), software development kits (SDKs), further tools for complementors, and documentation (Guo et al. 2021; Heimburg et al. 2022).

2.3 Governance of Decentralized Digital Platform Ecosystems

In decentralized DPEs, the role of platform owner, and therefore the privilege to govern the DPE is distributed across multiple organizations. Usually, these organizations are participants in the DPE (Zhao et al. 2022). Thus, in varying degrees, participants in decentralized DPEs collectively make decisions about platform governance (Chen et al. 2021; O'Mahony and Karp 2022).

Literature mainly distinguishes between two types of decentralized DPEs. Some scholars study decentralized DPEs whose decentralization is based on blockchain technology. Others study decentralized DPEs whose decentralization is based on collective decision-making (Sockin and Xiong 2023; Joglekar et al. 2022; O'Mahony and Karp 2022). The latter includes consortia that operate platforms (Hein et al. 2020).

The literature on the governance of decentralized DPEs does not provide a uniform understanding of the dimensions of governance mechanisms (Joglekar et al. 2022;

Zhao et al. 2022). While in centralized DPEs, a platform owner defines rules and incentives and controls boundary resources, literature does not define its equivalent in decentralized DPEs.

However, existing research scrutinizes the operational governance of decentralized DPEs based on an underlying blockchain. Unlike in centralized DPEs, operational governance can happen automatically, as rules and incentives are solidified in code. Compared to centralized platforms, this enables transparent visibility into all rules and incentives (Kamble et al. 2023).

3 Method

The purpose of this paper is to give an overview of current IS research on the governance of decentralized DPEs. To this end, we perform a structured literature review of high-impact Information Systems literature. Given the wealth of literature on digital platforms, we used two main criteria to decide which publications are relevant. For the first criterion, we focused on the decentralized orientation of a digital platform, which is our unit of analysis. For the second criterion, governance strategies should be central topics and be set in relation to the digital platform. Overall, we developed a uniform comparison that aims to examine how governance in decentralized DPEs is conceptualized in practice. In order to identify relevant literature and achieve a systematic comparison, we applied the guidelines of Webster and Watson (2002) and vom Brocke et al. (2009).

We limited our search to journals included in the Senior Scholars' Basket of Journals of the Association for Information Systems and the VHB JOURQUAL3 ranking A+ and A. Additionally, we completed this selection of journals with the proceedings of the International Conference on Information Systems (ICIS) (Webster and Watson 2002) (Table 1).

Table 1 illustrates our search string. We searched title, keywords, and abstract. We included the terms "ledger*" and "on-chain" in our search string to take into account that decentralization in DPEs is often implemented through blockchain technology (Zhao et al. 2022). We included the term "organization*" in our search string to acknowledge research on decentralized autonomous organizations, which emerged from an initial search. The initial search also showed that the term "blockchain" is too broad and does not address specific governance mechanisms. In total, the search query returned 195 journal articles and 114 conference articles.

Next, we selected a set of relevant research papers by going through each paper's abstract and identified 52 papers, which need to be examined in more detail (Webster and Watson 2002). In the selection process, we paid particular attention to ensuring that the publications concern (a) a decentralized platform structure and (b) potential governance mechanisms (Zhao et al. 2022). Hereafter, in line with vom Brocke et al. (2009), we performed a forward and backward search based on the selected articles. This resulted in finding two additional articles that are concerned with the topic but were not captured with the search terms.

Table 1 Summary of the literature search process

Outlet		Search	Hits	Selected
AIS basket of eight IS journals	ISR	decentral* or distributed* and platform* or ecosystem* or on-chain or ledger* or organization *	9	3
	JAIS		3	3
	MISQ		11	2
	JIT		9	2
	ISJ		8	2
	JSIS		3	2
	JMIS		11	1
	EJIS		4	0
VHB JQ3 A+ & A	Manage Sci		31	3
	POM		16	3
	Strateg Man J		7	2
	INFORMS JoC		5	2
	Others		78	16
ICIS conference			114	11
Forward and backward search				2
		Total	309	**54**

Following, we analyzed the 54 selected publications[1] to identify patterns and develop concepts (Webster and Watson 2002). We inductively coded dimensions of governance in an explorative coding process, which we repeated iteratively to develop conclusive coding constructs (Lacity et al. 2010).

4 Results

Table 2 illustrates five key dimensions we identified in the literature, which deal with different aspects of the governance of decentralized DPEs. We also identified different categories of most dimensions. For each category, the table provides illustrative articles.

Dynamic Roles. Dynamics of roles characterize the governance of decentralized DPEs. The distribution of participants with decision rights and platform participants without decision rights related to governance can be dynamic, and their roles do not map one-to-one on the prevalent platform participant roles platform owner, complementor, and end-user. In a sense, all participants with decision rights are fractional platform owners, while they can also be complementor and/or end-user (Hsieh and Vergne 2023; Tsoukalas and Falk 2020). Overall, evaluating the structure and degree of distribution of decision rights is essential for understanding a platform's decentralization of governance (Sockin and Xiong 2023; Shafiei Gol et al. 2019).

[1] Full list, including the articles not selected, available upon request.

Table 2 Key dimensions of governance of decentralized DPEs

Key dimension	Category	Illustrative articles
Roles	Dynamic roles	Hsieh and Vergne (2023), Sockin and Xiong (2023)
Boundary resources	Documentation	Zhao et al. (2022), Huberman et al. (2021)
	Distributed data infrastructure	Biais et al. (2019), Babich and Hilary (2020)
Decision rights	Distribution of power	Chen et al. (2021), Beck et al. (2018)
	Verification of transactions	Malhotra et al. (2020), Tsoukalas and Falk (2020)
Control	Definition	Shafiei Gol et al. (2019), Karunakaran et al. (2022)
	Entry barriers	Chod et al. (2022), Ziegler and Welpe (2022)
	Enforcing	Mini et al. (2021), Rossi et al. (2019), Benedict et al. (2022)
Involvement incentives	Monetary (e.g., token/crypto)	Ziolkowski et al. (2020), Beck et al. (2018)
	Non-monetary	Kuang et al. (2019), Russell et al. (2017)

Understanding the role of participants with decision rights is also critical to determine the process of the governance of decentralized DPEs. Some participants with decision-making rights may only be involved in establishing the platform and defining its governance. Others might join the platform later and participate to varying degrees in defining new or evolving existing governance mechanisms and rules. Also, it is possible they continuously participate in varying scopes and intensities (Beck et al. 2018).

Boundary resources. The allocation of boundary resources plays a role in the governance of decentralized DPEs (see Table 2).

Documentation helps ensure a high level of interaction, as the governance of decentralized DPEs is based on participation (Huberman et al. 2021). Zhao et al. (2022) discover a positive connection between a high degree of information sharing and the participation of stakeholders. Thus, interested platform participants can access detailed information on platform governance mechanisms and processes (Shafiei Gol et al. 2019). This positive relationship applies to blockchain-based organizations as well as other decentralized DPEs (Xiao et al. 2020; Babich and Hilary 2020).

Another important boundary resource is the data infrastructure in decentralized DPEs. Decentralized DPEs distribute data storage efficiently (Salvador and Madiedo 2021). Blockchain literature identifies this type of data infrastructure under the term *distributed ledger*. Distributed ledgers are digital systems for recording transactions in multiple locations simultaneously. It is a collection of, for example, transactions, records, and identities. A consensus mechanism, which we will present later, is essential for distributed ledgers (Rossi et al. 2019). Unlike traditional databases, distributed ledgers have no central data storage or management function (Babich and Hilary 2020; Biais et al. 2019).

Decision rights. The distribution of decision rights across platform participants determines the degree of decentralization of a DPE and accountability (Biais et al. 2019; Beck et al. 2018). We identify two subordinate categories that describe the allocation of decision rights (see Table 2).

In their nature, decision-making power is distributed in decentralized DPEs. Yet, the details are case-specific. The distribution of power to define or evolve the governance mechanisms and rules deduces from the ownership structure, distribution of governance tokens and/or bylaws of the decentralized DPE (O'Mahony and Karp 2022; Mini et al. 2021). Furthermore, the terms or protocol of the platform specify how the governance takes place. To this end, decentralized DPEs based on an underlying blockchain can exhibit off-chain or on-chain governance. Both alternatives concern defining or evolving the governance mechanisms and rules and not the validation of transactions, which we will discuss later. *Off-chain governance* allows for defining or evolving the governance mechanisms through a discussion process among participants (Werner 2023). *On-chain governance* allows a token-weighted voting approach to decide on proposed protocol changes (Tsoukalas and Falk 2020). The more tokens a participant holds, the more weight their vote holds. Thus, on-chain governance leads to a transparent and invariable election result (Chod et al. 2022; Stinner 2022). Both options can result in changes to the blockchain protocol, which contains the governance mechanisms and rules (Huberman et al. 2021; Zhao et al. 2022). Typically, participants must reach a consensus or adopt a hard fork with a subset of participants that reach a consensus (Chen et al. 2021).

Finally, the verification of transactions is a key category of decision rights. It typically happens by a majority vote of so-called validators. This has nothing to do with changes to the governance mechanisms and rules but is all about enforcing them. It is still relevant for understanding the governance of decentralized DPEs. Theoretically, participants could manipulate voting with a *majority attack* and thereby disregard the predefined governance mechanisms and rules (Stinner 2022). Thus, in some way, manipulated enforcement of governance has similarities with governance itself. For the verification of transactions in decentralized DPEs based on an underlying blockchain, the infrastructure of validators automatically validates each transaction in the DPE against the defined governance mechanisms and rules (Werner 2023). The validators are active participants in the DPEs that either show *proof-of-stake* of tokens or *proof-of-work* in solving hash puzzles. Only after a majority (typically) vote of the validators the transaction is adopted in all ledgers in all notes (Chod et al. 2022). In contrast, decentralized DPEs not based on an underlying blockchain mostly lack a predefined process that enforces that transactions follow the governance mechanisms and rules. Thus, literature refers to the potential complexities and inefficiencies of this process (O'Mahony and Karp 2022).

Control. Platform control refers to defining and enforcing the governance mechanisms and rules to guide a DPE's usage and trajectory (Beck et al. 2018). Throughout the lifecycle of a decentralized DPE, the distribution of decision rights among participants is decisive, as presented in the section on decision rights. All organizations with some part of the decision rights have partial control (Biais et al. 2019).

Before a decentralized DPE launches, a group of initial participants defines an initial set of governance mechanisms and rules. In the case of a DPE based on an underlying blockchain, the mechanisms and rules (e.g., on access conditions, voting processes, or verification of transactions) are partly defined and anchored in a blockchain protocol. The protocol and its history are recorded in the distributed ledger, visible to all participants (Wörner et al. 2022; Ziegler and Welpe 2022; Benedict et al. 2022). Regardless of whether the DPE is based on a blockchain, the details of the mechanisms and rules determine whether it is possible to adapt them after launch. If so, participants with decision rights may evolve the platform governance by suggesting or voting on changes to the governance mechanisms and rules (Zhao et al. 2022; Huberman et al. 2021; Ziegler and Welpe 2022). This process might happen on-chain or off-chain and typically by consensus, as described in the decision rights findings (Tsoukalas and Falk 2020; Werner 2023).

A major element of governance mechanisms and rules is the entry barriers of a decentralized DPE. Becoming a participant in a decentralized DPE is often permissionless. In contrast, as presented earlier, participating in shaping the governance mechanisms and rules typically depends on the ownership structure, the distribution of governance tokens and/or bylaws (Ziegler and Welpe 2022). Still, in the case of decentralized DPEs based on blockchain technology, the entry barriers are transparent, as they are explicit in the protocol (Kamble et al. 2023).

Next to the definition of governance mechanisms and rules, platform control also concerns enforcing the governance mechanisms and rules. The enforcement differs significantly across cases. Actors in decentralized DPEs not based on an underlying blockchain mainly enforce manually (O'Mahony and Karp 2022; Kornberger et al. 2017). In contrast, decentralized DPEs based on an underlying blockchain mainly rely on enforcing governance mechanisms and rules through code (Rossi et al. 2019; Mini et al. 2021). The decentralized blockchain infrastructure automatically validates every transaction in the DPE against the defined governance mechanisms and rules. This formalized distributed validation process ensures that enforcing the coded governance mechanisms and rules is distributed among participants. Thus, it cannot be manipulated by one participant or a minority group (Stinner 2022; Werner 2023).

Involvement incentives. Individual participants with few decision rights may have little influence in shaping and enforcing governance mechanisms and might consequently become less engaged (Chen et al. 2021). Therefore, many decentralized DPEs incentivize participation in governance activities (Shafiei Gol et al. 2019). We identify two types of incentives in the literature (see Table 2). On the one hand, incentives such as financial rewards. On the other hand, non-monetary incentives such as a valuation system. Extant research provides detailed insights regarding monetary incentives. Non-monetary incentives have received limited attention (Zhao et al. 2022; Tsoukalas and Falk 2020). In platforms based on blockchain technology, monetary incentives can base on token gains. For example, validators might automatically receive tokens for their participation in proof-of-stake or proof-of-work validations. Thus, financial rewards can be allocated without the evaluation of a managerial position (Xiao et al. 2020; Kuang et al. 2019; Ziolkowski et al. 2020).

While the majority of literature on incentives in the governance of decentralized DPEs focuses on tokenization within blockchain-based DPEs, non-monetary rewards also play a role. Mainly for non-blockchain platforms, rewards like membership level or rewards or prizes are also found as incentives (Kuang et al. 2019; Russell et al. 2017).

5 Discussion

The results illustrate the current state of research on the governance of decentralized digital platforms. We find five different key dimensions of governance and ten corresponding categories (Table 2). Our systematization may serve as a foundation for scholars and practitioners to understand the governance of decentralized digital platforms better. It also provides entry points for future studies. For example, it offers the opportunity to identify unfilled gaps or under-researched areas (e.g., decentralized DPEs not based on an underlying blockchain) and to consider them as targets for future research (Sockin and Xiong 2023; Joglekar et al. 2022; O'Mahony and Karp 2022).

Distributed and overlapping roles. The roles in the definition, evolution, and enforcement of platform governance in decentralized DPEs distinguish from existing findings on platform governance in centralized DPEs. In centralized DPEs, a single platform owner is responsible for the entire governance process. In contrast, the governance of decentralized DPEs requires multiple actors with decision rights to participate. One group of these actors defines the governance mechanisms before the launch of the decentralized DPE. We suggest calling such a role *platform founders* (Table 3). Another group of actors may evolve the governance mechanisms after the launch of the decentralized DPE. We propose to refer to such a role that suggests, votes on and implements evolvements as *platform enhancers* (Table 3). An event at a major scale that highlights this role is the change of Ethereum's consensus mechanism and the underlying architecture from proof-of-work to proof-of-stake (Dillet 2022). Such an event requires actors with decision rights (platform enhancers) to agree by consensus and participate in changing the governance mechanisms of a decentralized DPE. Moreover, the actors enforcing the governance mechanisms are *platform validators*, as discussed in existing literature (Sockin and Xiong 2023). The actors holding any of the roles described above in the governance of decentralized DPEs are *fractional platform owners* if they possess a part of the decision rights. In this way, we contribute to the discussion on the instability of roles in DPEs (Heimburg and Wiesche 2022).

Table 3 Governance mechanisms of centralized DPEs and decentralized DPEs

Governance mechanisms		Centralized DPEs	Decentralized DPEs
Roles	Type of roles	Platform owner: decides on rules, incentives, and boundary resources	Platform founders: initially define governance mechanisms
			Platform enhancers: evolve governance mechanisms
		Participants: Complementors on supply-side. End-users on demand-side. Both take advantage of demand on platform	Platform validators (*miners* in case of proof-of-work): enforce governance
			Participants: complementors and end-users. May also be founders, enhancers, and/or validators
	Ownership	Proprietary, usually by platform owner	Distributed, depends on platform
Boundary resources	Data infrastructure	Centralized	Often distributed
		Private access	Often public access
	Documentation	Proprietary, up to the platform owner	Shared across platform participants (distributed ledger)
Decision rights	Distribution of power	Centralized with a platform owner	Determined distribution of decision rights
	Accountability	As per the gusto of the platform owner	Distributed through voting mechanisms
	Enforcement of governance	Centralized, not transparent	Distributed verification of transactions, transparent
Control	Source of the control	Platform owner's decisions	Decisions of actors with decision rights
	Entry barriers	Up to platform owner. Not transparent	Participation often permission-less. Often transparent
	Permanence of governance	Flexibly adapted by platform owner	Fixed by design. Voting required to evolve, if possible
Incen-tives	Reward structure	Platform owner incentivized by platform success	Possibly monetary (token/crypto) incentives
			Non-monetary incentives

Collective decision-making. A fundamental principle of governance of decentralized DPEs is collective decision-making by actors with decision rights (Table 3). This differs from the central decision-making of a single platform owner in centralized

DPEs (Chen et al. 2022). However, this does not mean that the governance of decentralized DPEs is fully distributed across all platform participants. Some platform participants are rather "passive" without decision rights.

Nevertheless, the consequences of more collective decision-making affect the understanding of dependencies and power distribution in DPEs. Existing platform research that predominantly studies centralized DPEs finds high dependence of platform participants on the platform owner and power centralized with the platform owner (Cutolo and Kenney 2021; Hurni et al. 2022). While research emphasizes possible challenges with fairness, it also finds that centralized decision-making can be efficient (Smedlund and Faghankhani 2015). In decentralized DPEs, the structural power over the DPE is less centralized with a single platform owner as it is distributed across all the actors with decision rights. This suggests future research on the efficiency of governance of decentralized DPEs and the power distribution in DPEs with different designs and levels of decentralization. This could also open new directions for research on the fairness in DPEs or the government regulation of DPEs (Heimburg et al. 2023). Another option for future research is to study how to transform centralized DPEs to become more decentralized to solve issues with platform owner power.

Ex-ante definition rather than an evolution of governance. In decentralized DPEs, governance mechanisms must be defined ex ante, i.e., before the launch of the platform. This stems from the fact that the actors controlling the system must collectively agree on them, usually by consensus (Chen et al. 2021). In the case of decentralized DPEs based on an underlying blockchain, the mechanisms can be embedded in the blockchain protocol. This may enable enforcing the defined governance mechanisms automatically through a validation process (Ziegler and Welpe 2022). Although the actors with decision rights over a decentralized DPE must agree on the governance mechanisms ex ante, evolving the governance mechanisms is possible for most decentralized DPEs. In a way, governance of decentralized platforms is fixed by design, but not impossible to change. These characteristics of decentralized DPEs contrasts platform governance literature focused on centralized DPEs that assumes that governance is a process that is shaped over the lifecycle of the platform (Schreieck et al. 2022; Tan et al. 2015).

5.1 Practical Implications

Our findings also hold practical implications. We make organizations or consortia that consider establishing decentralized DPEs aware of the necessity to define governance mechanisms ex ante. This is especially important for decentralized DPEs based on an underlying blockchain. In the design of the principles, reasonable options for changing the governance mechanisms after the platform launch should be included. Furthermore, practitioners may consider the variations of power distributions across platforms, depending on the centralization, in their management or selection of a

DPE. We invite practitioners to use these insights to establish new decentralized DPEs.

5.2 Limitations

Our results underlie some limitations. The literature review might not cover all relevant publications due to the choice of outlets and keywords. In addition, coding differently, possibly recognizing distinctions in the type of decentralized DPEs, might generate different results. We invite fellow researchers to use our findings as a starting point for their research.

References

Babich, V.; Hilary, G. (2020): Distributed ledgers and operations: What operations management researchers should know about blockchain technology. In *Manufacturing and Service Operations Management* 22 (2), pp. 223–240. https://doi.org/10.1287/MSOM.2018.0752.

Beck, R.; Müller-Bloch, C.; King, J. L. (2018): Governance in the blockchain economy: A framework and research agenda. In *Journal of the Association for Information Systems* 19 (10), pp. 1020–1034. https://doi.org/10.17705/1jais.00518.

Benedict, Gayan; Sullivan, Clare; Gill, Asif (2022): Governance Challenges of AI-enabled Decentralized Autonomous Organizations: Toward a Research Agenda. In: ICIS 2022 Proceedings.

Benlian, A.; Hilkert, D.; Hess, T. (2015): How open is this platform? The meaning and measurement of platform openness from the complementors' perspective. In *J. Inf. Technol.* 30 (3), pp. 209–228. https://doi.org/10.1057/jit.2015.6.

Biais, B.; Bisière, C.; Bouvard, M.; Casamatta, C. (2019): The Blockchain Folk Theorem. In *Review of Financial Studies* 32 (5), pp. 1662–1715. https://doi.org/10.1093/rfs/hhy095.

Chen, Liang; Tong, Tony W.; Tang, Shaoqin; Han, Nianchen (2022): Governance and Design of Digital Platforms: A Review and Future Research Directions on a Meta-Organization. In *Journal of Management* 48 (1), pp. 147–184. https://doi.org/10.1177/01492063211045023.

Chen, Y.; Pereira, I.; Patel, P. C. (2021): Decentralized Governance of Digital Platforms. In *Journal of Management* 47 (5), pp. 1305–1337. https://doi.org/10.1177/0149206320916755.

Chod, J.; Trichakis, N.; Yang, S. A. (2022): Platform Tokenization: Financing, Governance, and Moral Hazard. In *Management Science* 68 (9), pp. 6411–6433. https://doi.org/10.1287/mnsc.2021.4225.

Chong, A.Y.L.; Lim, E.T.K.; Hua, X.; Zheng, S.; Tan, C.-W. (2019): Business on chain: A comparative case study of five blockchain-inspired business models. In *Journal of the Association for Information Systems* 20 (9), pp. 1308–1337. https://doi.org/10.17705/1jais.00568.

Cusumano, Michael A.; Gawer, Annabelle; Yoffie, David B. (2021): Can self-regulation save digital platforms? In *Industrial and Corporate Change* 30 (5), pp. 1259–1285. https://doi.org/10.1093/icc/dtab052.

Cutolo, Donato; Kenney, Martin (2021): Platform-Dependent Entrepreneurs: Power Asymmetries, Risks, and Strategies in the Platform Economy. In *Academy of Management Perspectives* 35 (4). https://doi.org/10.5465/amp.2019.0103.

de Reuver, M.; Sørensen, C.; Basole, R. C. (2018): The digital platform: A research agenda. In *Journal of Information Technology* 33 (2), pp. 124–135. https://doi.org/10.1057/s41265-016-0033-3.

Dillet, Romain (2022): Ethereum switches to proof-of-stake consensus after completing The Merge. In *TechCrunch*, 9/15/2022. Available online at https://techcrunch.com/2022/09/15/ethereum-switches-to-proof-of-stake-consensus-after-completing-the-merge, checked on 3/8/2023.

Ghazawneh, Ahmad; Henfridsson, Ola (2013): Balancing platform control and external contribution in third-party development: the boundary resources model. In *Information Systems Journal* 23 (2), pp. 173–192. https://doi.org/10.1111/j.1365-2575.2012.00406.x.

Guo, W.; Straub, D.; Zhang, P.; Cai, Z. (2021): How trust leads to commitment on microsourcing platforms: Unraveling the effects of governance and third-party mechanisms on triadic microsourcing relationships. In *MIS Quarterly: Management Information Systems* 45 (3), 1309–1348.

Halckenhaeusser, André; Foerderer, Jens; Heinzl, Armin (2020): Platform Governance Mechanisms: An Integrated Literature Review and Research Directions. In: ECIS 2020 Proceedings.

Heimburg, V.; van der Wal, N.; Wiesche, M. (2022): Professionalizing Small Complementors in a Heterogeneous Platform Ecosystem. A Logistics Case. In: Proceedings of 17th International Conference on Wirtschaftsinformatik.

Heimburg, Vincent; Schmitt, Julian; Wiesche, Manuel (2023): The Future of Digital Platform Design - The Case of the EU Platform Regulation Discourse. In: ECIS 2023 Proceedings.

Heimburg, Vincent; Wiesche, Manuel (2022): Relations Between Actors in Digital Platform Ecosystems: A Literature Review. In: ECIS 2022 Proceedings.

Hein, Andreas; Schreieck, Maximilian; Riasanow, Tobias; Setzke, David Soto; Wiesche, Manuel; Böhm, Markus; Krcmar, Helmut (2020): Digital platform ecosystems. In *Electron Markets* 30 (1), pp. 87–98. https://doi.org/10.1007/s12525-019-00377-4.

Hein, Andreas; Weking, Jörg; Schreieck, Maximilian; Wiesche, Manuel; Böhm, Markus; Krcmar, Helmut (2019): Value co-creation practices in business-to-business platform ecosystems. In *Electron Markets* 29 (3), pp. 503–518. https://doi.org/10.1007/s12525-019-00337-y.

Hsieh, Y.-Y.; Vergne, J.-P. (2023): The future of the web? The coordination and early-stage growth of decentralized platforms. In *Strategic Management Journal* 44 (3), pp. 829–857. https://doi.org/10.1002/smj.3455.

Huberman, G.; Leshno, J. D.; Moallemi, C. (2021): Monopoly without a Monopolist: An Economic Analysis of the Bitcoin Payment System. In *Review of Economic Studies* 88 (6), pp. 3011–3040. https://doi.org/10.1093/restud/rdab014.

Hurni, Thomas; Huber, Thomas L.; Dibbern, Jens (2022): Power dynamics in software platform ecosystems. In *Information Systems Journal* 32 (2), pp. 310–343. https://doi.org/10.1111/isj.12356.

Joglekar, N.; Anderson, E.G., Jr.; Lee, K.; Parker, G.; Settanni, E.; Srai, J. S. (2022): Configuration of digital and physical infrastructure platforms: Private and public perspectives. In *Production and Operations Management* 31 (12), pp. 4515–4528. https://doi.org/10.1111/poms.13865.

Kamble, V.; Shah, N.; Marn, D.; Parekh, A.; Ramchandran, K. (2023): The Square Root Agreement Rule for Incentivizing Truthful Feedback on Online Platforms. In *Management Science* 69 (1), pp. 377–403. https://doi.org/10.1287/mnsc.2022.4375.

Karunakaran, A.; Orlikowski, W. J.; Scott, S. V. (2022): Crowd-Based Accountability: Examining How Social Media Commentary Reconfigures Organizational Accountability. In *Organization Science* 33 (1), pp. 170–193. https://doi.org/10.1287/ORSC.2021.1546.

Kornberger, M.; Pflueger, D.; Mouritsen, J. (2017): Evaluative infrastructures: Accounting for platform organization. In *Accounting, Organizations and Society* 60, pp. 79–95. https://doi.org/10.1016/j.aos.2017.05.002.

Kretschmer, Tobias; Leiponen, Aija; Schilling, Melissa; Vasudeva, Gurneeta (2022): Platform ecosystems as meta-organizations: Implications for platform strategies. In *Strategic Management Journal* 43 (3), pp. 405–424. https://doi.org/10.1002/smj.3250.

Krijestorac, H.; Garg, R.; Mahajan, V. (2020): Cross-platform spillover effects in consumption of viral content: A quasi-experimental analysis using synthetic controls. In *Information Systems Research* 31 (2), pp. 449–472. https://doi.org/10.1287/ISRE.2019.0897.

Kuang, L.; Huang, N.; Hong, Y.; Yan, Z. (2019): Spillover Effects of Financial Incentives on Non-Incentivized User Engagement: Evidence from an Online Knowledge Exchange Platform. In *Journal of Management Information Systems* 36 (1), pp. 289–320. https://doi.org/10.1080/07421222.2018.1550564.

Lacity, Mary C.; Khan, Shaji; Yan, Aihua; Willcocks, Leslie P. (2010): A Review of the it Outsourcing Empirical Literature and Future Research Directions. In *J Inf Technol* 25 (4), pp. 395–433. https://doi.org/10.1057/jit.2010.21.

Malhotra, A.; Majchrzak, A.; Bonfield, W.; Myers, S. (2020): Engaging customer care employees in internal collaborative crowdsourcing: Managing the inherent tensions and associated challenges. In *Human Resource Management* 59 (2), pp. 121–134. https://doi.org/10.1002/hrm.21952.

Mini, Tobias; Eleunthia Wong Ellinger; Robert W. Gregory; Thomas Widjaja (2021): An Exploration of Governing via IT in Decentralized Autonomous Organizations. In: ICIS 2021 Proceedings.

Ofe, H. A.; Sandberg, J. (2023): The emergence of digital ecosystem governance: An investigation of responses to disrupted resource control in the Swedish public transport sector. In *Information Systems Journal* 33 (2), pp. 350–384. https://doi.org/10.1111/isj.12404.

O'Mahony, S.; Karp, R. (2022): From proprietary to collective governance: How do platform participation strategies evolve? In *Strategic Management Journal* 43 (3), pp. 530–562. https://doi.org/10.1002/smj.3150.

Ondrus, Jan; Gannamaneni, Avinash; Lyytinen, Kalle (2015): The Impact of Openness on the Market Potential of Multi-Sided Platforms: A Case Study of Mobile Payment Platforms. In *Journal of Information Technology* 30 (3), pp. 260–275. https://doi.org/10.1057/jit.2015.7.

Rossi, M.; Mueller-Bloch, C.; Thatcher, J. B.; Beck, R. (2019): Blockchain research in information systems: Current trends and an inclusive future research agenda. In *Journal of the Association for Information Systems* 20 (9), pp. 1388–1403. https://doi.org/10.17705/1jais.00571.

Russell, Nick; Barros, Alistair; Hofstede, Arthur ter (2017): Towards a Coordinative Theory for Flexible Work Collaboration. In: ICIS 2017 Proceedings.

Salvador, F.; Madiedo, J. P. (2021): Enabling Globally Distributed Projects: Effects of Project Interface Match and Related Technical Experience. In *Production and Operations Management* 30 (4), pp. 1052–1081. https://doi.org/10.1111/poms.13292.

Schreieck, Maximilian; Wiesche, Manuel; Krcmar, Helmut (2016): Design and Governance of Platform Ecosystems – Key Concepts and Issues for Future Research. In: ECIS 2016 Proceedings.

Schreieck, Maximilian; Wiesche, Manuel; Krcmar, Helmut (2022): From Product Platform Ecosystem to Innovation Platform Ecosystem: An Institutional Perspective on the Governance of Ecosystem Transformations. In *JAIS* 23 (6), pp. 1354–1385. https://doi.org/10.17705/1jais.00764.

Shafiei Gol, E.; Stein, M.-K.; Avital, M. (2019): Crowdwork platform governance toward organizational value creation. In *Journal of Strategic Information Systems* 28 (2), pp. 175–195. https://doi.org/10.1016/j.jsis.2019.01.001.

Smedlund, Anssi; Faghankhani, Hoda (2015): Platform Orchestration for Efficiency, Development, and Innovation. In: Proceedings of 48th Hawaii International Conference on System Sciences. 2015 48th Hawaii International Conference on System Sciences (HICSS). HI, USA, pp. 1380–1388.

Sockin, M.; Xiong, W. (2023): Decentralization through Tokenization. In *Journal of Finance* 78 (1), pp. 247–299. https://doi.org/10.1111/jofi.13192.

Stinner, Jona (2022): On the Economics of Bitcoin Mining: A Theoretical Framework and Simulation Evidence. In: ICIS 2022 Proceedings.

Tan, Barney; Pan, Shan; Lu, Xianghua; Huang, Lihua (2015): The Role of IS Capabilities in the Development of Multi-Sided Platforms: The Digital Ecosystem Strategy of Alibaba.com. In *JAIS* 16 (4), pp. 248–280. https://doi.org/10.17705/1jais.00393.

Tsoukalas, G.; Falk, B. H. (2020): Token-weighted crowdsourcing. In *Management Science* 66 (9), pp. 3843–3859. https://doi.org/10.1287/mnsc.2019.3515.

vom Brocke, Jan; Simons, Alexander; Niehaves, Bjoern; Niehaves, Bjorn; Reimer, Kai; Plattfaut, Ralf; Cleven, Anne (2009): Reconstructing the giant: On the importance of rigour in documenting the literature search process. In: ECIS 2009 Proceedings.

Webster, Jane; Watson, Richard T. (2002): Analyzing the Past to Prepare for the Future: Writing a Literature Review. In *MIS Quarterly* 26 (2), pp. xiii–xxiii. Available online at http://www.jstor.org/stable/4132319.

Werner, Johannes (2023): Blockchain Governance – A Systematic Literature Review. In Maria Papadaki, Paulo Rupino Da Cunha, Marinos Themistocleous, Klitos Christodoulou (Eds.): Information Systems, vol. 464. 1st ed. Cham: Springer (Lecture Notes in Business Information Processing), pp. 185–197.

Wörner, A.; Tiefenbeck, V.; Wortmann, F.; Meeuw, A.; Ableitner, L.; Fleisch, E.; Azevedo, I. (2022): Bidding on a Peer-to-Peer Energy Market: An Exploratory Field Study. In *Information Systems Research* 33 (3), pp. 794–808. https://doi.org/10.1287/isre.2021.1098.

Xiao, S.; Chen, Y.-J.; Tang, C. S. (2020): Knowledge sharing and learning among smallholders in developing economies: Implications, incentives, and reward mechanisms. In *Operations Research* 68 (2), pp. 435–452. https://doi.org/10.1287/opre.2019.1869.

Zhao, X.; Ai, P.; Lai, F.; Luo, X.; Benitez, J. (2022): Task management in decentralized autonomous organization. In *Journal of Operations Management* 68 (6-7), pp. 649–674. https://doi.org/10.1002/joom.1179.

Ziegler, Christian; Welpe, Isabell M. (2022): A Taxonomy of Decentralized Autonomous Organizations. In: ICIS 2022 Proceedings.

Ziolkowski, Rafael; Gianluca, Miscione; Gerhard, Schwabe (2020): Exploring Decentralized Autonomous Organizations: Towards Shared Interests and 'Code is Constitution'. In: ICIS 2020 Proceedings.

From Challenges to Solution Pathways for Industrial Data Ecosystems—A Socio-technical Perspective

Marc Brechtel, Dimitri Petrik, and Katharina Hölzle

Abstract Many industrial firms know that inter-firm data sharing holds tremendous potential for the creation of new economic value. However, most of them are not yet willing to share data multilaterally for joint value creation. Consequently, they do not participate in so-called data ecosystems. In our study, we address this issue from a socio-technical perspective and apply a two-step qualitative-empirical research design composed of a problem-centered interview study followed by solution-oriented workshops. We have identified and prioritized the perceived challenges and present first solution pathways. We were able to assign respective responsibilities for needed actions to major roles in data ecosystems. Among others, we can show that the core participants, i.e., data owner and data user, and the governance body need to resolve key challenges mostly in a separate but complementary manner to help industrial data ecosystems emerge.

Keywords Data ecosystems · Data sharing · Socio-technical systems

1 Introduction

Data has become a valuable asset for many firms. Inter-firm collaboration on a data level holds tremendous potential (Oliveira et al. 2019; Azkan et al. 2020) to significantly improve or create new business models (Yoo et al. 2010). The added value of digital services highly depends on the accessibility of data sets inside and between

M. Brechtel (✉)
University of Potsdam, Potsdam, Germany
e-mail: marc.brechtel@uni-potsdam.de

D. Petrik
Graduate School of Excellence Advanced Manufacturing Engineering, Stuttgart, Germany
e-mail: dimitri.petrik@bwi.uni-stuttgart.de

K. Hölzle
Fraunhofer Institute for Industrial Engineering, Stuttgart, Germany
e-mail: katharina.hoelzle@iao.fraunhofer.de

D. Beverungen et al. (eds.), *Transforming the Digitally Sustainable Enterprise*, Lecture Notes in Information Systems and Organisation 76,
https://doi.org/10.1007/978-3-031-80125-9_7

firms. Because the required data for offering a value-adding digital service for its intended beneficiaries are often not generated by only one firm, firms are increasingly looking for complementary data sets that other firms could provide (Gelhaar et al. 2021). This is why firms are starting to consider joining networks to share data with peers to collaborate on digital services (Pfähler et al. 2022). The resulting socio-technical networks aim at making data accessible across firms' boundaries are known as data ecosystems (Oliveira et al. 2019). To ensure a secure exchange of sensitive data between organizations, they have the political support of the European Commission (2020). Adopting the logic of established ecosystem literature (Adner 2017), data ecosystems are defined by multilateral relationships between different actors with a value proposition that is not decomposable into multiple bilateral relationships.

Literature has identified three major motives for firms participating in a data ecosystem (Bauer et al. 2022): First, existing products and (digital) services can be further improved with respect to productivity and efficiency. Second, firms are increasingly pressured by legislative movements (e.g., Supply Chain Act) demanding higher social and environmental sustainability. Third, data ecosystems provide room for the realization of new data-driven digital services, like collaborative condition monitoring. Here "data is not only shared bilaterally but multilaterally between all actors in an ecosystem" (Gelhaar et al. 2021, p. 127). Nevertheless, firms continue to shy away from sharing data with peers and keep data siloed (Gelhaar et al. 2023). Consequently, the business potential that data ecosystems hold cannot be leveraged (De Prieelle et al. 2020). Early supporters of the data ecosystem idea experience difficulties convincing other actors along the supply chain to join a data ecosystem due to the fear of releasing sensitive data (Bian et al. 2016; Zhiwei et al. 2021). Such obstacles are even recognized by European policy makers (European Commission 2018). Previous research has shown that it is important to ensure that all potential actors benefit from taking part in a data ecosystem (Gelhaar et al. 2021). Without a clear benefit, firms neglect the idea of data sharing along the supply chain (Gelhaar et al. 2021). This effect is even reinforced when firms consider data as business-sensitive, especially in traditional sectors (Gelhaar et al. 2021). Nevertheless, recent literature emphasizes the socio-technical nature of data ecosystems. For example, Oliveira et al. (2019) emphasize the need for holistic approaches to study data ecosystem evolvement, going beyond the technical challenges. Despite first insights on factors influencing data sharing from a game-theoretical perspective (Kraemer et al. 2021) or focus on data sharing between scientists (Devriendt et al. 2021), further empirical studies are needed to gain knowledge about the socio-technical design of industrial data ecosystems.

This study aims to reason the absence of data ecosystems by identifying and prioritizing the perceived challenges and giving the first indication about solution pathways to move forward the understanding of how to design and scale industrial data ecosystems from a socio-technical perspective. We enrich existing predominantly conceptual work by allocating selected responsibilities to the major roles in a data ecosystem based on empirical data (Oliveira et al. 2019; Otto and Lis et al., 2019; Otto and Steinbuss et al., 2019). To get there, we are guided by the following research questions: *What are the critical challenges industrial firms perceive while considering data ecosystems? What solution pathways may help to overcome these challenges and who should take action?* With our study, we empirically identify needed actions to address the prioritized challenges differentiating between the core participants, namely the data owner and the data user, plus the governance body of a data ecosystem in industry.

2 Fundamentals

2.1 Data Ecosystems as Socio-technical Networks

Prior research conceptualized the ecosystem construct to depict the connections and relations among partners that strive for a strong focal value proposition (Adner 2017). Drawing on the original concept of business ecosystems (Moore 1993), ecosystem types reach from innovation ecosystems (Adner 2006) to digital platform ecosystems (Hein et al. 2019). Data ecosystems are another manifestation of the ecosystem construct. They are defined as distributed socio-technical systems in which autonomous actors interact and collaborate to explore, analyze and interpret data mutually while aiming for joint innovation and value creation (Oliveira et al. 2019). The term socio-technical systems goes back to Emery and Trist (1960). They coined this term to "describe systems that involve a complex interaction between humans, machines and [...] environmental aspects" (Baxter and Sommerville 2011, p. 5). Thus, transferred to today's data ecosystems the original logic of interdependent technical and social elements still holds true and is frequently applied in the information systems (IS) discipline (Sarker et al. 2019).

The success of data ecosystems relies on its actors' active engagement (Heimstädt et al. 2015). The rationale is that more value can be created based on shared data than if each ecosystem actor computes his own data only. Thus, data ecosystems are seen as a driver for innovation in which the data sovereignty of each actor needs to be preserved (Otto and Lis et al., 2019; Otto and Steinbuss et al., 2019). Compared to centralized digital platforms known to promote power asymmetries, known as the winner-takes-it-all phenomenon (Van der Aalst et al. 2019), applications functionalities can be implemented in so called connectors to increase the level decentralization in data ecosystems (Otto and Jarke 2019).

Taking a socio-technical perspective helps to better manage and achieve positive outcomes of information systems (Bostrom and Heinen 1977). Recent work related to data ecosystems stresses that the consideration of the interdependence of socio-technical dimensions is critical for their success (Oliveira et al. 2019). Hence, following the traditional socio-technical system literature (Brandt and Cernetic 1998), successful data ecosystems need to consider the interrelation of technology, people, and the organization while aiming for joint value creation. More recently, some scholars even refer to data as as an additional element of socio-technical systems (Wallace 2015; Weber et al. 2021). Albeit "it is widely acknowledged that adopting a socio-technical approach to system development leads to systems that are more acceptable to end users and deliver better value. [...] such approaches are not widely practiced" (Baxter and Sommerville 2011, p. 4). This also holds true for the ongoing endeavors to establish data ecosystems in industry and latest research in this field (Brechtel and Petrik 2024). Scholars have mainly focused on a sub-set of the socio-technical dimensions of data ecosystems, namely technology (Oliveira and Lóscio 2018). Thus, we argue that a socio-technical view, determining the success or failure of data ecosystems, is required.

2.2 Data Ecosystem Roles

There are various roles actors, i.e., enterprises or institutions, can occupy in data ecosystems. A role is a function related to a set of duties occupied by a data ecosystem actor (Oliveira et al. 2019). Typically, a data ecosystem constitutes at least two roles, namely *data owners* and *data users* (Oliveira et al. 2019). These two roles need to be filled by actors every time data is exchanged—making them core participants (Otto and Lis et al., 2019; Otto and Steinbuss et al., 2019). However, additional roles can be filled in a data ecosystem (Oliveira et al. 2019). Another important role beside the core participants is responsible for creating the rules and policies. The International Data Spaces Association refers here to the *governance body* (Otto and Lis et al., 2019; Otto and Steinbuss et al., 2019). *Data owners* are defined as legal entities creating data and/or executing control over it. For example an industrial firm measuring parameters to assess the condition of its pump in the field might acts as a data owner. In contrast, a *data user* is a legal entity equipped with the right to use the data owned by different actors (Otto and Lis et al., 2019; Otto and Steinbuss et al., 2019). In our example, a data user, might be a maintenance provider making use of the pump data to improve the uptime. The *governance body* "makes sure that only compliant organizations are granted access" (Otto and Lis et al., 2019; Otto and Steinbuss et al., 2019, p. 25). The governance body is responsible for standardization, certifications, and governance (Catena-X 2022b), aiming for the interoperability, data sovereignty, and security of all data ecosystem participants. This body is comparable to the ecosystem designer taking care of the design and implementation, as introduced by Autio (2022) for innovation ecosystems. Data ecosystem founders or standardization institutions may assume this role (Oliveira et al. 2019).

3 Methodology

In our study, we applied a two-step qualitative-empirical research design composed of problem-centered interviews followed by a set of solution pathway workshops.

Step one: The challenges perceived by participating or at least interested stakeholders in data ecosystems, were investigated through problem-centered interview data collection (Döringer 2020). Our study put the focus on organizations integrated in an industrial supply chain either producing and selling physical goods, or providing services paving the way for inter-firm data sharing. Therefore, we searched for representatives from industrial firms with expertise in data ecosystems or data economy since making machine data available or utilizing such data from other organizations appears to be difficult (European Commission 2018). Our interview partners were mostly from German incumbent firms, which either actively participate or communicate interest in industrial data ecosystems, such as Catena-X—a data ecosystem dedicated to the automotive industry. SMEs and start-ups made up a smaller share of the data sample. We completed the relevant set of interview data until theoretical saturation, i.e., the iterative, open coding process did not reveal any new challenges, has been reached. In total, we interviewed 31 experts from 26 different firms between June and November 2021 (Table 1, available at bit.ly/interview_workshop_participants). We used a semi-structured format to discuss predefined topics and add follow-up questions to get valuable information related to the research goal. Details of the interviews and their processing have been described elsewhere (Brechtel and Petrik 2024), since this study is part of a superordinate research project. In brief, we asked for the perceived challenges related to data ecosystems first, before we touched upon first solution ideas. Every interview was recorded, transcribed and coded. Via axial coding we got from first-order concepts to second order themes (Corbin and Strauss 1988). To achieve objectivity, group discussions among the researchers were used to reach a consensus during coding. We used Gioia et al. (2013) to aggregate the codes guided by the three dimensions of the socio-technical framework by Brandt and Cernetic (1998) comprising technology, people, and organization. We added value as a fourth dimension, as it is a defining feature of ecosystems (Jacobides et al. 2020). We decided not to create an explicit dimension dedicated to data since data-related aspects are ubiquitios in the other four dimensions.

Step two: To further refine and add to our findings from the interview series, we organized workshops. We have decided for workshops as they provide room for stimulating discussions among experts (Ørngreen and Levinsen 2017) for the purpose to map solution pathways and assigning respective responsibilities. The workshop format comprised four steps (i.e., longlist reflection, narrowing down, prioritizing, and assigning responsibilities), incorporating qualitative research to distill consensus withing the group of experts. In doing so, the first three of the four workshop steps draw on a study design described and applied in previous IS research (Schmidt et al. 2001).

In total, one inter-firm and five intra-firm workshops were carried out. The intra-firm workshops were held with firms that already took part in the previous interview study. Thereby we achieved an acceptance rate of approx. 19% on a firm level. For the inter-firm workshop, we used an event where platform and data ecosystem knowledge carriers participated anyhow and applied the same workshop procedure as for the intra-firm setting. At least one researcher moderated the workshops, while another took notes on a shared MIRO board. We started our workshops by introducing the longlist of challenges, and asked each workshop participant to select the top five challenges. Using MIRO functionalities we brought the independent selection of participants together, and conducted dot voting. If a clear ranking could not be derived based on the distribution of votes within the group immediately, we took a decision on prioritization in the big round. Based on the prioritized challenges, we proceeded with each workshop group by elaborating possible solution pathways. Further, we stimulated group discussions among the participating experts (Myers 2013) regarding the assignment of responsibilities differentiating between the core participants and the governance body of a data ecosystem. The cross-workshop data analysis resulted in a shortlist of challenges (Table 1), enriched by needed actions per challenge and role (Table 2).

4 Results

Starting with a longlist of 29 socio-technical challenges related to collaboration on data in data ecosystems across firms' boundaries (Brechtel and Petrik 2024), the workshops enabled the researcher team to distill a shortlist of twelve challenges. Below we refer to aspects introduced by Brechtel and Petrik (2024) in Sect. 4.1, but limit ourselves to the shortlisted challenges, before we map solution pathways to them in Sect. 4.2.

Table 1 A shortlist of challenges related to data ecosystems

	Challenge group	Challenge	Prioritized in workshops
Tech.	Compatibility	Poor interoperability	#3, #5
	Digital readiness	Poor data availability	#2, #3, #4, #6
People	Knowledge	Lack of knowledge carriers	#2, #5
	Leadership	Poor venture-driven mindset	#1, #2, #4, #6
		Unsuitable incentive system	#1, #2, #6
	Trust	Lack of trust	#5
Org.	Culture	Silo thinking	#4
	Accountability	Unclear data responsibility	#1, #3
Value	Business	Unclear business value	#4, #5, #6
		Unclear data value	#1, #2, #4, #5, #6
	Profitability	Need of high initial investments	#3
	Use case	Poor accessibility of use cases	#1, #3

Table 2 Assignment of needed actions per challenge and role

	Challenge	Solution	Needed action	CP[a]	GB[b]
Tech.	Poor interoperability	Standards	Set and enforce rules/standards		✖
	Poor data availability	Data cataloging	Take stock of intra-firm data	✖	
			Provide data requirements		✖
People	Lack of knowledge carriers	Mentoring	Introduce mentoring program	✖	
			Establish an intra-firm data ecosystem community	✖	
	Poor venture-driven mindset	Top management support	Ensure direct reporting of project teams to sponsors	✖	
			Create a sense of urgency	✖	
			Install right-minded C-level	✖	
	Unsuitable incentive system	Long-term orientation	Set long-term incentivization	✖	
			Define clear deliverables	✖	
	Lack of trust	Data sovereignty	Establish and adopt zero-trust environment	✖	✖
			Introduce fair data mgmt. principles		✖
			Introduce governance model managed by a neutral entity		✖
Org.	Silo thinking	Cultural mind shift	Establish ecosystem thinking	✖	✖
	Unclear data responsibility	Data team	Establish intra-firm data team	✖	
			Introduce a project org	✖	
Value	Unclear business value	Value demonstration	Demonstrate added value	✖	
			Introduce mechanisms for value creation and value capture		✖
	Unclear data value	Data Valuation	Intra-firm data valuation based on case studies	✖	
			Introduce a data strategy	✖	
			Provide a data valuation catalog		✖
	Need of high initial investments	Subsidy	Provide initial cost coverage		✖
			Take care of SME requirements		✖
	Poor accessibility of use cases	Use case accessibility	Describe and modularize use cases		✖

[a]CP = Core Participants, [b]GB = Governance Body

4.1 Challenges

The social-technical perspective allows us to differentiate challenges for industrial data ecosystems into technology-, people-, organization- and value-related challenges.

Technology. Our data revealed two prioritized technology challenges in the emergence of industrial data ecosystems. First, industrial firms struggle with the poor interoperability of system landscapes within and across firms' boundaries. We witnessed different data standards and interfaces per application. As a consequence, we see different levels of data structure homogeneity across firms and especially across industries [#26]. According to our data, this is due to the fact that the industries' standardization efforts vary greatly. Second, our workshops highlighted that many firms, but especially SMEs, still suffer from *data availability* in general. Project activities are required to make this data accessible as the following statement underpins [#27]: "Currently, it is still a huge project business to get access to the data at all, with a huge investment."

People. Based on our workshop results, we add four people-related challenges to the shortlist. First, the *lack of knowledge carriers* seems to be an issue. Especially on the management level, firms lack knowledge carriers to assess the opportunities of data spaces as the underlying technologies and thought structures are distinct from anything that has been encountered previously [#27]. Second, the *poor venture-driven mindset* towards the mass adoption of industrial data ecosystems forms another issue. Our data highlights risk-averse behavior on the management level. Interviewee [#7] claimed that today's decision makers consistently seek to observe and replicate use cases. Following him, only a few are early adopters who are willing to establish data ecosystems. Third, a prioritized leadership-related issue is an *unsuitable incentive system*. Our data reveals that management is not incentivized to budget for data ecosystems [#1]. Hence, if at all, most CEOs stick to lip service only. Finally, the barrier of *mistrust* is also evident. As of today, the knowledge is power thought dominates across firms. Even though, more and more industrial firms acknowledge the necessity of obtaining data from others, the great majority still refrains from sharing data—mainly due to trust issues [#9].

Organization. Silo thinking and unclear data responsibility have been prioritized as organizational challenges. Today, most industrial firms stick to developing proprietary verticals aiming to enhance their solution offering by incorporating digital elements [#19]. Hence, *silo thinking* is omnipresent leading to many solutions emerging side by side. Further, missing intra- and inter-firm *data responsibilities* lead to entities claiming data ownership of the same data, even within a firm. The question of who is responsible for the data remains unresolved within most industrial firms [#26].

Value. Most of the prioritized challenges relate to the dimension of value. First, there are doubts about the added business values with current data ecosystem initiatives are perceived revolving mainly around technology. One interviewee [#19] states that "things are simply thrown together, and the business model consideration falls short." Second, firms shy away from becoming early adopters of data ecosystems, as they cannot estimate the value of their data yet. This is because firms are used to pricing products and services, but not data. Adding to this is the fact that data possesses no value per se [#25]: Its value only arises while being contextualized. However, the individual firm that may provide data often lacks knowledge about the problem context which in turn hinders the determination of the actual data value. Third, *high initial investments* build a hurdle. Preparing to enter the realm of data ecosystems often involves facing substantial financial commitments while not knowing the exact economic benefit [#28]. This is a key reason why many firms are reluctant about making such investments. Finally, the *poor accessibility of use cases* is also among the shortlisted challenges. Decision-makers are waiting to be inspired by accessible use cases as most data ecosystem use cases miss detailed descriptions and are nothing beyond buzzwords [#5].

4.2 Solution Pathways

In this section, we elaborate on suitable solution pathways to address the challenges using the previously introduced roles in data ecosystems as a structuring element.

Core Participants. Technology-related challenges that require the attention of the core participants, i.e., data owner and data user, concern the *need to take stock of available data* on a firm level. While doing so, labeling and clustering the respective data is mandatory to get toward a firm internal data catalog [#2, WS #4]. Further, workshop group #6 recommended "establishing advanced data management mechanisms" on a firm level. People-related challenges need attention from core participants in at least four cases. First, to address the lack of knowledge carriers the experts recommend establishing a *mentoring program* to take the people with you [#12]. Following workshop group #2 the "digital natives need to train experienced top managers how to cope with data ecosystems." Second, the challenge of the missing venture-driven mindset can only be addressed if firms aim for top management support. To get there, "firms need to ensure *direct access of operational teams* to high-level sponsors with decision-making competence" [WS #4]. Further, data ecosystem supporters within a firm need to *create a sense of urgency* by knowing the right people and identifying the best leverage point [WS #2]. One leverage point might be to install a *right-minded visionary C-level* representative [#7, #11, WS #6]. Third, the core participants need to adjust toward more long-term-oriented thinking. Based on our study results, the currently unsuitable incentive systems need to be replaced by creating and setting *long-term incentivization* [#6] bound to *clear deliverables* [WS #6]. Fourth, the lack of trust needs to be addressed by adopting a *zero-trust environment*. Here, one of our workshop groups recommends the core participants implement and use only certified solutions to get there [WS #5]. Organization-related challenges that the core participants need to address include silo thinking and unclear data responsibilities. For the former, it needs a cultural mind shift towards "*thinking in terms of the ecosystem* value on not only firm value" [WS #4]. Historically, this ecosystem thinking has been the case with all the consortia firms that are traditionally organized. However, "with respect to data we have lost that a bit. But now we have to get back on track and say let's [share data] under certain rules" [#9]. For the latter, our workshop participants recommend the establishment of a dedicated *data team* [WS #1]. Further, there is a need for a *project organization* over a line organization when it comes to intra- and inter-firm data sharing [#16, WS #3]. Other needed actions identified for the core participants concern unclear business and data value. Participation in lighthouse projects, such as Catena-X, for industrial data ecosystems, may prove beneficial to *demonstrate the added business value* [WS #5]. To better understand the value of data sets, our study shows that the core participants should apply a *case study-driven approach*. Workshop group #2 agreed that "the value of data must be identified over time". Interviewee #2 is convinced that "iterations will help to gain insights that help to interpret the value of data". A thinking that was confirmed in workshop #4. Further, our experts [WS #2] recommend *introducing a data strategy* on the firm level first, before strategic thinking is widened up towards data ecosystems.

Governance Body. Regarding the perceived technology-related challenges, the governance body is required to *set and enforce rules and standards* to improve inter-firm interoperability. Workshop group #3 agreed that the developments and standardization around connectors are crucial. Further, this group agreed that the governance body needs to define standards for how data is best shared—meaning which data format and technical solutions, i.e., systems and interfaces, need to be in place. To improve the given data availability the governance body should *provide clear data requirements*. What is needed is a "to-do list on data for all data ecosystem actors" [WS #4]. Actions by the governance body are also required when it comes to people-related challenges. To improve the level of trust among data ecosystem actors the governance body should foster the idea of a *zero-trust environment* [#26]. Again, the connector plays a crucial role in ensuring data sovereignty [WS #4]. Further, the introduction of *fair data management principles*, such as "previously established certification standards that the ecosystem commits to" [WS #5] may help here. To operationalize this thinking, a *governance model which is managed by a neutral entity* is proposed. Interviewee #11 underpins the need for such a neutral instance by claiming that only then fair conditions are met. To address the organization-related challenge of silo thinking "institutions who push for ecosystem value" [WS #4] are needed. The governance body can be interpreted as such an institution that needs to take responsibility for continuously demonstrating the benefit of *ecosystem thinking* over silo thinking. Value-related challenges ask for actions by the governance body in various fields. First, this body should set and enforce *mechanisms for joint value creation and value capture* among the different data ecosystem actors. Short-term, simple revenue sharing seems to be a conceivable solution approach. Long-term, one workshop group asked for an inter-firm business model [#6]. Further, the governance body "needs to provide support, e.g., by provisioning a *value catalog for data* exchange" [WS #4] which is based on an ecosystem-wide alignment indicating the value of each data point. Another aspect mentioned has been that the governance body should consider making the early adopters offer *initial cost coverage* until critical mass is reached [WS #3]. As SMEs often lack the resources to actively participate in data ecosystems, they need *special attention* from the governance body. This is especially true when considering that SMEs bridge the gap between major actors at the beginning and end of the automotive supply chain [WS #5]. Finally, we see that the governance body needs to better *describe and modularize use cases* to make them more accessible to the mass market. More specifically, it is recommended to introduce a syntax for the description of use cases related to industrial data ecosystems. Thereby the what and why from a firm and ecosystem perspective need to be especially addressed. "We need to move away from pure buzzwords. Instead, we should introduce a syntax for the use case description […]" [#18].

5 Discussion

Our study examines the challenges perceived by (potential) data ecosystem actors and indicates what is needed to overcome them. The assignment of responsibilities allows us to derive advice for the roles and activities that data ecosystems require.

The governance body should primarily focus on finding solutions for the remaining technology-related challenges. Our research confirms and adds to the obligations that come with the role of the governance body, conceptualized earlier, for example by Oliveira et al. (2019). We find support for the argument that the governance body needs to take responsibility for standardization inside a data ecosystem (Catena-X 2022b). Further, based on our study results we welcome the decision by the European Commission to invest in federated cloud infrastructures in the period of 2021–2027 (European Commission 2020). Further, we stress that the governance body needs to set and enforce rules "to encourage and to control the participation of actors" (Oliveira et al. 2019 p. 608). These rules need to be "commonly understood when it comes to articulating usage conditions on the data" (Otto 2022, p. 13). Further, our data confirms that the governance body needs to provide data-related requirements and specify technical components, i.e., the connector each data ecosystem actor needs to operate. As a major building block of data ecosystems, the connector serves as the "interface between the internal systems […] and the [data] ecosystem itself" (Pettenpohl et al. 2022, p. 32).

The core participants need to primarily find answers to the perceived people- and organization-related challenges. Our data indicates that it is paramount that the core participants need to take action to address people- and organization-related challenges. Considering people as enablers, we endorse the argumentation by Kitsios et al. (2017) that the core participants, esp. data providers, need to inform and educate about the significance and value of shared data. Our workshop findings indicate that mentoring and community building within firms may be a viable way to compensate the lack of knowledge carriers. This finding is complementary to the idea of a network of data stewards from across data-intensive organization, fostered by the European Commission (2020). Besides, top management support needs to be ubiquitous in the data-owning and the data-using organization. In line with previous research, we "have identified top management support in an organization as a critical factor that is positively related to technology adoption" (Wang and Lo 2020, p. 3). Even though both researchers and practitioners assume that data ecosystems will be an imperative rather than an option for the competitiveness of industrial firms (Oliveira and Lóscio 2018; Gelhaar et al. 2023), we can show that the core participants still need to better understand the long-term undertaking of data ecosystems. Finally, our study results underpin that trust among the core participants is central to leveraging the idea of data sharing (Gelhaar et al. 2021; European Commission 2020). Hence, they should have an intrinsic motivation to work towards a zero-trust environment aiming for data sovereignty: before data is shared among data owners and data user, the respective entities need to be authenticated, authorized, and continuously validated through set standards and mechanisms (Mehraj and Banday 2020). From the perspective of the organization, we support the arguments by Martin et al. (2021), claiming that ecosystem thinking by all data ecosystem actors is crucial to break existing data silos. In this regard, our data points to the need for a cultural mind shift. Further, we have indications that the core participants need to assign "a team responsible for external data sharing" (Zhiwei et al. 2021, p. 32) to ensure clarity regarding data ownership on a firm level.

Both, the governance body, and the core participants must take responsibility when it comes to value-related challenges. The interplay of actions taken by the governance body and the core participants is crucial. First, to tackle the prioritized challenge of unclear business value, both need to find the shoulder to meet the *quid pro quo* requirement: every actor who contributes to the data ecosystem, must also get something in return (Gelhaar et al. 2021). Second, we add to prior research regarding the need for joint data valuation mechanisms, e.g., considering benefit-based or combinatorial valuation approaches (Azkan et al., 2022). Our data says that a case study-driven approach by the core participants may help the governance body to get to a data valuation catalog valid for all data ecosystem actors. In line with the project of Transfer-X (Sauer and Pontes 2023), aiming for the engagement of SMEs in data ecosystems through an easily accessible information and knowledge platform, our data adds that the governance body should take care of the SMEs and their requirements to get towards mass adoption. Otherwise, projects like Catena-X, are likely to fail, as roughly 70% of the targeted actors are SMEs (Catena-X 2022a). Our data show that the governance body needs to make use cases accessible to current and future actors to further a joint value perspective among all data ecosystem actors. This would contribute towards "a shared understanding of the ecosystem's operations and goals" (Gelhaar et al. 2021, p. 131).

6 Contribution

This study contributes to the understanding of industrial data ecosystems and indicates what is needed to pave their mass adoption. Our study serves as the foundation to leverage socio-technical design know-how on data ecosystems. As our findings can be used for different abstraction levels of data ecosystem design, we argue that our work can be useful for researchers, practitioners, and even policy makers.

Taking the theoretical perspective, to the best of our knowledge, our study is one of the first that goes beyond conceptually designating data ecosystems as socio-technical systems. We adopt the logic of socio-technical system theory (Brandt and Cernetic 1998; Baxter and Sommerville 2011) to identify what is needed to engineer industrial data ecosystems sustainably. While researching the perceived challenges and giving examples for solution pathways based on our empirical data, we have found considerable proof that the multi-dimensional socio-technical perspective helps to analyze and manage the complexity of data ecosystems. Following Baxter and Sommerville (2011), we are convinced that the results of our socio-technical system analysis can form the basis of increased value perception regarding data ecosystems and subsequently improve the overall acceptance rate. Our structured approach to mapping prioritized challenges and selected solutions to the responsible actors across four system dimensions highlights the potential of researching data ecosystems from a socio-technical perspective in the future. We extend the predominantly conceptual knowledge on data ecosystem engineering (Oliveira et al. 2019; Otto and Lis et al., 2019; Otto and Steinbuss et al., 2019) by empirically revealing which responsibilities go along with a certain role. We also contribute empirical knowledge to the experimental insights presented by Kraemer et al. (2021). To our knowledge, our study is the first to empirically elicit which actors occupying major roles need to accept which responsibilities for stabilizing and nurturing the ecosystem.

For practitioners, we provide explanations for the absence of data ecosystems in industry. The shortlist of challenges helps to understand why industrial data ecosystems are not subject to mass adoption yet. At the same time, our study proposes needed actions on how to overcome these challenges based on an aggregation of practitioner views. By differentiating the major roles actors can occupy in a data ecosystem about the responsibilities for actions, practitioners benefit from knowing who needs to do what to make data ecosystems flourish. Our study gives support to the European data strategy (European Commission 2020). Based on our study results, we recommend European policy makers to further support the establishment of zero-trust environments in a business context to let core participants trust each other.

7 Limitations and Outlook

The results of our study are subject to limitations that should be considered. First, the generalizability of our results should be treated with caution. The sample was drawn from mostly German firms that are either actively participating or communicating interest in data ecosystems, which may result in a biased sample as data ecosystem averse firm positions have not been considered at all. Second, with respect to the needed actions and their allocation to the major roles it is worth mentioning that not all data ecosystem roles are considered. Third, concerning the needed actions, we focused on the prioritized challenges only. Addressing non-prioritized challenges could be also beneficial for the establishment of industrial data ecosystems. In that context, the number of conducted workshops can be explained by the novelty of data ecosystems, which are still in a seminal stage (Oliveira et al. 2019). Nevertheless, due to the use of the socio-technical lens, we are convinced that our results will prove helpful for both researchers and practitioners. The constraints outlined above indicate opportunities for research. Future research can further enrich and validate our findings by including data ecosystem averse firm positions as well. Thereby, an international comparison of positions seems to valuable as well. Narrowing down the scope to a single case study may help to identify already implemented solutions and still unaddressed challenges of the ones identified. Further, we propose considering the other roles data ecosystem actors (Oliveira et al. 2019) can occupy while allocating the needed actions. To mitigate another limitation of our study, we recommend not leaving out the non-prioritized challenges elaborated by Brechtel and Petrik (2024). We suppose that each single challenge as well as their complex interrelations can be decisive in the competition between ecosystems for valuable data owners. Regarding future research, we see the chance to map suitable solution pathways for these as well.

References

Autio, E. (2022) 'Orchestrating ecosystems: A multi-layered framework', *Innovation*, 24(1), 96–109.

Adner, R. (2006) 'Match Your Innovation Strategy to Your Innovation Ecosystem', *Harvard Business Review*, 84(4), 98–107.

Adner, R. (2017) 'Ecosystem as Structure: An Actionable Construct for Strategy', *Journal of Management*, 43(1), 39–58.

Azkan, C., Möller, F., Meisel, L., & Otto B. (2020) 'Service dominant logic perspective on data ecosystems - A case study based morphology', In: Quammah, A.E. (Ed.): Proceedings of the *European Conference on Information Systems*. Marrakesh, Morocco.

Azkan, C., Gür, I., Hupperz, M., Gelhaar, J., Gieß, A., Groß, T. et al. (2022) *Anreizsysteme und Ökonomie des Data Sharings - Handlungsfelder des unternehmensübergreifenden Datenaustausches und Status quo der deutschen Wirtschaft*. Dortmund: Fraunhofer Institut für Software und Systemtechnik.

Bauer, K., Bienel, M., Drost, M., Grüner, S., Haße, H., Hill, M. et al. (2022) *Multilateral data sharing in industry – Concept using 'collaborative condition monitoring' as a basis for new business models*. Berlin: Federal Ministry for Economic Affairs and Climate Action.
Baxter, G. & Sommerville, I. (2011) 'Socio-technical systems: From design methods to systems engineering', *Interacting with Computers*, 23(1), 4–17.
Bian, W., Shang, J., & Zhang, J. (2016) 'Two-way information sharing under supply chain competition', *International Journal of Production Economics*, 178, 82–94.
Bostrom, R.P., & Heinen, J.S. (1977) 'MIS Problems and Failures: A Socio-Technical Perspective. Part I: The Causes', *MIS Quarterly*, 1(3), 17–32.
Brandt, D. & Cernetic, J. (1998) 'Human-centred appraoches to control and information technology: European experiences', *AI & Society*, 12(1–2), 2–20.
Brechtel, M. & Petrik, D. (2024) 'Converging challenges: industrial data ecosystems and a vital business model', In: Baumann, S. (Ed.); *Handbook on Digital Platforms & Ecosystems in Manufacturing*. Cheltenham: Edward Elgar Publishing.
Catena-X (2022a) *Catena-X Automotive Network*, https://catena-x.net/fileadmin/user_upload/Vereinsdokumente/Catena-X_UEbersicht.pdf. Accessed: 06.03.2023
Catena-X (2022b) *Catena-X Operating Model Whitepaper*, https://catena-x.net/fileadmin/user_upload/Publikationen_und_WhitePaper_des_Vereins/CX_Operating_Model_Whitepaper_02_12_22.pdf. Accessed: 06.03.2023.
Corbin, J. & Strauss, A. (1988) *Basics of qualitative research - Techniques and procedures for developing grounded theory*. Thousand Oaks: SAGE Publications Inc.
De Prieelle, F., De Reuver, M., & Rezaei, J. (2020) 'The Role of Ecosystem Data Governance in Adoption of Data Platforms by Internet-of-Things Data Providers: Case of Dutch Horticulture Industry', *IEEE Transactions on Engineering Management*, 69(4), 940–950.
Devriendt, T., Borry, P. & Shabani, M. (2021) 'Factors that influence data sharing through data sharing platforms: A qualitative study on the views and experiences of cohort holders and platform developers', PLoS ONE., 16(7), e0254202.
Döringer, S. (2020) 'The problem-centred expert interview - Combining qualitative interviewing approaches for investigating implicit expert knowledge', *International Journal of Social Research Methodology*, 24(3), 265–278.
European Commission (2018) *Guidance on sharing private sector data in the European data economy*, Communications from the Commission to the European Parliament, the Council, the European economic and social Committee and the Committee of the Regions, Brussels.
European Commission (2020) *A European strategy for data*, Communications from the Commission to the European Parliament, the Council, the European economic and social Committee and the Committee of the Regions, Brussels.
Emery, F.E. & Trist, E.L. (1960) 'Socio-technical systems', In: Churchman, C.W. & Verhulst, M. (Eds.); *Management Science Models and Techniques*. 2nd ed. Oxford: Pergamon Press.
Gelhaar, J., Bergmann, N., Müller, P., & Dogan, R. (2023) 'Motives and Incentives for Data Sharing in Industrial Data Ecosystems: An Explorative Single Case Study', In: Bui, T.X. (Ed.); Proceedings of the *Hawaii International Conference on System Sciences*. Maui, Hawaii.
Gelhaar, J., Both, J., & Otto, B. (2021) 'Requirements For Incentive Mechanisms In Industrial Data Ecosystems', In: Herberger, D., & Hübner M. (Eds.); Proceedings of the *Conference on Production Systems and Logistics*. Hannover, Germany.
Gioia, D.A., Corley, K.G., & Hamilton, A.L. (2013) 'Seeking Qualitative Rigor in Inductive Research: Notes on the Gioia Methodology', *Organizational Research Methods*, 16(1), 15–31.
Heimstädt, M., Saunderson, F., & Heath, T. (2015) 'Conceptualizing Open Data Ecosystems: A timeline analysis of Open Data development in the UK', In: Edelmann, N., & Parycek, P. (Eds.); Proceedings of the *International Conference for E-Democracy and Open Government*. Krems, Austria.
Hein, A., Schreieck, M., Riasanow, T., Setzke, D., Wiesche, M., Böhm, M., & Krcmar, H. (2019) 'Digital platform ecosystems', *Electronic Markets*, 30(1), 87-98.

Jacobides, M.G., Cennamo, C., & Gawer, A. (2020) *Distinguishing platforms and ecosystems - Complementarities, value creation, and coordination mechanisms*, https://www.jacobides.com/_files/ugd/0b15b1_7e0678d2815541bb920c77ec41e4d305.pdf. Accessed: 02.03.2023

Kitsios, F., Papachristos, N., & Kamariotou, M. (2017) 'Business Models for Open Data Ecosystem: Challenges and Motivations for Entrepreneurship and Innovation', In: Loucopoulos, P. (Ed.); Proceedings of the *IEEE Conference on Business Informatics*. Thessaloniki, Greece.

Kraemer, J., Stüdlein, N., & Zierke, O. (2021) 'Data as a Public Good: Experimental Insights on the Optimal Design of B2B Data Sharing Platforms', *SSRN Electronic Journal*. (preprint)

Martin, S., Gautier, P., Turki, S., & Kotsev, A. (2021) *Establishment of sustainable data ecosystems: Recommendations for the evolution of spatial data infrastructures*. Luxembourg: Publications Office of the European Union.

Mehraj, S. & Banday, M.T. (2020) 'Establishing a Zero Trust Strategy in Cloud Computing Environment', In: Kalaiarasi, A. (Ed.); Proceedings of the *International Conference on Computer Communication and Informatics*. Coimbatore, India.

Moore, J.F. (1993) 'Predators and prey - A new ecology of competition', *Harvard Business Review*, 71(3), 75–86.

Myers, M.D. (2013) *Qualitative research in business & management*. 2nd ed. London: SAGE Publication Inc.

Oliveira, M.I.S., Lima, G. de F., & Lóscio, B.F. (2019) 'Investigations into data ecosystems - A systematic mapping study', *Knowledge and Information Systems*, 61(2), 589–630.

Oliveira, M.I.S. & Lóscio, B.F. (2018) 'What is a data ecosystem?', In: Janssen, M., Chun, S., Weerakkody, V., Zuiderwijk, A., & Hinnant, C. (Eds.): Proceedings of the *Annual International Conference on Digital Government Research*. Delft, Netherlands.

Otto, B., Lis, D., Jürjens, J., Cirullies, J., Opriel, S., Howar, F. et al. (2019) *Data Ecosystems - Conceptual Foundations, Constituents and Recommendations for Actions*. Dortmund: Fraunhofer Institute for Software and Systems Engineering.

Otto, B., Steinbuss, S., Teuscher, A., Lohmann, S., Auer, S., Bader, S. et al. (2019) *Reference Architecture Model*. Dortmund: International Data Spaces Association.

Otto, B. (2022) 'The evolution of data spaces', In: Otto, B., Ten Hompel, M., & Wrobel, S.: *Designing Data Spaces - The Ecosystem Approach to Competitive Advantage*. Cham: Springer.

Otto, B. & Jarke, M. (2019) 'Designing a multi-sided data platform: findings from the International Data Spaces case', *Electronic Markets*, 29, 561–580.

Ørngreen, R., & Levinsen, K. T. (2017). Workshops as a Research Methodology. *Electronic Journal of E- Learning*, 15(1), 70–81.

Pettenpohl, H., Spiekermann, M., & Both, J. (2022) 'International data spaces in a nutshell', In: Otto, B., Ten Hompel, M., & Wrobel, S. (Eds.): *Designing Data Spaces - The Ecosystem Approach to Competitive Advantage*. Cham: Springer.

Pfähler, K., Baars, H., Hiller, S., Morar, D., & Petrik, D. (2022) 'Data Analytics Services for Additive Manufacturing Ecosystems', In: Davis, G., Brown, S., & Subramani, M.: Proceedings of the *Americas Conference on Information Systems*. Minneapolis, USA.

Sarker, S., Chatterjee, S., Xiao, X., & Elbanna, A. (2019) 'The sociotechnical axis of cohesion for the IS discipline: Its historical legacy and its continued relevance', MIS Quarterly, 43(3), 695–719.

Sauer, O. & Pontes, U. (2023) *"Transfer-X" paves the way for SMEs into the data economy*, https://www.iosb.fraunhofer.de/en/press/press-releases/2023/transfer-x-transformation-medium-sized-data-economy.html. Accessed: 04.03.2023.

Schmidt, R., Lyytinen, K., Keil, M., & Cule, P. (2001) 'Identifying Software Project Risks: An International Delphi Study', *Journal of Management Information Systems*, 17(4), 5–36.

Van Der Aalst, W., Hinz, O., & Weinhardt, C. (2019) 'Big Digital Platforms: Growth, Impact, and Challenges', *Business & Information Systems Engineering*, 61(6), 645–648.

Wallace, P. (2015) *Introduction to Information Systems*. 2nd ed. Essex: Pearson Education Ltd.

Wang, H.-J., & Lo, J. (2020) 'Factors Influencing the Adoption of Open Government Data at the Firm Level', *IEEE Transactions on Engineering Management*, 67(3), 670–682.

Weber, M., Hacker, J., and Vom Brocke, J. (2021) 'Resilience in Information Systems Research-A Literature Review from a Socio-Technical and Temporal Perspective', In: Valacich, J. (Ed.); *Proceedings of the International Conference on Information Systems*. Austin, USA.
Yoo, Y., Henfridsson, O. and Lyytinen, K. (2010) 'The new organizing logic of digital innovation: An agenda for information systems research', *Information Systems Research*, 21(4), 724–735.
Zhiwei, J., Thieullent, A., Jones, S., Perhirin, V., Baerd, M., Shagrithaya, P. et al. (2021) *Data sharing masters - How smart organizations use data ecosystems to gain an unbeatable competitive edge*. New York: Capgemini Research Institute.

From Apathy to Algoactivism: Worker Resistance to Algorithmic Control in Food Delivery Platforms

Matthias Weber, Ulrich Remus, and Alexander de Jong

Abstract Platforms in the gig economy rely on algorithmic control to manage their workforce, but recent scientific evidence has shown that workers have begun to resist this control. Due to lacking focus and limited empirical data, the phenomenon of worker resistance to algorithmic control is still insufficiently understood. Based on a topic modeling approach with over 2 million text documents extracted from Reddit forums of different food-delivery platforms, we identify 14 resistance actions showing how food-delivery workers resist algorithmic control. Our study contributes to current research by expanding the understanding of resistance to algorithmic control in the gig economy, showing what resistant actions workers take, and discussing the concepts of individual opacity and collective knowledge as possible escalators and de-escalators of this resistance.

Keywords Algorithmic control · Resistance · Gig economy · Topic modeling

1 Introduction

The gig economy is booming around the globe. Not only in the US, where one in three working Americans already relies on income from platform-mediated work, or in the EU, where 11% of employees participate in the gig economy, but also in China, the number of gig workers could reach a projected 400 million by 2036, making gig work one of the most dynamic features of the global economy (Wong, 2022; Masiero, 2021; Cini, 2022). Among the fastest-growing sectors within the gig

M. Weber (✉) · U. Remus · A. de Jong
Department of Information Systems, Production and Logistics Management, University of Innsbruck, Innsbruck, Austria
e-mail: matthias.j.weber@uibk.ac.at

U. Remus
e-mail: ulrich.remus@uibk.ac.at

A. de Jong
e-mail: alexander.de-jong@uibk.ac.at

D. Beverungen et al. (eds.), *Transforming the Digitally Sustainable Enterprise*, Lecture Notes in Information Systems and Organisation 76,
https://doi.org/10.1007/978-3-031-80125-9_8

economy is food delivery, as part of the app-work sector (Yu et al., 2022). One of the enablers for this growth is the ability to manage large workforces using algorithms. This managerial use of algorithms is referred to as algorithmic management (AM), which describes a system of oversight, governance, and control practices based on algorithms that are responsible for making and executing automated decisions that affect the work process, and limit human involvement and oversight of the work process (Lee et al., 2015; Bucher et al., 2021; Duggan et al., 2020; Möhlmann and Zalmanson, 2017). A central part of AM is algorithmic control (AC), which includes large-scale collection and use of data to monitor and align workers' behavior with business objectives, previously performed by human managers (Cram and Wiener, 2020; Kellogg et al., 2020; Möhlmann et al., 2021).

The resulting continuous tracking and evaluation of worker behavior (Pregenzer et al., 2020) leads to several health issues such as anxiety (Jhaver et al., 2018), sleep deprivation and social isolation (Wood et al., 2019), frustration and burnout (Zhang et al., 2022), and many other impacts on workers' well-being. Most gig workers experience some form of algorithmic unfairness (Schulze et al., 2022) but feel powerless to stand up to the platform corporations (Jarrahi et al., 2020; Möhlmann and Zalmanson, 2017). As a consequence, recent studies have found that workers show resistant behavior toward AC practices (Anwar and Graham, 2020; Ferrari and Graham, 2021; Tassinari and Maccarrone, 2020; Woodcock, 2021). These resistance actions take on different forms. Some forms are highly covert, e.g., the creation of "hidden transcripts" (Yu et al., 2022), gaming or manipulating the algorithm (Bambauer and Zarsky, 2018, Cameron, 2022, Jarrahi and Sutherland, 2019, Wood et al., 2019). Some are more visible, like organizing in online forums (Pregenzer et al., 2021; Martin et al., 2014) to undertake collective actions (Chen, 2018; Rizzo and Atzeni, 2020; Lei, 2021) such as strikes (Vandaele, 2022), which can be summarized as "algoactivism" (Kellogg et al., 2020).

Although several studies uncovered various worker responses to AC, there is still a lack of dedicated theory-driven focus on uncovering worker resistance, as previous resistance-related findings emerged rather as a byproduct. The core focus so far has been on understanding AC as something workers are exposed to, overlooking the possibilities workers have in reacting to such a type of control (Bucher et al., 2021). There is still a gap in understanding the complex construct of resistance, its various manifestations (Curchod et al., 2020; Bucher et al., 2021), and how it escalates through phases (Jiang et al., 2021). Therefore, we propose the following research question: *How are food-delivery workers resisting algorithmic control and how does resistance escalate?*

We deliberately focus on food delivery as it is the fastest-growing gig economy sector, where workers are exposed to the most stringent AC mechanisms (Yu et al., 2022; Franke and Pulignano, 2022). Our study uses the novel Big Data topic modeling approach BERTopic, which allows us to analyze 33,864 text documents from food delivery-related Reddit forums. By identifying 14 resistance behaviors and discussing concepts that enable their escalation and de-escalation, we contribute to the understanding of resistance in the specific context of the gig economy.

2 Theoretical Background

What differentiates the gig economy from other economic forms can be summarized by three criteria: (1) the use of digital platforms, mechanisms, and processes (2) enabling the de/re-construction of work into smaller, distributable tasks ("gigs"), which in turn enables more (3) flexible, short-term, and heterogeneous working arrangements (Tan et al., 2021). The mentioned working arrangements differ depending on the gig work sector, which can be divided into capital platform work, crowd work, and app work, where food delivery is classified (Duggan et al., 2020). What makes the gig economy unique lies in the use of algorithmic technologies to automate various mechanisms and processes. These can be summarized as AM systems, e.g., systems of oversight, governance, and control practices that are based on algorithms with the responsibility for making automated decisions affecting labor, limiting human involvement and oversight of the labor process (Duggan et al., 2020; Möhlmann and Zalmanson, 2017; Bucher et al., 2021; Lee et al., 2015). The algorithms are often automated and self-learning to be able to transform input data into desired outputs (Gillespie, 2014). Besides algorithmic matching, AC is the main feature of AM (Möhlmann et al., 2021).

AC describes the managerial use of intelligent algorithms and advanced digital technology as a means to align worker behaviors with organizational objectives (Cram and Wiener, 2020; Kellogg et al., 2020). The central part in which AC differs from traditional forms of control is that decision-making and control may be exerted entirely through computerized systems or a technology interface rather than by a human manager (humans out of the loop), it may be subjected to human oversight (humans on the loop), or it may be used as a means to support human decision making and control (humans in the loop) (Danaher, 2016; Cram et al., 2020).

After we have laid the first part of our theoretical foundation and described AM and AC, we now turn our focus to resistance as a theoretical concept. The concept of resistance is difficult to grasp and comes in different forms and intensities (Woodcock, 2021). In the first step, we draw on the epistemological conceptualization of resistance by Hollander and Einwohner (2004), which is based on four core dimensions. The first core dimension of our resistance understanding, implied in nearly all scientific use of the term, is a sense of **action** (Hollander and Einwohner, 2004). Therefore, we consider the terms resistance and resistance action interchangeable since we always imply a behaviorist action and thus follow the terminological root of the word resistance, which the Oxford English Dictionary defines as the action of resisting (Laumer and Eckhardt, 2012). The second core dimension builds on the first, as action is **target-**oriented or directed against an opposition (Hollander and Einwohner, 2004). These resistance targets may vary from individuals to groups and organizations to institutions or social structures. Regarding resistance to AC, some studies found resistance to the algorithm itself, e.g., in the case of Upwork, where workers use a second monitor or a timer to circumvent automatic screenshots (Wood et al., 2019) or in the case of Uber, where drivers deactivate their GPS signal to become invisible for the algorithm (Möhlmann and Zalmanson, 2017). However, workers' resistance also targets the customer, as platforms outsource monitoring and task evaluation to the customer, making the worker dependent on the customer's evaluation (Shapiro, 2018; Wood et al., 2019). In the rather rare cases of algo-activism, which describes collectively organized actions such as strikes, workers' resistance is directed directly against the platforms or even the gig economy as a whole (Kellogg et al., 2020). The third dimension is the **recognition** of resistance. There is an ongoing discussion about the visibility of a resistant act, as visibility is a prerequisite for recognizing resistance (Hollander and Einwohner, 2004). On the one hand, scholars argue that an act of resistance must be visible and recognized by others to be considered resistance (Rubin, 1995). On the other hand, it is argued that recognition depends in part on the goals of the actor, which may consist either of an action to be recognized or of the deliberate concealment or disguise of an action (Hollander and Einwohner, 2004). Especially in the context of AC, the concept of transparency is essential, as platforms are concerned with managing transparency through the help of AM to maintain competitive advantages, protect intellectual property, and prevent malicious users from gaming the system (Eslami et al., 2019; Burrell, 2016; Tan et al., 2021). Because the employed AC mechanisms are deliberately created opaque, workers constantly feel like being under the "algorithmic gaze" (Newlands, 2021), which reinforces covert resistance practices (Hollander and Einwohner, 2004) or "invisibility practices" (Anteby and Chan, 2018) to escape the gaze and prevent recognition. The fourth dimension, namely **intent**, follows this. If workers intend to resist, their actions are considered resistance, regardless of whether they are recognized or achieve the intended result (Hollander and Einwohner, 2004). Often intent is a better sign of resistance in the case of highly covert resistance actions or when the desired effect is not achieved (Scott, 1985). From this follows that resistance requires: a subject of oppression or target and a recognizable expression of a desire to counter that oppression, which results in action intending to counter the targeted oppression (Leblanc, 1999).

Worker resistance to AC practices can vary widely, ranging from passive resistance, such as cynical comments and avoidance (Pregenzer et al., 2021), to more active forms of resistance, like gaming tactics (Rahman, 2021; Petre et al., 2019) or active manipulation of the algorithm (Jarrahi and Sutherland, 2019) to even more aggressive resistance, like mobilizing in online groups (Cini, 2022) to perform collective resistance actions (Chen, 2018; Rizzo and Atzeni, 2020; Lei, 2021) such as strikes (Vandaele, 2022). To help classify these escalating phases of resistance, we further adopt the categorization of resistance by Coetsee (1999) into apathy, passive resistance, active resistance, and aggressive resistance. Apathy involves inaction and disinterest, followed by more mild actions of passive resistance such as complaining, withdrawal, or excuses (Coetsee, 1999; Laumer and Eckhardt, 2012). Active resistance actions are characterized as strong but not destructive, such as voicing opinions, collectivizing, and asking others to intervene (Laumer and Eckhardt, 2012). Aggressive resistance actions have a destructive or at least disruptive nature and include threats, collective boycotts, and strikes (Lapointe and Rivard, 2005).

3 Method and Analysis

To gain insight into gig workers' acts of resistance to AC and the escalation of such acts in food delivery, we apply a topic modeling approach using BERTopic (Grootendorst, 2022) based on Reddit data. Topic modeling is well suited to understanding online audiences (Hannigan et al., 2019) and presents an efficient way to analyze large datasets compared to other qualitative methods (Schmiedel et al., 2019). Due to the collective settings in forums and the natural occurrence, social dynamics are more visible for analysis than in an interview setting (Aromaa et al., 2019). We, therefore, focused on active Reddit forums (subreddits), which were selected by searching Reddit with relevant terms and brands of food-delivery platforms. This resulted in the following forum selection: DoorDash (r/doordash_drivers), Deliveroo (r/deliveroos), Grubhub (r/grubhubdrivers), and a general forum for food-delivery workers (r/couriersofreddit) to achieve good data coverage and a homogeneous sample. The data was retrieved using the Pushshift API (Baumgartner et al., 2020) and its Python wrapper *pmaw* (Podolak, 2021) between October 2016 (by then, all four forums had been founded) and August 2022. Posts on subreddits consist of user *submissions,* including text or media and *comments* replying to them. We refer to them as *documents.* Submissions' titles and content sections were combined into a single document, and media submissions were excluded. Comments shorter than 15 words were also removed, as a random sample turned out to be not meaningful. Table 1 shows the initial size of the data set for every forum. As we are not concerned with platform-specific differences, the extracted forum data do not represent the respective platform but rather a homogeneous sample of food-delivery workers in general, and thus were intentionally not weighted the data for the final dataset. To further narrow down the selection of relevant documents, we searched the selected documents with a semantic keyword-based search consisting of a combination of Sentence-BERT (SBERT) (Reimers and Gurevych, 2019) and FAISS (Johnson et al., 2019). SBERT is a modification of the BERT (Devlin et al., 2019) technique to compare semantic sentence embeddings for similarity that allows using different pre-trained models. For this semantic search, we chose the *msmarco-distilbert-base-dot-prod-v3* (huggingface.co) model, which was trained on search queries in the Bing search engine and performs well at retrieving text passages relevant to keywords or search phrases. A set of 73 resistance-related keywords for search queries were derived from worker comments quoted in three highly relevant empirical studies in the AM research field (Lee et al., 2015; Möhlmann and Zalmanson, 2017; Möhlmann et al., 2021). Example keywords are "algorithm", "rules", and "resistance". The full keyword set can be provided on request. Using this search engine, we retrieved the 500 best search matches for each keyword. Since the results for some keywords overlapped, the final dataset contained 33,864 documents. Table 1 shows the number of documents from each source before (initial) and after (final) the keyword filter and Fig. 1 comprehensively summarizes all analysis steps.

Table 1 Composition of the dataset

Forum	r/doordash_drivers	r/deliveroos	r/grubhubdrivers	r/couriersofreddit
Initial	2,465,383	120,539	470,659	209,372
Final	24,510	4964	2506	1884

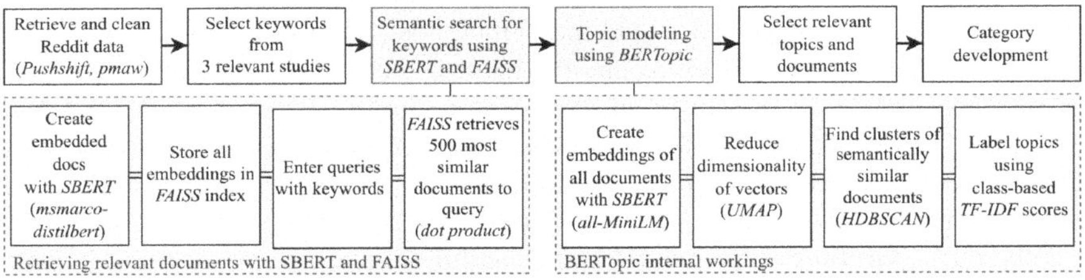

Fig. 1 Analysis steps

To analyze our final data set, containing 33,864 documents, we used the topic modeling approach BERTopic (Grootendorst, 2022). BERTopic sets itself apart from other topic modeling approaches by attempting to capture the semantics of texts using pre-trained large-language models. In contrast, most well-known topic modeling approaches, such as Latent Dirichlet Allocation (LDA), rely on a bag-of-words encoding that can only be used to consider the co-appearance likelihood of the individual words in a single dataset (Grootendorst, 2022). This makes BERTopic the most potent topic modeling method for analyzing text from social media (Egger and Yu, 2022). The next step involved labeling the resulting topics from the topic model. In addition to the automatic topic labels, we retrieved the most representative documents for each topic and followed an open coding approach to create the topic labels (Corbin and Strauss, 2014). The research team members independently coded and compared their labels to ensure intercoder reliability and minimize confirmation bias. To derive our 1st-order concepts, we clustered topic labels with similar or overlapping meanings using axial coding (Corbin and Strauss, 2014). To develop the 14 2nd-order themes representing resistance actions, the research team analyzed the representative documents of the 1st-order concepts and theorized, based on the four resistance dimensions (action, target, recognition, intent), whether and in what form resistance occurred. The found resistance action *coping*, for example, is intended to relieve work-related emotional stress, tension, and anxiety, has no specific target, usually goes unrecognized, and therefore resembles what Coetsee (1999) describes as apathetic or indifferent resistance behavior. The found resistance action *striking*, on the other hand, is intended to enforce workers' claims, gain public interest, and is targted against the platform itself, and recognized by almost all stakeholders resembling aggressive resistance. After theoretical saturation was reached through this process, the final 2nd-order themes were deductively allocated to the dimensions representing the phases of resistance by Coetsee (1999) (Glaser and Strauss, 2017; Gioia et al., 2013). Figure 2 shows the resulting data structure.

Illustrative Topics	1st-Order Concepts	2nd-Order Themes	Aggregated Dimensions
Topic 3: dd, just, app, orders Topic 17: Acceptance, acceptance rate, rate, orders Topic 66: memes, meme, send, sending Topic 56: robots, ai, automation, drone Topic 34: deactivated, appeal, account, fraud Topic 24: independent, contractors, contractors, independent contractors	Adaption to decrease tension	**Coping**	**Apathy**
	Detachment from involvement or responsibility	**Detaching**	
	Denying the algorithmic capabilities	**Denying**	
	Using irony, sarcasm, and cynicism	**Mocking**	**Passive Resistance**
	Figuring out how the algorithm works	**Sensemaking**	
	Independent contractors as position of power	**Empowering**	
Topic 25: multi, multi app, apping, multi apping	Complaints about lack of support and general	**Complaining**	
Topic 13: gig, gig work, work, gig workers	Working with given conditions to gain advantages	**Gaming**	**Active Resistance**
	Actions to avoid the algorithmic gaze	**Vanishing**	
	Deliberately changing conditions to gain advantages	**Manipulating**	
Topic 42: protest, protests, strike, protesting Topic 49: unions, union, unionize, workers	Threats against platform, customers, or restaurants	**Threatening**	**Aggressive Resistance**
	Collective execution of actions	**Collectivizing**	
	Collective organized stoppage of work	**Striking**	
	Quit the job and leave the platform	**Quitting**	

Fig. 2 Data structure

4 Findings

4.1 Apathy

From our analysis, we found that apathetic or indifferent resistance actions emerged in the form of *coping*, *detaching,* and *denying*. This form of resistance was mainly non-targeted and primarily recognized by other workers with the predominant intent to decrease work-related distress, tension, and anxiety.

Coping: Workers engaged in coping actions to decrease their emotional distress, tension, and anxiety caused by their work and exposure to opaque AC mechanisms. Through *coping*, workers maintain their ability to continue working.

> Yo dont quit your job but stop actively caring or stressing about it if you get fired your gonna cope that unemployment as long as you have been there for 3 months. Ive had shitty jobs and i just turn my brain off and we good.

Detaching: Apathetic actions of resistance were also found to be expressed in workers not taking responsibility or *detaching* from their identity as food-delivery workers and the emotional attachment that comes with it.

> […] Good luck. Get out while u can or multi app and save yourself the "lacking funds" headache. Dd [DoorDash] dont care about us. Time to keep that same energy when considering them.

Denying: Another way in which workers show their indifferent behavior towards the platform or the AC practices used is by denying the capabilities of the algorithm in terms of its control and matching capabilities.

> All you need is that one order to offer itself, who cares micromanaging your location compared to other dashers... the algorithm isn't as logical as you may expect it to be [...].

4.2 Passive Resistance

Actions of passive resistance emerged in the form of *mocking*, *sensemaking*, *empowering*, and *complaining*. This form of resistance was targeted against various actors (customer, algorithm, and platform) and also recognizable by them and other workers with the predominant intent to express dissatisfaction and gain knowledge about the functionality of the algorithm.

Mocking: *Mocking*, as a form of passive resistance, is targeted against the platform, customers, or restaurants by using irony, sarcasm, and cynicism to express dissatisfaction and undermine the platform's authority.

> I broke the algorithm matrix. Aka. How yo get orders if it's slow.: Every time. And I mean every time. When it's slow and I'm getting mid afternoon sleepy, I head into a parking lot and lean my seat back. As soon as I close my eyes, the alert chimes and an order roll in. Doordash knows when you are sleeping and when you're awake.

Sensemaking: Many workers use the analyzed forums to gather information and exchange with others to make sense of how the algorithm functions. Workers try to observe patterns and figure out why they receive specific orders and what behavior triggers the algorithm.

> The offers are all computer algorithms. Any algorithm will follow a set of rules. Just analyze the offers and look for patterns.

Empowering: Workers used their position as independent contractors as a position of power and leverage to formulate conditions and justify resistance actions. Workers strongly voice their opinions and are calling for outside actors to intervene.

> You're not a doordash driver, you're a self-employed independent contractor who controls their own income. [...] No, your location is your option. As an independent contractor you get to choose when and where you work. [...]

Complaining: A prominent theme that appeared was that various workers use the forums to express their dissatisfaction and complaint about the algorithm, the platform, customers, restaurants, or support.

> Support is a fucking joke.: A complete and utter waste of time...Unprofessional..slow.. literally worthless. Never trying to do the right thing for this bogus company ever again. They don't give a shit about any of us.

4.3 Active Resistance

Active forms of resistance emerged in our analysis in the form of *gaming, vanishing, and manipulating*. This form of resistance was targeted primarily against AC practices and mostly unrecognizable for the target with the predominant intent to gain advantages and actively sabotage the algorithm.

Gaming: Workers use various *gaming* practices to gain advantages. *Gaming* practices are characterized by the fact that the conditions imposed by the algorithm are not changed or manipulated but are dealt with by behavioral adaptation.

> I would assume they'd classify that under motorcycle but I'm not sure. Setting yourself to motorcycle gets the same short distance priority because the food still gets cold faster despite the same driving speed as a car. The problem is the algorithm. From what I understand if your set to bike it periodically checks your speed via GPS. If your going over a certain threshold it knows you can't be biking and flags you for fraud which can lead to deactivation. And we don't know what that threshold is...

Vanishing: Since most of the control mechanisms used are GPS-based, workers have developed specific circumvention tactics to hide from the algorithmic gaze to take unnoticed breaks, avoid low-paying orders, or avoid being monitored by customers.

> [...] Another little trick I just confirmed last week: Airplane mode on. Restart phone. Airplane mode off. It won't solve the problem of oversaturation but it gives a noticeable edge. That process resets your GPS and connections (ip address mac sim etc..)...also good to solve many other app issues with anything on your phone.

Manipulating: Workers try to manipulate the algorithm or the decisions made by the algorithm and, therefore, deliberately try to change the set conditions to gain advantages as an individual or a collective.

> There is a way to emulate "moving" to fool the algorithm into sending you orders without burning gas. Requires a computer though.

4.4 Aggressive Resistance

Aggressive resistance emerged in the form of *threatening, collectivizing, striking,* and *quitting*. It was targeted primarily against the platform with the predominant intent to force disruptive change and gain outsider attention.

Threatening: Workers try to *threaten* the platforms by announcing collective actions such as strikes, collectively declining orders which fall under a certain minimum payment, quitting, or even a class action lawsuit.

> Personally, I think this is a scam they are running at Doordash. It allows them to retain more income and is also in violation of minimum mileage payments that they promote to drivers. If we can get enough people to speak to being treated similarly, I think we can collectively address the problem. This can be done through state attorney's general and the threat of class action litigation.

Collectivizing: Most of the found active resistance actions had the potential to escalate into aggressive resistance actions by being performed by a collective rather than by an individual worker. For example, manipulation practices were much more impactful on a collective level. By forming a worker union, workers try to overcome the intentional individualization that the platform favors by managing workers separately.

> One thing im noticing, is that we as a community need to actually link up. I feel like we have the whole "gig-economy" filled to the brim with budding entrepreneurs but we're all sitting here.
>
> I wonder what would happen if we collectively started declining every order & clicked "order to small" I know they pause you but the algorithm should pick up that an entire region, or swaths of land go unclaimed. Any dasher out right now should click deny, reason, small order. Let's Wallstreet the system.

Striking: We found various calls for strikes and many signs that strikes have taken place. *Striking* is one of the most aggressive forms of resistance, as it involves high levels of organizing and planning, and a strong intent to take action and be recognized.

> DoorDash Strike Force—Means of Negotiation: I believe it's too early to put a date on a "strike" and I also believe that without any form of ongoing bargaining, and official discussion with DD [DoorDash] about rates, this tactic will be, largely, ineffective. For that reason, I've created a group whose goal it will be to gather enough drivers into one spot that we can then have enough power over their markets to inflict actual damage on their earnings. Once we've done that, the goal is to renegotiate with DD [DoorDash], as a group, with a council. [...]

Quitting: One of the most aggressive forms of resistance, which produces the most harm for the platforms but also the highest consequences for the workers, is *quitting*.

> [...] You have ZERO control of the outcome, but may look foolish in the process OR Quit and find another job that suits your needs. You have 100% control of this outcome.

5 Discussion

By mapping the 14 emerged resistance behaviors to the resistance categories (Apathy, Passive Resistance, Action Resistance, Aggressive Resistance) by Coetsee (1999) and discussing them based on the underlying resistance dimensions action, target, recoginition, and intent we showcase how our findings contribute to the more broad scientific discourse on resistance. Furthermore, we discuss concepts that potentially function as escalators or de-escalators for resistance in the gig economy context.

Apathy: When looking a the resistance behaviors *coping*, *detaching*, and *denying*, which we categorized as an apathetic or indifferent state of resistance, we find various similarities with resistance to IS or traditional management. Similar to service work systems, gig workers have to display certain behaviors or emotions (which may be inconsistent with their true feelings) in their customer contacts alongside the pressure to conform to an algorithm's requirements (Cameron, 2022; Shapiro, 2018). As a result, the workers focus more on their well-being by *coping* with work-related stress or feelings of powerlessness, which fits in with current findings that show that working in the gig economy leads to several health issues (Jhaver et al., 2018; Wood et al., 2019; Zhang et al., 2022). These *coping* tactics strongly resemble similar actions found by Jiang et al. (2021), such as comforting each other, as this also helps to keep emotions under control (Bucher et al., 2021) while working.

Passive Resistance: Workers express their dissatisfaction more openly by *mocking* and *complaining*. In regards to the *mocking* theme, we found that the workers have developed their language, e.g., referring to very good orders as "unicorns" or the DoorDash algorithm as "Tony" (in reference to the CEO Tony Xu). This resonates with a previous study, which also identified passive resistance actions such as using cynic language to mock the platform or the algorithm (Pregenzer et al., 2021). With a more strong intent, the actions are more target-oriented, and gaining knowledge about the algorithm's functionality becomes more important. This is found in *sensemaking* actions. *Sensemaking* describes a process that unfolds as a sequence in ongoing circumstances of workers organizing extracted cues from their work environment to make plausible sense (Weick et al., 2005). This can occur on the individual level or be extended to communities as collective sensemaking, referring to shared understanding arising from interactions within a social ecosystem (Chandra and Pal, 2019, Weick, 1995). Many workers, therefore, use forums to gather information, exchange with others, and share hints and advice (Jiang et al., 2021). Studies researching sensemaking of ride-hail drivers found that they engage in malevolent sensemaking, which includes beliefs with a negative assumption, and benevolent sensemaking, which refers to neutral or positive assumptions (Pregenzer et al., 2021). Furthermore, Möhlmann et al. (2022) theorized a new form of sensemaking—algorithm sensemaking—which describes how platform workers keep up with algorithmic instructions systematically. In our understanding, *sensemaking* serves three properties. It is a form of passive resistance, following Pregenzer et al. (2021)'s notion of malevolent sensemaking, it is a form of knowledge creation and gives workers a sense of *empowerment* as they become more knowledgeable.

Active Resistance: The feeling of *empowerment* and knowledge building through *sensemaking* can strengthen the intent. With more knowledge, workers can *vanish* from the algorithmic gaze, stay under the radar (Bucher et al., 2021), circumvent (Jarrahi and Sutherland, 2019), and avoid (Pregenzer et al., 2021) its continuous tracking. Workers constantly feel like being under the "algorithmic gaze" (Newlands, 2021), which reinforces covert resistance practices to escape the gaze and prevent recognition (Hollander and Einwohner, 2004). The forms of active resistance are mainly targeted against the algorithm or the implied AC mechanisms. The resistance intent behind the actions of *gaming* and *manipulating* is to gain a financial advantage, more freedom, and to harm the platform. This resembles what scholars describe as sabotage, which is defined as any behavior that deliberately undermines organizational goals (Brown, 1977). It is differentiated into "sabotage by direct action", which resembles *manipulating*, and "sabotage by circumvention", which is similar to *vanishing* (LaNuez and Jermier, 1994).

Aggressive Resistance: A central aspect of aggressive resistance is that workers *collectivize* to undertake resistance actions. Aggressive resistance is not targeted solely against the algorithm, but the target focus shifts to the platform. Targeting other actors, such as customers or restaurants, becomes rare. Also, the intent is to deliberately harm the platform by trying to organize a class action lawsuit or *collectively* decline orders which fall under a minimum threshold. Also, aggressive resistance actions are meant to be recognized by a wide range of actors and gain attention. Ultimately *striking* emerged as the second most aggressive form of resistance as it needs strong intent, a high degree of *collectivizing*, and a clear target. In our view, *quitting* is the most aggressive action of resistance because it harms the platform the most in the case of mass *quitting*. However, it also has high consequences for workers and thus requires the strongest intent.

Individual Opacity Versus Collective Knowledge: When looking at what differentiates AC from previous or more traditional forms of control, it comes down to the replacement of the human manager by an algorithm, which results in much tighter, less subjective, and more objective control due to the increased comprehensive, instantaneous, interactive, and opaque characteristics of AC (Kellogg et al., 2020). Especially the opacity of AM systems leads to difficulties in communicating with the platform or the algorithm, and the complexity of algorithmic decision-making lead workers to increasingly consider algorithms as "black boxes" (Shin, 2021; Rani et al., 2021; Eslami et al., 2019). This perception of algorithms as "black boxes" makes it difficult for workers to target their resistance actions as they encounter a depersonalized machine, which makes it almost impossible to estimate the impact of a specific resistance action. This opacity aspect helps to explain why workers begin to personify the algorithm by referring to it as "Tony" as a way to define a target against which they can direct their actions. Our findings are in line with other scholars who also identified opacity as a moderator of resistance Pregenzer et al. (2021) and fit in with the discussion about the transparency of AC and AM in current research (Weber et al., 2022; Schulze et al., 2022; Weiskopf and Hansen, 2022). Another key aspect of work in the gig economy is the isolation workers face as they operate highly individualized and separated from each other and the collective. As workers do not have personal contact with the platform or other workers and work independently from each other, this can lead to social isolation (Wood et al., 2019). Furthermore, workers can lose the ability to understand how their actions are perceived by others, whether their skills are satisfactory and improving, and how they contribute to the work of others as well as to the performance of the organization as a whole (Gal et al., 2020). Also, by interacting almost solely with a technology interface, workers are left with minimal human interactions. Consequently, in the gig economy, where algorithms mediate interpersonal relationships and communications, the ability of workers to create a community and a collective identity from which resistance actions could emerge is diminished (Gal et al., 2020). In summary, the interaction of these aspects forms the concept of individual opacity, which de-escalates or hinders resistance. In contrast to individual opacity, we present collective knowledge as a possible escalator for resistance. Collective knowledge emerged as a resistance escalator, as to perform resistance, workers need to gain knowledge about the algorithm. When looking at the similarities of the resistance actions *sensemaking*, *vanishing*, *manipulating*, and *gaming*, it emerged that knowledge about the target becomes a prerequisite to performing these actions. *Sensemaking* channels these efforts of knowledge creation. Furthermore, knowledge can help workers in an apathetic or indifferent state to form a stronger intent and better identify their target by learning more about it. Alongside knowledge, the community concept emerged as an integral part of resistance. The most characteristic theme of the community concept is *collectivizing*. We found that almost all of the aggressive resistance actions were carried out on a collective level. Therefore, the community seems amplifies passive or active forms of resistance to become aggressive forms of resistance. The impact of passive resistance actions such as *mocking* and *complaining* or active resistance actions such as *manipulating* or *gaming* could be strengthened and turned into aggressive resistance actions by acting as a collective.

6 Conclusion and Limitations

In conclusion, based on over 2 million text documents extracted from Reddit forums of different food-delivery platforms, we uncover 14 resistance actions showing how food-delivery workers resist algorithmic control. We further embed the found resistance behaviors in the current scientific resistance discourse and discuss possible concepts that function as escalators and de-escalators of resistance. By doing this, we contribute to current research in broadening the understanding of worker resistance against AC in the gig economy. Additionally, we developed an empirical use case for the topic modeling method BERTopic. The study design is limited in its ability to uncover apathy as workers who already participate in forums might already have a stronger resistance intent. Because our extracted forum data do not represent the respective platforms, but rather a sample of food-delivery workers, one or more platforms may be overrepresented, limiting the generalizability of the results. The identified escalators and de-escalators could serve as a first step toward better understanding the dynamics behind resistance. Therefore, the next steps are to track individual trajectories of resistance behavior over time and validate our findings by conducting focus group interviews.

Acknowledgements This research was funded in whole, or in part, by the Austrian Science Fund (FWF): P 35031-GBL. For the purpose of open access, the author has applied a CC BY public copyright license to any Author Accepted Manuscript version arising from this submission.

References

Anteby, M. & Chan, C. K. (2018). A self-fulfilling cycle of coercive surveillance: Workers' invisibility practices and managerial justification. *Organization Science,* 29, 247-263.

Anwar, M. A. & Graham, M. (2020). Hidden transcripts of the gig economy: labour agency and the new art of resistance among African gig workers. *Environment and Planning A: Economy and Space,* 52, 1269-1291.

Aromaa, E., Eriksson, P., Mills, J. H., Hiltunen, E., Lammassaari, M. & Mills, A. J. (2019). Critical sensemaking: challenges and promises. *Qualitative Research in Organizations and Management: An International Journal.*

Bambauer, J. & Zarsky, T. (2018). The algorithm game. *Notre Dame L. Rev.,* 94, 1.

Baumgartner, J., Zannettou, S., Keegan, B., Squire, M. & Blackburn, J. (2020). The Pushshift Reddit Dataset. arXiv.

Brown, G. (1977). Sabotage: A study in industrial conflict. *(No Title).*

Bucher, E. L., Schou, P. K. & Waldkirch, M. (2021). Pacifying the algorithm–Anticipatory compliance in the face of algorithmic management in the gig economy. *Organization,* 28, 44-67.

Burrell, J. (2016). How the machine 'thinks': Understanding opacity in machine learning algorithms. *Big data & society,* 3, 2053951715622512.

Cameron, L. D. (2022). "Making Out" While Driving: Relational and Efficiency Games in the Gig Economy. *Organization Science,* 33, 231-252.

Chandra, P. & Pal, J. Rumors and collective sensemaking: Managing ambiguity in an informal marketplace. Proceedings of the 2019 CHI Conference on Human Factors in Computing Systems, 2019. 1–12.

Chen, J. Y. (2018). Thrown under the bus and outrunning it! The logic of Didi and taxi drivers' labour and activism in the on-demand economy. *New media & society,* 20, 2691-2711.

Cini, L. (2022). Resisting algorithmic control: Understanding the rise and variety of platform worker mobilisations. *New Technology, Work and Employment.*

Coetsee, L. (1999). From resistance to commitment. *Public Administration Quarterly*, 204–222.

Corbin, J. & Strauss, A. (2014). *Basics of qualitative research: Techniques and procedures for developing grounded theory,* Sage publications.

Cram, W. A., Wiener, M., Tarafdar, M. & Benlian, A. Algorithmic Controls and their Implications for Gig Worker Well-being and Behavior. ICIS, 2020.

Cram, W. A. & Wiener, M. (2020). Technology-mediated control: Case examples and research directions for the future of organizational control. *Communications of the Association for Information Systems,* 46, 4.

Curchod, C., Patriotta, G., Cohen, L. & Neysen, N. (2020). Working for an algorithm: Power asymmetries and agency in online work settings. *Administrative Science Quarterly,* 65, 644-676.

Danaher, J. (2016). The threat of algocracy: Reality, resistance and accommodation. *Philosophy & Technology,* 29, 245-268.

Devlin, J., Chang, M.-W., Lee, K. & Toutanova, K. (2019). BERT: Pre-training of Deep Bidirectional Transformers for Language Understanding.

Duggan, J., Sherman, U., Carbery, R. & McDonnell, A. (2020). Algorithmic management and app-work in the gig economy: A research agenda for employment relations and HRM. *Human Resource Management Journal,* 30, 114-132.

Egger, R. & Yu, J. (2022). A Topic Modeling Comparison Between LDA, NMF, Top2Vec, and BERTopic to Demystify Twitter Posts. *Frontiers in Sociology,* 7, 886498.

Eslami, M., Vaccaro, K., Lee, M. K., Elazari Bar On, A., Gilbert, E. & Karahalios, K. User attitudes towards algorithmic opacity and transparency in online reviewing platforms. Proceedings of the 2019 CHI Conference on Human Factors in Computing Systems, 2019. 1–14.

Ferrari, F. & Graham, M. (2021). Fissures in algorithmic power: Platforms, code, and contestation. *Cultural Studies,* 35, 814-832.

Franke, L. M. & Pulignano, V. (2022). Labour Control and Commodification Strategies within a Food Delivery Platform in Belgium.

Gal, U., Jensen, T. B. & Stein, M.-K. (2020). Breaking the vicious cycle of algorithmic management: A virtue ethics approach to people analytics. *Information and Organization,* 30, 100301.
Gillespie, T. (2014). The relevance of algorithms. *Media technologies: Essays on communication, materiality, and society,* 167, 167.
Gioia, D. A., Corley, K. G. & Hamilton, A. L. (2013). Seeking qualitative rigor in inductive research: Notes on the Gioia methodology. *Organizational research methods,* 16, 15-31.
Glaser, B. G. & Strauss, A. L. (2017). *The discovery of grounded theory: Strategies for qualitative research,* Routledge.
Grootendorst, M. (2022). BERTopic: Neural topic modeling with a class-based TF-IDF procedure.
Hannigan, T. R., Haans, R. F., Vakili, K., Tchalian, H., Glaser, V. L., Wang, M. S., Kaplan, S. & Jennings, P. D. (2019). Topic modeling in management research: Rendering new theory from textual data. *Academy of Management Annals,* 13, 586-632.
Hollander, J. A. & Einwohner, R. L. Conceptualizing resistance. Sociological forum, 2004. Springer, 533–554.
huggingface.co. *sentence-transformers/msmarco-distilbert-base-dot-prod-v3* [Online]. Available: https://huggingface.co/sentence-transformers/msmarco-distilbert-base-dot-prod-v3 [Accessed].
Jarrahi, M. H., Sutherland, W., Nelson, S. B. & Sawyer, S. (2020). Platformic management, boundary resources for gig work, and worker autonomy. *Computer supported cooperative work (CSCW),* 29, 153-189.
Jarrahi, M. H. & Sutherland, W. Algorithmic management and algorithmic competencies: Understanding and appropriating algorithms in gig work. International Conference on Information, 2019. Springer, 578–589.
Jhaver, S., Karpfen, Y. & Antin, J. Algorithmic anxiety and coping strategies of Airbnb hosts. Proceedings of the 2018 CHI Conference on Human Factors in Computing Systems, 2018. 1–12.
Jiang, J., Adam, M. & Benlian, A. (2021). Algoactivistic Practices in Ridesharing-A Topic Modeling & Grounded Theory Approach.
Johnson, J., Douze, M. & Jégou, H. (2019). Billion-scale similarity search with gpus. *IEEE Transactions on Big Data,* 7, 535-547.
Kellogg, K. C., Valentine, M. A. & Christin, A. (2020). Algorithms at work: The new contested terrain of control. *Academy of Management Annals,* 14, 366-410.
LaNuez, D. & Jermier, J. M. (1994). Sabotage by managers and technocrats: Neglected patterns of resistance at work. *Resistance and power in organizations,* 219–251.
Lapointe, L. & Rivard, S. (2005). A multilevel model of resistance to information technology implementation. *MIS quarterly,* 461–491.
Laumer, S. & Eckhardt, A. (2012). Why do people reject technologies: a review of user resistance theories. *Information systems theory,* 63–86.
Leblanc, L. (1999). *Pretty in punk: Girls' gender resistance in a boys' subculture,* Rutgers University Press.
Lee, M. K., Kusbit, D., Metsky, E. & Dabbish, L. Working with machines: The impact of algorithmic and data-driven management on human workers. Proceedings of the 33rd annual ACM conference on human factors in computing systems, 2015. 1603–1612.
Lei, Y.-W. (2021). Delivering solidarity: Platform architecture and collective contention in China's platform economy. *American Sociological Review,* 86, 279-309.
Martin, D., Hanrahan, B. V., O'neill, J. & Gupta, N. Being a turker. Proceedings of the 17th ACM conference on Computer supported cooperative work & social computing, 2014. 224–235.
Masiero, S. Digital platform workers under COVID-19: A subaltern perspective. Proceedings of the 54th Hawaii International Conference on System Sciences, 2021. 6349.
Möhlmann, M. & Zalmanson, L. (2017). Hands on the wheel: Navigating algorithmic management and Uber drivers'. *38th ICIS Proceedings.*
Möhlmann, M., Zalmanson, L., Henfridsson, O. & Gregory, R. (2021). Algorithmic management of work on online labor platforms: When matching meets control. *MIS Quarterly.*

Möhlmann, M., de Lima Salge, C. A. & Marabelli, M. (2022). Algorithm Sensemaking: How Platform Workers Make Sense of Algorithmic Management. *Journal of the Association for Information Systems.*

Newlands, G. (2021). Algorithmic surveillance in the gig economy: The organization of work through Lefebvrian conceived space. *Organization Studies,* 42, 719-737.

Petre, C., Duffy, B. E. & Hund, E. (2019). "Gaming the system": Platform paternalism and the politics of algorithmic visibility. *Social Media+ Society,* 5, 2056305119879995.

Podolak, M. (2021). pmaw: A multithread Pushshift.io API Wrapper for reddit.com comment and submission searches. 2.1.3 ed.

Pregenzer, M., Remus, U. & Wiener, M. When Market Meets Bureaucracy: Toward an Integrative Framework of Technology-Mediated Control in the Gig Economy. ECIS, 2020.

Pregenzer, M., Wieser, F., Santiago Walser, R. & Remus, U. (2021). Obscure Oversight: Opacity Drives Sensemaking and Resistance Behavior in Algorithmic Management.

Rahman, H. A. (2021). The invisible cage: Workers' reactivity to opaque algorithmic evaluations. *Administrative Science Quarterly,* 66, 945-988.

Rani, U., Kumar Dhir, R., Furrer, M., Gőbel, N., Moraiti, A. & Cooney, S. (2021). *World employment and social outlook: the role of digital labour platforms in transforming the world of work,* International Labour Organisation.

Reimers, N. & Gurevych, I. (2019). Sentence-bert: Sentence embeddings using siamese bert-networks. *arXiv preprint* arXiv:1908.10084.

Rizzo, M. & Atzeni, M. (2020). Workers' power in resisting precarity: comparing transport workers in Buenos Aires and Dar es Salaam. *Work, Employment and Society,* 34, 1114-1130.

Rubin, J. W. (1995). Defining resistance: Contested interpretations of everyday acts. *Stud. L. Pol. & Soc'y,* 15, 237.

Schmiedel, T., Müller, O. & vom Brocke, J. (2019). Topic Modeling as a Strategy of Inquiry in Organizational Research: A Tutorial With an Application Example on Organizational Culture. *Organizational Research Methods,* 22, 941-968.

Schulze, L., Trenz, M., Cai, Z. & Tan, C.-W. (2022). Algorithmic Unfairness on Digital Labor Platforms: How Algorithmic Management Practices Disadvantage Workers.

Scott, J. C. (1985). *Weapons of the weak: Everyday forms of peasant resistance,* yale university Press.

Shapiro, A. (2018). Between autonomy and control: Strategies of arbitrage in the "on-demand" economy. *New Media & Society,* 20, 2954-2971.

Shin, D. (2021). The effects of explainability and causability on perception, trust, and acceptance: Implications for explainable AI. *International Journal of Human-Computer Studies,* 146, 102551.

Tan, Z. M., Aggarwal, N., Cowls, J., Morley, J., Taddeo, M. & Floridi, L. (2021). The ethical debate about the gig economy: A review and critical analysis. *Technology in Society,* 65, 101594.

Tassinari, A. & Maccarrone, V. (2020). Riders on the storm: Workplace solidarity among gig economy couriers in Italy and the UK. *Work, Employment and Society,* 34, 35-54.

Vandaele, K. (2022). Vulnerable food delivery platforms under pressure: protesting couriers seeking "algorithmic justice" and alternatives. *Forthcoming in Routledge Handbook of the Gig Economy, edited by I. Ness, New York, Routledge.*

Weber, M., Remus, U. & Pregenzer, M. (2022). A New Era of Control: Understanding Algorithmic Control in the Gig Economy.

Weick, K. E. (1995). *Sensemaking in organizations,* Sage.

Weick, K. E., Sutcliffe, K. M. & Obstfeld, D. (2005). Organizing and the process of sensemaking. *Organization science,* 16, 409-421.

Weiskopf, R. & Hansen, H. K. (2022). Algorithmic Governmentality and the Space of Ethics: Examples from'People Analytics'. *Human Relations.*

Wong, S. I. (2022). Job Crafting Can Help Digital Gig Workers Build Resilience. *Harvard Business Review.* https://hbr.org/2022/01/job-crafting-can-help-digital-gig-workers-build-resilience.

Wood, A. J., Graham, M., Lehdonvirta, V. & Hjorth, I. (2019). Good gig, bad gig: autonomy and algorithmic control in the global gig economy. *Work, Employment and Society,* 33, 56-75.
Woodcock, J. (2021). *The fight against platform capitalism: an inquiry into the global struggles of the gig economy*, University of Westminster Press.
Yu, Z., Treré, E. & Bonini, T. (2022). The emergence of algorithmic solidarity: unveiling mutual aid practices and resistance among Chinese delivery workers. *Media International Australia,* 183, 107-123.
Zhang, A., Boltz, A., Wang, C.-W. & Lee, M. K. Algorithmic Management Reimagined For Workers and By Workers: Centering Worker Well-Being in Gig Work. Proceedings of ACM CHI, 2022.

Introducing a Methodological Approach to Determine Value Shares in Digital Ecosystems

Cristina Mihale-Wilson, Simon Hagen, Tobias Kohl, Henrik Kortum, Fabian Illgen, Jonas Rebstadt, Oliver Thomas, and Oliver Hinz

Abstract Motivated by the critical yet unsolved task of fair value distribution in digital ecosystems (DEs), this study presents a methodological approach that allows us to determine ecosystem components' value share to the total co-created value. Our method takes a holistic perspective on DEs. It suggests that when viewing DEs as complex networks, the value share of a component to the total co-created value stems from the network size and the interaction between the network participants. We demonstrate the applicability of the proposed method in a simulation of a Smart Living service ecosystem. Our simulation shows that our method is suitable for unraveling hitherto hidden interconnectedness between value-co-creating ecosystem components. Components that offer a low structural contribution to the total value

C. Mihale-Wilson (✉) · T. Kohl · O. Hinz
Wirtschaftsinformatik und Informationsmanagement, Goethe Universität Frankfurt, Frankfurt, Germany
e-mail: mihale-wilson@wiwi.uni-frankfurt.de

T. Kohl
e-mail: tokohl@wiwi.uni-frankfurt.de

O. Hinz
e-mail: ohinz@wiwi.uni-frankfurt.de

S. Hagen · H. Kortum · F. Illgen · J. Rebstadt · O. Thomas
Deutsches Forschungszentrum für Künstliche Intelligenz GmbH, Osnabrück, Germany
e-mail: simon.hagen@dfki.de

H. Kortum
e-mail: henrik.kortum@dfki.de

F. Illgen
e-mail: fabian.illgen@dfki.de

J. Rebstadt
e-mail: jonas.rebstadt@dfki.de

O. Thomas
e-mail: oliver.thomas@dfki.de

D. Beverungen et al. (eds.), *Transforming the Digitally Sustainable Enterprise*, Lecture Notes in Information Systems and Organisation 76,
https://doi.org/10.1007/978-3-031-80125-9_9

can still play a crucial role in the network and have the most significant value share to the whole network.

Keywords Value decomposition · Value share · Co-created value · Digital ecosystem · Network theory

1 Introduction

In today's highly competitive business environment, companies increasingly recognize the importance of Digital Ecosystems (DEs) as a pathway to success and growth (Subramaniam et al. 2019). DEs are dynamic multi-agent environments in which interconnected digital services, goods, and platforms interact to create unique better products and services for their clients (Wang 2021). One of the biggest appeals of DEs is that they enable their participants to generate unique value that otherwise would not materialize (therein *co-created value*). Specifically, in DEs, the participants jointly contribute to the ecosystem's success by creating technologies, services, or tools that other ecosystem participants can recombine with other components to generate new complementary products and services (Floetgen et al. 2022).

Because in DEs co-created value emerges only through resource sharing and recombination of data and services, successful DEs demand extensive collaboration among their participants (Floetgen et al. 2022; Valdez-De-Leon 2019). Yet, to keep participants motivated to contribute, DEs must have adequate mechanisms for fair revenue allocation across partners (Valdez-De-Leon 2019). If the co-created value of the DE is not fairly distributed across contributing partners, the ecosystem is unattractive for new actors and, thus likely to fail (Valdez-De-Leon 2019; Wang 2021). Surprisingly, despite the importance of fair value distribution for DE's success, currently, it remains unclear how to achieve a fair value sharing mechanism.

Prior literature focuses predominantly on the value creation in DEs but remains silent on the distribution of the co-created value across the involved participants. One of the most probable reasons for this gap in the literature is the recombinant yet partly opaque nature of DEs. Although co-created value arises from the interconnectedness of the assets of various ecosystem participants, these interconnections often remain hidden. Accordingly, each participant's contribution to the total co-created value remains concealed. Viewing co-created value as the sum of value shares contributed by a variety of ecosystem components (e.g., products, data, services), a fair distribution of the total co-created value requires us to identify and quantify the contribution share of each participant. As of now, the critical task of determining each participant's value contribution share to the total of parts of the co-created value has yet to be solved. Our paper addresses this literature gap by addressing the question: *[RQ]: How can we determine the value shares of each contributor to the co-created value in DEs?*

2 Theoretical Background and Related Work

As the literature on DEs continues to develop across various disciplines, there is no widely established vocabulary to theorize various aspects of DEs. To avoid jingle-jangle fallacies stemming from the ambiguous use of our focal terms (e.g., participant, co-created value), in this section, we present insights from prior literature while clarifying the central terminology in our paper. First of all, for the sake of simplicity, we refer to any actors involved in the value-creation process as *participants*. Participants are typically providers of *components*. Depending on the DE domain, such components can be data, software artifacts, or hardware (e.g., Internet of Things devices). Whether participants are companies, organizations, independent developers, or individuals is not essential at this point. Similarly, whether a component is a data source, a trained Artificial Intelligence (AI) model, or a complex service is also unimportant. After all, we understand the *allocation of value to be fair* when it is not based on actors' size or available resources but rather based on the value that a component brings when it is combined with other components. Analogous to new products developments in a firm, where extant core-components of previous products are used for the development of new products and services (Mihale-Wilson et al. 2022), in digital ecosystems companies effectively integrate the functionalities and essential components of other products and services into their new offerings. This deliberate approach significantly shortens their time to market while substantially mitigating the risks of failure (Mihale-Wilson et al. 2022).

The most important characteristic of *components* is that they are tangible assets that can exist independently but simultaneously be part of a larger system. To illustrate the concept of components, let us assume an exemplary DE for AI-based services in Smart Living. The Smart Living concept (also often referred to as "smart home") envisions that by integrating technology (e.g., wearables, home sensors, intelligent transportation systems, and other AI-based systems), we can automate and optimize daily routines and activities to improve humans' comfort and quality of life. Hence, within the context of smart living DEs, various components are working together and form new complex products and services such as improved predictive maintenance of housing infrastructure (e.g., Lowin et al. 2021; Lowin and Mihale-Wilson 2021), or AI-based personal assistance (Mihale-Wilson et al. 2017, 2019). AI-based assistants can help individuals fulfill their personal and professional obligations easier. In the future, AI-based assistants will be able to perform tasks on their users' behalf, freeing up time for more meaningful activities (Meurisch et al. 2020). To this end, the ecosystem might, for instance, encompass an AI model that forecasts anomalous behavior in a heat sensor (call it <AI model>). This <AI model> can function on its own and predict heat sensor failures. Simultaneously, the same <AI model> can be combined with a particular dataset <dataset> and trained to generate a service <service> that predicts failures in more than one type of sensor and device. Based on our definition above, all three assets <AI model>, <dataset>, and <service> represent components. After all, <dataset> and <service> can again exist as independent entities on their own. Simultaneously, <dataset> and <service> can be combined with other data sets and services to generate more complex services. These examples illustrate the hierarchical relationship between components and, ultimately the participants in a DE. The fact that each component can exist in more than one version and is combinable with a multitude of other components which can also exist in more than one version complicates these relationships even further. Case in point: the <AI model> can exist in an initial version <_v_1> which is trained on a relatively small set of sensor data. Additionally, more elaborate versions of the <AI model> may exist <v_x>. Analogously, there might also be various versions of <dataset_v_x> and <service_v_x>. Assuming that there exist three versions <v_1>, <v_2>, and <v_3> of each of the three components <AI model>, <dataset>, and <service>, there are 27 possible recombinations. Clearly, in practice, there are more than three components and versions available to recombine with each other to co-create value. Against this background, we follow Kortum et al. (2022b) and suggest modeling and analyzing the complexly interwoven relationship between the components of a DE based on **network theory**.

Nascent in the field of mathematics network theory can be used to model and analyze a wide range of phenomena, including social networks, biological systems (Albert and Barabási 2002; Newman 2003), product and service systems (Hagen et al. 2019), and technological networks (Kortum et al. 2022a). The core idea of network theory is that actors within a network influence each other. Hence, the overall performance and behavior of the network depend not only on network size but also on the interactions in the network.

Following Newman (2003), a network consists of a set of items (in our case, components, which are also referred to as *nodes*) and the connections between them (also referred to as *edges*). Networks are often represented as graphs. The most parsimonious network entails a set of nodes joined by edges. More complex and sophisticated networks, however, can distinguish between more than one type of node and edges (Newman 2003). Circling back to our exemplary components (<AI model>, <dataset>, and <service>) and the network they build: The simplest form of the network would be to list the three components and link them to each other. More sophisticated representation of the network, however, would incorporate, for instance, the class of the AI model (i.e., decision tree, neural network), or directed or weighted edges to better describe the relationships between the nodes they connect.

While graphs allow visual investigations and inferences when the network under investigation is small and parsimonious, they are less visually informative as the number of nodes and edges and the level of detail increase (Newman 2003). Against this background, network theorists have developed various models and statistical methods to quantify large and complex networks. We use extant methods to model and document the **value chain within a DE**—i.e., the path of how independent components contribute to the total co-created value.

Central to the idea of *value chains* is that new value is generated when adding components to the chain. A value chain starts with an organic component—i.e., a component that is not the product of combining other components. We refer to the value-added when combining another component with the organic component as

Value Share (VS). We must clarify the term **value** at this stage, as it has several connotations across different research disciplines (Jimenez and Arenas 2021).

In essence, *value* can be defined in economic or more abstract terms. Most of the extant work investigating value contributions in complex networks such as DEs gravitates around economic value like revenue or pricing (e.g., Fricker and Maksimov 2017; Nguyen and Paczos 2020; Stoppel and Roth 2016). Nguyen and Paczos (2020), for instance, discuss approaches to measure the economic value of data, data monetization strategies for new business models, and how the value of data can be conceptualized and measured from a business perspective. Fricker and Maksimov (2017) analyze mechanisms used to evaluate the pricing of data products in data marketplaces. Stoppel and Roth (2016) transfer value-based pricing from the product to the service-oriented perspective. We acknowledge that the economic perspective on value is helpful on numerous occasions. However, for the purpose of this study, a more comprehensive perspective is needed. In this vein, revenue and pricing capture only the financial performance of the ecosystem, whereas a more abstract understanding of value can also entail non-financial, intangible benefits. Most recently, Jimenez and Arenas (2021) built on Grover and Kohli (2012) and used IT-based value to refer to the value generated when companies collaborate to implement joint IT-based products and services. In this study, we follow these scholars and comprehend *co-created value* as an abstract concept that can incorporate all types of utility generated through component recombination.

3 Methodological Approach for Value Decomposition in DEs

We process the various streams of literature to develop a method that allows us to decompose the co-created value in DEs. Our method exploits one of the many advantages of DEs—that they typically reveal (machine-readable) information on the relationships between individual components. Applying network theory to DEs and using the previously discussed nomenclatures, we can visualize components as nodes that are related to each other via directed edges. Components can form subnetworks. This representation allows new ways of calculating the value share each component contributes to the network or subnetwork (denoted by τ). Due to the network representation of the DE, one would immediately be tempted to determine that a node contributes to τ based on the node's position in the network (e.g., centrality) and other parameters. Although this approach is per se correct, it is incomplete, as it disregards the fact that nodes are recombinant, and thus the value of a node also depends on the value it generates for the subsequent nodes. Following this logic, our proposed method postulates that the value share that a node contributes to τ depends on *(i) the network size*—i.e., the amount of nodes and edges in the network and *(ii) its recombinant (or recursive) nature*.

We distinguish between *contributions* and *weights* of a node to τ. Contributions are generally computed within a (sub-)network while weights are typically parameters provided by domain experts. Besides, we also distinguish between the *structural* and *value-added* worth of a node within the entire network. The value-added stems from any value chains' central assumption that each component within the chain needs to add value to subsequent components of the chain. The structural value of a node, however, reflects that within a network there are interdependencies of components that need to be accounted for. After all, the interdependencies between components imply that the failure or malfunctioning of one component can have dire consequences for the entire network. We use this nomenclature to **describe the value shares that a node can have in a network**. We introduce **four core constructs**: *Structural Contributions (SC), Value-added Contributions (VC), Structural Weights (SW), and Value-added Weights (VW).* We elaborate on these core constructs individually.

The structural contribution (SC) of a component (i.e., node) is based on its location within the network. We explain based on a simplified example: A component that is located at the periphery (call it *periphery node*) of a network and thus has relatively few edges linking them with other components yields a comparatively small value for the network. In contrast, a component located at the center of the network (call it *central node*) with many edges that link it to various other components will yield a comparatively higher value to the network than the periphery node. The difference in value contribution of the exemplary periphery and central nodes stems from their relative importance for the network's overall performance. If the central node fails or malfunctions, large parts of the ecosystem will no longer be functional. In contrast, a failure of the periphery node is likely to have only minor effects on the overall performance of the ecosystem. Recently, Kortum et al. (2022b) identified possible metrics from network theory suitable for quantifying the relevance of a node within an ecosystem. In this work, the authors mention that PageRank is a popular method suitable for this purpose. PageRank evaluates the structural importance of a node based on the number and dependencies of other nodes in the network. This way, it provides insights on the underlying structure and importance of a node in relation to the network as a whole. In particular, PageRank uses the incoming edges to a node for calculating the importance of that node relative to the network as a whole. Thus, PageRank yields a network importance and ranks the nodes in an 'inverse' order compared to the aforementioned value chain contemplation. A node with a higher number of incoming edges are considered more important than edges with a low number of incoming edges.

In contrast to the structural contribution, the *Value Contribution (VC)* of a component (i.e., node) does not depend on its position in the network. It is determined directly from its value for one (or more) specific subsequent node(s). In this sense, a single node sometimes has several value contributions depending on the number of nodes that follow it. In technical terms, the value contribution represents the amount a node adds to the fulfillment of the task of its successor. This can be nicely illustrated based on the example of an AI-based component for the prediction of a value, which uses as input several services that provide or manipulate data.

Reusing the introduced nomenclature, imagine the following: An <AI model> is used by two different Services <S_1> and <S_2>. In both cases, <AI model> uses the same <dataset> for its training. Now, for <S_1>, the <AI model> is the only input and thereby has a high VC for <S_1>. In contrast, <S_2> has many different inputs, one being <AI model>. Clearly, the VC of <AI model> will probably be lower. If we assume that two <AI models> with the same functionality but from different providers are present in the DE, their VC for a <Service> might be different. To quantify their respective VC, different approaches are applicable. For example, the VC can be measured via the mean squared error (*MSE*). Generally speaking, the lower the MSE, the better the AI service. In this case, the MSE depends on the inputs ('features') provided by the predecessor node(s), here the <dataset>. A feature's specific contribution to the forecast's quality can be quantified using state-of-the-art statistical methods and represents the VC of the predecessor node for the AI service. For AI-based components, we can use, for example, SHapley Additive exPlanations (SHAP) values, permutation feature importance, or feature importance for trees. For non-AI services, other forms of contribution determination can be used (e.g., coefficient magnitude method, variance inflation factor (VIF), partial regression coefficient method).

We now turn to the *Structural* (SW) and *Value Weights* (VW), which should currently be determined by domain experts, who can evaluate the relative importance of SW and VW for the particular DE and within a specific domain. After all, every DE is marked by specific characteristics or manners dictated by the encompassing domain (e.g., Smart Living, production, etc.). These specific characteristics need to be accounted for, especially because these weights can vary greatly from application domain to application domain. In ecosystems with close links between services and few redundancies, for example, structural weights play a more important role than in ecosystems in which many substitutes exist for a particular service. Since both weights express relative importance, they must sum up to one.

All previous things considered, we formally propose that the value share (*VS*) of a component (*c*) to the overall network value τ ($\sum_1^n VS$) is calculated as:

$$VS_c = \frac{1}{\sum_1^n VS}\left(SW\frac{1}{n}\sum_1^n SC_c + VW\frac{1}{n}\sum_1^n VC_c\right) \quad (1)$$

where:

VS *denotes the value-added worth of a component (i.e., node) in the value chain to a related component (i.e., node).*

SW *is the structural weight of a node (i.e., represents a context-dependent weighing of the structural contribution of a node). SW together with the value weight (VW) add up to 1.*

SC *denotes the structural contribution of a node (i.e. the importance of a node in the value chain depending on its position in the (sub-)network).*

VW *refers to the value weight (i.e., calculated as a context-dependent weighting of the value contribution). VW together with the structural weight (SW) add up to 1.*
VC *is the value contribution of a node (i.e., the amount a component adds to the fulfillment of the task of its successor).*
c *denotes the focal component (i.e., node) for which the value share is computed.*
n *is the number of components (i.e., nodes) in the DE (i.e., network).*

$SW\frac{1}{n}\sum_1^n SC_c$ denotes the structural contribution of the component multiplied by its importance weight. This value does not change unless the structure of the DE changes. In contrast, $VW\frac{1}{n}\sum_1^n VC_c$ captures the value contribution of a component depending on the subnetwork evaluated. This value contribution might change in accordance with the value that that particular node adds to other services.

4 Simulation Study to Demonstrate Applicability

To demonstrate the applicability of the proposed method, we conduct a simulation study mimicking a DE in the Smart Living industry. The network was built with the Python package NetworkX (https://networkx.org/) and contains the relationships of components in the domain of Smart Living—e.g., *energy optimization* (i.e., appliance energy disaggregation, energy consumption recommendations), *user assistance* (e.g., smart access system, cooking assistance, nutrition value calculation, fridge inventory detection) and other *generic components* (e.g., face recognition, dataspace preprocessing, activity recognition or mold risk recognition). We generated a representation of the mentioned components (nodes) and their relations to each other (edges) and implemented Eq. (1) in Python. Figure 1 illustrates the simulated network and the assumed components and edges.

For our simulations, we randomly assume edge values (VC) between [0 and 5]—see Table lower left of Fig. 1. In a real DE, VCs can be estimated by using model-agnostic determined values such as SHAP. To calculate each node's structural contribution (SC) we used the previously mentioned PageRank method. To calculate the value shares of components such as services that do not offer any direct value to subsequent nodes in the network, we need only the structural contribution (SC)—in our case their PageRank. To calculate the value share (VS) of a node, we need the value and structural weights of the DE under scrutiny. Domain experts in Smart Living estimated the structural weight (SW) to 0.7 and the value weight (VW) to 0.3. Based on these parameters and Eq. (1), we first calculate each node's corresponding **value share (*VS*) to the co-created value in the entire network**. Table 1 presents the estimated value shares within the postulated network. As the VCs in the table reveal, the dataspace preprocessing component has the highest value share to the total network (VS = 0.178), followed by the cooking assistance component (VS = 0.096). The smart access system and energy consumption recommendations are on par (VS = 0.077).

Node	Pagerank
Face_Recognition	0.063029
Smart_Access_System	0.110549
Activity_Level_Apartment	0.063029
Mold_Risk_Prediction	0.089816
Energy_Consumption_Recommendation_on_Activity_Level	0.089816
Appliance_Energy_Disaggregation	0.063029
Energy_Consumption_Recommendation	0.110549
Fridge_Inventory_Detection	0.063029
Purchasing_Assistance	0.089816
Cooking_Assistance	0.137336
Nutri_Value_Calculation	0.063029
Dataspace_Preprocessing	0.056975

Source	Target	VC
Face_Recognition	Smart_Access_System	5
Activity_Level_Apartment	Mold_Risk_Prediction	4
Activity_Level_Apartment	Energy_Consumption_Recommendation_on_Activity_Level	5
Appliance_Energy_Disaggregation	Energy_Consumption_Recommendation	4
Fridge_Inventory_Detection	Purchasing_Assistance	4
Fridge_Inventory_Detection	Cooking_Assistance	4
Nutri_Value_Calculation	Cooking_Assistance	3
Dataspace_Preprocessing	Face_Recognition	4
Dataspace_Preprocessing	Mold_Risk_Prediction	4
Dataspace_Preprocessing	Activity_Level_Apartment	3
Dataspace_Preprocessing	Appliance_Energy_Disaggregation	3
Dataspace_Preprocessing	Fridge_Inventory_Detection	3
Dataspace_Preprocessing	Nutri_Value_Calculation	2
Dataspace_Preprocessing	Purchasing_Assistance	3
Dataspace_Preprocessing	Energy_Consumption_Recommendation_on_Activity_Level	3

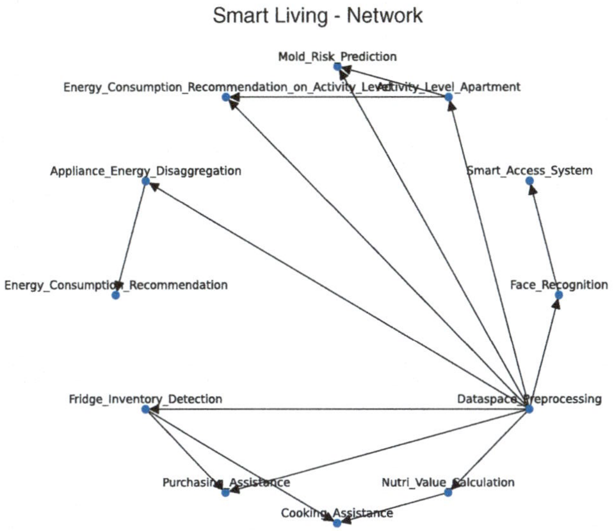

Fig. 1 Simulation of a DE for Smart Living services and assumed VC

Table 1 Value share (VS) to the total co-created value (per node)

Node	VS per node (computed)
Face_Recognition	0.072
Smart_Access_System	0.077
Activity_Level_Apartment	0.094
Mold_Risk_Prediction	0.063
Energy_Consumption_Recommendation_on_Activity_Level	0.063
Appliance_Energy_Disaggregation	0.066
Energy_Consumption_Recommendation	0.077
Fridge_Inventory_Detection	0.089
Purchasing_Assistance	0.063
Cooking_Assistance	0.096
Nutri_Value_Calculation	0.061
Dataspace_Preprocessing	0.179
Cumulated value	1.0

Interestingly although we set the value weight to only 0.3, which should in theory, result in a network value distribution still close to other current approaches, we end up with the node *Dataspace_Preprocessing* (VS = 0.178) having the highest value share contribution in the network. Even though, its structural importance is relatively small (SC = 0.056). This in turn, reiterates how important our methodology is to represent the added value in new DE. By giving a slight benefit to nodes that offer a high value to their subsequent nodes (VW = 0.3), components such as "data preprocessing" reveal their impact to the total co-created network value. This is important to encourage nodes that offer added value (e.g., enriched, data, preprocessing steps) to subsequent components in the value chain.

To verify the plausibility of the estimated VS, we assess the instantiation of the node *Activity_Level_Apartment* in more detail. Precisely, we first calculate the inner term of our formula ($SW\frac{1}{n}\sum_1^n SC_c + VW\frac{1}{n}\sum_1^n VC_c$), which represents the value-added by the node before considering the overall network to create the value share (VS). With our structural weight (SW) set to 0.7, the node *Activity_Level_Apartment* has a structural contribution (SC)—i.e., PageRank of ~ 0.063. The VC is computed by considering the nodes' contribution to all connected nodes, divided by the sum of the VC in this smaller sub-network.

With our set value weight factor (VW) at 0.3, the VC of our node 'Activity_Level_Apartment' is ~ 0.167. Now we can calculate our inner term in the formula to get the value-added ~ 0.094. Note that this value-added is not yet in relation to the network.

$$VS_{node} = \frac{1}{\sum_1^n VS'}(0.7 * 0.063 + 0.3 * 0.167)$$

To compute our overall value share (VS), we calculate the relative share of the value-added ~ 0.0941 in relation to the value co-created to the entire network. To this end, we divide ~ 0.0941 through the sum of all inner terms of all nodes in the network. In our simulated network this results in the overall network value-added at ~ 1.0. We compute VS_{node} as 0.094/1.0 = 0.094.

Next, we focus next on each node's **value share (*VS*) to the total co-created value within a sub-network—i.e., a node's corresponding value chain**(s). Let us consider the value chain of the component *Energy_Consumption_Recommendation.* Figure 2 highlights this path in red. In this example, the biggest contribution to creating the focal component *Energy_Consumption_Recommendation* comes from the *Appliance_Energy_Disaggregation* component. Next to the graphical network in Fig. 2, each network value chain is listed with its internal value shares for the nodes in its corresponding sub-network. These are also calculated based on Eq. (1). However, the co-created value under consideration is that of a sub-network rather than the entire network. This implies that to calculate the VC of a node, only subsequent nodes inside the value chain are considered. Likewise, to calculate the VS's of all nodes in the value chain, again, only the sum of the added value of the nodes inside this sub-network is considered. However, this approach allows for more in-depth analyses of specific value chains. Additionally, it can offer insights into diversifying a specific value chain.

To demonstrate the usefulness and functionality of the weights we also simulated other, contrary or more extreme allocations. In many occasions this leads the first and last node in the network to 'switch' importance, which is expected due to the underlying methods for value calculation. For the intermediary nodes it depends, obviously, on the structure of the network and their individual VC, but in general the changes are less significant compared to the first and last nodes. In the example given

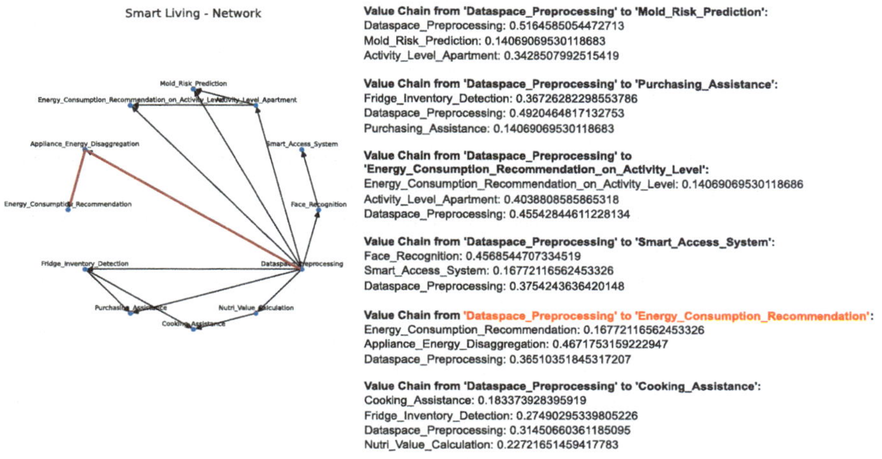

Fig. 2 Value distribution per value chain in the network

above these results are plausible and also in general suggest the comprehensiveness of the approach.

5 Discussion

In this work, we develop and present a methodological approach suitable to decompose the co-created value in (sub)networks. We demonstrate the applicability of the proposed methodology in a simulation with a Smart Living service ecosystem. This way, we present various contributions to theory and practice.

We highlight three of this study's main theoretical contributions. Firstly, our research closes the gap in the literature surrounding the question of how to achieve fair value allocation. Although various scholars (e.g., Valdez-De-Leon 2019; Wang 2021) emphasize the importance of fair value distribution across the ecosystem contributors for the DEs' long-term success, the corpus of literature presents a "blindspot" on this topic. The second main contribution of our work is its holistic perspective on co-created value. We suggest viewing DEs as complex entities for which we can model the value creation and relationship between its components based on constructs from network theory. This is not new per se. What is new, however, is our proposition to leverage the strengths of the network representation of the DE to account not only for structural interconnected relationships between DE components but also for the recombinant, recursive nature of these relationships. Earlier, we noted that components can exist alone and are part of more complex components. These more complex components can provide input and can be recombined with other components to generate even more sophisticated components. The recursive nature of DE components implies that the value contribution of a component is determined not only by its direct successors but also recursively by those components that build on the successors, and so on.

Based on the described recursivity and Wang's (2021) idea that DEs should be investigated not only in their parts but also as a whole, we argue that considering only structural interconnectivity would yield an incomplete and thus erroneous quantification of the contributors' value shares in the ecosystem. In contrast, our holistic approach will generate more accurate quantifications of components' value shares the co-created value. Ultimately, we contribute to the current corpus of literature by presenting a domain and component-agnostic approach to value decomposition. Extant literature investigated primarily data and value in economic terms (e.g., Fricker and Maksimov 2017; Nguyen and Paczos 2020). While we agree that the economic perspective on value is valuable in various contexts, the economic perspective is incomplete for complex and heterogeneous DEs that entail many types of digital species (e.g., data, software, and hardware). Our work rests upon the notion that fair value contribution implies that all types of tangible assets within an ecosystem need to be considered. In this vein, our method uses "component" as one of its core constructs. Thereby it is not crucial whether these components are data, hard- or software.

From a pure practice perspective, our methods represent a novel approach (1) to generate transparency of value contributions within an ecosystem, (2) to allocate the co-created value fairly across participants, and (3) ultimately increase the attractiveness of the DE for other potential contributors. Starting with the dual consideration of structural and value-added contributions to total co-created value: our approach will generate more accurate quantifications of components' individual shares on the total value created. Further, by considering each component's structural and value-added contribution (i.e., the value a component adds to the subsequent component), we can better understand the overall value distribution within the focal (sub-)network. By incorporating the structural and value contributions in our approach, we can also identify the value shares of components within a specific value chain. This can in turn, help us identify components that may be undervalued or underutilized. As mentioned, a common problem in DEs is that interconnections between components and their value contributions often remain hidden. Our approach allows us to unravel the previously hidden interconnections between contributors and generate hitherto unachieved transparency on value flows. Together, the transparency and the accurate quantification of components' value shares to the co-created value will enable DEs to distribute value equitably among all its participants. Because "fair" distribution of value will continuously attract potential new contributors into the ecosystem (Valdez-De-Leon 2019), our proposed method is essential to ensuring DE's long-term success.

Despite the numerous benefits our methodological approach affords, our work also features some **limitations** that can be addressed in **future research**. The most significant limitation of our proposed method is its "good faith" character which assumes provider honesty about the components a provider recombines to generate new components. Because this information is essential to compute VC, DEs need mechanisms to ensure the traceability of component recombination. Certifications, change logs, and audit trails can be helpful tools to motivate providers to be honest about the components they combine. This is particularly the case for established DEs but also for those in their inception. However, for the latter, DE designers should consider implementing dependency management tools (that track the recombination of components in a network), component metadata management, or component monitoring and logging. These tools will help increase transparency on recombining components within the DE without solely relying on stakeholders' honesty. Nonetheless, future research should develop other methods to ensure that the information needed to compute VC is derived automatically without providers' involvement.

One major challenge of formalizing the VC of a component is the discoverability of the value-added through each node for the subsequent nodes. This discoverability is directly linked to the accessibility of relevant data for the value determination of the subsequent nodes. For AI services, this could be based on model-agnostic determined values over the input variables. However, this would require fully open access to data concerning the inner workings of each service node. Such open access to such information is, in practice, unrealistic. Thus, our approach highlights the importance of data accessibility and discoverability for data ecosystems in determining their value contribution.

The domain experts' involvement in setting the structural and value weights as another potential limitation of our method. However, given the complexity and relative novelty of DEs in practice, reliance on domain experts is, at this stage, appropriate. In our simulation study, domain experts set the structural weight (SW) to 0.7 and the value weight (VW) to 0.3. As our discussion in Sect. 4 reveals, our method yields plausible value shares. We believe that domain experts can gauge the SW and VW values appropriate to describe the weights of the structural and value-added contributions. In the future, we encourage scholars to develop human-in-the-loop-based approaches to support domain experts in setting the SW and VW values. However, as long as these weights need to be defined by domain experts alone, we suggest that it is highly important to ensure the reliability and validity of the structural and value weights by (1) finding the right experts and (2) and deriving the correct weights by consolidating experts' opinions. On finding the right experts: it is important that these are familiar with the domain of the DE and the market developments within this domain. In this vein we deem experts to be appropriate if they are operating the ecosystem, they are part of a public entity or associations involved in the development and/or operation of the DE. Related to deriving the correct weights by consolidating experts' opinions: suitable methods include the Delphi method, structured workshops, and discussion rounds. Further, we note that our approach envisions only rigid values for the weights for all components of the network. Future research should try to develop methods or extend our approach to allow for varying weights across all different components entering the calculation of the value share. Ultimately, we like to mention that our simulation study was based on an exemplary smart service network in the Smart Living domain. However, our method is scalable and transferable to more complex and other types of DEs (e.g., AI-based components, libraries, data) in other domains. Future investigations should seek to extend our proposed method to more complex network structures from real-world ecosystems. Overall, given the importance of "fair" value distribution across participants as a driver for the long-term success of ecosystems, we expect to see significantly more research on the topic in the future.

Acknowledgements This research was conducted in the scope of the research project ForeSight, which is funded by the German Federal Ministry for Economic Affairs and Climate Action (BMWK). We would like to thank them for their support.

References

Albert, R., & Barabási, A.-L. (2002). Statistical mechanics of complex networks. *Reviews of Modern Physics*, *74*(1), 47.

Floetgen, R. J., Novotny, M., Hein, A., Weking, J., Urmetzer, F., Böhm, M., & Krcmar, H. (2022). *Digital Platform Ecosystem Performance: Antecedents and Interrelations.*

Fricker, S. A., & Maksimov, Y. V. (2017). Pricing of Data Products in Data Marketplaces. In A. Ojala, H. Holmström Olsson, & K. Werder (Hrsg.), *Software Business* (Bd. 304, S. 49–66). Springer International Publishing. https://doi.org/10.1007/978-3-319-69191-6_4

Grover, V., & Kohli, R. (2012). Cocreating IT value: New capabilities and metrics for multifirm environments. *MIS Quarterly*, 225–232.

Hagen, S., Brinker, J., Gembarski, P. C., Lachmayer, R., & Thomas, O. (2019). Integration von Smarten Produkten und Dienstleistungen im IoT-Zeitalter: Ein Graph-basierter Entwicklungsansatz. *HMD Praxis der Wirtschaftsinformatik*. https://doi.org/10.1365/s40702-019-00569-8

Jimenez, Y. O., & Arenas, A. E. (2021). Balancing Competition and Cooperation in IT Value Cocreation: The Case of Digital Platform Ecosystems. *AMCIS*.

Kortum, H., Hagen, S., Hühn, J., & Thomas, O. (2022a). *Analyzing Smart Services from a (Data-) Ecosystem Perspective: Utilizing Network Theory for a Graph-Based Software Tool in the Domain Smart Living*. https://doi.org/10.18420/INF2022_143

Kortum, H., Kohl, T., Hubertus, D., Hinz, O., & Thomas, O. (2022b). A Platform Framework for the Adoption and Operation of ML-Based Smart Services in the Data Ecosystem of Smart Living. *INFORMATIK 2022*.

Lowin, M., & Mihale-Wilson, C. (2021). Towards Predictive Maintenance as a Service in the Smart Housing Industry. *INFORMATIK 2021*.

Lowin, M., Kellner, D., Kohl, T., & Mihale-Wilson, C. (2021). From Physical to Virtual: Leveraging Drone Imagery to Automate Photovoltaic System Maintenance. *INFORMATIK 2021*.

Meurisch, C., Mihale-Wilson, C. A., Hawlitschek, A., Giger, F., Müller, F., Hinz, O., & Mühlhäuser, M. (2020). Exploring user expectations of proactive AI systems. *Proceedings of the ACM on Interactive, Mobile, Wearable and Ubiquitous Technologies*, *4*(4), 1–22. https://doi.org/10.1145/3432193

Mihale-Wilson, C., Zibuschka, J., & Hinz, O. (2017). About user preferences and willingness to pay for a secure and privacy protective ubiquitous personal assistant. *Proceedings of the 25th European Conference on Information Systems (ECIS)*. European Conference on Information Systems (ECIS), Guimarães, Portugal.

Mihale-Wilson, C., Zibuschka, J., & Hinz, O. (2019). User preferences and willingness to pay for in-vehicle assistance. *Electronic Markets*, *29*(1), 37–53.

Mihale-Wilson, C., Felka, P., Hinz, O., & Spann, M. (2022). The Impact of Strategic Core-Component Reuse on Product Life Cycles: The Case of Location-Based Games. *Business & Information Systems Engineering*, *64*(2), 223–237.

Newman, M. E. (2003). The structure and function of complex networks. *SIAM Review*, *45*(2), 167–256.

Nguyen, D., & Paczos, M. (2020). *Measuring the economic value of data and cross-border data flows*. https://www.oecd-ilibrary.org/content/paper/6345995e-en

Stoppel, E., & Roth, S. (2016). Value-Based Pricing im Kontext der Servicetransformation– Von produktzentrierten zu servicezentrierten Wertverständnissen undPreissystemen. In M. Bruhn & K. Hadwich (Hrsg.), *Servicetransformation* (S. 373–399). Springer Fachmedien Wiesbaden. https://doi.org/10.1007/978-3-658-11097-0_17

Subramaniam, M., Iyer, B., & Venkatraman, V. (2019). Competing in digital ecosystems. *Business Horizons*, *62*(1), 83–94.

Valdez-De-Leon, O. (2019). How to develop a digital ecosystem: A practical framework. *Technology Innovation Management Review*, *9*(8).
Wang, P. (2021). Connecting the parts with the whole: Toward an information ecology theory of digital innovation ecosystems. *MIS Quarterly*, *45*(1), 397–422.

Service Innovation, Engineering and Management

Digital Service Innovation for Sustainable Development: A Systematic Literature Review

Daniel Heinz, Mingli Hu, Carina Benz, and Gerhard Satzger

Abstract Creating and delivering products and services that promote sustainability is increasingly important in today's economy. Novel services based on digital technologies and infrastructure can significantly contribute to sustainable development, as demonstrated by digitally enabled car-sharing services where increased asset utilization reduces production-related greenhouse gas emissions. However, there is still limited knowledge on how digital service innovation can purposefully be applied to promote sustainability. To address this gap, we conduct a systematic literature review and perform a qualitative inductive analysis of 50 articles on the impact of digital service innovation on social, environmental, and economic sustainability. We provide a comprehensive overview of real-world applications and identify five underlying mechanisms through which innovation with digital services can drive sustainable development. In doing so, we aim to pave the way to purposefully conceive, design, and implement digital services for sustainability.

Keywords Sustainability · Sustainable development · Digital service innovation · Information systems · Systematic literature review

---

D. Heinz (✉) · M. Hu · C. Benz · G. Satzger
Karlsruhe Institute of Technology (KIT), Karlsruhe, Germany
e-mail: daniel.heinz@kit.edu

M. Hu
e-mail: mingli.hu@student.kit.edu

C. Benz
e-mail: carina.benz@kit.edu

G. Satzger
e-mail: gerhard.satzger@kit.edu

D. Beverungen et al. (eds.), *Transforming the Digitally Sustainable Enterprise*, Lecture Notes in Information Systems and Organisation 76,
https://doi.org/10.1007/978-3-031-80125-9_10

1 Introduction

As digital technologies and infrastructures offer powerful capabilities to promote economic, environmental, and social sustainability both in industrial activities and in citizens' daily life (de la Calle, Freije and Oyarbide, 2021), targeted innovation efforts in this area are critical for achieving sustainability goals. For instance, car sharing mediated by digital services can significantly reduce greenhouse gas (GHG) emissions by up to 0.58 tons per household per year (Duncan, 2011; Martin and Shaheen, 2011). Therefore, innovating digitally supported car-sharing services can help to develop sustainable transportation systems and support the Sustainable Development Goals (SDGs) proposed by the United Nations (2015). Similarly, telemedicine or remote diagnostics, which have gained importance during the COVID-19 pandemic, also bear significant potential to lower carbon emissions by reducing the need for travel, while promoting the well-being of citizens by improving healthcare quality and reducing patient waiting times (Ashford, 2017; Zimiles, 2020; Purohit, Smith and Hibble, 2021).

Achieving sustainability is a highly debated topic for policy makers due to pressing challenges such as climate change, global inequality, lack of financial inclusion, and discrepancies in access to healthcare (e.g., UN, 2015; Bundesregierung, 2021). As the examples above show, technology-driven innovation has been successful in promoting sustainable development and, thus, should form a key focus of information systems (IS) research (Malhotra, Melville and Watson, 2013; Pan et al., 2022). The IS discipline has a rich history of research on integrating economic, environmental, and social responsibility into organizations through information and communication technology (ICT) and methodological knowledge (e.g., vom Brocke et al., 2013; Gholami et al., 2016; Schoormann et al., 2023) and is well-suited to promote sustainable development due to its history of solving complex problems and driving advancements in software and hardware (Zeiss et al., 2021).

Designing and innovating digital services can significantly impact sustainable change (Saviano et al., 2017; Field et al., 2021), making it crucial for service research in the IS discipline to contribute to this discussion. However, there is neither a comprehensive understanding of the interplay between digital service innovation (DSI) and sustainable development nor a well-articulated research agenda to foster sustainable development with digital services. To address this issue, this article explores the following research question: *"How can digital service innovation promote sustainable development?"* To answer this question, we have conducted a systematic literature review to identify how digital services can help achieve sustainability based on the 17 SDGs (UN, 2015) and the Triple Bottom Line (Elkington, 1997). In particular, our study reveals five key mechanisms in which DSI may drive sustainable development: (a) promoting sustainable behaviors, (b) promoting social inclusion and integration, (c) improving citizens' daily life, (d) promoting sustainable economic growth, and (e) improving urban safety. These results should help to purposefully conceive, design, and implement novel services for sustainability benefits.

The article is structured as follows: The next section provides a brief overview of related work. Sect. 3 outlines our research method, before Sect. 4 presents the analytical results of the systematic literature review, including the key mechanisms of DSI's contribution to sustainable development. Finally, the study concludes by discussing potential negative aspects of DSI, pointing out the implications and limitations of our study, and suggesting directions for future research in form of a research agenda.

2 Background

Increased interest in service innovation by public and private organizations (Snyder et al., 2016), and the pervasive role of digital technologies in innovation processes and outcomes—as evident in emerging phenomena such as social media (Kaplan and Haenlein, 2010), the Internet of Things (Gubbi et al., 2013), and big data analytics (Hunke, Heinz and Satzger, 2022)—are driving research on digital services. While servitization and digitalization as global trends have been studied separately for some time (Vendrell-Herrero et al., 2017), recent research highlights their close interrelationship and introduces the concept of "digital servitization" (Kohtamäki and Rajala, 2016; Sklyar et al., 2019; Paschou et al., 2020). Digital servitization can be studied from multiple perspectives, such as strategy and partner orchestration, organizational transformation, and technological capabilities. Thereby, all of these interdisciplinary perspectives contribute to understanding how organizations and their employees can innovate digital services.

From an IS perspective, DSI can be defined as the use of digital technologies to create new or improve existing services (Rizk, Bergvall-Kåreborn and Elragal, 2017; Heinz et al., 2022), drawing on the literature on service innovation (e.g., Lusch and Nambisan, 2015) and digital innovation (e.g., Yoo, Henfridsson and Lyytinen, 2010). Rizk et al. (2017) identified three streams of DSI research that take different elements as their primary unit of analysis: the *digital service* as the artifact of innovation, the *innovation process* as the stages of how the innovation of a digital service unfolds, and *digital infrastructures* as enabling resources and networks for DSI. In our research we adopt this conceptualization for the search and selection of research articles.

In line with current publications by the United Nations (e.g., UN, 2018), we adopt Brundtland's (1987) notion of sustainability as meeting the needs of the present without compromising the ability of future generations to meet their own needs, which balances nature, production, and business (US Environmental Protection Agency, 1969). While sustainability rather represents a long-term goal, we refer to sustainable development as "the many processes and pathways to achieve it" (Jeronen, 2013, p. 2371). We ground our conceptual understanding of these two intertwined concepts in the Triple Bottom Line approach, which proposes three dimensions of sustainability: social, environmental, and economic (Elkington, 1997) as well as the UN's 17 Sustainable Development Goals (UN, 2015). Table 1 summarizes the 17 SDGs and maps them into the three dimensions of sustainability, building on previous studies (Vinuesa et al., 2020; Schoormann et al., 2023) and our own analysis.

3 Research Method

To answer our research question, we conduct a systematic literature review according to established methods in IS research (Webster and Watson, 2002; Vom Brocke et al., 2009). Our research process follows the five-step procedure suggested by vom Brocke et al. (2009), as described below.

First, we *define the review scope* using Cooper's (1988) taxonomy of literature reviews. Our focus is on systematizing theories as well as practices and applications explaining how DSI can promote sustainable development. The primary goal of our review is to integrate and synthesize existing literature on this topic. We conduct our review from a neutral perspective and aim for a representative rather than exhaustive coverage of the literature, given the far-reaching linkages of our topic. We employ techniques for conceptual synthesis and grouping of studies, and we reach out to general scholars as the audience of our review.

Second, we *conceptualize the topic* of our review to generate a search phrase by combining two main areas of focus: sustainability and digital service innovation. To conceptualize sustainability, we follow the approach of Schoormann et al. (2023) and draw on the Triple Bottom Line (Elkington, 1997) and the 17 SDGs (UN, 2015). Regarding DSI, we engage in an iterative process of constructing a search phrase that ultimately combined the term "digital" and synonyms such as "smart," "data-based," "analytics," and "data-driven" with the terms "service," "innovation," and "infrastructure," which we derive from the conceptualization of DSI by Rizk et al. (2017). The full search phrase is shown in Fig. 1.

Third, we conduct a *literature search* for articles in the IS discipline drawing on the VHB-JOURQUAL3 as a recognized rating of academic outlets. We searched the journals of the AIS Senior Scholars' Basket of Eight and the proceedings of major IS conferences (ICIS, ECIS, PACIS, AMCIS, HICSS, WI), which we consider to be a representative sample of high-quality research as well as the most recent research in the IS discipline. We consider only articles published after January 1, 2010, as DSI is an emerging phenomenon resulting from recent advances in digital technologies. Using the Web of Science, Scopus, and AISeL databases, we identified 386 articles, which we narrowed down to 369 after removing duplicates and incomplete articles.

We then perform an initial screening of the remaining articles based on their titles, abstracts, and keywords. We select articles that meet specific criteria, including those that (a) promote sustainable development and help achieve the 17 SDGs, (b) contribute to DSI through one of the three DSI research streams, (c) discuss digital technologies' implications on sustainability, and (d) are located at the intersection of DSI and sustainability. After the initial screening, we included 21 articles in the final sample, with 85 articles undergoing a second relevance assessment based on their full-text (Templier and Pare, 2018). Ultimately, 29 more articles were included

Table 1 SDGs classified into sustainability dimensions

SDGs	1	2	3	4	5	6	7	8	9
	No poverty	Zero hunger	Good health & well-being	Quality education	Gender equality	Clean water & sanitation	Affordable & clean energy	Decent work & economic growth	Industry, innovation & infrastructure
Social	●	●	●	●	●	●	●		
Environmental						○	●		
Economic								●	●

SDGs	10	11	12	13	14	15	16	17
	Reduces inequalities	Sustainable cities & communities	Responsible consumption & production	Climate action	Life below water	Life on land	Peace, justice & strong institutions	Partnerships for the goals
Social	○	●	●				●	
Environmental		●	●	●	●	●		
Economic	●							●

○ added based on our analysis, ● adopted from Vinuesa et al. (2020) / Schoormann et al. (2023)

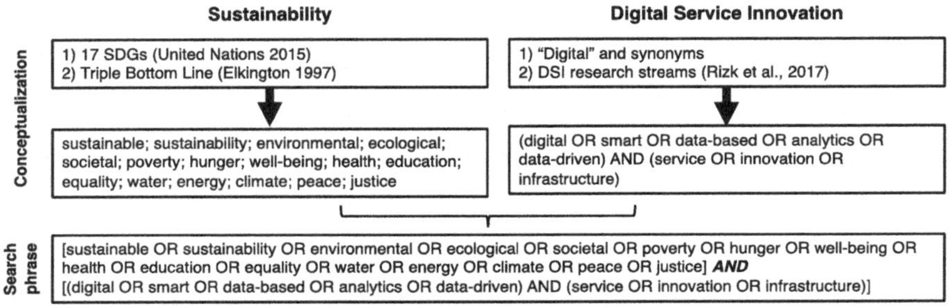

Fig. 1 Search phrase based on the conceptualization of the topic

in the final sample in this step, resulting in a total of 50 articles that are considered relevant to our study.

Fourth, we *analyze the literature*, beginning with a preliminary thematic analysis to familiarize ourselves with the dataset (Braun and Clarke, 2006) by extracting each article's research questions, methods, findings, and limitations and paraphrasing its contribution to sustainable development. Then, we apply qualitative inductive coding techniques to analyze how DSI promotes sustainable development. We follow the cascading approach of the Gioia methodology (Gioia, Corley and Hamilton, 2013; Gioia, 2021), which we apply to academic articles instead of empirical sources (similar to, e.g., Hund et al., 2021). In the first-order analysis, we search for similarities and differences across articles, using initial and in vivo coding. In the second-order analysis, we summarize the information and aggregate similar first-order concepts into second-order themes. Finally, we group second-order themes into aggregated dimensions that represent the key mechanisms of how DSI promotes sustainable development. We derived five key mechanisms, which we present in the next section. After the qualitative analysis, we interpret the mechanisms' impact on the 17 SDGs and the Triple Bottom Line. Two authors independently labelled the direct or indirect impacts of each mechanism on the SDGs. Both authors reached broad agreement, and the few discrepancies were resolved in a subsequent discussion.

Finally, we *develop future research directions* for service research in the IS discipline. Our goal in this phase is to promote a more comprehensive contribution of DSI research to sustainable development and to facilitate synergies between the IS discipline and long-term sustainability.

4 Mechanisms of How DSI Promotes Sustainable Development

In this section, we present the findings of our systematic literature review. As the results of our qualitative inductive analysis of the literature sample, we present five key mechanisms of how innovating digital services can promote sustainable development. After introducing the five mechanisms in detail, we map them to the 17 SDGs to explore the general potential of DSI to achieve sustainability.

4.1 Promote Sustainable Behaviors

As the first mechanism, DSI can "promote sustainable behaviors" ultimately leading to sustainable development (Radziszewski et al. 2021). Figure 2 depicts related concepts and themes, which we explain in more detail below.

Digital services can increase transparency and citizens' awareness of the consequences of their behavior. Two main applications in our literature sample are mobile health (mHealth) apps that use wearables and smartphones to provide real-time data on physical activity and physiological functions, such as daily steps or blood glucose (e.g., Hakkila et al., 2016; Ghose et al., 2022), and smart metering technologies that make energy consumption more transparent and allow users to identify ways to save energy (Lawson, Watson and Ramaswamy, 2015; Wunderlich, Veit and Sarker, 2019). This theme can also be applied to other domains, such as making the GHG emissions of different transportation modes transparent.

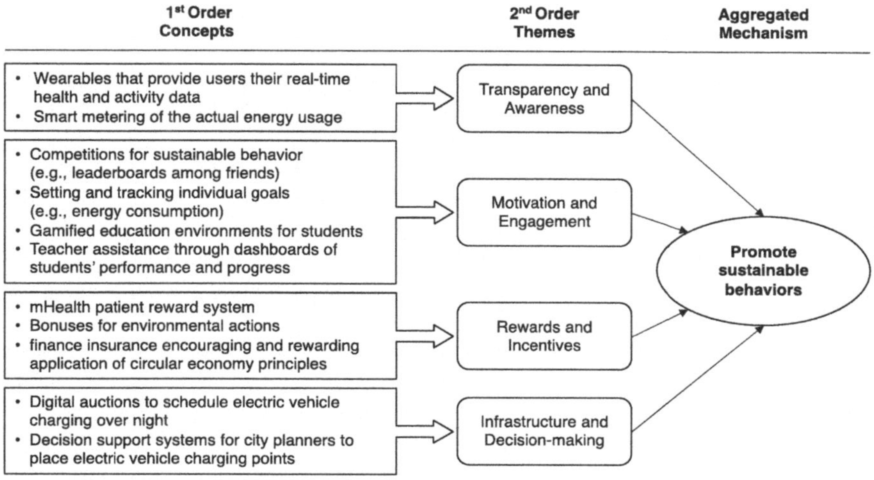

Fig. 2 Data structure for "promote sustainable behaviors" mechanism

Another way how digital services can promote sustainability is by motivating and engaging users through certain features. Many of these features "gamify" sustainable behavior, such as creating leaderboards for sports activities to compete among friends (Emerson et al. 2020), setting and tracking household goals for energy savings (Loock, Staake and Thiesse, 2013), or introducing gaming elements into workplace training to create a more engaging experience (Helms, Barneveld and Dalpiaz, 2015). Digital service features can also provide information for teachers or other in-person service providers to adjust their interactions with clients based on individual progress (Hakkila et al., 2016).

Third, digital services can serve as means to provide rewards and incentives for sustainable behaviors: For example, Bonazzi et al. (2017) designed an mHealth app that provides monetary rewards to diabetic patients who adhere to health goals set as part of their treatment, such as diet or exercise goals. Other articles propose other monetary reward systems for pro-environmental actions, such as bonus points that can be traded for sustainable products (Radziszewski, Weichbroth and Anacka, 2021) or benefits in insurance programs (Wood and Godsill, 2021).

Finally, DSI can provide an infrastructure for incorporating sustainability goals into decision-making. Two examples are digital services that provide a decision support system for city planners to optimize the placement of electric vehicle charging points (Wagner et al. 2014) or conduct digital auctions to schedule overnight vehicle charging based on renewable energy availability (Valogianni et al. 2019).

4.2 Promote Social Inclusion and Integration

The second mechanism describes how DSI promotes social inclusion and integration and, therefore, sustainable development. The respective concepts and themes are depicted in Fig. 3.

Digitalization of services can improve accessibility for citizens, especially for disadvantaged groups. For example, online banking can meet most financial service needs of citizens in poor areas without access to offline banking (Lagna and Ravishankar, 2022), and peer-to-peer lending platforms can virtually connect low-income individuals with lenders, enabling access to loans at low interest rates (Ravishankar, 2021). Telemedicine (Srivastava and Shainesh, 2015) and mHealth services (Lichtenberg et al., 2019; Ahuja, Chan and Krishnamurthy, 2023) address health issues in developing countries, e.g., by remotely consulting community health workers to properly treat patients.

Equal access to quality education is crucial for an inclusive society and free education services can support the integration of refugees into the host society. Digital services promoting this can be media platforms that connect refugees with the local community—which is especially beneficial when learning the new language— or e-learning platforms that make knowledge accessible for domain-specific trainings (e.g., programming) (Abujarour, 2020).

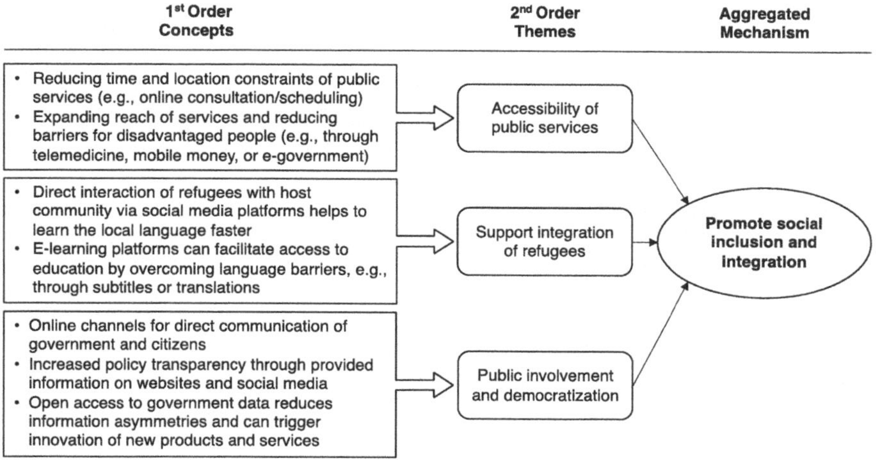

Fig. 3 Data structure for "promote social inclusion and integration" mechanism

In addition, digital services can promote public involvement in democratic processes. E-government service innovation can create new channels of communication between governments and citizens (Alawadhi and Scholl, 2016; Bernhard et al., 2019) and make policies more transparent by allowing citizens to obtain real-time information from local governments (e.g., vaccination policies, nuclear energy policies), ultimately increasing citizens' trust in the government (Chatfield et al. 2016). Furthermore, DSI enables governments to provide open access to government data, which can reduce information asymmetries and inform decision-making (e.g., in the real estate market). This data can also be used as a resource for innovating new products and services, such as mobile applications that provide real-time transportation information to navigate public transit systems (Jetzek et al., 2019).

4.3 Improve Citizens' Daily Life

DSI can improve citizens' daily life by providing convenience, quality care services, and a comfortable and safe environment, ultimately contributing to sustainable development in a society (Kjell, 2011). Examples of how DSI improves citizens' daily life and well-being are depicted in Fig. 4 and discussed in more detail below.

First, DSI can enhance citizen's daily lives with convenient services such as trip planning and parking assistance (Schreieck, Wiesche and Krcmar, 2016; Di Leo et al., 2019), online appointment scheduling (Thorseng and Blegind Jensen, 2015), remote professional services such as virtual medical consultations (Warren et al., 2020; Ghose et al., 2022), or financial services such as digital community currencies

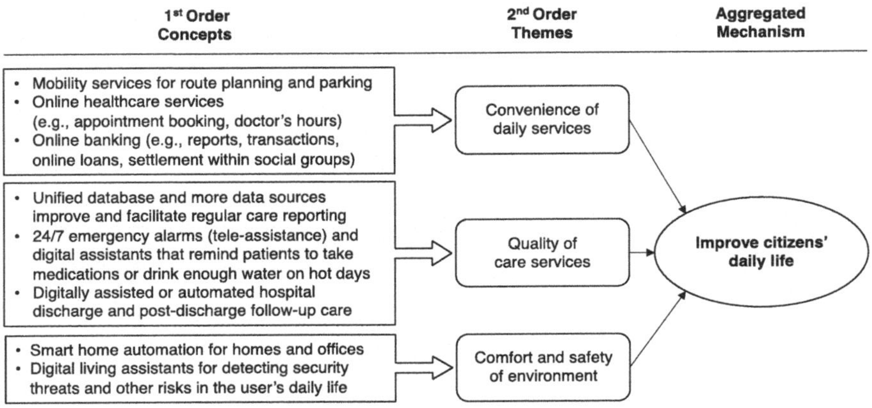

Fig. 4 Data structure for "improve citizens' daily life" mechanism

(Chasin, et al. 2020; Nan, 2021). Some digital services also combine different forms of assistance into a comprehensive "life coach" (Cazier and Green, 2016).

Second, DSI has great potential to improve the quality of services in health care and elderly care. DSI provides the means to scale digital components across local care facilities, improving accuracy while reducing the workload for standard processes like care reporting (Sahay et al., 2018), hospital discharge, and post-discharge communication (Tanniru et al. 2016; Lichtner et al. 2017), allowing caregivers to spend more time with patients. In addition, electronic devices coupled with digital services can protect elderly people with disabilities who live independently. Examples are teleassistance services that can send emergency alerts around the clock (Di Leo et al., 2019), or digital assistants that remind users to take their medication and provide dietary advice (e.g., water intake on a hot day) (Fernando et al., 2016).

Third, DSI can contribute to a comfortable and safe environment. This can be enabled, for example, by smart home technologies that enhance thermal or visual comfort and indoor air quality (Yassaee and Winter, 2017; Laing and Kühl, 2018). Furthermore, digital assistants can identify potential safety risks, such as external threats or unusual resident behavior that indicates a critical health risk (Fernando et al., 2016).

4.4 Promote Sustainable Economic Growth

Besides social and environmental sustainability, DSI also provides means to promote sustainable economic growth, as depicted in Fig. 5.

DSI can help improve production processes while reducing the environmental footprint. The manufacturing industry has been using digital technology and automation for years to increase efficiency, reduce costs, and minimize material usage. Two

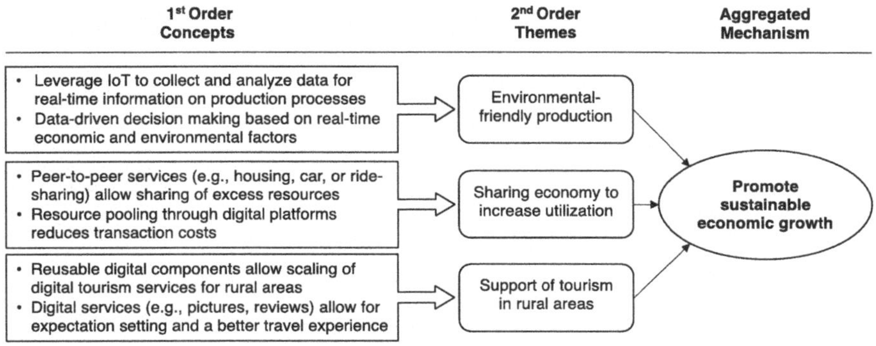

Fig. 5 Data structure for "promote sustainable economic growth" mechanism

articles in our sample focus on the benefits of smart agricultural services (Cu et al. 2017; Jacobs et al., 2017). These services allow farmers to use Internet-of-Things (IoT)-enabled technologies to adapt agricultural processes to actual environmental conditions, leading to increased productivity and environmental benefits (e.g., more targeted and thus less use of pesticides). Other industries, such as oil and gas, can also benefit from DSI by using IoT-based services to simplify the collection and analysis of data from connected, inaccessible equipment in the ground (Khan et al., 2017).

DSI has also given rise to the "sharing economy," in which digital platforms increase the utilization of assets. In particular, peer-to-peer service platforms (e.g., housing, car or ride sharing) can promote sustainability by enabling users to share excess resources at low transaction costs (Avital et al., 2014). However, the sharing economy can also have a negative impact on traditional economic networks. For example, an increase in Airbnb listings has been associated with a decrease in overall hotel revenues (Mody, et al. 2017).

Finally, DSI promotes local industry development and economic growth in rural areas. For instance, "Digital Wuyi" was a Chinese e-government initiative that developed an online channel to integrate tourism services, such as 3D images and online travel guides, to promote economic growth through tourism (Dong et al., 2012). Digital services in this context offer scalability by reusing components from other local areas. Digital services for less popular tourist destinations can also enable tourists to set their expectations in advance, leading to a better travel experience and sustainable growth of the local tourism industry (Dong et al., 2012).

4.5 Improve Urban Safety

The last mechanism DSI-promoted sustainable development focusses on improving urban safety, as depicted in Fig. 6.

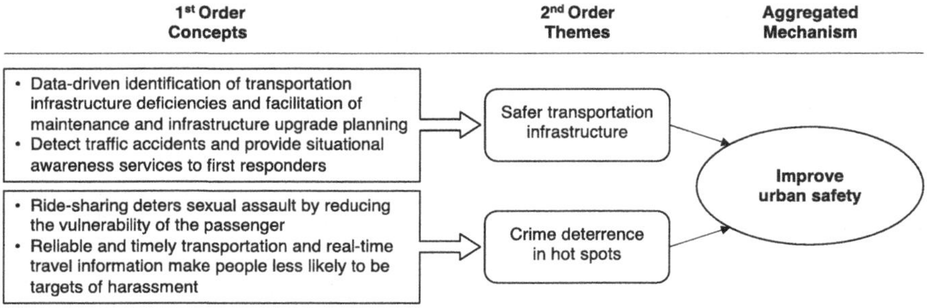

Fig. 6 Data structure for "improve urban safety" mechanism

DSI can enable governments to provide a safer traffic infrastructure: smart transportation systems can monitor road conditions and automatically identify deficiencies in transportation infrastructure based on road imagery (Chatterjee et al. 2018). This information can be integrated into decision support systems to facilitate necessary maintenance processes and plan infrastructure upgrades. In addition, mobile applications based on vehicular social networks can quickly detect traffic accidents and provide situational awareness services to first responders (Hu et al., 2015). DSI can also improve urban safety by deterring crime in hot spots. Ride-sharing, for example, has been shown to reduce the likelihood of sexual assault (Park et al., 2021). Moreover, DSI allows for more reliable and timely transportation and real-time travel information, reducing the likelihood of harassment at public transportation stations (Park et al., 2021).

5 Discussion and Conclusion

5.1 Impact of the Mechanisms on Sustainable Development

After deriving the five domain-spanning mechanisms of how DSI can promote sustainable development, we used the first-order concepts and second-order themes to interpret the mechanisms' respective impact on the 17 SDGs and the Triple Bottom Line. The complete mapping is depicted in Fig. 7. While discussing each relation would be beyond the scope of this article, we highlight key observations below.

Recent conference themes such as "Digital responsibility: social, ethical, ecological implications of IS" (WI 2023) or "Co-creating sustainable digital futures" (ECIS 2023) show that achieving sustainability is a high priority in the current academic IS discourse and should therefore also guide DSI research. The IS literature on DSI in our sample currently addresses 13 out of 17 SDGs, demonstrating the potential of DSI research to contribute to sustainable development. However, future studies should pay particular attention to the four omitted goals: SDG2 (zero hunger), SDG6

	Mechanisms / SDGs	Promote sustainable behaviors	Promote social inclusion & integration	Improve citizens' daily life	Promote sustainable econ. growth	Improve urban safety	Social	Environm.	Economic
1	No poverty		●		●		■		
2	Zero hunger						■		
3	Good health & well-being	●	●	●		●	■		
4	Quality education	●	●				■		
5	Gender equality		○		○		■		
6	Clean water						■	■	
7	Affordable & clean energy	○					■	■	
8	Decent work & economic growth			○	●				■
9	Industry/Innovation/Infrastructure				○				■
10	Reduced inequalities		●		○			■	■
11	Sustainable cities	○	○	●	○	○	■	■	
12	Responsible Consumption	●					■	■	
13	Climate change	●			●			■	
14	Life below water							■	
15	Life on land				●			■	
16	Peace and justice					●	■		
17	Global partnership								■

● *direct impact on SDG* ○ *indirect impact on SDG*

Fig. 7 Mapping of the five mechanisms to the SDGs and Triple Bottom Line

(clean water), SDG14 (life below water), and SDG17 (global partnership). Second, health services (SDG3) and digital services for smart sustainable cities (SDG11) are predominant themes in this area. In general, DSI research contributing to the social dimension of sustainability is the most common in our literature sample. In contrast, DSI research so far lacks a detailed discussion of how DSI can contribute to the environmental dimension helping to combat climate change and how achieving the SDGs correlates with sustainable economic growth.

5.2 Implications for Research, Policy, and Practice

Our research contributes to service research in the IS discipline and provides implications for research. First, our findings provide a broad picture of DSI application areas that relate to sustainable development. This comprehensive overview emphasizes the importance of service research in the scientific discussion on using digital technologies for sustainable development. Our aim is to mobilize future service research by enabling scholars to identify significant phenomena in terms of societal impact and relate their contributions to the SDGs and the Triple Bottom Line. Second, the derived mechanisms provide an analytical structure to conceptually explain the general role of DSI in promoting sustainable development in society. While we view our analytical results as a theory that "says what is" (Gregor, 2006), future research can build on our findings to explain why DSI promotes sustainable development as described. Finally, our findings have implications beyond service research within the IS discipline. They inform IS scholars about how service research complements other streams within IS research regarding their impact on sustainable development and sharpen the role of an IS perspective on service-related phenomena in an interdisciplinary context.

Our research has also implications for policy and practitioners. Highlighting the role of DSI for sustainable development, our research can benefit policymakers to allocate funding to DSI-related research projects that promote sustainable development. These projects can help to enact existing knowledge in local initiatives, improve scientific understanding by extending the scope of preliminary research findings, and generate new knowledge through long-term interaction and empirical insights. Moreover, managers can use the set of application areas as inspiration to identify ways to lead their organization towards contributing to sustainable development in its environment.

5.3 Limitations and Outlook

Given the nature of our study, there are limitations to our findings that should guide future research. First, our analysis deliberately analyzes the positive impact of DSI on sustainable development. However, it is important to consider that there are also many potentially negative impacts and unintended consequences of DSI. Some articles in our sample take a more critical stance on this issue, highlighting "dark sides" such as an increase in the digital divide within a society and between countries, a significant increase in privacy risks (e.g., for mHealth services) and other potentially threatening data security risks (e.g., for critical information infrastructures), or potential benefits of DSI for sustainable development not being realized (e.g., digital care services not leading to more time available for the patient but to less staffing). Second, we cannot claim that our sample is complete or representative as we limited it to a fixed set of journals and conference proceedings. Future research should validate and eventually extend our findings by discussing them in a broader context (e.g., beyond IS research). Finally, we again emphasize that we consider the proposed mechanisms to be analytical rather than explanatory, as we do not provide causal explanations for why DSI promotes sustainable development. Future research should therefore extend our findings in this regard.

References[1]

* Abujarour, S. (2020), Social inclusion of refugees through digital learning: Means, needs, and goals, *in* 'PACIS 2020 Proceedings'.

* Ahuja, S., Chan, Y.E. & Krishnamurthy, R. (2023), Responsible innovation with digital platforms: Cases in India and Canada, *Information Systems Journal,* **33**(1), pp. 76–129.

* Alawadhi, S. & Scholl, H.J. (2016), Smart Governance: A Cross-Case Analysis of Smart City Initiatives, *in* 'HICSS 2016 Proceedings', pp. 2953–2963.

---

[1] All articles included in the final sample of the literature review are marked with an asterisk (*).

Ashford, K. (2017), 1 In 5 People Would Switch Doctors for Video Visits, Forbes. Available at: https://www.forbes.com/sites/kateashford/2017/01/30/videodoctor/?sh=7b9b1f5510ce. Accessed: 21.06.2023.

* Avital, M., Andersson, M., Nickerson, J., Sundararajan, A., Van Alstyne, M. & Verhoeven, D. (2014), The collaborative economy: a disruptive innovation or much ado about nothing?, *in* 'ICIS 2014 Proceedings'.

* Bernhard, I., Gustafsson, M., Hedström, K., Seyferin, J. & Whilborg, E. (2019), A digital society for all?: meanings, practices and policies for digital diversity, *in* 'HICSS 2019 Proceedings', pp. 3067–3076.

* Bonazzi, R., Cimmino, F. & Blondon, K. (2017), Healthy lottery: An economically viable mobile system to increase compliance of individuals with diabetes, *in* 'HICSS 2017 Proceedings'. Available at: https://doi.org/10.24251/hicss.2017.176.

Braun, V. & Clarke, V. (2006), Using thematic analysis in psychology, *Qualitative Research in Psychology,* **3**(2), pp. 77–101.

Brundtland, G.H. (1987), Our Common Future - Call for Action, *Environmental Conservation*, **14**(4), pp. 291–294.

Bundesregierung (2021), Deutsche Nachhaltigkeitsstrategie - Weiterentwicklung 2021. Germany.

* Butler, T., & Hackney, R. (2015), Understanding Digital Eco-innovation in Municipalities: An Institutional Perspective, *in* 'ECIS 2015 Proceedings'.

de la Calle, A., Freije, I. & Oyarbide, A. (2021), Digital Product-Service Innovation and Sustainability: A Multiple-Case Study in the Capital Goods Industry, *Sustainability*, **13**(11).

* Cazier, J.A. & Green, J.A. (2016), Life coach: using big data and analytics to facilitate the attainment of life goals, *in* 'HICSS 2016 Proceedings', pp. 1000–1008.

* Chasin, F., Schmolke, F. & Becker, J. (2020), Design principles for digital community currencies, *in* 'HICSS 2020 Proceedings'. Available at: https://doi.org/10.24251/hicss.2020.504.

* Chatfield, A., Reddick, C. & Anggoro, Y. (2016), Indonesia's digital infrastructures for nuclear energy policy transparency, *in* 'AMCIS 2016 Proceedings'.

* Chatterjee, S., Brendel, A.B. & Lichtenberg, S. (2018), Smart infrastructure monitoring: Development of a decision support system for vision-based road crack detection, *in* 'ICIS 2018 Proceedings'.

Cooper, H.M. (1988), Organizing knowledge syntheses: A taxonomy of literature reviews, *Knowledge in Society*, **1**, pp. 104–126.

* Cu, T., Lamacchia, C. & Nguyen, T. (2017), The Internet of Things: Can a Tree Talk to You?, *in* 'AMCIS 2017 Proceedings'.

* Dong, X., Yu, Y., Wang, X. & Zhang Na, N. (2012), Leveraging e-government for city transformation: A case study of 'Digital Wuyi', *in* 'ECIS 2012 Proceedings'.

Duncan, M. (2011), The cost saving potential of carsharing in a US context, *Transportation*, **38**(2), pp. 363–382.

Elkington, J. (1997), *Cannibals with forks: The triple bottom line of 21st century business*. Stoney Creek, CT: New Society Publishers.

* Emerson, S., Heavin, C. & Power, D.J. (2020), Workplace health promotion: Effects of an mHealth application on employee behaviour and wellness, *in* 'HICSS 2020 Proceedings'. Available at: https://doi.org/10.24251/hicss.2020.419.

* Fernando, N., Tan, F.T.C., Vasa, R., Mouzaki, K. & Aitken, I. (2016), Examining digital assisted living: Towards a case study of smart homes for the elderly, *in* 'ECIS 2016 Proceedings'.

Field, J.M., Fotheringham, D., Subramony, M., Gustafsson, A., Ostrom, A.L., Lemon, K.N., Huang, M.-H. & McColl-Kennedy, J.R. (2021), Service Research Priorities: Designing Sustainable Service Ecosystems, *Journal of Service Research*, **24**(4), pp. 462–479.

Gholami, R., Watson, R.T., Hasan, H., Molla, A. & Bjorn-Andersen, N. (2016), Information Systems Solutions for Environmental Sustainability: How Can We Do More?, *Journal of the Association for Information Systems*, **17**(8). Available at: https://doi.org/10.17705/1jais.00435.

* Ghose, A., Guo, X., Li, B. & Dang, Y. (2022), Empowering patients using smart mobile health platforms: Evidence from a randomized field experiment, *MIS Quarterly*, **46**(1), pp. 151–192.

Gioia, D. (2021), A Systematic Methodology for Doing Qualitative Research, *The Journal of Applied Behavioral Science*, **57**(1), pp. 20–29.
Gioia, D.A., Corley, K.G. & Hamilton, A.L. (2013), Seeking Qualitative Rigor in Inductive Research: Notes on the Gioia Methodology, *Organizational Research Methods*, **16**(1), pp. 15–31.
Gregor, S. (2006), The nature of theory in information systems, *MIS Quarterly*, **30**(3), pp. 611–642.
Gubbi, J., Buyya, R., Marusic, S. & Palaniswami, M. (2013), Internet of Things (IoT): A vision, architectural elements, and future directions, *Future Generation Computer Systems*, **29**(7), pp. 1645–1660.
* Hakkila, J., Alhonsuo, M., Virtanen, L., Rantakari, J., Colley, A. & Koivumaki, T. (2016), MyData approach for personal health - A service design case for young athletes, *in* 'HICSS 2016 Proceedings'. Available at: https://doi.org/10.1109/hicss.2016.436.
Heinz, D., Breidbach, C., Benz, C., & Satzger, G. (2022), Towards Explaining Smart Service Innovation Events and Trajectories, *in* 'ICIS 2022 Proceedings'.
* Helms, R.W., Barneveld, R. & Dalpiaz, F. (2015), A Method for the Design of Gamified Trainings, *in* 'PACIS 2015 Proceedings'.
* Hopf, K., Sodenkamp, M., & Kozlovskiy, I. (2016), Energy Data Analytics for Improved Residential Service Quality and Energy Efficiency, *in* 'ECIS 2016 Proceedings'.
* Hu, X., Li, X., Ngai, E.C.H., Zhao, J., Leung, V.C.M. & Nasiopoulos, P. (2015), Health Drive: Mobile Healthcare Onboard Vehicles to Promote Safe Driving, *in* 'HICSS 2015 Proceedings', pp. 3074–3083.
Hund, A., Wagner, H.-T., Beimborn, D. & Weitzel, T. (2021), Digital innovation: Review and novel perspective, *The Journal of Strategic Information Systems*, **30**(4). Available at: https://doi.org/10.1016/j.jsis.2021.101695.
Hunke, F., Heinz, D., & Satzger, G. (2022), Creating customer value from data: foundations and archetypes of analytics-based services, *Electronic Markets*, **32**(2), pp. 503–521. Available at: https://doi.org/10.1007/s12525-021-00506-y.
* Jacobs, M., Cazier, J.A., Wilkes, J.T., Rogers, R.E.L. & Hassler, E.E. (2017), Building a business analytics platform for enhancing commercial beekeepers' performance: Descriptive validation of a data framework for widespread adoption by citizen scientists, *in* 'AMCIS 2017 Proceedings'.
Jeronen, E. (2013), Sustainability and Sustainable Development, in S.O. Idowu, N. Capaldi, L. Zu, & A.D. Gupta (eds.) *Encyclopedia of Corporate Social Responsibility*. Berlin, Heidelberg: Springer Berlin Heidelberg, pp. 2370–2378.
* Jetzek, T., Avital, M. & Bjorn-Andersen, N. (2019), The Sustainable Value of Open Government Data, *Journal of the Association for Information Systems*, **20**(6). Available at: https://doi.org/10.17705/1jais.00549.
Kaplan, A.M. & Haenlein, M. (2010), Users of the world, unite! The challenges and opportunities of Social Media, *Business Horizons*, **53**(1), pp. 59–68.
Khan, W.Z., Aalsalem, M.Y., Khan, M.K., Hossain, M.S. & Atiquzzaman, M. (2017), A reliable Internet of Things based architecture for oil and gas industry, *in* '2017 19th International conference on advanced communication Technology (ICACT)', pp. 705–710.
Kjell, O.N.E. (2011), Sustainable well-being: A potential synergy between sustainability and well-being research, *Review of General Psychology*, **15**(3), pp. 255–266.
Kohtamäki, M. & Rajala, R. (2016), Theory and practice of value co-creation in B2B systems, *Industrial Marketing Management*, **56**, pp. 4–13.
* Lagna, A. & Ravishankar, M.N. (2022), Making the world a better place with fintech research, *Information Systems Journal*, **32**(1), pp. 61–102.
* Laing, S. & Kühl, N. (2018), Comfort-as-a-service: Designing a user-oriented thermal comfort artifact for office buildings, *in* 'ICIS 2018 Proceedings'.
* Lawson, V.J., Watson, R.T. & Ramaswamy, L. (2015), C-SenZ-IS: A customizable sensor IS model for energy efficient SaaS, *in* 'HICSS 2015 Proceedings'. Available at: https://doi.org/10.1109/hicss.2015.411.
* Di Leo, G., Ferro, M., Liguori, C., Paciello, V. & Pietrosanto, A. (2019), Smart devices and services for Smart City, *in* 'HICSS 2019 Proceedings'.

* Lichtenberg, S., Greve, M., Brendel, A.B. & Kolbe, L.M. (2019), Towards the design of a mobile application to support decentralized healthcare in developing countries - The case of diabetes care in eSwatini, *in* 'AMCIS 2019 Proceedings'.
* Lichtner, V., Cornford, T. & Klecun, E. (2017), 'it's people heavy': A sociotechnical view of hospital discharge, *in* 'ECIS 2017 Proceedings'.
* Loock, C.-M., Staake, T. & Thiesse, F. (2013), Motivating energy-efficient behavior with green IS: An investigation of goal setting and the role of defaults, *MIS Quarterly*, **37**(4), pp. 1313–1332.
Lusch, R.F. & Nambisan, S. (2015), Service innovation: A service-dominant logic perspective, *MIS Quarterly*, **39**(1), pp. 155–175.
* Ma, T., & McGroarty, F. (2017), Social Machines: how recent technological advances have aided financialisation, *Journal of Information Technology,* **32**(3), pp. 234-250.
Malhotra, A., Melville, N.P. & Watson, R.T. (2013), Spurring Impactful Research on Information Systems for Environmental Sustainability, *MIS Quarterly*, **37**(4), pp. 1265–1274.
Martin, E.W. & Shaheen, S.A. (2011), Greenhouse gas emission impacts of carsharing in North America, *IEEE Transactions on Intelligent Transportation Systems*, **12**(4), pp. 1074–1086.
* McBride, N., & Liyala, S. (2023), Memoirs from Bukhalalire: a poetic inquiry into the lived experience of M-PESA mobile money usage in rural Kenya, *European Journal of Information Systems,* **32**(2), pp. 173–194.
Mody, M., Suess, C. & Dogru, T. (2017), Comparing apples and oranges? Examining the impacts of Airbnb on hotel performance in Boston, *Boston Hospitality Review*, **5**(2).
* Nan, W.V. (2021), Digital Infrastructure for Development: The Case of Mobile Money in Kenya, *in* 'AMCIS 2021 Proceedings'.
Pan, S.L., Carter, L., Tim, Y. & Sandeep, M.S. (2022), Digital sustainability, climate change, and information systems solutions: Opportunities for future research, *International Journal of Information Management*, **63**. Available at: https://doi.org/10.1016/j.ijinfomgt.2021.102444.
* Pantazos, K., & Vatrapu, R. (2016), Enhancing the professional vision of teachers: A physiological study of teaching analytics dashboards of students' repertory grid exercises in business education, *in* 'HICSS 2016 Proceedings', pp. 41–50.
* Park, J., Pang, M.-S., Kim, J. & Lee, B. (2021), The deterrent effect of ride-sharing on sexual assault and investigation of situational contingencies, *Information Systems Research*, **32**(2), pp. 497–516.
Paschou, T., Rapaccini, M., Adrodegari, F. & Saccani, N. (2020), Digital servitization in manufacturing: A systematic literature review and research agenda, *Industrial Marketing Management,* **89**, pp. 278–292.
Purohit, A., Smith, J. & Hibble, A. (2021), Does telemedicine reduce the carbon footprint of healthcare? A systematic review, *Future Healthcare Journal,* **8**(1), pp. e85–e91.
* Radziszewski, K., Weichbroth, P. & Anacka, H. (2021), Greencoin: a Proenvironmental Action-Reward System, *in* 'AMCIS 2021 Proceedings'.
* Ravishankar, M.N. (2021), Social innovations and the fight against poverty: An analysis of India's first prosocial P2P lending platform, *Information Systems Journal,* **31**(5), pp. 745–766.
Rizk, A., Bergvall-Kåreborn, B. & Elragal, A. (2017), Digital service innovation enabled by big data analytics - A review and the way forward, *in* 'HICSS 2017 Proceedings'.
* Sahay, S., Nielsen, P., Faujdar, D., Kumar, R. & Mukherjee, A. (2018), Frugal Digital Innovation and Living Labs: A Case Study of Innovation in Public Health in India, *in* 'ICIS 2018 Proceedings'.
* Sapraz, M., & Han, S. (2019), A Review of Electronic Government for Environmental Sustainability, *in* 'PACIS 2019 Proceedings'.
Saviano, M., Barile, S., Clinton, S.J. & Caputo, F. (2017), A service research contribution to the global challenge of sustainability, *Journal of Service Theory and Practice,* **27**(5), pp. 951–976.
Schoormann, T., Strobel, G., Möller, F., Petrik, D. & Zschech, P. (2023), Artificial Intelligence for sustainability—A systematic review of Information Systems literature, *Communications of the Association for Information Systems,* **52**(1), pp. 199–237.

* Schreieck, M., Wiesche, M. & Krcmar, H. (2016), Modularization of digital services for urban transportation, *in* 'AMCIS 2016 Proceedings'.

Sklyar, A., Kowalkowski, C., Tronvoll, B. & Sörhammar, D. (2019), Organizing for digital servitization: A service ecosystem perspective, *Journal of Business Research,* **104**, pp. 450–460.

Snyder, H., Witell, L., Gustafsson, A., Fombelle, P. & Kristensson, P. (2016), Identifying categories of service innovation: A review and synthesis of the literature, *Journal of Business Research,* **69**(7), pp. 2401–2408.

* Srivastava, S.C. & Shainesh, G. (2015), Bridging the service divide through digitally enabled service innovations, *MIS Quarterly,* **39**(1), pp. 245–268.

* Stryja, C., Satzger, G., & Dorner, V. (2017), A Decision Support System Design to Overcome Resistance towards Sustainable Innovations, *in* 'ECIS 2017 Proceedings'.

* Tanniru, M., Khuntia, J. & Weiner, J. (2016), Aligning digital health to services: A case of leadership for transformation, *in* 'AMCIS 2016 Proceedings'.

Templier, M. & Pare, G. (2018), Transparency in literature reviews: an assessment of reporting practices across review types and genres in top IS journals, *European Journal of Information Systems,* **27**(5), pp. 503–550.

* Thorseng, A. & Blegind Jensen, T. (2015), Building National Infrastructures for Patient-centred Digital Services, *in* 'ECIS 2015 Proceedings'.

UN (2015), Transforming our world: the 2030 agenda for sustainable development. A/RES/70/1.

UN (2018), The Sustainable Development Agenda, UN. United Nations: Sustainable Development Goals. Available at: https://www.un.org/sustainabledevelopment/development-agenda/. Accessed: 21.06.2023.

US Environmental Protection Agency (1969), The National Environmental Policy Act. Available at: https://www.epa.gov/sustainability/learn-about-sustainability. Accessed: 21.06.2023.

* Valogianni, K., Gupta, A., Ketter, W., Sen, S. & van Heck, E. (2019), Multiple Vickrey Auctions for Sustainable Electric Vehicle Charging, *in* 'ICIS 2019 Proceedings'.

Vendrell-Herrero, F., Bustinza, O.F., Parry, G. & Georgantzis, N. (2017), Servitization, digitization and supply chain interdependency, Industrial Marketing Management, 60, pp. 69–81.

Vinuesa, R., Azizpour, H., Leite, I., Balaam, M., Dignum, V., Domisch, S., Felländer, A., Langhans, S.D., Tegmark, M. & Fuso Nerini, F. (2020), The role of artificial intelligence in achieving the Sustainable Development Goals, Nature communications, 11(1). Available at: https://doi.org/10.1038/s41467-019-14108-y.

vom Brocke, J., Simons, A., Niehaves, Bjoern, Niehaves, Bjorn, Reimer, K., Plattfaut, R. & Cleven, A. (2009), Reconstructing the giant: On the importance of rigour in documenting the literature search process, *in* 'ECIS 2009 Proceedings'.

vom Brocke, J., Watson, R.T., Dwyer, C., Elliot, S. & Melville, N. (2013), Green Information Systems: Directives for the IS Discipline, *Communications of the Association for Information Systems,* **33**(1). Available at: https://doi.org/10.17705/1CAIS.03330.

* Wagner, S., Brandt, T. & Neumann, D. (2014), Smart city planning-developing an urban charging infrastructure for electric vehicles, *in* 'ECIS 2014 Proceedings'.

* Warren, J., Hopkins, S., Leung, A., Hetrick, S. & Merry, S. (2020), Building a digital platform for behavioral intervention technology research and deployment, *in* 'HICSS 2020 Proceedings'. Available at: https://doi.org/10.24251/hicss.2020.414.

Webster, J. & Watson, R.T. (2002), Analyzing the past to prepare for the future: Writing a literature review, *MIS Quarterly*, **26**(2), pp. xiii–xxiii.

* Wood, Z. & Godsill, P. (2021), Circular Insurance: customer-centric, data-driven services for the Circular Economy, *in* 'HICSS 2021 Proceedings'.

* Wunderlich, P., Veit, D.J. & Sarker, S. (2019), Adoption of sustainable technologies: A mixed-methods study of German households, *MIS Quarterly,* **43**(2), pp. 673–691.

* Yang, M., Li, Y., & Kiang, M. (2011), Uncovering social media data for public health surveillance, *in* 'PACIS 2011 Proceedings'.

* Yassaee, M. & Winter, R. (2017), Analyzing affordances of digital occupational health systems, *in* 'HICSS 2017 Proceedings'. Available at: https://doi.org/10.24251/hicss.2017.432.

Yoo, Y., Henfridsson, O. & Lyytinen, K. (2010), Research Commentary-The New Organizing Logic of Digital Innovation: An Agenda for Information Systems Research, *Information Systems Research,* **21**(4), pp. 724–735.

Zeiss, R., Ixmeier, A., Recker, J. & Kranz, J. (2021), Mobilising information systems scholarship for a circular economy: Review, synthesis, and directions for future research, *Information Systems Journal,* **31**(1), pp. 148–183.

Zimiles, A. (2020), Four new statistics that prove that telemedicine isn't just a pandemic fad," *Medical Economics,* **97**(11).

Managing Customer Data in Data-Driven Service Innovation: A Framework of Data Principles

Katharina Blöcher, Olaf Reinhold, and Rainer Alt

Abstract While customer data has been collected in enterprise systems since decades, the emerging consumer technologies create new sources of data. Although the need to co-create services with customers has been recognized, a systematic approach of how to include this sensitive source of innovation in the service innovation process ist still lacking. This research explores the potential of data governance practices for data-driven service innovation. Data principles for the governance of customer data are collected and assessed by practioners in order to provide conceptual support for organizations and to facilitate the service innovation process. The results of this research integrate data principles of different research streams and offer a framework of data principles that can be applied in the design and management of data-driven services.

Keywords Data governance · Customer data · Data-driven service innovation

1 Introduction

The rising number of digital touchpoints and smart devices in the consumers' everyday lives generate large amounts of digital traces (Lim et al. 2019). In these data-rich environments (Troilo et al. 2017), a wealth of customer data emerges via

K. Blöcher (✉) · R. Alt
Information Systems Institute, Leipzig University, Leipzig, Germany
e-mail: katharina.bloecher@uni-leipzig.de

R. Alt
e-mail: rainer.alt@uni-leipzig.de; rainer.alt@scrc-leipzig.de

O. Reinhold · R. Alt
Social CRM Research Center E. V., Leipzig, Germany
e-mail: olaf.reinhold@scrc-leipzig.de

O. Reinhold
University of Cooperative Education Saxony, Riesa, Germany

D. Beverungen et al. (eds.), *Transforming the Digitally Sustainable Enterprise*, Lecture Notes in Information Systems and Organisation 76,
https://doi.org/10.1007/978-3-031-80125-9_11

smart devices, social media, and various application systems and becomes a decisive factor for service innovation and new data-driven services. However, concepts and methods of how new services can be designed from this data is still developing. Although companies are eager to "cash in" on their data (Bitkom 2022; Wixom and Ross 2017), they often lack the knowledge of how to fully take advantage of data and analytics for expanding their portfolio with data-driven services (Hunke et al. 2022; Schüritz et al. 2017). Data-driven service innovation has emerged as a particular research stream putting data and analytics as driving resources in the innovation process (Lim et al. 2018; Engel and Ebel 2019; Schymanietz 2020). Yet, research on methodological support that integrates data and analytics into service innovation activities is still in its infancy (Engel and Ebel 2019; Fruhwirth et al., 2020). Further, organizations which strive to exploit customer data in particular, must comply with legal regulations, ensure privacy rights and guarantee trust in the communication with customers (Spiekermann et al. 2015; Schäfer et al. 2022).

Data governance as a cross-functional discipline addresses these challenges and aims at managing data as a strategic asset of an organization (Alhassan et al. 2019; Abraham et al. 2019). For this purpose, *data principles* define boundary requirements for data usage. They represent guidelines for data governance activities and provide directions for the use of data over its lifecycle (Khatri and Brown 2010; Brous et al. 2016; Alhassan et al. 2019). Organizations can benefit from data governance practices to leverage data and analytics opportunities for data-driven services (Mikalef et al. 2018, 2020; Potiguara et al. 2020). Yet, with the rising importance of the customer in producing and exchanging customer data with an organization, especially in the context of data-driven services (Lim et al. 2019), the question of how to deal with customer data comprehensively in data governance gains importance. Customers are not only "creators" of data anymore (Lim et al. 2019), but they adopt an active role in service configuration as well as service operations (Alt et al. 2019; Beverungen et al. 2019; Ostrom et al. 2015). If data governance should support the design of data-driven services using customer data, it must not only ensure data privacy and security, but also incorporate the active role of customers. Thus, data principles must ensure customer sovereignty (Nomura et al. 2020; Koskinen et al. 2019) in the production, management and consumption of their data (Chaudhry et al. 2015; Tapsell et al. 2018).

This research aims to identify and assess data principles for data-driven service innovation focusing specifically on customer data from both, a theoretical and practical perspective. For this purpose, the following research question guides the research activities: *How can data principles for customer data be incorporated into data-driven service innovation?* For answering this research question, data principles, as key requirements guiding the governance of customer data, are in a first step collected and classified into different groups of data principles. For this purpose, different literature streams are synthesized. In a second step, experts are interviewed to identify the relevance and challenges involved in putting these principles into practice. Finally, first conceptual knowledge is developed to assist organizations in data-driven service innovation initatives when working with customer data. The remainder of the paper is structured as follows. Sect. 2 outlines related work. Sect. 3 gives an overview of the research design. Sect. 4 outlines the data principles and the research results. Finally, contributions and research limitations are presented.

2 Theoretical Foundation

2.1 Data-Driven Service Innovation

Service innovation is defined as the "rebundling of diverse resources that create novel resources that are beneficial (i.e., value experiencing) to some actors" (Lusch and Nambisan 2015, p.161). The discpline represents a rather heterogenous research field with various sub-streams, such as service design, service engineering or new service development that attempt to develop and manage new services (Beverungen et al. 2018; Kurtmollaiev and Pedersen 2022; Patrício et al. 2018). Data-driven service innovation has emerged as a particular research stream. The discipline focuses on leveraging data and analytics within the entire process of service innovation and looks at data and analytics as an analytical unit for the exploration, validation or value generation of new services (Demirkan et al. 2015; Engel and Ebel 2019; Schymanietz 2020). Yet, research on methodological support that integrates data and analytics more deeply into service innovation activities is only about to gain momentum (Fruhwirth et al. 2020). As companies still lack the comprehensive knowledge of how to fully take advantage of data and analytics, more conceptual work is necessary that supports service organizations with the appropriate instruments to design and manage new data-driven services (Schüritz et al. 2017; Blöcher and Alt 2022).

2.2 Data Governance

Data governance represents a cross-functional framework for managing data as a strategic enterprise asset of an organization (Alhassan et al. 2019; Abraham et al. 2019; DAMA International 2009). The management approach takes care of the "valuation, creation, collection, analysis, distribution, storage, use and control of information" (Kooper et al. 2011, p. 196). Data governance practices consist of the definition of decision rights and accountabilities regarding the use of data (Khatri and Brown 2010; Abraham et al. 2019) and strive to maximize its value (Kooper et al. 2011; Tallon et al. 2013). Data principles in particular represent key requirements providing directions for decisions that affect the way data is managed, accessed, processed, distributed and valued (Abraham et al. 2019; Khatri and Brown 2010; Micheli et al. 2020). Due to the rising awareness of data as an organizational asset, the necessity for data governance has grown in the last years (Abraham et al. 2019; Legner et al. 2020). In parallel, AI governance is emerging as another layer of data governance, emphasizing the need for governance mechanisms allowing the trustworthy use of artificial intelligence (Cath 2018; Dafoe 2018; Fadler and Legner 2021; Papagiannidis et al. 2022). Data governance mechanisms have a positive impact on innovation capabilities in organizations (Mikalef et al. 2020). Thus, aspects, such as legal compliance, data quality and security must be taken into account from the beginning when designing new data-driven services (Kühne and Böhmann 2018; Sammon and Nagle 2017).

2.3 *Customer Data for Data-Driven Service Innovation*

Customer data, also called personal data, denote data that can be linked to a specific person (European Commission 2016a, b) and represent an essential part of the rising big data resources. Customer data include not only the customer's demographic or contact information, but also refer to behavioral data, such as the customer's purchase history or device usage data. Even if this type of data has long been applied by companies for CRM or data-driven marketing (Stone et al. 2004; Wedel and Kannan 2016), the use of this data as a design material for the customer's value creation represents a recent phenomenon (Lim et al. 2019; Saarijärvi et al. 2014; 2016; Seidelin et al. 2020). Personal assistants have emerged that transform personal data into valuable information or self-monitoring services to augment human capabilities and to improve the customers' quality of living (Alt et al. 2021; Demirkan et al. 2015). But, the use of customer data is associated with several requirements: Service providers must ensure privacy regulations as well as data security and need to create trust when working with this data (Huhtala 2018; Kunz et al. 2017; Spiekermann et al. 2015). With the rising importance of the customer in producing and exchanging data with an organization, the customer's sovereignty in the production, management and consumption of their data must be ensured (Tapsell et al. 2018; Nomura et al. 2020; Koskinen et al. 2019). Consequently, data governance principles should provide guidance on how to leverage the potential of data for the customer and consider under which conditions this data can be utilized.

3 Methodology

This research follows a two-stage research approach. In the first phase, a structured literature review (LR) is conducted to systematically analyse the literature for data principle identification as transparent and rigour as possible (Vom Brocke et al. 2009). The second research phase strives to assess the current relevance of the identified principles just as current challenges in their implementation by means of interviews. Table 1 presents the different steps of the structured LR. It took place in Q4 2020 in a sequential process focusing on different literature streams (cf. Table 3). For this purpose, the four bibliographic databases Emerald, IEEE, ACM Digital

Library, Springer were screened and a supplementary dedicated search on A + and A Ranked Journals in Information Systems and Marketing/Services was conducted to ensure a borad coverage of high quality sources and to refine the research results. For searching and filtering the databases and journals, a keyword-based approach was chosen. The first search strings strive to identify concrete data principles using the combinations *"Data Governance" AND "principle" AND "personal data" OR "customer data" OR "Information Governance" AND "principle" AND "personal data" OR "customer data"*. To broaden the search scope, another keyword search was performed using the combinations *"CRM"AND "personal data"OR "customer data;"CRM"AND "information management";"CRM"AND "data management"; "service" AND "personal data"OR "customer data"AND "information management" OR "data management"* related to data governance and service management. In the second step, the abstracts and titles were screened for filtering out potential contributions. Subsequently, the resulting articles were analyzed in detail for the presence of data principles or conceptual knowledge represented as *models, frameworks or patterns* related to *requirements, guidelines or success factor or even blueprints* for the management of customer data. The third step constitutes a back and forward research. After deduplication and the final investigation, 51 relevant papers emerged and a concept-centered analysis as suggested by Weber and Watson (2002) was performed to group the results into *legal, business and customer-orientated data principles*. When principles are grounded on regulatory requirements or laws (Alhassan et al. 2019), they are categorized as *legal-orientated principles*. Those relate to regulatory necessities and policy guidelines. In contrast, *business-orientated principles* are requested by IT or business stakeholders (Alhassan et al. 2019). They add another layer that and are mainly driven by business requirements. Finally, *customer-orientated principles* put the customer into the foreground of data management. They consider the customer's active role and strive to maximize data value for the customer (Table 2).

In the seconed research phase, semi-structured interviews (Myers and Newman 2007) with data and analytics experts in Q1/Q2 2021 were performed. For this purpose, a theoretical sampling approach was chosen. Interviewees (see Table 2) were selected due to their long-year experience in CRM, analytics and data governance (Eisenhardt and Graebner 2007). The interviews were conducted online with a duration of 90 min. The extracted data principles from the LR guided the semi-structured interviews. For each principle, three questions formed the basis, i.e., the understanding, the current implementation and the perceived relevance. The relevance for organizations and the personally perceived relevance of the interviewee were assessed with two structured questions using a likert-scale from 1 to 5 (Likert 1932) and two open questions. In respect to current practices, the surveyed consultants are asked how they advise their clients regarding the principles' implementation. The data has a descriptive function to gather knowledge around current organizational practices. A cross-case synthesis (Yin 2009) is conducted. The data is coded and analyzed along the dimensions (1) current practices (2) the perceived relevance of each data principles and (3) current drivers and challenges by two researchers in

Table 1 Overview of the literature review

Step 1: Key word-based search (*including both keyword combinations*)		
Source	*Restriction and settings*	*Results*
(1) Emerald	(1) Focus on journal articles, Book chapters, case studies (2) Date range: 2000–2020	922
(2) IEEE	(1) All metadata, (2) Date range: 2000–2020	243
(3) ACM	(1) Date range: 2000–2020	957
(4) Springer	(1) Include preview content only, (2) Data governance in title OR customer/personal data in title, (3) Date range: 2000–2020	233
(5) Journals	A + /A ranked journals in IS and marketing/service research based on VHB Joural Ranking	228
Step 2: Abstract and title reading		322
Step 3: Search for principles and conceptual knowledge		140
Step 4: Extension of the results set by forward and backward search		64
Step 5: Deduplication and final identification of data principles		**51**

Table 2 Overview of the interviewees

No.	Firm	Role	Industry
1	Consultant	Founder data/analytics consultancy	Media, public organizations
2	Enterprise	Product owner, data lake	Mobility
3	Enterprise	Director analytics	E-commerce
4	Consultant	Senior CRM consultant	E-commerce
5	Consultant	Teamlead architecture and solutions	E-commerce, energy, retail
6	Consultant	Principal consultant	Banking, insurances
7	Start-up	Teamlead analytics	Recruiting service provider

two independent rounds and one final joint discussion until their identified groups matched.

4 Results

4.1 Data Principles in Literature

Data principles characterize key guidelines of data governance activities (Khatri and Brown 2010; Brous et al. 2016; Alhassan et al. 2019). They must include shared decision-making over data assets and activities just as policies, standards and procedures (Brous et al. 2016; Ladley 2019; Wong et al. 2020). The data principles obtained from the LR are categorized in Table 4 *as legal-, customer- and business-orientated*

Table 3 Literature streams and identified relevant literature

Stream	References
Legal institutional frameworks and management frameworks	(1) AICPA 2020; (2) Code of Conduct of the Data And Marketing Association 2020; (3) European Commission 2022; (4) Federal Trade Commission 2012; (5) GDPR 2023; (6) Gellmann 2017; (7) Langford et al. 2022; (8) ISO 2019; (9) OECD 2022; (10) Sitra 2021; (11) The White House Report 2012; (12) TrustArc 2021 (13) LGPD Brazil 2023; (14) CCPA 2023
AI governance	(15) European Commission 2019; (16) IEEE 2022
CRM, IS and service literature	(17) Bose 2002; (18) Cavoukian 2009; (19) Cespedes and Smith 1993; (20) Chan 2005; (21) Cunningham et al. 2004; (22) Fan and Poole 2006; (23) Fellenz and Brady 2010; (24) Fischer et al. 2018; (25) Gebert et al. 2003; (26) Raj et al. 2018; (27) Häikiö et al. 2020; (28) Jayachandran et al. 2005; (29) Kumar et al. 2013; (30) Kumar and Reinartz 2006; (31) Lehrer et al. 2018; (32) Neslin et al. 2006; (33) Pan and Lee 2003; (34) Payne et al. 2015; (35) Payne and Frow 2005; (36) Park and Kim 2003; (37) Ranjan and Bhatnagar 2009; (38) Rowley 2002; (39) Stone et al. 2004; (40)Vesanen 2007; (41) Wulf 2020; (42) Xu and Walton 2005
PIMS and personal informatics	(43) Cena et al. 2018; (44) Crabtree and Mortier 2015; (45) Crabtree et al. 2018; (46) Li et al. 2010; (47) Mortier et al. 2014; (48) Poikola et al. 2020; (49) Rapp and Cena 2016; (50) Rooksby et al. 2014

principles representing key requirements for data-driven services. Table 3 provides an overview of identified literature grouped by the different literature streams. All in all, fifty contributions contain concrete or deducted data principles for customer data. Another paper (Culnan 2019) compares the previously identified principles and is therefore not explicitly listed.

Legal-orientated data principles can be identified in a variety of legal and institutional frameworks, guidelines, and regulations, but also in management frameworks or in marketing, IS or CRM literature (e.g., Payne et al. 2015; Trustarc 2021; Data and Marketing Association 2022). These data principles represent regulatory necessities and policy guidelines and originate from a set of self-regulatory programs that formed early privacy policies, e.g., the Code of Fair Information Practices (Culnan 2019; Gellman 2017). In Europe, the General Data Protection Regulation, GDPR) forms the legal ground for processing customer data. Other countries have recently institutionalized similar policies, such as the California Privacy Rights Act, the Virginia's Consumer Data Protection Act or the Brazilian General Data Protection Law (Erickson 2018). Even if the principles slightly differ in their wording, they are built upon central requirements, such as privacy by design, security, consent management, the need for accuracy and data quality, and transparency. Another central element is the customer's right to access their data just as the right for

Table 4 Identified data principles and respective literature

Legal-orientated Data Principles	
Privacy by design	2, 4, 5, 12, 15, 16
Accuracy and quality	1, 2, 5, 6, 9, 12, 13, 15, 19, 34
Information transparency	1, 2, 3, 4, 5, 6, 7, 9, 11, 12, 13, 14, 15, 16, 34
Purpose specification/ limitation	1, 5, 6, 9, 11, 12, 13, 34
Minimization of data collection and storage limitation	1, 2, 5, 6, 9, 11,12, 13, 14
Access of customer data	1, 3, 4, 5, 6, 9, 11, 12, 13, 14, 34
Restriction, rectification and deletion	1, 5, 9, 12, 13, 14, 34
Consent management	1, 4, 5, 9,12, 13, 14, 19, 34
End-to-end security	1, 2, 5, 6, 8, 9, 11,12, 13, 14, 15, 34
Legal authorization and accountability	2, 5, 6, 9, 11,12,13,14, 15, 34
Responsible Exchange with Service Partners	1, 2, 9, 12,13, 17, 24
Data Portability	3, 5, 7, 12 13, 43, 48
Business-orientated Data Principles	
Single View of the Customer	17, 20, 22, 23, 28, 33, 35
Meta-Data Management	12, 39
Company-wide integrated Data Access	17, 24, 25, 28, 32, 33, 38, 41
Analytical Capabilities for Customer Intelligence	20, 21; 23, 35, 41, 42
Personalization of Customer Interaction	22, 31, 33, 40, 42
Real-time Capabilities	24, 26, 37
Performance Assessment for Decision-Making	20, 30, 31, 35
Customer-orientated Data Principles	
Customer Feedback Loops	28, 36
Customer Control and Self-Management of Data	7, 10, 11, 15, 16, 44, 45, 47, 48, 49
Multi-operator Identity and Consent Management	16, 47, 48
Multi-operator Interoperability	10, 48
Traceability and Legibility	10, 27, 43, 44, 47, 49
Customer Value and Personal Analytics for Improving Life Value	2, 15, 16, 28, 37, 43, 46, 49, 50

restriction, rectification, or deletion of their data. AI governance frameworks, such as the Ethics Guidelines for Trustworthy AI (European Commission 2019) emphasize another layer of transparency, i.e., the need to explain certain results of algorithms and AI models. Furthermore, other core legal principles are authorization and accountability for the right data usage, the purpose specification of data or the collection and storage limitation principle. Moreover, the necessity for responsible data exchange with service partners is highlighted (e.g., GDRP 2023; AICPA 2020). Finally, data portability signifies the customer's right for data transmission from one organization to another (GDPR 2023; European Commission 2022). Besides legal regulatory requirements, data principles are also grounded on business requests. These *business-orientated data principles* can be mainly found in the CRM and service management literature that demand customer-centric information management for a successful application of customer data (Fellenz and Brady; Bose 2002; Chan 2005). One core requirement is the integration of all data sources into one single unified view (Payne and Frow 2005). This requires the integration of all interactions with customers and the resulting data across touchpoints (Payne and Frow 2005; Jayachandran et al. 2005). For this purpose, meta-data and master-data management are important to create a common understanding and semantic definitions of data models, types and repositories of customer data as a prerequisite of data integration (Stone et al. 2004; 2017; Dyché and Levy 2006). In addition, data governance practices should address the organisation's integrated data access for customer management. For this purpose, front-office and back-office applications must be linked (Bose 2002; Pan and Lee 2003), and an easy access to updated and integrated information of the customer must be available for relevant employees (Bose 2002; Jayachandran et al. 2005; Stone et al. 2017) just as an integrated knowledge management for a consistent customer experience (Wulf 2020; Neslin et al. 2006; Rowley 2002). Besides this, an encompassing governance approach must ensure analytical capabilities to generate customer intelligence, e.g., via descriptive, prescriptive or predictive modeling (Payne and Frow 2005; Chan 2005). Analytical capabilities are often interlinked with the principle of personalization which is grounded on accurate user profiling and segmentation functions (Xu and Walton 2005; Bose 2002). Customer data management must be set up in a way to achieve personal service offerings on an individual or segment level (Pan and Lee 2003; Fan and Poole 2006). Activities must allow trigger- and preference-based personalization just as automatic and human-based personalization when employees are involved (Lehrer et al. 2018). Two other core requirements are real-time capabilities and performance assessment. Principles must not only cover the development of performance metrics for strategic and tactical decision-making (Chan 2005; Kumar et al. 2013), several researchers also emphasize the need of real-time customer insights (Fischer et al. 2018; Ranjan and Bhatnagar 2009; Raj et al. 2018).

In contrast, *customer-orientated data principles* put the customer into the foreground. They underline the active role of the customer and the necessity to develop human-centered approaches of good data practices (Poikola et al. 2020). The principles are mainly anchored in the literature streams of PIMS and personal informatics, but also in the CRM literature. One central data principle is the consideration of customer feedback loops (Park and Kim 2003). Practices around customer data should allow the systematic collection, processing, and use of the customer's voice providing feedback to an organization. This requires processes for information reciprocity so that organizations can directly respond to the customer's feedback (Jayachandran et al. 2005). Research around PIMS strengthens the principles of data agency, human-centric control and self-management of customer data (e.g., Poikola et al. 2020; Mortier et al. 2014). Similarly, defined guidelines around AI governance (IEEE 2022; European Commission 2019) incorporate the aspects of control and agency. Closely involved are principles such as multi-operator identity and consent management. Customers must be able to manage multiple identities and even more important multiple consents for data usage across organizations and services (Poikola et al. 2020; IEEE 2022). Another related principle is the legibility of customer data processes. This includes transparency related to data processing, data visualizations, or the methods used for algorithms and related decisions (Mortier et al. 2014; Sitra 2021). Data presentation and visualization must help customers to make sense of their data and can incorporate a way of user-understandable data logging and auditing (Crabtree and Mortier 2015), or simple and engaging reports or suggestions (Rapp and Cena 2016; Häikiö et al. 2020). Moreover, the principle of interoperability across operators and organizations become more and more important (Langford et al. 2022; Sitra 2021). When customers are able to exchange their data between services and organizations, organizational, semantic, and technical interoperability are necessary (Langford et al. 2022). Finally, data governance practices should aim to add value to the customer and improve their wellbeing. This can range from improving understanding of the customer's needs and actions, to develop customer -specific products and services (Jayachandran et al. 2005), to improve the customer's life (Rooksby et al. 2014; European Commission 2019). For example, personal informatics support customers to "collect personally relevant information for the purpose of self-reflection and gaining self-knowledge" (Li et al. 2010, p. 558) and can include goal-driven, or diagnostic tracking (Rooksby et al. 2014).

4.2 Relevance of Data Principles in Practice

The interviews confirmed a practical relevance of the principles and several drivers and challenges for implementation. Some of the legal principles, such data quality, consent management, end-to-end security and legal authorization and accountability are assessed as critical for daily operations. Enablers to incorporate them into daily practices are customer expectations, but also guaranteeing process assurance, efficiency and competitive advantages. When specifically asking the experts about *customer-orientated principles*, the interviews demonstrate that data governance is still mainly organizational-driven and that these principles have not yet arrived in organizations. Even if the experts generally assess these principles as more important than currently operationalized in organizations, they still play a minor role due to missing organizational awareness. Similarly, the importance of data portability is generally rated as low by the experts. They remark that the relevance highly depends on the industry and the business model. In some areas, such as healthcare, insurances or banking, some respondents note a higher significance, but the low demand on customer side results in a low awareness for the organizations. Likewise, the principles of control and self-management just as traceability and legibility have a generally low relevance in organizations. Even if the experts see a positive value for customers, they remark the need for high transparency of all internal and external processes on the organization side to implement these guidelines. Moreover, the experts critically mention that not many customers currently demand functionalities related to the self-management of data so that organizations must weigh up whether the implementation is worthwhile. Other challenges are the technical complexity, but also related data security and privacy isssues, e.g., a secure customer identification for data access. In respect to the principle of data portability, some experts see external service providers as responsible for ensuring data portability for the customer rather than the organization itself. Multi-operator identity management plays, for example, a higher role in e-commerce, especially with the rise of federated identity solutions (Ehrlich et al. 2021), such as Facebook or Google Connect. Interviewees remark that organizations should collaborate with neutral solution providers for identity management that should not base their business model on the commercialization of customer data. Finally, the principles of customer value and personal analytics is perceived as important. Experts see the chance for organizations to improve customer-related processes and to develop competitive advantages focusing on customer value. Similarly, data standards represent an important driver to ensure interoperability and data portability. The experts see the potential for creating trust and value for customers and to meet customer expectations in the appropriate handling with their data. Yet, they also mention the need for internal data understanding and transparency and the organizational awareness for *customer-orientated principles.*

5 A Conceptual Framework of Data Principles for Data-Driven Service Innovation

Based on the identified principles from LR and interviews, this research suggests a first conceptual framework of data principles for data-driven service innovation. By incorporating data principles into data-driven service innovation, organizations can ensure the responsible and effective use of data, while building trust and delivering value to their customers. Data principles can thereby support in the actual service concept design and implementation just as the actual management of new data-driven services (cf. Beverungen et al. 2018). For example, they assist in the design of information collection, distribution and delivery just as relevant workflow processes and responsibilities for data-driven service implementation (Khatri and Brown, 2010; Lim et al. 2018). The proposed framework presented in Fig. 1 systematizes the presented data principles along the dimension of customer centricity. The customer has become the creator and a recipient of information so that customer-centered data governance approaches focusing on customer value and the self-management of customer data should receive more attention (Becerril 2018; Koskinen et al. 2019; Tapsell et al. 2018). However, the interviews revealed that the relevance of *customer-orientated principles* highly depends on the organizational awareness and

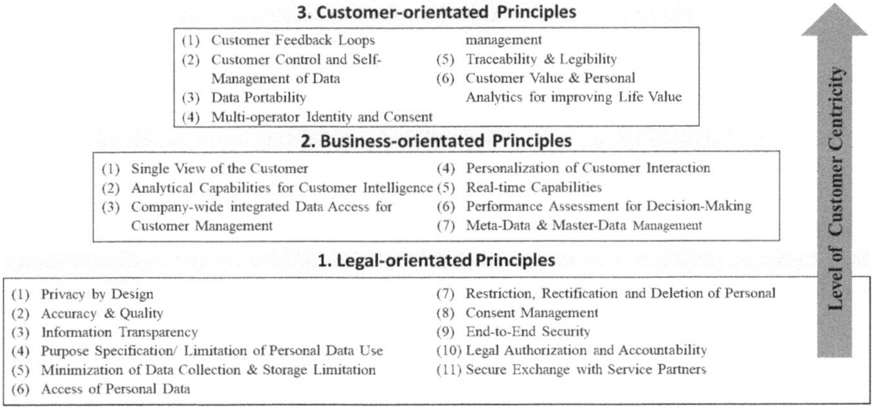

Fig. 1 Framework of data principles in data-driven service innovation

the maturity of the organization. This work follows the *Customer Dominant Logic* (Heinonen and Strandvik 2020) and conceives the customer as the overall data subject, still considering that a customer can represent different roles, such as a citizen, a user, or a client (Heinonen and Strandvik 2018). Thus, the framework underlines the need for legal guidance, but goes further and highlights the development towards strong *customer-orientated principles* for the design and management of data-driven services. The framework suggests starting with the implementation of *legal-orientated principles* as a basis when developing data-driven services, but to gradually expand activities to include *business and customer-orientated* principles. Where as the application of *legal-orientated principles* are mostly forced by law, organizations can gradually take advantage of *business and customer-orientated* data principles to increase the level of customer centricity. By following more and more *customer-orientated* principles, new types of services can be designed that allow the self-management and control of customer data.

6 Summary and Research Contribution

This paper extracts and categorizes several data principles for managing customer data for data-driven service innovation. For this purpose, it outlines the analysis of different research streams and discusses the resulting perspectives *of legal-, business- and customer-orientated* data principles with experts. Simarly to other researchers (Kühne and Böhmann, 2018; Sammon and Nagle, 2017), this research points toward the need for integrating data governance into the design of new services from the outset, rather than building procedures only as a part of operational activities. The results of this research provide practical and theoretical contributions. First, it adds value to the service innovation research stream by systematically incorporating data principles through the analysis of different academic streams. Second, practical knowledge is gathered regarding the implementation of the identified principles and the related maturity level. Third, existing data governance approaches are extended with a strong customer focus instead of a primary organizational perspective. Finally, practical guidance for taking advantage from the identified principles is provided as a toolbox for service providers. The presented framework proposes to increase the level of customer centricity by building up the management of customer data for data-driven services upon *legal-, business, and customer-orientated* data principles. Integrating data principles into the service innovation process has several potential benefits. First, it ensures compliance with regulatory requirements throughout the service innovation process, taking into account important guidelines as early as the conception of new services. Second, the gradual application of business and *customer-orientated principles* not only ensures the integration of business requirements, it allows the discourse for novel perspectives that strengthen personal data sovereignty of the customer in human-centered approaches of data-driven service innovation (Nomura et al. 2020; Koskinen et al. 2019).

Yet, this research has several limitations. Even if the first research results offer valuable knowledge for the design of a first conceptual framework, subsequent evaluation is required that actually demonstrate the usability and feasibility of the conceptual model when designing new data-driven services. This evaluation should occur in different industries or application fields to reach more confident and rigorous justification and generalization (Vom Brocke et al. 2020). The conceptual framework represents early conceptual knowledge to support organizations in the design of data-driven services. Further development must be discussed if the model can be further refined, e.g., in the form of design principles or certain process models (Gregor and Hevner 2013). Moreover, the conducted interviews can only offer first tendencies related to the relevance of the discussed principles. The analysis of the interviews already demonstrates several differences in the perceived relevance and implementation depending on the industry, size of the organization, and their maturity level. Accordingly, a more comprehensive survey is necessary to assess the current relevance of the principles in more detail. Finally, ethical guidelines representing values such as avoiding discrimination, ensuring human rights or fairness (Balasubramaniam et al. 2022; IEEE 2022) need to be more strongly integrated. While this contribution focused more on data principles for technical implementation, further research should also consider the relevance of ethical principles for data-driven service innovation, such as fairness or discrimination.

References

Abraham, R., Schneider, J.,Vom Brocke, J. (2019). Data governance: A conceptual framework, structured review, and research agenda. International Journal of Information Management 49, 424–438. https://doi.org/10.1016/j.ijinfomgt.2019.07.008.

AICPA (2020). AICPA Privacy Management Framework. https://us.aicpa.org/interestareas/informationtechnology/privacy-management-framework. Accessed: 22.02.2023.

Alhassan, I.,Sammon, D.,Daly, M. (2019). Critical success factors for data governance: A theory building approach. Information Systems Management 36 (2), 98–110. https://doi.org/10.1080/10580530.2019.1589670.

Alt, R.,Ehmke, J.F., Haux, R., Henke, T., Mattfeld, D.C., Oberweis, A.,Paech, B., Winter, A. (2019). Towards customer-induced service orchestration - requirements for the next step of customer orientation. Electronic Markets 29 (1), 79–91. https://doi.org/10.1007/s12525-019-00340-3.

Alt, R., Göldi, A., Österle, H., Portmann, E., Spiekermann, S. (2021). Life Engineering - Towards a new Discipline. Business & Information Systems Engineering 63 (2), 191-205.

Balasubramaniam, N.,Kauppinen, M., Hiekkanen, K.,Kujala, S. (2022). Transparency and Explainability of AI Systems: Ethical Guidelines in Practice. In: International Working Conference on Requirements Engineering: Foundation for Software Quality. Springer, Cham, 3–18.

Becerril, A. A. (2018). The value of our personal data in the Big Data and the Internet of all Things Era. ADCAIJ: Advances in Distributed Computing and Artificial Intelligence Journal, 7 (2), 2255–2863. https://doi.org/10.14201/ADCAIJ2018727180.

Beverungen, D., Lüttenberg, H., Wolf, V. (2018). Recombinant service systems engineering. Business & Information Systems Engineering 60 (5), 377–391. https://doi.org/10.1007/s12599-018-0526-4.

Beverungen, D., Müller, O., Matzner, M., Mendling, M.,Vom Brocke, J. (2019). Conceptualizing smart service systems. Electronic Markets 29 (1), 7–18. https://doi.org/10.1007/s12525-017-0270-5.

Bitkom. (2022). *Deutsche Unternehmen öffnen sich der Datenökonomie.* https://www.bitkom.org/Presse/Presseinformation/Unternehmen-oeffnen-sich-Datenoekonomie

Blöcher, K., Alt, R. (2022). The Potentials of Personal Data Management for Smart Service Innovation. In: Manfred Bruhn/Karsten Hadwich (Eds.). Smart Services. Band 1: Konzepte - Methoden, Prozesse. Springer Gabler, Wiesbaden, 335–362.

Bose, R. (2002). Customer relationship management: key components for IT success. Industrial Management & Data Systems 102 (2), 89–97. https://doi.org/10.1108/02635570210419636.

Brous, P.,Janssen, M.,Vilminko-Heikkinen, R. (2016). Coordinating Decision-Making in Data Management Activities: A Systematic Review of Data Governance Principles. In: Hans Jochen Scholl/Olivier Glassey/Marijn Janssen et al. (Eds.). Electronic Government. 15th IFIP WG 8.5 International Conference, EGOV 2016, Guimarães, Portugal, September 5–8, 2016, Proceedings, Cham, 2016. Cham, Springer International Publishing, pp. 115–125.

Cath, C. (2018). Governing Artificial Intelligence: Ethical, Legal and Technical Opportunities and Challenges. Philosophical transactions. Series A, Mathematical, physical, and engineering sciences 376 (2133). https://doi.org/10.1098/rsta.2018.0080.

Cavoukian, A. (2009). Privacy by design: The 7 foundational principles. Information and Privacy Commissioner of Ontario, Canada.

CCPA (2023). California Consumer Privacy Act. Available on https://oag.ca.gov/privacy/ccpa.

Cena, F., Rapp, A., Likavec, S., & Marcengo, A. (2018). Envisioning the Future of Personalization through Personal Informatics: A user study. International Journal of Mobile Human Computer Interaction (IJMHCI), 10(1), 52–66.

Cespedes, F.,Smith, H. J. (1993). Database marketing: New rules for policy and practice. Database marketing: New rules for policy and practice. Sloan Management Review 34(4), 7–22.

Chan, J. O. (2005). Toward a Unified View of Customer Relationship Management. Journal of American Academy of Business 6(1), 32-38.

Chaudhry, A., Crowcroft, J.,Howard, H.,Madhavapeddy, A., Mortier, R.,Haddadi, H., McAuley, D. (2015). Personal Data: Thinking Inside the Box. Critical Alternatives (1,1). https://doi.org/10.7146/aahcc.v1i1.21312.

Crabtree, A.,/Mortier, R. (2015). Human Data Interaction: Historical Lessons from Social Studies and CSCW. In: ECSCW 2015: Proceedings of the 14th European Conference on Computer Supported Cooperative Work, 19–23 September 2015, Oslo, Norway. Springer, Cham, 3–21.

Crabtree, A.,Lodge, T.,Colley, J., Greenhalgh, C., Glover, K., Haddadi, H.Amar, Y., Mortier, R., Li, Q., Moore, J., Wang, L., Yadav, P., Zhao, J., /Brown, A., Urquhart, L., McAuley, D. (2018). Building Accountability into the Internet of Things: the IoT Databox model. Journal of Reliable Intelligent Environments 4 (1), 39–55.

Cunningham, C.Song, I.,Chen, P. P. (2004). Data warehouse design to support customer relationship management analyses. In: Il-Yeol Song (Ed.). Proceedings of the 7th ACM international workshop on Data warehousing and OLAP, the 7th ACM international workshop, Washington, DC, USA, 11/12/2004 - 11/13/2004. New York, NY, ACM, 14.

Dafoe, A. (2018). AI governance: a research agenda. Centre for the Governance of AI, Future of Humanity Institute, University of Oxford.

DAMA International (2009). The DAMA Guide to The Data Management Body of Knowledge. New Jersey, Technics Publications, LLC.

Data and Marketing Association (2022). Code of conduct. Available online at https://dma.org.uk/the-dma-code.

Demirkan, H., Bess, C., Spohrer, J., Rayes, A., Allen, D., & Moghaddam, Y. (2015). Innovations with smart service systems: Analytics, big data, cognitive assistance, and the internet of everything. *Communications of the Association for Information Systems*(37,35), 733–752. https://doi.org/10.17705/1CAIS.03735

Dyché, J.,Levy, E. (2006). Customer data integration. Reaching a single version of the truth. Hoboken, N.J, John Wiley & Sons.

Ehrlich, T., Richter, D., Meisel, M.,Anke, J. (2021). Self-Sovereign Identity als Grundlage für universell einsetzbare digitale Identitäten. HMD Praxis der Wirtschaftsinformatik 58 (2), 247–270. https://doi.org/10.1365/s40702-021-00711-5.

Eisenhardt, K. M., Graebner, M. E. (2007). Theory Building From Cases: Opportunities And Challenges. Academy of Management Journal 50 (1), 25–32. https://doi.org/10.5465/amj.2007.24160888.

Engel, C., Ebel, P. (2019). Data-driven service innovation: A systematic literature review and development of a research agenda. (accessed 8/22/2019).

Erickson, A. (2018). Comparative Analysis of the EU's GDPR and Brazil's LGPD: Enforcement Challenges with the LGPD. Brook. J. Int'l L. 44,859.

European Commission (2016). The EU Data Protection Reform and Big Data Factsheet 2016. Available online at http://ec.europa.eu/justice/.

European Commission (2016). The EU Data Protection Reform and Big Data Factsheet 2016. Retrieved from European commission web. http://ec.europa.eu/justice/, Accessed: 22.01.2023.

European Commission (2019b). European data strategy. https://ec.europa.eu/info/strategy/priorities-2019-2024/europe-fit-digital-age/european-data-strategy_en. Accessed: 22.01.2023.

European Commission (2019a). Ethics guidelines for trustworthy AI Expertengruppe für künstliche Intelligenz 2018. Available online at https://ec.europa.eu/digital-single-market/en/news/ethics-guidelines-trustworthy-ai.

European Commission (2022). Proposal for a Regulation of the European Parliament and of the council on harmonised rules on fair access to and use of data (Data Act). https://eur-lex.europa.eu/legal-content/EN/TXT/?uri=COM%3A2022%3A68%3AFIN, Accessed: 22.01.2023.

Fadler, M., Legner, C. (2021). Toward Big Data and Analytics Governance: Redefining Structural Governance Mechanisms. In Proceedings of the 54th Hawaii International Conference on System Sciences, pp. 5696–5705.

Fan, H.,Poole, M. S. (2006). What Is personalization? Perspectives on the design and implementation of personalization in information systems. Journal of Organizational Computing and Electronic Commerce 16 (3-4), 179–202. https://doi.org/10.1080/10919392.2006.9681199.
Federal Trade Commission (2012). The 2012 Federal Trade Commission Privacy Framework. https://www.ftc.gov/sites/default/files/documents/reports/federal-trade-commission-report-protecting-consumer-privacy-era-rapid-change-recommendations/120326privacyreport.pdf, Accessed: 22.01.2023.
Fellenz, M. R., Brady, M. (2010). Managing Customer-Centric Information: The Challenges of Information and Communication Technology (ICT) Deployment in Service Environments. International Journal of Applied Logistics (IJAL) 1 (3), 88–105. https://doi.org/10.4018/jal.2010070105.
Fischer, M., Imgrund, F.,Friedrich-Baasner, G., Janiesch, C.,Winkelmann, A. (2018). Connected Enterprise Meets Connected Customer - A Design Approach. Hawaii International Conference on System Sciences 2018 (HICSS-51), pp. 4641–4650.
Fruhwirth, M., Ropposch, C., & Pammer-Schindler, V. (2020). Supporting Data-driven Business Model Innovations. *Journal of Business Models*, *8*(1), 7–25. https://doi.org/10.5278/ojs.jbm.v8i1.3529
GDPR.EU (2023). GDPR: Complete guide to GDPR compliance. https://gdpr.eu/, Accessed: 22.01.2023.
Gebert, H., Geib, M., Kolbe, L., Brenner, W. (2003). Knowledge-enabled customer relationship management: integrating customer relationship management and knowledge management concepts. Journal of Knowledge Management 7 (5), 107–123. https://doi.org/10.1108/13673270310505421.
Gellman, R. (2017). Fair information practices: A basic history. Available at SSRN.
Gregor, S.,Hevner, A. (2013). Positioning and Presenting Design Science Research for Maximum Impact. Management Information Systems Quarterly 37 (2), 337–355.
Häikiö, J., Yli-Kauhaluoma, S., Pikkarainen, M., Iivari, M., Koivumäki, T. (2020). Expectations to Data: Perspectives of Service providers and users of Future Health and Wellness Services. Health and Technology 10 (3), 621–636. https://doi.org/10.1007/s12553-020-00410-z.
Heinonen, K., Strandvik, T. (2020). Customer-dominant service logic. In E. Bridges & K. Fowler (Eds.), The Routledge Handbook of Service Research Insights and Ideas Routledge, 69–90.
Heinonen, K., Strandvik, T. (2018). Reflections on customers' primary role in markets. European Management Journal 36 (1), 1–11. https://doi.org/10.1016/j.emj.2017.09.005.
Huhtala, T. (2018). Using Personal Data to Advance Preventive Healthcare Services. Journal of Service Science Research 10 (1), 77–115. https://doi.org/10.1007/s12927-018-0003-0.
Hunke, F., Heinz, D., Satzger, G. (2022). Creating Customer Value from Data: Foundations and Archetypes of Analytics-based Services. Electronic Markets 32 (2), 503–521. https://doi.org/10.1007/s12525-021-00506-y.
IEEE (2022). Ethically Aligned Design, First Edition (EAD1e) - Principles of ethically aligned design for of autonomous and intelligent systems. Available online at https://standards.ieee.org/content/dam/ieee-standards/standards/web/documents/other/ead1e_principles_to_practice.pdf.
ISO (2019). ISO/IEC 27701:2019 Security techniques — Extension to ISO/IEC 27001 and ISO/IEC 27002 for privacy information management — Requirements and guidelines.
Jayachandran, S.,Sharma, S., Kaufman, P., Raman, P. (2005). The Role of Relational Information Processes and Technology Use in Customer Relationship Management. Journal of Marketing 69 (4), 177–192. https://doi.org/10.1509/jmkg.2005.69.4.177.
Khatri, V., Brown, C. V. (2010). Designing Data Governance. Communications of the ACM 53(1), 148-152.
Kooper, M. N., Maes, R., Lindgreen, E.E.O. Roos (2011). On the Governance of Information: Introducing a new Concept of Governance to support the Management of Information. International Journal of Information Management 31 (3), 195–200. https://doi.org/10.1016/j.ijinfomgt.2010.05.009.

Koskinen, J., Knaapi-Junnila, S.,Rantanen, M. M. (2019). What if we Had Fair, People-Centred Data Economy Ecosystems? In: 2019 IEEE SmartWorld, Ubiquitous Intelligence & Computing, Advanced & Trusted Computing, Scalable Computing & Communications, Internet of People and Smart City Innovation. SmartWorld/UIC/ATC/SCALCOM/IOP/SCI 2019: Leicester, United Kingdom, 19–23 August 2019 : Piscataway, NJ, IEEE, pp. 329–334.

Kühne, B.,Böhmann, T. (2018). Formative Evaluation of data-driven Business Models – The Data Insight Generator. Proceedings of the 53rd Hawaii International Conference on System Sciences, 427–236. https://doi.org/10.24251/HICSS.2020.053.

Kumar, V., Chattaraman, V., Neghina, C., Skiera, B., Aksoy, L., Buoye, A., Henseler, J. (2013). Data-driven Services Marketing in a Connected World. Journal of Service Management 24 (3), 330–352. https://doi.org/10.1108/09564231311327021.

Kumar, V., Reinartz, W.J. (2006). Customer Relationship Management: A Databased Approach, Wiley, Hoboken, NJ.

Kunz, W.,Aksoy, L., Bart, Y., Heinonen, K., Kabadayi, S., Ordenes, F.V. , Sigala, M., Diaz, D., Theodoulidis, B. (2017). Customer Engagement in a Big Data World. Journal of Services Marketing 31 (2), 161–171. https://doi.org/10.1108/JSM-10-2016-0352.

Kurtmollaiev, S.,Pedersen, P.E. (2022). Bringing together the Whats and Hows in the Service Innovation Literature: An Integrative Framework. International Journal of Management Reviews 24, 625–653. https://doi.org/10.1111/ijmr.12297.

Ladley, J. (2019). Data governance: How to design, deploy, and sustain an effective data governance program. Academic Press.

Langford, J.,Poikola, A., Janssen, W., Lähteenoja, V., Rikken, M. (2022). Understanding MyData Operators, https://www.mydata.org/publication/understanding-mydata-operators/. Accessed: 22.01.2023.

Legner, C., Pentek, T., Otto, B. (2020). Accumulating Design Knowledge with Reference Models: Insights from 12 Years' Research into Data Management. Journal of the Association for Information Systems 21 (3). https://doi.org/10.17705/1jais.00618.

Lehrer, C., Wieneke, A., Vom Brocke, J., Jung, R., Seidel, S. (2018). How Big Data analytics enables service innovation: Materiality, affordance, and the individualization of service. Journal of Management Information Systems 35 (2), 424–460. https://doi.org/10.1080/07421222.2018.1451953.

LGPD (2023). Lei Geral de Proteção de Dados. Available on http://usercentrics.com/de/knowledge-hub/brazil-lgpd-general-data-protection-law-overview/

Li, I., Dey, A., Forlizzi, J. (2010). A Stage-based Model of Personal Informatics Systems. In Proceedings of the SIGCHI Conference on Human Factors in Computing Systems. 557–566.

Likert, R. (1932). A technique for the measurement of attitudes. Archives of Psychology (22 140), 55.

Lim, C., Kim, M., Kim, K., Kim, K.J., Maglio, P (2019). Customer Process Management. Journal of Service Management 30 (1), 105–131. https://doi.org/10.1108/JOSM-02-2017-0031.

Lim, C. Kim, K, Kim, M., Heo, J., Kim, K.J., Maglio, P. P. (2018). From Data to Value: A nine-factor Framework for data-based Value Creation in Information-intensive Services. International Journal of Information Management 39, 121–135. https://doi.org/10.1016/j.ijinfomgt.2017.12.007.

Lusch, R. F., & Nambisan, S. (2015). Service innovation: A service-dominant logic perspective. MIS Quarterly, 39(1), 155–175. https://doi.org/10.25300/MISQ/2015/39.1.07

Micheli, M., Ponti, M., Craglia, M., Berti S. A. (2020). Emerging Models of Data Governance in the Age of Datafication. Big Data & Society 7 (2), 1-15. https://doi.org/10.1177/2053951720948087.

Mikalef, P., Boura, M., Lekakos, G., Krogstie, J. (2020). The Role of Information Governance in Big Data Analytics Driven Innovation. Information & Management 57 (7), 103361. https://doi.org/10.1016/j.im.2020.103361.

Mikalef, P., Krogstie, J., van de Wetering, R., Pappas, I., Giannakos, M. (2018). Information Governance in the Big Data Era: Aligning Organizational Capabilities. Proceedings of the 51st Hawaii

International Conference on System Sciences, pp. 4911–4920. https://doi.org/10.24251/HICSS.2018.615.
Mortier, R., Haddadi, H., Henderson, T., McAuley, D., Crowcroft, J. (2014). Human-Data Interaction: The Human Face of the Data-Driven Society.
Myers, M. D., Newman, M. (2007). The qualitative interview in IS research: Examining the craft. Information and Organization 17 (1), 2–26. https://doi.org/10.1016/j.infoandorg.2006.11.001.
Neslin, S. A., Grewal, D., Leghorn, R., Shankar, V., Teerling, M. L., Thomas, J. S., Verhoef, P. C. (2006). Challenges and Opportunities in Multichannel Customer Management. Journal of Service Research (9(2)), 95–112.
Nomura, S.,Sakamoto, H., Ishizuka, A., Katsuma, Y.,Akashi, H., Miyata, H. (2020). Ongoing debate on data governance principles for achieving Universal Health Coverage: a proposal to post-G20 Osaka Summit meetings. Global Health Action 13 (1), 1859822. https://doi.org/10.1080/16549716.2020.1859822.
OECD (2022). Privacy Expert Group Report on the Review of the 1980 OECD Privacy Guidelines, OECD Digital Economy Papers, No. 229, OECD Publishing, p. 1–12. Available online at https://www.oecd.org/sti/ieconomy/privacy.htm.
Ostrom, A. L.; Parasuraman, A., Bowen, D. E./Patrício, L., Voss, C. A. (2015). Service Research Priorities in a Rapidly Changing Context. Journal of Service Research 18 (2), 127–159. https://doi.org/10.1177/1094670515576315.
Pan, S, L., Lee, J.N. (2003). Using e-CRM for a unified View of the Customer. Communications of the ACM 46 (4), 95–99. https://doi.org/10.1145/641205.641212.
Papagiannidis, E., Enholm, I.M., Dremel, C., Mikalef, P., Krogstie, J. (2022). Toward AI Governance: Identifying Best Practices and Potential Barriers and Outcomes. Information Systems Frontiers, 1–19. https://doi.org/10.1007/s10796-022-10251-y.
Park, C. H./Kim, Y. G. (2003). A Framework of Dynamic CRM: Linking Marketing with Information Strategy. Business Process Management Journal 9 (5), 652–671. https://doi.org/10.1108/14637150310496749.
Patrício, L., Gustafsson, A., Fisk, R. (2018). Upframing Service Sesign and Innovation for Research Impact. Journal of Service Research 21 (1), 3–16. https://doi.org/10.1177/1094670517746780.
Payne, D., Landry, B., Dean, M. (2015). Data Mining and Privacy: An Initial Attempt at a Comprehensive Code of Conduct for Online Business. Communications of the Association for Information Systems 37 (1). https://doi.org/10.17705/1CAIS.03734.
Payne, A., Frow, P. (2005). A Strategic Famework for Customer Relationship Management. Journal of Marketing 69 (4), 167–176. https://doi.org/10.1509/jmkg.2005.69.4.167.
Poikola, A., Kuikkaniemi, K., Honko, H. (2020). Mydata a ordic Model for Human-centered Personal Data Management and Processing. Finnish Ministry of Transport and Communications.
Policy to Avoid a Privacy Disaster. Journal of the Association for Information Systems S20 (6). 10.r17705/1.jais.00554.
Potiguara C.A., Potiguara C., Fernanda/Dias C.E., Potiguara C., Pedro H. (2020). Big Data, Anonymisation and Governance to Personal Data Protection. In: Seok-Jin Eom (Ed.). The 21st Annual International Conference on Digital Government Research. New York, United States, Association for Computing Machinery, 185–195.
Raj, W., Malik, M., Kanioura, A. (2018). Real-Time Analytics: The Key to Unlocking Customer Insights & Driving the Customer Experience. Harvard Business Review Available online at https://www.sas.com/en/whitepapers/real-time-analytics-109676.html. https://doi.org/10.5278/ojs.jbm.v7i2.2482.
Ranjan, J., Bhatnagar, V. (2009). A Holistic Framework for mCRM – Data Mining Perspective. Information Management & Computer Security 17 (2), 151–165. https://doi.org/10.1108/09685220910964018.
Rapp, A., Cena, F. (2016). Personal informatics for everyday life: How users without prior self-tracking experience engage with personal data. International Journal of Human-Computer Studies 94, 1–17. https://doi.org/10.1016/j.ijhcs.2016.05.006.

Rooksby, J., Rost, M.,Morrison, A., Chalmers, M. (2014). Personal tracking as lived informatics. In: Matt Jones (Ed.). Proceedings of the SIGCHI Conference on Human Factors in Computing Systems, CHI '14: CHI Conference on Human Factors in Computing Systems, Toronto Ontario Canada, 2014. New York, NY, ACM, pp. 1163–1172.

Rowley, J. E. (2002). Reflections on Customer Knowledge Management in e-business. Qualitative Market Research: An International Journal 5 (4), 268–280. https://doi.org/10.1108/13522750210443227.

Saarijärvi, H., Grönroos, C., Kuusela, H. (2014). Reverse Use of Customer Data: Implications for Service-based Business Models. Journal of Services Marketing 28 (7), 529–537. https://doi.org/10.1108/JSM-05-2013-0111.

Saarijärvi, H., Kuusela, H., Kannan, P. K., Kulkarni, G., Rintamäki, T. (2016). Unlocking the Transformative Potential of Customer Data in Retailing. The International Review of Retail, Distribution and Consumer Research 26 (3), 225–241. https://doi.org/10.1080/09593969.2015.1105846.

Sammon, D., Nagle, T. (2017). The Data Value Map: A Framework for Developing Shared Understanding on Data Initiatives. ECIS 2017: 25th European Conference on Information Systems, 1439–1452.

Schäfer, F., Gebauer, H.,Gröger, C., Gassmann, O., Wortmann, F. (2022). Data-driven Business and Data Privacy: Challenges and Measures for Product Companies. Business Horizons. https://doi.org/10.1016/j.bushor.2022.10.002.

Schüritz, R., Seebacher, S., Satzger, G., Schwarz, L. (2017). Datatization as the next Frontier of Servitization: Understanding the Challenges for Transforming Organizations. In Proceedings of the 38th International Conference on Information Systems, South Korea, pp.1–21.

Schymanietz, M. (2020). Capabilities for Data-driven Service Innovation. Wiesbaden, Springer Fachmedien Wiesbaden.

Seidelin, C., Dittrich, Y., Grönvall, E. (2020). Foregrounding Data in Co-design – An Exploration of how Data may Become an Object of Design. International Journal of Human-Computer Studies 143, 102505. https://doi.org/10.1016/j.ijhcs.2020.102505.

Sitra (2021). IHAN Blueprint. https://www.sitra.fi/en/articles/ihan-blueprint/. Accessed: 22.01.2023.

Spiekermann, S.,Acquisti, A., Böhme, R., Lung H., K. (2015). The Challenges of Personal Data Markets and Privacy. Electronic Markets 25 (2), 161–167. https://doi.org/10.1007/s12525-015-0191-0.

Stone, M.,Bond, A., Foss, B. (2004). Consumer insight. How to use Data and Market Research to get closer to your Customer. Kogan Page Publishers.

Stone, M., Aravopoulou, E., Gerardi, G., Todeva, E., Weinzierl, L., Laughlin, P., Stott, R. (2017). How Platforms are Transforming Customer Information Management. The Bottom Line (30,3), 216–235. https://doi.org/10.1108/BL-08-2017-0024.

Tallon, P. P., Ramirez, R. V., Short, J. E. (2013). The Information Artifact in IT Governance: Toward a Theory of Information Governance. Journal of Management Information Systems 30 (3), 141–178. https://doi.org/10.2753/MIS0742-1222300306.

Tapsell, J. Akram, R. N., Markantonakis, K. (2018). Consumer Centric Data Control, Tracking and Transparency – A Position Paper. In: 2018 17th IEEE International Conference On Trust, Security And Privacy In Computing And Communications/ 12th IEEE International Conference On Big Data Science And Engineering 2018, pp. 1380–1385.

The White House Report (2012). Consumer Data Privacy in a networked World: A Framework for Protecting Privacy and romoting innovation in the Global Digital Economy. Journal of Privacy and Confidentiality 4 (2), 95–142.

Troilo, G., de Luca, L. M., Guenzi, P. (2017). Linking data-rich Environments with Service Innovation in incumbent Firms: A conceptual Framework and Research Propositions. Journal of Product Innovation Management 34 (5), 617–639. https://doi.org/10.1111/jpim.12395.

Trustarc (2021). Privacy & Data Governance Accountability Framework. https://trustarc.com/trustarc-privacy-data-governance-accountability-framework/.Accessed: 22.02.2023.

Vesanen, J. (2007). What is Personalization? A Conceptual Framework. European Journal of Marketing, *41*(5/6), 409-418.
Vom Brocke, J. V., Simons, A., Niehaves, B., Reimer, K., Plattfaut, R., Cleven, A. (2009). Reconstructing the giant: On the Importance of Rigour in Documenting the Literature Search Process. ECIS 2009 Proceedings. 161.
Vom Brocke, J., Winter, R., Hevner, A., Maedche, A. (2020). Special Issue Editorial – Accumulation and Evolution of Design Knowledge in Design Science Research: A Journey Through Time and Space. Journal of the Association for Information Systems 21 (3). https://doi.org/10.17705/1jais.00611.
Weber, J., Watson, R.T. (2002). Analyzing the Past to Prepare for the Future: Writing a Literature Review. MIS Quarterly 26(2).
Wedel, M.,Kannan, P. K. (2016). Marketing Analytics for Data-rich Environments. Journal of Marketing 80 (6), 97–121. https://doi.org/10.1509/jm.15.0413.
Wixom, B., Ross, J. (2017). How to Monetize Your Data. MIT Sloan Management Review 58(3).
Wong, D. H.-T., Maarop, N., Samy, G. N. (2020). Data Governance and Data Stewardship: A Success Procedure. In: 2020 8th International Conference on Information Technology and Multimedia (ICIMU), 2020, pp. 54–61.
Wulf, J. (2020). Development of an AHP Hierarchy for Managing Omnichannel apabilities: A Design Science Research Approach. Business Research 13 (1), 39–68. https://doi.org/10.1007/s40685-019-0095-5.
Xu, M., Walton, J. (2005). Gaining Customer Knowledge through Analytical CRM. Industrial Management & Data Systems 105 (7), 955–971. https://doi.org/10.1108/02635570510616139.
Yin, R. K. (2009). Case Study Research: Design and Methods. SAGE Publications.

Towards Designing a NLU Model Improvement System for Customer Service Chatbots

Daniel Schloß, Ulrich Gnewuch, and Alexander Maedche

Abstract Current customer service chatbots often struggle to meet customer expectations. One reason is that despite advances in artificial intelligence (AI), the natural language understanding (NLU) capabilities of chatbots are often far from perfect. In order to improve them, chatbot managers need to make informed decisions and continuously adapt the chatbot's NLU model to the specific topics and expressions used by customers. Customer-chatbot interaction data is an excellent source of information for these adjustments because customer messages contain specific topics and linguistic expressions representing the domain of the customer service chatbot. However, extracting insights from such data to improve the chatbot's NLU, its architecture, and ultimately the conversational experience requires appropriate systems and methods, which are currently lacking. Therefore, we conduct a design science research project to develop a novel arti-fact based on chatbot interaction data that supports NLU improvement.

Keywords Customer service · Chatbots · Analytics · Language understanding

D. Schloß (✉) · U. Gnewuch · A. Maedche
Human-Centered Systems Lab, Karlsruhe Institute of Technology, Karlsruhe, Germany
e-mail: daniel.schloss@kit.edu

U. Gnewuch
e-mail: ulrich.gnewuch@uni-passau.de

A. Maedche
e-mail: alexander.maedche@kit.edu

D. Beverungen et al. (eds.), *Transforming the Digitally Sustainable Enterprise*, Lecture Notes in Information Systems and Organisation 76,
https://doi.org/10.1007/978-3-031-80125-9_12

1 Introduction

Chatbot technology is now widely used in customer service to answer customer questions or handle concerns end-to-end (Schuetzler et al., 2021).

In the rather short conversations with customer service chatbots, customers place particular value on performance (Diederich et al., 2022; Følstad and Skjuve, 2019). However, as known from research and practice, many customers still have negative experiences with chatbots. This is often due to weaknesses in the chatbots' natural language understanding (NLU). In the worst case, customers experience a breakdown ("Sorry, I did not understand that") or a mismatch (an incorrect or inappropriate response) (Benner et al., 2021; Følstad and Taylor, 2021). To avoid this, various NLU improvements performed by chatbot managers are possible: The language model of a customer service chatbot can be supplemented with additional topics or training data. Additionally, the architecture of the NLU can be adapted or linguistic fine tuning can be performed (AI Multiple, 2022). However, with growing options in NLU training, chatbot managers must make very thoughtful decisions as these can affect the customer service experience of possibly thousands of customers. However, these decisions do not have to be made uninformed. As research as well as practical advice on chatbot and NLU development suggest, real-world interaction data is valuable for a "conversation-driven development" (Akhtar et al., 2019; Rasa, 2023). By "reviewing conversations on a regular basis" (Rasa, 2023), improvements, especially with regard to NLU and Dialog Man-agement (DM), can be discovered and conducted (Følstad and Taylor, 2021). However, it is still largely unknown how a system providing such insights based on real-world conversation data needs to be designed to enable the discovery of such improvement opportunities on a mass large scale and in a more automated manner (Chen and Beaver, 2022). To address this gap, we formulate the following research question:

RQ: *How ought a system for NLU model improvement*

Of Customer Service Chatbots to Be Designed?

Accordingly, the goal of the project presented in this paper is to generate (instantiated) design knowledge for a user-centric and usage data-based system for NLU model improvement. Regarding the usage data, we aim to provide a high degree of automation (compared to manual analytical approaches, e.g. Kvale et al., 2020). Regarding the users of the system, we reveal how and what descriptive as well as prescriptive insights into conversation data help NLU designers and chatbot managers on an aggregate as well as detailed level to improve their NLU (and DM). Additionally, to ensure practical relevance and user-centeredness, this research project is conducted as design science research (DSR) project in collaboration with an industry partner. The setup is presented in chapter three. Prior to this, we introduce and build on related research from the fields of chatbot analytics and communication theory. In chapter four we provide a first in-sight into our project and system. Chapter five concludes with a summary and outlook.

2 Related Work: Chatbots in Customer Service

In customer service, task-focused chatbots are used (Schuetzler et al., 2021). With these, customers typically have short conversations regarding specific concerns where they expect to be served fast and effectively (Diederich et al., 2022; Følstad and Skjuve, 2019). They answer questions, e.g. via texts or links or start guided dialogs in which multiple conversational "turns" takes place, for example, when asking prescripted questions to identify a user to ultimately process a business transaction.

While open domain chatbots like ChatGPT or Replika build on non-deterministic Natural Language Generation (NLG), the architecture of customer service chatbots is intent-based at its core (Open AI, 2023; Replika, 2023; Schuetzler et al., 2021). As Fig. 1 shows, customer utterances are classified to an intent with a probability by a Natural Language Understanding (NLU) system. Next, the dialog management (DM) controls the chatbots' actions based on the NLU information and defined logical rules. For customer service chatbots, the responses are then typically retrieved from a knowledge base (KB) (Kucherbaev et al., 2018). This deterministic approach has the advantage that the responses, which only need to cover certain topics, are fully controllable for service managers as opposed to probalistic NLG responses (Galitsky, 2019).

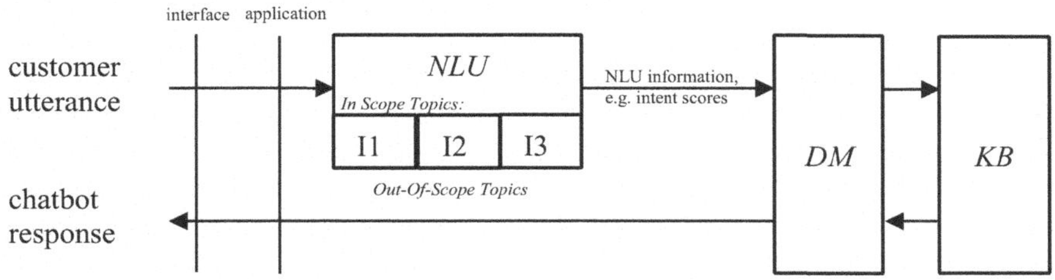

Fig. 1 Typical customer service chatbot architecture (Adamopoulou et al., 2020)

However, problems can arise with this language-based classification problem. In chatbot research, these are summarized as conversational or chatbot "breakdowns," i.e. situations in which the chatbot responds with "Sorry, I can't help you." (Benner et al., 2021). A large body of research has been devoted to the moderation and resolution of these situations within a conversation (e.g., Ashktorab et al., 2019), as they cause customer dissatisfaction and poor reputation for the technology and the company (Schuetzler et al., 2021; van der Goot et al., 2021). A breakdown is caused by the failure to succesfully detect a correct intent. In addition, an incorrect response, a so-called (intent) mismatch can occur as well (or false positive, Følstad and Taylor, 2021). Both types of errors must be corrected by a chatbot manager. This often requires manual review of conversations, as well as small adjustments within a large and difficult-to-manage set of intents, training data, and features (Beaver and Mueen, 2021). Large NLU systems, e.g., IBM Watson or Microsoft LUIS, do provide rudimentary reporting for NLU revision (Diederich et al., 2019). However, NLU improvement support is often based only on internal training data omitting detailed analysis of the real-world conversation data and specific interpretation capabilities. For this reason, user-friendly chatbot analytics systems can help to better understand conversational, specifically NLU, problems and suggest appropriate actions (Beaver and Mueen, 2020; Yaeli and Zeltyn, 2021).

3 Research Method

To address the problem of detecting and adequately resolving NLU problems in customer service chatbots, we are designing a data-driven NLU model improvement system following the design science research (DSR) paradigm (Gregor and Jones, 2007). To ensure the relevance of the project besides scientific rigor we collaborate with an industry partner (Hevner, 2007). Our industry partner is an IT and service provider for the utility industry, operating and maintaining customer service chatbots for over 25 small to very large utilities. The DSR project, shown in Table 1, follows the established structure of Kuechler and Vaishnavi (2008) and consists of two design cycles. The first design cycle (DC1) is dedicated to the descriptive analysis of chatbot log data (user messages and internal metrics). To this end, we first explored the problem space building on research on customer service chatbots and NLU. In the suggestion phase, we explored insights from (chatbot) analytics and communication research to outline methods for log data analysis for NLU optimization. Moreover, we had access to more 600.000 user messages and NLU log data. Based on this, we have drafted a first system and are currently in the development phase. Currently, it mainly contains descriptive exploration of chat data for NLU improvement, e.g. filter functions (e.g. according to intent scores) and corresponding visualizations. In the second step (DC2), we plan to upgrade the system for prescriptive analysis. By connecting the support system not only to the log data source but to the NLU system, we finally want to provide usage data-driven decision support and recommendations for the NLU, e.g. regarding training data. This will be guided by two evaluations

Table 1 Overview of the design science research project

	DC1: Log data analysis	DC2: Log—training data comparison
(1) Problem awareness	Chatbot and NLU research	
(2) Suggestion	Theory and sample dataset	Concept for data integration of system
(3) Developement	System prototype	Update: NLU/KB data integration
(4) Evaluation	Expert think-aloud sessions	Expert assessment of system guidance
(5) Conclusion	Refinement and planning DC2	Summary of design knowledge

we plan in both design cycles, first a think aloud study with experts of the industry partner, in DC2 an evaluation including external experts such as researchers and a case study where we evaluate the NLU performance, e.g. classification, ex ante and ex post implementing changes suggested by our system.

4 NLU Model Improvement System

4.1 Problem Awareness

If the NLU of a chatbot does not understand the customer's concern and the chatbot does not provide a relevant answer, it creates customer frustration and runs counter to the goal of automating customer service (Schuetzler et al., 2021; van der Goot et al., 2021). Therefore, chatbot managers need to continuously improve the NLU. But just like Large Language Models, intent-based NLU systems are often referred to as a "black box". Chatbot managers have only limited insight into the statistical operations of the NLU offered by the chatbot platforms (Diederich et al., 2019; Schuurmans and Frasincar, 2019). What they can control, is the selection and partitioning of training data, as well as the use of specific NLU features (Ruane et al., 2020). Since language understanding in intent-based (retrieval) chatbots is based on a classification problem, the performance of the model is often evaluated by means of precision, recall or F1 score, testing training utterances internally in the NLU (Rasa, 2023). Against this back-ground, there are different reasons why breakdowns (or mismatches) occur. First, it may be that a customer has simply entered (1) semantic nonsense (e.g., "Colorless green ideas sleep furiously," Chomsky and Lightfoot (2007)) or (2) grammatical nonsense (e.g., "sadsasdsde") the NLU does not need cover. However, it may also be that he or she expresses appropriately, but the topic addressed is (3) out-of-scope of the chatbot (Følstad and Taylor, 2021). In all cases, the actual tokens (e.g. "sleep") or the semantic meaning will intentionally be underrepresented in the NLU training data (Debortoli et al., 2016). It is also possible, as we observed in the provided log data, that customers use familiar words, but (4) formulate too short or verbose (Beaver and Mueen, 2020; Reinkemeier and Gnewuch, 2022). If all that is not the case and a breakdown occurred, it might be that (5a) the training data of the NLU may not be grammatically (i.e. syntactically) sufficient (e.g., "I want to cancel" vs. "Cancellation please) or (5b) lacks synonyms for equal semantics (e.g., "I want to buy a product" vs. "I want to purchase a product") (Jurafsky and Martin, 2009; Sperber and Wilson, 1986). In this case, chatbot managers need to add on the training data. Last, the NLU itself may have (6) super-vised learning performance issues such as imbalances (over-/underfitting) or poorly weighted linguistic features (Rasa, 2023). All of these causes ultimately lead to poor user experiences, but can be mitigated incrementally through informed NLU improve-ments, particularly based on real-world usage data (Diederich et al., 2019).

4.2 Suggestion

What can chatbot managers do to improve their language model to meet customer needs? To inform the design of our improvement system, we draw on the communication theories "Grounding in Communication" and "Communication Accommodation Theory" (Clark, 1996; Giles and Ogay, 2007). These theories propose the main components of communication:

Semantical: First, successful communication is characterized by all parties having a "common ground", i.e. a shared level of knowledge of the world (Clark, 1996). With regard to customer service chatbots, customers expect a broad knowledge base on all their concerns. Therefore an important component of the NLU Model Improvement System is the discovery of the situations where the chatbot violates the assumed common ground, see (3). These situations can be used as opportunities to create new intents and training data (Chen and Beaver, 2022). We have addressed this in the prototype shown on the next page by means of filter functions for unrecognized utterances and are also working on fast topic modeling for an easier overview of the unknown topics.

Syntactical: Second, according to "communication accommodation" good communication is characterized by the fact that a convergence of communication parties happens in a conversation. This can refer to social aspects or gestures, concerning text-based chatbots as in this stage of the project, this convergence needs to manifest in the applied language (understanding), see (4), (5a), (5b) (Giles and Ogay, 2007). Customer-friendly customer service chatbots must therefore not only choose their answers in the style of the customer, they also need to acquire the customer's understanding of the language (semantic and grammatical) over time. For our proposed system, this means that it must provide insight into the patterns of customers, especially with regard to utterances that are not yet well understood. This is represented by our initial filters, but also by linguistic metrics such as most frequent words or part-of-speech.

Structural: Third, there are internal technical premises of NLU systems that affect their performance independently of the specific semantics or syntax of the chosen train-ing data, see (6). An example of this is a "skewed" distribution of training data leading to imbalances (Ruane et al., 2020). We will address the analysis of these structural NLU improvement opportunities in DC2 when the NLU system is connected to our system.

4.3 Development

The prototype of the NLU improvement system, developed on the basis of python modules and connected to a MySQL log database, is built in a top-down design. This allows for generous filtering and mining of many customer utterances to apply detailed analysis for specific utterances (Beaver and Mueen, 2020). First, timestamps can be selected (due to NLU adaptations), but also intents can be filtered (left). In addition, the tool provides an overview on current intent utilization, since a too "long tail of intents" can also be cause of structural NLU performance problems (Greyling, 2022). Moreover, chatbot managers have the possibility of selecting the most interesting utterances via intent scores/thresholds or the text length as the first linguistic feature. After that, they can examine in-depth structural linguistic metrics of their selection or individual utterances (e.g. n-grams or Part-of-Speech, Manning et al., 2014). In DC2, it is planned to expand these metrics and compare them to NLU training data according to the customer service chatbot experts' input and requirements. Finally, the right-hand side of the system offers the possibility to apply parameterizable topic mining to an utterance selection. In this way, new (in-scope) topics can be discovered (Chen and Beaver, 2022) (Fig. 2).

5 Conclusion and Outlook

The NLU model improvement system we present addresses the current problem of imperformant customer service chatbots. We are planning the technical completion of the system in order to evaluate it with customer service experts in the next DSR stage. The descriptive and exploratory nature of the system, as applied to log data, will then be augmented with research and practical expertise to provide a stronger guiding function.

Fig. 2 Screenshot of the NLU model improvement system prototype

References

Akhtar, M., Neidhardt, J., and Werthner, H. (2019). The potential of chatbots: analysis of chatbot conversations. In 2019 IEEE 21st conference on business informatics (CBI) (Vol. 1, pp. 397–404). IEEE.

Beaver, I., and Mueen, A. (2020). Automated conversation review to surface virtual assistant misunderstandings: Reducing cost and increasing privacy. In Proceedings of the AAAI Conference on Artificial Intelligence (Vol. 34, No. 08, pp. 13140–13147).

Benner, D., Elshan, E., Schöbel, S., and Janson, A. (2021). What do you mean? A Review on Recovery Strategies to Overcome Conversational Breakdowns of Conversational Agents. ICIS 2021.

Chen, X., and Beaver, I. (2022). An Adaptive Deep Clustering Pipeline to Inform Text Labeling at Scale. Baltimore, Maryland, USA: Proceedings of the 39 th International Conference on Machine Learning.

Clark, H. H. (1996). Using language, Cambridge: Cambridge University Press.

Debortoli, S., Müller, O., Junglas, I., and Vom Brocke, J. (2016). Text mining for information systems researchers: An annotated topic modeling tutorial. Communications of the Association for Information Systems, 39(1), 7.

Diederich, S., Brendel, A. B., Morana, S., and Kolbe, L. (2022). On the design of and interaction with conversational agents: An organizing and assessing review of human-computer interaction research. Journal of the Association for Information Systems, 23(1), 96-138.

Diederich, S., Brendel, A. B., and Kolbe, L. M. (2019). Towards a Taxonomy of Platforms for Conversational Agent Design. Internationale Tagung, Wirtschaftsinformatik, Siegen, Germany.

Følstad, A., and Skjuve, M. (2019). Chatbots for customer service: user experience and motivation. In Proceedings of the 1st international conference on conversational user interfaces (pp. 1–9).

Følstad, A., and Taylor, C. (2021). Investigating the user experience of customer service chatbot interaction: a framework for qualitative analysis of chatbot dialogues. Quality and User Experience, 6(1), 6.

Galitsky, B. (2019). Developing enterprise chatbots. New York: Springer International Publishing.

Giles, H., and Ogay, T. (2007). Communication accommodation theory.

Van der Goot, M. J., Hafkamp, L., and Dankfort, Z. (2021). Customer service chatbots: A qualitative interview study into the communication journey of customers. In Chatbot Research and Design: 4th International Workshop, CONVERSATIONS 2020, Virtual Event, November 23–24, 2020, Revised Selected Papers 4 (pp. 190–204). Springer International Publishing.

Gregor, S., and Jones, D. (2007). The Anatomy of a Design Theory. Journal of the Association for Information Systems, 8(5), 312–335.

Greyling, C. (2022). Solving for the long tail of intent distribution. https://cobusgreyling.medium.com/solving-for-the-long-tail-of-intent-distribution-24daa372fcc, Accessed: 08.03.2023.

Hevner, A. R. (2007). A three cycle view of design science research. Scandinavian journal of information systems, 19(2), 4.

Jurafsky, D. and Martin, J. H. (2009). Speech and Language Processing, 2nd Edition, New Jersey: Prentice-Hall.

Kucherbaev, P., Bozzon and A., Houben, G. (2018). Human-Aided Bots. IEEE Internet Computing, Vol. 22, 6.

Kuechler, B., and Vaishnavi, V. (2008). On theory development in design science research: anatomy of a research project. European Journal of Information Systems, 17(5), 489-504.

Kvale, K., Sell, O. A., Hodnebrog, S., & Følstad, A. (2020). Improving conversations: lessons learnt from manual analysis of chatbot dialogues. In Chatbot Research and Design: Third International Workshop, CONVERSATIONS 2019, Amsterdam, The Netherlands, November 19–20, 2019, Revised Selected Papers 3 (pp. 187–200). Springer International Publishing.

Manning, C. D., Surdeanu, M., Bauer, J., Finkel, J. R., Bethard, S., & McClosky, D. (2014, June). The Stanford CoreNLP natural language processing toolkit. In Proceedings of 52nd annual meeting of the association for computational linguistics: system demonstrations, pp. 55–60.

AI Multiple, (2022). In-Depth Guide Into Chatbots Intents Recognition in 2023. https://research.aimultiple.com/chatbot-intent/, Accessed: 08.03.2023.
Open AI (2023). ChatGPT. https://chat.openai.com/chat, Accessed: 08.03.2023.
Rasa (2023). Conversation-Driven Development. https://rasa.com/docs/, Accessed: 08.03.2023.
Reinkemeier, F., and Gnewuch, U. (2022). Designing effective conversational repair strategies for chatbots. *ECIS 2022 Research Papers*
Replika (2023), The AI companion who cares. https://replika.ai/, Accessed: 08.03.2023
Ruane, E., Young, R., and Ventresque, A. (2020). Training a chatbot with Microsoft LUIS: effect of intent imbalance on prediction accuracy. In Proceedings of the 25th International Conference on Intelligent User Interfaces Companion (pp. 63–64).
Schuetzler, R. M., Grimes, G. M., Giboney, J. S., and Rosser, H. K. (2021). "Deciding Whether and How to Deploy Chatbots", MIS Quarterly Executive 20 (1), 1-15.
Schuurmans, J., and Frasincar, F. (2019). Intent classification for dialogue utterances. IEEE Intelligent Systems, 35(1), 82-88.
Sperber, D. and Wilson, D. (1986). Relevance: Communication and cognition, Vol. 142. Cambridge, MA: Harvard University Press.

IT Strategy, Governance and Management

Executive AI Literacy: A Text-Mining Approach to Understand Existing and Demanded AI Skills of Leaders in Unicorn Firms

Marc Pinski, Thomas Hofmann, and Alexander Benlian

Abstract Despite the growing relevance of artificial intelligence (AI) for businesses, there is a lack of research on how top-level executives must be skilled in AI. Drawing on upper echelons theory, this paper explores executive AI literacy, defined as the combined AI skills of top-level executives, and its relevance for different executive roles. We conducted a text-mining analysis of 1625 executives' online profiles and 1033 executive job postings from unicorn firms retrieved via web-scraping from an online professional social network. We find that AI skills are mostly required in product-related executive roles (vs. administrative roles). Thus, we provide an AI-specific perspective complementing prior information systems research on executives, which asserts that (non-AI) IT is driven by administrative executive roles. Our paper contributes to AI literacy literature by shedding light on the substance of executive AI literacy within firms. Lastly, we provide implications for AI-related information systems strategy.

Keywords Artificial intelligence · AI skills · Upper echelons · Executive roles · IS stratessgy

M. Pinski (✉) · T. Hofmann · A. Benlian
Technical University of Darmstadt, Information Systems and Electronic Services, Darmstadt, Germany
e-mail: pinski@ise.tu-darmstadt.de

T. Hofmann
e-mail: thomas.hofmann@stud.tu-darmstadt.de

A. Benlian
e-mail: benlian@ise.tu-darmstadt.de

D. Beverungen et al. (eds.), *Transforming the Digitally Sustainable Enterprise*, Lecture Notes in Information Systems and Organisation 76,
https://doi.org/10.1007/978-3-031-80125-9_13

1 Introduction

Information system (IS) academics and practitioners agree that recent developments regarding artificial intelligence (AI) have shaken up core assumptions within the research and business world (Schuetz and Venkatesh 2020; Tarafdar et al. 2019). While there is no unanimous AI definition, recent IS research characterizes AI as technology at the frontier of computational advancement, distinguishing itself through autonomy, the ability to learn, or its inscrutability (Berente et al. 2021). Some praise the multibillion-dollar value AI potentially unlocks through its novel and unique capacities compared to traditional technology (Manyika and Sneader 2018). However, others warn about an AI "hype" (Willcocks 2020) or point out difficulties yet to be solved—manifesting, for example, in a 75% failure rate of AI projects in organizations in the UK (Williams 2021). In any case, organizations must engage with AI, enabling them to judge how AI impacts them and how they can leverage AI to navigate its potential up- and downsides (Benbya et al. 2021; Li et al. 2021).

The primary barrier for many firms when implementing AI projects is a lack of AI skills, according to a survey of 3,000 executives (Brock and von Wangenheim 2019). The existing advances to explore, measure, and contextualize AI skills have formed under the term **AI literacy**. Multiple AI skills comprise AI literacy, that is, the ability to use and critically evaluate AI as well as communicate and collaborate effectively with AI (Long and Magerko 2020). So far, research approaches AI literacy from a stakeholder-agnostic (Ng et al. 2021) or a user-centric perspective (Wang et al. 2022). While IS researchers emphasize that a multistakeholder perspective on AI literacy is essential to understand its diverse facets (Arrieta et al. 2020), a decisive group within the organizational context has largely been neglected thus far: **top-level executives**.

IS research has shown that technology within the organizational context is no longer a side topic for managers (Bassellier et al. 2015; Baesens et al. 2016). Firms must have technology on their top agenda to stay competitive—already for a long time "business cannot afford technology-illiterate managers anymore" (Keen 1991). The tasks of executives differ significantly from the tasks of operational employees (e.g., developers) or middle management (e.g., product managers). For example, they are more long-term oriented to ensure that a firm can create value in the future (Hiller and Beauchesne 2013). AI's continuously evolving capacities upend core IS assumptions, such as functional transparency (Baird and Maruping 2021), and induce distinct organizational changes that can shift whole business models and ways of value creation (Li et al. 2021; Shollo et al. 2022). Hence, it remains unclear exactly how the AI literacy of executives should be composed to steer organizations effectively (Wamba-Taguimdje et al. 2020). While studies neglect AI-specific skills for managers, the urges to explore **executive AI literacy** are getting stronger: 0% of managers believe that AI will not have a significant impact on their industry (Davenport 2018), and Forbes Magazine recently called in a "change imperative" for more "Board Directors And CEO AI Literacy" (Gordon 2022). From an IS academic point of view, executive AI literacy constitutes a valuable additional perspective called for in AI literacy research (Long and Magerko, 2020; Tarafdar et al. 2019). We do not yet fully know what executive AI literacy looks like and which executive roles need it most to promote the purposeful deployment of AI while reducing the risk of failure. Therefore, we formulate the following research question: *What are the AI skills that executives (should) have, and how are they organized within the top management team (TMT)?*

Drawing on upper echelons theory and the attention-based view (ABV) of the firm (Hambrick and Mason 1984; Ocasio 2011), we analyzed observational skill data, i.e., skills disclosed in online profiles and job postings in an online professional social network ("LinkedIn.com"). We follow prior studies on executives that utilize social media data (e.g., Heavey et al. 2020) and leverage data from an online professional social network. This allows us to follow a text-mining approach, which is well-suited to explore a new construct like executive AI literacy. Furthermore, we focused on a data sample of unicorn firms (privately held firms with a valuation above one billion USD). We selected unicorn firms because the fast-paced startup environment requires quick adaptation, making it more likely that purposeful executive structures concerning the fast-evolving topic of AI are in place. The retrieved skill data were disclosed by executives in their online profiles ("existing perspective") and by firms in job postings for executives ("demand perspective"). While IS research has generally used the analysis of user-disclosed data (Heavey et al. 2020), IS skill research has hitherto almost exclusively leveraged the demand perspective (Anton et al. 2020; Debortoli et al. 2014; Gardiner et al. 2017). We performed a text-mining analysis (skill frequency and latent semantic analysis) to uncover the substance of executive AI literacy and its organization within the TMT. As a result, we identified specific executive AI skills and executive skill profiles (i.e., common skill combinations) related to AI and the respective executive roles these skill profiles represent.

This study makes the following contributions: (1) We complement the advances in AI literacy literature with a perspective on executives by identifying which AI skills exist and are demanded among executives. By examining existing and demanded AI skills, we also contribute a comparison of two viewpoints on AI skills, so far absent from prior AI literacy research. Furthermore, we uncover which executive roles within the TMT are commonly equipped with AI literacy. (2) Concerning practice, we provide guidance on how to set up an executive AI skill strategy, for example, through specific recruiting or upskilling policies.

The paper is organized as follows: First, we introduce the theoretical background, including upper echelons theory and related work on AI literacy. Then, we discuss the research design, including data retrieval and text mining analysis. After presenting the respective results, we synthesize the findings regarding AI-related IS strategy.

2 Theoretical Background

2.1 Upper Echelons Theory and Executive Research in IS

Upper echelons theory states that the decisions of a firm reflect how its top-level executives ("upper echelons") interpret the environment and how much attention they pay to it (Hambrick and Mason 1984). Thereby, the upper echelons theory emphasizes managerial attention, which links it closely to the ABV of the firm (Ocasio 1997, 2011). The central premise of the ABV is that a firm's behavior is determined by how it channels and distributes attention. Consequently, ABV states that the more managerial attention a topic receives within a firm, the more resources and support are allocated to the topic, which leads to the desired outcomes. According to upper echelons theory, such outcomes result from executives' decisions and reflect their characteristics (Hambrick and Mason 1984; Carpenter et al. 2016). Such characteristics include, among others, executives' values, perceptions, or skills (Klein and Harrison 2007). IS research found, for example, that executives' (general) IT skills affect their intention to challenge IT issues and foster a greater propensity to engage with IT units (Bassellier et al. 2015, 2003). In other words, executives' attention is channeled toward issues they are more skilled in.

In addition to the attributes of individual executives, a significant amount of executive research based on upper echelons theory is concerned with the TMT, also known as the board of directors (Carpenter et al. 2016). Research has examined diverse effects of the TMT, such as the presence of executive roles within the TMT, for example, the chief sustainability officer's presence on corporate social responsibility activities (Fu et al. 2019), or the characteristics of the whole TMT, for example, TMT diversity on firm performance (Simons et al. 1999). An acknowledged differentiation of such executive roles distinguishes two types according to their closeness to the firm's business domain: product-related roles (e.g., marketing, manufacturing, research & development [R&D]) and administrative roles (e.g., human resources [HR], finance, legal) (Guadalupe et al. 2014). Regarding IS, research has shown that the prevalence of administrative executive roles in TMTs has been associated with higher (general) IT investments and usage since administrative functions often centralize processes across different divisions, which leads to more technology usage (Guadalupe et al. 2014).

Many IS studies based on upper echelons theory predominantly investigated the roles of chief technology officers (CTO) and chief information officers (CIO) (Benlian and Haffke 2016). For example, CTO presence is associated with profitability increases (Cetindamar and Pala 2011), while CIO presence is associated with information quality increases (Ding et al. 2014) under certain conditions. Firms do not always separate CIO and CTO roles. However, if they are separated, the substantive distinction is that CIOs are rather focused inward (e.g., internal information flow), while CTOs are rather focused outward (e.g., customer information flow) (Hunts 2021).

2.2 Related Work on AI Literacy

A growing stream of IS literature does not focus on the technical features of AI to enhance human-AI collaboration but rather on the unique "features" of humans regarding AI—a concept coined AI literacy (Long and Magerko 2020; Anton et al. 2020; Pinski and Benlian 2023). AI literacy is distinct from prior technology literacies, such as digital or data literacy (Eshet-Alkalai 2004; Kerpedzhiev et al. 2020), because AI's new capacities break core IS assumptions, such as functional transparency or functional consistency (Berente et al. 2021). These capacities enable new use cases requiring new skills, such as evaluating the business risk from a functionally not transparent AI. The majority of research acknowledges that AI literacy not only refers to technical AI skills (e.g., programming) but also includes skills such as judging AI ethics, evaluating AI business value, or critically interpreting AI outputs (Cetindamar et al. 2022).

There is agreement in the literature that it is essential to take a multistakeholder perspective on AI literacy, which goes beyond developers and users and includes further stakeholders such as regulators, nontechnical employees, and executives (Meske et al. 2020; Arrieta et al. 2020; Benlian et al. 2022). While most studies approach AI skills' exploration, conceptualization, or measurement with a stakeholder-agnostic (Long and Magerko 2020) or user-centric approach (Wang et al. 2022), executives have been neglected. However, the tasks of executives differ significantly from those of other positions, which also necessitates a distinct skill set. Executives do not need information about every (technical) detail; they must have an overview of the entire AI process, enabling them to make informed decisions (Peifer et al. 2022). However, research has not yet explored how detailed such an overview should be for different executive roles. A potential executive AI skill might be the ability to make informed decisions on which activities should be taken over by humans and which should be carried out by AI. Taking such a decision requires being skilled in the strengths and weaknesses of AI and humans in the context of the respective use case (Peifer et al. 2022; Adam et al. 2022). In the long term, executives must ensure that their firm continues to create value, extending or securing its competitive position. Therefore, assessing how AI can create value should be a top priority of an executive (Shollo et al. 2022; Wamba-Taguimdje et al. 2020). In summary, executive AI literacy has potentially tremendous effects on organizations but remains a hitherto underexplored field in IS research.

3 Research Design

Our research design consists of two main phases. First, we retrieved the observational skill data (i.e., skills disclosed online) from an online professional social network (LinkedIn.com) via a web-scraping procedure. Then, we conducted a text-mining analysis to identify which AI skills executives have and which executive skill profiles contain those AI skills. Therefore, we analyzed executives' online profiles (OP) and firms' executive job postings (JP) through skill frequency and latent semantic analysis.

3.1 Data Retrieval and Preprocessing

We retrieved all observational skill data for this study from LinkedIn.com, a widely used online professional social network with several 100 million individual users and several 10 million firms. In this online professional social network, firms can publish JPs, and individuals can create OPs. Individuals populate their OPs with their skills in a dedicated skill section and link them to their current employer, while firms describe the required skills for their open positions in their JPs. Individuals use the network to connect to others and create a professional online presence. At the same time, firms leverage it to market their JPs or other firm-related information or announcements. Prior research has shown that executives engage with social media in meaningful ways, for example, to communicate with other business stakeholders (Heavey et al. 2020). Furthermore, previous studies showed that LinkedIn.com, as the worldwide largest professional social network, sends valid signals regarding user's personality traits (Fernandez et al. 2021), and skills disclosed by users are consistent with hiring managers' assessment of the respective users (Roulin and Levashina 2018). Given that research shows executives engaging meaningfully in social media to exchange with relevant business stakeholders, thus making potential false impressions costly, and studies on the validity of stated skills on LinkedIn.com, we deem the data source viable for our text-mining analysis. Furthermore, we also analyze the skill demand perspective as an additional cross-check since firms have little incentive to overstate their advertised jobs' required skills.

To answer our research question (What are the AI skills that executives (should) have, and how are they organized within the TMT?), we (1) selected a suitable data sample of unicorn firms and (2) retrieved the existing and demanded executives' skills of these firms: (1) We retrieved our sample from unicorn firms because the startup ecosystem is particularly suited to study a rapidly evolving phenomenon such as AI due to the fast-paced environment requiring contestants to adapt quickly to avoid being outcompeted (Pigola et al. 2022). Given the dynamic environment, firms seem likelier to implement novel and purposeful patterns among upper echelons more quickly. Furthermore, the survival in the startup ecosystem and the above-average valuation indicate that purposeful executive structures are in place. We retrieved an up-to-date list of unicorns from CB Insights in July 2022 (CB Insights 2022). There were no filters regarding the country of origin applied. From the list of unicorns, we included only those who publicly disclosed their executives on their company websites and where we were able to retrieve the skill data from at least three executives to only include TMTs, of which we likely have recorded a majority (average TMT size = 6 (Simons et al. 1999)). Of the selected firms, all were present on LinkedIn.com.

(2) We retrieved the executive skills of the selected unicorn firms from two perspectives: existing and demanded executive skills. While many studies on IS skills use the demand perspective through required skills in JPs (Verma et al. 2021; Gardiner et al. 2017; Debortoli et al. 2014; Föll et al. 2018), we integrate both complementing perspectives for a more holistic and rigorous picture of executive AI skills. The existing perspective gives insights into the available executive skills at the firm in question. Additionally, the demand perspective complements these insights with executive skills that firms believe to need but might not be present within the firm yet. The data retrieval via the two-sided professional social network (firms and employees are present) enabled the retrieval of the existing and demanded skill data from a single source. We filtered for JPs classified as "executives and directors" by the firms. Then, we extracted the relevant disclosed skill data of each executive's OP and each JP of the selected unicorn firms with a web-scraping procedure. Therefore, we first scraped a list of all skills disclosed in a dedicated "skill section" of the OPs. In this skill section of the OP, executives enter skills separately, which enabled us to retrieve a search list of skills. We recorded each skill exactly as the executives entered it in their profile's skill section. Since the skills in the dedicated skill section were already separated from the nonrelevant text in a tabular-like format, removing stopwords was unnecessary, and we were able to include skills that consisted of multiple words, such as "machine learning," because the executives entered them that ways in their skill section.

Subsequently, we used this list of skills to extract additional skills disclosed in additional text elements that can be used within OPs/JPs to describe the personal experience or job requirements in greater detail. The extracted text data have been lemmatized to unify the data set as recommended by the literature for text mining analysis (Anton et al. 2020; Kortum et al. 2022; Sidorova et al. 2008). Acronyms, such as "AI" for artificial intelligence, have been manually replaced with their full terms to unify skill labeling. As a result, we compiled a data set including 168 unicorn firms with 1625 unique executives (represented through their OPs) and 1033 executive JPs. In total, the executives disclosed 98,437 existing skills in their OPs, and the unicorn firms demanded 54,752 skills in their JPs. The combined skill corpus of existing and demanded skills consisted of 4520 unique skills. On average, we extracted 60.6 skills per OP. The existing and demanded skill data were retrieved between July and September 2022.

3.2 *Text Mining (1/2): Identification of Executive AI Skills*

We performed a skill frequency analysis to identify executive AI skills by their direct terms. Therefore, we used an AI skill taxonomy containing 78 AI skills provided by Burning Glass Technologies, which has already been used in prior AI job studies (Alekseeva et al. 2021), to identify AI skills within the developed skill corpus of existing and demanded skills. We identified all skills from the taxonomy in the data and computed their relative frequencies (for existing skills based on the total number of executives; for demanded skills based on the total number of JPs). Furthermore, we categorized the individual AI skills that occurred in the data by three independent raters to determine patterns in the data. Categories were independently formed inductively from the data set and subsequently discussed until the raters reached an agreement. The initial interrater agreement was satisfactory (Cohen's Kappa (K) = 0.80) (Landis and Koch 1977; Cohen 2016). Any deviations regarding the categorization of individual skills were discussed and resolved to achieve complete agreement.

3.3 Text Mining (2/2): Identification of Executive Profiles Related to AI

Since executives' tasks differ from the tasks of operational employees, their AI literacy might also have a different, potentially more complex shape. Hence, we aimed to complement the skill frequency analysis by identifying executive skill profiles related to AI. Considering whole skill profiles might give a more accurate picture of executive AI literacy because it uncovers which other skills are often paired with AI skills among executives. This way, we aimed to gain also a more holistic picture of the AI skills of executives. Therefore, we generated executive skill profiles through topic modeling via latent semantic analysis (LSA) to identify those executive skill profiles (respectively, the executive roles they represent) that contain AI skills.

Role titles in OPs/JPs can be ambiguous and not unified in the online professional social network. Therefore, we follow prior research by modeling the underlying roles based on their skills (Anton et al. 2020). The modeled profiles were cross-checked with common executive roles to ensure they represent actual executive roles. Topic modeling through LSA is a widely used unsupervised text-mining method in IS research (Anton et al. 2020; Sidorova et al. 2008; Jiang et al. 2021). We first discuss LSA's general functioning and provide the mathematical background at the end of the section. LSA aims to identify underlying topics in a skill corpus without an a priori theoretical model. LSA can, for example, identify synonyms (Landauer 2002) or metaphors (Kintsch and Bowles 2002). Similar to other factor analysis methods, LSA reduces the dimensionality of the data through singular value decomposition (SVD). The target number of topics (r), executive skill profiles in our context, is chosen ex-ante. Through SVD, each term (i.e., skill) in the corpus receives a factor loading for each topic (i.e., executive skill profile) describing the relevance of the skill for the latent executive skill profile (Kortum et al. 2022). To construct the executive skill profiles from the SVD, we selected the 50 skills with the highest factor loadings for each skill profile as suggested for a thorough exploration of the skill profiles by prior IS literature leveraging LSA (Debortoli et al. 2014). We classified each skill extracted via this method by two independent raters into skill categories to interpret the resulting executive skill profiles. Skills were first coded deductively into categories based on common executive functions (e.g., HR, Marketing) (Guadalupe et al.

2014). After the first coding iterations, we refined the coding structure until agreement among the raters was achieved. The interrater agreement exceeded commonly used thresholds (K = 0.93, (Cohen 2016)), and skills with disagreement between the raters were discussed individually until all disagreements had been resolved.

We followed established technical guidelines when performing the LSA (Sidorova et al. 2008). We conducted the LSA with the software "Python" (v 3.10) and specifically the Python package "scikit-learn" (v 1.1.2). The mathematical explanation of the methodology uses the general vocabulary "term" (for skill) and "document" (for OP/JP) for simplicity. First, a term-document matrix (**A**) is created with the frequency of each term within each document. The raw term frequency (tf_i) for each term (i) is weighted with the inverse document frequency ($idf_i = \log_2(N/n_i) + 1$, where N is the number of documents and n_i is the term frequency in the entire corpus). This results in the indicator *TF-IDF* (Salton and Buckley 1988; Han and Kamber 2006). *TF-IDF* promotes the occurrence of rare words and discounts the influence of common words, which generally leads to better results in SVD. The SVD of **A** is then expressed as $\mathbf{A} = \mathbf{TSD^T}$, where **T** is a *term-topic* matrix of eigenvectors of the square symmetric matrix of term covariances $\mathbf{AAT^T}$, **D** is the *document-topic* matrix of eigenvectors of the square symmetric matrix of document covariances $\mathbf{A^TA}$, and **S** is a *topic-topic* diagonal matrix containing the square roots of eigenvalues of $\mathbf{AAT^T}$ and $\mathbf{A^TA}$. **TS** is the matrix of interest for our study, as it contains the term factor loadings for each topic (Park et al. 2003).

4 Results

4.1 Skill Frequency Analysis

Eighteen AI skills were found in the skill corpus of existing and demanded skills from the taxonomy of 78 AI skills, which we grouped into five skill classes (Fig. 1). Within our unicorn firm sample, a significant share of executives (19%) has stated "artificial intelligence" as a general skill they possess. A look at the demand side of those firms for the same skill (13% of JP) confirms that the firms' executives not only state "artificial intelligence" as a byproduct that they picked up somewhere else but that the executive positions require the skill. The more differentiated skills appear with lower but nonnegligible frequencies. Therefore, the skills were categorized following the procedure stated above. All "specialized AI techniques" (e.g., Machine learning, Deep learning) together are almost as prevalent (14%) as general "artificial intelligence" (19%). AI application-specific skills, such as vision/images (4%) and natural language (3%), occur with almost equal frequencies and significantly less. The occurrence of AI software, on the other hand, is negligible. Overall, we find differentiated AI skills even among executives. Furthermore, we observed that the relative "existing frequency" is greater than the relative "demand frequency" for all skills.

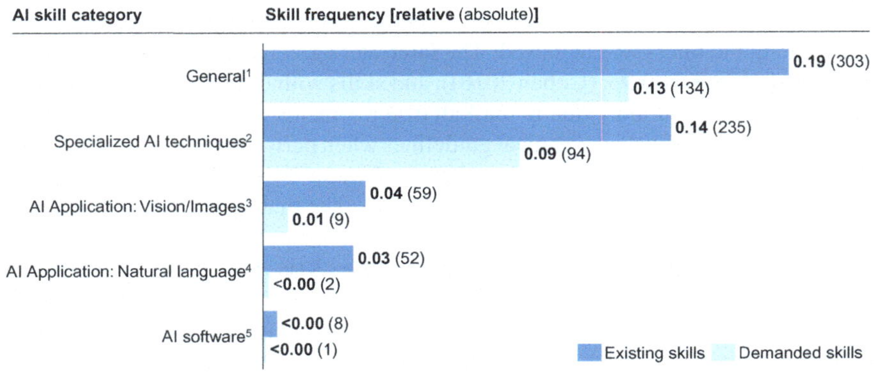

Included terms with existing / demanded frequencies [relative (absolute)]:

1. "Artificial Intelligence": 0.19 (303) / 0.13 (134)
2. "Machine Learning": 0.12 (198) / 0.09 (90), "Deep Learning": 0.02 (31) / 0 (4) , "Pattern Recognition": 0 (6) / 0 (0)
3. "Computer Vision": 0.02 (37) / 0.01 (9), "Image Processing": 0.01 (17) / 0 (0), "Object Recognition": 0 (3) / 0 (0), "Machine Vision": 0 (2) / 0 (0)
4. "Natural Language Processing": 0.02 (34) / 0 (2), "Tokenization": 0 (4) / 0 (0), "Text Mining": 0 (4) / 0 (0), "Chatbot": 0 (3) / 0 (0), "Speech Recognition": 0 (3) / 0 (0), "Language Models": 0 (2) / 0 (0), "Text to Speech": 0 (1) / 0 (0), "Sentiment Analysis": 0 (1) / 0 (0)
5. "Opencv": 0 (5) / 0 (0), "TensorFlow": 0 (3) / 0 (1)

Fig. 1 Frequencies of executive AI skills and AI skill categories

4.2 *Latent Semantic Analysis*

In the LSA, we included the 50 skills with the highest factor loadings for each skill profile.[1] All included skills were categorized as stated above (388 unique skills in total, excluding duplicates). Based on the categorization, we interpreted the skill profiles, inferred their executive role (e.g., CEO) and role type (administrative vs. product-related), and determined whether AI skills belonged to the skill profile (Fig. 2). We modeled $r = 8$ executive skill profiles because profiles beyond that could not be allocated to meaningful executive roles.

AI skills occurred in three of the eight modeled skill profiles (#2, #7, #8). In those profiles, AI skills occurred with a 2% frequency, which can still be considered significant since they are a very narrow, specialized skill class compared to broad executive skill classes like marketing, comprising much more skills in the corpus. Furthermore, there is a clear emphasis on general technology skills across all profiles (average share of 24%), consistent with prior research on the need for general technology skills for executives (Bassellier et al. 2015). Therefore, we will not explicitly mention general technology skills when evaluating each skill profile in detail below.

The eight extracted skill profiles closely mirror typical executive roles: Profile #1 is the broadest skill profile, with five skill categories containing more than 10% of the skills within the profile and all categories containing less than 30%. Given the strong focus on general (24%) and business development skills (16%), we infer the

[1] Since an LSA of the demanded and existing skill data are congruent at large, we proceed with a description of the existing perspective due to simplicity.

Skill profile ID	#1	#2	#3	#4	#5	#6	#7	#8	Avg.
Skills by category (%)									
AI	0%	2%	0%	0%	0%	0%	2%	2%	1%
General	24%	14%	6%	14%	16%	24%	18%	18%	17%
Business development	16%	4%	2%	16%	4%	6%	12%	10%	9%
Technology	26%	58%	22%	18%	12%	12%	20%	24%	24%
Finance & accounting	6%	0%	34%	2%	4%	6%	2%	2%	7%
Risk	0%	4%	4%	0%	0%	2%	0%	0%	1%
Marketing & sales	14%	4%	10%	46%	6%	18%	10%	32%	18%
Human resources	0%	4%	8%	2%	34%	6%	2%	2%	7%
Operations	10%	6%	12%	2%	12%	2%	2%	2%	6%
Legal	2%	4%	2%	0%	4%	22%	2%	4%	5%
Domain specific	2%	0%	0%	0%	8%	2%	30%	4%	6%
Number of significant categories (≥10%)	5	2	4	4	4	4	5	4	4.0
Inferred executive role	**Generalist ('CEO')**	**Technology ('CTO')**	**Finance & accounting ('CFO')**	**Marketing & sales ('CMO')**	**Human resources ('CHRO')**	**Legal specialist**	**Domain specialist**	**Marketing & Technology specialist**	
Inferred executive type	-	Admin. / Product	Admin.	Product	Admin.	Admin.	Product	Product	
AI skills included	No	Yes	No	No	No	No	Yes	Yes	

Fig. 2 Executive skill profiles based on existing skills

executive role of a "chief executive officer" (CEO). AI skills were not present in profile #1.

Profile #2 is highly driven by technology skills (58%) and does—intuitively—contain AI skills. We associate profile #2 with the type "chief technology officer" or "chief information officer" (the LSA was not able to discriminate between CIO and CTO; therefore, CTO is used for simplicity in the following). Depending on the underlying business, this executive type can be either administrative if IT is not the core business or product-related if the underlying core business is IT.

Profiles #3, #4, and #5 are driven by financial skills (34% in #3), marketing & sales skills (46% in #4), and human resources skills (34% in #5). We associate these skill profiles with the roles of a chief financial officer (CFO) for profile #3, a chief marketing officer (CMO) for profile #4, and a chief human resource officer (CHRO) for profile #5. While the CFO and CHRO play administrative roles, the CMO is product-related. None of the three roles (CFO, CMO, CHRO) have AI skills included in their profile.

Profiles #6 and #7 were driven by legal skills (22% in #6) and domain-specific skills (30% in #7). Since legal skills do not have a commonly used "chief"-title as the previous types, we chose the label "legal specialist," which is an administrative role. The legal specialist profile does not include AI skills. Domain-specific executives, who are executives specific to the industry a firm operates in and closer to the actual product of the firm, are often found on firm boards, for example, a chief research officer in pharmaceuticals or a chief manufacturing officer in industrials (Guadalupe et al. 2014). Therefore, we chose the industry-agnostic label "domain specialist" for profile #7. The domain specialist executive role is naturally product-related and does include AI skills.

Last, profile #8 included, apart from general skills, predominantly marketing and sales skills as well as technology skills. Interestingly, this product-related skill profile, which contains AI skills, is hitherto not found as often as in the traditional upper echelons literature compared to the other explored profiles (Guadalupe et al. 2014).

5 Discussion

5.1 Synthesis of Executive Skill Profile Findings

Based on the skill data, we modeled eight executive skill profiles, of which three profiles included AI skills: "CTO," "marketing & technology specialist," and "domain specialist." While it is intuitive that a **CTO** possesses AI skills, the association of AI skills with domain-specific and commercial skills is not immediately apparent. When analyzing the executive type (administrative vs. product-related) rather than individual roles, it can be observed that AI skills seem to occur in the product-related type rather than the administrative type. The only product-related executive role where we did not find AI skills is the CMO role. However, we find a distinct, nontraditional "**marketing & technology specialist**" executive role that emphasizes the relevance of AI regarding marketing through the emergence of a separate executive role.

The emergence of such a nontraditional executive role with AI skills is particularly interesting. The IS literature discusses the evolution of a role labeled the "chief data officer" (CDO), whose task is to integrate data from different data sources and draw actionable conclusions about new business opportunities (Lee et al. 2018). While we find that the label disappeared (only two executives with the job title CDO were found in the data), the underlying skill profile is still demanded. Our skill profile analysis adds that marketing & technology specialists have more weight on marketing (32%) than technology (24%) skills and are likely to be AI-literate. Such executives could leverage AI, for example, to exploit sales opportunities, optimize revenue streams, or predict demand—a potential focus area or starting point for firms seeking to use AI.

A combination of AI with domain-specific skills within the **domain specialist** role suggests that many AI projects are placed in the business context, such as drug discovery in health (Lou and Wu 2021) or autonomous driving in mobility (Rao and Frtunikj 2018), rather than in administrative functions, such as finance & auditing, legal, or HR. This must not mean that those roles generally do not need AI skills. It rather suggests that AI skills are more common in the former, product-related executive roles. We thus support prior research that finds a qualitative difference between product-related and administrative executive types regarding their relationship to IS (Guadalupe et al. 2014). However, we extend this line of research with our findings indicating that AI is driven by product-related functions, as opposed to general IT, which is driven predominantly by administrative functions (Guadalupe et al. 2014).

5.2 Contributions to Research and Practice

This paper set out to explore the substance of executive AI literacy and its organization in firms. Therefore, we retrieved skill data of 1,625 executives' OPs and 1,033 executive JPs from 168 unicorn firms via an online professional social network and analyzed the data with a text-mining approach. We find that 19% of executives have general AI skills, while 3–14% disclose more specialized AI skills. Regarding skill demand, 13% of executive jobs required general AI skills, while 1–9% required more specialized AI skills. Furthermore, we find AI more often associated with product-related rather than administrative executive roles. With those findings, we make two contributions to the AI literacy and upper echelons literature:

(1) *We complement existing AI literacy research with a perspective on executives from both an existing and demanded viewpoint on AI skills.* Prior IS research on AI literacy took a stakeholder-agnostic (Long and Magerko 2020; Heyder and Posegga 2021) or a user-centric view (Wang et al. 2022). By focussing on executives, we increase our understanding of which AI skills executives have and are required to have and which executive roles are most often associated with AI. We extend prior research by specifying the type of executive role (those with a product-related function) predominantly associated with AI skills. In contrast to non-AI IT, which is predominately driven by administrative functions (Guadalupe et al. 2014), our findings indicate that AI is more relevant in product-facing functions. Additionally, we extend prior IS skill research which almost exclusively used the demand perspective on skills (e.g., Debortoli et al. 2014) with a complementary approach that utilizes not only demanded but also existing skills, thus increasing the validity of the analysis. We could show that in the case of executives, existing and demanded AI skills frequencies were congruent at large. Therefore, we expose that executive AI literacy is not only a desired future state, but that executives started already acquiring AI skills requested from the market.

(2) *We provide guidance for firms about potential AI literacy strategies for executives.* While most AI-literate executives seem to have a general understanding, we show that it is not uncommon for executives also to have more profound application-specific AI skills. Most firms bundle AI with product-related rather than administrative executive roles, suggesting that application-specific AI skills should be developed combined with a product focus. Practitioners can leverage these insights, for example, to decide whom to recruit as their executives, how to upskill their executives, or how to structure their TMTs. Based on our findings, one could argue that a viable executive AI literacy strategy might require all executives to have a minimum of general AI literacy while requiring deeper application-specific AI literacy in product-related executive functions. Given that general technology skills are prevalent across all executive roles, it seems plausible that nearly all executives must obtain a minimum AI literacy in the future. Thus, firms should develop a process, routine, or requirement to let AI skills permeate into the TMT. Since such a process includes changing the skills of executives or replacing the executives who typically only report to a supervisory board, it can constitute a substantial challenge for an organization to implement such a process successfully.

5.3 Limitations and Future Research

This study has several limitations that pose potential future research directions: (1) All existing skills retrieved through the online professional social network were self-disclosed. Executives might overstate their skills to make a more favorable impression online. Future research could analyze the specific AI skills of executives in a smaller-scale survey design and leverage objective measurement tools to address the potential bias due to self-disclosure. (2) We specifically focused on unicorn firms suitable for studying a dynamic environment. However, it might also be of interest to investigate traditional SME or conglomerate firms and analyze whether this study's findings hold or how they differ. (3) Due to the quantitative research design, the investigated AI skills needed to be summarized under broader labels, such as "machine learning." A qualitative follow-up study might investigate what executives include exactly under such labels in more depth. (4) Furthermore, the skill taxonomy used was from 2019. Since AI skills evolve quickly, future studies might aim to update this or similar skill taxonomies. We encourage future research to further increase our understanding of more detailed aspects of executive AI literacy.

References

Adam, M., Roethke, K. and Benlian, A. (2022). "Human Versus Automated Sales Agents: How and Why Customer Responses Shift Across Sales Stages", *Information Systems Research* **0**.

Alekseeva, L., Azar, J., Giné, M., Samila, S. and Taska, B. (2021). "The demand for AI skills in the labor market", *Labour Economics* **71**.

Anton, E., Behne, A. and Teuteberg, F. (2020). The humans behind artificial intelligence - An operationalisation of AI competencies. *European Conference on Information Systems*. Virtual.

Arrieta, A. B., Díaz-Rodríguez, N., Del Ser, J., Bennetot, A., Tabik, S., Barbado, A., Garcia, S., Gil-Lopez, S., Molina, D., Benjamins, R., Chatila, R. and Herrera, F. (2020). "Explainable Artificial Intelligence (XAI): Concepts, taxonomies, opportunities and challenges toward responsible AI", *Information Fusion* **58**, 82–115.

Baesens, B., Bapna, R., Marsden, J. R., Vanthienen, J. and Zhao, J. L. (2016). "Transformational Issues of Big Data and Analytics in Networked Business", *MIS Quarterly* **40**(4), 807–818.

Baird, A. and Maruping, L. M. (2021). "The Next Generation of Research on IS Use: A Theoretical Framework of Delegation to and from Agentic IS Artifacts", *MIS Quarterly* **45**(1), 315–341.

Bassellier, G., Benbasat, I. and Reich, B. H. (2003). "The Influence of Business Managers' IT Competence on Championing IT", *Information Systems Research* **14**(4), 317–336.

Bassellier, G., Reich, B. H. and Benbasat, I. (2015). "Information Technology Competence of Business Managers: A Definition and Research Model", *Journal of Management Information Systems* **17**(4), 159–182.

Benbya, H., Pachidi, S. and Jarvenpaa, S. L. (2021). "Special Issue Editorial: Artificial Intelligence in Organizations: Implications for Information Systems Research", *Journal of the Association for Information Systems* **22**(2), 281–303.

Benlian, A. and Haffke, I. (2016). "Does mutuality matter? Examining the bilateral nature and effects of CEO–CIO mutual understanding", *The Journal of Strategic Information Systems* **25**(2), 104–126.

Benlian, A., Wiener, M., Cram, W. A., Krasnova, H., Maedche, A., Möhlmann, M., Recker, J. and Remus, U. (2022). "Algorithmic Management", *Business & Information Systems Engineering* **64**, 825–839.

Berente, N., Gu, B., Recker, J. and Santhanam, R. (2021). "Managing Artificial Intelligence", *MIS Quarterly* **45**(3), 1433–1450.

Brock, J. K.-U. and Von Wangenheim, F. (2019). "Demystifying AI: What Digital Transformation Leaders Can Teach You about Realistic Artificial Intelligence", *California Management Review* **61**(4), 110–134.

Carpenter, M. A., Geletkanycz, M. A. and Sanders, W. G. (2016). "Upper Echelons Research Revisited: Antecedents, Elements, and Consequences of Top Management Team Composition", *Journal of Management* **30**(6), 749–778.

Cetindamar, D., Kitto, K., Wu, M., Zhang, Y., Abedin, B. and Knight, S. (2022). "Explicating AI Literacy of Employees at Digital Workplaces", *IEEE Transactions on Engineering Management* **0**, 1–14.

Cetindamar, D. and Pala, O. (2011). "Chief technology officer roles and performance", *Technology Analysis & Strategic Management* **23**(10), 1031–1046.

Cohen, J. (2016). "A Coefficient of Agreement for Nominal Scales", *Educational and Psychological Measurement* **20**(1), 37–46.

Davenport, T. (2018). *The AI Advantage. How to Put the Artificial Intelligence Revolution to Work,* Cambridge: MIT Press.

Debortoli, S., Müller, O. and Vom Brocke, J. (2014). "Comparing Business Intelligence and Big Data Skills", *Business & Information Systems Engineering* **6**(5), 289–300.

Ding, F., Li, D. and George, J. F. (2014). "Investigating the effects of IS strategic leadership on organizational benefits from the perspective of CIO strategic roles", *Information & Management* **51**(7), 865–879.

Eshet-Alkalai, Y. (2004). "Digital literacy", *Journal of Educational Multimedia and Hypermedia* **13**(1), 93–106.

Fernandez, S., Stöcklin, M., Terrier, L. and Kim, S. (2021). "Using available signals on LinkedIn for personality assessment", *Journal of Research in Personality* **93**.

Föll, P., Hauser, M. and Thiesse, F. (2018). Identifying the Skills Expected of IS Graduates by Industry: A Text Mining Approach. *International Conference on Information Systems.* San Francisco, USA.

Fu, R., Tang, Y. and Chen, G. (2019). "Chief sustainability officers and corporate social (Ir)responsibility", *Strategic Management Journal* **41**(4), 656–680.

Gardiner, A., Aasheim, C., Rutner, P. and Williams, S. (2017). "Skill Requirements in Big Data: A Content Analysis of Job Advertisements", *Journal of Computer Information Systems* **58**(4), 374–384.

Gordon, C. 2022. *Board Directors And CEO AI Literacy - A Change Imperative.* Forbes Magazine. URL: https://www.forbes.com/sites/cindygordon/2020/08/03/why-board-directors-and-ceos-must-become-ai-literate/?sh=1ba1a7805036. Accessed: 28 February 2023.

Guadalupe, M., Li, H. and Wulf, J. (2014). "Who Lives in the C-Suite? Organizational Structure and the Division of Labor in Top Management", *Management Science* **60**(4), 824–844.

Hambrick, D. C. and Mason, P. A. (1984). "Upper Echelons: The Organization as a Reflection of Its Top Managers", *The Academy of Management Review* **9**(2).

Han, J. and Kamber, M. (2006). *Data Mining: Concepts and Techniques,* San Francisco: Morgan Kaufmann.

Heavey, C., Simsek, Z., Kyprianou, C. and Risius, M. (2020). "How do strategic leaders engage with social media? A theoretical framework for research and practice", *Strategic Management Journal* **41**(8), 1490–1527.

Heyder, T. and Posegga, O. (2021). Extending the foundations of AI literacy. *International Conference on Information Systems.* Austin, USA

Hiller, N. and Beauchesne, M.-M. (2013). "Executive Leadership: CEOs, Top Management Teams, and Organizational-Level Outcomes", in: Day, D. V. (eds.) *The Oxford Handbook of Leadership and Organizations*, New York: Oxford University Press.

Hunts, A. 2021. *CTO vs. CIO – Who do I need?* URL: https://rocketloop.de/en/blog/cto-vs-cio/. Accessed: 28 February 2023.

Cb Insights. 2022. *The Complete List Of Unicorn Companies*. URL: https://www.cbinsights.com/research-unicorn-companies. Accessed: 24 July 2022.

Jiang, J., Adam, M. and Benlian, A. (2021). Algoactivistic Practices in Ridesharing - A Topic Modeling & Grounded Theory Approach. *European Conference on Information Systems*. Virtual.

Keen, P. G. W. (1991). *Shaping the Future: Business Design through Information Technology*, Boston: Harvard Business School Press.

Kerpedzhiev, G. D., König, U. M., Röglinger, M. and Rosemann, M. (2020). "An Exploration into Future Business Process Management Capabilities in View of Digitalization", *Business & Information Systems Engineering* **63**(2), 83–96.

Kintsch, W. and Bowles, A. R. (2002). "Metaphor Comprehension: What Makes a Metaphor Difficult to Understand?", *Metaphor and Symbol* **17**(4), 249–262.

Klein, K. J. and Harrison, D. A. (2007). "On the Diversity of Diversity: Tidy Logic, Messier Realities", *Academy of Management Perspectives* **21**(4), 26–33.

Kortum, H., Rebstadt, J. and Thomas, O. (2022). Dissection of AI Job Advertisements: A Text Mining-based Analysis of Employee Skills in the Disciplines Computer Vision and Natural Language Processing. *Proceedings of the 55th Hawaii International Conference on System Sciences*. Virtual.

Landauer, T. K. (2002). "On the computational basis of learning and cognition: Arguments from LSA", *Psychology of Learning and Motivation* **41**, 43–84.

Landis, J. R. and Koch, G. G. (1977). "The Measurement of Observer Agreement for Categorical Data", *Biometrics* **33**(1).

Lee, Y., Madnick, S., Wang, R., Zhang, H. and Wang, F. (2018). "A Cubic Framework for the Chief Data Officer: Succeeding in a World of Big Data", *MIS Quarterly Executive* **13**(1).

Li, J., Li, M., Wang, X. and Bennett Thatcher, J. (2021). "Strategic Directions for AI: The Role of CIOs and Boards of Directors", *MIS Quarterly* **45**(3), 1603–1644.

Long, D. and Magerko, B. (2020). What is AI Literacy? Competencies and Design Considerations. *2020 CHI Conference on Human Factors in Computing Systems*. Honolulu, USA.

Lou, B. and Wu, L. (2021). "AI on Drugs: Can Artificial Intelligence Accelerate Drug Development? Evidence from a Large-Scale Examination of Bio-Pharma Firms", *MIS Quarterly* **45**(3b), 1451–1482.

Manyika, J. and Sneader, K. (2018). AI, automation, and the future of work: Ten things to solve for. *Briefing note, prepared for the Tech4 Good Summit, Organized by the French Presidency*. McKinsey Global Institute.

Meske, C., Bunde, E., Schneider, J. and Gersch, M. (2020). "Explainable Artificial Intelligence: Objectives, Stakeholders, and Future Research Opportunities", *Information Systems Management* **39**(1), 53–63.

Ng, D. T. K., Leung, J. K. L., Chu, S. K. W. and Qiao, M. S. (2021). "Conceptualizing AI literacy: An exploratory review", *Computers and Education: Artificial Intelligence* **2**.

Ocasio, W. (1997). "Towards an Attention-Based View of the Firm", *Strategic Management Journal* **18**(S1), 187–206.

Ocasio, W. (2011). "Attention to Attention", *Organization Science* **22**(5), 1286–1296.

Park, H., Jeon, M. and Rosen, J. B. (2003). "Lower Dimensional Representation of Text Data based on Centroids and Least Squares", *Bit Numerical Mathematics* **43**(2), 427–448.

Peifer, Y., Jeske, T. and Hille, S. (2022). "Artificial Intelligence and its Impact on Leaders and Leadership", *Procedia Computer Science* **200**, 1024–1030.

Pigola, A., Da Costa, P. R., Van Der Poel, N. and Yamaçake, F. T. R. (2022). "New perspectives for dynamic capabilities in meeting needs of startups' survival", *Journal of Entrepreneurship in Emerging Economies.*

Pinski, M. and Benlian, A. (2023). AI Literacy - Towards Measuring Human Competency in Artificial Intelligence. *56th Hawaii International Conference on System Sciences.* Lahaina, USA.

Rao, Q. and Frtunikj, J. (2018). Deep learning for self-driving cars. *1st International Workshop on Software Engineering for AI in Autonomous Systems.* Gothenburg, Sweden.

Roulin, N. and Levashina, J. (2018). "LinkedIn as a new selection method: Psychometric properties and assessment approach", *Personnel Psychology* **72**(2), 187–211.

Salton, G. and Buckley, C. (1988). "Term-weighting approaches in automatic text retrieval", *Information Processing & Management* **24**(5), 513–523.

Schuetz, S. and Venkatesh, V. (2020). "Research Perspectives: The Rise of Human Machines: How Cognitive Computing Systems Challenge Assumptions of User-System Interaction", *Journal of the Association for Information Systems* **21**(2), 460–482.

Shollo, A., Hopf, K., Thiess, T. and Müller, O. (2022). "Shifting ML value creation mechanisms: A process model of ML value creation", *The Journal of Strategic Information Systems* **31**(3).

Sidorova, Evangelopoulos, Valacich and Ramakrishnan (2008). "Uncovering the Intellectual Core of the Information Systems Discipline", *MIS Quarterly* **32**(3).

Simons, T., Pelled, L. H. and Smith, K. A. (1999). "Making Use of Difference: Diversity, Debate, and Decision Comprehensiveness in Top Management Teams", *Academy of Management Journal* **42**(6), 662–673.

Tarafdar, M., Beath, C. M. and Ross, J. W. (2019). "Using AI to Enhance Business Operations", *MIT Sloan Management Review* **60**(4), 37–44.

Verma, A., Lamsal, K. and Verma, P. (2021). "An investigation of skill requirements in artificial intelligence and machine learning job advertisements", *Industry and Higher Education* **36**(1), 63–73.

Wamba-Taguimdje, S.-L., Fosso Wamba, S., Kala Kamdjoug, J. R. and Tchatchouang Wanko, C. E. (2020). "Influence of artificial intelligence (AI) on firm performance: the business value of AI-based transformation projects", *Business Process Management Journal* **26**(7), 1893–1924.

Wang, B., Rau, P.-L. P. and Yuan, T. (2022). "Measuring user competence in using artificial intelligence: validity and reliability of artificial intelligence literacy scale", *Behaviour & Information Technology*, 1–14.

Willcocks, L. (2020). "Robo-Apocalypse cancelled? Reframing the automation and future of work debate", *Journal of Information Technology* **35**(4), 286–302.

Williams, C. 2021. *Four reasons your AI plan is failing (and how to fix them).* International Business Machines (IBM). URL: https://www.ibm.com/blogs/think/uk-en/four-reasons-your-ai-plan-is-failing-and-how-to-fix-them/. Accessed: 28 February 2023.

Empowering Leadership, Job Satisfaction, and the Moderating Effect of Individual Ambidexterity of Information Technology Workers

Kristina Kusanke and Till J. Winkler

Abstract Effective leadership is crucial for developing and sustaining ambidexterity, which involves engaging in both exploratory and exploitative activities. Empowering leadership behaviors, which foster trust and discipline to create engaged employees, have been identified as facilitators of contextual ambidexterity. However, there is still a lack of understanding of how individual outcomes are affected by these leadership styles in ambidextrous information technology (IT) work environments. This study investigates the impact of empowering leadership on job satisfaction among IT workers and whether the level of individual ambidexterity moderates this relationship. Analyzing survey data from 553 IT workers, we find a positive direct effect of empowering leadership on job satisfaction and, contrary to our hypothesis, a negative moderating effect of individual ambidexterity. Our study contributes to the leadership and ambidexterity literatures in Information Systems by highlighting the need for nuanced approaches to leadership in ambidextrous IT organizations.

Keywords Individual ambidexterity · Empowering leadership · Job satisfaction · Information technology (IT) worker

1 Introduction

Dynamic competitive conditions have forced companies to adapt their organizational structures by creating ambidextrous work environments that focus on both exploration of innovative ideas and exploitation of the known (Haffke et al. 2017). This

K. Kusanke (✉) · T. J. Winkler
FernUniversität in Hagen, Hagen, Germany
e-mail: kristina.kusanke@fernuni-hagen.de

T. J. Winkler
e-mail: till.winkler@fernuni-hagen.de

T. J. Winkler
Department of Digitalization, Copenhagen Business School, Frederiksberg, Denmark

D. Beverungen et al. (eds.), *Transforming the Digitally Sustainable Enterprise*, Lecture Notes in Information Systems and Organisation 76,
https://doi.org/10.1007/978-3-031-80125-9_14

phenomenon is especially relevant in information technology (IT) organizations, as they play a crucial role in digitization and innovation, while ensuring stable and reliable IT operations (Gerster 2017; Leonhardt et al. 2017). To manage the contradictory goals and potential paradoxes of exploitation and exploration, academia and practice are searching for measures that help organizations and individuals cope (Jöhnk et al. 2019). Regarding facilitating factors of ambidexterity, a growing body of research indicates that the role of leadership in organizations and specific leadership styles, such as empowering leadership, can be beneficial (von Assen 2020).

In line with further calls for research (Tang et al. 2020) we examine empowering leadership, a leadership style in which leaders provide support, resources, and autonomy to their team members, allowing them to take ownership of their work and make decisions (Tang et al. 2020). Research on empowering leadership in adjacent disciplines, including the study of empowering leadership in the context of ambidexterity, has been increasing. There is a particular focus on innovation, which represents the exploratory side of ambidexterity (Caniëls et al. 2017). In addition, empowering leadership is assumed to influence perceptual, attitudinal, motivational, and behavioral outcomes in employees (e.g., Kim et al. 2018). Several studies and two meta-analyses have linked empowering leadership to, among other things, positive employee work behavior (e.g., Kim et al. 2018) and firm performance (e.g., Srivastava et al. 2006; Carmeli et al. 2011). Given the notion that leadership must be evaluated contextually (Tigre et al. 2022), we still lack insight into the influence of empowering leadership on job satisfaction in the IT context.

Job satisfaction significantly affects business-critical outcomes, such as organizational business performance (e.g., Chi and Gursoy 2009) and turnover intentions (e.g., Alam and Asim 2019). The importance of job satisfaction is fueled by the current shortage of information systems (IS) professionals, creating a highly competitive labor market for IT workers (Prommegger et al. 2019). Given the dynamic nature of the global marketplace and the pace of change, attracting, motivating, and retaining employees is critical to an organization's continued success (e.g., Venkatesh et al. 2017).

Although a correlation between empowering leadership and contextual ambidexterity has been confirmed by previous research (von Assen 2020), it is unknown whether individual ambidexterity, encountered through one's work environment, has a moderating effect of empowering leadership on job satisfaction. Therefore, we aim to contribute to the existing knowledge base by posing the following research question: *How does empowering leadership affect job satisfaction in ambidextrous IT work environments?* Specifically, we examine the interplay between individual ambidextrous behavior, empowering leadership, and job satisfaction, shedding light on the combined effects of supervisors and employee behavior within challenging work environments.

Our analysis of survey data from 553 IT workers reveals a positive direct effect of empowering leadership on job satisfaction. This reinforces the notion that a leadership style that empowers employees and fosters trust and discipline can lead to more engaged and satisfied workers. However, contrary to our hypothesis, we also found a negative moderating effect of individual ambidexterity. These results highlight the importance of considering individual differences in ambidexterity when examining the effects of leadership on job satisfaction in IT organizations.

We contribute to the current research on (empowering) leadership by investigating the context (i.e., individual ambidexterity) in which and the extent to which empowering behaviors can be considered beneficial. Simultaneously, we contribute to the ambidexterity literature by adding potential measures (i.e., empowering leadership) that could help build and maintain successful individual ambidexterity. The remainder explains the theoretical foundations, methods, and results, before closing with a discussion of the findings, limitations, implications for future research, and a brief conclusion.

2 Background and Hypotheses

This section reviews the theoretical foundations of job satisfaction, individual ambidexterity and empowering leadership, which are core constructs of this research.

2.1 *Job Satisfaction*

Job satisfaction is *"a pleasurable or positive emotional state resulting from the appraisal of one's job or job experiences"* (Locke 1976, p. 1300). Job satisfaction remains one of the most studied work attitudes in industrial and organizational psychology and organizational behavior theory (Judge et al. 2020). Academics and practitioners have recognized the value of job satisfaction due to its usefulness in predicting the efficiency and effectiveness of business organizations. Further, employee job satisfaction is often considered a significant predictor of organizational business performance (Chi and Gursoy 2009; De Leaniz and Rodríguez 2015) and turnover intention (Ali 2008; Alam and Asim 2019) in the literature. Judge et al. (2020) presented a detailed review of job satisfaction outcomes (performance, effectiveness, organizational citizenship behavior, counterproductive work behavior, and withdrawal). Their review also concluded that, especially in today's turbulent climate with high turnover rates, *"satisfied employees are more likely to be loyal champions, ambassadors, and advocates for their organizations"* (Judge et al. 2020, p. 1). Thus, companies are interested in creating and maintaining organizational and structural conditions conducive to employee satisfaction.

2.2 *Ambidexterity*

The need to adapt organizationally and structurally to changing economic conditions is as inevitable as the ongoing and intensifying struggle for resources in the

IT industry (e.g., Prommegger et al. 2019). Ambidexterity (i.e., the simultaneous performance of two seemingly contradictory activities, such as exploitation and exploration) helps organizations meet this challenge and has become increasingly popular with multiple applications in IS research (Werder and Heckmann 2019; Birkinshaw et al. 2016). While ambidexterity describes the general ability to pursue two different goals simultaneously, it also includes combining capabilities from these two conflicting dimensions (Cao et al. 2009; Gibson and Birkinshaw 2004).

Organizational ambidexterity encompasses the notion that organizations can adapt to their environment and achieve long-term success by simultaneously exploring new opportunities and exploiting existing capabilities (Andriopoulos and Lewis 2010). In other words, exploitation refers to the efficient use of existing resources and capabilities through known processes, whereas exploration refers to discovering how to combine resources and capabilities in new ways to create new capabilities and further opportunities (March 1991). Accordingly, in the context of IS research, IT ambidexterity is viewed as the ability of an IT function to simultaneously explore new IT resources and practices (IT exploration) and exploit current IT resources and practices (IT exploitation; Gregory et al. 2015; Napier et al. 2011). In addition, IT utilization reflects the ability of the IT function to manage existing IT assets well and to improve the effectiveness and efficiency of deployed IT resources to ensure their best use. In contrast, IT exploration reflects the ability of the IT function to devote resources to learning about and experimenting with new technologies, methodologies, and capabilities to select those of the highest value to the organization (Leonhardt 2017).

The literature generally distinguishes between structural, temporal, and contextual ambidexterity. Structural ambidexterity achieves two conflicting goals using two separate subunits, such as through bimodal IT, each of which pursues a different goal (Tushman and O'Reilly 1996, Kusanke and Winkler 2022). Temporal ambidexterity suggests that a unit is capable of working on conflicting goals simultaneously over time. Contextual ambidexterity suggests that paradoxical demands can be resolved by providing an organizational context that enables employees to behave ambidextrously (Gibson and Birkinshaw 2004). Thus, exploitation and exploration are simultaneously organized in an organizational unit based on a context-specific combination of social support, performance management, structure, and capabilities to create alignment (i.e., coherence among all activity patterns) and adaptability (i.e., the ability to quickly reconfigure activities to meet changing demands in the task environment; van Assen 2020; Meglio et al. 2015).

From a contextual ambidexterity perspective, individual ambidexterity refers to an employee's behavior to balance, coexist, and nest two extreme ambidextrous activities (Birkinshaw and Gibson 2004). This can be achieved through aligning the current goals with performance and adaptability to a changing environment and future performance in the context of an individual's daily work (Zhang et al. 2019). The combination of these two distinct behaviors, stemming from exploitation and exploration, is conceptualized as individual ambidexterity (e.g., Mom et al. 2009). Good and Michel (2013) argue theoretically, that ambidextrous individuals should be proficient in both exploratory and exploitative activities, with high skill levels in each. In practice, individual ambidexterity is challenging because individuals tend to be biased toward either exploratory or exploitative behaviors, potentially creating inter- and intrapersonal conflicts (Smith and Tushman 2005; Schnellbächer et al. 2019).

Thus, at the department, group, and even individual level it is necessary to determine when and how conflicting activities and corresponding goals can best be pursued, depending on the specific context (van Assen 2020). Consequently, contextual and, thus, individual ambidexterity requires a supportive organizational context that enables and encourages employees to make judgments about allocating their time between the conflicting demands of alignment and adaptability (van Assen 2020). Organizational factors that support individual ambidexterity are proposed to be support and trust to provide employees with the security and assistance they may need to perform (Gibson and Birkinshaw 2004). This supportive environment inspires people to work together and feel free to engage in conflicting ambidextrous behaviors (Zhang et al. 2019). Extending this approach, scholars have begun to discuss the active role of operational managers in reconciling tensions between exploration and exploitation (e.g., Mom et al. 2009). Effective leaders could help organizations and individuals balance exploration and exploitation, creating a culture that fosters innovation and continuous improvement.

2.3 *Empowering Leadership*

Leadership style plays an important role in developing and maintaining contextual ambidexterity throughout organizational ambidexterity (Havermans et al. 2015; Junni et al. 2013) by implementing and maintaining mechanisms of differentiation and integration (Andriopoulos and Lewis 2010; Raisch et al. 2009). As part of a qualitative study exploring leadership in project-based organizations, Havermans et al. (2015) examined the role of adaptive leadership in enabling contextual ambidexterity by exploring the daily practices that leaders enact to promote exploration and exploitation and shift dynamically between them. Similarly, Gibson and Birkinshaw (2004) found that appropriate leadership behaviors to enable contextual ambidexterity are based on facilitating trust and discipline to create engaged and empowered employees.

Although research on empowering leadership is at a relatively early stage (Kim and Beehr 2021), the number of publications outside the IS field is growing. Empowering leadership is considered "*the process of enhancing an individual's or group's capacity to make purposive choices and to transform those choices into desired actions and outcomes*" (Alsop et al. 2005, p. 1). It refers to a leadership style that empowers employees to take control of their work, make decisions, and solve problems independently. Empowering leaders provides employees with the authority, resources, and support they need to achieve their goals and develop their skills and abilities (Tang et al. 2020). Empowering leadership is a set of leadership behaviors characterized by the following (Kirkman and Rosen 1999; Sharma and Kirkman 2015; Knippenberg 2017):

(1) Trust: Empowering leaders trust their followers to take responsibility for their work and make decisions in the best interest of the organization (Caniëls et al. 2017).
(2) Collaboration: Empowering leaders encourage collaboration and teamwork and create a supportive and inclusive work environment.
(3) Delegation: Empowering leaders delegate responsibility and authority to their followers, allowing them to take ownership of their work and develop their skills.
(4) Coaching: Empowering leaders provide support and coaching to their followers, helping them overcome challenges and achieve their goals (Arnold et al. 2000).
(5) Empowerment: Empowering leaders empower their followers to take control of their work, make decisions, and solve problems independently.

Kim et al. (2018) meta-analyzed 55 independent samples to examine the relationship between empowering leader behaviors and subordinate responses, confirming positive associations of empowering leadership, among others, with employee motivation and attitudes such as job satisfaction. Subordinates who were subjected to empowering leadership displayed increased job satisfaction, likely due to the emphasis placed by empowering leaders on granting them autonomy in establishing objectives and determining work methods. This approach facilitates employees' comprehension and execution of complete tasks, ultimately enabling subordinates to find purpose in their work (Amundsen and Martinsen 2014). Given the importance of retaining IT workers, which is largely influenced by job satisfaction, we seek to replicate these findings and validate previous findings within the research setting of IT workers. Consequently, we pose:

Hypothesis H1: *Empowering Leadership Has a Positive Direct Effect on Job Satisfaction in IT Workers.*

Empowered employees are more proactive, continually searching for methods to improve and revise work processes and seeking innovative solutions to work problems (Kirkman Rosen 1999). Because employee empowerment is associated with higher levels of self-efficacy and self-confidence and makes employees feel free to take risks and solve problems in novel ways, it is thought to support exploratory learning (van Knippenberget al. 2004). In addition, employee empowerment is associated with higher commitment and motivation to perform work most efficiently and effectively; thus, it is assumed to support exploitative learning (Kirkman and Rosen 1999). Accordingly, appropriate leadership behaviors to facilitate contextual ambidexterity include employee empowerment (Caniëls et al. 2017). This finding is supported by other studies confirming that empowerment is positively associated with contextual ambidexterity (van Assen 2020; Yu et al. 2012), including in an IT context (Siachou and Gkorezis 2018) and software developer context (Xu and Shen 2018). As individuals strive to manage and balance the two potentially conflicting and, in any case, opposing work styles of exploration and exploitation, tensions may arise (March 1991). Empowering leadership could help resolve these conflicting demands. Consequently, we hypothesize that the more an individual must balance the conflicting demands of exploration and exploitation, the greater the influence of empowering leadership on job satisfaction. In other words, employees who need to balance both exploration and exploitation perceive higher job satisfaction if they receive support and guidance through empowering leadership from their supervisor than employees who do not face these conflicting demands. This leads to our second hypothesis:

Hypothesis H2: *The Influence of Empowering Leadership on Job Satisfaction is Moderated by the Individual Ambidexterity Level.*

3 Research Method

3.1 Sample and Procedure

We conducted an online survey to assess the hypotheses and collected data in April and May of 2022. A pretest ($n = 12$) was performed to ensure the comprehensibility and technical functioning of the online questionnaire. Survey data were collected by a market research company. Participants were part of an online panel in Germany and received a small compensation for their participation. The participants were preselected and confirmed that they worked in the IT department of a company, participated in IT projects, or were employed or self-employed as IT professionals. At the beginning of the questionnaire, we guaranteed confidentiality to reduce social desirability bias. After data collection, we applied data cleaning procedures. All incoming datasets were filtered for data quality based on consistency checks in the respondents' response behavior. We received a total of $n = 553$ datasets. Of the 553 participants included in the analysis, 348 were male (63%), and 201 were female (36%). The age of the participants ranged from 21 to 70 years, with a mean of 44 years. The participants came from IT work environments in a variety of industries, including professional services (18%), public services (10%), and electronics and high technology (9%). Over 50% of respondents had been with their company for over 5 years.

3.2 Measures

Following Judge et al. (1998), we measured job satisfaction with five items adapted from the Brayfield-Rothe (1951) measure of job satisfaction. These items included the statements "*I feel fairly satisfied with my current job*" and "*I find real enjoyment in my work.*" These and all subsequent items in this study were translated from English to German in a collaborative, iterative process, as suggested by Douglas and Craig

(2007), and tested for applicability at the level of an IT employee. This approach is superior to the method of back-translation because it also considers issues of conceptual equivalence (Douglas and Craig 2007). We measured responses on a five-point scale ranging from 1 (strongly disagree) to 5 (strongly agree). Cronbach's alpha was calculated for the reliability analysis. The internal consistency is satisfactory, with a Cronbach's alpha job satisfaction of 0.79.

We measured empowering leadership with ten items from the empowering leadership questionnaire developed by Arnold et al. (2020). These items aim to measure employees' perceived level of empowering leadership behaviors exhibited by a direct supervisor. The scale included the statements "*My supervisor encourages team members to point out ideas and suggestions*" and "*My supervisor encourages team members to solve problems together.*" We measured responses on a five-point scale ranging from 1 (strongly disagree) to 5 (strongly agree). The internal consistency is highly satisfactory, with a Cronbach's alpha score for empowering leadership of 0.95.

To measure the individual level of ambidexterity experienced in the work environment, we used two 7-item scales by Mom et al. (2009), who validated these scales in the financial services industry (exploration $\acute{\alpha} = 0.85$ and exploitation $\acute{\alpha} = 0.81$). The authors developed a measure of exploration and exploitation consisting of exploration and exploitation activity items. Thus, we asked respondents about the extent to which they engaged in certain work-related activities (e.g., activities in which considerable experience was accumulated). We measured responses on a five-point scale ranging from 1 (never) to 5 (always). While some scholars, such as March (1991), viewed exploration and exploitation as two opposite ends of a continuum, with ambidexterity being the exact midpoint, more recent scholars have begun to characterize exploration and exploitation as more orthogonal. This way, firms and individuals could increase their exploration or exploitation levels without compromising. Following this line of reasoning, we followed previous authors and multiplied the exploration and exploitation measures to obtain the magnitude to construct the measure of individual ambidexterity (see Gibson and Birkinshaw 2004; Cao et al. 2009; Mom et al. 2009, 2015). This approach reflects the argument that these two abilities are non-substitutable and interdependent.

We included several covariates to control for their direct effect on job satisfaction. Specifically, we tested for the influence of age and gender, the respondents' affiliation with the business or IT department, tenure (measured in years associated with the company currently employed), leadership responsibility, company size and IT department size. Harman's single-factor test was applied to test for common method variance. The factor analysis results (33.9%) are below the 50% threshold, suggesting that common method bias is not an issue in the data.

4 Results

A moderation analysis was performed using the PROCESS macro by Hayes (2013), which has become widely used by researchers interested in testing hypotheses about moderation (Hayes and Rockwood 2017). We tested whether the interaction between empowering leadership and individual ambidexterity significantly predicts job satisfaction. The PROCESS method uses ordinary least squares regression, yielding unstandardized coefficients for all effects. Bootstrapping with 5000 samples and heteroscedasticity-consistent standard errors were employed to compute the confidence intervals.

The overall model (Fig. 1; Table 1) was significant, $F(10, 509) = 20.4, p < 0.001$, predicting 28.62% of the variance. The analysis reveals a significant direct effect of empowering leadership on job satisfaction ($0.57, p < 0.001$). Thus, H1 is supported. In addition, the moderation analysis indicates that individual ambidexterity significantly moderates the effect between empowering leadership and job satisfaction, $\Delta R2 = 1.25\%, F(1, 509) = 6.15, p = 0.01$. Despite the modest level of significance, there is support for Hypothesis 2. Furthermore, the data reveal that the interaction coefficient is negative (– 0.02). If the direction (indicated by the sign) of the interaction coefficient is the same as that of the main effect (positive sign), then the interaction variable strengthens the main effect. An opposite (negative) direction means the main effect is weakened. Therefore, the data shows a negative moderation effect.

Of the control variables we included, only age had a significant direct effect on job satisfaction, indicating that older IT workers in our sample had higher job satisfaction. Regarding the moderating effect, we find that as the level of ambidexterity increases, the effect size of moderation decreases (Table 2).

The interaction effect was significant. We used the Johnson-Neyman technique to identify the points along the continuous moderator where the relationship between the independent variable and outcome variable transitions from being statistically significant to insignificant or vice versa. Based on the multiplicative interaction effect model, the Johnson-Neyman technique uses a regression line where the effect of the predictor on the outcome is regressed on the moderator to demonstrate how the effect changes with changes in the moderator. The Johnson-Neyman technique also uses 95% confidence bands around the simple regression line to determine

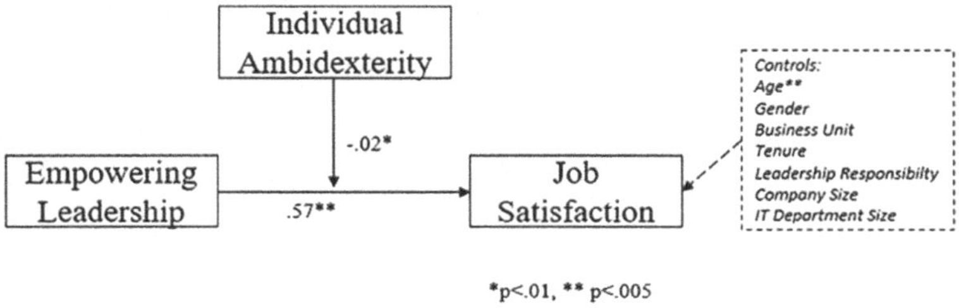

Fig. 1 Model results

Table 1 Moderation model output

		Coeff	SE	t	*p*	LLCI	ULCI
–	Constant	0.184	0.461	0.399	0.690	– 0.721	1.09
H1	Empowering Leadership (EL)	0.572**	0.106	5.38	< 0.001	0.363	0.780
–	Level of Ambidexterity (IA)	0.109**	0.031	3.50	< 0.001	0.048	0.170
H2	Interaction (EL × IA)	– 0.020*	0.008	– 2.48	0.010	– 0.035	– 0.005
C	*Gender*	*0.006*	*0.064*	*0.094*	*0.925*	*– 0.12*	*0.132*
o n	*Age*	*0.018***	*0.003*	*6.62*	*< 0.001*	*0.013*	*0.024*
t	*Business Unit*	*0.105*	*0.066*	*1.59*	*0.110*	*– 0.024*	*0.234*
r	*Tenure*	*0.005*	*0.023*	*0.205*	*0.837*	*– 0.04*	*0.050*
o l	*Leadership Responsibility*	*0.065*	*0.061*	*1.07*	*0.284*	*– 0.054*	*0.185*
s	*Company Size*	*0.001*	*0.016*	*0.053*	*0.957*	*– 0.031*	*0.033*
	IT Department Size	*– 0.009*	*0.017*	*–0.543*	*0.588*	*– 0.043*	*0.024*

$^{*}p < 0.01$, $^{**}p < 0.005$

Table 2 Conditional effects of the focal predictor at values of the moderator

Individual ambidexterity	Effect	SE	*p*	LLCI	ULCI
9.05	0.4	0.04	< 0.001	0.31	0.48
12.45	0.33	0.03	< 0.001	0.26	0.4
16.53	0.25	0.04	< 0.001	0.16	0.34

the region of significance. When one of the confidence bands crosses the *x*-axis, the corresponding value of the moderator is the dividing point between a region of significance and a region of nonsignificance. By finding the transition points within the observed data, this method allows us to understand the patterns of significance across the moderator range (Montoya 2019). The analysis results reveal that the positive effect of empowering leadership on job satisfaction became insignificant when the ambidexterity score was > 20.7.

We used the data to visualize the conditional effect of individual ambidexterity, the focal predictor (Fig. 2). The graphs depict that, within the corridor of significance, the interaction effect is negative, and the effect size decreases. Thus, when exposed to the same level of empowering leadership, higher scores of individual ambidexterity generally lead to higher job satisfaction. However, this effect decreases with elevated individual ambidexterity.

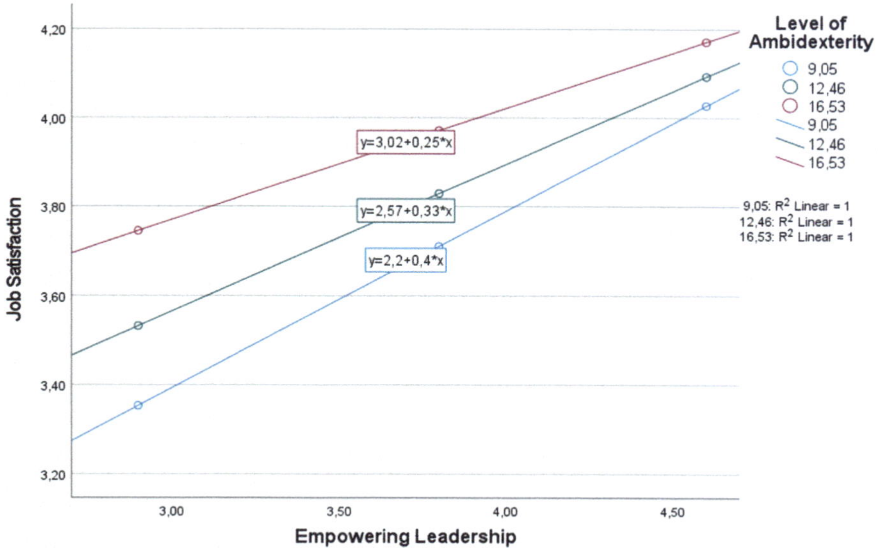

Fig. 2 Visualized interaction effects

5 Discussion

While the relationship between empowering leadership and ambidexterity has been investigated by previous research outside the IT domain, this study assesses the extent to which empowering leadership facilitates job satisfaction of on IT workers and the role of individual ambidexterity in this relationship. We hypothesized that empowering leadership influences job satisfaction (H1) and that individual ambidexterity is a moderator that positively amplifies this relationship (H2). While our findings confirm H1, we found an opposing moderating effect regarding H2: higher levels of individual ambidexterity reduce the effect of empowering leadership on job satisfaction. Consequently, our contribution is two-fold.

Our finding regarding H1 supports the notion that empowering leadership behaviors are associated with positively connotated outcomes such as, increased employee motivation, performance, and creativity (e.g., Srivastava et al. 2006; Lee et al. 2018). This finding adds to the empowering leadership literature by adding job satisfaction to the outcomes and consequences and encourages organizations to promote and facilitate empowering leaders.

This research also expands the knowledge base on ambidexterity, the simultaneous occurrence of exploitation and exploration, and empowering leadership in the IT context. As individuals strive to manage and balance the two potentially conflicting and, in any case, opposing work styles, tensions may arise (March 1991). Empowering leadership can assist individuals in managing the conflicting demands of explorative and exploitative tasks by providing them with the autonomy and support necessary to navigate these dual responsibilities effectively (von Assen 2020). This, in turn, may positively influences job satisfaction as individuals feel supported and empowered to strike a balance between exploration and exploitation, ultimately enhancing their ability to cope with these conflicting demands. Although we hypothesized that the greater the level of ambidexterity, the greater the need for and effect of empowering leadership on job satisfaction, we found the opposite.

We, therefore, argue that our specific contribution regarding H2 is a further evaluation of the contextual facilitators and, ultimately, the potential limitations of empowering leadership styles. The need for organizations to build more dynamic and exploratory capabilities while ensuring efficient operations through exploitation is undeniable, resulting in the need to implement ambidextrous structures through bimodal IT (Haffke et al. 2017), for example, or foster contextual and, thus, individual ambidexterity. To this end, we evaluated whether individual ambidexterity moderates the relationship between empowering leadership and job satisfaction in IT workers. Due to the non-hypothesized direct effect of ambidexterity on job satisfaction, IT workers with the same perceived empowering leadership report higher job satisfaction at higher levels of individual ambidexterity. However, the effect of empowering leadership on job satisfaction diminishes with increasing levels of ambidexterity (see Fig. 2) until it becomes insignificant (ambidexterity score > 20.7). The data, therefore, indicates a moderate negative moderation effect of the interaction of individual ambidexterity and empowering leadership. Thus, the moderator weakens the main effect of empowering leadership on job satisfaction.

A potential explanation for this effect can be found in previous studies that have suggested that empowering leadership could also yield negative outcomes, potentially due to the emphasis on granting high autonomy in decision-making and task delegation, which might consequently amplify task uncertainty (Kim et al. 2018) or job induced tension (Cheong et al. 2016). Our findings underscore the existence of potentially two distinct aspects of empowering leadership: the well-studied positive aspect and the paradoxical or contrasting negative aspect.

These results have interesting practical implications. Although organizations should generally encourage empowering leadership, this may lose its power when individuals are confronted with very high levels of ambidexterity because, as the level of ambidexterity increases, the tension and potential for intrapersonal and interpersonal conflict may become too high for the individual to manage alone. In this case, the individual may be more likely to seek guidance than empowerment and trust. From a different point of view, Kim and Beehr (2021) suggested that empowering leadership may be construed as a source of stress for employees who desire structure and have a low need for autonomy. This line of thinking is supported by literature that seeks the boundaries of empowering leadership and encourages researchers to explore the less positive outcomes of empowering leadership (Sharma and Kirkman 2015).

Consequently, individual characteristics should continue to be considered potential moderators when examining the outcomes of empowering leadership (Kim and Beerh 2021). For future research, we propose including the construct of person-job fit in this research model. Person-job fit refers to the relationship between employee characteristics and job characteristics (Kristof-Brown et al. 2005) and includes the question of whether employees would agree that their abilities fit the demands of the job and whether they believe that they are the right type of person for that type of job (Lauver and Kristof-Brown 2001). From a survey sample of 6179 employees of a technology company in China, Cai et al. (2018) concluded that empowering leadership has a positive, indirect effect on employee work engagement through person-job fit. Therefore, it is reasonable that person-job fit may also play a role in the individual assessment of job satisfaction.

This study is not without limitations. Job satisfaction is a multidimensional concept that includes personality traits and environmental factors (Ilies and Judge 2013). Thus, examining the relationship between empowering leadership and job satisfaction by accounting for the level of ambidexterity may fall short if other potential influencing factors, such as personality traits, teamwork, or performance, are neglected. In addition, we do not account for any learning effects because we did not ask about or account for the length of time someone is led by empowering leadership.

6 Conclusion

Leadership styles that promote trust, discipline, and employee empowerment are crucial in fostering and maintaining ambidexterity. Therefore, we aimed to investigate whether empowering leadership has an effect on job satisfaction among IT workers and whether individual ambidexterity moderates this relationship. The findings contribute to existing research by demonstrating that empowering leadership affects IT employees' perceived job satisfaction. In addition, the data suggest that individual ambidexterity negatively moderates these relationships in that higher levels of individual ambidexterity reduce the effect of empowering leadership on job satisfaction. We explained this finding by potential interpersonal and intrapersonal conflicts arising from the conflicting work modes of exploration and exploitation, which may lead individuals to seek guidance and structure rather than trust and empowerment. Altogether, our paper contributes to the empowering leadership and ambidexterity literature in IS by highlighting the need for nuanced approaches to leadership in ambidextrous IT organizations.

References

Alam, A., & Asim, M. (2019). Relationship between job satisfaction and turnover intention. International Journal of Human Resource Studies, 9(2), 163.

Ali, N. (2008). Factors affecting overall job satisfaction and turnover intention. Journal of Managerial Sciences, 2(2), 239–252.

Alsop, R., Bertelsen, M. and Holland, J. (2005), Empowerment in Practice: From Analysis to Implementation, The World Bank, Washington, DC.

Amundsen, S., & Martinsen, Ø. L. (2014). Empowering leadership: Construct clarification, conceptualization, and validation of a new scale. Leadership Quarterly, 25, 487–511.
Andriopoulos, C. & Lewis, M. W. (2010). Managing innovation paradoxes: Ambidexterity lessons from leading product design companies. Long Range Planning, 43, 104–122
Arnold, J. A., Arad, S., Rhoades, J. A., & Drasgow, F. (2000). The empowering leadership questionnaire: The construction and validation of a new scale for measuring leader behaviors. Journal of organizational behavior, 21(3), 249–269.
Birkinshaw, J., Zimmermann, A., & Raisch, S. (2016). How do firms adapt to discontinuous change? Bridging the dynamic capabilities and ambidexterity perspectives. California Management Review, 58(4), 36–58.
Brayfield, A. H., & Rothe, H. F. (1951). An index of job satisfaction. Journal of applied psychology, 35(5).
Cai, D., Cai, Y., Sun, Y., & Ma, J. (2018). Linking empowering leadership and employee work engagement: The effects of person-job fit, person-group fit, and proactive personality. Frontiers in psychology, 9, 1304.
Caniëls, M. C., Neghina, C., & Schaetsaert, N. (2017). Ambidexterity of employees: the role of empowerment and knowledge sharing. Journal of Knowledge Management, 21(5), 1098–1119
Cao, Q., Gedajlovic, E. R., & Zhang, H. (2009). Unpacking organizational ambidexterity: Dimensions, contingencies, and synergistic effects. Organization Science, 20, 781–796
Carmeli, A., Schaubroeck, J., & Tishler, A. (2011). How CEO empowering leadership shapes top management team processes: Implications for firm performance. The Leadership Quarterly, 22(2), 399–411.
Cheong, M., Spain, S. M., Yammarino, F. J., & Yun, S. (2016). Two faces of empowering leadership: Enabling and burdening. The Leadership Quarterly, 27(4), 602–616.
Chi, C.G., & Gursoy, D. (2009). Employee satisfaction, customer satisfaction and financial performance: An empirical examination. International Journal of Hospitality Management, 28(2), 245–253.
De Leaniz, P.M.G., & Rodriguez, I.R.D.B. (2015). Exploring the antecedents of hotel customer loyalty: A social identity perspective. Journal of Hospitality Marketing Management, 24(1), 1–23.
Douglas, S. P., & Craig, C. S. (2007). Collaborative and iterative translation: An alternative approach to back translation. Journal of International Marketing, 15(1), 30–43
Gerster, Daniel, "Digital Transformation and IT: Current State of Research" (2017). PACIS 2017 Proceedings. 133.
Gibson, C. B. & Birkinshaw, J. (2004). The antecedents, consequences, and mediating role of organizational ambidexterity. The Academy of Management Journal, 47, 209–226.
Good, D., & Michel, E. J. (2013). Individual ambidexterity: Exploring and exploiting in dynamic contexts. The Journal of psychology, 147(5), 435–453
Gregory, R. W., Keil, M., Muntermann, J., and Mähring, M. 2015. "Paradoxes and the nature of ambidexterity in IT transformation programs," Information Systems Research (26:1), 57–80.
Haffke, I., Kalgovas, B., and Benlian, A. (2017). Options for Transforming the IT Function Using Bimodal IT. MIS Quarterly Executive, 16, 2, 101–120
Havermans, L. A., Den Hartog, D. N., Keegan, A., & Uhl-Bien, M. (2015). Exploring the role of leadership in enabling contextual ambidexterity. Human Resource Management, 54(S1), 179–200.
Hayes, A. F., & Rockwood, N. J. (2017). Regression-based statistical mediation and moderation analysis in clinical research: Observations, recommendations, and implementation. Behaviour research and therapy, 98, 39–57.
Hayes, A. F. (2013). Introduction to Mediation, Moderation, and Conditional Process Analysis, Second Edition (Methodology in the Social Sciences). Guilford Press.
Jöhnk, J., Oesterle, S., Winkler, T. J., Nørbjerg, J., & Urbach, N. (2019). Juggling the Paradoxes–Governance Mechanisms in Bimodal IT Organizations.

Judge, T. A., Locke, E. A., Durham, C. C., & Kluger, A. N. (1998). Dispositional effects on job and life satisfaction: the role of core evaluations. Journal of applied psychology, 83(1), 17.
Judge, T.A., Zhang S., & Glerum, D. R. (2020). Job Satisfaction. In Essentials of job attitudes and other workplace psychological constructs (pp. 3–12). Routledge.
Junni, P., Sarala, R. M., Taras, V., & Tarba, S. Y. (2013). Organizational Ambidexterity and Performance: A Meta-Analysis. The Academy of Management Perspectives, 27, 299–312.
Kim, M., & Beehr, T. A. (2021). The power of empowering leadership: Allowing and encouraging followers to take charge of their own jobs. The International Journal of Human Resource Management, 32(9), 1865–1898.
Kim, M., Beehr, T. A., & Prewett, M. S. (2018). Employee responses to empowering leadership: A meta-analysis. Journal of Leadership & Organizational Studies, 25(3), 257–276.
Kirkman, B. L., & Rosen, B. (1999). Beyond self-management: Antecedents and consequences of team empowerment. Academy of Management journal, 42(1), 58–74.
van Knippenberg, D. (2017). Team leadership. In E. Salas, R. Rico, & J. Passmore (Eds.), The Wiley Blackwell handbook of the psychology of team working and collaborative processes (pp. 345–368). Chichester, UK: Wiley. https://doi.org/10.1002/9781118909997.ch15
Kristof-Brown, A. L., Zimmerman, R. D., and Johnson, E. C. (2005). Consequences of individual's fit at work: a meta-analysis of person-job, person-organization, person-group, and person-supervisor fit. Pers. Psychol. 58, 281–342.
Kusanke, K. and Winkler, T. J., (2022). "Structural Ambidexterity through Bimodal IT – A Literature Review and Research Agenda" (2022). Wirtschaftsinformatik 2022 Proceedings. 5.
Lauver, K. J., & Kristof-Brown, A. (2001). Distinguishing between employees' perceptions of person--job and person--organization fit. Journal of Vocational Behavior, 59(3), 454–470.
Lee, A., Willis, S., & Tian, A. W. (2018). Empowering leadership: A meta-analytic examination of incremental contribution, mediation, and moderation. Journal of Organizational Behavior, 39(3), 306–325.
Leonhardt, D., Haffke, I., Kranz, J., & Benlian, A. (2017). Reinventing the IT function: The Role of IT Agility and IT Ambidexterity in Supporting Digital Business Transformation. In ECIS (Vol. 63, pp. 968–984).
Meglio, O., King, D. R., & Risberg, A. (2015). Improving Acquisition Outcomes with Contextual Ambidexterity. Human Resource Management, 54, 29–43.
Mom, T. J. M., Van Den Bosch, F. A. J., & Volberda, H. W. (2009). Explaining variation in managers' ambidexterity: Investigating direct and interaction effects of formal structural and personal coordination mechanisms. Organization Science, 20, 812–828.
Mom, T. J., Fourné, S. P., & Jansen, J. J. (2015). Managers' work experience, ambidexterity, and performance: The contingency role of the work context. Human Resource Management, 54(S1), 133–153.
Montoya, A. K. (2019). Moderation analysis in two-instance repeated measures designs: Probing methods and multiple moderator models. Behavior research methods, 51, 61–82.
Napier, N. P., Mathiassen, L., and Robey, D. 2011. "Building contextual ambidexterity in a software company to improve firm-level coordination," European Journal of Information Systems (20:6), 674–690.
Prommegger, B., Huck-Fries, V., Wiesche, M., & Krcmar, H. (2019). Agile and attached: The impact of agile practices on agile team members' affective organisational commitment. Proceedings of the 14th International Conference on Wirtschaftsinformatik.
Raisch, S., Birkinshaw, J., Probst, G., & Tushman, M. L. (2009). Organizational ambidexterity: Balancing exploitation and exploration for sustained performance. Organization Science, 20, 685–695.
Schnellbächer, B., Heidenreich, S., & Wald, A. (2019). Antecedents and effects of individual ambidexterity–A cross-level investigation of exploration and exploitation activities at the employee level. European Management Journal, 37(4), 442–454.

Sharma, P. N., & Kirkman, B. L. (2015). Leveraging leaders: A literature review and future lines of inquiry for empowering leadership research. Group & Organization Management, 40(2), 193–237.

Siachou, E., & Gkorezis, P. (2018, April). Empowering leadership and organizational ambidexterity: a moderated mediation model. In Evidence-based HRM: a Global Forum for Empirical Scholarship. Emerald Publishing Limited.

Smith, W. K., & Tushman, M. L. (2005). Managing strategic contradictions: A top management model for managing innovation streams. Organization Science, 16(5), 522–536.

Srivastava, A., Bartol, K. M., & Locke, E. A. (2006). Empowering leadership in management teams: Effects on knowledge sharing, efficacy, and performance. Academy of management journal, 49(6), 1239–1251.

Tang, G., Chen, Y., van Knippenberg, D., & Yu, B. (2020). Antecedents and consequences of empowering leadership: Leader power distance, leader perception of team capability, and team innovation. Journal of Organizational Behavior, 41(6), 551–566.

Tigre, F. B., Curado, C., & Henriques, P. L. (2022). "Digital Leadership: A Bibliometric Analysis," Journal of Leadership & Organizational Studies, 15480518221123132.

van Assen, M. F. (2020). Empowering leadership and contextual ambidexterity–The mediating role of committed leadership for continuous improvement. European Management Journal, 38(3), 435–449.

van Knippenberg, D., Van Knippenberg, B., De Cremer, D., & Hogg, M. A. (2004). Leadership, self, and identity: A review and research agenda. The Leadership Quarterly, 15(6), 825–856.

Venkatesh, V., Windeler, J. B., Bartol, K. M., & Williamson, I. O. (2017). Person–Organization and Person–Job Fit Perceptions of New IT Employees. Mis Quarterly, 41(2), 525–558.

Werder, K., & Heckmann, C. S. (2019). Ambidexterity in information systems research: overview of conceptualizations, antecedents, and outcomes. Journal of Information Technology Theory and Application (JITTA), 20(1), 2.

Xu, P. and Shen, Y. (2018). "The Role of Leadership in Agile Software Development" (2018). International Research Workshop on IT Project Management 2018. 12.

Yu, T., Patterson, P. G., & de Ruyter, K. (2012). Achieving service-sales ambidexterity. Journal of Service Research, 16, 52–66.

Zhang, Y. I., Wei, F., & Van Horne, C. (2019). Individual ambidexterity and antecedents in a changing context. International Journal of Innovation Management, 23(03).

Low-Coders, No-Coders, and Citizen Developers in Demand: Examining Knowledge, Skills, and Abilities Through a Job Market Analysis

Björn Binzer and Till J. Winkler

Abstract The emergence of low-code/no-code (LCNC) platform technologies and the resulting increase in citizen development programs are facilitating the democratization of the design, development, and deployment of digital solutions. *Citizen developers*, non-technical employees who leverage LCNC platforms, are at the heart of this trend. While many firms perceive LCNC and citizen development as a crucial component of their digital transformation strategy, little is known about the evolving roles in this field or the necessary knowledge, skills, and abilities (KSA). To address this knowledge gap, we processed 113,106 job postings published on Indeed.com. Our topic modeling methodology identified 34 KSA topics and classified them into the three domains *platform*, *business*, and *technology*. We contribute to research by empirically demonstrating which competencies are required to successfully work in the LCNC field. Our findings can guide individual professionals and organizations alike.

Keywords Low-code/no-code skills · Citizen developer · Topic modeling · Job postings analysis

1 Introduction

> (…) the future of coding is no coding at all.— Chris Wanstrath, former CEO at GitHub (Swinhoe 2017; Peterson 2017)

B. Binzer (✉) · T. J. Winkler
University of Hagen, Hagen, Germany
e-mail: bjoern.binzer@fernuni-hagen.de

T. J. Winkler
e-mail: till.winkler@fernuni-hagen.de

T. J. Winkler
Copenhagen Business School, Department of Digitalization, Frederiksberg, Denmark

D. Beverungen et al. (eds.), *Transforming the Digitally Sustainable Enterprise*, Lecture Notes in Information Systems and Organisation 76,
https://doi.org/10.1007/978-3-031-80125-9_15

While driving the digital transformation is a top priority for organizations of all types (Matt et al. 2016), only few initiatives achieve their intended goals (Forth et al. 2020; Wade and Shan 2020). Firms struggle to meet the ever-increasing demands for digital solutions and automation whilst facing a shortage of digital talent (Breaux and Moritz 2021; Carroll and Maher 2023). To address this challenge, the concept of citizen development has gained momentum in practice and academia. Citizen development empowers non-IT professionals within organizations to design, develop, and deploy lightweight digital solutions to solve specific work-related problems based on IT tools that are provided, recommended, or at least tolerated by core IT units (Binzer and Winkler 2022). These IT tools are popularly referred to as low-code or no-code (LCNC) platforms (e.g., Carroll et al. 2021). Employees who leverage these LCNC platforms but work outside of IT functions are often called *citizen developers*. Digital solutions built on LCNC platforms can range from small business transactional applications (e.g., booking management) to more sophisticated enterprise-wide solutions (Johannessen and Davenport 2021). Notably, business process and workflow automation are also closely linked to LCNC and citizen development (Johannessen and Davenport 2021; Lebens et al. 2021; Eggers et al. 2023).

According to recent market analyses, the global LCNC platform market size is expected to reach between US$ 94.8 and US$ 169.2 billion by 2030 (Fortune Business Insights 2022; GreyViews 2023). More than two-thirds of all new applications in organizations are likely to be based on low-code platforms by 2025 (Gartner 2021). It is thus hardly surprising that the number of citizen developers is rising and expected to exceed the number of professional developers by a factor of four in 2024 (Drakos and Wong 2021). As evidenced by industry reports, firms are actively training their workforce to become LCNC users (e.g., Kappeyne 2021). Moreover, recent job postings indicate that firms are explicitly seeking candidates with LCNC qualifications in the job market. In light of these developments, the significance of LCNC and citizen development in the broader context of digital transformation becomes evident.

Despite the increasing relevance of the phenomenon, the literature is still limited in terms of the knowledge and skillset of citizen developers (Binzer and Winkler 2022). While citizen developers are often referred to as non-technical business users that leverage LCNC platforms to address operational pain points and inefficiencies (Carroll et al. 2021), they have also been characterized as tech-savvy coders with specialized IT expertise (Steele 2021). Contrasting with this, McKendrick (2017) noted that the majority of citizen developers are actually power users and professional developers embedded within business units. Given these conflicting portrayals and the limited exploration of the required knowledge, skills, and abilities (KSA) in prior studies, there exists a gap in understanding the profiles of the evolving roles in the context of LCNC. No research has yet placed emphasis on unraveling KSAs that are demanded from individual LCNC users. Building on this observation, we aim to contribute to research by addressing the following research question:

RQ: What knowledge, skills, and abilities do employers seek in prospective employees for effective utilization of low-code and no-code technologies?

We pursued this question by processing a large collection of crawled job postings published at Indeed.com. Job postings are useful sources of information because they represent the most important and valued characteristics about a candidate (i.e., KSAs) from the viewpoint of organizations (Walsh et al. 1975; Todd et al. 1995; Cegielski and Jones-Farmer 2016). As a result, we identified 34 KSA topics with our topic modeling approach, classified into three domains: platform, business, and technology. Our findings suggest that organizations currently require a broad spectrum of business and technical expertise to successfully approach the LCNC and citizen development field.

The remainder of this study is structured as follows: The next section describes related work. Section 3 illustrates our research methodology. Next, in Sect. 4, we present our results. In Sect. 5, we discuss our work by addressing implications and limitations before highlighting our theoretical and practical contributions in Sect. 6.

2 Background

2.1 Low-Code/No-Code and Citizen Development

Low-code and *citizen development* are practice-driven phenomena that are closely intertwined. While the term *low-code development platform* was first introduced by Forrester Research in 2014 (Richardson and Rymer 2014), the term *citizen development* has already been coined in 2009 by Gartner (Weisinger 2011). Since then, the innovativeness and relevance of the concepts have been debated (Bock and Frank 2021; Di Ruscio et al. 2022). However, researchers also acknowledge the new emerging potential (Tisi et al. 2019; Phalake and Joshi 2021), which is occasionally justified by recent advances in technologies such as artificial intelligence or machine learning (Carroll and Maher 2023). As commonly defined, low-code platforms represent cloud-based environments that provide features such as advanced graphical user interfaces, visual representations, drag-and-drop functionality, reusable components, and declarative languages (e.g., Tisi et al. 2019; Sahay et al. 2020).

The basic idea behind both concepts is to hide the complexity of coding through a high level of abstraction while ensuring full functionality of the code (Sahay et al. 2020; Carroll et al. 2021). This, in turn, leads to an enhanced ease-of-use allowing subject matter experts with minimal or no coding skills to design, develop, and deploy their own lightweight applications (Sahay et al. 2020; Carroll and Maher 2023). In this context, and to reinforce the idea of empowering employees without any IT-knowledge, the term *no-code* has recently emerged. However, low- and no-code are conceptually closely related, which is why they are regularly used interchangeably or combined under LCNC (e.g., Carroll and Maher 2023). Against this backdrop, citizen development can be understood as an organizational strategy, that strives to democratize digital solution delivery through the large-scale adoption of LCNC (Binzer and Winkler 2022).

More recently, research on citizen development and LCNC has gained increasing momentum. Binzer and Winkler (2022) conducted a multivocal literature review to identify dominant themes and propose an agenda for future citizen development research. Other studies investigated organizational factors that influence citizen development adoption decisions (Hoogsteen and Borgman 2022), explored potential challenges that may occur during the implementation and ongoing use of LCNC (Prinz et al. 2022), and identified the key building blocks for establishing a citizen development program as part of a digital transformation initiative (Carroll and Maher 2023).

2.2 Previous Research Analyzing Job Postings

Management research has long recognized job postings as an important source of information for the analysis of occupational qualifications and skills (Walsh et al. 1975; Todd et al. 1995). Online job platforms such as Indeed and Monster, and the emergence of advanced text-mining algorithms, recently fueled the interest of researchers to study increasingly large collections of job postings. Such an approach bears the potential to identify relevant KSAs that employers value most in a particular domain. In this context, text-mining research can be classified into three categories (Pejic-Bach et al. 2020): (1) developing classification schemes, (2) improving matching quality with potential candidates, and (3) exploring skillsets and developing job profiles.

Since our study falls into the third category, we focus on previous studies within this research stream in the following. Debortoli et al. (2014), for example, developed a taxonomy of big data and business intelligence competencies by analyzing a corpus of 1807 job postings. Studies from the recent past demonstrate that scholars similarly approached related fields such as Industry 4.0 (Pejic-Bach et al. 2020), analytics (Handali et al. 2020), and data science (Michalczyk et al. 2021). While their applied methodological approaches are partly different, topic modeling techniques such as Latent Dirichlet Allocation (LDA) are particularly popular (e.g., Michalczyk et al. 2021). The basic assumption behind topic modeling is that text documents can be expressed in terms of a specific number of underlying topics that the algorithm is striving to uncover (Řehůřek and Sojka 2010). In the context of job postings, these identified topics are then believed to represent required job qualifications and knowledge domains.

3 Methodology

By drawing on prior text-mining research, in particular on the works of Debortoli et al. (2016) and Michalczyk et al. (2021), we analyzed current job market demands around LCNC and citizen development. We therefore have chosen a multi-stage

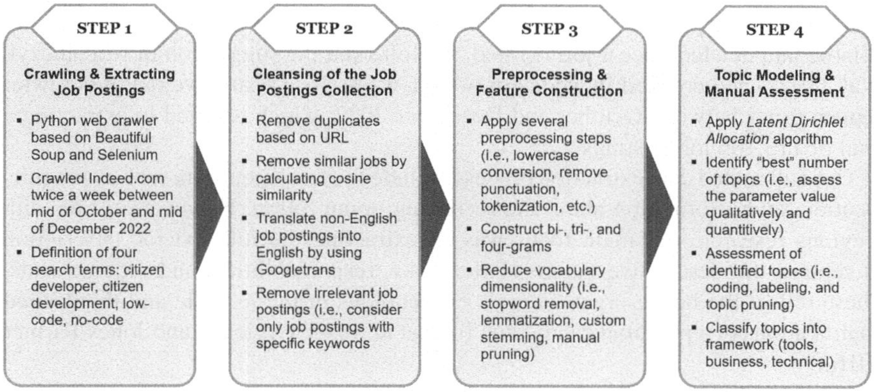

Fig. 1 Topic modeling pipeline

methodological approach as illustrated in our topic modeling pipeline in Fig. 1. The subsequent sections explain the steps of our topic modeling pipeline.

3.1 *Crawling, Collecting, and Extracting the Job Postings*

We started our research by seeking relevant and appropriate job titles in the context of LCNC and citizen development. By screening common online job platforms and examining diverse combinations of keywords, we came up with a set of six search terms that delivered satisfying search results. Accordingly, our set of search terms consists of *citizen developer, citizen development*, *low-code*, *no-code, low code*, and *no code.*

To retrieve online job postings, we developed a web crawler in Python using the packages *Beautiful Soup* (Richardson 2022) for the purpose of web scraping and Selenium (2022) as web driver and browser automation framework. As job platform, we selected *Indeed.com* which is one of the largest platforms for job seekers and recruiters from all over the world (Michaeli 2023; Polner 2023). Previous studies have demonstrated the suitability and usefulness of Indeed.com for research (e.g., Michalczyk et al. 2021; Sainju et al. 2021; Kortum et al. 2022). To gain a global perspective and to avoid any country-specific bias from crawling only one online job platform, we considered all 62 subdomains of Indeed.com.[1] By manually querying our six pre-defined search terms, we found that Indeed.com's search engine also considered the non-hyphenated counterparts ('low code' and 'no code') when searching for the hyphenated words ('low-code' and 'no-code'), and vice versa. Thus, we limited our set of search terms to four (*citizen developer*, *citizen development*, *low-code*, *no-code*). All four search terms have been queried individually and in quotation marks

[1] https://www.indeed.com/worldwide.

and have been applied to the full text of the job postings. As job postings are highly volatile and deleted once a job is filled, we followed the suggestion of Michalczyk et al. (2021) and crawled Indeed.com twice a week. As a result, we ran our crawler sixteen times between October and December 2022, which resulted in extracting a total of 113,106 job postings.

Our automated data extraction process included several meta data such as job title, location, and information about the recruiting organization. However, in line with previous research, our main focus was on extracting the full-text job description to capture the descriptive nature of the tasks, responsibilities, and requirements. These reflect the hiring organization's expectations of the job role and the desired qualifications of a potential candidate (Todd et al. 1995; Cegielski and Jones-Farmer 2016).

3.2 Cleansing and Preparing of Extracted Job Postings

After completing our crawling and extraction activities, we merged our separate datasets into one large dataset. Overall, we relied on the Python package of *pandas* (pandas 2022) for data preparation, data analysis, and data visualization. As we crawled Indeed.com twice a week, we started our cleansing process by removing redundant exact matches based on the extracted URL of the job postings. As a result, our dataset of job postings was reduced from 113,106 to 21,085. However, since some of the URLs were parameterized and therefore inherently unique, removing duplicates based on the URL was only of partial utility. Therefore, we additionally assessed the similarity of job postings by calculating the cosine similarity (Manning et al. 2009; Jurafsky and Martin 2023). For calculation, we relied on the in-built *pairwise.cosine_similarity* function of *Scikit-learn* (Pedregosa et al. 2011). Whilst testing different thresholds, we identified a threshold of 0.9 as best-fitting for our dataset. This means that all pairs with a similarity of more than 90% were treated as duplicates and one of them was removed randomly, resulting in a set of 8902 unique job posting documents.

While text mining studies often tend to filter out non-English documents to rely on a common language, we aimed to reflect a global perspective. Thus, we first identified the language of each job posting and then translated all non-English job postings into English using the Python library *Googletrans* (2021). Our cross-checking of translations yielded sufficient results to accept this approach as reasonable.

Lastly, while we became more familiar with our dataset, we noticed job postings that were not relevant to our research endeavor. After manual investigation, we identified several false-positive phrases such as '*no Code of Conduct*', '*jobtarget code: no code*', '*low code locations*', or '*dress no code*'. Moreover, similar to Debortoli et al. (2014), we observed that our search terms often only appeared in the company description (e.g., '*we are building a no-code solution*'), indicating that these firms were not looking for candidates that are intended to work with LCNC, but for a communications specialist or customer success manager, for example. We therefore decided to consider only job postings that included specific keywords in their job title. These keywords comprise *low-code, no-code, citizen dev**, and the names of the 25 most famous LCNC platforms[2] (Richardson and Rymer 2014; Sahay et al. 2020; Bratincevic and Koplowitz 2021). Following this procedure narrowed down our collection of job postings to a total of 1632 unique documents that remained for further analysis.

3.3 Preprocessing and Feature Construction

Next, we performed the feature construction step of our topic modeling pipeline. Since traditional data mining techniques are not designed to deal directly with textual data, feature construction serves to convert raw textual data into mathematical representations (Brank et al. 2011; Verdonck et al. 2021). In this study, each job posting is represented as a vector of frequencies of each term, thus assuming the principles of the vector space model (Manning et al. 2009; Jurafsky and Martin 2023). However, since this approach discards the words' grammatical ordering and focus solely on the frequencies of words within a document (i.e., bag-of-words assumption), we followed the procedure of previous text mining studies (e.g., Wallach 2006; Debortoli et al. 2016; Michalczyk et al. 2021; Jurafsky and Martin 2023) and constructed bi-, tri-, and four-grams in addition to unigrams (i.e., single words). Thus, we take contextual information into account, resulting in the inclusion of more meaningful features[3] such as *software_development* (bi-gram) or *analytical_problem_solving* (tri-gram).

Before constructing the bi-, tri-, and four-gram features, we applied several common data preprocessing steps (Silva et al. 2021). First, we converted all text to lowercase. We furthermore tokenized the text, removed punctuation, and replaced all non-alphanumeric characters. Second, we removed irrelevant standard stop words such as '*you*', '*this*', and '*any*' using the *NLTK* package (Bird et al. 2009). The resulting vocabulary was then systematically reviewed to correct unambiguous typos such as *developpment*, and to separate words written together, such as *softwaredevelopment*. Next, a lemmatization dictionary (Měchura 2017) was applied to account for the dictionary form of the words (Manning et al. 2009). For instance, *analyze* is the lemma of *analyze, analyzes,* and *analyzed*. In addition, because our collection included both American English and British English words (e.g., *analyse* versus *analyze*), we harmonized our vocabulary by converting all spellings to American English. Finally, to reduce the feature dimension of the remaining vocabulary, we normalized similar features by grouping them together under a new custom lemma (Manning et al. 2009; Michalczyk et al. 2021; Silva et al. 2021). For example,

[2] We encountered a lot of specialized job postings (e.g., *power platform* or *mendix developer*).

[3] Following common naming conventions of text-mining research (e.g., Manning et al. (2009); Jurafsky and Martin (2023)), we use the overarching term *feature* for referring to both, single words (i.e., unigrams) and word phrase patterns (i.e., bi-, tri-, and four-grams).

we merged *entrepreneurial*, *entrepreneurship*, and *entrepreneur* into the lemma *entrepreneu*, which is still open to human interpretation. While our initial non-processed vocabulary would have contained more than 1.4 million unique features, our described preprocessing steps reduced the amount to a total of 1.1 million.

Next, to further trim the number of uninformative features, we followed the recommendations of previous research (e.g., Grimmer and Stewart 2013; Debortoli et al. 2014; Carter et al. 2016; Székely and vom Brocke 2017; Michalczyk et al. 2021). Consequently, we decided to drop all features that are present in less than 1% and in more than 50% of the analyzed job postings. While the lower limit of 1% ensures that a larger number of uncommon and sparse features (e.g., headquarter location) are not included in the subsequent analysis, the upper limit of 50% suppresses the inclusion of prevalent and non-differentiating job posting features (e.g., *experience*, *work*, or *business*). The remaining vocabulary contained 6199 unique features, which we then manually reviewed to identify and exclude irrelevant features to the field of LCNC and citizen development. This final pruning process is a common and effective technique in topic modeling studies (e.g., Debortoli et al. 2014; Székely and vom Brocke 2017). Overall, the manual review and cleansing resulted in 1952 highly relevant features, which were then used as the final dictionary for applying the topic modeling algorithm.

3.4 Topic Modeling and Topic Coding

Following the data preprocessing, we chose to analyze our job postings dataset using *Latent Dirichlet Allocation* (LDA; Blei et al. 2003) as topic modeling approach. LDA is an probabilistic unsupervised machine learning algorithm that strives to discover hidden topics by running through a set of text documents (Blei 2012). The algorithm generally assumes that (1) each document can be characterized by a mixture of different (latent) topics, and (2) each topic, in turn, can be represented by a certain distribution of features, while each individual feature may occur in more than one single topic (Blei et al. 2003; Airoldi et al. 2008; Debortoli et al. 2016). Prior research has used LDA in various contexts (e.g., Lukins et al. 2010; Chen et al. 2016; Yang et al. 2017), thereby demonstrating LDA's capability to extract semantically meaningful topics from large amounts of text (Debortoli et al. 2016). In this study, we applied the online variational Bayes algorithm (Hoffman et al. 2010) by using *gensim* (Řehůřek and Sojka 2010).

The most crucial parameter when running the LDA topic modeling is the number of topics to obtain (*num_topic*). When setting *num_ topic* too high, the algorithm might disclose a plenty of minimally distinct and meaningless topics; on the other side, when setting *num_ topic* too low, there is a risk to severely constrain the exploratory potential of the LDA algorithm (Debortoli et al. 2016; Diegmann et al. 2018). Researchers have therefore proposed different approaches to identify the optimal number of topics (Griffiths and Steyvers 2004; Cao et al. 2009; Arun et al. 2010; Mimno et al. 2011), but there is no general rule to apply. We followed the recommendations as proposed by Debortoli et al. (2016). Hence, we qualitatively evaluated different numbers of topics (i.e., we trained various models and gradually increased *num_topic* from 10 to 80). While 30 topics describe our dataset imprecisely, 50 topics lead to numerous meaningless topics. Therefore, qualitatively evaluating the meaningfulness of the different models resulted in defining the ideal number of topics at *num_topic* = 38.

Next, we manually assessed and interpreted each topic by searching for patterns and assigning meaningful topic labels based on the associated features. In general, we used the visualization tool *pyLDAvis* for our explorative analysis (Sievert and Shirley 2014). As suggested by Diegmann et al. (2018), we reviewed not only the most *frequent* features, but also examined the relatively most *salient* (relevant) features. Salient features are those that have the highest frequency within a particular topic compared to all other topics. Similar to previous studies, we discarded five topics that were irrelevant for our context, resulting in 33 relevant topics. Building upon the classification of Todd et al. (1995), we then grouped our labeled topics into the three domains: *platform, business*, and *technology*. Here, we applied *pattern-coding* to group our KSA topics into meaningful 'summative labels' (Saldaña 2021). Apart from that, one topic contained both business-related and technology-related components. Therefore, we split this topic into two (see BR12 and TR7) and report a total of 34 relevant KSA topics in this study.

4 Results

4.1 Platform-Specific *Knowledge, Skills, and Abilities in Demand*

As shown in Table 1, our analysis revealed nine platform-specific topics. Most of them point relatively clearly to a specific LCNC platform. For example, we derived topic P1 (Microsoft Power Platform) from its highest-loading features *power_platform*, *microsoft*, and *power_apps*. Features such as *dataverse* and *virtual_agent* supported our assumption. We similarly identified ServiceNow, OutSystems, Mendix, Oracle APEX, Salesforce, Pega, Appian, and SAP as predominant platform topics in our job postings collection. While multiple high-loading features within the topics P1 to P8 indicate their respective topic label, we derived P9 mainly from its highest-loading feature.

Table 1 Identified platform-specific KSA topics in LCNC and citizen development

Topic label	High-loading features (excerpt)
P1: Microsoft power platform	power_platform, microsoft, power_apps, power_automate, dataverse, canvas, virtual_agent, power_bi, consultant, flow
P2: ServiceNow platform	servicenow, servicenow_platform, service_management, integrate, workflow, lead, script, module, itil, servicenow_developer
P3: Oracle APEX	sql, database, oracle, programming, apex, web, pl_sql, oracle_apex, server, erp, java, software_development
P4: Salesforce platform	salesforce, cloud, integrate, lightning, apex, salesforce_developer, practice, component, salesforce_platform, mulesoft, visualforce
P5: OutSystems platform	outsystems, outsystems_developer, consultant, dutch, learn, budget, agile, challenge, scrum, outystems_platform, consult
P6: Pega Platform	pega, business_process_mangement, process_management, architect, system_architect, pega_system, sap, lead, pega_platform
P7: Appian platform	appian, innovate, business_process, lead, empower, experience_appian, business_application, business_process_management
P8: Mendix platform	mendix, scrum, mendix_developer, innovate, challenge, dutch, user, expert, enthusiasm, consultant, experience_mendix
P9: SAP	sap, innovate, management_system, operational, active, sustainable, specialist, challenge, process_technology, audit

4.2 Business-Related *Knowledge, Skills, and Abilities in Demand*

Table 2 presents the twelve business-related topics that emerged from our analysis. BR1 and BR2 highlight work and educational experience through high-loading features such as *+_year_work_experience*, *bachelor,* and *master_degree*. Topics BR3 and BR4 refer to interpersonal KSAs. For topic BR3, we interpret the high-loading features *cooperate*, *partner*, *exchange*, and *interdisciplinary* as essential work collaboration, in which professional language skills in English and German are required. BR4 complements this by highlighting appropriate communication skills and problem-solving abilities. Next, topic BR5 relates to the adoption and scaling of LCNC and citizen development, indicated by features such as *adoption*, *ensure*, and *center_excellence*. The following four topics, "Change Management" (BR6), "Business Analysis & Project Management (BR7), "Consulting" (BR8), and "Business Understanding" (BR9) were derived through their respective high-loading features. Further, due to the features *marketing*, *web_interaction*, and *customer_* *relationship_management*, we labeled BR10 as "Marketing & Customer Relationship Management". Finally, as topic BR11 contains the features *startup*, *entrepreneu*, and *business_development*, we labeled this topic "Entrepreneurial Mindset". Similarly, the high-loading features *enthusiasm*, *creative*, *creative_problem_solve*, and *creativity* lead us to the assumption to name topic BR12 "Enthusiasm & Creativity". In summary, while topics BR1, BR2, BR3, BR4, BR11 and BR12 highlight skills, abilities, and personal traits, topics BR5 to BR10 can be considered as business functions and knowledge areas in which LCNC and citizen development, as our results reveal, plays an important role.

4.3 Technology-Related *Knowledge, Skills, and Abilities in Demand*

We identified 13 technology-related KSA topics as depicted in Table 3. The first topic (TR1) refers to automation. In particular, the highest-loading features *automation*, *process_automation*, and *intelligent_automation* justify our assumption. Next, topic TR2 represents the related field of robotic process automation. While *rpa* itself is a high-loading feature, this topic also includes platform-specific features around RPA (e.g., *uipath*, *blue_prism*, and *automation_anywhere*). The next topic, TR3, was labeled "Data Analytics & Business Intelligence" due to several high-loading features such as *dashboard*, *report*, *sql*, and *business_intelligence*, thus clearly referring to common keywords within these two analytical disciplines. We titled TR4 "Computer Science & Programming Skills" due to the features *computer_science*, *programming*, *software_developer*, *programming_language*, and *learn*. Similarly, the features *scrum*, *agile*, *product_owner*, *agile_method_scrum*, and *scrum_master* led us to the decision to label TR5 "Agile Methodology". The subsequent three topics TR6, TR7, and TR8 relate to software development. As TR6 contains the features *html*, *web*, *css*, *code*, and *javascript*, we labeled this topic "Web Development". We identified TR7 as a related field and labeled it "Mobile Application Development". Moreover, we identified topic TR8 as "User Experience & User Interface" and TR9 as "DevOps & Continuous Integration/Delivery" because the highest-loading features represent the same. The architecture-related features in TR10 and TR11 encouraged us to label these topics with "Digital Solution Design & Architecture" and "Cloud Architecture". While TR10 refers to *architect*, *solution_architect*, and *technical_architect*, topic TR11 contains features such as *cloud*, *azure*, and *infrastructure*, thus supporting our assumption. Finally, the features *test*, *quality*, *framework*, *qa*, and *test_automation* underline the labeling of the topic TR12 as "Testing & Quality Management". Lastly, we labeled TR13 "Integration Knowledge" because of its high-loading features *odata*, *integration*, *soap*, *soap_rest*, and *knowledge_integration*. In summary, our 13 technology-related KSA topics highlight the need for automation knowledge

Table 2 Business-related KSA topics in LCNC and citizen development

Topic label	High-loading features (excerpt)
BR1: Professional work experience	+_year, two_+_year, two_+, test, deliver, microsoft, user, +_year_experience, +_year_work_experience, power_apps
BR2: Academic education	master, master_degree, bachelor_master, bachelor_master_degree, bachelor, user, digital_ product, function, bank, degree
BR3: Collaboration and professional language skills	consultant, microsoft, cooperate, german, specialist, innovate, english, partner, concept, advice, exchange, interdisciplinary
BR4: Communication and problem-solving ability	lead, application_development, solve, excellent_ write, outsystems, problem_solve, communication_skill, analytic_problem_solve
BR5: Adoption and governance	power_platform, architect, adoption, microsoft, ensure, strategy, center_excellence, cloud, lead, community, stakeholder, governance
BR6: Change management	change, agile, ensure, user, method, monitor, change_management, analyst, improvement, operation, risk, agile_method
BR7: Business analysis and project management	analyst, manager, business analyst, project manager, user, internal, airtable, learn, project_ management, autonomous, agile
BR8: Consulting	consultant, consult, multidisciplinary, analytic_ skill, combine, german, architecture, agile, specialist, strategy, senior_consultant
BR9: Business understanding	architecture, data, security, zerocode, code, understand_business, architecuture_design, meet_business, understand_business_need
BR10: Marketing and customer relationship management	marketing, automation_specialist, google, customer_relationship_management, web_ design, web, interaction, master_business
BR11: Entrepreneurial mindset	english, startup, consultant, internal, programming, fluent, plan, problem_solve, communicate, entrepreneu, business_ development
BR12: Enthusiasm and creativity	web, enthusiasm, software_developer, ict, solve, mobile, creative, creative_problem_solve, creativity, mobile_application, web_app

(TR1, TR2), analytical skills (TR3), computer science and (agile) software development (TR4, TR5, TR6, TR7), customer-facing applications (TR8), and software practices (TR9, TR12). Moreover, architecture (TR10, TR11) and integration (TR13) seem to play an important role in LCNC.

Table 3 Technology-related KSA topics in LCNC and citizen development

Topic label	High-loading features (excerpt)
TR1: Automation	automation, intelligent_automation, learn, process_automation, lead, business_process, artificial_intelligence, machine_learn, deliver
TR2: Robotic process automation	rpa, uipath, rpa_developer, power_automate, robot, blue_prism, analyst, automation_anywhere, business_process, artificial_intelligence
TR3: Data analytics and business intelligence	data, report, power_bi, data_analytic, partner, manage, visualization, business_intelligence, data_model, dashboard, sql, aws, data_science
TR4: Computer science and programming skills	appian, programming, challenge, software_developer, creativity, java, collaboration, learn, programming_language, computer_science
TR5: Agile methodology	mendix_developer, scrum, innovation, dutch, expert, challenge, agile, agile_scrum, product_owner, agile_method_scrum, scrum_master
TR6: Web development	web, javascript, css, html, frontend, html_css, user, code, framework, practice, api, react, fullstack, development_experience, backend
TR7: Mobile application development	web, enthusiasm, software_developer, ict, solve, mobile, creative, creative_problem_solve, creativity, mobile_application, web_app
TR8: User experience and user interface	user, interface, user_interface, user_experience, manager, product_manager, plan, bubble, user_experience_design, react_javascript
TR9: DevOps and continuous integration/delivery	continuous, integration, delivery, devops, continuous_integration, cloud, continuous_delivery, agile, quality, azure, programming, git
TR10: Digital solution design and architecture	architect, solution_architect, leadership, lead_team, manage, technical_architect, cloud_solution, architecture_solution, modernization
TR11: Cloud architecture	microsoft, cloud, azure, integration, microsoft_azure, azure_cloud, azure_service, javascript_typescript, infrastructure, manage, deploy
TR12: Testing and quality management	test, test_automation, quality, automate, automation_engineer, framework, qa, automate_test, script, test_automation_engineer, selenium
TR13: Integration knowledge	odata, outsystems_consultant, integration, degree, solve, complex, web, knowledge_integration, soap_rest, integration_system, soap

5 Discussion

Given the lack of empirical research on the knowledge and skillset of individual citizen developers in the area of LCNC, we shed light on much demanded KSAs associated with the field. Our three-pronged framework covering platforms, business, and technology supports the understanding of these KSAs. We identified that LCNC users should have a substantial professional and academic background (BR1, BR2). Consistent with prior findings (e.g., Whitmore 2021), LCNC users are valued for their creativity and problem-solving abilities. Additionally, as intermediaries between business and IT (e.g., Krejci et al. 2021), successful utilization of LCNC tools relies on collaboration (BR3), effective communication (BR4), and a profound understanding of business functions and activities (BR7, BR9). However, our findings also reveal that employers primarily demand general KSAs, rather than requiring KSAs that are specific to the domain of LCNC technologies. For instance, KSAs in change and project management, consulting, or familiarity with agile methodologies are prevalent and characteristic for various professional IT roles (Todd et al. 1995; McMurtrey et al. 2008; Gallagher et al. 2010). In turn, this raises the discussion on whether and how LCNC-related jobs are distinct from other IT-related professions.

Furthermore, our findings challenge the claims made by numerous LCNC vendors by revealing that LCNC is associated with a wide spectrum of technical expertise. This implies that utilizing LCNC platforms requires specialized technical knowledge or, in some cases, even programming experience (TR3-TR12). Consequently, the notion of non-IT professionals building digital solutions by solely leveraging LCNC platforms is being questioned. This contributes to the ongoing discourse surrounding the extent to which LCNC platforms truly fulfill the envisioned promise of "democratization of IT", highlighting the findings of prior research (e.g., Sahay et al. 2020; Luo et al. 2021; Hoogsteen and Borgman 2022). Moreover, our topic modeling approach revealed "Integration" (TR13) as a standalone topic, which is seen as difficult challenge in the LCNC area (Al Alamin et al. 2021). This finding further indicates the presence of diverse LCNC user types, including professionals, semi-professionals, and citizen developers.

Lastly, it is important to note that due to the absence of unified standards (e.g., language), each LCNC platform possesses its own distinctive features and peculiarities that users must acquaint themselves with (Sahay et al. 2020). Our identification of nine distinct platform-specific topics reinforces this observation, underlining the fact that the LCNC job market currently necessitates a profound understanding and proficiency in platform-specific knowledge and skills. This finding, again, contrasts the claims put forth by vendors that LCNC platforms are easy to use without requiring prior knowledge or experience.

We also recognize the limitations of this work. Limitations of our study arise from our applied crawling strategy and the topic modeling methodology itself. We may have missed jobs that are not in scope of our keyword search strategy. For instance, scholars began to use terms such as *zero-code, hyperautomation,* or *citizen automation* (Luo et al. 2021; Herm et al. 2022). Second, although we carefully cleaned our dataset by following best practices and previous research recommendations, there is always a risk of bias. Third, the LDA parameter settings we used may have biased the results of our topic modeling approach. Lastly, other scholars may have interpreted, labeled, and grouped the topics differently than we did.

6 Conclusion

In summary, the contribution of this work is two-fold. Our theoretical contribution lies in the empirical investigation of a large dataset of job postings in the area of LCNC and citizen development. Hence, we respond to calls for exploring the nature of LCNC users (Prinz et al. 2021; Binzer and Winkler 2022). This study is thus the first empirical work that focuses solely on individual LCNC users, thereby extending the literature with a framework of 34 identified KSA topics.

However, since our findings revealed a broad spectrum of demanded KSAs, we encourage future research to examine (1) which types of LCNC users exist, and (2) how these types utilize and leverage the respective LCNC platforms. In addition, our findings emphasize the importance of automation in the context of LCNC and citizen development. Further research on bringing these literature streams into harmony may thus be an important and useful avenue.

From a practical viewpoint, we highlight much demanded KSAs in which individual professionals may upskill in order to successfully leverage LCNC platforms and prepare for new emerging job opportunities. Moreover, organizations can utilize our framework of identified KSAs to effectively identify and evaluate their workforce needs when defining citizen development strategies. On this basis, existing employees can be trained, or new ones be recruited. In addition, academic institutions can use our findings to design innovative course programs for teaching the field of LCNC and citizen development.

References

Airoldi, E. M., Blei, D. M., Fienberg, S. E. & Xing, E. P. (2008) Mixed Membership Stochastic Blockmodels. *Journal of Machine Learning Research* **9** (65), 1981–2014.

Al Alamin, M. A., Malakar, S., Uddin, G., Afroz, S., Haider, T. B. & Iqbal, A. (2021) An Empirical Study of Developer Discussions on Low-Code Software Development Challenges. In: *18th International Conference on Mining Software Repositories (MSR)*. IEEE.

Arun, R., Suresh, V., Veni Madhavan, C. E. & Narasimha Murthy, M. N. (2010) On Finding the Natural Number of Topics with Latent Dirichlet Allocation: Some Observations. In: Hutchison, D., Kanade, T. & Kittler, J. et al. (eds.) *Advances in Knowledge Discovery and Data Mining: 14th Pacific-Asia Conference*, Berlin, Heidelberg, pp. 391–402.

Binzer, B. & Winkler, T. J. (2022) Democratizing Software Development: A Systematic Multivocal Literature Review and Research Agenda on Citizen Development. In: Carroll, N., Nguyen-Duc, A., Wang, X. & Stray, V. (eds.) *Proceedings of the 13th International Conference on Software Business (ICSOB)*. Springer, Cham, pp. 244–259.

Bird, S., Loper, E. & Klein, E. (2009) Natural Language Processing with Python. https://www.nltk.org/book/. Accessed: 01.02.23.
Blei, D. M. (2012) Probabilistic topic models. *Communications of the ACM* **55** (4), 77–84.
Blei, D. M., Ng, A. Y. & Jordan, M. I. (2003) Latent Dirichlet Allocation. *Journal of Machine Learning Research* **3** (Jan), 993–1022.
Bock, A. C. & Frank, U. (2021) Low-Code Platform. *Business & Information Systems Engineering* **63** (6), 733–740.
Brank, J., Mladenić, D. & Grobelnik, M. (2011) Feature Construction in Text Mining. In: *Encyclopedia of Machine Learning*. Springer, Boston, MA, pp. 397–401.
Bratincevic, J. & Koplowitz, R. (2021) The Forrester Wave™: Low-Code Development Platforms For Professional Developers, Q2 2021. https://www.forrester.com/report/The-Forrester-Wave-LowCode-Development-Platforms-For-Professional-Developers-Q2-2021/RES161668. Accessed: 10.02.23.
Breaux, T. & Moritz, J. (2021) The 2021 software developer shortage is coming. *Communications of the ACM* **64** (7), 39–41.
Cao, J., Xia, T., Li, J., Zhang, Y. & Tang, S. (2009) A density-based method for adaptive LDA model selection. *Neurocomputing* **72** (7-9), 1775–1781.
Carroll, N. & Maher, M. (2023) How Shell Fueled a Digital Transformation by Establishing DIY Software Development. *MIS Quarterly Executive* **22** (2), 99–127.
Carroll, N., Móráin, L. Ó., Garrett, D. & Jamnadass, A. (2021) The Importance of Citizen Development for Digital Transformation. *Cutter IT Journal* **34** (3), 5–9.
Carter, J. D., Brown, J. & Rahmani, A. (2016) READING THE HIGH COURT AT A DISTANCE: TOPIC MODELLING THE LEGAL SUBJECT MATTER AND JUDICIAL ACTIVITY OF THE HIGH COURT OF AUSTRALIA, 1903–2015. *UNSW Law Journal* **39** (4), 1300–1354.
Cegielski, C. G. & Jones-Farmer, L. A. (2016) Knowledge, Skills, and Abilities for Entry-Level Business Analytics Positions: A Multi-Method Study. *Decision Sciences Journal of Innovative Education* **14** (1), 91–118.
Chen, C., Huang, E. & Yan, H. (2016) Detecting the association of health problems in consumer-level medical text. *Journal of Information Science* **44** (1), 3–14.
Debortoli, S., Müller, O. & vom Brocke, J. (2014) Comparing Business Intelligence and Big Data Skills. *Business & Information Systems Engineering* **6** (5), 289–300.
Debortoli, S., Müller, O., Junglas, I. & vom Brocke, J. (2016) Text Mining for Information Systems Researchers: An Annotated Topic Modeling Tutorial. *Communications of the Association for Information Systems* **39**, 110–135.
Di Ruscio, D., Kolovos, D., Lara, J. de, Pierantonio, A., Tisi, M. & Wimmer, M. (2022) Low-code development and model-driven engineering: Two sides of the same coin? *Software and Systems Modeling* **21** (2), 437–446.
Diegmann, P., Dreesen, T., Binzer, B. & Rosenkranz, C. (2018) Journey Towards Agility: Three Decades of Research on Agile Information Systems Development. In: *Proceedings of the 39th International Conference on Information Systems (ICIS)*.
Drakos, N. & Wong, J. (2021) *Future of Work Trends: Tinkerers Become Mechanics*.
Eggers, J., Wewerka, J., Viljoen, A. & Krcmar, H. (2023) Supporting Subject Matter Experts as Developers: Towards a Framework for Decentralized Robotic Process Automation Development. In: *Proceedings of the 56th Annual Hawaii International Conference on System Sciences (HICSS)*.
Forth, P., Laubier, R. de, Reichert, T. & Chakaborty, S. (2020) Flipping the Odds of Digital Transformation Success. https://www.bcg.com/de-de/publications/2020/increasing-odds-of-success-in-digital-transformation. Accessed: 10.03.23.
Fortune Business Insights (2022) Low Code Development Platform Market. https://www.fortunebusinessinsights.com/low-code-development-platform-market-102972. Accessed: 17.02.23.
Gallagher, K. P., Kaiser, K. M., Simon, J. C., Beath, C. M. & Goles, T. (2010) The requisite variety of skills for IT professionals. *Communications of the ACM* **53** (6), 144–148.

Gartner (2021) Gartner Says Cloud Will Be the Centerpiece of New Digital Experiences: Global Cloud Revenue to Total $474 Billion in 2022, Up from $408 Billion in 2021. https://www.gartner.com/en/newsroom/press-releases/2021-11-10-gartner-says-cloud-will-be-the-centerpiece-of-new-digital-experiences. Accessed: 17.02.23.
Googletrans: Free and Unlimited Google translate API for Python — Googletrans 3.0.0 documentation (2021). https://py-googletrans.readthedocs.io/en/latest/. Accessed: 11.02.23.
GreyViews (2023) Low Code Development Platform Market– Growth | Global Analysis to 2030. https://greyviews.com/reports/low-code-development-platform-market/578. Accessed: 17.02.23.
Griffiths, T. L. & Steyvers, M. (2004) Finding scientific topics. *Proceedings of the National Academy of Sciences of the United States of America* **101** (Suppl 1), 5228–5235.
Grimmer, J. & Stewart, B. M. (2013) Text as Data: The Promise and Pitfalls of Automatic Content Analysis Methods for Political Texts. *Political Analysis* **21** (3), 267–297.
Handali, J., Schneider, J., Dennehy, D., Hoffmeister, B., Conboy, K. & Becker, J. (2020) INDUSTRY DEMAND FOR ANALYTICS: A LONGITUDINAL STUDY. In: *Proceedings of the 28th European Conference on Information Systems (ECIS).*
Herm, L.-V., Janiesch, C., Helm, A., Imgrund, F., Hofmann, A. & Winkelmann, A. (2022) A framework for implementing robotic process automation projects. *Information Systems and e-Business Management*, 1–35.
Hoffman, M. D., Blei, D. M. & Bach, F. (2010) Online learning for Latent Dirichlet Allocation. In: *Proceedings of the 23rd International Conference on Neural Information Processing Systems*, pp. 856–864.
Hoogsteen, D. & Borgman, H. (2022) Empower the Workforce, Empower the Company? Citizen Development Adoption. In: *Proceedings of the 55th Hawaii International Conference on System Sciences (HICSS).*
Johannessen, C. & Davenport, T. H. (2021) When Low-Code/No-Code Development Works — and When It Doesn't. https://hbr.org/2021/06/when-low-code-no-code-development-works-and-when-it-doesnt. Accessed: 16.02.23.
Jurafsky, D. & Martin, J. H. (2023) Speech and Language Processing: An Introduction to Natural Language Processing, Computational Linguistics, and Speech Recognition. https://web.stanford.edu/~jurafsky/slp3/. Accessed: 09.02.23.
Kappeyne, N. (2021) Citizen software development | Shell Global. https://www.shell.com/energy-and-innovation/digitalisation/news-room/do-it-yourself-software-development-the-power-is-in-your-hand.html. Accessed: 17.02.23.
Kortum, H., Rebstadt, J. & Thomas, O. (2022) Dissection of AI Job Advertisements: A Text Mining-based Analysis of Employee Skills in the Disciplines Computer Vision and Natural Language Processing. In: *Proceedings of the 55th Hawaii International Conference on System Sciences (HICSS).*
Krejci, D., Iho, S. & Missonier, S. (2021) Innovating with employees: an exploratory study of idea development on low-code development platforms. *ECIS 2021 Research Papers.*
Lebens, M., J Finnegan, R., C Sorsen, S. & Shah, J. (2021) Rise of the Citizen Developer. *Muma Business Review* **5**, 101–111.
Lukins, S. K., Kraft, N. A. & Etzkorn, L. H. (2010) Bug localization using latent Dirichlet allocation. *Information and Software Technology* **52** (9), 972–990.
Luo, Y., Liang, P., Wang, C., Shahin, M. & Zhan, J. (2021) Characteristics and Challenges of Low-Code Development. In: Lanubile, F. (ed.) *Proceedings of the 15th ACM / IEEE International Symposium on Empirical Software Engineering and Measurement (ESEM).* ACM, New York, NY, USA, pp. 1–11.
Manning, C., Raghavan, P. & Schütze, H. (2009) Introduction to Information Retrieval. https://nlp.stanford.edu/IR-book/information-retrieval-book.html. Accessed: 08.02.23.
Matt, C., Hess, T., Benlian, A. & Wiesbock, F. (2016) Options for Formulating a Digital Transformation Strategy. *MIS Quarterly Executive* **15** (2).

McKendrick, J. (2017) The Rise of the Empowered Citizen Developer. https://dbta.com/DBTA-Downloads/ResearchReports/THE-RISE-OF-THE-EMPOWERED-CITIZEN-DEVELOPER-7575.pdf. Accessed: 05.08.22.

McMurtrey, M. E., Downey, J. P., Zeltmann, S. M. & Friedman, W. H. (2008) Critical Skill Sets of Entry-Level IT Professionals: An Empirical Examination of Perceptions from Field Personnel. *Journal of Information Technology Education: Research* **7**, 101–120.

Měchura, M. (2017) Machine-readable lists of lemma-token pairs in 23 languages. https://github.com/michmech/lemmatization-lists. Accessed: 08.02.23.

Michaeli, A. (2023) Indeed Cements its Lead as the Most Popular Job Search App. https://appfigures.com/resources/insights/20230203?f=2. Accessed: 13.02.23.

Michalczyk, S., Nadj, M., Maedche, A. & Gröger, C. (2021) Demystifying Job Roles in Data Science: A Text Mining Approach. In: *Proceedings of the 29th European Conference on Information Systems (ECIS).*

Mimno, D., Wallach, H., Talley, E., Leenders, M. & McCallum, A. (2011) Optimizing Semantic Coherence in Topic Models. *Proceedings of the 2011 Conference on Empirical Methods in Natural Language Processing*, 262–272.

pandas (2022) pandas documentation — pandas 1.5.1 documentation. https://pandas.pydata.org/docs/index.html. Accessed: 30.10.22.

Pedregosa, F., Varoquaux, G. & Gramfort, A. et al. (2011) Scikit-learn: Machine Learning in Python. *Journal of Machine Learning Research* (12), 2825–2830.

Pejic-Bach, M., Bertoncel, T., Meško, M. & Krstić, Ž. (2020) Text mining of industry 4.0 job advertisements. *International Journal of Information Management* **50**, 416–431.

Peterson, B. (2017) The CEO of GitHub, which caters to coders, thinks automation will bring an end to traditional software programming. *Business Insider,* October 11. https://www.businessinsider.com/github-ceo-wanstrath-says-automation-will-replace-software-coding-2017-10. Accessed: 16.02.23.

Phalake, V. S. & Joshi, S. D. (2021) Low Code Development Platform for Digital Transformation. In: *Information and Communication Technology for Competitive Strategies (ICTCS 2020).* Springer, Singapore, pp. 689–697.

Polner, E. (2023) Best Job Search Websites. https://www.thebalancemoney.comtop-best-job-websites-2064080. Accessed: 13.02.23.

Prinz, N., Rentrop, C. & Huber, M. (2021) Low-Code Development Platforms – A Literature Review. In: *Proceedings of the 27th Americas Conference on Information Systems (AMCIS).*

Prinz, N., Huber, M., Riedinger, C. & Rentrop, C. (2022) Two Perspectives of Low-Code Development Platform Challenges – An Exploratory Study. In: *Proceedings of the 26th Pacific Asia Conference on Information Systems (PACIS).*

Řehůřek, R. & Sojka, P. (2010) Software Framework for Topic Modelling with Large Corpora. In: *Proceedings of the LREC 2010 Workshop on New Challenges for NLP Frameworks*, pp. 45–50.

Richardson, C. & Rymer, J. (2014) New Development Platforms Emerge For Customer-Facing Applications. https://www.forrester.comreport/New-Development-Platforms-Emerge-For-CustomerFacing-Applications/RES113411. Accessed: 15.02.23.

Richardson, L. (2022) Beautiful Soup Documentation — Beautiful Soup 4.9.0 documentation. https://www.crummy.comsoftware/BeautifulSoup/bs4/doc/ Accessed: 23.10.22.

Sahay, A., Indamutsa, A., Di Ruscio, D. & Pierantonio, A. (2020) Supporting the understanding and comparison of low-code development platforms. In: *2020 46th Euromicro Conference on Software Engineering and Advanced Applications (SEAA).* IEEE, pp. 171–178.

Sainju, B., Hartwell, C. & Edwards, J. (2021) Job satisfaction and employee turnover determinants in Fortune 50 companies: Insights from employee reviews from Indeed.com. *Decision Support Systems* **148**, 113582.

Saldaña, J. (2021) *The coding manual for qualitative researchers,* 4e. SAGE, Los Angeles, London, New Delhi, Singapore, Washington DC, Melbourne.

Selenium (2022) The Selenium Browser Automation Project. https://www.selenium.dev/documentation/. Accessed: 11.02.23.

Sievert, C. & Shirley, K. (2014) LDAvis: A method for visualizing and interpreting topics. In: Chuang, J., Green, S., Hearst, M., Heer, J. & Koehn, P. (eds.) *Proceedings of the Workshop on Interactive Language Learning, Visualization, and Interfaces*. Association for Computational Linguistics, Stroudsburg, PA, USA, pp. 63–70.

Silva, C. C., Galster, M. & Gilson, F. (2021) Topic modeling in software engineering research. *Empirical Software Engineering* **26** (6).

Steele, T. (2021) Democratizing Innovation: Low-Code / No-Code Platforms & The Citizen Developer. https://www.capco.com/intelligence/capco-intelligence/democratizing-innovation. Accessed: 17.02.23.

Swinhoe, D. (2017) GitHub CEO: "The future of coding is no coding at all". https://www.idgconnect.com/article/3578431/github-ceo-the-future-of-coding-is-no-coding-at-all.html. Accessed: 17.02.23.

Székely, N. & vom Brocke, J. (2017) What can we learn from corporate sustainability reporting? Deriving propositions for research and practice from over 9,500 corporate sustainability reports published between 1999 and 2015 using topic modelling technique. *PloS one* **12** (4), e0174807.

Tisi, M., Mottu, J. M. & Kolovos, D. S. et al. (2019) Lowcomote: Training the next generation of experts in scalable low-code engineering platforms. In: *Software Technologies, Applications and Foundations (STAF 2019)*.

Todd, P. A., McKeen, J. D. & Gallupe, R. B. (1995) The Evolution of IS Job Skills: A Content Analysis of IS Job Advertisements from 1970 to 1990. *MIS Quarterly* **19** (1), 1.

Verdonck, T., Baesens, B., Óskarsdóttir, M. & vanden Broucke, S. (2021) Special issue on feature engineering editorial. *Machine Learning*, 1–12.

Wade, M. & Shan, J. (2020) Covid-19 has accelerated digital transformation, but may have made it harder not easier. *MIS Quarterly Executive* **19** (3), 199–211.

Wallach, H. M. (2006) Topic modeling: Beyond Bag-of-Words. In: Cohen, W. W. & Moore, A. W. (eds.) *Proceedings of the 23rd International Conference on Machine Learning*. ACM, New York, pp. 977–984.

Walsh, J., Johnson, M. & Sugarman, M. (1975) *Help wanted: Case studies of classified ads*. Olympus Pub. Co, Salt Lake City.

Weisinger, D. (2011) Open Data: Rise of the Rogue Citizen Developer and End-User Application Development. https://formtek.com/blog/open-data-rise-of-the-rogue-citizen-developer/. Accessed: 15.02.23.

Whitmore, R. (2021) Citizen Development Insights: Citizen Development Part 2: Getting Started. https://www.projectmanagement.com/blog/blogPostingView.cfm?blogPostingID=69464&thisPageURL=/blog-post/69464/citizen-development-part-2--getting-started#_=_. Accessed: 05.03.23.

Yang, X., Lo, D., Li, L., Xia, X., Bissyandé, T. F. & Klein, J. (2017) Characterizing malicious Android apps by mining topic-specific data flow signatures. Information and Software Technology 90, 27–39.

Design Principles for Institutionalized Data Ecosystems—Results from a Series of Case Studies

Patrick Weber, Maximilian Werling, and Henning Baars

Abstract Sharing and collaborating on data across organizational boundaries is increasingly important for building a comprehensive data foundation for a variety of relevant analytical models and reports. We argue that a formalized set of rules and responsibilities—data governance—is needed to guide such data sharing activities and thus provide the foundation for an institutionalized data ecosystem. To this end, we propose a set of design principles. Based on three case studies from different application domains, we derive the design principles using Service-Dominant Logic as our theoretical lens. We distinguish between dynamic and static design principles. Our approach supports the delineation and specification of data governance structures for data ecosystems.

Keywords Data ecosystem · Data governance · Service-Dominant Logic · Data collaboration

1 Introduction

Data sharing across organizational boundaries has become increasingly important as it is recognized as a powerful opportunity for value creation, especially in the context of the Internet of Things (IoT) (Lehrer et al. 2018). This has led to the design and establishment of trusted and secure data infrastructures, so-called data spaces (Pretzsch et al. 2020; Braud et al. 2021). However, building and deploying infrastructures is not enough. In an increasing number of cases, it has become apparent

P. Weber (✉) · M. Werling
Ferdinand Steinbeis Institute, Stuttgart and Heilbronn, Germany
e-mail: patrick.weber@ferdinand-steinbeis-institut.de

M. Werling
e-mail: maximilian.werling@ferdinand-steinbeis-institut.de

H. Baars
Chair of Information Systems I, University of Stuttgart, Stuttgart, Germany
e-mail: henning.baars@bwi.uni-stuttgart.de

D. Beverungen et al. (eds.), *Transforming the Digitally Sustainable Enterprise*, Lecture Notes in Information Systems and Organisation 76,
https://doi.org/10.1007/978-3-031-80125-9_16

that it is advisable to embed data spaces in holistic Information Systems (IS) that also consider non-technical aspects (Reiberg et al. 2022). Data governance is a central aspect of such IS, providing the shared institutional logics that govern data sharing (Baars et al. 2021; Gelhaar and Otto 2020; Vargo and Lusch 2016).

The topic of data spaces has attracted the attention of management and IS researchers and is discussed under the term *data ecosystems*. However, the solutions discussed in research are rarely found in practice: There, many data sharing projects do not get beyond the prototype phase due to the lack of a framework for binding collaboration (Weber et al. 2022). In this paper, we examine three different data ecosystems that have moved beyond this stage. The focus is on the rules and regulatory structures—data governance—that have been established in these cases. Following the research gap outlined above, this paper focuses on the following two Research Questions (RQ):

- RQ1: *What are data governance design principles for the creation of an institutionalized data ecosystem?*
- RQ2: *How can design principles be grouped for the purpose of providing a structure for an institutionalized data ecosystem?*

The next section presents a literature review that provides the conceptual background and current state of research on the topic. The next section presents our methodology and an overview of our case studies. We then propose our data governance design principles. We conclude with a discussion of the limitations of this study and our contributions to theory and practice.

2 Related Work and Background

To gain a better understanding of the current state of research on our topic, we conducted a systematic literature search (Levy and Ellis 2006; Vom Brocke et al. 2009). The search process was documented according to PRISMA 2020 (Page et al. 2021). We searched titles and abstracts for the keywords "*data*" AND "*ecosystem*" AND "*governance*" in the following databases: AIS eLibrary, ScienceDirect, and IEEE eXplorer. Since we use the Service-Dominant Logic (SDL) as our theoretical lens, we conducted a second search to identify publications that also use it. The following keywords were used: "*service-dominant logic*" AND "*governance*", searched in the title and abstract, respectively. The results of both searches were checked for title and abstract relevance.

A total of 172 accessible publications were identified in both searches. Of these, 72 were excluded because of obvious irrelevance (especially in the second search). A further 54 titles were excluded after evaluation of the abstracts and 3 as duplicates. A total of 41 publications were examined in more detail, of which 6 were finally eliminated in this step. The following sections provide an overview of the relevant publications.

2.1 Data Ecosystems: An SDL Perspective

Recent developments around the IoT and the increasing availability of smart objects in value-added processes provide new opportunities for companies to offer innovative digital services (Lehrer et al. 2018). Smart objects continuously generate status data, which forms the basis for improved processes and digital services (Porter and Heppelmann 2014). However, for many companies, such efforts are accompanied by various technical and organizational challenges that they can hardly overcome on their own (Gelhaar and Otto 2020; Weber et al. 2020). This leads to the need to collaborate across company boundaries, building partnerships that are often rooted in a cooperative value proposition that aligns the economic activities and resources of the actors (Adner 2017; Shipilov and Gawer 2020). Digital ecosystems that focus on the aspect of data sharing are referred to as data ecosystems. Organizations are connected to each other cooperatively and/or competitively through digital platform infrastructures, often referred to as data spaces, for their value creation activities (de Reuver et al. 2022; Oliveira and Lòscio 2018). Data spaces are a form of digital platform infrastructure, providing a trust-based space for the exchange or transaction of data (Reiberg et al. 2022).

To better understand these phenomena, we use the Service-Dominant Logic (SDL) as our theoretical lens. The SDL originated in marketing (Vargo and Lusch 2004, 2008), but is increasingly used in IS research, especially in conceptualizing data ecosystems (Azkan et al. 2020; Kannan et al. 2022; Blaschke et al. 2019; Hein et al. 2018; Lehrer et al. 2018). Instead of product offerings, SDL focuses on the exchange of service, where one actor uses its capabilities to benefit another actor (Lusch and Nambisan 2015). Lusch and Nambisan provide a framework for describing collaborative service innovation based on three key concepts: the service ecosystem, the service platform, and value co-creation (Lusch and Nambisan 2015).

Service ecosystem: The service ecosystem refers to a set of "*[...] of mostly loosely coupled social and economic (resource-integrating) actors connected by shared institutional logics and mutual value creation through service exchange*" (Lusch and Nambisan 2015, p. 162). As a conceptual pillar of our paper, we interpret a data ecosystem as a variant of a service ecosystem.

Service platform: The value creation activities are facilitated by the service platform, which is defined as "*[a] modular structure that consists of tangible and intangible components (resources) and facilitates the interaction of actors and resources [...]*" (Lusch and Nambisan 2015, p. 162). In our case, the service platform is the digital platform infrastructure that facilitates the exchange of data and information between actors in the ecosystem (de Reuver et al. 2022).

Value co-creation: Value co-creation is defined as "[t]he processes and activities that underlie resource integration and incorporate different actor roles in the service ecosystem" (Lusch and Nambisan 2015, p. 162). In our understanding, value is created by actors who collect and share data, generate new insights by applying their specific know-how to the data, and use these insights to contribute to the collaborative value proposition of the data ecosystem (Adner 2017; Weber et al. 2020).

2.2 An SDL Perspective on Data Governance

The SDL emphasizes the importance of shared institutional logics within service ecosystems. Shared institutional logics facilitate both the exchange of service and the creation of added value. They also support the development of network effects: The more actors adhere to shared logics, the greater the potential benefits (Vargo and Lusch 2016). We argue that inter-organizational data governance is not only enabled by such logics, but that they form its backbone.

Data governance generally refers to the distribution of decision rights and responsibilities for data-related decisions (Weill and Ross 2004). Historically, the scope of data governance was mostly limited to a single organization (intra-organizational data governance). More recently, the literature has shifted towards the study of data governance in a decentralized ecosystem setting (inter-organizational data governance) (Abraham et al. 2019; Lis and Otto 2021). A relevant data governance needs to facilitate the creation of a collaborative environment in which all actors act in accordance with, and further benefit from, the shared values of the ecosystem (van den Broek and Fleur van Veenstra 2015).

Data governance challenges in service ecosystems: Data governance for an ecosystem setting must ensure that members behave in a manner consistent with collective goals, prevent or resolve conflicts between actors, and ensure that collective resources—in particular, shared data—are used effectively and transparently. Ownership and valuation of shared data, considering the interests of the ecosystem and its individual members, is a challenge that governance needs to address (Lis and Otto 2021).

Data governance challenges regarding service platforms: A key challenge is the distribution of decision rights over which actors use the platform infrastructures and how. This translates into the task of finding an appropriate mix of centralized and decentralized approaches. Key platform-oriented data governance issues include data security and quality, standardization, regulation of competition among members, and questions of revenue distribution (Scholz et al. 2022; Perscheid et al. 2020).

Data governance challenges regarding value co-creation: In the context of value co-creation, there are four main challenges that inter-organizational data governance must address: First, it is imperative to define the roles of each partner in the value creation process. Second, since all activities in the data value chain process require an investment and thus generate costs, but revenues are only generated in a data exploitation phase that is often not fully predictable, an appropriate mechanism needs to be put in place to compensate actors for their (data) contributions (Badewitz et al. 2020; Martens et al. 2020). Finally, data providers often do not know which data with which properties (especially in terms of format, latency and quality, etc.) are

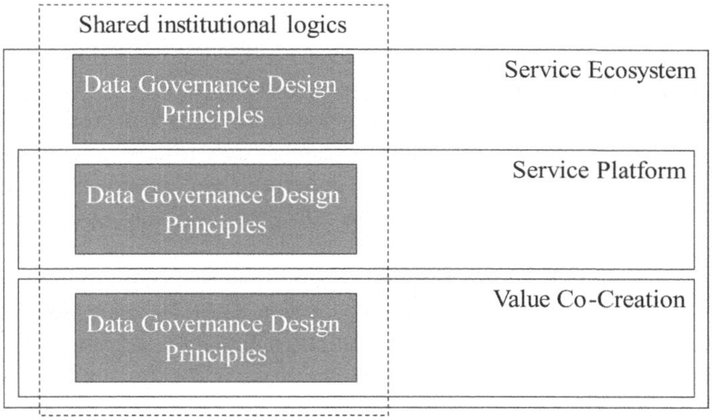

Fig. 1 Conceptual framework, based on Lusch and Nambisan (2015)

needed by other actors, so tools for describing data supply and demand need to be established (Fernandez et al. 2020; Susha et al. 2017).

Figure 1 illustrates the conceptual framework of our work. The conceptual framework forms the basis for the development of our observation protocols as well as for the analysis of the results. It reflects our research questions and the related work section.

3 Research Design

We followed a multiple case study design (Yin 2018), in which we accompanied three consortia, each of which included three companies. Each consortium was followed through the establishment of a cooperative business unit as a separate legal entity, and the design and implementation of a supporting data governance. In all cases, the collaborations followed four steps: (1) building the partner network, (2) defining a cooperative goal, (3) establishing a shared unit as a legal entity, (4) prototyping the data sharing solutions for storage and analysis. The timeframes ranged from 9 to 24 months.

To elicit our design principles, we followed the approach of Action Design Research (ADR). In ADR, an organizational-technical solution is developed as an "ensemble artifact" in continuous cycles involving the participating companies and the research consortium (Sein et al. 2011). The ensemble artifact included running pilot systems, each of which was iteratively developed, applied, and evaluated in multiple cycles. Our personal involvement as researchers ensured that the state of the art in data ecosystems, data governance, and SDL was considered in both design and evaluation. It should be emphasized that the (non-funded) companies involved in the design and evaluation functioned as the final authority for the specific solution design, and that all ecosystems continued to collaborate, develop, and adopt the prototypes after the research projects were completed.

For data collection, we primarily conducted workshops with relevant company representatives and at least two researchers. The researchers participated as observers and documented all workshop outcomes in written and photographic protocols. These were later analyzed on the basis of the conceptual framework using Mayring's structured content analysis (Mayring 2014).

A total of 15 case studies were initiated as part of our research activities. However, only three of these led to the formal specification of governance aspects and the institutionalization of a separate legal entity. The fact that only 3 of the 15 initiatives reached this stage is not an unusual ratio. The reasons for this are barriers to data sharing, as described by Fassnacht et al. (2023). While the three successful cases form the empirical basis for this paper, similar patterns were observed in the other cases. The following sections describe the three cases in more detail:

Case Study 1 (CS1)—Coolant Management: Coolant is used in metalworking to lubricate and cool tools and workpieces. Heavily contaminated coolant not only causes equipment wear and degrades product quality (e.g., by causing rust), but also potentially creates toxic fumes that pose a risk to life and limb (Evans et al. 2020). The companies in CS1 defined a cooperative value proposition based on a data-driven reorganization of the supply and management of coolant processes. To achieve this, digital services (e.g., continuous monitoring of coolant or optimization of the coolant ordering process) were defined and implemented both technically and organizationally. The associated data and information requirements were defined and the relevant reports and analyses were implemented—initially as a prototype by the researchers and later permanently by a professional software development company. The focus was on status data (e.g., pH values, coolant concentration, coolant temperature) of smart objects relevant to the coolant process (e.g., coolant, coolant tanks, shop floor environment). The digital data was transferred to a data space. Between August 2020 and August 2022, a total of seven workshops were conducted as part of the case study, each lasting two to three hours. In addition, several bilateral discussions were held with each of the companies. The participating companies are shown in Table 1.

Case Study 2 (CS2)—Risk Mitigation in the Wood Processing Industry: In CS2, a sawmill, a wholesaler, and a risk broker worked together to stabilize supply chains

Table 1 CS1 participating companies

Company	Employees	Main representatives
Metalworking Company	~ 60	Managing Directors
Wholesaler and Service Provider for Coolant	~ 75	Head of Strategic Development, Head of Operational Coolant Business
Manufacturer of Cleaning Machines for Coolant	~ 10	Managing Director

Table 2 CS2 participating companies

Company	Employees	Participant
Sawmill	~ 30	Managing Director
Wholesaler	~ 30	Managing Director
Insurance Broker	~ 10	Managing Director

and detect critical conditions in assets (mainly fire hazards in the sawmill) to increase operational readiness and promote risk reduction. Smart saw blades and machines measure status data (e.g. temperatures, residual currents, and power consumption volumes) and transfer them to a data space. Prototypical digital services have been implemented with partners to monitor and analyze the electric motors of band saws, shredders, and transport motors. Among other things, an alarm is triggered when certain relevant thresholds are exceeded. This allows risks to be identified at an early stage and damage to be prevented. A total of five workshops were held with the participating companies, as well as several bilateral meetings with each company. All workshops and discussions took place between March and December 2022. Table 2 provides a summary.

Case Study 3 (CS3)—Improving Energy Efficiency in an Industrial Laundry: The third case study brought together an industrial laundry, a textile machinery manufacturer, and a gas burner manufacturer with the common goal of improving the energy efficiency and machine uptime of laundry finishing processes. Laundry finishing is a particularly energy-intensive process in which large laundry finishing machines use gas burners to quickly and gently heat air to dry laundry items. Given the focus on gas as an energy source at the time, the three companies decided to focus on this process first and investigate the potential for reducing energy consumption. Again, status data was collected from key assets in the processes and transferred to a data space; data from the conveyor system leading to the laundry finishing machine (e.g., current number and quality of laundry items), the laundry finishing machine itself (e.g., target and actual temperature, gas consumption), and the laundry shop floor (e.g., temperature and humidity). The data was then monitored and analyzed to gain insight into the common goal. In total, three workshops were held with the participating companies, as well as several bilateral discussions with each of the companies. All workshops and discussions took place between January and September 2022. Table 3 provides a summary of the participants.

4 Results

The case studies served as the basis for the derivation of the design principles (DP) and thus the answer to RQ1. Each design principle was identified in one or more workshops in the context of one or more case studies. Using the conceptual framework, the design principles were derived from the field notes and observation protocols.

Table 3 CS3 participating companies

Company	Employees	Participant
Industrial Laundry	~ 100	Managing Director, Expert for Machine Control Systems
Machine Manufacturer for Textile Machines	~ 25	Managing Director, Head of Construction, Expert for Machine Control System
Manufacturer of Gas Burners	~ 10	Managing Director

They are abstractions from the cases and were evaluated in the final workshops. The identified DPs will be structured to answer RQ2.

4.1 Design Principles for Institutionalizing Data Ecosystems

The case studies show that it is important for all partners in the ecosystem to share a common goal, while at the same time aligning their own company-specific goals. In particular, the common purpose is needed to ensure the coherence of all subsequent governance measures. In the textile cleaning case study (CS3), the cooperative value proposition defined by the partners at the end of the second workshop was as follows "*Create a data space that enables ecosystem partners to improve energy efficiency and machine uptime in the laundry finishing process based on data-driven insights.*" Our experience supports the conclusion that this goal is abstract enough to allow the ecosystem to evolve as intended. It also sets the stage for the formulation of more concrete rules and regulations, all of which must feed into the provision of appropriate inputs to the data space, as well as the provision of the data space itself. The other two case studies supported this by providing similar insights.

DP1: Establish a cooperative value proposition for the actors in the data ecosystem.

In all three case studies, the participating companies considered the preservation of their legal autonomy as an irrevocable prerequisite for entering the ecosystem. This is particularly important for companies when a separate legal entity is established to provide the shared data space on a permanent and binding basis (as was the case in all three cases). It was considered critical that this entity only provide the digital platform infrastructure. The members were strongly opposed to a scenario where the separate legal entity operates independently in the market as a joint venture. CS2 is a telling example: the insurance broker is not only interested in better risk assessment based on shared data to calculate more appropriate risk premiums. It also promotes a reduction in business interruptions at the sawmill, enabling a new type of service for the broker. For this to happen, however, the broker must have full access to the data—but not at the expense of the sawmill's independence, as was made clear in workshops three and four. The data governance framework should preserve the legal autonomy of all partner companies.

DP2: Protect the legal autonomy of the actors in the data ecosystem.

In CS1, partners stated that it was critical to be able to flexibly exit the collaboration at will to avoid lock-in. For the manufacturer of coolant cleaning machines, the ability to bring additional partners into the collaboration was seen as critical to the long-term success of the data ecosystem. Therefore, data governance should address the rules for joining and leaving the collaboration. The ability of the collaboration to scale is important to create and maintain a broad and deep data base for analysis, and this includes the ability to replace partners.

DP3: Provide regulations for the entry and exit of actors in the data ecosystem.

In all three cases, there were initial concerns about the lack of transparency about what the other partners in the ecosystem might do with the data transferred to the data space. For this reason, the initial workshops focused on jointly developing the cooperative value propositions and intended data uses. Transparency about who uses what data in what way and how it benefits them was created through visualization and group discussion. The companies considered status data (e.g., coolant temperature, current temperature in the laundry finisher, etc.) to be less critical than contextual information (e.g., physical location of machines or machine type, etc.). As a result, rules were established that the data space would be used primarily for sharing status data, and other use cases would require separate negotiations.

DP4: Provide rules establishing transparency about the intended use of shared data for the actors in the data ecosystem.

The partners in the three cases argued that the cooperative value propositions can only be realized if all partners make a binding commitment to contribute data of adequate quality. The cases showed that responsibilities for data provision need to be defined quantitatively and qualitatively. Our observations also suggest that in addition to quality, granularity and transfer rate need to be made explicit. Upon closer examination, most partners realized that the time criticality was less than expected. In summary, data governance needs to address the quality, granularity, and transfer rate of shared data.

DP5: Provide regulations that specify data quality, granularity, and transfer rate for shared data in the data ecosystem.

An important question regarding the DP3 regulations is what happens to the data of a partner who leaves the collaboration. Based on the discussions in the workshops, it was determined that the status data that a partner has contributed up to the point of leaving the data ecosystem will remain in the data space. Conversely, contextual information should be immediately deleted or anonymized. However, there are reasons why analytic models, templates for analytic models, benchmarks and results developed or computed with the contributed data can usually remain in the data ecosystem. This DP could be observed in Workshop 3 of CS1 and was repeatedly mentioned in the following workshops.

DP6: Provide regulations that govern the handling of data when an actor leaves the data ecosystem.

In the course of our research project, it became increasingly clear that the step towards a pilot implementation is a relevant challenge. CS1 and CS2 showed that acceptance of the implementation can be increased if the implementation itself is carried out in small steps and cycles as a continuous and PoC process. Participants emphasized that such a process allows an early assessment of whether the value proposition can be realized and what technical and organizational challenges are associated with the later implementation. In addition, the financial risk of implementation is lower in such an environment, and a cyclical approach is helpful for companies because it enables continuous synchronization with parallel digitization initiatives. As mentioned in the description of the case study above, the implementation of the required technical infrastructures was driven in each consortium, initially by the scientists in a prototypical manner, and in the later course of the collaboration in a leading role by a specialized service provider. After initial evaluations by the participating companies, there was a growing willingness to expand the implementation. Accordingly, data governance should provide rules for the continuous development of a proof of concept (PoC). We found that, despite claims to the contrary, the infrastructure required to capture, transfer, and store data of adequate quality is not always available or sufficient. For this reason, the governance frameworks developed in the case studies do not specify the form in which the data is to be collected, while at the same time allowing for at least temporary (semi-)manual entry (e.g. with spreadsheets) in case the automatically collected measurement data does not meet the requirements. For example, in CS1, at first only status data of the shop floor environment of the metalworking company (e.g., temperature and humidity), and of the coolant (e.g., temperature and pH value) could be made available. Later, other smart objects were added, such as coolant tanks (providing fill levels) and, later, coolant concentration measurements. After that, additional contextual information such as visualizations of machine locations, machine types, machine manufacturers, and machine ages were added to the data space. This led to the conclusion that the data ecosystem should be designed to be flexible enough to continuously add new types of data. Only through an iterative approach can acceptance be created for the technical implementation and development of the infrastructure.

DP7: Provide regulations for the continuous development of a PoC in the data ecosystem.

The rules for joint decision making in the context of data sharing became clear in CS1 and 2, especially during the final workshops. To achieve the cooperative value proposition, all partners need to contribute data and resources, so it is important that relevant decisions are made jointly and by majority vote. In CS1 and 2, it was bindingly agreed that fundamental decisions would be made in a general meeting where all members have equal voting rights. Examples of such decisions include responsibility for the implementation and operation of the IS, changes in billing and fee models, or in the underlying software tools and system environments. In terms of data governance, this means that bodies need to be created that allow such decisions to be made. This was particularly evident in CS2. Within the structures created there, individual companies were able to make joint decisions about the integration of additional data sources. Each member had a voice, which ensured trustworthiness for both data sharing and joint development of the data ecosystem.

DP8: Provide regulations ensuring the capability for shared decision making in the data ecosystem.

For the governance structure, it is crucial to clearly define which partner of the data ecosystem takes which role. As the data space is implemented and integrated into day-to-day operations, the need for clearly defined responsibilities becomes paramount. This includes, for example, the maintenance of sensors or data transfer services. A clear assignment of roles is particularly important in the context of liability issues. Roles should be defined and assigned within an independent legal entity of the ecosystem. Roles identified in CS2 (Workshops 3 and 4) include: the data provider contributes status data related to the band saw (e.g. temperature, fault currents); the knowledge provider provides industry-specific know-how when needed to perform specific analyses. The decision on which contextual information and industry-specific expertise to contribute is left to the individual company. While the case studies have emphasized the need to consider the different roles, they are subject to the specifics of each data ecosystem and its value proposition. Established role models from the literature can be used as a starting point, see e.g. Böhm et al. (2010), Yoo et al. (2010) and Baars et al. (2022). Depending on the value proposition and the partners, the level of detail of the specification can vary.

DP9: Provide regulations to assign roles, responsibilities, and liability to actors of the data ecosystem.

4.2 Grouping and Characterization the Design Principles

To answer RQ2, we grouped and characterized the identified DPs based on our conceptual framework, based on Lusch and Nambisan (2015) (see Fig. 1): service ecosystem, service platform, and value co-creation. We see that DP1, DP2, and DP3 support ecosystem formation, DP4, DP5, DP6, and DP7 govern data sharing on the digital platform infrastructure, and DP8, DP9 govern value co-creation activities (see Table 4). Our results suggested another dimension for structuring the design principles, namely a temporal one. Our observations and discussions with the participating companies from the different CS indicated that some of the identified DPs are relatively stable and require only few adjustments—such DPs are referred to as "static elements". Other DPs need to be constantly and quickly adapted to changes, "dynamic elements". We first assigned the DPs individually according to these dimensions and then consolidated the results. DP1, DP2, DP3, DP6, and DP8 were classified as static

DPs, while we consider DP5 and DP9 to be dynamic. DP4 and DP7 combine static and dynamic elements (see Table 4). This distinction is also reflected in the types of legal documents developed.

Table 4 Data governance design principles

#	Data governance design principles	CS	SDL	Static/dynamic
DP1	Establish a cooperative value proposition for the actors in the data ecosystem	CS1, CS2, CS3	Service ecosystem	Static
DP2	Protect the legal autonomy of the actors in the data ecosystem	CS1, CS2, CS3		Static
DP3	Provide regulations for the entry and exit of actors in the data ecosystem	CS1		Static
DP4	Provide rules establishing transparency about the intended use of shared data for the actors in the data ecosystem	CS1, CS2, CS3	Service platform	Static/dynamic
DP5	Provide regulations that govern the handling of data when an actor leaves the data ecosystem	CS1, CS2, CS3		Dynamic
DP6	Provide regulations that govern the handling of data when an actor leaves the data ecosystem	CS1		Static
DP7	Provide regulations for the continuous development of a PoC in the data ecosystem	CS1, CS2		Static/dynamic
DP8	Provide regulations ensuring the capability for shared decision making in the data ecosystem	CS1, CS2	Value co-creation	Static
DP9	Provide regulations to assign roles, responsibilities, and liability to actors of the data ecosystem	CS1, CS2, CS3		Dynamic

5 Discussion

Essential aspects of a governance structure in the context of a data ecosystem have not been adequately addressed in existing work (Weber et al. 2022; Pretzsch et al. 2020; Baars et al. 2021; Gelhaar and Otto 2020). Furthermore, our literature review supports the conclusion that more precise recommendations are still lacking. This paper contributes to this research gap by abstracting insights from three case studies and deriving DPs that guide the design of data governance. By using SDL as a theoretical lens, we were able to place our findings within a larger theoretical construct. In this way, data governance measures contribute to the establishment of a shared institutional logic and thus provide the framework for collaboration in the sense of SDL. Previous work has pointed out that collaboration in data ecosystems is fluid and often not based on fixed structures (Gelhaar and Otto 2020). To address this, this paper provides a specification of DPs that distinguishes between static and dynamic DPs. First initiatives in science and practice have started to work on the selection of adequate legal forms for data ecosystems (Reiberg et al. 2022; Pretzsch et al. 2020; Weber et al. 2022). The static and dynamic design principles identified in this paper support such activities by delineating aspects that need to be considered. A relevant line of further research is a deeper exploration of DPs and their mapping to different legal forms.

6 Conclusion and Limitations

The paper provides a contribution to the service innovation framework in the context of institutionalizing data governance aspects in data ecosystems. This is relevant for both academia and practice. For the scientific community, the paper adds value by identifying nine design principles based on the discussions on data governance in data ecosystems. The identified dynamic and static design principles can be used as a basis for further research to determine which design principles can be mapped to which documents of different legal forms. The added value of our paper for practice is that it provides a basis for companies to decide which governance aspects they should address in a data ecosystem.

The paper has several limitations: First, as an ADR project, the researcher was involved in the observed social system, which carries a risk of bias (Cassell and Symon 2004). Second, the DPs are not free of overlap. Third, as a qualitative study, the proposed DPs and conclusions are of a preliminary nature and would require further rigorous testing—we make no claim to completeness regarding the DPs. Fourthly, the companies in the study are mainly located in southern Germany, which may lead to a geographical bias. The chosen research design does not yet allow us to assess how important individual DPs are for the institutionalization of data ecosystems. Further cases will be initiated to answer this question. In addition, these cases will also help to increase the resilience of the DPs.

Acknowledgements The case studies described in this paper were conducted in the context of the research project "Digitale Datenräume zur Kooperation von KMUs unter Einsatz von KI zur Schaffung von Wettbewerbsvorteilen gegenüber ausländischem Wettbewerb, der auf Datenplattformen setzt", which was funded by the Ministry of Economy, Labor and Tourism Baden-Württemberg.

References

Abraham, R., Schneider, J. & Vom Brocke, J. (2019), Data governance: A conceptual framework, structured review, and research agenda, *in* 'International Journal of Information Management', **49**, pp. 424–438.

Adner, R. (2017), Ecosystem as structure: An actionable construct for strategy, *in* 'Journal of Management', **43**(1), pp. 39–58.

Azkan, C., Möller, F., Meisel, L. & Otto, B. (2020), Service dominant Logic Perspective on Data Ecosystems - a Case Study based Morphology, *in* 'Proceedings 28th European Conference on Information Systems'.

Baars, H., Tank, A., Weber, P., Kemper, H. G., Lasi, H., & Pedell, B. (2021), Cooperative approaches to data sharing and analysis for industrial internet of things ecosystems, *in* 'Applied Sciences', **11**(16), 7547.

Baars, H., Weber, P. & Tank, A. (2022), Institutionalizing Analytic Data Sharing in SME Ecosystems - A role-based Perspective, *in* 'Proceedings 55th Hawaii International Conference on System Sciences'.

Badewitz, W., Kloker, S. & Weinhardt, C. (2020), The Data Provision Game: Researching Revenue Sharing in Collaborative Data Networks, *in* 'Proceedings 22th IEEE Conference on Business Informatics (CBI)'.

Blaschke, M., Riss, U., Haki, K. & Aier, S. (2019), Design principles for digital value co-creation networks: a service-dominant logic perspective, *in* 'Electronic Markets' **29**, pp. 443–472.

Böhm, M., Koleva, G., Leimeister, S., Riedl, C. & Krcmar, H. (2010), Towards a generic value network for cloud computing, *in* 'International workshop on grid economics and business models', Springer, pp. 129–140.

Braud, A., Fromentoux, G., Radier, B. & Le Grand, O. (2021), The road to European digital sovereignty with Gaia-X and IDSA, *in* 'IEEE Network', **35**(2), pp. 4–5.

Cassell, C. & Symon, G. (2004), Essential guide to qualitative methods in organizational research, SAGE.

De Reuver, M., Ofe, H., Agahari, W., Abbas, A. E. & Zuiderwijk, A. (2022), The openness of data platforms: a research agenda, *in* 'Proceedings 1th International Workshop on Data Economy', pp. 34–41.

Evans, R. D., Hooijman, J. J. & van der Veer, J. M. (2020), Advances in cooling and lubrication for high speed machining, *in* 'High Speed Machining', Elsevier, pp. 97–125.

Fassnacht, M., Benz, C., Heinz, D., Leimstoll, J. & Satzger, G. (2023), Barriers to Data Sharing among Private Sector Organizations, *in* 'Proceedings 56th Hawaii International Conference on Systems Sciences'.

Fernandez, R. C., Subramaniam, P. & Franklin, M. J. (2020), Data market platforms: Trading data assets to solve data problems, *in* 'Proceedings of the VLDB Endowment', **13**(12), pp 1933–1947.

Gelhaar, J. & Otto B. (2020), Challenges in the Emergence of Data Ecosystems, *in* 'Proceedings 23th Pacific Asia Conference on Information Systems'.

Hein, A., Scheiber, M., Böhm, M., Weking, J., Rocznik, D. & Krcmar, H. (2018), Towards a Design Framework for Service Platform Ecosystems, *in* 'Proceedings 26th European Conference on Information Systems'.

Kannan, V., Mathew, S. K. & Lehner, F. (2022), Digitally Enabled Shrimp Farming: A Service-Dominant Logic View, *in* 'Proceedings Americas Conference on Information Systems'.

Lehrer, C., Wieneke, A., vom Brocke, J. A. N., Jung, R. & Seidel, S. (2018), How big data analytics enables service innovation: materiality, affordance, and the individualization of service, *in* 'Journal of Management Information Systems', **35**(2), pp. 424–460.

Levy, Y. & Ellis, T. J. (2006), A systems approach to conduct an effective literature review in support of information systems research, *in* 'Informing Science Journal', **9**, pp. 181–213.

Lis, D. & Otto, B. (2021), Towards a taxonomy of ecosystem data governance, *in* 'Proceedings 54th Hawaii International Conference on System Sciences'.

Lusch, R. F. & Nambisan, S. (2015), Service innovation: A service-dominant logic perspective, *in* 'MIS quarterly' **39**(1), pp. 155–176.

Martens, B., de Streel, A., Graef, I., Tombal, T. & Duch-Brown, N. (2020), Business-to-Business data sharing: An economic and legal analysis, JRC Digital Economy Working Paper, No. 2020-05, European Commission, Joint Research Centre (JRC).

Mayring, P. (2014), Qualitative content analysis: theoretical foundation, basic procedures and software solution.

Oliveira, M. I. S. & Lòscio, B. F. (2018), What is a data ecosystem? *in* 'Proceedings 19th International Conference on Digital Government Research: Governance in the Data Age'.

Page, M. J., McKenzie, J. E., Bossuyt, P. M., Boutron, I., Hoffmann, T. C., Mulrow, C. D., Shamseer, L., Tetzlaff, J. M., Akl, E. A., Brennan, S. E., Chou, R., Glanville, J., Grimshaw, J. M., Hróbjartsson, A., Lalu, M. M., Li, T., Loder, E. W., Mayo-Wilson, E., McDonald, S., McGuinness, L. A. & Moher, D. (2021), The PRISMA 2020 statement: an updated guideline for reporting systematic reviews, *in* 'International Journal of Surgery', **88**.

Perscheid, G., Ostern, N. K. & Moormann, J. (2020), Determining Platform Governance. Framework for Classifying Governance Types, *in* 'Proceedings 41th International Conference on Information Systems'.

Porter, M. E. & Heppelmann, J. E. (2014), How smart, connected products are transforming competition, *in* 'Harvard Business Review', **92**(11), pp. 64–88.

Pretzsch, S., Drees, H. & Rittershaus, L. (2020), MOBILITY DATA SPACE. EIN SICHERER DATENRAUM FÜR DIE SOUVERÄNE UND PLATTFORM ÜBER GREIFENDE BEWIRTSCHAFTUNG VON MOBILITÄTSDATEN, https://mobility-dataspace.eu/solutions-features. Accessed: 08.03.2023.

Reiberg, A., Niebel, C. & Kraemer; P. (2022), What is a Data Space?, White Paper.

Scholz, N., Wieland, J. & Schäffer, T. (2022), Towards a Framework for Enterprise & Platform Ecosystem Data Governance, *in* 'Proceedings Americas Conference on Information Systems'.

Sein, M. K., Henfridsson, O., Purao, S., Rossi, M. & Lindgren, R. (2011), Action design research, *in* 'MIS Quarterly', **31**(1), pp. 37–56.

Shipilov, A. & Gawer, A. (2020), Integrating research on interorganizational networks and ecosystems, *in* 'Academy of Management Annals', **14**(1), pp. 92–121.

Susha, I., Janssen, M., & Verhulst, S. (2017), Data collaboratives as a new frontier of cross-sector partnerships in the age of open data: Taxonomy development, *in* 'Proceedings 50th Hawaii International Conference on System Sciences'.

Van den Broek, T. & Fleur van Veenstra A. (2015), Modes of governance in inter-organizational data collaborations, *in* 'Proceedings 23th European Conference on Information Systems'.

Vargo, S. L. & Lusch, R. F. (2004), The four service marketing myths: remnants of a goods-based, manufacturing model, *in* 'Journal of Service Research' **6**(4), pp. 324–335.

Vargo, S. L. & Lusch, Robert F. (2008), Service-dominant logic: continuing the evolution, *in* 'Journal of the Academy of Marketing Science', **36**, pp. 1–10.

Vargo, S. L. & Lusch, R. F. (2016), Institutions and axioms: an extension and update of service-dominant logic, *in* 'Journal of the Academy of Marketing Science', **44**, pp. 5–23.

Vom Brocke, J., Simons, A., Niehaves, B., Niehaves, B., Reimer, K., Plattfaut, R. & Cleven, A. (2009), Reconstructing the giant: On the importance of rigour in documenting the literature search process, *in* 'Proceedings 17th European Conference on Information Systems'.

Weber, P., Hiller, S. & Lasi, H. (2020), Identifying Business Potentials within an IoT Ecosystem – An Explorative Case Study in the Industrial Domain, *in* 'Proceedings Americas Conference on Information Systems'.

Weber, P., Werling, M., Tank, A. & Baars, H. (2022), Institutionalisierung digitaler Ökosysteme in der Rechtsform einer Genossenschaft: Case Study im produzierenden Kontext, *in* 'HMD Praxis der Wirtschaftsinformatik', **59**(5), pp. 1353–1365.

Weill, P. & Ross, J. W. (2004), IT governance: How top performers manage IT decision rights for superior results, Harvard Business Press.

Yin, R. K. (2018), Case study research and applications. Design and methods, **6**, SAGE.

Yoo, Y., Henfridsson, O. & Lyytinen, K. (2010), Research commentary - the new organizing logic of digital innovation: an agenda for information systems research, *in* 'Information Systems Research' **21**(4), pp. 724–735.

Unpacking the Black Box: A Cognitive Process Model of Escalation of Commitment in IS Project Management

Carolin Marx and Falk Uebernickel

Abstract In the plethora of challenges associated with managing Information Systems (IS), deciding when to persist or withdraw from a distressed IS project is of utmost importance. Distressed IS projects are particularly prone to Escalation of Commitment (EoC)—the tendency to persist with failing courses of action. To better understand how the cognitive "black box" behind this tendency unfolds, we uncovered 13 cognitive reasoning patterns and a cognitive process model based on 270 text-based reflections of 56 participants during a sequential decision-making simulation. Cognition differs between the four escalation phases regarding the temporal focus (retrospective, introspective, prospective), the underlying mechanism (starting momentum, path dependency, denial, perceived completion proximity), and the combination of cognitive reasoning patterns. The cognitive process model of EoC helps detangle the complexities of managing IS. Our findings also support IS managers in identifying signs of escalation and selecting the appropriate actions to turn distressed projects around.

Keywords Escalation of Commitment · Process model · Cognition · IS project management

1 Introduction

IS projects play a crucial role in shaping organizations' strategic directions and helping them to gain and sustain a competitive advantage through successful IS management and governance (Baghizadeh et al. 2020). Still, they are observed to

C. Marx (✉) · F. Uebernickel
Hasso Plattner Institute, University of Potsdam, Potsdam, Germany
e-mail: carolin.marx@hpi.de

F. Uebernickel
e-mail: falk.uebernickel@hpi.de

D. Beverungen et al. (eds.), *Transforming the Digitally Sustainable Enterprise*, Lecture Notes in Information Systems and Organisation 76,
https://doi.org/10.1007/978-3-031-80125-9_17

fail at exceptionally high rates, run over budget, and frequently extend past schedules (Keil and Mähring 2010; Doherty et al. 2012). Recognizing and appropriately addressing Escalation of Commitment (EoC)—the tendency to persist with failing courses of action—might determine whether a distressed project can be turned around (Sitaw 1976; Marx and Uebernickel 2022). Distressed IS projects are particularly prone to EoC (Marx and Uebernickel 2022). Thus, increasing the decision quality behind deciding when to persist or withdraw from a distressed IS project by understanding how EoC unfolds over time is of utmost practical relevance.

Also, academic interest regarding EoC has long since spread from psychology to management and IS providing researchers and practitioners with a long and well-established list of antecedent factors, moderators, mediators and consequences of escalating behavior in the context of project distress (Marx and Uebernickel 2022).

However, when looking at existing research, there is a mismatch between the fact that EoC is consistently described as a process that unfolds over time (Staw and Ross 1987; Brockner 1992) and the predominance of factor model research, which might account for the enduring challenge to detect and handle escalation. We, therefore, argue that an understanding of escalation as a process not only brings us closer to its nature but also increases the chances of discovering effective countermeasures. EoC is widely recognized as a lifecycle phenomenon encompassing a beginning, a developmental trajectory over time, and a set of outcomes (Brockner 1992; Montealegre and Keil 2000). Thus, employing a framework that reflects this characterization is imperative for understanding how EoC evolves. Research has started to analyze the process behind EoC. Based on a case study of an IT project, Mähring and Keil (2008), for instance, proposed that EoC is a gradual process characterized by a phase of drifting, a phase of unsuccessful incremental adaptation, and a phase of rationalized continuation.

While unpacking the behavioral stages of the escalation process greatly advances our understanding of how this phenomenon unfolds in practice, the underlying cognitive mechanisms accounting for the behavioral changes still remain a "black box". Theoretical positions on cognition converge on the idea that understanding human behavior necessitates the consideration of mental representations and processes that involve thoughts, beliefs, and emotions (Russell et al. 2020). Hence, applying a cognitive perspective for unpacking the "black box" behind the process of EoC has promising potential to advance the predominantly behavior-centered discourse and contribute to synthesizing theoretical perspectives for explaining escalation. Thus, the following research question is posed: *How does a decision-maker's cognition change during the process of EoC in the context of IS project distress?*

We address this question by identifying a set of cognitive reasoning patterns underlying EoC, from which we develop a cognitive process model of escalation. The findings are based on replicating the most common vignette study setting from behavioral EoC research while adding the measurement of cognition by asking the participants to share their thought processes during the decision-making process.

2 Theoretical Background

2.1 EoC in the Context of IS Project Management

The EoC phenomenon has its roots in the theory that individuals allocate additional resources to a previously chosen but failing course of action, among others, due to personal responsibility (Staw 1976). Distressed IS and IT projects are particularly prone to incurring more resources than initially anticipated due to their explorative nature and uncertain environment, the rapid pace of technological advancement, and their complexity, making it difficult to evaluate progress and predict success (Keil et al. 1994; Baghizadeh et al. 2020). Another factor contributing to the managerial challenges of deciding when to persist with or withdraw from a troubled IS project is the high level of interdependence visible in integrating different systems, technologies, and other projects (Bathallath et al. 2016). Also, the shift from plan-based to agile and product-centered management in IS development unintendedly increases the chances of escalation behavior. Klingebiel and Esser (2020), for instance, revealed how innovation projects at Sony Ericson escalated through a stage-gate process that was meant to minimize initial commitment. On a similar line, evidence shows that self-organized agile teams are even more likely to escalate than individual decision-makers (Whyte 1993). Ultimately, this enduring proneness to EoC in IS project management can lead to a waste of resources, missed opportunities, and a negative impact on the company's competitive advantage.

The potentially negative impact of EoC on an organization's efforts to remain competitive highlights the importance of better understanding how this phenomenon evolves. Staw and Ross (1987) suggested that the factors determining escalation are likely to be differentially important, depending upon the stage of the escalation process. Such determinants include decision-specific factors such as feedback information and decision risk, external factors like market complexity and environmental uncertainty, and individual factors like optimism, risk perception, and personality (Sleesman et al. 2012; Marx and Uebernickel 2022). Brockner (1992) concluded that to explain escalation behavior more completely, several concepts and theoretical perspectives are needed, which most likely differ in their explanatory power depending on the stage of escalation. One major cognitive concept accounting for escalation behavior is the sunk cost effect—the tendency to continue an endeavor once an investment in money, effort, or time has been made even though those "sunk" costs should be disregarded (Arkes and Blumer 1985). Another key concept touching upon the cognition behind escalation is self-justification. The Self-Justification Theory posits that decision-makers continue to commit resources to self-justify an earlier decision and minimize cognitive dissonance (Staw 1976; Brockner 1992). Additional theories which can explain EoC are the prospect theory (Tversky and Kahneman 1981) highlighting the role of risk-seeking as a result of loss framing, expectancy theory (Vroom 1964) focusing on expectations and the perceived proximity of reaching a goal, and the decision dilemma theory (Bowen 1987) emphasizing economic considerations, curiosity, or experimentation over the need to self-justify.

2.2 Cognition

The term cognition refers to the mental processes that involve "using, modifying, enacting, recalling, storing, sensing, and transforming knowledge in a dynamic and recursive manner" (Brymer et al. 2011, p. 121). In contrast to behaviorism and related perspectives, which contend that mental states are merely unobservable intervening variables, the cognitive perspective posits that attitudes, motivations, and other mental states can be regarded as constructs that exist in the mind (Sternberg and Ben-Zeev 2001). A critical assumption of the cognitive perspective is that the environment is enacted and represented through cognitions. During cognitive processes, decision-makers' personal beliefs and mental models incorporate knowledge and an understanding of current events and predictions of future developments (Russell et al. 2020).

3 Methodology

Our main interest lies in the changes in the cognition of individual decision-makers during escalation situations, for which replicating the EoC effect is necessary but assumes a secondary role. Consequently, a laboratory environment with decision-making simulations was chosen over real-world settings. This controlled setting allows for exploration regarding changes in cognitive patterns while mitigating potential confounding factors associated with projects or contexts, enhancing replicability, and facilitating the analysis of multiple decisions and decision-makers within the same controlled setting. Moreover, the simulated study environment promotes a "safe space" for genuine introspection. 73 Master- and MBA-level business students with a minimum of 2 years working experience in a related field (mean age = 26 years; mean professional experience = 3.5 years; 61% female) were presented with a series of decision-making scenarios and were asked to make decisions based on the information provided. On average, each participant spent 37 min on the computer-based simulation, which included preparation and debriefing.

The participants were assigned the role of a senior manager responsible for deciding on the continuation of an IS development project in the aviation industry. The decision-making vignettes and feedback prompts were adopted from the "blank radar plane" case (Arkes and Blumer 1985). The participants received negative feedback multiple times, such as a competitor launching a further developed system or significant project delays due to technical difficulties. In five sequential decisions, participants had to decide whether to continue the project and, if so, how much money to invest within a predefined budget range. For each decision, the participants were asked to explain in written form (minimum of 30 words), as detailed as possible, the reasoning and thought processes behind their decision to continue with the troubled project (see Moser et al. 2013 for a similar procedure). To analyze changes in cognition during the escalation scenario, we disregarded 16 participants who did not show any sign of EoC. The remaining 57 participants exceeded the given budget and chose at least once to invest further in the troubled project yielding a total of 170 decisions to persist.

As a foundation for developing the process model, we first examined the text data of the 170 decisions with regard to the reasoning behind persisting using open coding. We then used axial coding to draw connections between the codes and to generate categories. We used selective coding as a third step, focusing on categories with the most supportive data. After iterations between the authors, 13 cognitive sub-patterns (codes) and six cognitive patterns (categories) remained. As part of the selective coding procedure, we identified the temporal mode of cognition as an overarching category and core narrative that connects the patterns and the subpatterns. In contrast to factor models, process models focus on the sequences of events and the mechanisms and reasons for the evolution of these processes (Langley 1999; Langley et al. 2013). We chose the lifecycle archetype for the process model as it is most consistent with the nature of the EoC phenomenon (Mähring and Keil 2008). Following the punctuated equilibrium model (Tushman and Romanelli 1985), we included periods of stability (cognitive phases) and events (cognitive phase-changing triggers) in the process model. The identification and delineation of phases were determined by detecting the periods within which the cognitive reasoning patterns identified in the previous step of behaviors were more uniform than across phases and by the timeline of negative feedback prompts and key decisions given by the simulation (Langley et al. 2013). By iterating between the coding of the cognitive reasoning patterns and the process model development, we further identified for each phase the driving mechanism that sustained the current state. We then identified cognitive events that served as phase-changing triggers, initiating a shift in the importance and combination of cognitive reasoning patterns.

4 Results

4.1 *Cognitive Reasoning Patterns*

Based on 267 explanations given by the participants for 170 decisions to persist, we identified 13 distinct sub-patterns, which can be further summarized in six overarching cognitive reasoning patterns during EoC to a failing project. We mapped those clusters based on their temporal focus into retrospective, prospective, and introspective cognition. The six cognitive reasoning patterns underlying escalating behavior are *past investments, past performance, problem assessment, decision assessment, trust and belief in the project and people*, and *anticipated outcomes* (Fig. 1).

Retrospective Cognition is characterized by a temporal focus on the past. We identified reasoning with past investments, including past monetary and past time investment, and past project and decision success as key reasoning patterns associated with retrospective cognition.

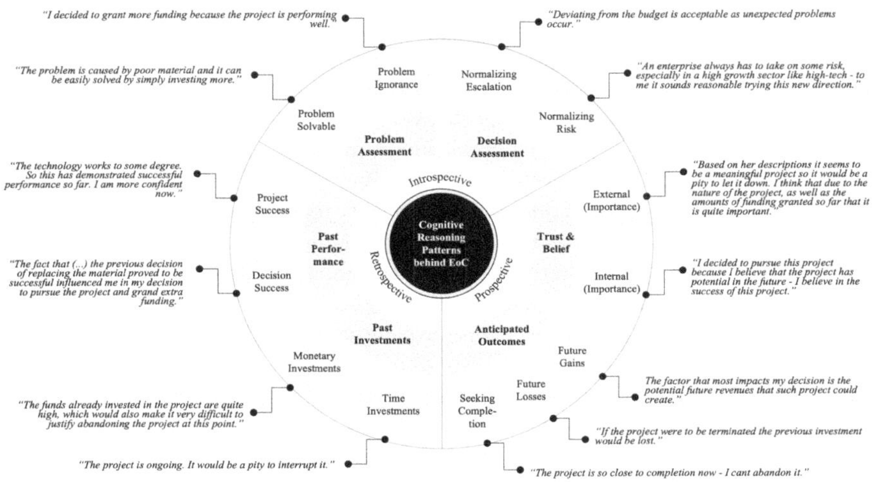

Fig. 1 Cognitive reasoning patterns behind EoC

Past Investments: This cognitive pattern can be divided into past monetary and past time investments. People frequently justify their escalating behavior with the amount of money or time already invested in the current path, making this pattern one of the most mentioned reasons for persisting. Participants described feeling locked in the current path of action due to past monetary investments with statements like "for all the previous amounts invested in this project, it would be disappointing to come to the end of the project". Similarly focused on the existing monetary investments made in the past, decision-makers note the increasing difficulty of changing courses: "The funds already invested in the project are quite high, which would also make it very difficult to justify abandoning the project at this point". Besides monetary investments, time is mentioned as a resource invested in the past that impacts the current decision: "The project is ongoing. It would be a pity to interrupt it". While sunk costs should be disregarded, most participants relied on past investments of time and money when deciding to continue, as this cluster is the most frequent reasoning overall.

Past Performance: Also categorized as retrospective cognition, we identified a stream of argumentation that focused on the project's past success even though the feedback about the project performance was negative in all cases. Decision-makers directly point out apparent past project success and use this to justify not deviating from their previous decisions: "First successes are visible. So this made me invest extra money even though our budget is exceeded." Even when the project feedback clearly stated severe problems regarding the project performance, decision-makers evaluated the current state as successful and gained confidence in their decision to continue investing in the failing project: "The technology works to some degree. So this has demonstrated successful performance so far. I am more confident now." Within the same cluster on past success, we found decision-makers justifying additional investments with the previous success of their own decisions: The fact that (...) the previous decision of replacing the material proved to be successful influenced me in my decision to pursue the project and grand extra funding.

Introspective Cognition is characterized by a temporal focus on the present and the self. We identified cognitive processes related to assessing the problem, such as denial and minimization, as well as normalizing escalation and risk as part of assessing the decision as key introspective cognitive patterns during project escalation.

Problem Assessment: While utilizing previous project success or invested resources signals retrospective cognition, arguments regarding assessing the problem and the reactive focus more on the present state and internal factors. Biased problem assessment mainly manifests in two ways: Either the problem is being denied, and the project is falsely interpreted as running smoothly despite objectively negative feedback, or the problem is acknowledged but downplayed in its severeness and overstated in its solvability. Regarding the former, participants escalated because their assessment of the current situation was erroneous. "I feel excited about the project and I am looking forward to the new product" is an excellent example of how objectively negative project performance is not only being ignored but also transfigured to the contrary. The perception that the project is running smoothly is widespread among decision-makers, especially in later phases of the decision sequences: "Now the project seems well on its way. I decided to grant more funding because the project is performing well". When looking at the second manifestation of faulty problem assessment—downplaying the problem—decision-makers have argued that "adding the software to take care of the additional problem should be a minor problem". Other decision-makers gave similar insights into their cognitive reasoning stating that "the problem seems to be solvable with additional investments".

Decision Assessment: Similar to potentially faulty assessments of the current project performance and the interpretation of the severity and solvability of the problems, the category decision assessment is based on a misjudgment but targeted at the decision that is being made, not the problem. In this case, decision-makers normalize exceeding budget and time or taking unreasonable risks by further investing. The costs of the decision to continue with the troubled projects are thereby understated. As one of the participants put it: "It often takes a little more money than expected because unforeseen events can happen. (...) The project seems very complex. Therefore, it's normal that during the process of developing the technology needed, there will be a few issues that will require more funding than initially required". Also, taking more risk with the decision to continue investing is assessed as being ordinary or necessary: "An enterprise always has to take on some risk, especially in a high growth sector like high-tech - to me it sounds reasonable trying this new direction".

Prospective Cognition is characterized by a temporal focus on the future. We identified cognitive processes related to internally and externally created trust and belief in the project and other people, as well as the anticipation of future outcomes, including anticipated future losses and gains as key prospective cognitive patterns.

Trust and Belief: This category of cognitive clusters associated with reasoning during escalating behavior is focused on future events, predictions, and anticipation. Several participants associated their approval of more funding for the failing project with its importance and the general belief and trust in future success. We identified two types of attributed importance within this cluster: Externally and internally created importance. The former refers to external indicators of importance, like the range of possible funding amounts, the complexity of the project, or the perceptions of others. Participants, for instance, stated that "The Vice President seemed confident about the development. (…) Based on [her] descriptions, it seems to be a meaningful project, so it would be a pity to let it down. Also, I think that due to the nature of the project, as well as the amounts of funding granted so far that it is quite important". This externally created perception of project importance and the general belief in the project is also related to the trust decision-makers have in other stakeholders associated with the project: "I believe in the engineer. (…) Also, I am trusting my employees to turn this around". Internally created perceptions of project importance refer to the belief people have in the project and its success. This subjectively attributed, performance-independent value is used to justify a continuation of the investment: "I decided to pursue this project because I believe that the project has potential in the future".

Anticipated Outcomes: The second pattern related to future-oriented cognition is the anticipation of outcomes. Within this cluster, we identified three types of reasoning: Continuing to invest in the failing project to maximize future gains, to minimize future losses, and to reach completion. While focusing on potential future gains and goal completion is related to anticipated positive emotions, hope, and optimism, avoiding future losses is fear-based and more pessimistic. Hope-based anticipation of future gains included statements like "I am still hoping the project will be successful" and "Once the product is on the market, we will be able to compete and gain a lot". Here, anticipated joy, hope, and picturing the potential future gains motivated the decision-makers to keep investing despite negative performance feedback. The foundation for this type of reasoning is optimism and overly focusing on benefits while neglecting the possibility of costs and risks associated with the decision to continue. On the other hand, anticipated regret and fear of losing resources by not continuing funding is reflected in statements like: "It is worth to continue also with all the problems - otherwise there will be a total loss of all the investments", and "The additional investment result to be the best option to avoid a complete waste of the already invested 12 million". In contrast to anticipated joy out of future gains, the foundation for this type of reasoning is anticipated regret, fear, and the urge to avoid future losses. The third type of outcome anticipation relates to striving for completion. As one participant put it: "The project is so close to completion now - I can't abandon it". Seeking completion and the anticipated pleasure it will bring makes it more difficult for the decision-makers to abandon the failing project: "It will be very difficult to market the product, but it must be finished". It should be noted that while ambiguity concerning the actual completion rate of the project was

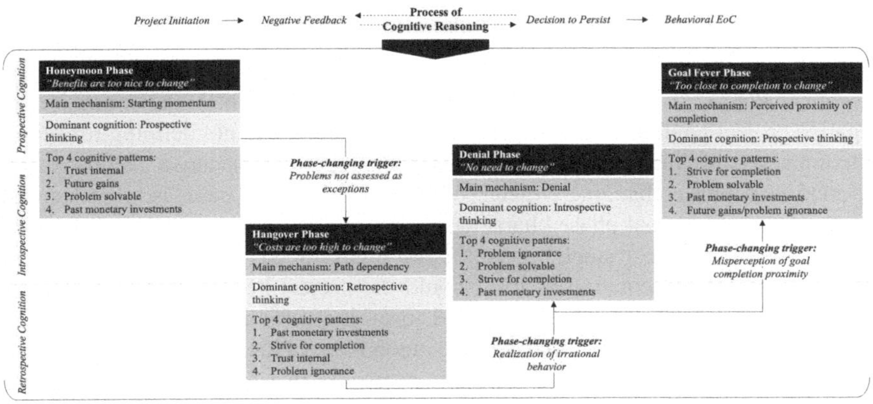

Fig. 2 Cognitive process model of EoC

intentional, most participants interpreted the project completion as being in very close reach after the second decision round and used this as a key foundation of their reasoning: "Only one small step seems to be missing to get the project ready without errors. (…) I don't want to abandon now that we are almost there".

4.2 *Cognitive Process Model*

We developed a process model of cognition (Fig. 2) that shows different reasoning patterns for different phases of the process and reveals distinct phase-changing triggers.

Honeymoon Phase ("Benefits are too nice to change"): The "Honeymoon Phase" is characterized by optimism and a high level of intrinsic belief about the promising potential of the project driven by the recency of just having started the course of action. Hence, one of the main mechanisms fostering escalation behavior in this phase is starting momentum—"the energy associated with persisting with or extending the current trajectory" (Jansen 2004, p. 277). The most dominant cognitive cluster underlying this phase is *internal trust and belief*—the internally created perceptions of project importance, like people's general belief in the project and its success. Also the second most crucial cognitive sub-cluster in this phase—*the prospect of future gains*—belongs to the category of anticipated outcomes and signifies prospective cognition. This focus on potential future benefits stemming from generally believing in the project overshadows potential costs and makes it appear rational to the decision-maker to keep investing more budget and time. Hence, the force or energy that propels the endeavor forward at the beginning leads to overly optimistic assessments of future project developments and the solvability of the problems arising. During the Honeymoon Phase, problems are seen as exceptions on an overall successful and promising trajectory with no or only minor effects on future gains. The reasoning is further driven by general, unspecific trust, enthusiasm, and positive emotions.

Hangover Phase ("Costs are too high to change"): While in the Honeymoon Phase, negative project feedback was interpreted as exceptional and not defining for future outcomes, a shift in this assessment based on repetitive negative feedback can function as a phase-changing trigger. What follows, in this case, is what we call the *Hangover Phase*—a phase characterized by retrospective cognition. Decision-makers find themselves "stuck" given the resources already invested in the project and the resulting anticipation of loss should the project be abandoned. The cost-benefit assessment is accordingly skewed towards overemphasizing the potential abandonment costs compared to the Honeymoon Phase. Hence, the dominant mechanism is path dependence, which refers to a process in which a decision-maker's range of available options is gradually reduced over time and eventually becomes locked in (Schreyögg et al. 2011). The central idea of path dependence is that positive feedback on past decisions encourages similar decisions. While previous positive decision feedback might seem counterintuitive in the given context, path dependence can still occur as decision-makers assess the problems in the project performance as not severe or even nonexistent in this phase: Problem ignorance is among the top 4 cognitive clusters in the Hangover Phase. Additionally to becoming locked in through past investments and a misjudgment of the problem, the Hangover Phase can be characterized by partially realizing bad decision-making. Decision-makers start to distance themselves from the project, indicated by first doubts and a general shift towards more rational and external-focused arguments.

Denial Phase ("No need to change"): Following the Hangover Phase, the escalation process transitions into a *Phase of Denial*, triggered by the partial realization of irrational behavior. Denying that the project is not running ideally at this stage or understating the problem's severeness and overstating its solvability—the cognitive subclusters associated with problem assessment—are representative of the Denial Phase and indicate a shift from retrospective to introspective thinking. Escalating behavior is driven by a mismatch of the decision-maker's reaction to the partial realization of irrationality triggering this phase: The unpleasant realization of the project going sideways reaches a point where overstating potential costs would not justify continuing anymore. However, the reaction to this shift in decision awareness is not behavior change but denial and the minimization of the troubled situation. As a result, decision confidence increases, and priorly rising doubts diminish.

Goal Fever Phase ("Too close to completion to change"): Decision-makers escalating their commitment find themselves in a Phase of Denial until project completion or any other overarching goal is assessed to be in close reach. When this tipping point has been reached, the Phase of Denial transitions into what we call the *Goal Fever Phase*. A strong strive for completion characterizes cognition in this phase that overshadows potential arguments for changing the course of action. Hence, introspective cognition shifts towards prospective cognition, focusing on future-oriented thinking, anticipation, and forecasting. While, compared to the Denial Phase, problem awareness increases and problems are acknowledged, they are still misjudged as solvable or not severe. This focus on the solvability of specific problems differs from the first prospective phase (Honeymoon Phase), where the general belief in the project and a generic positive future assessment dominated thinking patterns. Further, in the Goal Fever Phase, emotions play a more crucial role than in the previous phases: Regret and negative emotions arise, which is related to the partial realization of previous decision mistakes. However, this realization does not translate into action, as decision-makers feel unable to stop given the proximity of potential completion. Contributing to the strength of the goal completion effect dominating this phase is social pressure and the perception that not completing or changing the course is seen as giving up.

5 Discussion

Our findings show that decision-makers use different cognitive reasoning patterns to justify escalating behavior. Those reasoning patterns change over time during the process of escalation, indicating a typical sequence of four different cognitive phases: Honeymoon, Hangover, Denial, and Goal Fever Phase. Decision-makers' cognition differs between those phases with regards to its temporal focus (retrospective, introspective, or prospective thinking), its dominant mechanisms (starting momentum, path dependency, denial, or perceived proximity of completion), and with regards to which combination of cognitive reasoning patterns dominates (Fig. 1). The transitioning between phases is triggered by changes in the problem assessment, the degree of realizing irrational behavior, and the misperception of the goal proximity.

The cognitive reasoning patterns identified in this study correspond to and extend existing academic knowledge about the mechanisms underlying escalation behavior. For instance, the reasoning pattern *problem assessment* can be related to Staw and Ross (1987), who suggested that decision-makers are more likely to escalate when they perceive problems as temporary and easily solvable. Minimizing or denying the problem as part of this cognitive reasoning cluster can further be related to the decision-dilemma theory (Bowen 1987), for example, applied by Priandi et al. (2020) in the context of EoC as a potential force for good. Another example is the cognitive reasoning pattern associated with considering past monetary and time investments during the decision-making process—*past investments*. This pattern is in line with the sunk cost effect (Arkes and Blumer 1985). Along the same lines, the cognitive pattern of *anticipated outcomes* can be linked to well-established psychological concepts: What we observed mainly in the Goal Fever Phase, where people assumed close project completion, can be related to the planning fallacy—the tendency to underestimate the time, costs, and risks of future actions and at the same time overestimate the benefits of the same actions—and the general tendency to strive for the positive feeling of completing something (Kahneman and Tversky 1979; Lovallo and Kahneman 2003). Within the same cognitive reasoning cluster, Kahneman and

Tversky's (1979) prospect theory, including the aversion of losses compared to seeking equivalent gains, can be linked to the cognitive reasoning pattern of *future losses*. Here, the anticipation of future losses and the strive to avoid these losses drives escalation in phases of prospective cognition. A last example is the Hangover Phase, characterized by doubts, first signs of regret, and decreasing decision confidence. This description also matches the indicators for cognitive dissonance—the underlying psychological tension and state of discomfort that has been used to explain EoC (Pepitone and Festinger 1959; Brockner 1992).

Our cognitive process model builds on and advances existing process research (e.g., Mähring and Keil 2008) by adding a cognitive perspective. We could further validate elements of Mähring and Keil's (2008) phase of unsuccessful incremental adaptation, where problems are assessed as easily solvable without changing the course and their phase of rationalized continuation, which corresponds to parts of the Hangover Phase. Additionally, we can derive four general contributions bridging the academic discourses on EoC and IS project management: Firstly, our results confirm that for people escalating their commitment, further investing in the troubled project seems rational. This view aligns with Drummond's (1996) observation that discrete individual decisions may have underlying rationality, while the irrational escalation lies in the cumulative effect of those decisions over time. It further supports Mähring and Keil's (2008) argument that the escalation process is not based on a failure to respond to problems but on a mismatch between problem and response. Conventional wisdom favors rationality over intuition to increase decision quality. On the other hand, and in line with cognitive dissonance theory, there exists evidence that rational, not intuitive thinking can increase escalation behavior (Wong et al. 2008). Our findings add to that latter view, as even when consciously reflecting on the decision, decision-makers continued to escalate during the simulation. Secondly, our findings show that not one cognitive factor accounts for escalation behavior, but multiple patterns, which co-occur, can interact and differ in their importance and intensity depending on the escalation phase. Finding evidence for a whole plethora of cognitive mechanisms within the same escalation situation can be seen as support for Brockner's (1992) argument that self-justification theory can only partially explain escalation behavior and needs to be complimented by multiple theoretical perspectives. Our findings add to this theoretical progress by showing that the underlying cognitive mechanisms are a combination of retro-, intro-, and prospective thinking, all linked to different theoretical explanations and all differing in their temporal importance during the different stages of escalation. Thirdly, we saw that EoC does not necessarily mean being completely unaware of irrational tendencies and potentially harming the decision quality. While not visible when looking at behavior, cognition during escalation is also influenced by partial realization, doubts, and regret. Hence, we call for a more complex view of EoC that accounts for the potential of "subjective rationality" related to the explanations given by decision-dilemma theory. And fourthly, while we were primarily interested in decision-makers' cognition during project escalation, our findings also point toward the role of emotions in understanding EoC. When looking at prospective thinking, we found that emotions like fear, hope, and anticipated joy and regret play a crucial role during cognitive processes leading to further escalation. This aligns with research on the interaction of emotion and cognition during decision-making and its reciprocal impact on attitudes and behavior (Healey and Hodgkinson 2017).

For managing IS projects under distress, our findings underline the importance of paying attention to early signs of escalation, especially when using agile project management methods. This might be particularly challenging but also most promising regarding the potential to de-escalate during the initial Honeymoon Phase, which kicks off the process of "getting stuck in the mud". Warning signs could be overly optimistic forecasts and misplaced enthusiasm downplaying the potential risks associated with continuing the course of action during project update meetings. In general, creating awareness for the potential risks of EoC during IS project management, for the strength of the cognitive mechanisms underlying escalation behavior, and for the fact that the reasons for escalating commitment change during the process of escalation is a good starting point to turn distressed IS projects around.

6 Conclusion

This study aimed to understand how cognition changes during the process of EoC in the context of IS project distress. To reach this goal, we identified 13 cognitive reasoning patterns underlying escalation behavior grouped into six categories and three cognition modes. We further provided a cognitive process model of escalation, which includes four phases with distinct patterns of cognitive reasoning and phase-changing triggers. Our main academic contribution lies in breaking down the cognitive reasoning patterns that allow for a better understanding of the underlying belief structures and thought processes behind the behavioral dimension of escalation. Opening up the cognitive "black box" and further breaking down the escalation process into different phases provides a more nuanced understanding of how decision-makers get "stuck in the mud" and how cognitive reasoning changes during the process of escalation. While the hypothetical decision simulation using students could be criticized for lacking external validity, for instance as real-life alternatives like changing the project team were not available, our approach allowed for a more controlled setting, increased replicability, and enabled the analysis of multiple decisions and decision-makers simultaneously. From a project management perspective, EoC is highly relevant in transforming processes, managing IT and IS projects, managerial decision-making, and strategy formulation. Hence, unpacking the cognition behind that phenomenon helps to distinguish between healthy, entrepreneurial persistence and irrational EoC that potentially harms the entire organization. The cognitive reasoning patterns and the process model can help IT and IS managers identify the current escalation phase and choose the appropriate countermeasures that increase decision quality and help turn distressed projects around.

References

Arkes, H.R. and Blumer, C. (1985) 'The psychology of sunk cost', *Organizational Behavior and Human Decision Processes*, 35(1), pp. 124–140.

Baghizadeh, Z., Cecez-Kecmanovic, D. and Schlagwein, D. (2020) 'Review and critique of the information systems development project failure literature: An argument for exploring information systems development project distress', *Journal of Information Technology Impact*, 35(2), pp. 123–142.

Bathallath, S., Smedberg, Å. and Kjellin, H. (2016) 'Managing project interdependencies in IT/IS project portfolios: a review of managerial issues', *International Journal of Information Systems and Project Management*, 4(1), pp. 67–82.

Bowen, M.G. (1987) 'The Escalation Phenomenon Reconsidered: Decision Dilemmas or Decision Errors?', *The Academy of Management Review*, 12(1), pp. 52–66.

Brockner, J. (1992) 'The Escalation of Commitment to a Failing Course of Action: Toward Theoretical Progress', *The Academy of Management Review*, 17(1), pp. 39–61.

Brymer, R.A., Hitt, M.A. and Schijven, M. (2011) 'Cognition and human capital: the dynamic interrelationship between knowledge and behavior'. Oxford University Press.

Doherty, N.F., Ashurst, C. and Peppard, J. (2012) 'Factors affecting the successful realisation of benefits from systems development projects: Findings from three case studies', *Journal of Information Technology*, 27(1), pp. 1–16.

Drummond, H. (1996) *Escalation in Decision-Making: The Tragedy of Taurus*. Oxford University Press.

Healey, M.P. and Hodgkinson, G.P. (2017) 'Making Strategy Hot', *California Management Review*, 59(3), pp. 109–134.

Jansen, K.J. (2004) 'From Persistence to Pursuit: A Longitudinal Examination of Momentum During the Early Stages of Strategic Change', *Organization Science*, 15(3), pp. 276–294.

Kahneman, D. and Tversky, A. (1979) 'Prospect theory: An analysis of decision under risk', *Econometrica: Journal of the Econometric Society*, 47(2), p. 263.

Keil, M. and Mähring, M. (2010) 'Is Your Project Turning into a Black Hole?', *California Management Review*, 53(1), pp. 6–31.

Keil, M. *et al.* (1994) 'Understanding Runaway Information Technology Projects: Results from an International Research Program Based on Escalation Theory', *Journal of Management Information Systems*, 11(3), pp. 65–85.

Klingebiel, R. and Esser, P. (2020) 'Stage-gate escalation', *Strategy Science*, 5(4), pp. 311–329.

Langley, A. (1999) 'Strategies for Theorizing from Process Data', *The Academy of Management Review*, 24(4), pp. 691–710.

Langley, A. *et al.* (2013) 'Process Studies of Change in Organization and Management: Unveiling Temporality, Activity, and Flow', *Academy of Management Journal*, 56(1), pp. 1–13.

Lovallo, D. and Kahneman, D. (2003) 'Delusions of success', *Harvard Business Review*, 81(7), pp. 56–63.

Mähring, M. and Keil, M. (2008) 'Information technology project escalation: A process model', *Decision Sciences*, 39(2), pp. 239–272.

Marx, C. and Uebernickel, F. (2022) 'How to Turn Around: Escalation of Commitment in the Context of ISD Project Distress', *International Conference on Information Systems (ICIS) 2022 Proceedings*.

Montealegre, R. and Keil, M. (2000) 'De-Escalating Information Technology Projects: Lessons from the Denver International Airport', *The MIS Quarterly*, 24(3), pp. 417–447.

Moser, K., Wolff, H.-G. and Kraft, A. (2013) 'The de-escalation of commitment: Predecisional accountability and cognitive processes', *Journal of Applied Social Psychology*, 43(2), pp. 363–376.

Pepitone, A. and Festinger, L. (1959) 'A Theory of Cognitive Dissonance', *The American Journal of Psychology*, 72(1), p. 153.

Priandi, M., Fernandez, W. and Sandeep, M.S. (2020) ''escalation of commitment' as a force for good? Evidence from an Indonesian digital government project', *Hawaiian International Conference on System Sciences (HICSS) 2020 Proceedings.*

Russell, K. *et al.* (2020) 'A cognitive model of digital transformation and IS decision making', *Journal of Decision Systems*, pp. 1–18.

Schreyögg, G., Sydow, J. and Holtmann, P. (2011) 'How history matters in organisations: The case of path dependence', *Management & Organizational History*, 6(1), pp. 81–100.

Sleesman, D.J. *et al.* (2012) 'Cleaning up the big muddy: A meta-analytic review of the determinants of escalation of commitment', *Academy of Management Journal*, 55(3), pp. 541–562.

Staw, B.M. (1976) 'Knee-deep in the Big Muddy: A study of escalating commitment to a chosen course of action', *Organizational behavior and human performance*, 16(1), pp. 27–44.

Staw, B.M. and Ross, J. (1987) 'Behavior in escalation situations: Antecedents, prototypes, and solutions', *Research in Organizational Behavior*.

Sternberg, R.J. and Ben-Zeev, T. (2001) *Complex cognition: The psychology of human thought*. Oxford University Press.

Tushman, M.L. and Romanelli, E. (1985) 'Organizational evolution: A metamorphosis model of convergence and reorientation', *Research in Organizational Behavior*, 7, pp. 171–222.

Tversky, A. and Kahneman, D. (1981) 'The framing of decisions and the psychology of choice', Science, 211(4481), pp. 453–458.

Vroom, V. (1964) 'Work and motivation', *New York: Wiley*.

Whyte G. (1993) 'Escalating commitment in individual and group decision making: A prospect theory approach', *Organizational Behavior and Human Decision Processes*, 54(3), pp.430–455.

Wong, K.F.E., Kwong, J.Y.Y. and Ng, C.K. (2008) 'When thinking rationally increases biases: The role of rational thinking style in escalation of commitment', *Applied Psychology*, 57(2), pp. 246–271.

Digital Industry and Retailing

Designing In-Store Navigation Systems in Physical Retail

Bijan Khosrawi-Rad, Lea Sophie Fischer, Carolin Kaiser, and Susanne Robra-Bissantz

Abstract Physical retail faces the challenge of remaining attractive to customers in the age of e-commerce. In-store navigation systems are one way to mitigate this issue. These software systems allow customers to be navigated through the retail store. We derive design requirements (DRs) for in-store navigation systems based on eight interviews with customers and employees of furniture stores. We illustrate the implementation of the DRs in a conceptual prototype designed with the platform "Hololink." Initial evaluation results (n = 20) show that customers perceive such a solution for physical retail as mainly positive. We contribute to research and practice by showing how to design in-store navigation systems.

Keywords In-store navigation · Augmented reality · Retail · Requirement

1 Introduction

Due to the rise of e-commerce, physical retail got under pressure (Hagberg et al. 2016; Northington et al. 2021). Retailers get into economically difficult situations. Sales move into cyberspace, and shops in cities are closing down or moving to the outside areas of the cities (Deckert and Wohllebe 2021). Customers get used to the convenience of online shopping; thus, they also expect hassle-free shopping

---

B. Khosrawi-Rad (✉) · L. S. Fischer · S. Robra-Bissantz
Institut für Wirtschaftsinformatik, TU Braunschweig, Braunschweig, Germany
e-mail: b.khosrawi-rad@tu-braunschweig.de

L. S. Fischer
e-mail: lea.fischer@tu-braunschweig.de

S. Robra-Bissantz
e-mail: s.robra-bissantz@tu-braunschweig.de

C. Kaiser
Nürnberg Institut für Marktentscheidungen e.V., Nürnberg, Germany
e-mail: carolin.kaiser@nim.org

D. Beverungen et al. (eds.), *Transforming the Digitally Sustainable Enterprise*, Lecture Notes in Information Systems and Organisation 76,
https://doi.org/10.1007/978-3-031-80125-9_18

and rich user experiences in physical retail (Barann et al. 2022; Betzing et al. 2019). Studies show that customers are frustrated when they cannot find products in the store or service personnel are unavailable to help them (Alexander and Alvarado 2017; Riegger et al. 2021). In-store navigation is a solution to counteract this frustration and to meet the customer expectation of hassle-free shopping to improve customer experience. Such systems enable customers to quickly find the products they are searching for by showing the customer directions within the store (Deckert and Wohllebe 2021). Betzing et al. (2019) mirrored different e-services for physical retail and investigated customers' likelihood of using them. The study shows that 80% of customers are likely to use in-store navigation systems in physical retail (Betzing et al. 2019). For future research, they suggest building upon the discovered insights by designing pilots of those promising technologies. We pick up on this research gap and aim to identify factors that promote the use of an in-store navigation system and to capture these as initial design requirements (DRs) that aim to guide future developments of in-store navigation systems. Since in-store navigation offers added value, especially in large stores where products are not easy to find, we use furniture retail as a use case. We address the following **research question (RQ)**: *How can an indoor navigation system for furniture retail be designed to foster user experience and customer satisfaction?* We focus on user experience (UX) because it is a critical success factor for accepting this novel technology (Robier 2015). We assess customer satisfaction because this variable is crucial for retailers, affecting customers' retention and loyalty toward a store (Inman and Nikolova 2017). In this research-in-progress, we showcase the application of our DRs in a conceptual prototype and provide the first results of its evaluation.

2 Research Background and Related Work

In-store navigation systems are digital software products applied in (large) retail stores aiming to simplify locating specific departments or items, which may reduce customers' dissatisfaction with being unable to find what they are searching for (Merkle 2020). Studies show that the likelihood of customers using search and navigation systems, including in-store navigation, product exploration, and product recommendation, is high (Betzing et al. 2019; Márquez and Ziegler 2023; Merkle 2020). In-store navigation systems often rely on augmented reality (AR) to offer a live view of additional information or virtual objects in physical environments (Merkle 2020; Tan et al. 2022; Xue et al. 2023). They help to visualize non-existent, virtual objects in the physical world, e.g., via cameras. This enables a live view of the real environment complemented with movement-responsive virtual elements (Tan et al. 2022). In-store navigation systems with AR can be used from tablets, smartphones, head-up displays, or AR-Glasses (Cesinger et al. 2020; Tan et al. 2022). While the first commercial in-store navigation solutions exist, they are not widely implemented. According to a representative study by Linzbach et al. (2019), only 32% of German consumers know such systems and only 10% have ever used them.

Despite the outlined potentials, prescriptive design knowledge of in-store navigation systems is lacking (Betzing et al. 2019). A recent review shows that in-store applications are rarely considered in the literature on AR in retail and do not focus on navigation but on other features like product presentation (Riar et al. 2021). Some studies deal with the technical requirements of in-store navigation systems (e.g., Cruz et al. 2019; Molina et al. 2018), but there are yet no design science research (DSR) studies that propose DRs while highlighting users' and retailers' needs. We take a first step toward reducing this research gap.

3 Methodology

We follow DSR by first deriving DRs (as a level 2 artifact) and showing how they can be conceptually implemented (as a level 1 artifact) (Gregor and Hevner 2013). We chose first to derive DRs rather than design principles (prescriptive rules for a proposed design) because DRs are often considered the starting point of DSR because they reflect the target audience's needs and issues (e.g., Möller et al. 2020). We aim to contribute to solving a practical problem (challenges in retail) and present an innovative solution (Hevner 2007). We conducted guided interviews with customers and retailers lasting 30–59 min (Stier 2013). We chose to survey both customers and retailers because researchers emphasize that DSR should involve multiple stakeholders to design artifacts relevant to practice (e.g., Hevner 2007). The interview guide consisted of questions regarding shopping habits in the physical retail, customer needs, and wishes for the design of an in-store navigation system. We interviewed four customers (one director, one manager, and two students) and four experts from a furniture manufacturer (a sales assistant, the head of sales, the retail development director as an expert on store design, and the head of business development). Two participants had prior experience with AR in retailing. We deliberately decided to include the views of people without prior AR experience to identify together with our target group factors that would encourage them to actually utilize AR-based in-store navigation systems. We analyzed the interviews qualitatively, according to Mayring (2015). We created one category system for the customer interviews and one for the retailer interviews to examine the results separately. We deductively created a coding guide based on our interview guide containing decision criteria and anchor examples for each category to enable a match with our RQ, and added categories inductively (Mayring 2015). The category system for the customers consisted of the main categories "shopping behavior," "functionalities of the solution," "limitations of the solution," "impact of the solution," as well as "presentation and accessibility of the solution." The category system for the retailers consisted of the main categories "customers and their behavior," "measures to ensure customer satisfaction," and "new technological solutions." After separately evaluating the results from both category systems, we reviewed them and formulated DRs that summarize the stated needs. The retail experts stated that their customers can be divided into three groups: **value/bargain hunters** (customers that are driven by good deals), **solution seekers** (customers that want to buy the complete solution in one place), and **easy shoppers** (customers that come to a store for a very specific product). We assigned the results according to which DRs apply to all groups (overlapping) and to individual groups. Finally, we exemplify our DRs in a UX prototype, which, according to Richter et al. (2016), should visualize how functions desired by interviewees can be realized to fulfill the mentioned goals instead of focusing on the visual design of the user interface.

4 Results

We clustered the final DRs into six categories: **navigation, recommendations, information, assistance, general DRs, and adaptation to customer needs** (Fig. 1). The main functionality of the software system is **navigation**. Participants desired that products could be found quickly to not cause frustration (DR1.1), e.g., "If you want a specific duvet, then it's annoying going down to the duvets and then it's not there, and you have to find a sales assistant and then back and forth." Retailers reported that customers often ask where to find products and want an efficient shopping experience. The in-store navigation system should hence calculate the shortest route (DR1.2). Easy shoppers should have the option to get guided to the relevant products directly (DR1.3). Retailers emphasized that the system should integrate features to highlight products of interest on the shelf to reduce stress if customers have many items on the shopping list.

In addition, customers and retailers wished to receive product **recommendations** from the system and be inspired to buy new products. This can counteract that some customers are frustrated by an overwhelming assortment. This feature requires an analysis of customer needs (DR2.1). The interviewees stated that it is beneficial for bargain hunters when the system gives special offers of reduced products, even though they did not plan on buying the product (DR2.2). This feature particularly appeals to customers with low loyalty to individual providers (Merkle 2020). The system could, for instance, recommend cheaper alternatives to the chosen product. Furthermore, recommendations can be given for style-matching and complementary products, e.g., by suggesting a bedsheet when a mattress is purchased (DR2.3). Matching products is vital because otherwise, customers get frustrated when they do not buy the right product: "And for the negative, I think it's when you don't find something. Or, as I mentioned earlier, you bought something, and then later, you think there was something even better for me, and I did not see it." The system should include product **information**, e.g., how to use the product and the opportunity to compare products (DR3.1). One retailer emphasized that only relevant information should be displayed to avoid cognitive overload (Robier 2015) (DR3.2). Providing information is relevant so that physical retail can cope with the information diversity of online shopping, including usage tips or construction instructions (Merkle 2020) (DR3.3). According to the retailers, **assisting functions** are helpful throughout the customer journey (DR4.1), i.e., providing information, finding the right product,

Category	Requirement	Customer Type
Navigation	**1.1** The system should offer navigation through the store.	Overlapping
	1.2 The system should navigate on the shortest way.	Overlapping
	1.3 The system should always allow the user to be guided to a product directly.	Easy shoppers
	1.4 The system should highlight the right products on the shelf.	Overlapping
Recommendations	**2.1 The system should show recommendations based on the customers' needs (e.g., a cheaper product).**	Bargain Hunter / Solution Seeker
	2.2 The system should show special offers.	Bargain Hunter
	2.3 The system should offer inspiration.	Solution Seeker
Information	**3.1** The system should provide basic product information.	Overlapping
	3.2 The system should be limited in the amount of information.	Overlapping
	3.3 The system should provide additional product information if required.	Overlapping
Assistance	**4.1** The system should provide assistance.	Overlapping
	4.2 It should be possible to notify the sales personnel if personal advice is needed.	Overlapping
General	**5.1** The system should cover all in-store processes.	Overlapping
	5.2 The system should be intuitive to use.	Overlapping
	5.3 The main functionality should not be disturbed.	Overlapping
	5.4 The system should provide clarity.	Overlapping
Adaptation to customer needs	**6.1 The system should analyze the customers' needs.**	Overlapping
	6.2 The system should offer different functionalities based on the customers' needs.	Overlapping
	6.3 The system should be adaptable to the customers' needs.	Overlapping

Fig. 1 Requirements for in-store navigation systems

ordering products from stock, and paying. It should be possible to call sales staff for help if necessary by clicking a button, similar to what further studies demonstrated (Meyer et al. 2021) (DR4.2). One customer said: "When I go into the store, I don't need a person right there. I would like to go around, but I would like the possibility of getting the help." Furthermore, **general wishes** were expressed regarding UX. The system should take into account all in-store processes (DR5.1), enable intuitive use with not too many choice options (DR5.2) to not impair the main functionalities of the application (DR5.3), and provide clarity (DR5.4). To address the DRs, the system should enable **adaptivity** (Bontcheva 2002) by collecting data about the customer to enable appropriate recommendations (DR6.1) and multiple functions to address individual customer needs (DR6.2). It should be possible to deactivate functions, e.g., undesired product recommendations (DR6.3). This is vital because retailers emphasized that shopping needs vary: "Some customers just want to be inspired, and some have a fixed goal: I need a bedspread. Another has an even firmer goal: I need the bedspread from page four in the newspaper." We instantiated the DRs with a low-fidelity prototype as a smartphone app using the AR platform "Hololink" (Fig. 2). Our UX design focuses on translating the desired DRs into concrete functionalities, thus instantiating design knowledge rather than focusing on the visual representation of the prototype.

First, users can select the desired experience (in line with the customer types): "as quick as possible," "inspire me," and "cheap, please!" Users who select "as fast

Fig. 2 Excerpts of our conceptual prototype

as possible" receive quick navigation based on a pre-defined shopping list. With the "inspire me" option, the system recommends, e.g., matching products purchased by others with similar preferences. The route is adjusted if the customer adds one of the suggested products to the shopping list. The app uses a short questionnaire on customers' preferences to make appropriate recommendations. For bargain hunters, the app points out when a similar product is offered at a lower price. The system includes a shopping map and a feature to calculate the shortest route. Customers can capture products with their cameras to see additional product information displayed as an overlay, including basic product information, product ratings, and further images. Once they select a product, it is added to the shopping list. Users then see that the chosen product on the shopping list is checked, and the app proceeds to navigate to the following product on the list. If customers need help, they can click a help button. Customers can choose to receive help in the app or by notifying an employee. When seeking help in the app, they can fill out a questionnaire. For instance, when searching for a duvet, the app asks whether the user prefers to sleep warm, normal, or cold and suggests a suitable product. The app includes payment processes and orders from stock. When ordering a product from stock, the app informs the customer that it will be sent to the checkout. When selecting the payment, the customer can go to the checkout or pay in the app. We evaluated the prototype with 20 participants (13 female, seven male) using video demonstrations of a possible shopping experience. We used the user experience questionnaire (UEQ) (Laugwitz et al. 2008) with 26 items distributed over six scales and a three-item scale for customer satisfaction (Lin and Wang 2006) (7-point Likert scale for all items). We calculated reliability and conducted a confirmatory factor analysis to validate our data set. We only had to remove four UEQ items because of too low corrected item-scale correlation (< 0.3) or Cronbach's alpha (< 0.7) (Hair et al. 2014; Nunnally and Bernstein 1994). We will report the mean values (MV) and standard deviations (SD) in the following. Regarding the UEQ, we assessed attractiveness (MV = 5.65; SD = 1.11), understandability (MV = 6.13; SD = 1.01), efficiency (MV = 5.25; SD = 1.09), dependability (MV = 5.23; SD = 1.56), stimulation (MV = 5.34; SD = 1.14), and novelty (MV = 5.44; SD = 1.34). Customer satisfaction was rated with MV = 5.53 and SD = 1.34. Overall, participants tended to rate the prototype positively, with all MV > 5. Open-ended questions indicated that they liked the following aspects: different experiences for different needs (fast, cheap, inspiration), the guided tour, the recommendations, opportunities for additional information like product reviews, and the feature of getting assistance from the salesperson. Improvement ideas were: customizability of the shopping list while shopping, recalculation of the route when leaving the route, setting a maximum budget for shopping, customer profiles, and audio guidance from a voice assistant. Participants moreover mentioned that holding a smartphone while shopping could be annoying, so smartphone holders for shopping carts would be necessary.

5 Conclusion and Outlook

In-store navigation systems could create a convenient customer experience in physical retail. We have derived DRs for in-store navigation systems that aim to support researchers and practitioners in designing them. The evaluation of our conceptual prototype (n = 20) shows that customers perceive such a system mainly positively. We admit the limitations of our study. So far, we could only give preliminary results from a small group of respondents. The prototype is only conceptual, and the evaluation focused on video demonstrations. As a next step, we conduct a larger-scale online survey to ask customers about their shopping behavior and preferences for (in-store) digital shopping technologies to identify which consumer groups are most likely to use such technologies and for which purposes to gain a better understanding of the issues to be solved. We further plan to validate and refine our DRs in a follow-up interview study and extend the DRs, e.g., with additional functions such as integrating a voice assistant.

References

Alexander, B. and Alvarado, D.O. (2017), "Convergence of Physical and Virtual Retail Spaces: The Influence of Technology on Consumer In-Store Experience", *Advanced Fashion Technology and Operations Management*, IGI Global, pp. 191–219.

Barann, B., Betzing, J.H., Niemann, M., Hoffmeister, B. and Becker, J. (2022), "Exploring customers' likeliness to use e-service touchpoints in brick and mortar retail", *Electronic Markets*, Vol. 32, No. 2, pp. 523–545.

Betzing, J.H., Niemann, M., Barann, B., Hoffmeister, B. and Becker, J. (2019), "Mirroring E-service for Brick and Mortar Retail: An Assessment and Survey", *Proceedings of the Wirtschaftsinformatik Conference*, Siegen, Germany.

Bontcheva, K. (2002), "Adaptivity, adaptability, and reading behaviour: some results from the evaluation of a dynamic hypertext system", *Proceedings of the Adaptive Hypermedia and Adaptive Web-Based Systems*, Malaga, Spain.
Cesinger, B., Kulas, C., Lienbacher, E. and Vallaster, C. (2020), "Virtual Reality Augmented Reality im Handel", https://www.fh-salzburg.ac.at/fileadmin/fhs_daten/forschung/bwl-kmu/documents/Brosch%C3%BCre_AR_VR_FHS_web.pdf. Accessed: 16.06.2023.
Cruz, E., Orts-Escolano, S., Gomez-Donoso, F., Rizo, C., Rangel, J.C., Mora, H. and Cazorla, M. (2019), "An augmented reality application for improving shopping experience in large retail stores", *Virtual Reality*, Vol. 23, No. 3, pp. 281–291.
Deckert, R. and Wohllebe, A. (2021), *Digitalisierung Und Einzelhandel*, Springer.
Gregor, S. and Hevner, A.R. (2013), "Positioning and Presenting Design Science Research for Maximum Impact", *MIS Quarterly*, Vol. 37, No. 2, pp. 337–355.
Hagberg, J., Sundstrom, M. and Egels-Zandén, N. (2016), "The digitalization of retailing: an exploratory framework", *International Journal of Retail & Distribution Management*, Vol. 44, No. 7, pp. 694–712.
Hair, J.F., Black, W.C., Babin, B.J. and Anderson, R.E. (2014), *Multivariate Data Analysis*, 7th ed., Pearson.
Hevner, A.R. (2007), "A three cycle view of design science research", *Scandinavian Journal of Information Systems*, Vol. 19, No. 2, pp. 87–92.
Inman, J.J. and Nikolova, H. (2017), "Shopper-facing retail technology: A retailer adoption decision framework incorporating shopper attitudes and privacy concerns", *Journal of Retailing*, Vol. 93, No. 1, pp. 7–28.
Laugwitz, B., Held, T. and Schrepp, M. (2008), "Construction and evaluation of a user experience questionnaire", *HCI and Usability for Education and Work Proceedings*, Graz, Austria.
Lin, H.-H. and Wang, Y.-S. (2006), "An examination of the determinants of customer loyalty in mobile commerce contexts", *Information & Management*, Vol. 43, No. 3, pp. 271–282.
Linzbach, P., Inman, J.J. and Nikolova, H. (2019), "E-commerce in a Physical Store: Which Retailing Technologies Add Real Value?", *NIM - Nuremberg Institute for Market Decisions*, Vol. 11, No. 1, pp. 43–47.
Márquez, J.O.Á. and Ziegler, J. (2023), "Creating Omni-Channel In-Store Shopping Experiences through Augmented-Reality-Based Product Recommending and Comparison", *International Journal of Human–Computer Interaction*, pp. 1–26.
Mayring, P. (2015), *Qualitative Inhaltsanalyse: Grundlagen und Techniken*, 12th ed., Beltz Verlag.
Merkle, W. (2020), *Erfolgreich Im Stationären Einzelhandel – Wege Zur Konsequenten Profilierung Im Digitalen Zeitalter*, Springer.
Meyer, M., Siemon, D. and Robra-Bissantz, S. (2021), "Emotion-based IS support for Customer-Salesperson Interaction", *Proceedings of the Hawaii International Conference on System Sciences*, Kauai, USA.
Molina, B., Olivares, E., Palau, C. and Esteve, M. (2018), "A Multimodal Fingerprint-Based Indoor Positioning System for Airports", *IEEE Access*, Vol. 6, pp. 10092–10106.
Möller, F., Guggenberger, T.M. and Otto, B. (2020), "Towards a method for design principle development in information systems", *Proceedings of the International Conference on Design Science Research in Information Systems and Technology*, Kristiansand, Norway.
Northington, W.M., Gillison, S.T., Beatty, S.E. and Vivek, S. (2021), "I don't want to be a rule enforcer during the COVID-19 pandemic: Frontline employees' plight", *Journal of Retailing and Consumer Services*, Vol. 63.
Nunnally, J. and Bernstein, I. (1994), *Psychometric Theory*, 3rd ed., McGraw-Hill.
Riar, M., Korbel, J.J., Xi, N., Zarnekow, R. and Hamari, J. (2021), "The Use of Augmented Reality in Retail: A Review of Literature", *Proceedings of the Hawaii International Conference on System Sciences*, Kauai, USA.
Richter, M., Flückiger, M.D., Richter, M. and Flückiger, M.D. (2016), "Usability und UX", *Usability Und UX Kompakt: Produkte Für Menschen*, Springer, pp. 7–19.

Riegger, A.-S., Klein, J.F., Merfeld, K. and Henkel, S. (2021), "Technology-enabled personalization in retail stores: Understanding drivers and barriers", *Journal of Business Research*, Vol. 123, pp. 140–155.

Robier, J. (2015), *Das Einfache Und Emotionale Kauferlebnis: Mit Usability, User Experience Und Customer Experience Anspruchsvolle Kunden Gewinnen*, Springer.

Stier, W. (2013), *Empirische Forschungsmethoden*, Springer.

Tan, Y.-C., Chandukala, S.R. and Reddy, S.K. (2022), "Augmented reality in retail and its impact on sales", *Journal of Marketing*, Vol. 86, No. 1, pp. 48–66.

Xue, L., Parker, C.J. and Hart, C.A. (2023), "AR In-Store Solutions for Different Fashion Retail Environments: Retailers' Perspectives", *Proceedings of the International XR Conference*, Lisbon, Portugal.

Smart Cities and Digital Government

What Measures Can Government Agencies in Germany Take Against Digital Disinformation? A Systematic Literature Review and Ethical-Legal Discussion

Stefan Stieglitz, Jennifer Fromm, Alexander Kocur, Frauke Rostalski, Michelle Duda, Alison Evans, Jonas Rieskamp, Luzia Sievi, Maria Pawelec, Wulf Loh, Jessica Heesen, Christoph Fuchss, and Kaan Eyilmez

Abstract Disinformation campaigns spread rapidly through social media and can cause serious harm, especially in crises, ranging from confusion about how to act to a loss of trust in government agencies. Therefore, the prevention of digital disinformation campaigns represents an important research topic and concern that needs to

---

S. Stieglitz (✉) · A. Kocur
Faculty of Economics and Social Sciences, University of Potsdam, Potsdam, Germany
e-mail: stefan.stieglitz@uni-potsdam.de

A. Kocur
e-mail: alexander.kocur@uni-potsdam.de

J. Fromm
Faculty of Engineering, University of Duisburg-Essen, Duisburg, Germany
e-mail: jennifer.fromm@uni-due.com

F. Rostalski · M. Duda · A. Evans
Faculty of Law, University of Cologne, Cologne, Germany
e-mail: frauke.rostalski@uni-koeln.de

M. Duda
e-mail: michelle.duda@uni-koeln.de

A. Evans
e-mail: alison.evans@uni-koeln.de

J. Rieskamp
Faculty of Business Administration and Economics, University of Paderborn, Paderborn, Germany
e-mail: jonas.rieskamp@uni-paderborn.de

L. Sievi · M. Pawelec · W. Loh · J. Heesen
International Center for Ethics in the Sciences and Humanities, University of Tuebingen, Tuebingen, Germany
e-mail: luzia.sievi@izew.uni-tuebingen.de

M. Pawelec
e-mail: maria.pawelec@izew.uni-tuebingen.de

D. Beverungen et al. (eds.), *Transforming the Digitally Sustainable Enterprise*, Lecture Notes in Information Systems and Organisation 76,
https://doi.org/10.1007/978-3-031-80125-9_19

be considered by government agencies to protect public security. However, previous research in the field of information systems focused on the technical possibilities to detect and combat disinformation (e.g., by social bots). In this article, we synthesize information systems literature on disinformation prevention measures by government agencies and discuss these measures from an ethical and legal perspective. We conclude by proposing questions for future research on the prevention of disinformation campaigns by government agencies from an IS, ethical, and legal perspective. Thereby, we contribute to a balanced discussion on the prevention of digital disinformation campaigns and encourage interdisciplinary collaboration in future research.

Keywords Disinformation campaigns · Social media · Ethical implications · Legal implications · Government agencies

1 Introduction

Early in the COVID-19 pandemic, the documentary *Plandemic* (Plandemic 2022) falsely claimed that the global elite had planned the coronavirus to control the population. The creators encouraged viewers to share the video on social media and thus acted strategically to spread misleading information (Nazar and Pieters 2021). This strategic or coordinated action to mislead an audience with false information in a digital environment is commonly referred to as a digital disinformation campaign. It can take place on any digital medium that allows for the exchange of information. Some users deliberately pollute the information climate, e.g., to worsen an opponent's political image or to spread ideologies and manipulate public opinion (Meel and Vishwakarma 2020). The *Plandemic* disinformation campaign increased engagement with anti-vaccination content and reduced the willingness to comply with containment measures (Nazar and Pieters 2021). This illustrates how disinformation can have severe consequences in humanitarian crises, such as confusion, loss of trust, emotional suffering, economic costs and mortal danger (Tran et al. 2019). Furthermore, disinformation campaigns can challenge societal cohesion, democratic processes and the rule of law (Arayankalam 2020).

W. Loh
e-mail: wulf.loh@izew.uni-tuebingen.de

J. Heesen
e-mail: jessica.heesen@izew.uni-tuebingen.de

C. Fuchss · K. Eyilmez
Virtimo AG, Berlin, Germany
e-mail: christoph.fuchss@virtimo.de

K. Eyilmez
e-mail: kaan.eyilmez@virtimo.de

During the 2018 general elections in Brazil, coordinated efforts of a few top users to spread misinformation in multiple groups (Nobre et al. 2021) showing that influential spreaders often act strategically to get disinformation to the widest possible audience. In addition, a study on Twitter communication during the COVID-19 pandemic found that 20.5% of highly active users could be classified as bot accounts; however, these retweeted both information and misinformation (Marx et al. 2020). Bots are computer algorithms that automatically create content and interact with social media users, attempting to mimic and influence human behavior (Ferrara et al. 2016). Measures to prevent digital disinformation aim to counteract the belief and spread of false information. Balakrishnan et al. (2021) identified altruism and ignorance as the strongest motivators for spreading fake news suggesting that many spreaders are unaware of the falsity of the information. Accordingly, literature on disinformation prevention highlights media literacy as a preventive measure (Apuke and Omar 2021). Regarding users' belief of misinformation, researchers found that fake news flags increase cognitive activity, but are unable to influence the subjects' beliefs (Moravec et al. 2019). Thus, social media users are more likely to believe information that supports their own political views, a phenomenon also known as "confirmation bias" (Nickerson 1998).

Previous research also emphasizes the central role of official actors such as government agencies, e.g., showing that a single tweet from official sources can be sufficient to counter misinformation (Vraga and Bode 2017). Therefore, our contribution focuses on those agencies, specifically on authorities tasked with protecting public security such as disaster control authorities and police departments. In this vein, the Munich police department received high praise for their social media activities during the 2016 shooting in Munich (Germany) because it actively countered rumors (Akkaya et al. 2019). However, the effectiveness thereof depends heavily on the politicization of the issue. During the COVID-19 pandemic, many did not listen to official sources such as the police (Jarolimek and Melzer 2022). Besides corrective statements, research recommends collaboration between trusted actors on social media as a prevention measure (Crook et al. 2016). In addition, government agencies could use social bots to automatically disseminate verified information or answer questions from the public (Brachten et al. 2018; Hofeditz et al. 2019). However, governmental agencies in liberal democracies face conflicting demands concerning their engagement with disinformation: While they must ensure security, they must also protect fundamental rights such as the freedom of expression. This ethical and legal dilemma needs to be considered with regard to measures against disinformation.

Most related articles in information systems (IS) research focus on *technical* issues such as detection algorithms (e.g., Al-Asadi and Tasdemir 2022; da Cardoso Durier Silva et al. 2019; Lahby et al. 2022). Ethical and legal issues are seldom addressed. Rare exceptions are e.g., contributions on ethical issues surrounding algorithmic content moderation (Gorwa et al. 2020) and ethical-legal implications of new laws to fight disinformation (Ivanova 2019; Nagasako 2020; Radu 2020). Additionally, there is a lack of research evaluating preventive measures for government agencies. More interdisciplinary research is needed that equally discusses technical, ethical, and legal issues in the prevention of disinformation (Piccolo et al. 2021). We address this shortcoming and focus on an ethical-legal discussion of measures taken by government agencies, especially government agencies ensuring the safety of citizens.

To do so, we first briefly present our definition of disinformation. Thereafter, we present the methodology and results of a systematic review synthesizing the current state of IS research on disinformation prevention measures. We then discuss the identified measures from an ethical and legal perspective, focusing on democratic states, and Germany, specifically. Finally, we then propose open questions for future research on the prevention of disinformation campaigns from an IS, ethical, and legal perspective, and synthesize our findings in a brief conclusion.

2 Definition of Disinformation

IS research often uses the terms misinformation, disinformation, fake news, and rumors interchangeably (Kapantai et al. 2021). However, there have been attempts at a clearer distinction based on the dimensions of falseness, harm, and the intention to deceive (Allcott and Gentzkow 2017; DiFonzo and Bordia 2007; Fallis 2009; Wardle and Derakhshan 2017). For example, rumors are understood as "unverified and instrumentally relevant information statements in circulation that arise in contexts of ambiguity, danger or potential threat, and that function to help people make sense and manage risk" (DiFonzo and Bordia 2007). Furthermore, Wardle and Derakhshan (2017) conceptualized both misinformation and disinformation as false information, with disinformation being deliberately shared to cause harm. This aligns with Fallis (2009) who defined disinformation as "misleading information that is intended to be (or at least foreseen to be) misleading". Fake news could be considered a subset of disinformation focusing on news articles "that are intentionally and verifiably false and could mislead readers" (Allcott and Gentzkow 2017). In this article, we focus on disinformation because it offers a particular challenge for prevention, as it is created to mislead and cause harm.

3 Systematic Literature Review

3.1 Method

To find out which measures IS literature suggests preventing the spread of digital disinformation, we conducted a systematic literature review (Webster and Watson 2002). We selected the following databases for our search: (1) AIS eLibrary and (2) litbaskets.io (based on SCOPUS). While the former yields a comprehensive set of AIS conferences, the litbaskets.io interface provides access to 847 relevant to IS to obtain journal articles (Boell and Wang 2019). Hence, this selection of databases offered a comprehensive review of the IS literature. We obtained the relevant articles from the databases using a keyword search, followed by forward and backward searches.

The following search string was specified for the literature retrieval: *abstract: ((prevent* OR counter* OR block* OR debunk* OR prebunk* OR combat*) AND (misinformation OR disinformation OR "fake news" OR infodemic)).* Test searches indicated that further synonyms (e.g., rumor or hoax) did not improve the relevance of the retrieved articles. We defined the following inclusion and exclusion criteria to assess the relevance of the search results based on a manual assessment of the title and abstract: (1) The article describes one or more measures to prevent digital disinformation and (2) the measure described must possess a preventive character (i.e., it must not be applied after disinformation is already spread). We excluded articles with a focus on (1) factors contributing to the spread of disinformation and (2) the technical implementation of detection algorithms. The query resulted in 70 articles (no duplicates were found) of which eleven articles remained after applying the inclusion and exclusion criteria. Subsequently, we performed forward and backward searches (vom Brocke et al. 2015; Webster and Watson 2002), resulting in a final set of 18 relevant articles.

3.2 Results of Measures to Prevent Digital Disinformation in the IS Literature

Our qualitative analysis adhered to the concept-centric literature synthesis according to Webster and Watson (2002). We employed an inductive approach that led to four dimensions along which we synthesized the literature. Articles including more than one prevention measure were assigned to every corresponding concept. Table 1 depicts the concept matrix.

Firstly, we distinguished the prevention measures according to the actors. Most prevention measures are designed for the platform operator with only a few measures proposed for implementation by government agencies. Moreover, journalists and media outlets, or individual users are suggested to act. Secondly, there are differences in the degree of automation. Although there are no completely autonomous measures, many can be executed partially automatically. Conversely, certain measures require manual execution. Thirdly, we discovered that the measures differ in terms of whom they address. Respectively, we distinguish between initial creators, multipliers, and audience of disinformation. Creators initially post disinformation and multipliers are users who play a role in its diffusion while the audience is reached by the information without spreading.

Finally, we summarized the type of measure into six groups. The first group comprises policies and regulations enacted by the platform operator such as the introduction of an "activity-capping policy" intended to reduce harmful actions (Jeong

Table 1 Concept matrix

Actor	Government agencies	Eccles et al. (2021), Seo et al. (2021) and Vemprala et al. (2021)
	Platform operators	Amoruso et al. (2020), Cao et al. (2015), Eccles et al. (2021), Figl et al. (2020), Gimpel et al. (2021), Hasan and Salah (2019), Jeong et al. (2020), Jin et al. (2016), Kim and Dennis (2019), Ng et al. (2021), Nguyen et al. (2020), Ozturk et al. (2015) and Wang et al. (2021)
	Individuals	Eccles et al. (2021) and Seo et al. (2021)
	Media and journalists	Chen et al. (2020), Eccles et al. (2021), Narayan and Attili (2021), Saad et al. (2019) and Seo et al. (2021)
Automation	Partially	Amoruso et al. (2020), Cao et al. (2015), Eccles et al. (2021), Hasan and Salah (2019), Jin et al. (2016), Kim and Dennis (2019), Narayan and Attili (2021), Nguyen et al. (2020), Ozturk et al. (2015) and Seo et al. (2021)
	Manually	Chen et al. (2020), Eccles et al. (2021), Gimpel et al. (2021), Jeong et al. (2020), Ng et al. (2021), Saad et al. (2019), Vemprala et al. (2021) and Wang et al. (2021)
Addressee	Creator	Cao et al. (2015), Chen et al. (2020), Eccles et al. (2021), Hasan and Salah (2019) and Wang et al. (2021)
	Multiplier	Amoruso et al. (2020), Cao et al. (2015), Eccles et al. (2021), Figl et al. (2020), Gimpel et al. (2021), Hasan and Salah (2019), Jeong et al. (2020), Jin et al. (2016), Kim and Dennis (2019), Narayan and Attili (2021), Ng et al. (2021), Nguyen et al. (2020), Vemprala et al. (2021) and Wang et al. (2021)
	Audience	Cao et al. (2015), Eccles et al. (2021), Figl et al. (2020), Gimpel et al. (2021), Hasan and Salah (2019), Jin et al. (2016), Kim and Dennis (2019), Narayan and Attili (2021), Ng et al. (2021), Nguyen et al. (2020) and Vemprala et al. (2021)
Type	Policy	Jeong et al. (2020)
	Technical	Amoruso et al. (2020), Chen et al. (2020), Hasan and Salah (2019), Jin et al. (2016), Kim and Dennis (2019), Narayan and Attili (2021), Ng et al. (2021), Nguyen et al. (2020), Ozturk et al. (2015), Saad et al. (2019) and Wang et al. (2021)
	Social/ psychological	Eccles et al. (2021) and Gimpel et al. (2021)
	Education	Eccles et al. (2021) and Seo et al. (2021)
	Debunking	Cao et al. (2015) and Vemprala et al. (2021)
	Moderation	Figl et al. (2020) and Ng et al. (2021)

et al. 2020). The group of technical measures includes algorithms (e.g., identification of the disinformation's origin (Amoruso et al. 2020)), changes in the structure of the platform (e.g., source ratings (Kim and Dennis 2019; Ng et al. 2021), identity verification (Wang et al. 2021), displaying counter information (Jin et al. 2016; Ozturk et al. 2015), limitation of forwarding postings (Ng et al. 2021)) and additional information systems that inhibit the diffusion of false information (e.g., blockchain-based solutions (Chen et al. 2020; Hasan and Salah 2019; Narayan and Attili 2021; Saad et al. 2019)). Moreover, we observed measures addressing social and/or psychological levels (e.g., emphasizing social norms (Gimpel et al. 2021), psychological inoculation (Eccles et al. 2021)). Additionally, we found measures aimed at improving users' media literacy in dealing with false information (e.g., Seo et al. 2021). In contrast, measures with a debunking character provide information that directly corrects specific false information (e.g., Cao et al. 2015; Vemprala et al. 2021). Lastly, moderating measures comprise efforts to mark false information or to delete respective postings (e.g., Figl et al. 2020; Ng et al. 2021).

4 Discussion

Only few measures are proposed specifically for government agencies. Firstly, government agencies can create and conduct *educational* programs to teach digital *media literacy* (Eccles et al. 2021; Seo et al. 2021). Secondly, they can engage in *debunking* false information (Vemprala et al. 2021). However, government agencies could take further steps that are not explicitly designed for them. Specifically, they could incorporate the *psychological inoculation* theory in the creation of their content and in media literacy training (Eccles et al. 2021). Similarly, they could create content that highlights *descriptive and injunctive social norms* (Gimpel et al. 2021). Further, government agencies could draw upon *technical* support, e.g., by using *social bots to debunk and provide content automatically* (Hofeditz et al. 2019) or to improve *education* with media literacy on false information with a chatbot (Kocur et al. 2023). Given computational facilities, they could employ *algorithms* to trace down the origin of a specific false information and place debunking messages strategically (Amoruso et al. 2020). Beyond this analytical step, government agencies could take the initiative to provide additional information systems to support or enable prevention measures. Our literature review reveals the ability of blockchain technology to verify the authenticity of content (Chen et al. 2020; Hasan and Salah 2019; Narayan and Attili 2021; Saad et al. 2019).

In sum, government agencies have options for preventing the spread of digital disinformation, but few measures are explicitly designed for them. However, it is important to reflect these ethically and legally—aspects that IS literature often neglects.

4.1 Ethical Discussion of Government Measures Against Disinformation

In pluralistic democracies, the public sphere, including social media, performs important functions (Puppis 2014): Public debates inform citizens, enable them to develop political interests, and to translate these into the political sphere (Habermas 2022; Warren 2017). Publicly voiced opinions and information can expose governmental deficits. This enables citizens to control political institutions (Loh 2021). A democratic state must thus ensure that the opinion-forming process can take place without major distortions (Habermas 2022; Heesen 2021) and must safeguard the freedom of speech, opinion and expression, access to relevant and reliable information, freedom of the press, independence of the media, and the right to privacy (Reporters without Borders 2018). Interference in public communication by government agencies requires a special degree of justification and is only legitimate if the functioning of the public sphere is seriously endangered. Digital disinformation campaigns—by governments, the private sector, or political groups—can cause such serious disruptions (Farkas 2018; Giusti and Piras 2021; Tenove 2020). They distort opinion formation through false or misleading information (Brown 2018). They also impede the translational function of the public sphere by "morally denigrat[ing] certain groups" (McKay and Tenove 2021), helping others gain disproportionate attention, or discouraging victims e.g., of deepfakes from political participation (Pawelec 2022). Disinformation also leads to a loss of trust in public agencies (European Parliament et al. 2021; Wardle 2019). In so doing, it inhibits the media and civil societies' ability to control and criticize governmental actions.

Therefore, the challenge for democratic states and government agencies is to contain the harmful effects of disinformation without undermining democratic values like the freedom of speech, of information, and of the press, and privacy rights. In fact, civil liberties were originally developed as defensive rights against the state (Plattner 1999), and there is always a danger that the state will use its power and resources to suppress unpopular opinions (Kaul 2022). The literature frequently advises *educational* and empowering measures to improve citizens and state employees' *digital media literacy* and critical faculties (Apuke and Omar 2021; Eccles et al. 2021; Seo et al. 2021; Vese 2022). This aligns with the democratic concept of free and equal citizens participating in the political process, and it is an important task for democracies to encourage their citizens to become well informed and critical (Kellner and Share 2007). However, one strategy of disinformation actors is to assert that they are the 'real' critical thinkers who decry state policies and ideologies. Thus, for Jarvis (2017), "our problem isn't 'fake news.' Our problem is trust". People tend to believe right-wing populists because "of a lack of basic trust in liberal institutions" (Mounk 2017). Therefore, educational strategies should include why certain media and agencies can be trusted more than others (e.g., due to (self-)regulation, institutional standards, established scientific and journalistic methods), and how to identify trustworthy sources. Government security agencies themselves can increase citizens' trust through trustworthy communication. Such communication by public authorities is fair, responsible, transparent, appreciative, empowering, and reliable (Gabel and Krüger 2020). This also holds true if *psychological inoculation* becomes part of media literacy trainings by government agencies. People should agree to it beforehand, and government agencies should be transparent. The highlighting of *descriptive and injunctive social norms* is, however, problematic: In democracies, government agencies can communicate laws, regulations, and democratic norms, but they should be cautious when promoting social behaviors. It may be perceived as patronizing and disadvantage groups, e.g., if users are encouraged to report disinformation (Gimpel et al. 2021), this could increase reports of certain minority opinions.

Debunking (e.g., publishing corrections) by government agencies can directly counter disinformation. In a democracy, this must not undermine the public opinion-forming process (requirement of objectivity, no exaggerated evaluative tendency, see Ferreau (2020) and the legal perspectives). In any case, agencies must create transparency about the source of information. There is also the risk that debunking will be abused for propaganda or to discredit and suppress legitimate opinions with state resources and authorities. Fact-checking institutions should therefore be independent (Ferreau 2020).

As a *technical measure*, government agencies can employ *detection algorithms* to identify disinformation automatically. However, monitoring citizens' communication may violate privacy and data protection, requiring special justification. In addition, citizens may feel restricted in their freedom of expression: The mere uncertainty as to whether disadvantages could arise from automated monitoring can reduce political participation (Loh 2021). Besides, automatic detection should be transparent and the affected must be able to appeal against potential false positives. *Social bots* could also automate debunking and informing the public. Bots operate on a large scale and are widely used by states and political groups to influence public opinion (Woolley 2020). Their use is highly controversial. Arguments range from ideas on how "good" bots can counter misinformation to a complete ban on bots used by states (Ferreau 2020).

4.2 Legal Discussion of Government Measures Against Disinformation

The use of *technical measures* to detect and prevent disinformation raises several legal issues (Milker 2018). The evaluation of these in this paper, considering the sovereignty of European nation states, can only refer to the German legal system and German legal literature. Here, the focus is on the German Basic Law, the foundation of a functioning democratic constitutional state, as this is the standard against which state action by the government agencies focused on in this project is to be measured (Starck 2005; Schmidt-Jortzig 2009). Especially where *social bots* are used by government agencies, a violation of various German Basic Law may ensue. Above all, the right to freedom of expression, protected by Article 5 (1) of the German Basic Law, which guarantees individuals the right to express themselves (publicly) according to their individual views, can be violated (on this already in the previous (ethical) section; Bethge 2021; Müller-Franken 2013). Whether a statement is protected or not depends on whether it is considered a value judgment or a statement of fact (Holznagel 2018; Starck and Paulus 2018). Intentionally made, untrue statements of fact as well as value judgments, which sole purpose is to defame another person, do not fall within the remit of protection of Art. 5 sec. 1 GG (Schulze-Fielitz 2013; Starck and Paulus 2018; Hillgruber 2016). All other statements fall within the scope of freedom of expression (Holznagel 2018). In addition to protecting freedom of expression, this fundamental right also protects the freedom to form opinions, i.e. the right to obtain information from all publicly accessible sources (Bethge 2021; Schmidt-Jortzig 2009; Starck and Paulus 2018; Kloepfer 2005).

The prevention of disinformation by governmental agencies may infringe the freedom of expression in different ways. It is commonly accepted, that the mere dissemination of information by the state to its citizens—e.g., regarding a roadblock due to an ongoing protest—does not amount to an infraction of freedom of opinion (Tschorr 2020). However, *debunking* by publishing corrections by the government agencies may violate freedom of expression if it relates to a specific person and his or her previous statement that differs from the state's communication content, as it may lead to stigmatization of that person, which in turn may affect social reputation (Schoch 2011).

Based on those distinctions, different requirements must be met by the government agencies. Where a basic law is violated, the reservation of the law (Art. 20 sec. 3 GG) requires that the government agencies may only act, where it was enabled to do so by an Act of Parliament (Grzeszick 2021; Kokott 2004). In the context of *debunking*, the state must further adhere to the principles of neutrality, objectivity, and correctness (Tschorr 2020; Starck and Paulus 2018; Battis and Edenharter 2022; Masing 2012; Ingold 2017; on the requirement of objectivity see in the previous section). More recent case law found *debunking* by the government agencies to be a functional equivalent of the "classic" violation of a basic right, if it equals such in its aim and effects (Schoch 2011; Ingold 2017). As well as regarding the use of *social bots* an infringement must be considered separately against the background in each individual case—under consideration of the problematic content and its ability to affect the basic rights of individuals.

It must further be taken into account, that *debunking* by the government agencies aims to enable independent opinion forming and participation in social matters—however without formative influence by the government agencies (Tschorr 2020; Starck and Paulus 2018; Kloepfer 2005; Müller-Franken 2013; Hillgruber 2016; Masing 2012). If and to what extent this can be realized by using *social bots* must be analyzed critically. Especially when considering that the state uses its own far-reaching social media accounts, this may be regarded as an infringement on the citizens' freedom to voice an opinion (Milker 2018). The same applies, where government agencies *correct* statements made by third parties using *social bots* (Sachs 2021). However, violations of the freedom of expression may be constitutionally justified. This is determined by the principle of reasonableness, whereby a violation of freedom may be acceptable if it is suitable, necessary, and appropriate to achieve a legitimate aim (Kotzur 2021; Battis and Edenharter 2022; BVerfGE 65, 1 (54)). In addition, the agencies must openly declare the use of *social bots* (Laude 2021) and limit its action to the person who poses a threat to public safety and order (Goldhammer 2021; Herzog 2006).

5 Open Research Questions

Based on our systematic review of IS research on disinformation prevention as well as the ethical and legal discussion above, we outline key questions for further research.

5.1 IS Research Questions Regarding Measures Against Disinformation

From an IS perspective, the questions of how disinformation spreads on social networks and what content and network characteristics can be used to automatically detect disinformation are of particular interest. Nevertheless, the scientific literature lacks more detailed analyses to identify (influential) spreaders to prevent the dissemination process. While previous studies also revealed that personal dispositions such as the user's online trust, self-disclosure, or fear of missing out are positively associated with intentionally sharing fake news (Talwar et al. 2019), it remains an open question what and how further information about a user can be automatically inferred from their historical and behavioral social media data to predict likely spreaders of disinformation. Furthermore, the question arises as how to address these users appropriately.

Moreover, countering disinformation raises the fundamental question of which design elements can encourage users to engage critically with the information. However, while there are promising results demonstrating the effectiveness of fact-checking flags (Gaozhao 2021), there are also conflicting results (Moravec et al. 2019) which suggests that further research is required. In addition, labeling assessments made by professional fact-checkers or through crowdsourcing have been found to be equally influential (Gaozhao 2021) but the question of the acceptance and influence of automated fact-checking, e.g., by bots, remains unanswered. With respect to social bots, Guzmán Rincón et al. (2022) included them as spreaders in simulation environments to analyze and educate in behavioral patterns of disinformation for decision making, but the authors address the need to deepen various analyses and to complement this educational simulation model. In this regard, it remains of interest to not only examine how governmental agencies can strategically employ social bots to spread verified information but also how bots can be integrated in an educational simulation environment to support decision-making processes by also evaluating the accountability of algorithmic decision-making. In doing so, further research questions such as how psychological strategies can be implemented to reach social media users should be considered.

5.2 Ethical Questions Regarding Measures Against Disinformation

There is a broad debate about disinformation harming democracy (for a summary thereof see McKay and Tenove 2021). Likewise, observers fear that measures to counter disinformation can also negatively affect democracy (Vese 2022; European Parliament et al. 2021). Government agencies thus need more research as to whether they should counter specific pieces of disinformation or not. We raise fundamental ethical questions that government agencies should always consider anew and context-specifically when countering disinformation. More case-specific research—e.g., in form of best practices—is needed to help government agencies with these fundamental questions.

The first question for government agencies is who gets to decide what counts as disinformation. Are automated algorithmic decision-making mechanisms suitable here, or do humans ultimately have to decide? The second question is how actors can distinguish disinformation from legitimate expressions of opinion in a pluralistic society. Next, they must decide whether a specific piece of disinformation restricts the democratic functions of the public sphere or whether it is merely an expression of pluralism and the freedom of opinion in the "marketplace of ideas" (Mill 1859). A functioning deliberative democracy should be able to withstand some false or misleading statements because it "filters out and discards the worst ideas" (Mansbridge 1999). Such statements may even serve a function, e.g., by raising the tensions that motivate political debates (Mouffe 2005). In any case, decision-makers must communicate their decisions transparently, and in a way that allows those affected to appeal against them.

To decide whether to counter disinformation, actors need to conduct a context-sensitive evaluation in each case to determine potential value conflicts. Open questions are how can decision-makers balance value conflicts between the functioning of the public sphere, freedom (including free speech), security, privacy, personal expression, and transparency? E.g., may they restrict freedom rights in the name of security when false information endangers life? Under which circumstances would this be justified? Do they consider broader dimensions, such as balancing individual and collective interests? The fundamental question here is how government agencies can strengthen the resilience of the open society against disinformation without sacrificing the principle of tolerance that is central to liberal democracies. Finally, beyond considering citizens' defensive and protective rights, citizens should also be enabled to use the digital space productively in the sense of informational self-determination and empowerment.

5.3 *Legal Research Questions Regarding Measures Against Disinformation*

After a view over the German Basic Law, which sets the ground rules for government agencies' action, it can be said that the constitutional state should be a guarantee for freedom on the one hand, but also for security on the other (Starck 2005). The individual's freedom finds its limits where it inappropriately curtails another's. The German state is granted a monopoly of force to meet this security objective (Papier 2017; Herzog 2006). Though, this objective may not run counter to the liberal and freedom-guaranteeing function of the state. The state must thus limit itself (Kloepfer 2005; Volkmann 2004). For the sake of a functioning democratic constitutional state, the source of voluntary loyalty to the law must be located and, if necessary, strengthened, or at least prevented from weakening. To bring about such acceptance of the laws and the rule of law among the population, reliance is placed on the communicative reason of the individual, derived from communicative action (Habermas 1998; Hill 1988).

If society relies too strongly on the government agencies' duty to protect in the fight against and prevention of disinformation campaigns, it will come at the expense of the citizens' self-responsibility. A central question (from an ethical and legal perspective) is therefore how much individual responsibility should be transferred to the state in dealing with disinformation campaigns. The goal in preventing disinformation, including the tools used (e.g., *social bots*), should not be to limit the individual's autonomy, but to enhance it (Mafi-Gudarzi 2019); "self-defensive democracy" as called by Bayer et al. (2021); also "informational self-determination" as in the previous (ethical) section (Müller-Franken 2013; Hillgruber 2016; Masing 2012).

A first and controversial (German) national approach to deal with disinformation is the passage of the Network Enforcement Act (Netzwerkdurchsetzungsgesetz = NetzDG). This legislation is to be used to fight against criminal fake news and hate speech on *social media* networks (BT-Drs. 18/12356): Social network providers are obligated to produce an effective and transparent procedure to deal with illegal content. Content, which is obviously illegal, must be *removed* within 24 h, other illegal content within 7 days acc. to the NetzDG. This approach is criticized for shifting the responsibility to ensure public order onto private social networks (Guggenberger 2017; Dankert 2018). Another important point of criticism is, that it gives rise to the risk that content containing opinions are deleted by provider "preventatively" as the NetzDG stipulates high monetary fines but simultaneously very short time frames for deletion (Papier 2017; Rostalski 2017). Thus, even with the passage of the NetzDG, the state runs the risk that it opens the scope for invasive infringement of the basic rights of users and the creation of a "censorship authority" (Guggenberger 2017). This must be considered when creating means to fight disinformation campaigns. Following on from this, the Digital Services Act (DSA, COM (2020) 825 final) of November 16, 2022, is intended to contribute to a safe, predictable and trustworthy online environment at European level from February 17,

2024, by imposing due diligence obligations and liability exclusions for intermediary services such as online platforms. This includes, for example, a Europe-wide uniform design of procedures for reporting and prompt removal of illegal content, as well as additional due diligence requirements for very large online platforms and search engines. The focus is on a form of *regulated self-regulation* by platform operators in which the role of state actors in action against illegal content remains an indirect one, for example through the preferential treatment of reports from various (also state) actors when they are qualified as "trusted flaggers" (Article 19).

6 Conclusion

This article identified measures government agencies can apply to counter digital disinformation campaigns based on a systematic literature review of IS research. It then discussed these measures from an ethical and legal perspective. Due to the nature of systematic literature reviews, our study has some limitations. Subjective decisions regarding the selection of databases, keywords, and exclusion criteria may have resulted in a neglect of relevant articles. Furthermore, the ethical discussion on democratic states and the legal discussion focusing on German law cannot be directly applied to other political and legal systems. Lastly, further research is needed to apply our findings to real-world disinformation campaigns, tracing their origin and spread and discussing government agencies' responses combining IS, legal, and ethical perspectives.

Notwithstanding, our paper contributes to a nuanced discussion of measures against disinformation in IS research, but also in practice, with a focus on government agencies. As shown, the literature discusses only few preventative measures explicitly designed for government agencies, so there is a need for more research on measures against disinformation suitable for government agencies. From a technical view, open research questions include how psychological insights can be used to, e.g., strategically employ social bots for educational purposes, to spread verified information or counter disinformation. From an ethical and legal perspective, government agencies must contribute to a safe, predictable, and trustworthy online environment at the national, but also the European level and strengthen the self-defensive democracy. At the same time, they must consider the risks that countering disinformation may constitute an invasive infringement of users' basic rights and create a censorship authority. Government agencies thus need to balance value conflicts between the functioning of the public sphere, freedom, security, privacy, and personal expression.

References

Akkaya, C., Fedorowicz, J. & Krcmar, H. (2019). Successful Practices for Using Social Media by Police Departments: A Case Study of the Munich Police. *European Conference on Information Systems.*

Al-Asadi, M. A. & Tasdemir, S. (2022). Using Artificial Intelligence Against the Phenomenon of Fake News: A Systematic Literature Review. In M. Lahby, A.-S.K. Pathan, Y. Maleh & W.M.S. Yafooz (Hrsg.), *Studies in Computational Intelligence. Combating Fake News with Computational Intelligence Techniques* (S. 39–54). Springer.

Allcott, H. & Gentzkow, M. (2017). Social media and fake news in the 2016 election. *Journal of Economic Perspectives, 31* (2), 211–236.

Amoruso, M., Anello, D., Auletta, V., Cerulli, R., Ferraioli, D. & Raiconi, A. (2020). Contrasting the Spread of Misinformation in Online Social Networks. *Journal of Artificial Intelligence Research, 69*, 847–879.

Apuke, O. D. & Omar, B. (2021). Modelling the antecedent factors that affect online fake news sharing on COVID-19: The moderating role of fake news knowledge. *Health Education Research, 35* (7), 490–503.

Arayankalam, J. (2020). Disinformation as a strategic weapon: Roles of societal polarization, government's cybersecurity capability, and the rule of law. *International Conference on Information Systems.*

Balakrishnan, V., Ng, K. S. & Rahim, H. A. (2021). To share or not to share – The underlying motives of sharing fake news amidst the COVID-19 pandemic in Malaysia. *Technology in Society, 66.*

Battis, U., Edenharter, A. (2022). Einführung in das Verfassungsrecht, 291 f., 335 ff.

Bayer, J., Holznagel, B., Lubianiec, K., Pintea, A., Schmitt, J. B., Szakács, J. et al. (2021). *Disinformation and propaganda: impact on the functioning of the rule of law and democratic processes in the EU and its Member States - 2021 update.* Brussels. Available at: https://www.europarl.europa.eu/RegData/etudes/STUD/2021/653633/EXPO_STU(2021)653633_EN.pdf (Accessed: 01 March 2023).

Bethge, H. (2021). Art. 5 GG, Rn.18, 24. *Grundgesetz Kommentar* (9. Auflage). Sachs.

Boell, S. & Wang, B. (2019). www.litbaskets.io, an IT Artifact Supporting Exploratory Literature Searches for Information Systems Research. *Australian Conference on Information Systems.*

Brachten, F., Mirbabaie, M., Stieglitz, S., Berger, O., Bludau, S. & Schrickel, K. (2018). Threat or Opportunity? - Examining Social Bots in Social Media Crisis Communication. *Australasian Conference on Information Systems.*

Brown, É. (2018). Propaganda, Misinformation, and the Epistemic Value of Democracy. *Critical Review, 30* (3), 194–218.

Cao, C., Hu, Y. & Yu, L. (2015). Containment of Rumors Under Limit Cost Budget in Social Network. *Wuhan International Conference on E-Business.*

Chen, Q., Srivastava, G., Parizi, R. M., Aloqaily, M. & Al Ridhawi, I. (2020). An incentive-aware blockchain-based solution for internet of fake media things. *Information Processing & Management, 57* (6), 102370.

Crook, B., Glowacki, E. M., Suran, M., K. Harris, J. & Bernhardt, J. M. (2016). Content Analysis of a Live CDC Twitter Chat During the 2014 Ebola Outbreak. *Communication Research Reports, 33* (4), 349–355.

da Cardoso Durier Silva, F., Vieira, R. & Garcia, A. C. (2019). Can Machines Learn to Detect Fake News? A Survey Focused on Social Media. *Hawaii International Conference on System Sciences.*

Dankert, K. (2018). Verfälschung von Datenbeständen durch Social Bots. In W. Hoffmann-Riem (Hrsg.). Big Data - Regulative Herausforderungen, 157–166.

DiFonzo, N. & Bordia, P. (2007). *Rumor Psychology: Social and Organizational Approaches.* Washington, DC: American Psychological Association.

Eccles, D., Kurnia, S., Dingler, T. & Geard, N. (2021). Three Preventative Interventions to Address the Fake News Phenomenon on Social Media. *Australian Conference on Information Systems.*

European Parliament, Directorate-General for External Policies of the Union, Colomina, C., Sánchez Margalef, H., Youngs, R. et al. (2021). *The impact of disinformation on democratic processes and human rights in the world*. European Parliament, 2021, https://data.europa.eu/doi/10.2861/59161.

Fallis, D. (2009). A conceptual analysis of disinformation. *iConference*.

Farkas, J. (2018). Disguised Propaganda on Social Media. Addressing Democratic Dangers and Solution. *Brown Journal of World Affairs, 25* (1), 1–16.

Ferrara, E., Varol, O., Davis, C., Menczer, F. & Flammini, A. (2016). The rise of social bots. *Communications of the ACM, 59* (7), 96–104.

Ferreau, F. (2020). Desinformation aus rechtswissenschaftlicher Perspektive. In J. Möller, M. Hameleers & F. Ferrau (Hrsg.), *Typen von Desinformation und Misinformation. Verschiedene Formen von Desinformation und ihre Verbreitung aus kommunikationswissenschaftlicher und rechtswissenschaftlicher Perspektive* (S. 44–78). ALM GbR.

Figl, K., Kießling, S., Rank, C. & Vakulenko, S. (2020). Fake News Flags, Cognitive Dissonance, and the Believability of Social Media Posts. *International Conference on Information Systems*.

Gabel, F. & Krüger, M. (2020). Leitfaden für eine ethisch reflektierte Krisenkommunikation - Eine Analyse wertbezogener Spannungsfelder in der Krisenkommunikation. *Materialien zur Ethik in den Wissenschaften, Band 15*. IZEW.

Gaozhao, D. (2021). Flagging fake news on social media: An experimental study of media consumers' identification of fake news. *Government Information Quarterly, 38* (3).

Gimpel, H., Heger, S., Olenberger, C. & Utz, L. (2021). The Effectiveness of Social Norms in Fighting Fake News on Social Media. *Journal of Management Information Systems, 38* (1), 196–221.

Giusti, S. & Piras, E. (2021). *Democracy and Fake News: Information Manipulation and Post-Truth Politics*. Routledge.

Goldhammer, M. (2021). Verantwortlichkeit im Polizeirecht. *Juristische Ausbildung, 43* (6), 638–650.

Gorwa, R., Binns, R. & Katzenbach, C. (2020). Algorithmic content moderation: Technical and political challenges in the automation of platform governance. *Big Data and Society, 7* (1).

Grzeszick, B. (2021). Art. 20 GG, Rn. 81. *Grundgesetz Kommentar*. Dürig/Herzog/Scholz.

Guggenberger, N. (2017). Das Netzwerkdurchsetzungsgesetz – schön gedacht, schlecht gemacht. *Zeitschrift für Rechtspolitik, 98*, 89–101.

Guzmán Rincón, A., Carrillo Barbosa, R. L., Segovia-García, N. & Africano Franco, D. R. (2022). Disinformation in Social Networks and Bots: Simulated Scenarios of Its Spread from System Dynamics. *Systems, 10* (2).

Habermas, J. (1998). Faktizität und Geltung. Beiträge zur Diskurstheorie des Rechts und des demokratischen Rechtsstaats. Frankfurt a. M.: Suhrkamp.

Habermas, J. (2022). Reflections and hypotheses on a further structural transformation of the political public sphere. *Theory, Culture & Society, 39*(4), 145–171.

Hasan, H. R. & Salah, K. (2019). Combating Deepfake Videos Using Blockchain and Smart Contracts. *IEEE Access, 7*, 41596–41606.

Heesen, J. (2021). Responsible Freedom. The Democratic Challenge of Regulating Online Media. In L.T. Price, K. Sanders & W.N. Wyatt (Hrsg.), *The Routledge Companion to Journalism Ethics* (S. 435–442). Routledge.

Herzog, R. (2006). § 72 Ziele, Vorbehalte und Grenzen der Staatstätigkeit. In J. Isensee, P. Kirchhof (Hrsg.). Handbuch des Staatsrechts, Band IV, 38 f., 47, 49.

Hill, H. (1988). Akzeptanz des Rechts — Notwendigkeit eines besseren Politikmanagements, *Juristen Zeitung* (377–381).

Hillgruber, C. (2016). Meinungsfreiheit als Grundrecht der Demokratie: Der Schutz des demokratischen Resonanzbodens in der Rechtsprechung des BVerfG, *Juristen Zeitung* (495–501).

Hofeditz, L., Ehnis, C., Brachten, F. & Stieglitz, S. (2019). Meaningful Use of Social Bots? Possible Applications in Crisis Communication During Disasters. *European Conference on Information Systems*.

Holznagel, B. (2018). Phänomen "Fake News" – Was ist zu tun? *Multimedia und Recht, 18*, 18–22.
Ingold, A. (2017). »Polizei 2.0«: Grenzen der behördlichen Öffentlichkeitsarbeit in sozialen Netzwerken, *Verwaltungsarchiv* (240–265).
Ivanova, Y. (2019). Can EU Data Protection Legislation Help to Counter "Fake News" and Other Threats to Democracy? *International Conference on e-Democracy.*
Jarolimek, S. & Melzer, A. (2022). Öffentliche Kommunikation, Polizei und Corona. In H.-J. Lange (Hrsg.), *Politik zwischen Macht und Ohnmacht, Studien zur inneren Sicherheit* (S. 341–361). Wiesbaden: Springer.
Jarvis, J. (2017, Juni 12). Our problem isn't 'fake news.' Our problems are trust and manipulation. *Medium.* Zugriff am 13.6.2022. Verfügbar unter: https://medium.com/whither-news/our-problem-isnt-fake-news-our-problems-are-trust-and-manipulation-5bfbcd716440.
Jeong, D., Han, S.-P., Park, S. & Lee, S. K. (2020). Fighting Abuse while Promoting Free Speech: Policies to Reduce Opinion Manipulation in Online Platforms. *Hawaii International Conference on System Sciences.*
Jin, Z., Cao, J., Zhang, Y. & Luo, J. (2016). News Verification by Exploiting Conflicting Social Viewpoints in Microblogs. *AAAI Conference on Artificial Intelligence.*
Kapantai, E., Christopoulou, A., Berberidis, C. & Peristeras, V. (2021). A systematic literature review on disinformation: Toward a unified taxonomical framework. *New Media & Society, 23* (5), 1301–1326.
Kaul, V. (2022). Freedom of speech in liberal and non-liberal traditions. *Philosophy & Social Criticism, 48*(4), 460–472.
Kellner, D., & Share, J. (2007). Critical media literacy: Crucial policy choices for a twenty-first-century democracy. *Policy Futures in Education, 5*(1), 59–69.
Kim, A. & Dennis, A. R. (2019). Says Who? The Effects of Presentation Format and Source Rating on Fake News in Social Media. *MIS Quarterly, 43* (3), 1025–1039.
Kloepfer, M. (2005). § 42 Öffentliche Meinung, Massenmedien. In J. Isensee, P. Kirchhof (Hrsg.). Handbuch des Staatsrechts, Band III, 11 f., 44 f., 51.
Kocur, A., Clausen, S., Hofeditz, L., Brünker, F., Fromm, J., Stieglitz, S. 2023. Fighting False Information - Designing a Conversational Agent for Public Sector Organizations. *European Conference on Information Systems.*
Kokott, J. (2004). § 22 Grundrechtliche Schranken und Schrankenschranken. In D. Merten, H.-J. Papier (Hrsg.), Handbuch der Grundrechte, Band I, 20 f.
Kotzur, M. (2021). Art. 20 GG, Rn. 163. *Grundgesetz Kommentar* (7. Auflage). Münch/Kunig.
Lahby, M., Pathan, A.-S. K., Maleh, Y. & Yafooz, W. M. S. (2022). *Combating Fake News with Computational Intelligence Techniques* (M. Lahby, A.-S.K. Pathan, Y. Maleh & W.M.S. Yafooz, Hrsg.). Springer.
Laude, L. (2021). *Automatisierte Meinungsbeeinflussung: Der Schutz des Kommunikationsprozesses in sozialen Online-Netzwerken.* Mohr Siebeck.
Loh, W. (2021). Soziale Medien. In M.G. Festl (Hrsg.), *Handbuch Liberalismus* (S. 543–551). Metzler.
Mafi-Gudarzi, N. (2019). Desinformationen: Herausforderungen für die wehrhafte Demokratie. *Zeitschrift für Rechtspolitik, 3*, 65–68.
Mansbridge, J. (1999). Everyday Talk in the Deliberative System. In S. Macedo (Hrsg.), *Deliberative Politics: Essays on Democracy and Disagreement* (S. 1–211). Oxford University Press.
Marx, J., Brünker, F., Mirbabaie, M. & Hochstrate, E. (2020). 'Conspiracy Machines' – The Role of Social Bots during the COVID-19 "Infodemic". *Australasian Conference on Information Systems.*
Masing, J. (2012), Meinungsfreiheit und Schutz der verfassungsrechtlichen Ordnung, *Juristen Zeitung* (585–592).
McKay, S. & Tenove, C. (2021). Disinformation as a Threat to Deliberative Democracy. *Political Research Quarterly, 74* (3), 703–717.

Meel, P. & Vishwakarma, D. K. (2020). Fake news, rumor, information pollution in social media and web: A contemporary survey of state-of-the-arts, challenges and opportunities. *Expert Systems with Applications, 153*. Elsevier Ltd.

Milker, J. (2018). Die Polizei auf Twitter – Brauchen wir ein Social-Media-Gesetz für staatliche Stellen? *Neue Zeitschrift für Verwaltungsrecht, 23*, 1751–1758.

Mill, J. S. (1859). *On Liberty*. Hackett Publishing Company.

Moravec, P., Minas, R. & Dennis, A. R. (2019). Fake News on Social Media: People Believe What They Want to Believe When it Makes No Sense at All. *MIS Quarterly, 43* (4), 1343–1360.

Mouffe, C. (2005). *On the Political*. Routledge.

Mounk, S. (2017, Juli 13). Rechtspopulismus. Anti. Autoritär. *Zeit-Online*. Available at: https://www.zeit.de/2017/29/rechtspopulismus-bildung-neue-rechte (Accessed 13 June 2022).

Müller-Franken, S. (2013). *Meinungsfreiheit im freiheitlichen Staat*, 27, 51, 53.

Nagasako, T. (2020). A Consideration of the Case Study of Disinformation and Its Legal Problems. *IFIP International Conference on Human Choice and Computers*.

Narayan, S. & Attili, V. S. P. (2021). Combating the spread of fake news on social media through a blockchain-led intervention. *American Conference on Information Systems*.

Nazar, S. & Pieters, T. (2021). Plandemic Revisited: A Product of Planned Disinformation Amplifying the COVID-19 "infodemic". *Frontiers in Public Health, 9*.

Ng, K. C., Tang, J. & Lee, D. (2021). The Effect of Platform Intervention Policies on Fake News Dissemination and Survival: An Empirical Examination. *Journal of Management Information Systems, 38* (4), 898–930.

Nguyen, H. T., Cano, A., Vu, T. & Dinh, T. N. (2020). Blocking Self-Avoiding Walks Stops Cyber-Epidemics: A Scalable GPU-Based Approach. *IEEE Transactions on Knowledge and Data Engineering, 32* (7), 1263–1275.

Nickerson, R. S. (1998). Confirmation Bias: A Ubiquitous Phenomenon in Many Guises. *Review of General Psychology, 2* (2), 175–220.

Nobre, G. P., Ferreira, C. H. G. & Almeida, J. M. (2021). A Hierarchical Network-Oriented Analysis of User Participation in Misinformation Spread on WhatsApp. *Information Processing & Management, 59* (1).

Ozturk, P., Li, H. & Sakamoto, Y. (2015). Combating Rumor Spread on Social Media: The Effectiveness of Refutation and Warning. *Hawaii International Conference on System Sciences*.

Papier, H.-J. (2017). Rechtsstaatlichkeit und Grundrechtsschutz in der digitalen Gesellschaft. *Neue Juristische Wochenschrift, 42*, 3025–3031.

Pawelec, M. (2022). Deepfakes and Democracy (Theory): How Synthetic Audio-Visual Media for Disinformation and Hate Speech Threaten Core Democratic Functions. *Digital Society, 1* (19), 1–37.

Piccolo, L. S. G., Bertel, D., Farrell, T. & Troullinou, P. (2021). Opinions, Intentions, Freedom of Expression, ..., and Other Human Aspects of Misinformation Online. *Conference on Human Factors in Computing Systems*.

Plandemic. (2022). Plandemic – 100% Censored. 0% Debunked. *Plandemic*. Zugriff am 30.5.2022. Verfügbar unter: https://plandemicseries.com/.

Plattner, M.F. (1999). From Liberalism to Liberal Democracy. *Journal of Democracy 10*(3), 121–134.

Puppis, M. (2014). The regulation of political communication. In C. Reinemann (Hrsg.), *Political communication. Series: Handbooks of Communication Science* (S. 39–62). De Gruyter Mouton.

Radu, R. (2020). Fighting the 'Infodemic': Legal Responses to COVID-19 Disinformation. *Social Media and Society, 6* (3).

Reporters without Borders. (2018). Global communication and information space: a common good of humankind. *Reporters without Borders*. Zugriff am 13.6.2022. Verfügbar unter: https://rsf.org/en/global-communication-and-information-space-common-good-humankind.

Rostalski, F. (2017). "Fake News" und die "Lügenpresse" – ein (neuer) Fall für das Straf- und Ordnungswidrigkeitenrecht? *Rechtswissenschaft, 4*, 436–460.

Saad, M., Ahmad, A. & Mohaisen, A. (2019). Fighting Fake News Propagation with Blockchains. *IEEE Conference on Communications and Network Security.*

Sachs, M. (2021). Art. 20 GG, Rn. 113. *Grundgesetz Kommentar* (9. Auflage). Sachs.

Schmidt-Jortzig, E. (2009). § 162 Meinungs- und Informationsfreiheit. In J. Isensee, P. Kirchhof (Hrsg.). Handbuch des Staatsrechts, Band VII, 9, 22, 33 f.

Schoch, F. (2011). Die Schwierigkeiten des BVerfG mit der Bewältigung staatlichen Informationshandelns. *Neue Zeitschrift für Verwaltungsrecht, 4*, 193–197.

Schulze-Fielitz, H. (2013). Art. 5 Abs. 1–2 GG. *Grundgesetz Kommentar* (3. Auflage). Dreier.

Seo, H., Thorson, S., Blomberg, M., Appling, S., Bras, A., Davis-Roberts, A. et al. (2021). Country Characteristics, Internet Connectivity and Combating Misinformation: A Network Analysis of Global North-South. *Hawaii International Conference on System Sciences.*

Starck, C. (2005). § 33 Grundrechtliche und demokratische Freiheitsidee. In J. Isensee, P. Kirchhof (Hrsg.). Handbuch des Staatsrechts, Band III, 14 f., 8 f., 11.

Starck, C, Paulus, A. (2018). Art. 5. In H. v. Mangoldt, F. Klein, C. Starck, Grundgesetz Band 1, 76, 81 ff, 166, 169.

Talwar, S., Dhir, A., Kaur, P., Zafar, N. & Alrasheedy, M. (2019). Why do people share fake news? Associations between the dark side of social media use and fake news sharing behavior. *Journal of Retailing and Consumer Services, 51*, 72–82.

Tenove, C. (2020). Protecting democracy from disinformation: Normative threats and policy responses. *The International Journal of Press/Politics*, 25(3), 517–537.

Tran, T., Valecha, R., Rad, P. & Rao, & H. R. (2019). An Investigation of Misinformation Harms Related to Social Media during Two Humanitarian Crises. *International conference on secure knowledge management in artificial intelligence era.*

Tschorr, S. (2020). Verfassungsrechtliche Grenzen der twitternden Polizei im Rahmen von Großveranstaltungen und Versammlungen. *Neue Juristische Wochenschrift*, 3755–3759.

Vemprala, N., Gudigantala, N. & Chaganti, R. (2021). Debunking Misinformation Using a Game Theoretic Approach. *American Conference on Information Systems.*

Vese, D. (2022). Governing Fake News: The Regulation of Social Media and the Right to Freedom of Expression in the Era of Emergency. *European Journal of Risk Regulation, 13* (3), 477–513.

Volkmann, U. (2004). Sicherheit und Risiko als Probleme des Rechtsstaats, *Juristen Zeitung (696–703).*

vom Brocke, J., Simons, A., Riemer, K., Niehaves, B., Plattfaut, R. & Plattfaut, R. (2015). Standing on the Shoulders of Giants: Challenges and Recommendations of Literature Search in Information Systems Research. *Communications of the Association for Information Systems, 37* (9), 205–224.

Vraga, E. K. & Bode, L. (2017). Using Expert Sources to Correct Health Misinformation in Social Media. *Science Communication, 39* (5), 621–645.

Wang, S. (Ada), Pang, M.-S. & Pavlou, P. A. (2021). Cure or Poison? Identity Verification and the Posting of Fake News on Social Media. *Journal of Management Information Systems, 38* (4), 1011–1038.

Wardle, C. (2019). A New World Disorder. *Scientific American, 321* (3), 88–93.

Wardle, C. & Derakhshan, H. (2017). *INFORMATION DISORDER: Toward an interdisciplinary framework for research and policy making Information Disorder Toward an interdisciplinary framework for research and policymaking.* Zugriff am 1.3.2023. Verfügbar unter: https://rm.coe.int/information-disorder-toward-an-interdisciplinary-framework-for-researc/168076277c.

Warren, M. E. (2017). A Problem-Based Approach to Democratic Theory. *American Political Science Review*, 111(1), 39–53.

Webster, J. & Watson, R. T. (2002). Analyzing the Past to Prepare for the Future: Writing a Literature Review. *MIS Quarterly, 26* (2), 13–23.

Woolley, S. C. (2020). Bots and Computational Propaganda: Automation for Communication and Control. In N. Persily & J.A. Tucker (Hrsg.), *Social media and democracy. The state of the field, prospects for reform* (S. 89–110). Cambridge University Press.

Toward Government as a Platform: An Analysis Method for Public Sector Infrastructure

Peter Kuhn, Liudmila Zavolokina, Dian Balta, and Florian Matthes

Abstract Government as a Platform (GaaP) is a promising approach to the digital transformation of the public sector. In practice, GaaP is realized by platform-oriented infrastructures. However, despite successful examples, the transformation toward platform-oriented infrastructures remains challenging. A potential remedy is the analysis of existing public infrastructure regarding its platform orientation. Such an analysis can identify the gaps to an ideal platform-oriented infrastructure and, thus, support the transformation toward it. We follow the design science research methodology to develop a four-dimensional analysis method. We do so in three iterations, and, after each iteration, evaluate the method by its application to infrastructures in practice. With regard to theory, our results suggest extending GaaP conceptualizations with a specific emphasis on platform principles. With regard to practice, we contribute an analysis method that creates proposals for the improvement of infrastructures and, thus, supports the transformation toward GaaP.

Keywords Government as a Platform · e-government · Digital government

P. Kuhn (✉) · D. Balta
Research Institute of the Free State of Bavaria, fortiss GmbH, Munich, Germany
e-mail: pkuhn@fortiss.org

D. Balta
e-mail: balta@fortiss.org

L. Zavolokina
Digital Society Initiative, University of Zurich, Zurich, Switzerland
e-mail: zavolokina@ifi.uzh.ch

P. Kuhn · D. Balta · F. Matthes
School of CIT, Technical University of Munich, Munich, Germany
e-mail: matthes@tum.de

D. Beverungen et al. (eds.), *Transforming the Digitally Sustainable Enterprise*, Lecture Notes in Information Systems and Organisation 76,
https://doi.org/10.1007/978-3-031-80125-9_20

1 Introduction

Government as a Platform (GaaP) envisions the public sector as an open platform where people inside and outside government can innovate and contribute to co-create better public services (O'Reilly 2011). The approach fosters higher efficiency (Janssen and Estevez 2013) and increases the user-friendliness of public services (Cordella and Paletti 2019). Today, when human-centric digital transformation is part of the strategic goals of governments (European Commission 2022), GaaP is of high priority for policymakers and governmental institutions. On a technical level, GaaP is realized by modular and open IT infrastructures (Bender and Heine 2021; Brown et al. 2017; Pope 2019). The modularization of infrastructure leads to more flexible interconnections and, thus, enables shared services (Brown et al. 2017; Tiwana 2013). Openness allows for the participation and co-creation of digital services by users and third parties (Millard 2018; Soto Setzke et al. 2019). In other sectors, such infrastructures have been coined "platform-oriented infrastructures" (Bygstad and Hanseth 2018).

However, the transition toward platform-oriented infrastructures can be challenging (Kuhn et al. 2022a), particularly given the complexity of existing public infrastructures. For example, the platform boundary is hard to define since it concerns numerous components across several organizations and different levels of government. Public sector literature provides first conceptualizations (e.g. Bender and Heine 2021; Brown et al. 2017) and individual examples of GaaP (e.g. Cordella and Paletti 2019; Smorgunov 2021), but defining the boundaries of a platform-oriented infrastructure is not explicitly addressed. More general, it remains unclear what makes a public sector infrastructure platform-oriented and how to transition toward, which may even hinder the digital transformation of the public sector at large (Kuhn et al. 2022a).

A potential remedy for this challenge is the analysis of public infrastructures regarding their platform orientation. Public sector infrastructures arguably do not start their "platformization" (Bygstad and Hanseth 2018) efforts from scratch. Thus, to navigate the GaaP transition effectively, governments need to understand the current state of their infrastructures. Only then they are able to outline a path to GaaP. An analysis of public sector infrastructures regarding their platform orientation is therefore a basis for the required transition and serves as a starting point toward ideal platform orientation.

We formulate the following research question: *How can public sector infrastructure be analyzed regarding its platform orientation?*

We follow the design science research methodology (Peffers et al. 2007) to develop a four-dimensional analysis method. The method development is conducted in three iterations, each evaluated by its application to public sector infrastructures. With regard to theory, we propose extending GaaP conceptualizations with a specific emphasis on platform principles. We contribute to practice by providing a method that can be used to analyze public sector infrastructure and, thus, support the transformation of infrastructure toward GaaP. The paper is structured based on Gregor and Hevner (2013).

2 Theoretical Background and Objective for a Solution

2.1 Government as a Platform

In his seminal contribution "Government as a Platform", Tim O'Reilly imagined the government as an open platform on which people inside and outside the government can innovate and contribute so that better public services can be co-created (O'Reilly 2011). Over the years, several different perspectives on and conceptualizations of this idea have been developed—for example, GaaP as an approach to digital public infrastructure (Pope 2019) and GaaP to co-create public value (Cordella and Paletti 2019). Scholars have highlighted the benefits of GaaP, in particular, cost reduction (Janssen and Estevez 2013), service orientation (Vestues et al. 2021), and better outcomes regarding user-friendliness (Millard 2018). With GaaP, governments can "[do] more with less" (Janssen and Estevez 2013) by providing infrastructure that enables others to build upon existing structures instead of building from scratch. This notion has been described as leveraging (Millard 2018) and harnessing "the power of its users (…) to co-create (…) its offerings" (O'Reilly 2011, p. 13). While the exact definition and conceptualization of GaaP are still subject to research (Seo and Myeong 2020), the idea of leveraging is one of the central principles that underlie the approach. Other principles are openness (O'Reilly 2011; Seo and Myeong 2020) and participation (Millard 2018; O'Reilly 2011). Crucially, with GaaP, the government's role changes from a service provider to a platform owner (Fishenden and Thompson 2013; Millard 2018; O'Reilly 2011). This and the aforementioned principles make "Government as Platform" more than a "Platform for Government" but a holistic approach to the digital transformation of the public sector (Brown et al. 2017).

2.2 Platforms and Platform-Oriented Infrastructures

In general IS literature, scholars investigate the phenomenon of platforms in numerous publications (de Reuver et al. 2018; Hein et al. 2020; Jacobides et al. 2018; Tiwana 2013; Van Alstyne et al. 2016). Platforms can be described as modular architectures with a core and a periphery (Baldwin and Woodard 2008) on which actors are brought together and coordinated to innovate and compete (Gawer 2014). The link between the core and the periphery is facilitated and managed by so-called "boundary resources", which play an important role in the regulation of the openness of the platform (Boudreau 2010; Ghazawneh and Henfridsson 2013; Karhu et al. 2018). The modular structure and the boundary resources foster the emergence of ecosystems. Taken together, a digital platform ecosystem "comprises a platform owner that implements governance mechanisms to facilitate value-creating mechanisms on a digital platform between the platform owner and an ecosystem of autonomous complementors and consumers" (Hein et al. 2020, p. 4). Digital infrastructures are an integral part of platforms (Constantinides et al. 2018). With "their ability to collect, store, and make digital data available across a number of systems and devices" (Constantinides et al. 2018, p. 2) they provide platforms with a backbone. Existing frameworks for the design and development of platform infrastructures are from domains like health care (Bygstad and Hanseth 2018; Herman et al. 2020) or mobility (Weiss et al. 2020), sometimes using the term "platform-oriented infrastructure". Since there is no established definition, for the scope of this paper, we adopt the infrastructure focus of other domains and define GaaP as the adoption of platform orientation to a public sector infrastructure.

2.3 Challenges of GaaP in Practice

In practice, GaaP is applied by numerous countries, including Italy (Cordella and Paletti 2019), Russia (Styrin et al. 2022) and the UK (Brown et al. 2017) and is pursued on a supranational level (European Commission 2018). To achieve successful public value creation, GaaP needs to be properly orchestrated and "configured" (Cordella and Paletti 2019). There is no "one-size-fits-it-all" approach to transforming a government toward GaaP. Several publications provide hints on how to approach practical challenges (Bender and Heine 2021; Brown et al. 2017; Cordella and Paletti 2019; Millard 2018; O'Reilly 2011), some focusing on the analysis of practical GaaP applications. For example, Brown et al. propose an assessment framework that distinguishes between the dimensions "organizational form," "market dynamic," and "architectural structure" (Brown et al. 2017). Bender and Heine describe constituting elements of public service platforms based on the categories "platform foundation & ecosystem," "platform architecture," and "platform governance" (Bender and Heine 2021). While these conceptualizations provide the first groundwork, they are not designed to be applied to infrastructure in particular and are not targeted at practitioners.

2.4 Objective for a Solution

Based on this gap, our objective for a solution is to create an analysis method for public sector infrastructure that supports the application of GaaP in practice. To ensure its support capability, we further specify the objective by means of requirements for the method. We draw from Kuhn et al. (2022a), who find five barriers that can hinder the application of GaaP in practice. The authors find that it remains unclear for practitioners what GaaP actually means in practice. From this, we infer the need for some form of structure in the application of GaaP and formulate requirement 1 as **Req 1: The method should provide a comprehensive framework of what to consider when applying GaaP in practice**. In particular, the solution should consider the various dimensions of GaaP elaborated in literature, including the architecture and principles of platform-oriented infrastructures. Second, Kuhn et al. (2022a) find that the aim of implementing structural changes, such as the application of GaaP, is confronted with limited personnel and time in the public sector. Practitioners in these situations lack the resources for trial and error approaches or extensive preparation. Instead, there is a need for pragmatic solutions and hands-on tools. From this, we formulate **Req 2: The method should be applicable with little resources**. In particular, the solution should address the limitations of digital agencies that were founded recently and are not yet established. Third, many aspects of GaaP are not completely new and have already been considered in the public sector. Examples include the ideas of modularity and shared services, but also the government as an infrastructure provider (O'Reilly 2011). However, the existing, organically developed IT infrastructures typically contain numerous areas for improvement, which makes it challenging for practitioners to prioritize. There is the need for support to determine which areas are already close to the GaaP approach and which are not. From this, we formulate **Req 3: The method should identify gaps of the infrastructure with regard to GaaP**. In particular, the gaps should be suitable for the development of actionable proposals for improvement of the infrastructure. Fourth, while there are certain commonalities among GaaP implementation across countries, the approach needs to be adopted to its context (Smorgunov 2021). Given the identified gaps, there is a need for context-specific design to fill them. From this, we formulate **Req4: The method should create actionable proposals for the improvement of the infrastructure toward GaaP**. In particular, the proposals should be implementable by the digital agency itself, that is, should be specific for the infrastructure in question.

3 Methodology

To achieve our objective of creating a method for the analysis of public sector infrastructure regarding its platform orientation, we follow the design science research (DSR) paradigm (Hevner et al. 2004). Designing a method is an artifact of DSR that aims at creating solutions for real-world problems (Hevner et al. 2004). Given the real-world relevance of this research, we follow this paradigm. More specifically, we follow the well-established and widely used six-step design science research methodology (Peffers et al. 2007) and go through three design iterations, as shown in Table 1.

First iteration. Agency A is a digital agency in Germany, responsible of the architecture management of federal e-government infrastructure. Based on a literature review and a case study of the GaaP approach of Agency A, the first iteration yielded a three

Table 1 Overview over the three iterations of the artefact development

Iteration	Time	Design and development	Demonstration and evaluation
1st	06/2020–06/ 2021	Based on literature review and case study (Agency A)	Two applications of the method to infrastructures from Agency A
2nd	12/2021–04/ 2022	Based on evaluation results and three practitioner interviews (Agency A)	Three applications of the method to infrastructures from Agencies A, B, and C
3rd	11/2022–03/ 2023	Based on evaluation results	Two applications of the method to infrastructures from Agencies A and D

dimensional framework. For evaluation, the framework was applied to two infrastructures of Agency A. The first iteration was communicated in Kuhn et al. (2022b), which is why we focus on reporting iteration two and three in the following.

Second iteration. The *objective for a solution* was iterated based on the evaluation results and three interviews with IT architects from Agency A in December 2021. The interviews were semi-structured and lasted between 37 and 54 min. The *design and development* was conducted between January and March 2022 in several workshops among the authors, in which the framework was specified into a method. For example, we split the dimension "elements and roles" into two separate dimensions, renaming the first one "architecture". In addition, the first version had only one step, the application of a platform perspective to the infrastructure. Based on problems with the applicability, the second version was expanded to four steps, adding two steps for decomposing the infrastructure and a final step for assessing the results. For the *demonstration* and ex-post *evaluation* of the second iteration, we applied the method to three infrastructures from Agencies A, B, and C in the beginning of 2022. Agency B is an IT service provider that provides municipalities and states with an infrastructure for digital public service delivery including the corresponding business processes. Agency C is a small municipality. The corresponding workshops for the application of the method lasted a total of 7.75 h and took place in a virtual collaborative setting, using the Miro online collaboration tool. They were conducted in the participant's mother tongue. Three to five experts (IT architects and strategists) from the respective agencies participated. After a short introduction, the workshops consisted of the application of the method, i.e. the application of each step in each dimension. The workshops were concluded with a summary and a feedback section. The collected data include the recordings of the workshops, the workshop results on the online collaboration board and written as well as oral feedback from the participants.

Third iteration. Conducted at the end of 2022 and in the first quarter of 2023, the third iteration aimed at incorporating the evaluation insights from the second iteration. In the *design and development*, the method was extended by a theoretical part before the analysis to clarify the motivation for and the terminologies of GaaP; and by a design part after the analysis to improve the method's ability to infer proposals for improvement from the identified gaps. Some renaming happened to align the dimensions with participant's intuition. The steps of the analysis part remained the same. Moreover, based on the evaluation data, the principles dimension was simplified to be more consistent with the other dimensions. Finally, examples from successful GaaP countries were added to inspire the design of proposals for improvement. For the *demonstration* and ex-post *evaluation* of the resulting third iteration, we applied the method in two workshops, lasting a total of 9.5 h, to infrastructures of Agencies A and D. Agency D is the federal agency for public administration, and, among others, responsible for the infrastructure that allows the retrieval of register data. One workshop took place in a virtual collaborative setting, the other in person. Both were using the Miro online collaboration tool[1] and were conducted in the participant's mother tongue. To account for the extended method and based on feedback from iteration two, the duration of the workshops was expanded from three to five hours. One and two experts (IT architects and strategists) from the respective agencies participated. After a short introduction, the workshops started with a theoretical input by the researchers on GaaP. Then, the analysis followed dimension by dimension and step by step. After the analysis, the workshop was concluded by the overall assessment of the infrastructure and a feedback section. The collected data includes the recordings of the workshop, the results on the online collaboration board and written as well as oral feedback from the participants.

4 The GaaP Infrastructure Analysis Method

4.1 Dimensions

The GaaP infrastructure analysis method consists of four dimensions. The dimensions and their characteristics are based on literature and were refined in the course of the iterative development process. Since we adopt an infrastructure-focused definition of GaaP, we use an architecture dimension to analyze the technical aspects of a GaaP approach. Then, regarding IT governance and IT management (Pereira and da Silva 2012), we consider the actors of the infrastructure and their platform roles, the underlying principles to engage them and finally the special role of the platform owner.

GaaP Architecture. Following Brown et al. (2017) and Bender and Heine (2021), we propose an architectural dimension concerned with the elements of GaaP infrastructure and their interactions. The elements are software components such as payment or authentication. The characteristics are based on literature on constituting parts of platforms: the platform core, the platform boundary resources, and the platform ecosystem (Baldwin and Woodard 2008; Ghazawneh and Henfridsson 2013). The dimension aims to identify the components of the infrastructure in question and to

[1] The Miro board template can be found here: https://miro.com/app/board/uXjVPgMwvlo=/.

map them to the platform parts. This helps to identify inconsistencies, double entries, or the absence of components in the overall architecture of the infrastructure.

GaaP Actors. Based on Hein et al. (2020), we propose an organizational dimension concerned with the actors of the infrastructure and their roles. The actors are organizations and individuals such as administrative entities or IT service providers. The characteristics of this dimension are based on typical roles in platforms: the platform owner, the complementors, and the users (Hein et al. 2020). This dimension aims to identify actors of the infrastructure and map them to their respective platform roles. This helps to identify inconsistencies, double entries, or the absence of roles.

GaaP Principles. Based on the importance of platform principles such as openness, participation and co-creation (Cordella and Paletti 2019; Janssen and Estevez 2013; Millard 2018), we propose a dimension concerned with the engagement of users and complementors into the GaaP approach. Users and complementors are central to the ecosystem of a platform and, therefore, the dimension considers their perspective. The characteristics of the dimension are the discussed principles openness, participation, and co-creation. This helps to identify shortcomings in the ecosystem of the platform.

GaaP Activities. Based on Brown et al. (2017) and Millard (2018), we propose a dimension concerned with the infrastructure owner and its activities, especially the orchestration of platform actors by the infrastructure owner(s) (Cordella and Paletti 2019). Orchestration is the coordination of actors via the planning, implementation, and maintenance of infrastructure components and related resources such as documentation. The characteristics of the dimension are those proposed by Millard (2018): facilitation and orchestration provision of tools, and management of assets. The dimension aims to identify the management activities of the infrastructure owners to map them to the characteristics. This helps to identify inconsistencies, overlapping responsibilities, and missing elements in the infrastructure management from a platform perspective.

4.2 Method

The proposed method provides a procedure for analyzing public sector infrastructure regarding its platform orientation. For the analysis, the method's dimensions and characteristics are broken down into a theory, an analysis, and a consolidation part. The analysis part is again subdivided into four steps. Table 2 depicts the method.

The **Theory part** of the method aims at communicating the knowledge prerequisites for the analysis to the participants. The part includes a presentation of central concepts of GaaP along the dimensions of the method. For example, for the architecture dimension the difference between platform core and platform periphery are discussed.

Table 2 The GaaP infrastructure analysis method

	GaaP architecture	GaaP actors	GaaP principles	GaaP activities
Theory	Learn and discuss central concepts of GaaP and its dimensions			
Analysis				
1. Status quo	Identify the major components of the infrastructure	Identify the major actors of the infrastructure	Identify the major usage scenarios for the users and complementors	Identify the activities of the infrastructure owner(s)
2. Infrastructure decomposition	Classify the components to the infrastructure core use cases	Classify the actors by their role	Classify the scenarios by infrastructure services	Classify the activities by actors
3. Platform interpretation	Map the components to the platform core, boundary resources, and ecosystem	Map the actors to the roles of platform owner, complementor, and user	Map the infrastructure services to openness, participation, and co-creation	Map the activities to facilitation, tool provision, and asset management
4. Assessment	Identify gaps to ideal platform orientation	Identify gaps to ideal platform orientation	Identify gaps to ideal platform orientation	Identify gaps to ideal platform orientation
Consolidation	Consolidate the identified gaps and develop actionable proposals inspired by examples from other countries			

The **Analysis part** of the method follows the notion of decomposition and recomposition. For each dimension of the method, the method provides two steps for the decomposition of the current infrastructure into its sub-aspects and then two steps for the recomposition of those subparts from a platform perspective. The rationale for the notion of decomposition and recomposition and the four steps is its gradual development. The analysis starts from the status quo and progresses, step by step, to the final assessment. The status quo at the start makes the method relevant and the step-by-step approach makes it understandable. Both are supposed to increase the direct applicability in practice. **1. Status quo**. The first analysis step of each dimension is capturing the status quo. Its goal is to identify all relevant elements of this dimension. In the dimension architecture, for example, these elements are the major components of the infrastructure. The step lays the basis for the analysis that follows by defining the object of analysis, that is its scope and granularity. **2. Infrastructure decomposition**. The second analysis step of each dimension is infrastructure decomposition. Its goal is to classify the identified elements into categories. In the dimension architecture, the categories distinguish between components that are core parts of the infrastructure, supporting components, and external components. This step aims to break up the existing way of thinking, that is the current categories that are used when working with the architecture. **3. Platform interpretation**. The third analysis step of each dimension is platform interpretation. Its goal is to map the identified elements into a platform-oriented schema. In the dimension architecture, this schema is the platform core, boundary resources, and ecosystem. The step aims to apply a platform perspective to the infrastructure. **4. Assessment**. The fourth analysis step of each dimension is assessment. Its goal is to process the insights from the previous steps and infer gaps. In the dimension architecture, this can be, for example, two components with the same functionality.

The **Consolidation Part** of the method aims at converting insight from the analysis into actionable proposals. This part includes a presentation of examples from GaaP implementations of other countries, which serves as inspiration for the consolidation.

5 Demonstration

To demonstrate the presented method, we elaborated on the application of the third iteration to an infrastructure of Agency A. The infrastructure supports the online portals of the German states with information on available services, the jurisdiction, and the routing information to that jurisdiction. In the following, we exemplarily describe what the analysis yielded for the "GaaP Actors" dimension of Agency A's infrastructure.

The **Theory Part** introduced the GaaP Actors dimension with a brief overview of typical platform roles—such as users, complementors and platform owners—and their differentiation. This included the association of those roles with the typical architecture components, for instance, the platform owner being directly occupied with the platform core. The concepts were discussed using private sector examples.

The **Analysis Part** of the "GaaP Actors" dimension (see Table 3) started with identifying the major actors of the infrastructure. The participants did this autonomously and by means of sticky notes. The actors of Agency A's infrastructure are numerous since it historically was owned by another entity and several states and working groups are involved in its development. In the second step of the analysis part, the identified actors were categorized along their roles. The categories included "Who decides about new components?" and "Who uses the components?". While the former is true only for Agency A and an IT service provider which is commissioned with the coding of the infrastructure, the latter includes eight types of actors. The third step focused on the reconstruction. Here the categories from step two were used as a first guess. For instance, the actors who decided about components were assigned as platform owners and the actors who use the components were assigned as users. In the consecutive discussion, these assignments were refined. While Agency A kept its assignment as platform owner, the IT service provider was omitted to reflect that it serves only as an agent of Agency A and, thus, does ultimately not own the infrastructure. In the final step of the analysis, the participants and the researchers discussed the reconstruction and generated insights regarding gaps towards GaaP. One of those insights was that in theory the roles of the infrastructure are quite close to GaaP and also clear. However, in practice, Agency A cannot always enforce ownership.

Table 3 Excerpt from the analysis part of the exemplary application

	GaaP actors
Analysis	
1. Status quo	Relevant stakeholders: Agency A, IT service provider A, editorial offices of the states, owners of online services, developers of online services, operators of online portals, the states, online service providers, federal ministry of the interior, citizens, working groups
2. Infrastructure decomposition	Who decides about new components?: Agency A, IT service provider A Who develops and deploys components?: IT service provider A Who uses the components?: Editorial offices of the states, owners of online services, developers of online services, operators of online portals, the states, online service providers, federal ministry of the interior, citizens Who is responsible for the infrastructure as a whole?: Agency A, board of CIOs, board of department heads, integration group
3. Platform interpretation	Platform owner: Agency A, board of CIOs, board of department heads, integration group Complementors: Editorial offices of the states, owners of online services, developers of online services, operators of online portals, the states, online service providers, federal ministry of the interior Users: Companies, citizens
4. Assessment	* The platform owner is kind of clear, how can this be enforced in practice? * Agency A is not always able to decide about API standards [that are central to the infrastructure] * Consolidation of working groups? * Who is setting standards? The complementors or legacy boards? * How can the relationship between owner and complementors be better defined? […]

The **Consolidation Part** built on the insights of the analysis and aimed at inferring context-specific proposals for improvement. To inspire this process, the researchers presented examples from other countries such as the UK, Italy and Estonia. Then, the insights of the analysis of the four dimensions were consolidated in a discussion. For example, the aforementioned insight regarding enforcement resulted in the recommendation to clarify the relationship between owner and complementors.

6 Evaluation

To evaluate the presented method, we consider the collected data from the application workshops of the third iteration and analyze them along the defined requirements for the method.

Comprehensiveness. The presented method is organized along four dimensions. The dimensions are based on literature, combining existing sets of dimensions to include all relevant aspects. Namely, we integrate the dimension of platform principles which play a central role in literature (Millard 2018; O'Reilly 2011) but are not explicitly included in other proposed sets of dimensions, for example (Brown et al. 2017). Regarding the steps of the method, the analysis part proved stable after iteration two, with the procedure of decomposition and recomposition being perceived as helpful from the participants. ("*It was interesting to compile the status quo of our infrastructure and then deconstruct and reconstruct it*", Agency C). In iteration three, the newly added theory part, with the motivation for GaaP, and the consolidation part, with examples from practice, were highlighted by the participants.

Applicability. All steps in all dimensions were successfully performed in the application workshops. The workshops concluded with gaps and proposals. This speaks to the general applicability of the artefact, and was also reflected by the participants ("*Where do I see myself and where is our system in this context—that has obviously worked well*", Agency D). Moreover, the method proved to be applicable in a short amount of time (five hours) and with few participants compared to the size of GaaP as a transformation effort. Given the considerable output of the workshops, this speaks to the efficiency of the method. However, the actual application of the method was conducted under the researchers' supervision. As recorded in the observations, this supervision was necessary to explain the steps and make the application efficient.

Identification of gaps. The workshops created 15 (Agency A) and nine (Agency D) insights on gaps for the respective infrastructures. Those gaps mainly became apparent in the recomposition step, which introduced the platform perspective and, thus, a focus on specific aspects of the infrastructure. Other insights were created through the combined consideration of the different dimensions, leading to back and forth discussions. An example for this is the consideration of the platform owner in the dimension GaaP Activities, which in one example led to the reconsideration of the set of core components ("*Because we cannot dictate that, we do not own our own platform. That might also be an important revelation*", Agency A). Several participants saw the structured approach of the method as a key reason for its capability to create these insights. ("*The structure is quite good. That helps already [...] to think differently about it*", Agency D).

Creation of proposals. Already the second iteration received good feedback regarding the transferability and value of the results for the participants ("*I can derive many things for my own work*", Agency B). However, not many proposals where explicitly developed within the workshop. For iteration three, the workshops created four (Agency A) and nine proposals (Agency D) respectively, for example "clarification of the relationship between owner and complementors" (Agency A) and "focus on an API instead of the dashboard" (Agency D). The improvements were created either directly during the analysis or in the final consolidation part of the workshop. For the latter, the examples from other countries were perceived as particularly helpful, suggesting that the changes from iteration two to three were effective.

7 Discussion and Conclusion

Based on the evaluation we would argue that the presented method meets the defined requirements and, by extension, the objective for a solution. In the following, we discuss the implications for theory and practice as well as the limitations of this research.

For successful public value creation, a GaaP approach needs to be properly orchestrated and "configured" (Cordella and Paletti 2019). We find that a decomposition and recomposition procedure can organize the analysis and guide its user. For practitioners, that means that while there are barriers to applying GaaP in practice (Kuhn et al. 2022a), tools such as methods can help to overcome them. In addition, our method is structured along multiple dimensions. While there are existing sets of dimensions (Brown et al. 2017), our research suggests that a dimension concerned with platform's principles such as openness (Millard 2018; Soto Setzke et al. 2019) can complement them. Further research should investigate the role of platform principles in GaaP.

Public sector infrastructures play a fundamental part in GaaP (Bender and Heine 2021; Brown et al. 2017; Pope 2019). The method shows that focusing on their platform orientation can be a rewarding starting point for GaaP endeavors in practice. However, our method builds on both GaaP/E-Government (e.g., Brown et al. 2017; Millard 2018) and general IS platform literature (Baldwin and Woodard 2008; Ghazawneh and Henfridsson 2013; Hein et al. 2020). While GaaP literature proved helpful for determining the dimensions, the IS platform literature was able to fill those dimensions with characteristics. For the ongoing conceptualization efforts of GaaP, this means that further integration with IS platformization literature, especially that with a focus on infrastructure (e.g. Bygstad and Hanseth 2018; Törmer and Henningsson 2020), has potential. The importance of infrastructure is also relevant to policymakers who have to justify investments into backend capabilities that are not directly visible in the frontend. Our method can help them communicate the actual dimensions and characteristics of platform-oriented infrastructures and, thus, the GaaP approach.

Finally, we find that theoretical conceptualizations of GaaP can be challenging to apply in practice. Concepts like openness or leveraging help to develop an understanding of the general idea of GaaP, but they need to be supported with examples and implemented by skilled personnel. Governments planning to apply GaaP should consider successful examples to make the transformation more effective. In addition, professionals with specific "platformization" expertise and skills are necessary.

We see the strength of our artefact in its relevance to practitioners. However, while we tested our method with different cases, we acknowledge that the proposed method was only applied to infrastructures within one European country. This calls for future research that applies the method across other contexts. A similar limitation concerns the evaluation concept of the method. The evaluation data speaks to the impact of the method on the participants and not on the infrastructure itself. While a positive impact on the participants arguably can have a positive impact on the infrastructure as well, this needs to be further investigated. Finally, the researchers' guidance was required to apply the method. This calls for further research that considers improvements in the applicability of the method without expert guidance and beyond single workshops. While limitations exist, we believe that our research is valuable to both theory and practice. In particular, we hope to further the application of GaaP in practice.

Acknowledgements We thank the University of Zurich and the Digital Society Initiative for partially financing this study under the DIZH postdoc fellowship of Liudmila Zavolokina. We thank Micha Lutz and Efstratios Pahis for their support and our reviewers for their comments.

References

Baldwin, C.Y., Woodard, C.J., 2008. The Architecture of Platforms: A Unified View. SSRN Journal. https://doi.org/10.2139/ssrn.1265155

Bender, B., Heine, M., 2021. Government as a Platform? Constitutive Elements of Public Service Platforms, in: Kö, A., Francesconi, E., Kotsis, G., Tjoa, A.M., Khalil, I. (Eds.), Electronic Government and the Information Systems Perspective, Lecture Notes in Computer Science. Springer International Publishing, Cham, pp. 3–20. https://doi.org/10.1007/978-3-030-86611-2_1

Boudreau, K., 2010. Open Platform Strategies and Innovation: Granting Access vs. Devolving Control. Management Science 56, 1849–1872. https://doi.org/10.1287/mnsc.1100.1215

Brown, A., Fishenden, J., Thompson, M., Venters, W., 2017. Appraising the impact and role of platform models and Government as a Platform (GaaP) in UK Government public service reform: Towards a Platform Assessment Framework (PAF). Government Information Quarterly 34, 167–182. https://doi.org/10.1016/j.giq.2017.03.003

Bygstad, B., Hanseth, O., 2018. Transforming Digital Infrastructures through Platformization, in: ECIS 2018 Research Papers.

Constantinides, P., Henfridsson, O., Parker, G.G., 2018. Introduction—Platforms and Infrastructures in the Digital Age. Information Systems Research 29, 381–400. https://doi.org/10.1287/isre.2018.0794

Cordella, A., Paletti, A., 2019. Government as a platform, orchestration, and public value creation: The Italian case. Government Information Quarterly 36, 101409. https://doi.org/10.1016/j.giq.2019.101409

de Reuver, M., Sørensen, C., Basole, R.C., 2018. The Digital Platform: A Research Agenda. Journal of Information Technology 33, 124–135. https://doi.org/10.1057/s41265-016-0033-3

European Commission, 2018. Digital Platform for Public Services. DG Joint Research Centre.

European Commission, 2022. Declaration on European Digital Rights and Principles | Shaping Europe's digital future [WWW Document]. URL https://digital-strategy.ec.europa.eu/en/library/declaration-european-digital-rights-and-principles (accessed 2.16.22).

Fishenden, J., Thompson, M., 2013. Digital Government, Open Architecture, and Innovation: Why Public Sector IT Will Never Be the Same Again. Journal of Public Administration Research and Theory 23, 977–1004.

Gawer, A., 2014. Bridging differing perspectives on technological platforms: Toward an integrative framework. Research Policy 43, 1239–1249. https://doi.org/10.1016/j.respol.2014.03.006

Ghazawneh, A., Henfridsson, O., 2013. Balancing platform control and external contribution in third-party development: the boundary resources model. Information Systems Journal 23, 173–192. https://doi.org/10.1111/j.1365-2575.2012.00406.x
Gregor, S., Hevner, A.R., 2013. Positioning and presenting design science research for maximum impact. MIS quarterly 37, 337–355.
Hein, A., Schreieck, M., Riasanow, T., Setzke, D.S., Wiesche, M., Böhm, M., Krcmar, H., 2020. Digital platform ecosystems. Electron Markets 30, 87–98. https://doi.org/10.1007/s12525-019-00377-4
Herman, H., Grobbelaar, S.S., Pistorius, C., 2020. The design and development of technology platforms in a developing country healthcare context from an ecosystem perspective. BMC Medical Informatics and Decision Making 20, 55. https://doi.org/10.1186/s12911-020-1028-0
Hevner, A., R, A., March, S., T, S., Park, Park, J., Ram, Sudha, 2004. Design Science in Information Systems Research. Management Information Systems Quarterly 28, 75.
Jacobides, M.G., Cennamo, C., Gawer, A., 2018. Towards a theory of ecosystems. Strategic Management Journal 39, 2255–2276. https://doi.org/10.1002/smj.2904
Janssen, M., Estevez, E., 2013. Lean government and platform-based governance—Doing more with less. Government Information Quarterly, ICEGOV 2011 Supplement 30, S1–S8. https://doi.org/10.1016/j.giq.2012.11.003
Karhu, K., Gustafsson, R., Lyytinen, K., 2018. Exploiting and Defending Open Digital Platforms with Boundary Resources: Android's Five Platform Forks. Information Systems Research 29, 479–497. https://doi.org/10.1287/isre.2018.0786
Kuhn, P., Buchinger, M., Balta, D., Matthes, F., 2022a. Barriers of applying Government as a Platform in Practice: Evidence from Germany, in: Proceedings of the 55th Hawaii International Conference on System Sciences. Presented at the Hawaii International Conference on System Sciences. https://doi.org/10.24251/HICSS.2022.328
Kuhn, P., Dallner, S., Buchinger, M., Balta, D., 2022b. Towards "Government as a Platform": An analysis framework for public sector infrastructure, in: Wirtschaftsinformatik 2022 Proceedings. Presented at the WI 2022.
Millard, J., 2018. Open governance systems: Doing more with more. Government Information Quarterly, Platform Governance for Sustainable Development 35, S77–S87. https://doi.org/10.1016/j.giq.2015.08.003
O'Reilly, T., 2011. Government as a Platform. Innovations: Technology, Governance, Globalization 6, 13–40. https://doi.org/10.1162/INOV_a_00056
Peffers, K., Tuunanen, T., Rothenberger, M.A., Chatterjee, S., 2007. A Design Science Research Methodology for Information Systems Research. Journal of Management Information Systems 24, 45–77. https://doi.org/10.2753/MIS0742-1222240302
Pereira, R., Silva, M.M. da, 2012. Designing a New Integrated IT Governance and IT Management Framework Based on Both Scientific and Practitioner Viewpoint. IJEIS 8, 1–43. https://doi.org/10.4018/jeis.2012100101
Pope, R., 2019. Playbook: Government as a Platform.
Seo, H., Myeong, S., 2020. The Priority of Factors of Building Government as a Platform with Analytic Hierarchy Process Analysis. Sustainability 12, 5615. https://doi.org/10.3390/su12145615
Smorgunov, L., 2021. Governability and a technocratic approach to government as a platform: critics using the Russian case. International Journal of Electronic Governance 13, 4–20. https://doi.org/10.1504/IJEG.2021.114298
Soto Setzke, D., Böhm, M., Krcmar, H., 2019. Platform Openness: A Systematic Literature Review and Avenues for Future Research. Wirtschaftsinformatik 2019 Proceedings.
Styrin, E., Mossberger, K., Zhulin, A., 2022. Government as a platform: Intergovernmental participation for public services in the Russian Federation. Government Information Quarterly 39, 101627. https://doi.org/10.1016/j.giq.2021.101627
Tiwana, A., 2013. Platform Ecosystems: Aligning Architecture, Governance, and Strategy. Morgan Kaufmann.

Törmer, R.L., Henningsson, S., 2020. Platformization and Internationalization in the LEGO Group, in: HICSS Proceedings. Presented at the HICSS. https://doi.org/10.24251/HICSS.2020.709

Van Alstyne, M.W., Parker, G.G., Choudary, S.P., 2016. Pipelines, platforms, and the new rules of strategy. Harvard business review 94, 54–62.

Vestues, K., Mikalsen, M., Monteiro, E., 2021. Using digital platforms to promote a service-oriented logic in public sector organizations: A case study. Presented at the Hawaii International Conference on System Sciences. https://doi.org/10.24251/HICSS.2021.269

Weiss, N., Wiesche, M., Schreieck, M., Krcmar, H., 2020. Learning to be a Platform Owner: How BMW Enhances App Development for Cars. IEEE Transactions on Engineering Management 1–17. https://doi.org/10.1109/TEM.2020.3017051

Gender and Mobility—A Literature Review on Women's (Non-)Use of Shared Mobility Services

Jennifer Kendziorra, Michelle Barmann, Kristina Kusanke, and Anne-Katrin Witte

Abstract In the context of the development of smart cities, the number and types of shared mobility solutions, such as carsharing and bikesharing, have increased in recent years. While the services are generally becoming more popular, there are comparatively few women among the users. With a view to gender-equitable mobility, this literature review explores gender-specific reasons for this low use of shared mobility solutions. Based on 35 relevant studies from multiple databases and disciplines, we identified four overarching barriers related to: security, availability, simplicity, and costs. By identifying these barriers and the reasons for them, and by linking them in a self-developed conceptual model with starting points for potential actions to address these issues, this literature review contributes to gender-equitable mobility.

Keywords Shared mobility · Smart cities · Gender differences · Gender equity · Literature review

1 Introduction

The development of smart cities is revolutionizing urban planning by using technology and data-driven approaches to improve many aspects of urban life in an efficient and sustainable way, including transportation (Benevolo et al. 2016; Nikitas

---

J. Kendziorra (✉) · M. Barmann · K. Kusanke · A.-K. Witte
Chair of Information Management, FernUniversität in Hagen, Hagen, Germany
e-mail: jennifer.kendziorra@fernuni-hagen.de

M. Barmann
e-mail: michelle.barmann@studium.fernuni-hagen.de

K. Kusanke
e-mail: kristina.kusanke@fernuni-hagen.de

A.-K. Witte
e-mail: anne-katrin.witte@fernuni-hagen.de

D. Beverungen et al. (eds.), *Transforming the Digitally Sustainable Enterprise*, Lecture Notes in Information Systems and Organisation 76,
https://doi.org/10.1007/978-3-031-80125-9_21

et al. 2017; Singh 2019). The integration of advanced information and communication technologies in transportation has given rise to innovative 'smart' mobility solutions, which are recognized as a crucial component in improving the quality of services for all citizens (Giffinger et al. 2007; Orlowski and Romanowska 2019; Singh 2019). One of the main smart mobility innovations is shared mobility services (Butler et al. 2020) such as bikesharing, e-scooters, carsharing, and ridesharing, where multiple users share the same transportation options on a pay-per-use basis (Nikitas et al. 2017). Despite the associated potential benefits of creating more sustainable and accessible transportation systems, studies have revealed a considerable gender gap in the adoption and usage of these services. User data shows that across different types of shared mobility, country contexts, and providers, the proportion of female users remains consistently low, typically ranging from 20 to 40% (Ramboll Smart Mobility 2021; Reidl 2021; Valentiner 2021).

Previous research on mobility and transportation has shown that gender is an influential variable, affecting transportation mode choice, with significant differences prevailing between women and men (Duchène 2011; Ramboll Smart Mobility 2021). Women often have more complex travel patterns, combining multiple routes with short stops in between, for example, to take children to daycare on the way to work or to run other errands. Men are more likely to move linearly from A to B, e.g., to and from work (Gerecht Mobil, n.d.; Ramboll Smart Mobility 2021). However, due to the fact that decision-making in this sector is conducted almost exclusively by men for decades (Stanković and Nikolić 2021) with only 22% of workers in the transport sector in Europe being women today (Hortelano et al. 2021), transportation systems and mobility solutions tend to be geared toward the average man and his needs and travel patterns (Ramboll 2021), not taking gender differences in travel needs and patterns into account (ITF 2021; Ramboll Smart Mobility 2021; Women in Mobility 2022). As a consequence, feminist urban planning has developed as a research field that aims to address the limitations of traditional urban planning. It recognizes the importance of considering the diverse needs and experiences of all individuals regardless of gender, age, and origin and challenges the male-oriented "one size fits all" approach (Majdoub 2023).

In line with this perspective and in order to design a truly gender-neutral transport sector that is equally accessible to all genders, it is important to examine the reasons for the above-mentioned gap, which may be rooted in different mobility behaviors and needs, as well as gender-specific barriers. Identifying and addressing these points will help to design and enable more equal transportation systems in the present and future. Thus, the goal of this paper is to identify possible causes for the low female usage rate of shared mobility services and to answer the following research question (RQ) and two sub-questions (SQ):

- RQ: Why are women less likely to use shared mobility services?
  - SQ1: Which gender-specific differences exist in mobility behavior?
  - SQ2: What barriers do women face when using shared mobility services?

To answer these research questions, a systematic literature review was conducted. Considering the increasing number of publications in past years, this method allows us to thoroughly examine previous research, consequently gaining a broad perspective and valuable insights into our area of interest. Therefore, relevant literature was identified and reviewed according to the works of vom Brocke et al. (2009) and Webster and Watson (2002). The current state of knowledge will be explored to find correlations between mobility use and gender in order to identify possible starting points for bridging the gender mobility gap in shared mobility services.

This paper is structured as follows: Sect. 2 establishes a theoretical basis, explaining relevant key terms related to shared mobility. Section 3 addresses the research methodology and its process. Section 4 presents the research findings and Sect. 5 interprets them, pointing out possible links for future research. Finally, in the conclusion, the most important findings are briefly summarized.

2 Theoretical Background

Transportation is a key factor in determining the quality of life (Jiao 2021). The digital age has created new business models that integrate mobility with technology (Jiao 2021), starting in the late 1990s with websites that helped drivers and passengers to connect and organize joint trips (Guyader et al. 2021). Driven by the advancement of information and communication technologies and an increased environmental orientation, shared mobility services were developed, which belong to the "sharing economies" and encompass business models that focus on collaborative or shared consumption providing access to goods or services without the costs and environmental impacts associated with personal ownership (Karbaumer and Metz 2022; Krämer and Bongaerts 2019). "Shared mobility", the sharing of a vehicle, bicycle, or other modes of transportation, is a growing sector of the sharing economy, where smartphone interactions and intermediary platforms create innovative services and bring user groups together (Jie et al. 2021; Mourey and Köhler 2017), providing short-term access to transportation on demand (Shaheen et al. 2017a).

Shared mobility is often found in the context of smart cities as one important topic among other "smart mobility" solutions, such as intelligent transport systems, alternate fuel systems, or driving automation systems (Butler et al. 2020). The smart city concept describes a concept where communication and information technology are used in cities in an intelligent and sustainable way (Wawer et al. 2022), with the overarching goal to improve various sectors such as economy, governance, and mobility, and to enhance citizens' quality of life (Benevolo et al. 2016; Giffinger et al. 2007). However, not all of these smart solutions seem to reach women to the same extent as men (Singh 2019), considering the gender usage gap mentioned above and the often applied "one size fits all" approach in the mobility sector. This issue has already been recognized by previous research which tries to address these inequalities and promote gender equality within urban environments (e.g. Hudson and Rönnblom

2020; Ortiz Escalante and Gutiérrez Valdivia 2015; Singh 2019), including transportation. By adopting a feminist, gender-neutral, perspective on urban planning, smart cities should be designed in an inclusive, safe, and accessible way for everyone (Hudson and Rönnblom 2020; Majdoub 2023; Singh 2019).

Smart mobility, as one of the most important aspects of smart cities (Benevolo et al. 2016), and shared mobility, as one aspect of smart mobility, thus play a fundamental role in improving the lives of women and other underrepresented groups in the context of feminist urban planning (Singh 2019; Zehba and Firoz 2022), but the use of these transportation options is still limited compared to men (Reidl 2021; Valentiner 2021; Ramboll Smart Mobility 2021). In order to explore the reasons for women's lower use of shared mobility services, it is important to first have an understanding of the different forms of shared mobility.

Two overarching forms of shared mobility can be distinguished: "vehicle sharing" and "trip sharing" (Karbaumer and Metz 2022; Shaheen et al. 2017a). "Vehicle sharing" includes carsharing and shared micromobility (Karbaumer and Metz 2022). Ridesharing and on-demand ride services fall under the umbrella term "trip sharing" (Karbaumer and Metz 2022). There are numerous forms and characteristics for the respective forms of shared mobility. To facilitate understanding, the different forms of shared mobility solutions have been summarized in Fig. 1, with the shared mobility types focused on in the analysis marked in bold.

Carsharing allows the use of locally available cars for any period of time (Karbaumer and Metz 2022). The vehicles are owned by a provider and payment is usually per hour and per kilometer (Karbaumer and Metz 2022; Krauss et al. 2021). The use of small vehicles, such as bicycles, scooters, and mopeds, powered by muscle power or electricity, falls under "*shared micromobility*" (Karbaumer and Metz 2022). Such offerings include for example bikesharing, scootersharing, and mopedsharing (Karbaumer and Metz 2022). They are freely accessible in public spaces, can be unlocked and locked via smartphone at the beginning and the end of the ride, and billing is usually per minute (Krauss et al. 2021). For vehicle sharing, further distinctions can be made regarding the usage specifications, e.g., whether the vehicles have to be picked up and returned at the same place (roundtrip) or whether

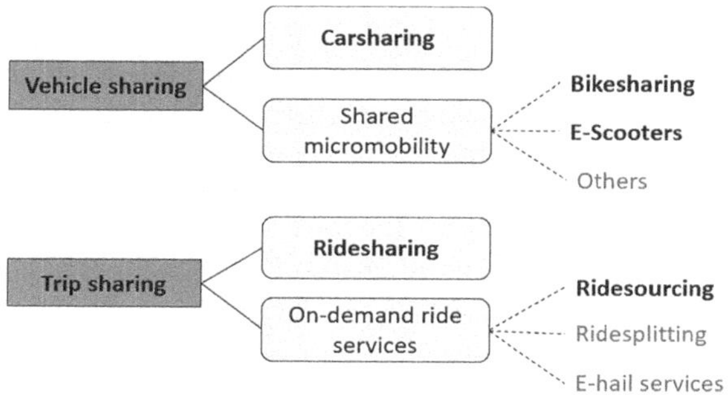

Fig. 1 Forms of shared mobility (based on Karbaumer and Metz 2022)

the return location expands to a specific operating zone defined by the provider (one-way) (Karbaumer and Metz 2022; Shaheen et al. 2017a).

Through *Ridesharing*, several people share a single vehicle. The start and end destinations are recorded within the intermediary platform or app and passengers agree on a pick-up location before the trip begins (Karbaumer and Metz 2022). In contrast to such formal ridesharing models that connect services and user groups via a platform, ridesharing services can also be created through own networks (informal ridesharing model). The latter ones are, however, not part of our analysis. *On-demand ride services* differ from ridesharing in that the driver acts as the chauffeur; the driver and passenger do not share a common start and end destination (Shaheen et al. 2017a; Weber 2020). This includes the following models: ridesourcing, ridesplitting, and e-hail services (Karbaumer and Metz 2022; Shaheen et al. 2017a). *Ridesourcing* providers, also called "ride hailing" and "ride booking", use online platforms to match passengers in need of a ride with a private driver (Shaheen et al. 2017a). Drivers typically work on a freelance basis, they are not directly employed by the service provider and are not licensed cab drivers (Karbaumer and Metz 2022). Compared to traditional cabs, operators of ridesourcing companies are not bound to regulated fares and payments are cashless via an app (Weber 2020). Ridesourcing services offer various vehicles, such as vehicles with car seats, wheelchair-accessible vehicles, SUVs, etc. (Shaheen et al. 2017a). These include providers such as "Uber" and "Lyft". *Ridesplitting* is a further development of the ridesourcing concept, where users with similar origins and destinations are assigned a ride in real-time (Karbaumer and Metz 2022). The trip and trip costs are shared amongst the users (Shaheen et al. 2017a). Ridesplitting services are operated by ridesourcing companies, such as "Uber-POOL" and "Lyft Line". Due to competition from ridesourcing providers, cab services have developed so-called "*e-hail services*" (Shaheen et al. 2017a), which are operated either by a cab company or a third party. This allows travelers to book a cab electronically through a service app (Shaheen et al. 2017a), such as "taxi.eu" and "Bolt" (Karbaumer and Metz 2022).

3 Methodology

As the aim of this paper is to identify possible causes for the low female usage rate of shared mobility services, a systematic literature review was conducted to summarize the current state of research on this topic and to find possible starting points for gender equitable mobility. We followed the approach of vom Brocke et al. (2009), which requires rigorous documentation and presentation of the literature review and search process by applying five sequential steps.

In the first step, the scope of the literature review was defined. In our study, the focus of this paper was on empirical findings (research outcomes) and concepts. The aim of the literature analysis was to analyze the results of various studies on gender-specific differences in mobility behavior and gender-specific mobility requirements and to synthesize the existing results and theoretical approaches to the given research question. The selection of literature was based on predefined selection criteria. The literature to be examined was presented conceptually and viewed from a neutral position. This work can be relevant for general scholars as well as for practitioners. The conceptualization of the topic (step two) was conducted as part of Sect. 2 by providing an overview of shared mobility and thus enabling a common understanding of the relevant concepts. The approach to the literature search and analysis (steps three and four) is explained within this section. The results were then classified and presented using a concept matrix according to Webster and Watson (2002), which ensures reusability. Possible starting points or questions for future research (step five) are discussed in Sect. 5.

To optimize the search process and find sources containing all specified search terms, we used the advanced search function and the Boolean operators "AND" and "OR". Key terms were enclosed in quotation marks to search for groups of words and exact matches. Depending on the database, the search strings had to be partially adjusted. The literature search was limited to the period 2017–2022 in order to collect the most recent data in a rapidly evolving sector, but at the same time not to limit the results too much. Due to the background of the authors, English and German literature was considered. Thus, we searched the selected databases (see Fig. 2) for the following two search strings that should appear in the abstract:

- "shared mobility" OR "transport" AND "gender" for English literature
- "shared mobility" OR "geteilte mobilität" AND "geschlecht" for German literature.

The literature databases and the selection of relevant publications are presented in Fig. 2.

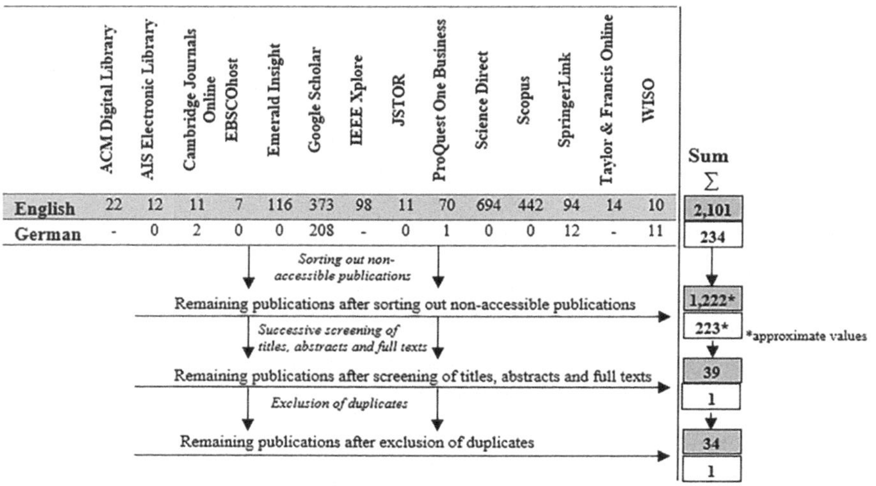

Fig. 2 Selection of relevant publications (own representation)

Three of the examined databases did not support German literature (see databases with "-"). Some results had to be excluded due to a lack of accessibility, which reduced the number of sources that we analyzed for content. In two databases this restriction was not clearly determinable, so the values with the * can only be understood as approximate values. The total number of the remaining literature decreased due to the lack of relevance to the research question. Search results were sorted out sequentially, first based on the title, then by reading the abstract. In the English search string, "transport" was included as a search term to ensure that literature where the authors may not explicitly use the term "shared mobility", but (in part) discuss this type of mobility, could be found. As expected, this also resulted in many irrelevant search hits, which were therefore excluded (e.g., men and women were asked about mobility, e.g., women's opinion on using public transportation during COVID-19). All papers with relevant abstracts were subjected to a full-text screening, leaving 40 sources. After removing five duplicates, a total of 34 English sources and one German source remained. Some of the identified sources did not specifically focus on shared mobility, but their concepts could nevertheless still be applied to shared mobility (e.g., the lack of bicycle infrastructure or street lights in public spaces also affects the use of bikesharing services). Our final dataset includes studies from different countries and continents, as there were no cultural or country-based exclusion criteria. In the next step, the relevant sources were analyzed for their content and structured using a concept matrix (see Table 1) based on their answers to the research questions.

4 Results

Our systematic literature review shows that gender differences in shared mobility are already being recognized and studied. Of the 35 references considered, 27 were published within the last three years and only 8 are from 2017 and 2019, highlighting the growing importance of this research field. The results of the literature review are presented in an overarching concept matrix (see Table 1). The 35 sources are numbered as in the reference list. The first major column 'Focus' shows which types of shared mobility and/or whether general shared mobility was discussed in the paper. In addition, the specific types of shared mobility were numbered with superscripts (Carsharing^1, Bikesharing^2, E-Scooters^3, Ridesharing^4, Ridesourcing^5) to enable a more precise analysis with regard to SQ2. The second column refers to SQ1, i.e., an examination of the female-specific characteristics in mobility behavior found in the literature. Here, an 'x' has been inserted, when a specific category is mentioned by a reference. The third column shows the barriers preventing women from using shared mobility services (SQ2), which are also marked with an 'x'. In order to provide a more detailed overview and to be able to better derive practical implications in the discussion, we additionally marked when certain barriers were mentioned in relation to a specific type of shared mobility (e.g. for reference 5, the barrier 'transport choice' was mentioned in relation to bikesharing and the barrier 'affordability' in relation

Table 1 Concept matrix: state of research on gender differences in shared mobility services

	Focus						Mobility behavior (SQ1)					
							Travel characteristics			Role characteristics		
	Carsharing[1]	Bikesharing[2]	E-Scooters[3]	Ridesharing[4]	Ridesourcing[5]	General shared mobility	Short distances	Trip chaining	Walking	Caregiver	Part-time	Feminine constructions
[1]		x					x	x		x		
[2]		x										x
[3]						x						
[4]						x	x					
[5]		x			x	x				x		
[6]						x						
[7]		x	x									
[8]		x										
[9]						x						
[10]			x							x		x
[11]		x				x	x	x			x	
[12]						x						
[13]		x				x	x	x		x		
[14]						x	x	x		x	x	
[15]		x				x	x	x		x		
[16]				x								
[17]						x				x		
[18]	x	x	x	x								

(continued)

Table 1 (continued)

	Focus						Mobility behavior (SQ1)					
							Travel characteristics			Role characteristics		
	Carsharing[1]	Bikesharing[2]	E-Scooters[3]	Ridesharing[4]	Ridesourcing[5]	General shared mobility	Short distances	Trip chaining	Walking	Caregiver	Part-time	Feminine constructions
[19]		x				x		x		x		
[20]	x					x				x		
[21]						x		x	x	x		
[22]		x								x		
[23]	x	x		x	x							
[24]						x	x	x	x	x		
[25]			x			x						
[26]						x	x	x	x	x		
[27]		x				x	x	x		x		x
[28]	x	x	x	x	x	x	x	x	x	x	x	
[29]						x	x		x			
[30]			x									
[31]	x	x				x						
[32]	x	x				x	x	x	x	x	x	
[33]			x									
[34]	x	x										
[35]		x										x
∑	7	18	7	4	5	22	12	12	6	16	4	4

(continued)

Table 1 (continued)

	Barriers (SQ2)										
	Security				Availability			Simplicity		Costs	
	Transport options	Street lighting	Ergonomics	Gender preferences	Lacking infrastructure	Parking zone	Coverage	Registration	Digital skills	High costs for families	Affordability
[1]	x^2				x^2						
[2]	x^2		x^2		x^2						
[3]											
[4]		x									
[5]	x^2										x^5
[6]									x		x
[7]	$x^{2,3}$		$x^{2,3}$		$x^{2,3}$						
[8]					x^2			x^2			
[9]									x		
[10]	x^3	x^3	x^3		x^3	x^3	x^3	x^3	x^3		
[11]	x^2							x	x		x
[12]											
[13]	x^2										
[14]											x
[15]				x^5			x^2				
[16]				x^4							
[17]		x			x		x		x		

(continued)

Table 1 (continued)

	Barriers (SQ2)										
	Security				Availability			Simplicity		Costs	
	Transport options	Street lighting	Ergonomics	Gender preferences	Lacking infrastructure	Parking zone	Coverage	Registration	Digital skills	High costs for families	Affordability
[18]					$x^{1,2,3,4}$						
[19]	x^2									x^2	x^2
[20]	x^1						x^1			x^1	
[21]											
[22]		x^2									
[23]				$x^{1,4,5}$							
[24]		x								x	x
[25]		x			x^3						
[26]											
[27]		x^2	x^2		x^2						
[28]	x^2	x		x^2	$x^{1,2}$					$x^{1,4,5}$	x^1
[29]											
[30]	x^3		x^3		x^3			x^3			
[31]					$x^{2,5}$	x^2	x		x^1		$x^{1,5}$
[32]	$x^{1,2}$										$x^{1,2}$
[33]		x^3			x^3						x^3
[34]						$x^{1,2}$	$x^{1,2}$				
[35]					x^2						
∑	12	9	5	4	14	3	6	4	7	4	10

Source Own representation

to ridesourcing). The last row of the concept matrix shows the sum of how many references are mentioned in each of the categories.

The differences found in the mobility behavior of men and women are mainly ascribed to the prevailing gender roles and lead to different travel patterns (e.g., Oviedo et al. 2020; Singh 2019). Almost half of the publications highlighted the still rather traditional role distribution, with women more often taking on domestic or caring roles, as opposed to men taking on the role of the breadwinner (Joshi et al. 2022; Oviedo et al. 2020). The prevalence of feminine constructions was also evident in the literature, where cultural expectations of women and "feminine" behavior were mentioned (Carboni et al. 2021, p. 3; Wild et al. 2021, p. 7). These distinct gender roles seem to shape the mobility behavior between men and women (Lecompte and Bocarejo 2017; Singh 2019), making women's travel behavior more complex due to different responsibilities and work roles (AitBihiOuali and Klingen 2022). Women are more likely to work part-time due to family obligations or responsibilities and are more likely to be responsible for housework, children, and elderly relatives (Hortelano et al. 2021; Ramboll Smart Mobility 2021). As a result, they are also more likely to have luggage, children, or other passengers with them (Ramboll Smart Mobility 2021). One study shows that women make twice as many trips for domestic tasks, such as taking children to school, compared to men (Hortelano et al. 2021).

The imbalance of domestic tasks puts a strain on women's time budgets: They travel shorter distances, drive less, use public transportation more often, walk more often, travel during off-peak hours, and resort to trip chaining (adding several short stops along their journey) (Ramboll Smart Mobility 2021; Saigal et al. 2021; Singh 2019).

Men, on the other hand, tend to travel longer distances and primarily travel for work-related activities (Lenz et al. 2019), and are more likely to exhibit a linear travel pattern from A to B (Ramboll Smart Mobility 2021). Research shows that women are more likely to work closer to home and thus travel shorter distances to work (Nasrin and Bunker 2021; Singh 2019). For example, women were found to be twice as likely to walk to work (28%) as men (14%) (Singh 2019).

In a second step, the publications were examined for gender-specific barriers that (may) lead to a gender imbalance in the use of shared mobility services. During the analysis of the relevant literature, four factors emerged that influence people's mobility decisions and behavior, namely: security (i.e., how safe one feels when using the vehicle), availability (i.e., how accessible and flexible the mode of transportation is at the time of need), simplicity (i.e., the ease of use), and costs (i.e., what costs incur). For this reason, it seemed useful to analyze the literature with regard to these four factors and to classify the barriers mentioned in this way. Therefore, the barriers were first recorded individually and then grouped into the four overarching categories (see Table 1).

Women tend to be more concerned about security than men (Levin 2019; Meyer and Shaheen 2017). Security is a high priority when choosing a mode of transportation, especially at night or in remote locations (Cassitas Hino and Cunha 2019; Haddad et al. 2022). Fear of assault and harassment strongly influences the route and transportation choices: For example, women often opt for longer routes if they perceive them to be safer or better lit at night (Cassitas Hino and Cunha 2021; Parnell et al. 2022). Considering this, and the sometimes long time it takes to unlock bikesharing bikes and e-scooters, the lack of street lighting at their stations is considered a barrier resulting in the non-use of such services (Haddad et al. 2022; Meyer and Shaheen 2017). While one of the main security-related barriers of micromobility solutions tends to relate to the fact that women are alone when using them, further barriers arise even in a more social setting, as seen with ridesourcing and ridesharing. Here, in both cases, women are in an enclosed vehicle with another person, typically a stranger (Nagy and Csiszár 2022). Particularly, the lack of the option to specify gender preferences was identified as a reason for the low female usage rate. Women prefer female drivers, however, only 5% of ridesourcing drivers are women (ITF 2021).

One barrier that has been mentioned in relation to all types of shared mobility services is the limited transportation and carrying capacity (12 mentions). While bikesharing and e-scooters are generally not suitable for carrying children, additional passengers, strollers, or luggage/food (Esztergár-Kiss and Lopez Lizarraga 2021; Ramboll Smart Mobility 2021), shared mobility services as a whole typically lack child seats and there is no way to check via the app whether the vehicles are equipped with them (lack of availability and convenience) (Carboni et al. 2021; Lenz et al. 2019; Ramboll Smart Mobility 2021). Lastly, the rather masculine-oriented design of the transport services was mentioned, especially in relation to bikesharing and e-scooters. For example, women perceive the weight of the vehicle as very heavy, thus making it difficult to move and maneuver, resulting in a lack of security (Haddad et al. 2022). In addition, parts of the female wardrobe (e.g., dresses or high heels) are rather impractical and risky for the use of certain shared mobility solutions (Haddad et al. 2022).

A second type of barrier is the availability and convenience of transport services and it is in part connected to security issues. Women are more risk averse; they perceive a significantly higher risk of being run over by a car while cycling (AitBihiOuali and Klingen 2022) and express fear of running over pedestrians or being hit by other drivers when riding e-scooters (Nathanail et al. 2021; Sanders et al. 2020). The high speed of e-scooters, coupled with the lack of helmets, and riding on the sidewalk or sharing traffic with cars and bikes, is viewed negatively (Nathanail et al. 2021). As can be seen in Table 1, the lack of infrastructure was the most frequently mentioned issue (14 mentions), especially for bikesharing. Women are less likely than men to bike when there is no or poor bike infrastructure (Ramboll Smart Mobility 2021). The limitation of carsharing and micromobility in zoned areas is another barrier. If stations are full at the end of the trip, users must travel to more distant stations to drop off the vehicle (Shaheen et al. 2017b; Wang et al. 2020). In addition, such mobility services are largely limited to central urban areas (lack of availability) (Lenz et al. 2019). These two aspects lead users to rely on other modes of transportation for the first and last mile, if necessary (Shaheen et al. 2017b), making the trips less convenient.

A third type of barrier is related to the perceived simplicity of using shared mobility, which was the least frequently mentioned. First, the complex and time-consuming registration process for micromobility solutions is seen as a barrier. Registration usually takes three to five minutes and requires a lot of information such as name, address, phone number, and bank details (Fan et al. 2019). Technical problems, such as system errors and failures, require re-registration (Fan et al. 2019). Also, the multitude of operators, all running their own app, creates confusion and can be overwhelming (Shaheen et al. 2017b). Overall, the use of car sharing and micromobility solutions requires digital skills, such as extensive knowledge of how to use a smartphone and location-based services (Durand et al. 2022) and knowledge regarding cashless payment systems with access to bank and credit cards (Golub et al. 2022). This primarily excludes people with low incomes and lower digital literacy (Golub et al. 2022; Horjus et al. 2022), which comparatively affects women more often than men (Singh 2019).

Lastly, the cost of technology and shared mobility solutions can be seen as a barrier. Since women are more likely to work part-time, they are more dependent on the affordability of transportation (Hail and McQuaid 2021; Hu 2021), and research shows that women primarily use low-cost modes of transportation such as walking or public transit (Ramboll Smart Mobility 2021; Singh 2019). However, micromobility, carsharing, and ridesourcing services are not considered easily affordable modes of transportation (Chowdhury 2019; Ramboll Smart Mobility 2021), which is reflected in the fact that this barrier is mentioned 10 times. Ridesharing services are especially costly for families since they charge per person and do not offer family tickets (Ramboll Smart Mobility 2021). This aspect is mainly prevalent for households with many children.

5 Discussion

From our literature review, we derived a conceptual model (see Fig. 3) that provides an overview of the conditions and barriers found as explained in Sect. 4. However, understanding and recognizing the gender-specific barriers and requirements is only the first step toward gender-equitable mobility. A logical next step would now be to put this knowledge into practice by developing and testing possible solutions. Therefore, the third building block of our conceptual model is *Actions*.

Based on our findings, it is now up to various parties in the transportation sector to develop solutions to the existing and perceived barriers in order to make shared mobility more inclusive and the smart city concept more equitable. Clearly, some issues are easier to address than others, and the responsibility is distributed among service providers, developers, public authorities, individual users, and so forth. Involving women in the design and development of shared mobility solutions, as well as early attempts and initiatives by service providers, can already be seen in practice. They show that the approaches can differ in nature by either making existing solutions more gender-equitable for women or by creating new gender-specific solutions. In

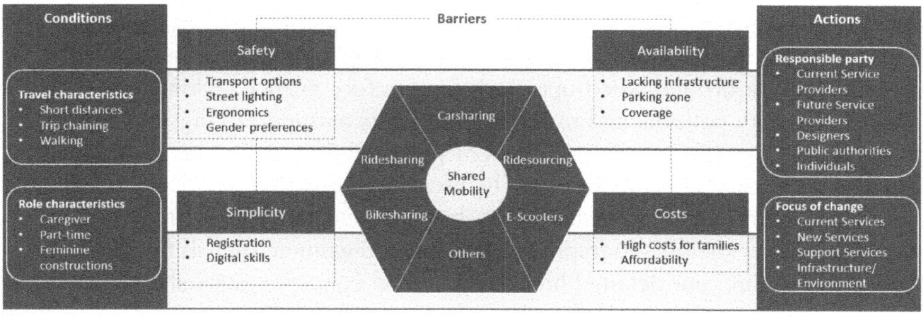

Fig. 3 Conceptual model for achieving gender-equitable shared mobility services (own representation)

the case of e-scooters, for example, the provider TIER found that women would feel more comfortable riding at night if certain product features and vehicle adaptations were provided (e.g., alarms on the vehicle or in the app, the ability to share their route with family and friends, etc.) (TIER 2022). In contrast, the North American ridesourcing company "Wilma"[1] has only female drivers, thus directly addressing a second security-related barrier. An additional approach would be to make the job of a driver more attractive to women and, from the user's perspective, to be able to select a female driver in the app (ITF 2021; Jain and Krishnamurthy 2020).

With regard to the often-mentioned barriers lacking infrastructure and street lighting (see Table 1), the municipality or local government plays an important role, as it is responsible for a city's infrastructure, transportation planning, and parking policy (Shaheen et al. 2016). Here, a collaboration with the service providers could be useful to jointly address some of the security and infrastructural barriers. Another possible solution would be the implementation of car-free spaces, as non-users wish for separate paths and the opportunity to familiarize themselves with the modes of transport before using them (Haddad et al. 2022). Other barriers are related to the characteristics of the transport mode, such as the limited carrying capacity of shared bikes. Here, providers could try to develop special offers (e.g., tandems) with extra space for objects or a second seat for children, for example.

Limitations to the validity of our findings result from the restriction of the literature search to 14 databases in the years 2017–2022, as well as the restriction by the selected search words in the two languages German and English. Furthermore, our findings regarding 'gender-specific' barriers and 'feminine' mobility behavior must be viewed with caution, as women are not a homogeneous group. For example, the lack of child seats is unlikely to be a barrier for women without young children, and the complex registration process may be more of a barrier for older women than for younger tech-savvy women. In addition, the country and cultural context also needs to be taken into account in a more in-depth analysis, as the various barriers that we identified based on papers across different continents may be weighted differently

[1] Company website: https://getwilma.app/.

in different countries (e.g. Nasrin and Bunker (2021) highlighting harassment—i.e., a security barrier—specifically for India), which will influence the actions to be derived. A more differentiated approach is therefore needed, taking into account different mobility patterns and usage requirements and identifying and addressing the specific barriers for different groups of potential female users across the globe. Therefore, we encourage researchers to use, validate and expand our conceptual model in its entirety including conditions, barriers, and actions in different (cultural) contexts for other sociodemographic groups beyond women, such as the older generation. Furthermore, our detailed breakdown in the concept matrix shows that some types of shared mobility solutions have been studied differently in the literature and that barriers seem to be more or less important for each type. Further research is needed to assess these differences in more detail. Since our literature review primarily yielded results for the first two aspects of our conceptual model (i.e., conditions and barriers), focusing on the implementation of certain solutions might provide interesting insights. In this sense, the model can also be used by practitioners to gain in-depth knowledge and to create a more (gender-)inclusive mobility sector.

6 Conclusion

The aim of this systematic literature review was to identify barriers to the low female usage rate of shared mobility services. Our literature search in 14 databases yielded 35 relevant papers that were published between 2017 and 2022. Our literature analysis identified gender-specific differences in mobility behavior and four different types of barriers that prevent women from using shared mobility solutions. These barriers are related to security (e.g., sharing a car with strangers), availability (e.g., restricted drop-off zones), simplicity (e.g., complex registration processes), and costs (e.g., high costs of use). In part, the limiting effects of these barriers can be attributed to differences in travel behavior between men and women, which in turn can be attributed to prevailing gender roles and the unequal distribution of household responsibilities that still exist to some extent. Understanding and recognizing these barriers can be a starting point for making shared mobility services more gender equitable and increasing their usage amongst women.

References

[1] AitBihiOuali, L. & Klingen, J. (2022), 'Inclusive roads in NYC: Gender differences in responses to cycling infrastructure'. *Cities*, 127, pp. 1–13.

Benevolo, C., Dameri, R. P., & D'auria, B. (2016). Smart mobility in smart city: Action taxonomy, ICT intensity and public benefits, In Empowering organizations: Enabling platforms and artefacts (pp. 13–28). Springer International Publishing.

Butler, L., Yigitcanlar, T., & Paz, A. (2020), Smart urban mobility innovations: A comprehensive review and evaluation. *IEEE Access*, 8, 196034–196049.

[2] Carboni, A., Pirra, M., Costa, M. & Kalakou, S. (2021), 'Gender perceptions of active mobility: Insights from three European cities', *European Transport\Trasporti Europei*, 85(9), pp. 1–14.
[3] Cassitas Hino, M. & Cunha, M. A. (2019), Study of Individual Differences in the Behavior of Mobile Technology Users in the Context of Urban Mobility, *in* T. X. Bui (ed.), Proceedings of the 52nd Annual Hawaii International Conference on System Sciences, pp. 3315–3324.
[4] Cassitas Hino, M. & Cunha, M. A. (2021), Female lens in urban mobility: technology-use behavior and individual differences. *Information Technology & People*, 34(4), pp. 1370–1397.
[5] Chowdhury, S. (2019), Women and Urban Mobility: Where to from Here? Perspectives on Equity. Institute of Transportation Engineers. *ITE Journal*, 89(11), pp. 24–25.
Duchène, C. (2011), Gender and Transport. Available at https://www.itf-oecd.org/sites/default/files/docs/dp201111.pdf.
[6] Durand, A., Zijlstra, T., Oort, N., Hoogendoorn-Lanser, S. & Hoogendoorn, S. (2022), Access denied? Digital inequality in transport services. *Transport Reviews*, 42(1), pp. 32–57.
[7] Esztergár-Kiss, D. & Lopez Lizarraga, J. C. (2021), Exploring user requirements and service features of e-micromobility in five European cities. Case Studies on Transport Policy, 9(4), pp. 1531–1541.
[8] Fan, A., Chen, X. & Wan, T. (2019), How Have Travelers Changed Mode Choices for First/Last Mile Trips after the Introduction of Bicycle-Sharing Systems: An Empirical Study in Beijing, China. Journal of Advanced Transportation, pp. 1–16.
Gerecht Mobil. (n.d.), *Was braucht es für eine gendergerechte Mobilität*? https://gerecht-mobil.de/was-braucht-es-fuer-eine-gendergerechte-mobilitaet/.
Giffinger, R., Fertner, C., Kramar, H., & Meijers, E. (2007), City-ranking of European medium-sized cities. Centre of Regional Science. Vienna UT, 9(1), 1–12.
[9] Golub, A., Brown, A., Brakewood, C., MacArthur, J., Lee, S. & Ziedan, A. (2022), Equity and exclusion issues in cashless fare payment systems for public transportation. Transportation Research Interdisciplinary Perspectives, 15, pp. 1–8.
Guyader, H., Friman, M. & Olsson, L. E. (2021), Shared Mobility: Evolving Practices for Sustainability. *Sustainability*, 13(21), pp. 1–14.
[10] Haddad, H., Sanderson, N. & Goodman, J. (2022), Shared e-scooters and gender equity: Learning from women's perceptions and experiences. https://www.voi.com/wp-content/uploads/2022/05/Voi_Gender-Equity-Report_2022-1.pdf.
[11] Hail, Y. & McQuaid, R. (2021), The Concept of Fairness in Relation to Women Transport Users. *Sustainability*, 13(5), pp. 1–15.
[12] Horjus, J. S., Gkiotsalitis, K., Nijënstein, S. & Geurs, K. T. (2022), Integration of shared transport at a public transport stop: mode choice intentions of different user segments at a mobility hub. *Journal of Urban Mobility*, 2, pp. 1–15.
[13] Hortelano, A. O., Grosso, M., Haq, G. & Tsakalidis, A. (2021), Women in Transport Research and Innovation: A European Perspective. Sustainability, 13(12), pp. 1–18.
[14] Hu, L. (2021), Gender differences in commuting travel in the U.S.: interactive effects of race/ethnicity and household structure. *Transportation*, 48(2), pp. 909–929.
Hudson, C. & Rönnblom, M. (2020), Is an 'other' city possible? Using feminist utopias in creating a more inclusive vision of the future city, *Futures*, 121.
[15] ITF. (2021). Transport Innovation for Sustainable Development: A Gender Perspective. OECD Publishing.
[16] Jain, A. & Krishnamurthy, S. (2020), A Study to Understand Behavioral Influencers Related to Carpooling in India. In C. Stephanidis & M. Antona (ed.), HCI International 2020 - Posters: 22nd International Conference, HCII 2020, Copenhagen, Denmark, July 19–24, 2020, Proceedings, Part III (1st ed.). Springer International Publishing.
Jiao, J. (ed.). (2021), Shared Mobility. Elsevier.
Jie, F., Standing, C., Biermann, S., Standing, S. & Le, T. (2021), Factors affecting the adoption of shared mobility systems: Evidence from Australia. *Research in Transportation Business & Management*, 41.

[17] Joshi, S., Roy, S., Mowri, S. & Bailey, A. (2022), Devising gender-responsive transport policies in South Asia. *Gender & Development*, 30(1–2), pp. 59–76.

Karbaumer, R. & Metz, F. (2022), Ein Planerleitfaden durch die Welt der Shared Mobility, Available at https://share-north.eu/wp-content/uploads/2022/05/Shared-Mobility-Guide_DEUTSCH.pdf.

Krämer, A. & Bongaerts, R. (2019), Shared Mobility: Wege aus der Nische? Marketing Review St. Gallen (5), pp. 888–895.

[18] Krauss, K., Scherrer, A., Burghard, U., Doll, C., Schuler, J. & Niessen, P. (2021), SHARED MOBILITY FACTS: WIE LASSEN SICH (GETEILTE MOBILITÄTSDIENSTE ERFOLGREICH IN KOMMUNALE MOBILITÄTSSYSTEME INTEGRIEREN – UND WER NUTZT SIE?, Available at https://www.isi.fraunhofer.de/content/dam/isi/dokumente/ccn/2021/shared_mobility_facts.pdf.

[19] Lecompte, M. C. & Bocarejo, S. J. P. (2017), Transport systems and their impact con gender equity. Transportation Research Procedia, 25, pp. 4245–4257.

[20] Lenz, B., Kolarova, V. & Stark, K. (2019), Gender Issues in the Digitalized 'Smart' Mobility World - Conceptualization and Empirical Findings Applying a Mixed Methods Approach. In H. Krömker (ed.), Lecture notes in computer science: vol. 11596. HCI in mobility, transport, and automotive systems: First international conference, MobiTAS 2019, held as part of the 21st HCI international conference, HCII 2019, Orlando, FL, USA, July 26–31, 2019: proceedings (pp. 378–392). Springer.

[21] Levin, L. (2019), How to Integrate Gender Equality in the Future of "Smart" Mobility: A Matter for a Changing Planning Practice. In H. Krömker (ed.), Lecture notes in computer science: vol. 11596. HCI in mobility, transport, and automotive systems: First international conference, MobiTAS 2019, held as part of the 21st HCI international conference, HCII 2019, Orlando, FL, USA, July 26–31, 2019: proceedings (pp. 393–412). Springer.

Majdoub, S. (2023), Women in Urbanism, Perpetuating the Bias? The shortfalls of feminist reactions to traditional urban planning and design, *The Palgrave Encyclopedia of Urban and Regional Futures* (pp. 2279–2283). Springer International Publishing.

[22] Meyer, G. & Shaheen, S. [Susan] (Ed.) (2017), Disrupting Mobility: Impacts of Sharing Economy and Innovative Transportation on Cities. Springer.

Mourey, T. & Köhler, D. (2017), Gemeinsam Nutzen bringt Dich weiter. https://www.umweltbundesamt.de/sites/default/files/medien/3298/dokumente/emw2017_thematicguideline_de_170519-digit_0.pdf.

[23] Nagy, S. & Csiszár, C. (2022), Assessment Methods for Comparing Shared Mobility and Conventional Transportation Modes in Urban Areas. *Periodica Polytechnica Social and Management Sciences*, 30(2), pp. 158–166.

[24] Nasrin, S. & Bunker, J. (2021), Analyzing significant variables for choosing different modes by female travelers. Transport Policy, 114, pp. 312–329.

[25] Nathanail, E. G., Adamos, G. & Karakikes, I. (2021), Advances in Mobility-as-a-Service Systems: Proceedings of 5th Conference on Sustainable Urban Mobility, Virtual CSUM2020, June 17–19, 2020, Greece (1st ed). Springer International Publishing; Imprint Springer.

Nikitas, A., Kougias, I., Alyavina, E., & Njoya Tchouamou, E. (2017), How can autonomous and connected vehicles, electromobility, BRT, hyperloop, shared use mobility and mobility-as-a-service shape transport futures for the context of smart cities? *Urban Science*, 1(4), 36.

Orlowski, A., & Romanowska, P. (2019), Smart cities concept: Smart mobility indicator. *Cybernetics and Systems*, 50(2), 118–131.

Ortiz Escalante, S. & Gutiérrez Valdivia, B. (2015), Planning from below: using feminist participatory methods to increase women's participation in urban planning, *Gender & Development*, 23:1, 113–126.

[26] Oviedo, D., Duarte, N. V. & Pinto, A. M. A. (ed.). (2020), Transport and Sustainability Ser: v. 12. Urban Mobility and Social Equity in Latin America: Evidence, Concepts, Methods. Emerald Publishing Limited.

[27] Parnell, K. J., Pope, K. A., Hart, S., Sturgess, E., Hayward, R., Leonard, P. & Madeira-Revell, K. (2022), 'It's a man's world': a gender-equitable scoping review of gender, transportation, and work. *Ergonomics*, 65(11), pp. 1537–1553.

Ramboll. (2021), Gender & (Smarte) Mobilität: Studie bestätigt unterschiedliche Reisemuster bei Frauen und Männern. https://de.ramboll.com/media/rde/gendermobilitaet.

[28] Ramboll Smart Mobility. (2021), GENDER AND (SMART) MOBILITY: GREEN PAPER 2021. https://ramboll.com/-/media/files/rgr/documents/markets/transport/g/gender-and-mobility_report.pdf.

Reidl, A. (2021), Brauchen wir Geschlechtergerechtigkeit in der Mobilität? https://web.de/magazine/auto/geschlechtergerechtigkeit-mobilitaet-36071598.

[29] Saigal, T., Vaish, A. K. & Rao, N. V. M. (2021), Gender and class distinction in travel behavior: evidence from India. *Ecofeminism and Climate Change*, 2(1), pp. 42–48.

[30] Sanders, R. L., Branion-Calles, M. & Nelson, T. A. (2020), To scoot or not to scoot: Findings from a recent survey about the benefits and barriers of using E-scooters for riders and non-riders. Transportation Research Part A: Policy and Practice, 139, pp. 217–227.

Shaheen, S., Cohen, A., & Zohdy, I. (2016), Shared mobility: current practices and guiding principles (No. FHWA-HOP-16-022). United States. Federal Highway Administration. https://ops.fhwa.dot.gov/publications/fhwahop16022/fhwahop16022.pdf.

Shaheen, S [S.], Bansal, A., Chan N. & Cohen, A. (2017a), Mobility and the Sharing Economy: Industry Developments and Early Understanding of Impacts. https://escholarship.org/content/qt96j5r729/qt96j5r729_no-Splash_0142bc9770d3aab46cd58cd499858c01.pdf.

[31] Shaheen, S [S.], Bell, C., Cohen, A. & Yelchuru, B. (2017b), Travel Behavior: Shared Mobility and Transportation Equity. https://www.fhwa.dot.gov/policy/otps/shared_use_mobility_equity_final.pdf.

[32] Singh, Y. J. (2019). Is smart mobility also gender-smart? *Journal of Gender Studies*, 29(7), pp. 832–846.

Stanković, M. & Nikolić, V. (ed.). (2021), Proceedings of the 3rd Virtual International Conference Path to a Knowledge Society - Managing Risks and Innovation.

[33] TIER. (2022), How making micromobility safer for women can achieve safer cities for everyone. Available at https://production.web.cms.tier.exu.dev/uploads/2022-03-TIER-Mobility_Safe-the-City-report-summary-for-International-Womens-Day.pdf.

Valentiner, V. (2021), Damit Carsharing kein Männerding bleibt. Available at https://future-moves.com/shared-mobility-gender-bias/.

vom Brocke, J., Simons, A., Niehaves, B., Reimer, K., Plattfaut, R. & Cleven, A. (2009), RECONSTRUCTING THE GIANT: ON THE IMPORTANCE OF RIGOUR IN DOCUMENTING THE LITERATURE SEARCH PROCESS. ECIS 2009 Proceedings. 161.

[34] Wang, G., Vaish, H. R., Sun, H., Wu, J., Wang, S. & Zhang, D. (2020), Understanding User Behavior in Car Sharing Services Through The Lens of Mobility. Proceedings of the ACM on Interactive, Mobile, *Wearable and Ubiquitous Technologies*, 4(4), pp. 1–30.

Wawer, M., Grzesiuk, K. & Jegorow, D. (2022), Smart Mobility in a Smart City in the Context of Generation Z Sustainability, Use of ICT, and Participation. *Energies*, 15(13).

Weber, J. (2020), *Bewegende Zeiten: Mobilität der Zukunft*. Springer. Available at https://e-bookcentral.proquest.com/lib/kxp/detail.action?docID=6318133.

Webster, J. & Watson, R. T. (2002), Analyzing the Past to Prepare for the Future: Writing a Literature Review. *MIS Quarterly*, 26(2), xiii–xxiii.

[35] Wild, K., Woodward, A. & Shaw, C. (2021), Regular Issue. Active Travel Studies, 1(1).

Women in Mobility. (2022), *Female Mobility*. Available at https://www.womeninmobility.org/femalemobility.

Zehba M. P. & Firoz C., M. (2022). Understanding Women's Perspective of Quality of Life in Cities. In: Brears, R.C. (ed) The Palgrave Encyclopedia of Urban and Regional Futures. Palgrave Macmillan, Cham.

Navigating Within the Digitalization Journey: Results and Implications of the First Maturity Assessment of German Public Health Agencies

Anna Lina Kauffmann, Maria Neubauer, Felix Reinsch, Melina Schreiter, Doreen Schick, Jeannette Stark, Katja Bley, Nick Heidmann, and Torsten Eymann

Abstract The COVID-19 pandemic revealed the need for Public Health Agencies to mature digitally. To help those agencies with their digitalization endeavor, a public health agency maturity model (PHAMM) has been developed, evaluated, and employed by 366 institutions to determine their digital maturity and to prioritize actions within digitalization projects. This paper discusses the digital maturity of

A. L. Kauffmann · M. Schreiter · D. Schick (✉) · T. Eymann
Branch Business and Information Systems Engineering of Fraunhofer FIT, Bayreuth, Germany
e-mail: doreen.schick@fit.fraunhofer.de

FIM Research Center, Bayreuth, Germany

University of Bayreuth, Bayreuth, Germany

A. L. Kauffmann
e-mail: anna-lina.kauffmann@fit.fraunhofer.de

M. Schreiter
e-mail: melina.schreiter@fit.fraunhofer.de

T. Eymann
e-mail: torsten.eymann@uni-bayreuth.de

M. Neubauer · F. Reinsch · J. Stark · K. Bley · N. Heidmann
TU Dresden, Dresden, Germany
e-mail: maria.neubauer@tu-dresden.de

F. Reinsch
e-mail: felix.reinsch@mailbox.tu-dresden.de

J. Stark
e-mail: jeannette.stark@tu-dresden.de

K. Bley
e-mail: katja.bley@tu-dresden.de

N. Heidmann
e-mail: nick.heidmann@mailbox.tu-dresden.de

D. Beverungen et al. (eds.), *Transforming the Digitally Sustainable Enterprise*, Lecture Notes in Information Systems and Organisation 76,
https://doi.org/10.1007/978-3-031-80125-9_22

German public health institutions and derives first insights into components spanning the PHAMM dimensions. Public health agencies can use these components to leverage their digital maturity in future digitalization projects. Implications are discussed for how digitalization projects with an enhanced impact can be defined and for future maturity modeling research.

Keywords Maturity model · Public health agency · Component analysis · Digital maturity · PHAMM

1 Introduction

The German public health service (PHS) and its approximately 375 public health agencies (PHAs) are essential in protecting the population's health (Arnold and Teichert 2021). In addition to the visible areas of responsibility, such as infection tracking, PHAs are responsible for diverse tasks, including monitoring hygiene in public facilities, checking drinking water quality, and offering citizens a wide range of counseling services (Rechel et al. 2018). Despite playing an essential role in the German PHS, PHAs have been underfunded for decades leading, for example, to a lack of resources, e.g., in terms of employees or IT equipment, as well as non-existent interoperable systems (Behnke and Zimmermann 2020; Schreyögg 2020). These shortcomings became apparent during the COVID-19 pandemic. In the awareness that PHAs need to be better prepared to respond to potential future crises, we developed a maturity model (MM) to support their digitalization efforts, referred to as the Public Health Agency Maturity Model (PHAMM). The PHAs first used it in 2022 to determine their digital maturity. Institutions planned digitalization projects to achieve higher maturity levels based on this as-is digital maturity. The government financially supports these digitalization projects through a €4 billion pact, of which €800 million are intended to fund the digitalization of PHAs (Federal Ministry of Health 2020). The €800 million funding for the digitization of the public health system is part of the German Reconstruction and Resilience Plan (Deutscher Aufbau- und Resilienzplan; DARP), which is in turn part of the EU's NextGenEU. The PHAMM serves as a reference indicator for milestones defined by the DARP. To receive funding, the PHAs must define projects enabling digital maturing for at least two maturity levels in two dimensions (Bundesgesundheitsministerium 2022). This work uncovers the digital maturity level of PHAs prior to governmental funding, thereby providing a baseline for PHA digital maturity. This baseline serves as a reference for future evaluations, assisting in determining the efficacy of granted funds. Thus, this work engages in answering the following research question (RQ):

RQ1: What is the baseline level of digital maturity within public health agencies?

After establishing the baseline level of digital maturity within PHAs, we delve deeper into understanding the intricate connections between various digitalization practices across different digitalization areas (dimensions) defined in the PHAMM.

We tackle this interconnectedness in a second RQ using a principal component analysis (PCA):

> RQ2: How can the interconnectedness of practices within different dimensions be leveraged to define digitalization projects with multi-dimensional impacts?

The aim of this paper is twofold. First, we report on the digital maturity of 366 public health institutions, especially PHAs, who participated in surveying the digital maturity. Second, we discuss six overarching components spanning the eight dimensions that PHAs can use to leverage their digital maturity in follow-up digitalization projects.

2 Background

2.1 Governmental Public Health Service

The PHS is a component of the public administration sector in Germany, consisting of public health institutions at the federal level (e.g., Robert Koch Institute), state level (e.g., state health ministries), and local level (e.g., PHAs). In particular, the 375 PHAs faced acute challenges during the pandemic suffering from high staff shortages and insufficient digital infrastructure. To cope with these challenges, they resorted to self-made isolated solutions and outdated communication tools such as fax machines for receiving laboratory reports. This led to delays and inaccuracies in outbreak detection (Schreyögg 2020), unnecessary documentation efforts, and loss of information, for example, in contact person management (Gerlach et al. 2021). In response to these deficiencies, the Public Health Service Pact was adopted in 2020, aiming to not only "somehow survive" (Spahn 2020) but also to sustainably strengthen the PHS and acknowledge its relevance politically (Arnold and Teichert 2021). Following this vision, the pact seeks to promote establishing standards regarding digital applications (Federal Ministry of Health 2020). A key element for implementing these digitalization measures is the development of a MM, which enables PHAs to assess their level of digitalization, sets minimum requirements, provides development paths, and allows for the allocation of funding from the Pact (Federal Ministry of Health 2020).

2.2 Maturity Model for Assessing the Digitalization of Public Health Agencies

MMs are long-proven tools for supporting digitalization efforts (Subba et al. 2003; Mehta et al. 2007; Becker et al. 2009). They enable the assessment and understanding of an organization's capabilities and the identification of potential for enhancement. MMs guide digitalization by supporting prioritizing, tracking progress, and allocating resources (Becker et al. 2009; De Bruin et al. 2005; Doctor et al. 2023). Although MMs were initially developed for private organizations, MMs are recommended for federally organized institutions like PHAs, as they help negotiate a shared objective and steps toward it (Doctor et al. 2023). MMs exist in many areas, including IT management (Becker et al. 2009), knowledge management (Freeze and Kulkarni 2005), business process management (Rosemann and De Bruin 2005; Hammer 2007), or e-government (Layne and Lee 2001; Andersen and Henriksen 2006; Yildiz 2007; Klievink and Janssen 2009). While MMs have their advantages, they are also often subject to some critics. For example, the MM development field tends to lack an empirical and theoretical foundation due to its reliance on deductive methods and literature-derived concepts, which may not always align with practical needs (Pereira and Serrano 2020). Additionally, MMs can oversimplify reality (Solli-Sæther and Gottschalk 2010), limiting their usefulness and hindering organizational development. They also exhibit limited applicability in diverse organizational structures and have not been widely used for budget allocation.

Given the limitations and the demand for a guided digital PHA transformation, developing a new MM was crucial. We based the development process on a widely adopted model for MM development (Becker et al. 2009) and included build-and-evaluate cycles and a collaborative approach involving PHA practitioners and government stakeholders from all federal states. The development process incorporated four interview rounds, three workshops, and a survey leading to the creation of the PHAMM. The PHAMM is designed to address the limitations of previous MMs: It is applicable across a broad range of federally structured public institutions, aims to decrease the structural discrepancies among PHAs, and offers a means for budget allocation to the PHAs. More information about the development can be found in Doctor et al. (2023). The PHAMM comprises 355 digitalization criteria (practices), classified into 27 subdimensions subsumed into eight dimensions (bold in Table 1). For each dimension and subdimension, five maturity levels are distinguished (levels 0–4), and each includes various practices. The practices in the PHAMM can be directly implemented in digitalization projects, serving as criteria for measuring the level of digitalization (Doctor et al. 2023). One practice in the dimension *of IT security* is, for example, "Reporting channels for security-relevant events are regularly checked, tested, and updated." The PHAs rate practices on a three-level scale as "applies," "is being implemented," or "does not apply". The PHA must evaluate all 355 practices. A maturity level for a dimension is achieved when at least 80% of its practices are applied. In the example of the subdimension *dealing with IT security risks and attacks*, a PHA at maturity level 0, for example, meets a few of the desirable practices for preventing, detecting, and responding to IT security risks and attacks. At higher levels, suitable measures for preventing, detecting, and responding to IT security risks and attacks exist and are continuously evaluated as part of a success-control measurement. As part of the funding appeal of the Federal Ministry of Health, a general goal is to reach maturity level 3 in all eight dimensions by 2025, thus reaching the mission statement of "Gesundheitsamt 2025" (Bundesgesundheitsministerium 2022).

Table 1 Dimensions of the PHAMM (Doctor et al. 2023)

Dimension	Description, including **subdimension**
Digitalization strategy	This dimension comprises (1) **the definition, communication, and implementation** of the digitalization strategy, (2) **the definition of responsibilities**, and the planning of (3) the **digitalization budget** for the PHAs' tasks
Employees	This dimension includes (1) **sensitization** and (2) **participation** of the employees in digitalization activities and the aspects of (3) **training**
Process digitalization	This dimension includes the extent to which processes are (1) **documented**, (2) **IT-supported**, and the extent to which there are (3) **overlapping processes** to be addressed via cross-process coordination. Finally, we lay out practices for the (4) **evaluation of processes**
IT security	This dimension includes the scope of (1) **IT security management**. It also addresses concrete measures for (2) **dealing with IT security risks and attacks** and (3) **identity and access management**
IT provision	This dimension includes the equipment of the (1) **IT workplace** (hardware and operating systems), the (2) **organization of the IT procurement**, the (3) **IT infrastructure**, and the (4) **application of IT service processes**
Citizen focus	This dimension includes considering the (1) **interaction** with citizens and orientation and design of the available information and (2) **preferences**
Cooperation	This dimension includes (1) **cooperation within the PHAs**, (2) **cooperation between PHAs and provincial offices**, and (3) **cooperation with external stakeholders**
Software, data, and interoperability	This dimension includes the (1) **use of specialist applications**, their (2) **technical interoperability**, (3) **data analysis, and reporting**, (4) **requirements and documentation** of specialist applications, and (5) the **protection of data**

3 Methods

3.1 Data Collection[1]

In early 2022, the Federal Ministry of Health issued its inaugural call for project funding (Bundesgesundheitsministerium 2022). Applicant institutions had to evaluate their digital maturity via the PHAMM and provide justifications for funding based on the practices. The PHAMM is implemented as an online survey available to determine digital maturity from May to July 2022. Beyond the classification into the PHAMM, the online survey included demographic data such as type of institution, number of employees, and professional background of the management. It

[1] The results listed here are based on the data collected in the first collection period (May–July 2022). By now, there is more data available as in the second collection period (December 2022–February 2023) additional institutions provided answers, also for the first time-period.

also included questions about the quality of each PHAMM dimension and user-friendliness using 18 of the 19 items from the scale by Lewis (2002). To ensure high data quality, we provided participating institutions with additional material, such as a glossary. At the beginning of the assessment period, several online workshops took place. The public health institutions then answered the survey using an individual link. So, participating institutions could fill in the survey in several sessions an also forward the link to stakeholders. We advised including relevant stakeholders within the assessment procedure to secure identifying their most appropriate state of digital maturity. The coordination of the assessment procedure was entrusted to the management of the institutions. User-friendliness of the PHAMM was assessed on a scale from 1 to 7 (1 representing higher user-friendliness). Overall, the PHAs and related institutions rated the usability as good (mean of 2.51). The tool was rated as easy to learn and helpful. The open-ended questions revealed that the dimensions, digitalization strategy, IT security, and IT provision required input from the institution in which the PHA is embedded. The results suggest that despite the high volume of questions, and the focus on PHAs, completion was generally feasible.

3.2 Sample

A total of 366 institutions participated in the first survey wave, including 330 PHAs. Table 2 summarizes all participating institutions, which we included in our sample, and which play an essential role within the public health service. On average participating institutions have M = 106.6 employees (min: 18, max: 1500). The catchment area of 86 institutions was mixed, 70 institutions had an urban and 156 had a rural catchment area, 54 did not respond.

Table 3 summarizes the professional background of the management, showing that a medical background is the most common. Only 128 participating institutions stated that they employ an IT specialist within their organization, 149 noted that no IT specialist was employed, 15 were unsure or replied "others", and 54 did not respond.

Table 2 Number of participating institutions in the 2022 maturity measurement

	Health department	Other local authority	Institution/body under the auspices of a federal state	State	Other
Type of institution[a]	330	4	3	8	17

[a] The data were evaluated manually. Four institutions did not provide any information

Table 3 Number of institutions by the professional background of the head of the office

	Medical	Legal	Commercial	Project management/ digitalization staff	Health-economic	Psychological
Professional background[a]	298	19	14	6	12	3

[a] The data were evaluated manually. 14 institutions did not provide any information

4 Results of the Current Digital Maturity Status Nationwide

The current nationwide state of digital maturity of German PHAs and related institutions is shown in Fig. 1. The lowest level of digital maturity is level 0. This level was achieved on the median across all participating institutions in five dimensions. In three dimensions ("digitalization strategy," "process digitalization," and "software, data, and interoperability"), no digital maturity level at all was achieved in the median nationwide, meaning that the digitalization in these dimensions is at the very beginning.

A more detailed breakdown of the results is provided in Table 4, which indicates the percentage and absolute number of participating institutions that have reached the respective maturity level for the dimensions. The proportion of participating institutions that have not yet reached a level is highest for "process digitalization" at 89.6%. Level 0 was most frequently achieved in the "employees" dimension.

Fig. 1 Overview of the results of the first survey wave. *Note* − 1 = no level achieved

Table 4 Count and percentage of the 366 institutions by level per dimension

Dimension		Levels reached					
		No level	Level 0	Level 1	Level 2	Level 3	Level 4
Digitalization strategy	Quantity	237	104	22	2	0	1
	Percentages (%)	64.8	28.4	6.0	0.5		0.3
Employees	Quantity	126	214	24	2	0	0
	Percentages (%)	34.4	58.5	6.6	0.5		
Process digitization	Quantity	328	28	10	0	0	0
	Percentages (%)	89.6	7.7	2.7			
IT security	Quantity	165	98	59	32	7	5
	Percentages (%)	45.1	26.8	16.1	8.7	1.9	1.4
IT provision	Quantity	160	81	68	38	17	2
	Percentages (%)	43.7	22.1	18.6	10.4	4.6	0.5
Citizen focus	Quantity	94	188	82	1	1	0
	Percentages (%)	25.7	51.4	22.4	0.3	0.3	
Cooperation	Quantity	44	193	120	9	0	0
	Percentages (%)	12.0	52.7	32.8	2.5		
Software, data, and interoperability	Quantity	184	117	48	15	2	0
	Percentages (%)	50.3	32.0	13.1	4.1	0.5	

5 Results of the Exploratory Component Analysis

Once we analyzed the baseline level of digital maturity, we delved deeper into the intricate interplay between the practices of the dimension, aiming to comprehend how they mutually influence each other. We were particularly interested in these interrelations as the dimensions of the PHAMM are formative constructs, meaning that they are fully defined and influenced by their respective subdimensions and practices (cf. Freeze and Raschke 2007). Though, interviews with PHAs and the content of some practices imply that some practices might also influence practices from other dimensions. For example, improved interoperability could lead to better cooperation internally and externally. Given the interconnected nature of the content of practices across different dimensions, enhancing one area could potentially have a ripple effect, influencing others. This interconnection presents an opportunity: instead of viewing the challenge of advancing digitalization projects to impact two maturity levels in two dimensions as a hurdle, we can see it as a chance to aim for practices that could have broader, multi-dimensional effects. Therefore, these interrelations might hint at other higher-level latent and reflective constructs influenced by the practices (Freeze and Raschke 2007). Thus, we conducted an exploratory analysis to gain insight into the relations between the different practices. Hence, we provide insights on how (1) relations between dimensions might be assessed and (2) give a first idea of how to address several dimensions using these higher-level constructs. To

assess if there are overarching fields of action (components) within the PHAMM, we calculated a PCA using SPSS (IBM Corp. 2021). To conduct the PCA, we used 354 of the 355 PHAMM practices (we excluded one practice due to its lack of variance) and used a Varimax-rotation method. Practices were all rated on a three-point Likert Scale from 0 (does not apply), and 1 (is being implemented) to 2 (applies). Moreover, we used the Scree-Test (Bortz and Schuster 2011) to identify the correct number of components. This criterium describes the right number of components as the point where the Scree-Plot shows a kink, meaning that the following components have substantially less eigenvalue than the ones before. For the interpretation and analysis of the retrieved components, we used the common cut-off point of 0.300 for retaining the criteria in a respective component (Field 2013). The Kaiser, Meyer, and Olkin (KMO) criteria, the Bartlett-Tests as well as the inverse correlation matrix could not be calculated due to the high number of variables and the comparatively small number of cases.

Conducting the PCA, we identified six higher-level components that account for a total of 28.58% of the explained variance and that can be interpreted as follows: (1) digitalization potentials awareness, (2) security awareness, (3) resource usability, (4) rule awareness, (5) IT efficiency, and (6) process and data awareness. For interpreting the components, we considered practices part of the component they loaded the highest on. Table 5 gives an overview of the six components, their means, standard deviation (Table 5), eigenvalues, and variance explained by them. A more detailed overview, including components, loadings for respective practices of the PHAMM, and their full text, can be seen in the online attachment.

Component 1—Digitalization Awareness. The central theme of this component is enhancing awareness of digitalization and its potential. For this component, practices of the dimensions "digitalization strategy", "process digitization", and "employees" load most heavily, such as the practice "*Individual, organizational units derive short-, medium- and long-term digitization measures from the digitization strategy*" from the dimension digitalization strategy. Applying this strategy leads to enhanced digitalization awareness. For example, through applying the digitalization strategy employees visit "*Regular workshops on digitalization*".

Component 2—Security Awareness. This component primarily contains practices from the "IT security" dimension. The central theme is to increase security awareness, e.g., by "*Defining, establishing and propagating a procedure for handling*

Table 5 Overview of the six components (comp.)

	Comp. 1	Comp. 2	Comp. 3	Comp. 4	Comp. 5	Comp. 6
Min	– 1.49	– 2.36	– 2.39	– 3.33	– 3.46	– 2.46
Max	5.97	3.12	2.74	2.28	1.99	2.94
Initial eigenvalue	48.57	16.23	11.03	10.21	8.17	6.97
Total variance explained (%)	13.72	4.58	3.12	2.89	2.31	1.97

Note $n = 322$; mean for all components = 0; SD for all components = 1

and evaluating security incidents" and "*Selecting authentication mechanisms on an as-needed basis according to the need for protection*". Although this component mainly includes practices of the "IT security" dimension, it also spans practices of other dimensions with the potential to enhance security awareness.

Component 3—Resource Usability. As in component 2, component 3 includes practices mostly from one dimension (IT provision). This component's central theme is enhancing resource usability by providing appropriate and retrievable resources for the tasks at hand. In this regard, this component spans practices that allow scaling up resources if required, such as "*Storage for large amounts of data is kept ready*" in case of necessity, and also focuses on practices that provide those resources with the potential to support all specialist applications best.

Component 4—Rule Awareness. Practices from several dimensions load on this component. The central theme of this component is to enhance rule awareness so that digitalization potential can be leveraged. In this regard, "*Reporting channels for safety-relevant events are defined and adhered to*" (IT security), "*The requirements of the federal government and the state concerning digitalization are specified in the digitalization strategy*" (digitalization strategy), and "*The IT service processes according to ITIL standard are known to the person responsible for IT*" belong to this component.

Component 5—IT Efficiency. This component mainly includes practices from the dimension "software, data, and interoperability" and, to a smaller extent, the dimensions "IT security", "citizen focus," and "IT provision". The central theme of this component is IT efficiency in the sense that practices need to allow efficient employment of the whole software system and digital technologies used in the organization. In this regard, "*informal or formal processes to report features and new ideas for enhancing business applications*" help to make IT more efficient so that the IT and, in particular, "*(…) specialist applications best support business processes*".

Component 6—Process and Data Awareness. This component spans several dimensions, including "software, data, and interoperability" as well as "process digitalization", "cooperation", and "digitalization strategy". The central theme of this component is to enhance awareness of processes and data and how to use them best. In this regard, "*Reporting/data is used for forecasting and decision support*" and "*A (partially) automated production of daily metrics*" occurs.

To get a deeper insight into the components, we calculated the correlations of the components with each PHAMM dimension (see Table 6). Component 1 has the strongest positive correlation with six PHAMM dimensions. This means that an increase in component 1 should lead to an improvement in the six dimensions. The two dimensions that do not correlate with component 1 correlate most strongly with components 2 and 3. Component 2 (security awareness) correlates most strongly with "IT security" and component 3 (resource usability) with "IT provision". Component 4 (rule awareness) correlates significantly with all PHAMM dimensions. This hints that awareness of compliance with rules and documentation positively affects all eight dimensions and seems to play a role in improving digital maturity. Component 5 (IT

efficiency) correlates most strongly with the dimensions "cooperation", "software, data, and interoperability", and component 6 (process and data awareness) correlates significantly only with the dimension "cooperation" ($p < 0.001$).

6 Discussion

The results suggest that, referring to RQ1, PHAs are at the beginning of their digitalization journey and that the most potential for development is in the dimensions of "process digitization", "digitalization strategy", and "software, data, and interoperability". Also, the results show above-average participation in the survey and, thus, the willingness to develop digitally. Some institutions have already achieved PHAMM levels 3 and 4 for individual or several dimensions, thus demonstrating the feasibility of digitalization. Achieving PHAMM-level 3 in all dimensions by 2025, as agreed on as a mid-term digitalization goal for PHAs by the federal states, is considered achievable and desirable. This survey will continue until 2026 so that improvements in digital maturity can be addressed in subsequent phases. This survey also revealed that PHAs needed to involve experts from the institutions in which they are embedded, especially for the dimensions of IT security, IT provision, and digitalization strategy. These areas are often managed by other administrations, and advancing in them thus often requires actions in governmental institutions outside the PHAs.

Furthermore, using an exploratory PCA to address RQ2 allowed identifying six higher-level action fields (components) that can be seen as overarching perspectives of PHA digitalization. These perspectives offer an additional lens on implementing and combining MM practices in digitalization projects. As an overarching construct, the concept of 'awareness' was identified. A related concept is situation awareness, defined as "the perception of the elements in the environment within a volume of time and space, the comprehension of their meaning, and the projection of their status in the near future" (Endsley 1995, p. 37). Comparing this definition with the characteristics of MMs and the specific requirements of PHA digitalization, the perception of awareness can be transferred to and even included in the conceptual operation mode of MMs. In contrast to existing research that considers *digitalization awareness* as an initial maturity level, thereby labeling it as a temporally closed element to overcome (Klötzer and Pflaum 2017), our results hint towards the importance of maintaining digitalization on all maturity levels and dimensions during the digitalization process (Fig. 2). Considering the definition of situation awareness, the PHA management needs to identify and understand the related elements of digitalization (i.e., strategy, processes, employees) and what their effects are in its current and future state. Given the sensitive character of health data and the respective processes, the components of *security* and *rule awareness* mirror the responsibility related to the maturation process of a PHA. Like MMs, which focus on cyber security (Yigit Ozkan et al. 2021) or information security (Spruit and Röling 2014; Mijnhardt et al. 2016), both perspectives focus on necessary elements of a secure and reliable PHA

Table 6 Correlations between components and dimensions of the PHAMM

Dimension of the PHAMM	Component 1		Component 2		Component 3		Component 4		Component 5		Component 6	
Digitalization strategy	0.30	***	– 0.05		0.12	*	0.45	***	– 0.16	**	0.13	*
Employees	0.36	***	0.06		0.13	*	0.53	***	– 0.03		0.04	
Process digitalization	0.37	***	– 0.04		0.10		0.22	***	0.07		0.06	
IT security	0.09		0.53	***	0.05		0.53	***	0.04		– 0.11	*
IT provision	0.08		0.20	***	0.60	***	0.28	***	0.11		– 0.08	
Citizen focus	0.22	***	– 0.05		0.10		0.34	***	0.12	*	0.14	**
Cooperation	0.21	***	0.11	*	0.26	***	0.15	**	0.21	***	0.27	***
Software, data, and interoperability	0.26	***	0.06		0.31	***	0.30	***	0.33	***	0.14	**
Overall digitalization status	0.34	***	0.24	***	0.4	***	0.59	***	0.16	**	0.08	

Note *** = $p < 0.001$; ** = $p < 0.01$; * = $p < 0.05$

environment. However, in contrast to models which focus merely on security as the primary objective within organizations, the PHAMM incorporates security as an underlying perspective in different dimensions. The remaining components, which are relevant for the provision of necessary resources (*resource usability*), the functionality of the IT infrastructure (*IT efficiency*), and the productivity and efficiency of organizational tasks (*process and data awareness*), can be understood as providing the infrastructural components necessary for a PHA to operate digitally.

Thus, our results strengthen digitalization as a multifaceted phenomenon (Park et al. 2020). By conducting a PCA, we included a perspective for the derivation of actions on a managerial level and comprised elements of the situation awareness theory (Endsley 1995). We keep the dimensional PHAMM structure, characterized by many items depicting the complexity of PHAs, but add six awareness perspectives to guide managerial decisions. For example, when developing a project to achieve specific PHAMM practice, PHA's management could evaluate the project before implementation using the six perspectives. Suppose a project aims to model essential processes in the PHA. In that case, the management could consider how the six perspectives can be integrated into the project, widening the project's impact. The management could take into account, e.g., what particular security aspects need to be considered (*security awareness*) or if and how a specific process modeling software can be used best (*resource usability* and *IT efficiency*), or how IT artifacts can be aligned more efficiently with the processes (*IT efficiency*). Considering the different perspectives is necessary due to highly interrelated and interdependent processes, technologies, and stakeholders.

7 Conclusion

Digitalizing PHAs is a socially relevant and complex issue. To support the PHAs in digitalization, we developed the PHAMM. Using this MM, the current digital maturity of the PHAs nationwide was measured in the Summer of 2022. This study presents the results of this measurement. Furthermore, we analyzed the data to find higher-level perspectives between the PHAMM practices using a PCA leading to six components. Taking these six components into account in digitalization projects might help to reduce the complexity of digitalization to the necessary extent and make digitalization particularly efficient. This study thereby increases the knowledge about the digital maturity of PHAs as part of the public administration and proposes concrete components to simplify digitalization. We, thus, answer the call for research by Mendoza-Silva (2021) for MMs that balance theory and practical applicability.

However, our study has some limitations. Regarding the data assessment, some PHAMM practices did not apply to other public healthcare institutions other than PHAs. Thus, our data might have some minor distortions. Though, they should not compromise our results too much, as we conducted our analyses on an aggregated level. Also, not all PHAs participated in this self-assessment survey. It is conceivable that the level of digitalization influences participation. The self-assessment could

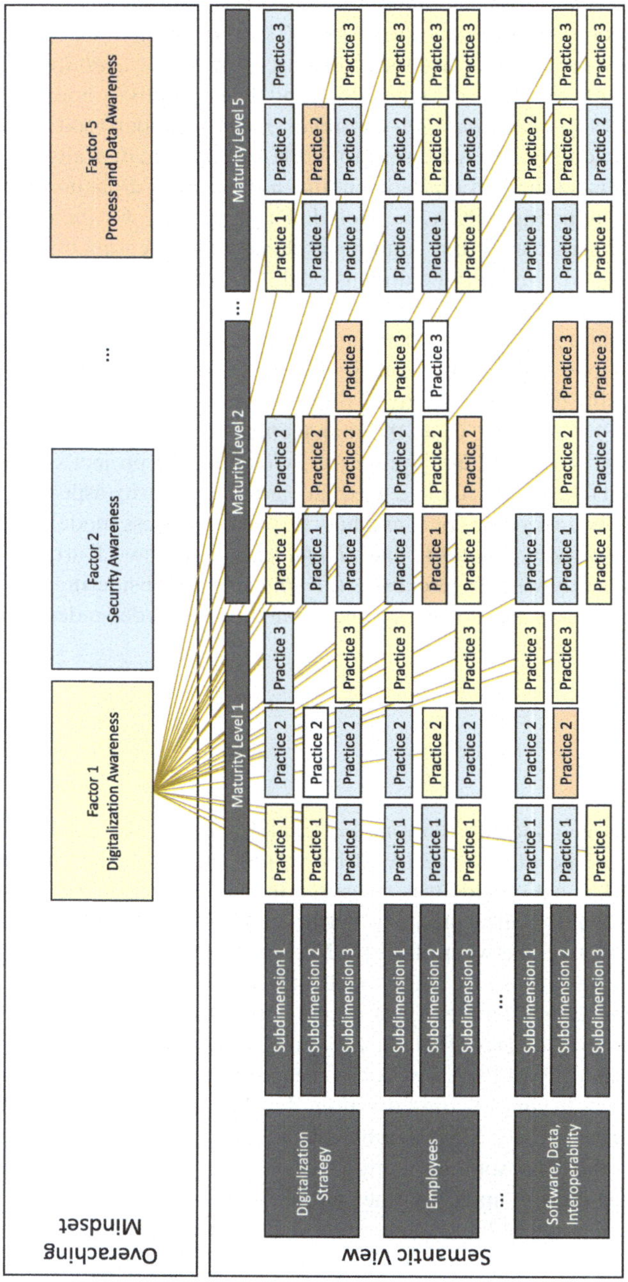

Fig. 2 Conceptual overview of PHAMM's dimensions and components perspectives

also lead to misjudgments if the person doing it is not fully informed about all areas. We tried to minimize this by advising PHAs to include relevant stakeholders in the assessment process. Furthermore, the survey was linked to financial support, and some PHAs might have assessed their digital maturity more conservatively to achieve funding.

Regarding the PCA, it should be noted that these are the preliminary results of an exploratory method, which should be interpreted and used cautiously until validated with a more confirmatory method (e.g., confirmatory factor analysis; CFA). The KMO criteria, the Bartlett-Test, and the inverse correlation matrix could not be calculated. This means that the data set is not ideal for performing a PCA. From our point of view, however, the PCA yielded interpretable results but must be carried out again in the future with more cases. A new calculation is especially important as our sample is relatively small, considering the number of items (practices), our factors only account for a rather small percentage of the total variance explained, and practices of higher levels were only reached by a few institutions causing little variance within them. As the recording of the digital maturity of PCAs continues until 2026, we are confident to use a more significant sample soon to apply more reliable analysis methods. We encourage future research to evaluate the possibility of finding overarching perspectives within MMs to help theory and practice better understand what needs to be addressed to achieve a coherent digitalization. Also, future research should consider evaluating our six overarching perspectives within other governmental institutions to test if those perspectives can be used as general principles when implementing eGovernment projects.

References

Andersen, K.V. & Henriksen, H.Z. (2006), 'E-government maturity models: Extension of the Layne and Lee model', *Government Information Quarterly*, **23**(2), pp. 236–248.

Arnold, L. & Teichert, U. (2021), 'Politischer Reformprozess im Zuge der COVID-19-Pandemie: Der Pakt für den Öffentlichen Gesundheitsdienst', in *Public Health Forum*. De Gruyter, pp. 47–50.

Becker, J., Knackstedt, R. & Pöppelbuß, J. (2009), 'Developing maturity models for IT management', *Business & Information Systems Engineering*, **1**(3), pp. 213–222.

Behnke, N. & Zimmermann, M. (2020), 'Notlage des öffentlichen Gesundheitsdienstes im ländlichen Raum', *VM Verwaltung & Management*, **26**(4), pp. 169–182.

Bortz, J. & Schuster, C. (2011), *Statistik für Human- und Sozialwissenschaftler: Limitierte Sonderausgabe*. Berlin, Heidelberg, New York: Springer-Verlag.

Bundesgesundheitsministerium (2022), *Digitales Gesundheitsamt: Förderaufruf 2022*. Available at: https://gesundheitsamt-2025.de/foerderung/foerderleitfaden (Accessed: 25 May 2022).

De Bruin, T., Rosemann, M., Freeze, R. & Kaulkarni, U. (2005), 'Understanding the main phases of developing a maturity assessment model', in *Australasian Conference on Information Systems (ACIS)*. Australasian Chapter of the Association for Information Systems, pp. 8–19.

Doctor, E., Eymann, T., Fürstenau, D., Gersch, M., Hall, K., Kauffmann, A.L., Schulte-Althoff, M., Schlieter, H., Stark, J. & Wyrtki, K. (2023), 'A Maturity Model for Assessing the Digitalization of Public Health Agencies', *Business & Information Systems Engineering*. https://doi.org/10.1007/s12599-023-00813-y.

Endsley, M.R. (1995), 'Toward a theory of situation awareness in dynamic systems', *Human Factors*, **37**(1), pp. 32–64.

Federal Ministry of Health (2020), *Pakt für den öffentlichen Gesundheitsdienst*. Available at: https://www.bundesgesundheitsministerium.de/service/begriffe-von-a-z/o/oeffentlicher-gesundheitsheitsdienst-pakt.html (Accessed: 17 January 2022).

Field, A. (2013), *Discovering statistics using IBM SPSS statistics*. London England: Sage.

Freeze, R. & Kulkarni, U. (2005), 'Knowledge management capability assessment: validating a knowledge assets measurement instrument', in *Proceedings of the 38th Annual Hawaii International Conference on System Sciences*. IEEE, pp. 251a–251a.

Freeze, R. & Raschke, R.L. (2007), 'An assessment of formative and reflective constructs in IS research'. *ECIS 2007 Proceedings. 171*.

Gerlach, F., Greiner, W., Jochimsen, B., Von Knalle, C., Meyer, G., Schreyögg, J. & Thürmann, P. (2021), 'Digitalisierung für Gesundheit–Ziele und Rahmenbedingungen eines dynamisch lernenden Gesundheitssystems', *Sachverständigenrat zur Begutachtung der Entwicklung im Gesundheitswesen, Bonn* [Preprint].

Hammer, M. (2007), 'The process audit', *Harvard Business Review*, **85**(4), p. 111.

IBM Corp. (2021), *IBM SPSS Statistics for Windows*. NY: Armonk.

Klievink, B. & Janssen, M. (2009), 'Realizing joined-up government-Dynamic capabilities and stage models for transformation', *Government Information Quarterly*, **26**(2), pp. 275–284.

Klötzer, C. & Pflaum, A. (2017), 'Toward the development of a maturity model for digitalization within the manufacturing industry's supply chain'. *Proceedings of the 50th Hawaii international Conference on System Sciences (HICSS) 2017*.

Layne, K. & Lee, J. (2001), 'Developing fully functional E-government: A four stage model', *Government Information Quarterly*, **18**(2), pp. 122–136.

Lewis, J.R. (2002), 'Psychometric evaluation of the PSSUQ using data from five years of usability studies', *International Journal of Human-Computer Interaction*, **14**(3–4), pp. 463–488.

Mehta, N., Oswald, S. & Mehta, A. (2007), 'Infosys Technologies: improving organizational knowledge flows', *Journal of Information Technology*, **22**(4), pp. 456–464.

Mendoza-Silva, A. (2021), 'Innovation capability: a systematic literature review', *European Journal of Innovation Management*, **24**(3), pp. 707–734.

Mijnhardt, F., Baars, T. & Spruit, M. (2016), 'Organizational characteristics influencing SME information security maturity', *Journal of Computer Information Systems*, **56**(2), pp. 106–115.

Park, Y., Fiss, P.C. & El Sawy, O.A. (2020), 'Theorizing the multiplicity of digital phenomena: The ecology of configurations, causal recipes, and guidelines for applying QCA', *Management of Information Systems Quarterly*, **44**, pp. 1493–1520.

Pereira, R. & Serrano, J. (2020), 'A review of methods used on IT maturity models development: A systematic literature review and a critical analysis', *Journal of Information Technology*, **35**(2), pp. 161–178.

Rechel, B., Maresso, A., Sagan, A., Hernandez-Quevedo, C., Williams, G., Rechardson, E., Jakubowski, E. & Nolte, E. (2018), *Organization and financing of public health services in Europe: country reports*. Health Policy Series.

Rosemann, M. & De Bruin, T. (2005), 'Towards a business process management maturity model', in *ECIS 2005 Proceedings of the thirteenth European Conference on Information Systems*. Verlag and the London School of Economics, pp. 1–12.

Schreyögg, J. (2020), 'Corona-Krise trifft auf Strukturprobleme im Gesundheitswesen', *Wirtschaftsdienst*, **100**(4), pp. 226–227.

Solli-Sæther, H. & Gottschalk, P. (2010), 'The modeling process for stage models', *Journal of Organizational Computing and Electronic Commerce*, **20**(3), pp. 279–293.

Spahn, J. (2020), *Digitales Gesundheitsamt: Leitbild*. Available at: https://gesundheitsamt-2025.de/digitalisierung/leitbild (Accessed: 21 June 2023).

Spruit, M. & Röling, M. (2014), 'ISFAM: the information security focus area maturity model'. *Twenty Second European Conference on Information Systems, Tel Aviv 2014*.

Subba, R., Metts, G. & Monge, M. (2003), 'Electronic commerce development in small and medium sized enterprises: A stage model and its implications', *Business Process Management Journal* [Preprint].
Yigit Ozkan, B., van Lingen, S. & Spruit, M. (2021), 'The cybersecurity focus area maturity (CYSFAM) model', *Journal of Cybersecurity and Privacy*, **1**(1), pp. 119–139.
Yildiz, M. (2007), 'E-government: initiatives, developments, and issues', *Government Information Quarterly*, **24**, pp. 646–665.

AI in Government: A Study on Explainability of High-Risk AI-Systems in Law Enforcement and Police Service

Fabian Walke, Lars Bennek, and Till J. Winkler

Abstract Law enforcement and police service are, related to the proposed AI Act of the European Commission, part of the high-risk area of artificial intelligence (AI). As such, in the area of digital government and high-risk AI systems exists a particular responsibility for ensuring ethical and social aspects with AI usage. The AI Act also imposes explainability requirements on AI, which could be met by the usage of explainable AI (XAI). The literature has not yet addressed the characteristics of the high-risk area law enforcement and police service in relation to compliance with explainability requirements. We conducted 11 expert interviews and used the grounded theory method to develop a grounded model of the phenomenon AI explainability requirements compliance in the context of law enforcement and police service. We discuss how the model and the results can be useful to authorities, governments, practitioners and researchers alike.

Keywords XAI · Artificial intelligence · AI Act · Requirements · Compliance

1 Introduction

Artificial Intelligence (AI), such as ChatGPT and other advanced AI models, have taken the topic of AI and machine learning (ML) to a new level, attracting the interest of both experts and laypeople. The term AI encompasses various research

---

F. Walke (✉) · L. Bennek · T. J. Winkler
Faculty of Business Administration and Economics, University of Hagen, Hagen, Germany
e-mail: fabian.walke@fernuni-hagen.de

L. Bennek
e-mail: lars.bennek@studium.fernuni-hagen.de

T. J. Winkler
e-mail: till.winkler@fernuni-hagen.de

T. J. Winkler
Department of Digitalization, Copenhagen Business School, Frederiksberg, Denmark

D. Beverungen et al. (eds.), *Transforming the Digitally Sustainable Enterprise*, Lecture Notes in Information Systems and Organisation 76,
https://doi.org/10.1007/978-3-031-80125-9_23

areas, including ML, natural language processing (NLP), speech, vision, and robotics (Mukhamediev et al. 2022), without having a standard definition (Buxmann and Schmidt 2019). Politicians have also taken notice of this technology, which is shown through the publication of the AI strategies of the European Commission (2018) and the German Federal Government (2020), and the proposal of the 'Artificial Intelligence Act' (AIA) by the European Commission (EC) (2021). The AIA categorizes AI into four different risk levels: unacceptable risk, high risk, low risk, and minimal risk. Unacceptable-risk systems are prohibited, and high-risk systems must comply with various requirements, including transparency and interpretability. Law enforcement authorities, which include state police authorities, federal police, customs investigation authorities, tax investigation, the federal criminal police office and prosecutors' authorities, are included in the high risk sector according to AIA Appendix III. The ethics guidelines of the EC (2019) go into more detail about the requirements: The entire decision-making process must be recorded and documented, and an "understandable explanation of the algorithmic decision-making processes" is required, as far as possible. Art. 13 (1) AIA stipulates with regard to transparency that users must be able to interpret and use the results appropriately. The corresponding field of research is called 'Explainable Artificial Intelligence' (XAI), which focuses on ensuring transparency and interpretability of AI systems. The high-risk sector is subject to the explainability requirements of the AIA, making law enforcement and police services (LEPS) subject to XAI and explainability requirements. XAI is of great importance for digital responsibility, as it allows decision-making processes of AI systems to be traced and understood, ultimately leading to greater accountability and transparency. Additionally, XAI has significant social implications, as it can help mitigate potential risks associated with biases, discrimination, and other negative impacts on individuals and society. In terms of ethical and environmental considerations, XAI can play a critical role in ensuring that AI is developed and used in a manner that aligns with ethical principles and sustainability goals.

So far, the literature has not yet examined the characteristics of the high risk area law enforcement and police service in terms of compliance with AI explainability requirements. The literature has only dealt with topics such as general legal requirements on explainability in ML (Bibal et al. 2021), metrics to measure explainability (Sovrano et al. 2021, 2022; Sovrano and Vitali 2023) and technical and ethical dimensions of XAI (McDermid et al. 2021). This leads to the research question (RQ) of this study: "*Which characteristics determine AI explainability requirements compliance in law enforcement and police service?*" The objective of this paper is to determine those characteristics and represent them in a grounded model.

We applied an explorative and qualitative research approach, using the grounded theory method (GTM), by conducting 11 expert interviews. The grounded theory method and exploratory approach were chosen because this specific research area of law enforcement and police service in terms of AI explainability requirements compliance has not been explicitly addressed in the literature so far. As compliance of AI explainability requirements in the high risk area law enforcement and police services is an emerging topic in the field of digital government, we have an abbreviated review of the literature in this study. In the next sections, we outline our grounded theory method (2), our findings (3), we discuss the findings, outline the limitations of this study and the implications for research and practice (4).

2 Methodology

In this research, we applied the grounded theory methodology (GTM) (Glaser and Strauss 1967) following the paradigm described by Strauss and Corbin (Strauss and Corbin 1990; Corbin and Strauss 2015) and the GTM procedure described by Wiesche et al. (2017). The context of this study is the European Union (EU) whereby Germany was selected as the focal case with its multiple embedded units of analysis, represented by various law enforcement authorities, including police. Germany is a particularly critical case in the EU regarding successful digital government (Walke et al. 2023), because it ranks the penultimate place out of 39 countries in terms of digital competitiveness in Europe and North America (ECDC 2021) and there are still significant discrepancies between the status quo of e-government services and the requirements of the Online Access Act (OZG) in Germany (Hölscher et al. 2021). By choosing Germany and the high risk area of AI, we applied a critical case selection in our study, as part of an information-oriented selection, which describes the counterpart of random selection. A critical case can be defined as having strategic importance in relation to the general problem and achieves information, that permits logical deductions of the type (Flyvbjerg 2006). Since in Germany the need for a successful digital government is particularly high and law enforcement and police service are particularly critical areas of AI, we expect characteristics for the grounded model, which could be particularly evident.

The study pursued an exploratory qualitative research approach by conducting expert interviews and analyzing them qualitatively. The study took place over a period of four months from November 2022 to February 2023. Methodologically, this study was based on nine steps regarding GTM described by Wiesche et al. (2017). During the steps of theoretical sampling (1) and role of prior theory (2), and in addition to identifying the research gap, deriving the research questions and data acquisition, we used Strauss and Corbin's GTM paradigm (Strauss and Corbin 1990) to define a GTM study model and to design our interview guidelines for the expert interviews. Our GTM study model (Fig. 1) consists of the categories causal conditions, phenomenon, context, influence factors (divided in general, drivers and barriers), action strategies, intervening conditions and consequences. In our GTM study model the influence factors are referred to the action strategies. To address a wide range of possible action strategies, reference was made within the category of action strategies to the quality dimensions technology, information, human, process and system (Walke and Winkler 2022; Walke et al. 2023; Walke and Winkler 2024; Walke 2024). The experts for the interviews (Table 1) were recruited from the public and private sector. A total of 11 experts were interviewed. The interviews were processed with open and explorative questions related to the given GTM study model category. The prerequisite for selection were expertise in the use, planning or development of AI systems that are or will be used in the field of law enforcement and police services. The data analysis steps of open coding (3), axial coding (4), selective coding (5), theoretical coding (6), constant comparison (7) and memoing (8) described by Wiesche et al. (2017) have been performed using MAXQDA Software and were based on the coding system of the GTM study model (Fig. 1). The coding paradigm, the phenomenon (AI explainability requirements compliance) and the relations between the categories have already been predetermined by the GTM study model. The step of the final connection to the coding paradigm (9) was used to develop the final grounded model.

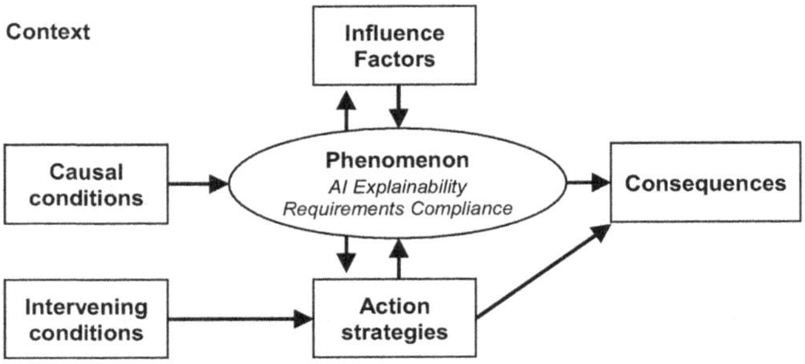

Fig. 1 GTM study model, adapted from Corbin and Strauss (2015)

Table 1 Overview of expert interviewees

#	Sector	Area	Position	Work experience (years)	Age
1	Public	Justice	Senior Prosecutor	> 15	40–49
2	Private	Public Sector Consultancy	Senior Manager	> 15	40–49
3	Private	Public Sector Consultancy	Big Data Scientist	> 3	20–29
4	Private	Public Sector Consultancy	Senior Consultant	> 5	30–39
5	Public	Research	PhD Candidate	> 5	30–39
6	Private	Lawyer Criminal Law	Partner	> 15	40–49
7	Private	Public Sector Consultancy	Leading Consultant	> 5	20–29
8	Public	Administration of Justice	Head of Unit	> 5	40–49
9	Public	Police Authority	IT employee	> 15	40–49
10	Public	Administration of Justice	Advisor	> 15	40–49
11	Public	Police University	Professor	> 25	50–59

3 Findings

We present the findings of this study successively based on the categories of the GTM study model and by separating the findings in three coding steps: axial coding, selective coding and theoretical coding (TC; asterisk* in the following tables means equal to selective coding), especially to provide a logical chain of evidence. The presentation of the coding results is based on the explanations of Williams and Moser (2019). The step of open coding is described textually and provides an excerpt of critical and relevant characteristics that were expressed by the expert interviewees. Additionally, we highlight relevant findings of the general coding process with expressive and direct citations from the expert (abbreviated as E1, E2, E3 etc.).

With the methodological restriction to the field of LEPS, the *context* was determined in relation to the phenomenon. In the course of coding, the special features of LEPS were assigned to the context. E11 emphasizes the higher requirements in law enforcement for the use of AI by describing that errors due to insufficient accuracy could "*completely destroy entire families*". Accordingly, AI systems are also classified as high-risk AI systems in the AIA, which in the opinion of E8 is too sweeping. E6 notes that there are hardly any concrete AI use cases in the area of law enforcement, but that these are "*very much*" discussed. Another special feature in the context of criminal prosecution is the judicial free assessment of evidence according to § 62 of the Code of Criminal Procedure (StPO), according to which a judge "*can make his own subjective conviction the basis of a guilty verdict on the basis of objective facts*" (E6). E8 adds to judicial independence: "*[...] the judge must not submit to an algorithm. And that is in principle our guiding principle*". The findings regarding context are summarized in Table 2.

Within the frame of selective coding, various *causal conditions* were summarized as "Legal AI requirements". AI explainability requirements itself was regularly named as the cause. E10 describes that the AIA specifies in the abstract that an AI decision must be comprehensible and verifiable. E4 emphasizes the importance of XAI metrics to identify misstatements. E6 sees metrics as a decision criterion for AI tool selection: "*Well, at the end of the day, you need some kind of tool*". The findings regarding causal conditions are summarised in Table 3.

Table 4 lists neutral (general), positive (drivers) and negative (barriers) *influence factors*. A neutral influence was used to code the actors mentioned, such as judges, prosecutors, defence lawyers, defendants, developers and users. Various technological dependencies were also noted, such as metric dependency to use cases, to the

Table 2 Context and its coding

Axial coding	Selective C.	TC
LEPS as a high-risk sector; Low penetration and use of AI in LEPS; Control by judges; Higher requirements in LEPS	LEPS specifics	*

Table 3 Causal conditions and their coding

Axial coding	Selective C.	TC
Objectivity; Decision factor in tool selection; Human limitations; Transparency requirement; Control over AI; AI explainability requirements; Black box; Identify erroneous explanations; Verifiability; Jurisdiction; No additional AIA requirements; European Law; Procedural rights; Judicial free assessment of evidence; Fundamental rights; Duty to state reasons; AIA; Burden of proof	Legal AI requirements	*

AI models or to XAI methods. E9 sees possible positive impacts on AI from technologies such as ChatGPT, as they could increase people's awareness in this regard. The complexity of some AI models is seen as a negative factor. E8 sees the danger, especially with neural networks, that only a "*best possible metric*" is realistic, but he cannot imagine an always correct metric. The availability and maturity of existing metrics was mentioned a total of nine times by five interviewees (E1, 3, 4, 7 and 8). It was noted that the topic was new (E3), that no metrics were known (E4) or that metrics were difficult to find (E8). In addition, bias and potential dependence on technology providers were mentioned. The influence of regulation was assessed differently. In the interviews, both insufficient or no regulation and partly too restrictive regulation were pointed out: "*Yes, and lumping all AI systems of police authorities together is absolutely not helpful.*" (E9); "*Let's take a look at these big language models GPT etc. Hardly anything comes from Europe these days. That's just the point. We can regulate everything very well, but then the technology simply moves away and we can't use it as a public sector.*" (E8). According to E5, clear requirements for a certain level of explainability would also have a driving effect. Regulation can also have a neutral effect if neither a positive nor a negative influence is associated with it. The findings regarding influence factors are summarized in Table 4 and have been condensed during theoretical coding to "Dependencies", "Future perspectives" and "Complexity".

In the following, the *action strategies* are listed along the five quality dimensions technology, information, human, process and system (Walke et al. 2023; Walke and Winkler 2022). The action strategies in the *technology* dimension are condensed to "Technological preconditions creation" (Table 5). A compromise between precision and explainability seems necessary. E3 states that in law enforcement, very complex models that deliver very high precision and high recall are not the primary goal. Rather, one tries to find a kind of trade-off between the quality of the model in relation to the current reference system and the simplicity of the explanatory power. This means that one tries to improve the quality minimally, but at the same time to achieve maximum explanatory power and simplicity of the model. Regarding preventing recalculability, E1 mentions: "*So far, we have focused on the question of the technical framework conditions and the recalculability of the AI models in order to ensure that a delivered AI cannot be used later to generate child pornography itself*".

Table 4 Influence factors and their coding

Axial coding	Selective C.	TC
General influence factors (neutral)		
Dependence metric with use case/AI model/XAI-method; Dependence AI model and XAI method; AI model quality criteria; Dependence on technology providers	Technological dependencies	Dependencies
Abstract requirements; Case law; Basic law	Regulation	
Injured party; Accused; Professionals; Developer; Experts; User; Defence lawyers; Prosecutor; Judges	Actors	
Drivers (positive)		
Future perspectives on AI; ChatGPT hype; Clear regulation as a potential driver	Future perspective	*
Barriers (negative)		
Lack of legal requirements; Lack of standards; Lack of legal clarity; Restrictive regulation; Data protection	Insufficient regulation	Complexity
ChatGPT as an example of complexity; Explainability not achievable or meaningful; Paradigm shift/system complexity; Complex models; Limits of measurability; Defining requirements for metrics is complex; Complexity of digital products	Complexity	
Availability of metrics; Maturity of metrics	Metrics maturity	
Bias	Bias	

When developing AI models, care must be taken to ensure that they cannot be used to generate prohibited content themselves. An AI that has been trained to recognize specific content could also generate it. Within the *information* dimension and during selective coding we identified "Support intelligibility" as a major action strategy. E2 points out that explainability is there for people and that corresponding metrics must also be understood by them. In his statement, E1 emphasizes the importance of being able to explain the technical framework conditions in a comprehensible way even to a person who does not have an affinity for technology.

One possible action strategy within the *human* dimension is to promote acceptance, benefit and trust. It must be possible to trust the result of a black box (E11). In addition, there must also be a certain acceptance of errors for AI, as it cannot achieve 100% accuracy (E9). Additionally, the action strategy "Building competencies" was identified. E7 assumes that decisions can be made better with a basic understanding of AI. E8 also argues for a decentralized anchoring of this knowledge and sees the development of digital competences through further training as necessary. We condensed the selective codes during theoretical coding to the action strategy "AI-focused education".

With regard to the *process* dimension and selective coding, we identified the following action strategies: "Development optimization", "Traceability assurance" and "Requirements through standards". According to E8, an interdisciplinary approach that takes both professional and technical aspects into account is necessary

Table 5 Action strategies and their coding

Axial coding	Selective C.	TC
Technology		
Compromise precision/explainability; Preventing recalculability; Barrier-free; Use transparent models; Do not use ready-made solutions	Technological preconditions creation	*
Information		
Use of domain language; Understandable explainability; Understandable metrics; Understandable regulation	Support intelligibility	*
Human		
Acceptance; Error acceptance; Usability; Trust; Highlighting benefits; Publish models used by the state; Create awareness; Create mindset; Motivation; Take away fears; Change	Promoting acceptance, benefit and trust	AI-focused education
AI literacy; Data literacy; Technological understanding; Training; Education	Building competencies	
Process		
In-house development; Interdisciplinarity; Involvement of relevant stakeholders in the development process; Integrate metrics in the development process; Paradigm shift; Quality assurance; Carry out simulations; Test procedures; Transparency through traceability; Holistic approach	Development optimization	Normed and optimized XAI development
Monitoring in use; Logging; Retraceability; Versioning; Traceability	Traceability assurance	
Benchmarks; Best practices (e.g. GDPR); Provide explanatory methods; Recommendations for action; Software repositories; Standardization; Mandatory legal requirements and voluntary standards; Certification; Standardized auditing process	Requirements through standards	
System		
Exchange with other departments; Promotion of research; Promotion of open source software; Publication of certified systems; Exchange with science; Workshops	Overarching exchange	Structural and cultural organization
Agility; AI as a central component of an organization; Organizational policy	Creating AI culture	
Risk management; Auditing unit; Supervision; Federal-state intergovernmental approach; Expert committee; AI commission; Taskforce; Certification institute	Building AI organizations	

to ensure the successful development of XAI. The metrics must already be integrated in the development process (E4) and the same applies to the users of the AI in question (E3). E1 also points out that, in his view, AI can only be used in the justice system if the justice system has a formative influence on it during the development phase, rather than adopting a solution from a manufacturer or scientific team: "*In my opinion, an AI in the justice system can hardly be used in the situation that a manufacturer or a scientific team presents us a solution and says that it can be used in this way; instead, we have to exert a formative influence in the development phase.*" E9 stresses the importance of clearly defined standards to ensure the reliability of AI systems. To this end, he suggests that independent bodies carry out and publish certifications for certain systems in order to achieve standardization. Another important factor is a standardized auditing process carried out by an external institution to check the traceability and reproducibility of the systems. E8 suggests that the definition of standards should focus on both general criteria and specific requirements for certain areas of application. A panel of experts could be used for the general part, while a case-by-case approach would be necessary for specific requirements. The development and updating of the standards could be carried out on the basis of practical experience. We condensed the action strategies of the selective coding during theoretical coding to "Normed and optimized XAI development". Regarding the *system* dimension, we identified during selective coding the action strategies the action strategies "Overarching exchange", "Creating AI culture" and "Building AI organizations". Aspects such as the promotion of open source software (E5) or research on XAI and metrics (E4) were mentioned here. E1 also emphasized the reason for taking part in the interview, in order to achieve a "*higher degree of formalization also in the area of explainability*" through dialogue and scientific support. With regard to the development of organizational structures for AI systems, a cross-federal state approach is called for (E8) and, for example, a certification institute (E8). We condensed the action strategies of the selective coding during theoretical coding to "Structural and cultural organization". All action strategies are summarized in Table 5.

The action strategies are based on *intervening conditions*, which in turn were coded along the previous quality dimensions technology, human, process and system. Regarding the information dimension, we found no relevant intervening condition. Regarding *technology* and "Technology preconditions", E10 makes clear that AI systems should be comprehensible in order to make their decision-making verifiable. However, it still has to be defined how this traceability is implemented technically. In the framework of the AIA, traceability is taken into account as an abstract requirement, however, there will be no concrete regulations on how traceability is to be technically implemented. Regarding the *human* dimension, "Psychosocial factors" appear as intervening conditions. E7 believes that metrics are particularly necessary in the justice system because of the principle-based thinking and the high level of responsibility. E8 and E9 state that 100% accurate AI will not exist and that this should be acceptable as humans also make mistakes (E8, E9). In addition, E8 emphasizes that no corresponding metric would exist for humans either, because their decisions themselves are not comprehensible. A *processual* intervening condition is the "Use type of AI". There is the uncritical use as an aid, for example, in the context of file processing (E8) or the decision-supporting use, in which investigations are supported by an AI, but the decision is made by a human (E9). E11 emphasizes: "*[…] the AI itself, no matter how good the metrics are, can never have the sole and final decision.*" E8 states that before the judiciary can enter the high-risk area particularly regulated by the AIA, there is still some groundwork to be done, such as business process automation and metadata extraction. Several expert interviewees stress that the introduction of a metric for XAI raises further questions.

For example, how the system arrives at the underlying metric (E8) or whether there is a need to evaluate the metric: "*[…] there is a category of explainability metrics. Yes, and one says score 80, the other says score 50. Then I will always take the one with the score 80. So the requirement, the driver for us is to keep control of the tool. That is the driver for us as lawyers. And it should also be the driver for the judiciary. And what is an obstacle? Well, of course, the question is then again: don't you also have to assess the metrics? So the assessment of the assessment.*" (E6). Regarding the *system* dimension, E8 wonders, in terms of resources, "*who do you call or where do you get these people?*" At the same time, he sees the opportunities: "*[…] this technology offers great potential to strengthen the state, to strengthen the rule of law, to relieve personnel and to make us really fit.*" (E8). The selective codes have been condensed during theoretical coding to "AI Quality preconditions" (Table 6).

E8 emphasizes that the introduction of an XAI assessment would bring a considerable gain in acceptance, as many reservations on the part of citizens and colleagues could be eliminated as a result. Such a development would also be advantageous from the perspective of the rule of law. E4 sees the possibility of a restriction of AI use if

Table 6 Intervening conditions and their coding

Axial coding	Selective C.	TC
Technology		AI quality preconditions
Quality of the input data; Robustness; Evaluation of the assessment; Lack of technological basis	Technological preconditions	
Human		
Rejectionism; Coziness, laziness; Age-related factors; Motivational factors; Avoidance of mistakes; Lack of awareness of the need; People also make mistakes; Human black box	Psychosocial factors	
Process		
Field of application; Independent decisions; Decision preparation, support; Consequences of decisions; Intended use	Use-type of AI	
System		
Resources; Cost recovery; Employee availability regarding staff shortage; Lack of time; Expenditure; Intervening regulation	Resources	

too high demands are made, including on metrics. These positive, neutral and negative consequences have been condensed during theoretical coding to "Antagonistic impact". The coding of the consequences can be found in Table 7.

Potential metrics were assigned to the category of the *phenomenon* "AI explainability requirements compliance", which is predetermined by the study model (Fig. 1). During selective coding we identified "Qualitative metrics", "Quantitative metrics", "Metrics visualization" and "Objectives of metrics". E2 sees a clear need for quantitative metrics, as qualitative metrics would leave the realm of AI and this always meant simplification. E1 can also imagine "*random parallel evaluations*". The results for the phenomenon can be seen in Table 8.

Due to the high importance of the measurability of the phenomenon, we additionally compared the literature on XAI metrics (Sovrano et al. 2021, 2022; Sovrano and Vitali 2023) with the metrics mentioned by the experts. We come to the conclusion that, of the 16 metrics mentioned by the experts, eight could be connected to the metrics mentioned in the literature. The other eight metrics (stress test, anchors, distance to tipping point of a decision, number of decision core components, explainable yes/no, meteor, BLEU and word error rate) have not yet been mentioned in the XAI literature we considered (Sovrano et al. 2021, 2022; Sovrano and Vitali 2023).

Table 7 Consequences and their coding

Axial coding	Selective coding	TC
Building trust; Reduction of reservations; Increasing acceptance	Trust and acceptance	Antagonistic impact
Enabling the appealability of decisions; Compliance with legal requirements	Legal compliance	
Innovation inhibition	Innovation inhibition	

Table 8 Phenomenon and its coding

Axial coding	Selective coding	TC
Charts; Dashboards	Metrics visualization	AI explainability requirements compliance
Human evaluation, survey; Stress test	Qualitative metrics	
Anchors; Distance to the tipping point of a decision; Reference corpus/reference model/ground truth; Feature importance; Accuracy; F1 score; Number of decision core components; Explainable: yes/no; Precision; Recall; Randomization; Meteor; BLEU; Word error rate	Quantitative metrics	
Objectives of metrics	Objectives of metrics	

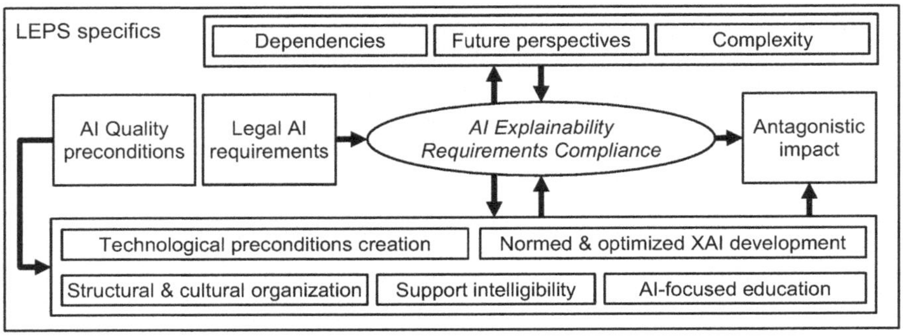

Fig. 2 Grounded model of AI explainability requirements compliance

Using the insights gained from the interviews and the subsequent coding, the grounded model (Fig. 2) was developed based on the study model (Fig. 1), which contains the theoretical coding's.

4 Discussion and Conclusion

In this study we followed an exploratory and qualitative research approach regarding the phenomenon—*AI explainability requirements compliance*—using the grounded theory method. The research question was addressed by discovering the characteristics of the phenomenon in the context of LEPS and by representing the characteristics in a grounded model. Dependencies, future perspectives and complexity were identified as key influence factors, and the creation of technological prerequisites, normed and optimized XAI development, structural and cultural organization, supporting intelligibility, and AI-focused education as action strategies. Intervening conditions of action strategies are AI quality preconditions. The cause of the phenomenon are legal AI requirements and the consequence of the phenomenon is an antagonistic impact.

The results of this paper show that the use of AI systems in LEPS is subject to further special requirements, as errors due to insufficient accuracy can lead to serious consequences. It is therefore important that they are designed in such a way that they meet the requirements of the rule of law, the requirements of criminal procedure and, in the future, the requirements of the AIA, while at the same time ensuring a high level of accuracy and reliability. The AI systems used must be transparent and comprehensible in order to ensure that judges and other actors can make their decisions on the basis of objective facts, or can review and challenge them if necessary. The action strategies indicate ways in which compliance with AI explainability requirements can be achieved. Since no metrics in use could be named during the interviews and AI has so far tended to be used in non-critical areas, metrics play a decisive role. The establishment of organizational structures for AI, the creation of certification institutes and, in particular, the provision of standards, are of great importance. Ideally, users must already be involved in the development process. Through co-design, a kind of transparency or comprehensibility can arise even with black-box AI, since the underlying logic can be co-developed and understood. At the same time, AI explainability requirements can be taken into account, including relevant metrics. In this context, it is important that users have the competences to understand the basic features of AI. This can be achieved by building AI and data literacy competencies through training and education. Awareness of such a need can also be raised through public awareness as a result of technologies such as ChatGPT, as people see what AI can be capable of. Skill enhancement and change management can help foster trust and acceptance in AI systems, providing a foundation for the development of XAI metrics. These metrics can, in turn, help to improve XAI and thus further increase trust and acceptance in these systems. It can furthermore be stated that a use of XAI metrics in the field of law enforcement, at least in the field of interview partners, does not seem to happen yet. AI applications are already in use or in development and explainability also plays a role in these, but their measurement or assessment does not seem to be considered yet.

Within the frame of the free assessment of evidence, a judge must in any case form his or her own opinion about the credibility and reliability of evidence, regardless of whether it comes from AI systems or not. This realization leads to the assumption that metrics can support the judge in this free assessment of evidence. It can be assumed that various degrees of freedom through the combination and free selection of metrics could contribute to this, but ultimately the judge decides to what extent he or she takes these metrics into account. In addition, the question of the explainability of the metric itself was raised, and whether it should not be evaluated itself.

A total of 11 expert interviews were conducted from the judiciary, judicial administration, police, research and private sector, which seemed sufficient to achieve theoretical saturation. However, this limited number of interviewees could be increased in future research. The decision to select LEPS as the critical focal case was based on the recognition that AI systems in this domain are likely to be classified as high-risk AI systems and are therefore subject to particular challenges. However, it could be, that this is precisely why AI systems are still comparatively rarely used in LEPS and thus there may be less expertise and experience in the development and use of AI systems than in other areas. The analysis of another sector could therefore lead to different results with regard to the general aspects. One approach for further research would be to carry out a sector comparison in order to examine the differences and similarities with regard to XAI and their assessment by means of metrics. This could provide insights that go beyond the field of LEPS and may also be applicable to other high-risk AI systems. Specificities in the field of LEPS are highlighted and it is found that challenges exist in the implementation of AI systems and XAI metrics. In order to meet these challenges, the phenomenon was considered holistically by applying a grounded-theory-approach.

This paper examined the specifics of compliance with the explainability requirements of AI systems in the context of law enforcement and police service. In this way, the paper contributes to the discussion about the impact of AI systems on law enforcement and police service and shows that the use of AI systems in this context is associated with special requirements and challenges. The identified characteristics of this high risk area can contribute to the academic discussion, the practical development of AI systems in high risk areas and can help authorities and governments create appropriate conditions for the use of AI.

References

Bibal, A., Lognoul, M., Streel, A. de and Frénay, B. (2021), "Legal requirements on explainability in machine learning", *Artificial Intelligence and Law*, Vol. 29 No. 2, pp. 149–169.

Buxmann, P. and Schmidt, H. (2019), *Künstliche Intelligenz*, Springer Gabler, Berlin, Heidelberg.

Corbin, J.M. and Strauss, A.L. (2015), *Basics of qualitative research: Techniques and procedures for developing grounded theory*, 4th ed., Sage, Los Angeles, Calif.

ECDC (2021), *Digital Riser Report 2021*, ESCP Business School, available at: https://digital-competitiveness.eu/wp-content/uploads/Digital_Riser_Report-2021.pdf.

European Commission (2018), *Künstliche Intelligenz für Europa*, available at: https://eur-lex.europa.eu/legal-content/DE/TXT/?uri=CELEX:52018DC0237 (accessed 28 October 2023).

European Commission (2019), *Mitteilung der Kommission an das Europäische Parlament, den Rat, den Europäischen Wirtschafts- und Sozialausschuss und den Ausschuss der Regionen Schaffung von Vertrauen in eine auf den Menschen ausgerichtete künstliche Intelligenz*, available at: https://eur-lex.europa.eu/legal-content/DE/TXT/?uri=CELEX:52019DC0168 (accessed 29 October 2022).

European Commission (2021), *Proposal for a regulation of the European Parliament and of the Council laying down harmonised rules on artificial intelligence (Artificial Intelligence Act) and amending certain union legislative acts*, available at: https://eur-lex.europa.eu/legal-content/DE/TXT/?uri=CELEX:52019DC0168 (accessed 29 October 2022).

Flyvbjerg, B. (2006), "Five Misunderstandings About Case-Study Research", *Qualitative Inquiry*, Vol. 12 No. 2, pp. 219–245.

German Federal Government (2020), *Strategie Künstliche Intelligenz der Bundesregierung. Fortschreibung 2020*, available at: https://www.ki-strategie-deutschland.de/files/downloads/201201_Fortschreibung_KI-Strategie.pdf (accessed 28 October 2022).

Glaser, B.G. and Strauss, A.L. (1967), *The discovery of grounded theory: Strategies for qualitative research, Observations*, Aldine, New York, NY.

Hölscher, I., Opiela, N., Tiemann, J., Gumz, J.D., Goldacker, G., Thapa, B. and Weber, M. (2021), "Deutschland-Index der Digitalisierung 2021. Kompetenzzentrum Öffentliche IT", available at: https://www.oeffentliche-it.de/documents/10181/14412/Deutschland-Index+der+Digitalisierung+2021.

McDermid, J.A., Jia, Y., Porter, Z. and Habli, I. (2021), "Artificial intelligence explainability: the technical and ethical dimensions", *Philosophical Transactions. Series A, Mathematical, Physical, and Engineering Sciences*, Vol. 379 No. 2207, p. 20200363.

Mukhamediev, R.I., Popova, Y., Kuchin, Y., Zaitseva, E., Kalimoldayev, A., Symagulov, A., Levashenko, V., Abdoldina, F., Gopejenko, V., Yakunin, K., Muhamedijeva, E. and Yelis, M. (2022), "Review of Artificial Intelligence and Machine Learning Technologies: Classification, Restrictions, Opportunities and Challenges", *Mathematics*, Vol. 10 No. 15, p. 2552.

Sovrano, F. and Vitali, F. (2023), *An Objective Metric for Explainable AI: How and Why to Estimate the Degree of Explainability*.

Sovrano, F., Sapienza, S., Palmirani, M. and Vitali, F. (2021), "A Survey on Methods and Metrics for the Assessment of Explainability Under the Proposed AI Act", 8–10 December, Vilnius, Lithuania.

Sovrano, F., Sapienza, S., Palmirani, M. and Vitali, F. (2022), "Metrics, Explainability and the European AI Act Proposal", *J*, Vol. 5 No. 1, pp. 126–138.
Strauss, A.L. and Corbin, J.M. (1990), *Basics of qualitative research: Grounded theory procedures and techniques*, Sage Publications, Inc.
Walke, F. (2024), Digital Transformation of the Public Sector [Dissertation, University of Hagen]. University Library Hagen. https://doi.org/10.18445/20240624-114639-0
Walke, F. and Winkler, T.J. (2022), "The TIHP Framework – An Instrument for Measuring Quality of Hybrid Services".
Walke, F. and Winkler, T.J. (2024), Assessing Omnichannel Service Quality in the Public Sector. Public Administration. https://doi.org/10.1111/padm.13038
Walke, F., Winkler, T.J. and & Le, M. (2023), "Success of Digital Identity Infrastructure: A Grounded Model of eID Evolution Success.", *Proceedings of the 56th Hawaii International Conference on System Sciences*, Vol. 56.
Wiesche, M., Jurisch, M., Yetton, P. and Krcmar, H. (2017), "Grounded Theory Methodology in Information Systems Research", *Management Information Systems Quarterly*, Vol. 41 No. 3, pp. 685–701.
Williams, M. and Moser, T. (2019), "The Art of Coding and Thematic Exploration in Qualitative Research", *International Management Review*, Vol. 15 No. 1, pp. 45–55.

Decoding the Landscape of Smart City Platforms: A Taxonomy Approach

Kenneth Richter, Markus P. Zimmer, and Kristina Lemmer

Abstract The notion of Smart Cities (SCs) has gained significant attention in recent years as cities become increasingly connected, integrated, and technologically advanced. Smart City Platforms (SCPs) are an important element of this movement representing the backbone for collecting, processing and analyzing urban data streams from peripheral devices and systems in a city. This study seeks to identify the key dimensions and characteristics of SCPs. Based on existing literature, we craft a taxonomy following Nickerson et al.'s (Eur J Inf Syst 22:336–359, 2013) guidelines. The resulting SCP taxonomy contributes to the literature on SCs by offering a set of characterizations of SCPs that provide a framework to analyze SCPs and identify types of SCPs.

Keywords Smart city · Smart city platform · Taxonomy

1 Introduction

City management faces issues of traffic jams, environmental pollution, energy consumption, and social cohesion. Issues which the increasing urbanization will intensify (Bibri 2020; Kaluarachchi 2022). The smart city (SC) phenomenon seeks to address these problems (Batty 2013). SCs are socio-technical systems that utilize information and communication technology (ICT) to collect, store, and process vast amounts of data to stimulate human- and social capital while improving the quality of life (QOL) for citizens (Bibri 2019; Fahmideh and Zowghi 2020; Hollands 2008).

K. Richter (✉) · M. P. Zimmer · K. Lemmer
Institute of Information Systems, Leuphana University Lüneburg, Lüneburg, Germany
e-mail: kenneth.richter@leuphana.de

M. P. Zimmer
e-mail: markus.zimmer@leuphana.de

K. Lemmer
e-mail: kristina.lemmer@leuphana.de

D. Beverungen et al. (eds.), *Transforming the Digitally Sustainable Enterprise*, Lecture Notes in Information Systems and Organisation 76,
https://doi.org/10.1007/978-3-031-80125-9_24

Thus, based on the notion of the Internet of Things (IoT), SCs comprise several interconnected ICTs, such as physical infrastructure, communication systems, and sensors which create smart city platforms (SCPs) (Albino et al. 2015; Bibri 2018). The European Innovation Partnership on Smart Cities and Communities define SCPs as the backbone for the integration and management of various technological solutions, data collection and analysis, and the delivery of services to citizens (EIP-SCC 2016).

SCPs enable different components of SCs to communicate with each other and share data, thereby enabling cities to operate more efficiently and effectively (Bouskela et al. 2016). The utilization of ICTs for conducting assignments within a social system has been found to result in a significant transformation in the socio-technical system of a city (Fahmideh and Zowghi 2020; Lyytinen and Newman 2008). As such, SCPs constitute high complexity and challenges for cities, i.e., through their deep embedding in the cities' infrastructure, heterogeneous systems and technologies must coexist and interact with several stakeholders (Yigitcanlar et al. 2018). Thus, SCPs are vital for bridging social and technical aspects of SCs and facilitating interactions among city stakeholders (Ballon et al. 2011; Patti and Acquaviva 2016; Santana et al. 2018).

Hitherto, several studies acknowledge different requirements for SCPs. However, they root these requirements in different SCP types (Anttiroiko et al. 2014; Javed et al. 2020; Santana et al. 2018). Thus, missing a typification of SCPs can cause issues in mapping requirements to the right SCP type (Mijuskovic et al. 2021; Santana et al. 2018). Further, the absence of a typification—a theory of analysis clarifying what something is (Gregor 2006)—limits our ability to compare findings from previous research and to make theoretical generalizations based on respective comparisons. That is, if we cannot identify two SCPs as the same type, how can we deduce insightful propositions about these SCPs? Therefore, we suggest that a profound classification is necessary for IS researchers to aggregate existing knowledge about SCPs; the initial point for platform design, the explanation of interdependencies, and the assessment of risks, patterns, and characteristics (Schermuly et al. 2019). Hence, to bridge the identified research gap and foster a comprehensive understanding of the research field concerning SCPs, this paper develops a SCP taxonomy.

In doing so, we decided to use an inductive-deductive research approach following Nickerson et al.'s (2013) taxonomy development method combined with Wolfswinkel et al. (2013) guidelines for systematic literature reviews. Based on a systematic literature review on SCPs, we develop a SCP taxonomy that comprises 4 meta-dimensions and 12 dimensions. This taxonomy contributes to the literature by providing a conceptual basis for understanding and differentiating SCPs. Thus, the taxonomy enables future research and theorizing of SCPs by establishing comparability among different SCP types. After this introduction, we outline the research background on SCs and SCPs. Section 3 describes our literature search and taxonomy building before we outline, in Sect. 4, the developed SCP taxonomy. We close the article by discussing the SCP taxonomies contribution, limitations, and avenues for future research.

2 Research Background

Over the past two decades, SCs have garnered considerable research and policy interest. Although extensively discussed in the literature, the term SC remains a concept with blurred boundaries and varying interpretations (Nastjuk et al. 2022). SCs are a growing phenomenon in urban development, leveraging ICTs to surge the human- and social capital to fuel sustainable economic growth and improve the QOL of their residents (Yigitcanlar et al. 2018). SC phenomena rely on SCP deployment, as a backbone for collecting, processing, and analyzing urban data streams from peripheral devices and systems within a city (Cheng et al. 2015; Gaur et al. 2015). In that vein, previous research investigated the distinct requirements for the design of SCPs. In the literature, the requirements are structured into functional and non-functional requirements (Da Cruz et al. 2018; Shapsough and Zualkernan 2019). The functional requirements mentioned most often in the literature are security and privacy, data management, standardization, interfaces, data visualization, and resource discovery (Fersi 2015; Mijuskovic et al. 2021; Oliveira et al. 2016). On the other hand, non-functional requirements encompass interoperability, scalability, real-time processing, timeliness, modularity, context awareness, and quality of service (Agarwal and Alam 2020; Al-Fuqaha et al. 2015; Mijuskovic et al. 2021). However, the requirements can broadly vary based on the distinct type of SCP they study. For instance, due to the lack of a uniform standard, Koo and Kim (2021) highlight the interoperability issues for horizontal SCPs. Advanced interoperability is crucial for horizontal SCPs, which are designed to be flexible, scalable, and capable of integrating diverse applications from various domains (Mijuskovic et al. 2021). In contrast, vertical SCPs differ in terms of scope, functionality, and intended use. Identifying valid requirements for diverse application scenarios on SCPs is challenging due to the heterogeneous array of applications and respective SCP types (El-Ghalayini and Al-Kandari 2020; Zanella et al. 2014). Therefore, major issues arise in identifying and considering relevant requirements for different types of SCPs. Existing classifications, e.g. Santana et al. (2018), suggest SCP types by enabling ICTs: Cyber-Physical Systems, IoT, Big Data, and Cloud Computing. This classification can offer instructions for implementing SCPs based on these ICTs but lacks insights into SCP characteristics or types. That is, SCP requirements stem not only from the underlying ICT but the broader context of the application.

Hence, while important features of SCPs are well understood, we lack a systematic classification of SCPs (Santana et al. 2018). We argue that the development of a taxonomy is necessary to effectively highlight and examine the SCP phenomenon from a systematic perspective. A taxonomy of SCPs illustrates the distinct and multi-faceted characteristics and enables the potential for new approaches for platform design, patterns, associations, and causal relationships (Lueg et al. 2022; Schermuly et al. 2019). Moreover, it captures transparency and enables an assignment of the requirements to the respective SCP types. Highlighting the diverse dimensions and characteristics of SCPs may facilitate further, leading to a deeper understanding and comprehensive analysis of the phenomenon (Nickerson et al. 2013).

3 Methodology

3.1 Data Collection and Data Analysis

We conducted a systematic literature review based on Wolfswinkel et al. (2013) and followed Nickerson et al.'s (2013) taxonomy development approach to assemble a SCP taxonomy. This method has been widely recognized in IS research and includes predefined phases for creating a structured taxonomy (Bailey 1994). Taxonomies embody a valid instrument to guide various disciplines to "*bring order to complex areas*" (Nickerson et al. 2013, p. 535). This is done by categorizing dimensions or traits and highlighting similarities among a subject being studied (Bailey 1994).

The data collection is based on a systematic literature review of SCPs and is consistent with the suggestions of Wolfswinkel et al. (2013). First, we conducted various search inquiries to obtain a common understanding of the phenomenon in the literature. The data collected in the databases utilized the search strings shown in Table 1. We built these search strings around the terms "Smart City" and synonyms for "Platform", and "Requirements" as well as the application context of SCs. We deliberately decided to not include search terms that refer to concepts related to SCs and SCPs (e.g., Big Data) to narrow the search results to existing literature that may deal with these related concepts but only within the context of SCs and SCPs.

This yielded 623 papers initially. In the beginning, we filtered the articles by examining the title and the abstract. Afterward, we read the full paper and eliminated papers that were not confirmed with the subsequent criteria. The focus is on SCPs, thus, we excluded papers that did not entail detailed information about the key characteristics of SCPs. Articles that applied a vague definition of SCPs, were also excluded. Second, only articles with a focus on SCPs were considered. Hence, solely papers restricted to the SC phenomena were excluded. In addition, due to the interwoven relationship between IoT and SCs, papers about IoT platforms in the context of SCs were considered as well. Furthermore, only articles written in English are considered. Lastly, a forward and backward search was performed to enrich the literature sample. We outline the article selection and filtering process in Fig. 1. During the data collection, we gathered information including the type of

Table 1 Search strings for data collection

Search string	Applied database
"Smart City" AND "Platform" OR "Middleware" OR "Data Platform" OR "Smart City Platform" AND "Characteristics" AND "Requirements"	Web of Science, ACM Digital Library, IEEE, AIS Electronic Library, ScienceDirect, and Google Scholar
"Smart City Services" OR "Smart City Application" AND "IoT"	
"Smart City" AND "Service" OR "Application" AND "IoT"	

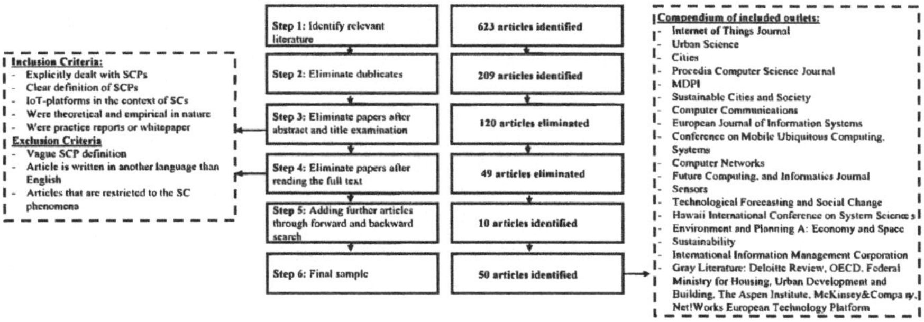

Fig. 1 Article selection and filtering process

articles. We differenced between scientific papers, and gray literature (e.g., practice reports or whitepapers). In general, whitepapers are characterized by an elaboration of a case and the gathered experience. In total, 50 articles form the baseline for our study.

3.2 *Taxonomy Development*

The taxonomy development process followed the iterative steps outlined by Nickerson et al. (2013). In the beginning, we determined our meta-characteristic. The meta-characteristics represent the basis for selecting the characteristics of the taxonomy (Nickerson et al. 2013; Pinto and Martins 2004). As our goal is to typify SCPs, we established the following meta-characteristic: "Key characteristics of SCPs". Accordingly, we devised objective and subjective ending conditions based on Nickerson et al. (2013) advocacy. We developed the following objective ending conditions: (1) All objects have been thoroughly scrutinized, (2) At least one object is classified under every characteristic of every dimension, (3) No new dimension was added in the last iteration and (4) Every dimension is unique within its dimension and is not repeated (Nickerson et al. 2013). In addition, Nickerson et al. (2013) suggest the ending condition that all characteristics are mutually exclusive. However, crafting our taxonomy, we encountered instances when restricting the taxonomy to mutually exclusive characteristics lead to information loss (Berger et al. 2018). Furthermore, removing these characteristics would contradict the motive of taxonomies to be sparing and holistic (Bailey 1994; Nickerson et al. 2013). Thus, we decided against this ending condition. Lastly, we determined subjective ending conditions—comprehensive, extendible, explanatory, concise, and robust—following Nickerson et al. (2013).

The taxonomy development comprised three iterations. Given the body of prior work on SCPs, we chose an empirical-to-conceptual (E2C) approach and first analyzed the scientific papers (Nickerson et al. 2013; Pinto and Martins 2004). Coding these papers, we identified common characteristics of SCPs and ordered them hierarchically (Gioia et al. 2013). Extending our analysis to non-scientific papers, we concluded that the taxonomy misses the defined ending conditions. We thus conducted a second iteration.

In the second iteration, we chose the conceptual-to-empirical (C2E) approach (Nickerson et al. 2013; Pinto and Martins 2004). We thus analyzed the identified whitepapers continuing the coding schema from the first iteration. This produced validation of existing characteristics and dimensions but also extension and specification of the taxonomy. Since we identified new dimensions and characteristics, we conducted a third iteration (Nickerson et al. 2013).

In the third iteration, we conducted an E2C approach and analyzed the entire literature sample again. Since we analyzed all items and did not identify additional characteristics or dimensions, we concluded that the taxonomy meets the ending conditions (Nickerson et al. 2013). Lastly, we evaluated the taxonomy's functionality by applying it to the Smart Santander case study by Sanchez et al. (2014) and Santana et al. (2018).

4 Smart City Platform Taxonomy

In the following, we elaborate on the taxonomy for SCPs in detail. Table 2 displays the final version characterizing SCPs. Based on our implied theoretical lens, the taxonomy consists of 12 dimensions within 4 meta-dimensions. The right column, displays, whether the characteristics are mutually exclusive (E) or non-mutually exclusive (N).

4.1 Meta-Dimension Smart City Platform Strategy

The strategy pays specific attention to the approach and strategic alignment to initiate SCPs and is divided into four dimensions (Bagheri et al. 2021). The dimension of **Platform Positioning** regards the holistic nature of SCPs. This dimension encompasses two distinct modes. First, SCPs can embody a specialized platform consisting of multiple fragmented systems (Khan et al. 2017; Kitchin and Moore-Cherry 2021). Specialized SCPs typically focus on a narrow set of services or functions and rely on specific data sources or stakeholders (Anttiroiko 2016; Stehlin et al. 2020). Common specialized SCPs include transportation, energy, and health platforms (Anttiroiko 2016; Bibri and Krogstie 2020; Massana et al. 2017). However, specialized SCPs may encounter challenges in interoperability, scalability, and sustainability, and require coordination and integration with other platforms and stakeholders (Bibri and Krogstie 2020; Correia and Wünstel 2011; Koo and Kim 2021). Second, SCPs represent one central system called integrative. This requires interoperable interfaces, open standards, and common governance frameworks that enable different SCPs to communicate and collaborate (Correia and Wünstel 2011; Koo and Kim

Table 2 Taxonomy for smart city platforms

Dimensions		Characteristics								E/N
Smart city platform strategy	Platform positioning	Integrative				Specialized				E
	Value proposition	Software-as-a-Service				Platform-as-a-Service				E
	Application domain	Public administration	Living	Economy	People	Mobility	Environment			N
	Software access	Open source				Proprietary				E
Smart city platform stakeholders	Platform owner	Government	Private company	Non-governmental org.	Private-public partnership					E
	External partners	Open platform				Closed platform				E
	Technical operator	Single operator				Multi-operator				E
Technical infrastructure	Development approach	Citizen-centric	Technology-centric	Institution-centric	Information-centric					E
	Data format	Numerical	Textual	Audio	Video	Geospatial				N
	Cloud mode	Public cloud	Private cloud	Hybrid cloud						E
Governance	Cybersecurity	Encryption	Access control	Anonymization						N
	Data management	Collection	Aggregation	Analysis	Sharing	Transmission	Visualization	Simulation	Storage	N

2021; Zanella et al. 2014). Therefore, empowering a specialized SCP to evolve into an integrative SCP represents a key strategy for creating a more integrated SC (Correia and Wünstel 2011; Khan et al. 2022; Zanella et al. 2014). The **Value Proposition** dimension refers to the benefits or advantages that SCPs offer to their users and stakeholders (Frow et al. 2014). Bibri and Krogstie (2020) argue that the London DataStore, based on raw urban data, can engage developers to create disruptive apps. In exchange for the data and platform usage, the operator receives a certain fee. In the literature, it is called Platform-as-a-Service (PaaS) (Ray 2016; Santana et al. 2018). Highly related to PaaS is Software-as-a-Service (SaaS). The main difference between those two is, that SaaS provides customers access to pre-build software applications, while PaaS provides a platform for developers to build and deploy their applications (Ballon et al. 2011; Mineraud et al. 2016). Due to different priorities and issues, the choice of which value proposition SCPs choose is strongly influenced by the **Application Domain** for which it is being designed. Based on the literature we follow Giffinger and Gudrun (2010) and consider six SCP application avenues: mobility, people, living, environment, economy, and public administration. SCPs in the mobility domain focus on optimizing and improving the existing transportation infrastructure within a city (Alavi et al. 2018; Hunter et al. 2019). While the people domain refers to the human and social needs of citizens, the living domain relies more on the physical and environmental components of city life (Kaluarachchi 2022). SCPs in the environmental domain refer to managing and mitigating environmental risks and improving the sustainability of urban environments (Giffinger and Gudrun 2010). Further, the economy domain emphasizes supporting economic growth in urban areas (Giffinger and Gudrun 2010; Kaluarachchi 2022). In addition, SCPs in the public administration domain focus on improving the efficiency, transparency, and effectiveness of government operations and services (Anttiroiko et al. 2014; OECD 2019). The previously mentioned application domains are in line with several other authors (Čukušić et al. 2019; Kaluarachchi 2022; OECD 2019). Finally, the dimension of **Software Access** concerns the ability or permission granted to users and stakeholders to interact with, utilize, or modify the software or platform. For instance, the City of Barcelona provides the open-source platform Sentilo, to collect, aggregate, and analyze the deluge of urban data (Bibri and Krogstie 2020). However, the provision of a proprietary platform is also possible (Woods and Citron 2020).

4.2 Meta-Dimension Smart City Platform Stakeholders

This meta-dimension defines the distinct components and traits of stakeholders that make up SCPs and interact with each other to create the whole system (EIP-SCC 2016; Lyytinen and Newman 2008). The dimension **Platform Owner** regards the question of who owns the platform. Santana et al. (2018), Lee et al. (2014) and Anttiroiko et al. (2014) note that SCPs can be owned by governments, private companies, non-governmental organizations (NGOs), or by private–public-partnerships

(PPPs). Each ownership model can have significant implications on the requirements of SCPs. For instance, while private ownership of a SCP may prioritize profit-making, a government owner may emphasize stricter regulations and oversight to ensure transparency and equal access (Anttiroiko et al. 2014; Mineraud et al. 2016). The dimension of **External Partners** relates to the engagement of actors beyond the city government who have a direct or indirect impact on SCPs and their operations (Ballon et al. 2011). On the one hand, actors outside of the city government, such as private sector companies, NGOs, and academic and research institutions support the development and implementation of SCPs (Bagheri et al. 2021; Sanchez et al. 2014). Some cases emphasized that external partners are engaged in a long-term business relationship and provide the whole IT-Infrastructure for SCPs. This expression is entitled an open platform (Ballon et al. 2011; Bouskela et al. 2016). In contrast, a closed platform is characterized by no involvement of external stakeholders (Ballon et al. 2011; Hunter et al. 2019). Finally, the dimension **Technical Operator** is closely related to the previous dimension. It relates to the complex and multifaceted right to control and administrate SCPs. Two significant approaches could be identified. First, several cases highlighted that the operator of SCPs also embodies the provider of the IT infrastructure (Deloitte 2020). This can occur for example when the city takes on both roles. This scenario is entitled as a single operator. Second, the operator of SCPs may contract with a private company or consortium to provide the IT infrastructure. Thus, we assume that tightly coupled business relationships between two distinct stakeholders lead to a multi-operator scenario (Deloitte 2020; Javed et al. 2020; Lee 2019).

4.3 Meta-Dimension Technical Infrastructure

The meta-dimension technical infrastructure encompasses the underlying infrastructure and attributes of the utilized data on SCPs (Mineraud et al. 2016). The dimension **Development Approach** outlines different methods to design and implement SCP initiatives (Ballon et al. 2011). We observed primarily citizen-centric approaches, which highlight the necessity to actively engage the citizens in the development process of SCPs to address their needs (Bollier 2016; von Radecki and Dieguez 2022). Frequently mentioned as well, was the technology-centric approach. While a citizen-centric approach emphasizes the needs and perspectives of citizens, a technology-centric approach emphasizes the usage of technology to solve city challenges and streamline the performance of city services (Belli et al. 2020; Chen and Chan 2023; von Radecki and Dieguez 2022). City services constitute digital tools designed to enhance the effectiveness and accessibility of public services in urban areas (Bollier 2016). Further, information- and institution-centric were also identified. While an information-centric SCP development approach outlines the means to collect, analyze and provide data to improve decision-making, institution-centric SCPs address the government institution's perspective such as city departments and agencies, leading to more efficient and effective management of the city (Belli et al.

2020; Woetzel et al. 2018). The Dimension **Data Format** pays attention to the structure and organization of data on SCPs, including the arrangement of data so that it can be easily understood and processed. Through our analysis, we identified four different data formats on SCPs. First, numerical data format relies on data that consists of numbers, such as integers, decimals, or floating-point numbers. The numerical data format can be used to represent a wide range of information, including measurements, quantities, and statistical data (Eggers et al. 2017). Second, textual data refers to data that consist of textual information, such as words, sentences, or paragraphs (Eggers et al. 2017). Third, audio and video data format relates to how audio and video data is represented and stored in a digital format. Audio and video data can be captured from a variety of sources such as microphones and cameras. Further, both can be stored in a variety of file formats, which depends on the nature of audio and video data and the requirements of the application (Al Nuaimi et al. 2015; Syed et al. 2021). In total, the data format used in SCPs is a significant component in platform design and implementation, as it can impact the platform requirements interoperability, security, and performance (Al Nuaimi et al. 2015; Eggers et al. 2017; Syed et al. 2021). Finally, the dimension **Cloud Mode** describes how SCPs are deployed and managed in a cloud computing environment (Bibri 2020; Ray 2016). A public cloud may be a suitable option for SCPs that require scalability, cost-effectiveness, and access to a wide range of cloud services and applications. Further, public clouds offer the advantage of economies of scale, access to a vast pool of computing resources, and the ability to scale up or down quickly based on demand (Nakhuva and Champaneria 2015; Ray 2016). Thus, it makes it easier for SCPs to add new features and services. However, a public cloud may not be suitable for SCPs that require high levels of security, data privacy, and customization. In that vein, a private cloud may be a better option for SCPs that require higher levels of security, data privacy, and customization (Woetzel et al. 2018). Private clouds offer the advantages of dedicated infrastructure, exclusive access to resources, and a higher level of control over the infrastructure (Syed et al. 2021; Zhang et al. 2017). However, private clouds provide limited scalability capabilities and are less cost-effective than public clouds. Therefore, a hybrid cloud model is possible as well (Mineraud et al. 2016; Santana et al. 2018). This setting provides SCPs the ability to leverage the scalability, agility, and cost-effectiveness of public cloud resources, while maintaining control over sensitive data in the private cloud (Ballon et al. 2011; Bibri 2018; Mineraud et al. 2016). Overall, the choice between public-, private- and hybrid cloud model, depends on the specific needs and requirements of SCPs.

4.4 Meta-Dimension Governance

The meta-dimension governance describes a set of principles, policies, and processes that govern the use and management of SCPs (Barns 2018). Recently, **Cybersecurity** on SCPs surged in significant interest and attention and refers to maintaining the confidentiality, truthfulness, and availability of information (Von Solms and Von

Solms 2018). During our analysis of SCPs, we identified that the value of cybersecurity primarily unfolds across the trifecta of encryption, anonymization, and access control. Encryption highlights the usage of cryptographic techniques to secure sensitive data that is transmitted and stored within SCPs (Fortino et al. 2022). It can be implemented in several areas and represent a crucial mechanism to maintain trust among the stakeholders (Fortino et al. 2022; Zhang et al. 2017). The anonymization method contributes to increasing the public trust in SCPs and is characterized by removing any identifiable information from the collected data such as name and address (Lupi 2019; Mineraud et al. 2016). In addition, several cases illustrated the implementation of access controls to manage access to sensitive data, resources, and functionalities within SCPs (Ballon et al. 2011; Mineraud et al. 2016). Overall. the elaborated cybersecurity techniques aim to foster acceptance and maintain trust in SCPs (Lupi 2019; Mineraud et al. 2016). Lastly, the **Data Management** dimension relates to the processes and operations of SCPs performed on the data collected from several sources within the city (Barns 2018; Mineraud et al. 2016; von Radecki and Dieguez 2022). Managing this data effectively is crucial for developing and implementing solutions that address the issues of the city (Da Cruz et al. 2018; Santana et al. 2018). As noted by several authors data management in SCPs can be categorized into eight main areas. First, the collection of data involves various data sources, such as sensors, cameras, and other IoT devices (von Radecki and Dieguez 2022). SCPs leverage storage systems, such as databases to store and manage the collected data in a way that is organized, secure, and easily accessible. Predominantly, cloud environments are used for the storage of urban data streams (Gaur et al. 2015; Mineraud et al. 2016). Afterward, data aggregation refers to the process of combining multiple data points into a single summary (Angelidou et al. 2018; Qiu et al. 2019). The main added value of data does not come from aggregating data, but rather from data analysis. Data analysis refers to the process of examining and interpreting data to extract useful information and insights (Correia and Wünstel 2011; Syed et al. 2021). Accordingly, features for visual representations, as well as simulations of the extracted information, are two important auxiliary instruments on SCPs to understand and interpret data and enable stakeholders to make informed decisions (Correia and Wünstel 2011; Gaur et al. 2015). SCPs can provide access to this extracted information and share it with others (Bibri and Krogstie 2020; Kim et al. 2020). In that vein, data transmission is a critical component enabling the sharing of information. The transmission process may be affected by several factors such as the type of encoding and decoding methods used on SCPs (Correia and Wünstel 2011).

4.5 Taxonomy Application

In this section, we apply the SCP taxonomy to the Smart Santander platform (SSP) presented by Sanchez et al. (2014) and Santana et al. (2018). Table 3 summarizes the taxonomy's application to this case. This application illustrates the usefulness of the taxonomy to typify SCPs.

Table 3 The smart Santander platform

Dimensions		Characteristics								E/N
Smart city platform strategy	Platform positioning	**Integrative**				Specialized				E
	Value proposition	**Software-as-a-Service**				Platform-as-a-Service				E
	Application domain	Public administration		**Living**	Economy	People	**Mobility**	**Environment**		N
	Software access	**Open source**				Proprietary				E
Smart city platform stakeholders	Platform owner	Government		Private company		Non-governmental org.		**Private-public partnership**		E
	External partners	**Open platform**				Closed platform				E
	Technical operator	Single operator				**Multi-operator**				E
Technical infrastructure	Development approach	Citizen-centric		**Technology-centric**		Institution-centric		Information-centric		E
	Data format	**Numerical**	Textual	Audio		Video		**Geospatial**		N
	Cloud mode	Public cloud			Private cloud		**Hybrid cloud**			E
Governance	Cybersecurity	**Encryption**			**Access control**		**Anonymization**			N
	Data management	**Collection**	Aggregation	**Analysis**	**Sharing**	Transmission	**Visualization**	Simulation	**Storage**	N

Smart City Platform Strategy. The SSP represents an integrative system. Moreover, both articles display that the SSP captures value based on a SaaS business model (Sanchez et al. 2014; Santana et al. 2018). Being integrative, the SSP addresses various application domains. These are in the living, mobility, and environmental domains. Sanchez et al. (2014) and Santana et al. (2018) did not emphasize the software access factor in their articles. However, Sanchez et al. (2014) highlight that the purpose of the SSP is the development of novel IoT-enabled applications. Based on this, we assume that the platform is open and accessible to the public, allowing developers and researchers to access and use the platform's data and services to develop new applications and services. Therefore, we deduce that the SSP constitutes an open-source platform to enable collaborative solutions.

Smart City Platform Stakeholders. The University of Cantabria collaborated in the development and implementation of the SSP with both private and public organizations, which speaks to PPP ownership (Sanchez et al. 2014; Santana et al. 2018). The involvement of external partners (e.g., private companies, agencies) makes the SSP an open platform (Sanchez et al. 2014). Sanchez et al. (2014) and Santana et al. (2018) reveal little about the technical operator. Since ownership is PPP, we assume that the IT provider differs from the SSP operator.

Technical Infrastructure. The Smart Santander testbed represents a research and technology-driven facility. This reflects a technology-centric development approach. The SSP primarily collects urban data streams comprising numerical and geospatial data formats (Santana et al. 2018). The SSP is hosted on a hybrid cloud (Sanchez et al. 2014; Santana et al. 2018).

Governance. The SSP implements encryption, access control, and anonymization as measures for cybersecurity (Santana et al. 2018). Both articles characterize the SSP's data management as involving collection, analysis, visualization, storage, and sharing of data (Sanchez et al. 2014; Santana et al. 2018).

5 Discussion, Limitations, and Future Research

Our conducted study was motivated by our observation that SCs gain much attention in recent years but lack a systematic framework about what SCPs truly are and how they vary. Already existing research primarily addresses specific requirements of SCPs or emphasis the architecture without a profound classification of characteristics (Koo and Kim 2021; Santana et al. 2018). This hinders the comparability of existing SCPs and the possibility to deduce conceptual abstractions from the result (Gregor 2006). In addition, we challenge the customary approach of investigating and applying the phenomena of SCPs through commonly held and simplified assumptions, which presume the clarity and absence of difficulties within the SCP construct (Lueg et al. 2022).

We argue that a profound classification is necessary for IS researchers to assemble aggregative knowledge about SCPs; the initial point for platform design, the explanation of interdependencies, assessment of risks, patterns, and characteristics (Schermuly et al. 2019). The conducted study provides this systematic classification of SCPs in the form of a taxonomy following Nickerson et al. (2013) based on a systematic literature review. Therefore, we contribute to academia by providing a framework based on the existing knowledge about the characteristics of SCPs. Our developed taxonomy distinguishes SCPs based on 4 meta-dimensions and 12 related dimensions.

By developing the taxonomy about the characteristics of SCPs we seek to fill this gap and thereby make a relevant contribution in the following respects; First, based on our taxonomy we structure the broad and complex knowledge about SCPs and provide a profound scheme of the multifaceted character of SCPs. By considering various layers, we go beyond current classifications and tackle a phenomenon that is characterized by its interdisciplinary and intricate nature (Lohoff 2022). Further, thereby, we can gain a profound understanding of the unique dynamics of SCPs and their necessary traits to attract further stakeholders to join the ecosystem. Second, we contend that our taxonomy aids in exploring SCP initiatives, as it offers means of classification and enables a structured examination of a wider context. Lastly, our structured classification enables comparability and captures transparency about what SCPs are and how SCPs conceptually differ, thereby we can identify and assign the relevant requirements for each respective SCP type. In that vein, we can make theoretical generalizations and provide the baseline for the development of better SCPs in the future.

From the practitioner's lens, the devised taxonomy outlines, that SCPs are not linear nor is there an archetypal model. Thus, practitioners can harness this taxonomy as an instrument to analyze and distinguish SCPs. A better understanding of embedded SCPs and their requirements supports cities to surge human- and social capital, fostering sustainable economic growth, and improving dwellers' QOL (Hollands 2008). Furthermore, the taxonomy embodies a beneficial instrument to ease and improve the development of SCPs, due to the interwoven and complex associations (Lueg et al. 2022).

Nevertheless, this study faces some limitations. First, due to the static nature of our taxonomy and the rapidly evolving field, our systematic literature review only offers a snapshot of SCPs. Hence, we cannot guarantee the exhaustiveness of the dimensions and characteristics. Second, we did not scrutinize possible interrelationships between single characteristics and dimensions. Third, we acknowledge that some dimensions, e.g., cybersecurity, may reveal little benefit in distinguishing different SCP types, because of the nature of their characteristics. That is, all SCPs should have the mentioned cybersecurity measures. However, we kept this dimension to highlight that cybersecurity is critical and that future work on SCPs should reveal more detailed information on their cybersecurity to allow for better differentiation of, e.g., implementations of access control. Finally, even though we followed Nickerson et al. (2013) guidelines and conducted an E2C and C2E approach, additional proof with empirical cases is needed to verify the taxonomy. Future research might concentrate on the deduction of SCP archetypes to permit an underlying classification of SCPs. By examining the identified archetypes, it could be possible to further explore if certain archetypes exhibit higher levels of efficacy than others, thus yielding to the derivation of design principles for SCPs (Gelhaar et al. 2021). Furthermore, scrutinizing the relationships between each dimension and their related characteristics may provide further insights into the design and the performance of SCPs.

References

Agarwal, P., & Alam, M. (2020). Open Service Platforms for IoT. In M. Alam, K. A. Shakil, & S. Khan (Hrsg.), Internet of Things (IoT) (S. 43–59). Springer International Publishing. https://doi.org/10.1007/978-3-030-37468-6_3

Al Nuaimi, E., Al Neyadi, H., Mohamed, N., & Al-Jaroodi, J. (2015). Applications of big data to smart cities. Journal of Internet Services and Applications, 6(1), 25. https://doi.org/10.1186/s13174-015-0041-5

Alavi, A. H., Jiao, P., Buttlar, W. G., & Lajnef, N. (2018). Internet of Things-enabled smart cities: State-of-the-art and future trends. Measurement, 129, 589–606. https://doi.org/10.1016/j.measurement.2018.07.067

Albino, V., Berardi, U., & Dangelico, R. M. (2015). Smart Cities: Definitions, Dimensions, Performance, and Initiatives. Journal of Urban Technology, 22(1), 3–21. https://doi.org/10.1080/10630732.2014.942092

Al-Fuqaha, A., Guizani, M., Mohammadi, M., Aledhari, M., & Ayyash, M. (2015). Internet of Things: A Survey on Enabling Technologies, Protocols, and Applications. IEEE Communications Surveys & Tutorials, 17(4), 2347–2376. https://doi.org/10.1109/COMST.2015.2444095

Angelidou, M., Psaltoglou, A., Komninos, N., Kakderi, C., Tsarchopoulos, P., & Panori, A. (2018). Enhancing sustainable urban development through smart city applications. Journal of Science and Technology Policy Management, 9(2), 146–169. https://doi.org/10.1108/JSTPM-05-2017-0016

Anttiroiko, A.-V. (2016). City-as-a-Platform: The Rise of Participatory Innovation Platforms in Finnish Cities. Sustainability, 8(9), 922. https://doi.org/10.3390/su8090922

Anttiroiko, A.-V., Valkama, P., & Bailey, S. J. (2014). Smart cities in the new service economy: Building platforms for smart services. AI & SOCIETY, 29(3), 323–334. https://doi.org/10.1007/s00146-013-0464-0

Bagheri, S., Brandt, T., Sheombar, H., & Van Oosterhout, M. (2021). Value Creation through Urban Data Platforms: A Conceptual Framework. Hawaii International Conference on System Sciences. https://doi.org/10.24251/HICSS.2021.302

Bailey, K. D. (1994). Typologies and taxonomies: An introduction to classification techniques. Sage Publications.

Ballon, P., Glidden, J., Kranas, P., & Menychtas, A. (2011). Is there a Need for a Cloud Platform for European Smart Cities? EChallenges E-2011 Conference Proceedings Paul Cunningham and Miriam Cunningham (Eds.) IIMC International Information Management Corporation.

Barns, S. (2018). Smart cities and urban data platforms: Designing interfaces for smart governance. City, Culture and Society, 12, 5–12. https://doi.org/10.1016/j.ccs.2017.09.006

Batty, M. (2013). Big data, smart cities and city planning. Dialogues in Human Geography, 3(3), 274–279. https://doi.org/10.1177/2043820613513390

Belli, L., Cilfone, A., Davoli, L., Ferrari, G., Adorni, P., Di Nocera, F., Dall'Olio, A., Pellegrini, C., Mordacci, M., & Bertolotti, E. (2020). IoT-Enabled Smart Sustainable Cities: Challenges and Approaches. Smart Cities, 3(3), 1039–1071. https://doi.org/10.3390/smartcities3030052
Berger, S., Denner, M.-S., & Röglinger, M. (2018). The Nature of Digital Technologies – Development of a Multi-layer Taxonomy. 26th European Conference on Information Systems, Portsmouth, UK.
Bibri, S. E. (2018). Smart Sustainable Cities of the Future. Springer International Publishing. https://doi.org/10.1007/978-3-319-73981-6
Bibri, S. E. (2019). The anatomy of the data-driven smart sustainable city: Instrumentation, datafication, computerization and related applications. Journal of Big Data, 6(1), 59. https://doi.org/10.1186/s40537-019-0221-4
Bibri, S. E. (2020). Advances in the Leading Paradigms of Urbanism and their Amalgamation: Compact Cities, Eco–Cities, and Data–Driven Smart Cities. Springer International Publishing. https://doi.org/10.1007/978-3-030-41746-8
Bibri, S. E., & Krogstie, J. (2020). The emerging data–driven Smart City and its innovative applied solutions for sustainability: The cases of London and Barcelona. Energy Informatics, 3(1), 5. https://doi.org/10.1186/s42162-020-00108-6
Bollier, D. (2016). The City as Platform—How Digital Networks are Changing Urban Life and Governance. https://www.aspeninstitute.org/wp-content/uploads/2016/03/CityAsPlatform.pdf
Bouskela, M., Casseb, M., Bassi, S., De Luca, C., & Facchina, M. (2016). The Road toward Smart Cities: Migrating from Traditional City Management to the Smart City. Inter-American Development Bank. https://doi.org/10.18235/0000377
Chen, Z., & Chan, I. C. C. (2023). Smart cities and quality of life: A quantitative analysis of citizens' support for smart city development. Information Technology & People, 36(1), 263–285. https://doi.org/10.1108/ITP-07-2021-0577
Cheng, B., Longo, S., Cirillo, F., Bauer, M., & Kovacs, E. (2015). Building a Big Data Platform for Smart Cities: Experience and Lessons from Santander. 2015 IEEE International Congress on Big Data, 592–599. https://doi.org/10.1109/BigDataCongress.2015.91
Correia, L. M., & Wünstel, K. (2011). Smart Cities Applications and Requirements. https://grow.tecnico.ulisboa.pt/wp-content/uploads/2014/03/White_Paper_Smart_Cities_Applications.pdf
Čukušić, M., Jadrić, M., & Mijač, T. (2019). Identifying challenges and priorities for developing smart city initiatives and applications. Croatian Operational Research Review, 10(1), 117–129. https://doi.org/10.17535/crorr.2019.0011
Da Cruz, M. A. A., Rodrigues, J. J. P. C., Al-Muhtadi, J., Korotaev, V. V., & De Albuquerque, V. H. C. (2018). A Reference Model for Internet of Things Middleware. IEEE Internet of Things Journal, 5(2), 871–883. https://doi.org/10.1109/JIOT.2018.2796561
Deloitte. (2020). 5G smart cities whitepaper. https://www2.deloitte.com/content/dam/Deloitte/cn/Documents/technology-media-telecommunications/deloitte-cn-tmt-empowering-smart-cities-with-5g-white-paper-en-200702.pdf
Eggers, W. D., Guszcza, J., Greene, M., & Lee, I. D. (2017). How citizens' collective intelligence can guide better decision making. 20, 139–154.
EIP-SCC. (2016). EIP-SCC Urban Platform Management Framework. https://smart-cities-marketplace.ec.europa.eu/sites/default/files/EIP_Mgnt_Framework.pdf
El-Ghalayini, Y., & Al-Kandari, H. (2020). Big Data Regulatory Legislation: Security, Privacy and Smart City Governance. Journal of Law, Policy and Globalization, 95, 19–26. https://doi.org/10.7176/JLPG/95-03
Fahmideh, M., & Zowghi, D. (2020). An exploration of IoT platform development. Information Systems, 87, 1–44. https://doi.org/10.1016/j.is.2019.06.005
Fersi, G. (2015). Middleware for Internet of Things: A Study. 2015 International Conference on Distributed Computing in Sensor Systems, 230–235. https://doi.org/10.1109/DCOSS.2015.43
Fortino, G., Guerrieri, A., Pace, P., Savaglio, C., & Spezzano, G. (2022). IoT Platforms and Security: An Analysis of the Leading Industrial/Commercial Solutions. Sensors, 22(6), 1–17. https://doi.org/10.3390/s22062196

Frow, P., McColl-Kennedy, J. R., Hilton, T., Davidson, A., Payne, A., & Brozovic, D. (2014). Value propositions: A service ecosystems perspective. Marketing Theory, 14(3), 327–351. https://doi.org/10.1177/1470593114534346

Gaur, A., Scotney, B., Parr, G., & McClean, S. (2015). Smart City Architecture and its Applications Based on IoT. Procedia Computer Science, 52, 1089–1094. https://doi.org/10.1016/j.procs.2015.05.122

Gelhaar, J., Groß, T., & Otto, B. (2021). A Taxonomy for Data Ecosystems. Hawaii International Conference on System Sciences. https://doi.org/10.24251/HICSS.2021.739

Giffinger, R., & Gudrun, H. (2010). Smart cities ranking: An effective instrument for the positioning of the cities? ACE: Architecture, City and Environment, 4(12), 7–26. https://doi.org/10.5821/ace.v4i12.2483

Gioia, D. A., Corley, K. G., & Hamilton, A. L. (2013). Seeking Qualitative Rigor in Inductive Research: Notes on the Gioia Methodology. Organizational Research Methods, 16(1), 15–31. https://doi.org/10.1177/1094428112452151

Gregor. (2006). The Nature of Theory in Information Systems. MIS Quarterly, 30(3), 611–642. https://doi.org/10.2307/25148742

Hollands, R. G. (2008). Will the real smart city please stand up?: Intelligent, progressive or entrepreneurial? City, 12(3), 303–320. https://doi.org/10.1080/13604810802479126

Hunter, M., Guensler, R., Guin, A., Saroj, A., & Roy, S. (2019). SMART CITIES ATLANTA - NORTH AVENUE. https://realtime.ce.gatech.edu/RenewAtlanta-GeorgiaTech-Final-Report.pdf

Javed, A., Malhi, A., Kinnunen, T., & Framling, K. (2020). Scalable IoT Platform for Heterogeneous Devices in Smart Environments. IEEE Access, 8, 211973–211985. https://doi.org/10.1109/ACCESS.2020.3039368

Kaluarachchi, Y. (2022). Implementing Data-Driven Smart City Applications for Future Cities. Smart Cities, 5(2), 455–474. https://doi.org/10.3390/smartcities5020025

Khan, M., Woo, M., Nam, K., & Chathoth, P. (2017). Smart City and Smart Tourism: A Case of Dubai. Sustainability, 9(12), 2279. https://doi.org/10.3390/su9122279

Khan, F., Chaturvedi, S., & Jaswal, A. (2022). Smart City Implications of the Internet of Things. Stallion Journal for Multidisciplinary Associated Research Studies, 1(1), 22–31. https://doi.org/10.55544/sjmars.1.1.4

Kim, J., Jang, S., Jee, D., Ko, E., Choi, S. H., & Kyong Han, M. (2020). 5G Based SmartCity Convergence Service Platform for Data sharing. 2020 International Conference on Information and Communication Technology Convergence (ICTC), 1522–1524. https://doi.org/10.1109/ICTC49870.2020.9289155

Kitchin, R., & Moore-Cherry, N. (2021). Fragmented governance, the urban data ecosystem and smart city-regions: The case of Metropolitan Boston. Regional Studies, 55(12), 1913–1923. https://doi.org/10.1080/00343404.2020.1735627

Koo, J., & Kim, Y.-G. (2021). Interoperability requirements for a smart city. Proceedings of the 36th Annual ACM Symposium on Applied Computing, 690–698. https://doi.org/10.1145/3412841.3441948

Lee, J. (2019). 2019 Smart Cities Index Report. https://smartcitiesindex.org/smartcitiesindexreport2019

Lee, J. H., Hancock, M. G., & Hu, M.-C. (2014). Towards an effective framework for building smart cities: Lessons from Seoul and San Francisco. Technological Forecasting and Social Change, 89, 80–99. https://doi.org/10.1016/j.techfore.2013.08.033

Lohoff, L. (2022). A Taxonomy for Digital Process Innovation. Pacific Asia Conference on Information Systems 2022 Proceedings.

Lueg, R., Zimmer, M. P., & Drews, P. (2022). Dividing Apples and Pears: Towards a Taxonomy for Agile Transformation. Pacific Asia Conference on Information Systems 2022 Proceedings.

Lupi, L. (2019). City Data Plan: The Conceptualisation of a Policy Instrument for Data Governance in Smart Cities. Urban Science, 3(3), 91. https://doi.org/10.3390/urbansci3030091

Lyytinen, K., & Newman, M. (2008). Explaining information systems change: A punctuated socio-technical change model. European Journal of Information Systems, 17(6), 589–613. https://doi.org/10.1057/ejis.2008.50

Massana, J., Pous, C., Burgas, L., Melendez, J., & Colomer, J. (2017). Identifying services for short-term load forecasting using data driven models in a Smart City platform. Sustainable Cities and Society, 28, 108–117. https://doi.org/10.1016/j.scs.2016.09.001

Mijuskovic, A., Ullah, I., Bemthuis, R., Meratnia, N., & Havinga, P. (2021). Comparing Apples and Oranges in IoT Context: A Deep Dive Into Methods for Comparing IoT Platforms. IEEE Internet of Things Journal, 8(3), 1797–1816. https://doi.org/10.1109/JIOT.2020.3016921

Mineraud, J., Mazhelis, O., Su, X., & Tarkoma, S. (2016). A gap analysis of Internet-of-Things platforms. Computer Communications, 89–90, 5–16. https://doi.org/10.1016/j.comcom.2016.03.015

Nakhuva, B., & Champaneria, T. (2015). Study of Various Internet of Things Platforms. International Journal of Computer Science & Engineering Survey, 6(6), 61–74. https://doi.org/10.5121/ijcses.2015.6605

Nastjuk, I., Trang, S., & Papageorgiou, E. I. (2022). Smart cities and smart governance models for future cities: Current research and future directions. Electronic Markets, 32(4), 1917–1924. https://doi.org/10.1007/s12525-022-00609-0

Nickerson, R. C., Varshney, U., & Muntermann, J. (2013). A method for taxonomy development and its application in information systems. European Journal of Information Systems, 22(3), 336–359. https://doi.org/10.1057/ejis.2012.26

OECD. (2019). Enhancing the Contribution of Digitalisation to the Smart Cities of the Future. https://www.oecd.org/cfe/regionaldevelopment/Smart-Cities-FINAL.pdf

Oliveira, A., Melo, D., Silva, G., & Gregório, T. (2016). Comparing IoT Platforms under Middleware Requirements in an IoT Perspective. The Tenth International Conference on Mobile Ubiquitous Computing, Systems, Services and Technologies, 138–143.

Patti, E., & Acquaviva, A. (2016). IoT platform for Smart Cities: Requirements and implementation case studies. 2016 IEEE 2nd International Forum on Research and Technologies for Society and Industry Leveraging a Better Tomorrow (RTSI), 1–6. https://doi.org/10.1109/RTSI.2016.7740618

Pinto, H. S., & Martins, J. P. (2004). Ontologies: How can They be Built? Knowledge and Information Systems, 6(4), 441–464. https://doi.org/10.1007/s10115-003-0138-1

Qiu, R. G., Zu, T., Qian, Y., Qiu, L., & Badr, Y. (2019). Leveraging Big Data Platform Technologies and Analytics to Enhance Smart City Mobility Services. In P. P. Maglio, C. A. Kieliszewski, J. C. Spohrer, K. Lyons, L. Patrício, & Y. Sawatani (Hrsg.), Handbook of Service Science, Volume II (S. 567–587). Springer International Publishing. https://doi.org/10.1007/978-3-319-98512-1_25

Ray, P. P. (2016). A survey of IoT cloud platforms. Future Computing and Informatics Journal, 1(1–2), 35–46. https://doi.org/10.1016/j.fcij.2017.02.001

Sanchez, L., Muñoz, L., Galache, J. A., Sotres, P., Santana, J. R., Gutierrez, V., Ramdhany, R., Gluhak, A., Krco, S., Theodoridis, E., & Pfisterer, D. (2014). SmartSantander: IoT experimentation over a smart city testbed. Computer Networks, 61, 217–238. https://doi.org/10.1016/j.bjp.2013.12.020

Santana, E. F. Z., Chaves, A. P., Gerosa, M. A., Kon, F., & Milojicic, D. (2018). Software Platforms for Smart Cities: Concepts, Requirements, Challenges, and a Unified Reference Architecture. ACM Computing Surveys, 50(6), 1–37. https://doi.org/10.1145/3124391

Schermuly, L., Schreieck, M., Wiesche, M., & Krcmar, H. (2019). Developing an Industrial IoT Platform – Trade-off between Horizontal and Vertical Approaches.

Shapsough, S., & Zualkernan, I. (2019). Requirements for an IoT Middleware for Utility-Scale Distributed Solar Farms. 2019 Sixth International Conference on Internet of Things: Systems, Management and Security (IOTSMS), 51–57. https://doi.org/10.1109/IOTSMS48152.2019.8939251

Stehlin, J., Hodson, M., & McMeekin, A. (2020). Platform mobilities and the production of urban space: Toward a typology of platformization trajectories. Environment and Planning A: Economy and Space, 52(7), 1250–1268. https://doi.org/10.1177/0308518X19896801

Syed, A. S., Sierra-Sosa, D., Kumar, A., & Elmaghraby, A. (2021). IoT in Smart Cities: A Survey of Technologies, Practices and Challenges. Smart Cities, 4(2), 429–475. https://doi.org/10.3390/smartcities4020024

von Radecki, A., & Dieguez, L. (2022). Data Strategies for a Common Good-oriented Urban Development. https://www.smart-city-dialog.de/wp-content/uploads/2022/01/Publication-Data-Strategies-for-Common-Good-oriented-Urban-Development-Int.pdf

Von Solms, B., & Von Solms, R. (2018). Cybersecurity and information security – what goes where? Information & Computer Security, 26(1), 2–9. https://doi.org/10.1108/ICS-04-2017-0025

Woetzel, J., Remes, J., Boland, B., Lv, K., Sinha, S., Strube, G., Means, J., Law, J., Cadena, A., & von der Tann, V. (2018). Smart Cities: Digital Solutions for a more Livable Future. https://www.mckinsey.com/~/media/McKinsey/Industries/Public%20and%20Social%20Sector/Our%20Insights/Smart%20cities%20Digital%20solutions%20for%20a%20more%20livable%20future/MGI-Smart-Cities-Executive-summary.pdf

Wolfswinkel, J. F., Furtmueller, E., & Wilderom, C. P. M. (2013). Using grounded theory as a method for rigorously reviewing literature. European Journal of Information Systems, 22(1), 45–55. https://doi.org/10.1057/ejis.2011.51

Woods, E., & Citron, R. (2020). The Evolution of Smart Cities: Delivering on the Promise. https://www.verizon.com/business/resources/whitepapers/evolution-of-smart-cities-delivering-on-the-promise.pdf

Yigitcanlar, T., Kamruzzaman, Md., Buys, L., Ioppolo, G., Sabatini-Marques, J., Da Costa, E. M., & Yun, J. J. (2018). Understanding 'smart cities': Intertwining development drivers with desired outcomes in a multidimensional framework. Cities, 81, 145–160. https://doi.org/10.1016/j.cities.2018.04.003

Zanella, A., Bui, N., Castellani, A., Vangelista, L., & Zorzi, M. (2014). Internet of Things for Smart Cities. IEEE Internet of Things Journal, 1(1), 22–32. https://doi.org/10.1109/JIOT.2014.2306328

Zhang, K., Ni, J., Yang, K., Liang, X., Ren, J., & Shen, X. S. (2017). Security and Privacy in Smart City Applications: Challenges and Solutions. IEEE Communications Magazine, 55(1), 122–129. https://doi.org/10.1109/MCOM.2017.1600267CM

Digital Education and Learning

Decide Wisely: Interactive Videos as Appealing Educational Element to Attract Students to Information Security

Martin Brehmer

Abstract Educational videos play an important role in university education. However, they are often not designed to foster active learning and the learning process is not immersive. Interactive digital storytelling is a promising game design element but requires a rigorous evaluation to avoid negative side effects. Therefore, we adopt a design science research approach to design and evaluate an interactive video that includes interactive storytelling and real-world recordings. The proposed artifact aims to raise information security awareness among bachelor students at a German university about malicious USB sticks and the reporting of incidents. In our evaluation, we focus on the students' level of knowledge before and after using the video as well as qualitative feedback about the experience with the learning object. Our results show that videos that are based on interactive choice-based storytelling can foster an active and immersive process, and significant learning outcomes.

Keywords Interactive video · Interactive digital storytelling · Information security · Awareness · University

1 Introduction and Problem Motivation

Although videos are hardly indispensable in today's university education, designing effective educational videos is still a major challenge because inappropriate video designs can decrease students' motivation to watch them and lead to comprehension problems, or students perceive videos as stressors, monotonous, and thus, not engaging and boring (Beheshti et al. 2018; Chouhan 2021; Croasdell et al. 2018; Wang 2022). Hence, it is crucial that the design of the video supports active learning, e.g., by using game design elements, such as a narrative and the inclusion of interaction opportunities (Beheshti et al. 2018; Chouhan 2021; Wang 2022). Thereby,

---

M. Brehmer (✉)
Faculty of Business and Economics, University of Augsburg, Augsburg, Germany
e-mail: martin.brehmer@uni-a.de

D. Beverungen et al. (eds.), *Transforming the Digitally Sustainable Enterprise*, Lecture Notes in Information Systems and Organisation 76,
https://doi.org/10.1007/978-3-031-80125-9_25

appropriate gamification fosters motivating, interactive, and immersive learning environments and the achievement of learning goals (Deterding et al. 2011; Hamari et al. 2014). Conversely, inappropriate gamification can cause negative effects, such as not reaching the learning goals or fostering feelings of aversion and boredom (Almeida et al. 2021). Thus, current research calls for rigorous evaluations of gamified approaches, such as an interactive video that relies on interactive digital storytelling. In particular, the evaluation should include whether learning outcomes are reached and, in addition, discuss motivational aspects regarding the learners' engagement with the system. (Chen et al. 2018; Hamari et al. 2014; Melcer et al. 2020) This article aims to address this gap by evaluating a novel instance of an interactive educational video that aims to build information security awareness (ISA) among university students. Therefore, we answer the following research questions in the following sections by applying a mixed-method approach:

> ***RQ1**: To what extent does the level of information security awareness change after using an educational video which includes interactive digital storytelling?*
> ***RQ2**: What are crucial design factors of the learning object that should be improved or remain within future design cycles?*

We focus on students' ISA because they represent a great share of IT users at universities, where security awareness is often low (Ulven and Wangen 2021). Furthermore, security education is still ineffective, often perceived as burdensome, and demotivating (D'Arcy et al. 2014; Hu et al. 2021). Universities also face a high number of severe cyberattacks that, e.g., threaten human life, put down IT infrastructure, and lead to leaks of confidential data (Knop 2023; Martin 2023; Ralston 2021). Thus, we strive to design an interactive educational video that suits user preferences in security education (Abawajy 2014), overcomes some limitations of non-interactive videos, and is based on a scalable delivery method (Croasdell et al. 2018; Rajadell and Garriga-Garzón 2017). Furthermore, our research aims to contribute to current research streams as a complement to realistic security education interventions by leveraging the effects of interactive storytelling and an immersive user experience (Fertig et al. 2022; Ulsamer et al. 2021). We chose 'reporting of security incidents' in combination with 'malicious USB sticks', called bad USB sticks, as a learning subject because they are an often neglected tremendous threat to universities' information security. For instance, many end user are not aware how to report security incidents at universities (Ulven and Wangen 2021). Tischer et al. (2016) further reveal that deployed and prepared USB sticks have been hardly reported but picked up and plugged in by finders in up to 98%. Recently, the FBI also warned that bad USB sticks are now being used to spread ransomware (Tung 2022). Thus, there is a need for educating and raising ISA for bad USB sticks and the reporting of incidents effectively for universities. This article is part of a larger design science research project that follows the Design Science Research Methodology (Peffers et al. 2007). The overarching goal is to develop innovative and effective educational approaches using information systems, e.g., a learning management system (LMS) as well as game design elements, to increase the level of ISA. Thereby, this article represents an additional design cycle that builds on our previous research in improving security education (Brehmer et al. 2021), in particular analyzing the effect of gamification on learning outcomes, e.g., by implementing a narrative (Brehmer and Reinelt 2023). Thus, we apply a within-subjects design to overcome our previous limitations whether a gamified learning object (LO) is able to foster learning progress. We focus on developing and evaluating another novel artifact, which is an interactive video with real-world scenarios and an underlying choice-based narrative. We outline the problem motivation for this article in this section. Within the next section, we depict the theoretical knowledge base that influenced our design decisions. The contribution of this artifact will be evaluated in Sect. 4 by following Venable et al. (2012), proving its utility and purpose, identifying weaknesses and areas of improvement, but also outlining negative side effects. With this, we contribute to existing design science research by following the suggestion of Nguyen and Pham (2020) to contribute to research by (a) extending the pedagogical body of knowledge for security education in regard to building ISA, and (b) sharing insights about an empirically proven effective artifact.

2 Knowledge Base and Related Work

Linking interactions with information systems and storytelling is known as ***interactive digital storytelling***. Thereby, a player is able to influence a storyline (Murray 2018) by making meaningful choices through interactions with an information system (Melcer et al. 2020). Furthermore, Murray (2018) depicts interactive digital storytelling as a rapid evolving field of both, research (e.g., see the annual '*International Conference on Interactive Digital Storytelling*') and university education that includes several decades of research knowledge to date and multiple facets of representations, e.g., **interactive videos**, games, simulations and augmented reality approaches. Within the context of interactive educational videos, digital storytelling offers several pedagogical advantages (Baldwin and Ching 2017; Shelton et al. 2016): E.g., it promotes learning by conveying complex topics through rich information streams. But it also connects students emotionally with the learning content or enables them to check their understanding while navigating through the story of the video. This supports students in active learning as it increases, e.g., curiosity and flow within the learning process. Thus, interactive storytelling is discussed among many educational fields, e.g. history, STEM and ethics (Grasse et al. 2022a). Current literature connects educational interactive storytelling to the ***self-determination theory*** of Ryan and Deci (2000) and highlights that intrinsic motivation is a crucial factor for achieving learning outcomes that should be addressed by fostering the feeling of autonomy and competence within the learning process, but also immersion and relatedness, e.g., by implementing real-world scenarios (Grasse et al. 2022a, b). In turn, role play and narratives are game design elements that support the feeling of relatedness: They address intrinsic as well as extrinsic motivational preferences by creating a state of flow, which is a 'highly focused psychological state of mind, where an individual experiences high enjoyment and is intrinsically motivated while executing any specific and even difficult task at hand', according to the ***theory of flow*** (Brehmer and Reinelt 2023; Csikszentmihalyi 1990; Deci and Ryan 2000; Grasse et al. 2022a). Thus, within the context of effective ISA trainings, branching narratives that include role play, e.g., based on "choose your own adventure" approaches are promising, as they combine the concept of interactivity with storytelling as a game design element (Dincelli and Chengalur-Smith 2020). Nevertheless, the literature review that we have conducted using the term "*(security-education OR information-security-awareness-training OR cyber-security-awareness-training OR "SETA") AND (storytelling OR narrative OR choose-your-own-adventure OR video) AND (interactive * OR immersive)*" (data fields: Abstract, Title; excluded articles contain full video games and lacked a narrative) in the databases of AISeL, IEEE Xplore, and WebOfScience only provided two articles. These articles show that educational videos can support a change in attitudes and behavior related to individual ISA through realistic immersive scenarios (Dincelli and Chengalur-Smith 2020; Ulsamer et al. 2021). Thus, interactive choice-based storytelling within videos further addresses known ***success factors for security education and training awareness programs*** to a great extent namely, e.g.: (a) applying gamification and using rich media, (b) providing immersive learning content which supports autonomy in the learning process for a specific target group, (c) provide feedback through the opportunity of choices and their consequences (Alyami et al. 2022; Brehmer et al. 2021; Hu et al. 2021; Kirova and Baumöl 2018; Yoo et al. 2018). From the perspective of educational practice, gamification is already reported to work well with students (Hamari et al. 2014). In conclusion, interactive digital storytelling is promising as it enables the experience of realistic training through game play, e.g., including simulated real-world decision situations.

However, as previously mentioned, meaningful learning content is crucial. Thus, we utilize the ***Human Aspects of Information Security Questionnaire (HAIS-Q)*** from Parsons et al. (2017) as a guideline for content details. This questionnaire is well accepted and validated (McCormac et al. 2016). It is also consistent with standards, e.g., NIST SP 800-50 (Wilson and Hash 2003). The questionnaire is furthermore a useful tool to measure the level of individual ***information security awareness (ISA)*** among varying contexts (Parsons et al. 2014; Wahyudiwan et al. 2017) as well as assessing ISA among students (Salem et al. 2021). Here, ISA is a representation of someone's knowledge about security procedures (dos and don'ts) in specific focus areas, e.g., 'incident reporting', but also the attitude towards following common standards or compliance guidelines, and in addition, the actual behavior of the person (Parsons et al. 2017). Aligning the educational video to the HAIS-Q facilitates a rigorous evaluation of specific learning outcomes, which also addresses current calls for research (see Sect. 1). Thus, the HAIS-Q serves as prescriptive theoretical design knowledge for our approach as well as an evaluation methodology. However, the HAIS-Q lacks the opportunity for important qualitative feedback regarding the design of the LO itself, such as user experience and perceived usefulness for learning. The interactive video presented in the following section can be considered as a LO, thus, it will be additionally evaluated qualitatively (see Sect. 4). In this context, a learning object is an "interactive web-based tool[s] that support[s] the learning of specific concepts" (Kay and Knaack 2009).

3 Designing the Artifact—An Interactive Choice-Based Video

The overall theme of our interactive video is "how to deal with USB sticks which are found on the university campus and how to report threats and incidents". We used items of the HAIS-Q (Parsons et al. 2017) as the theoretical basis for developing the learning content, included focus areas are 'Incident Reporting' and 'Information Handling' (only subarea 'inserting removable media'). In order to ensure scalability in terms of sharing the video with other faculties or universities, we used the H5P-software framework and created an 'interactive video' (see https://h5p.org/interactive-video), because H5P-modules can be integrated into some LMS, such as Moodle or to some extent in Stud.IP-based systems. We uploaded only one video that contains jump labels, to head from decisions to the next video scene. The video was recorded on the university campus and to make the video as realistic looking and immersive as possible we recorded video material in a first-person perspective. One full-time employee and 3 part-time employees were necessary to play the roles and create the video. The storyline and decision options have been documented using a process diagram to ensure transferability for later projects and independence from technology. The narrative starts with a student (protagonist, first-person view) who is receiving an e-mail with instructions to go to the university. Once there, he finds a USB stick (labeled with "contracts") and has to decide, within multiple decision situations, how to deal with the stick and upcoming situations. Afterward, the student has to deal with the decision, of whether or not to report that he plugged in the stick, or in case he makes a different decision beforehand (represents another decision path), whether or not to report that fellow students found USB sticks but did not report them. In the end, the decisions lead to the scenario that the university gets hacked (try again) or the cyberattack can be averted. Further design details can be found in Table 1 (or see Brehmer 2023).

4 Evaluation of the Artifact

4.1 Evaluation Procedure and Sample Description

The sample for the quantitative evaluation consists of **n = 60** completed surveys from **13 female and 47 male bachelor students** at a university in Germany (invalid surveys are excluded, e.g., incomplete datasets). The majors of these students vary. Most participants are business information systems engineering students (n = 29),

Table 1 Characteristics of the developed interactive video

Shortest/longest possible walk-through/video material in total	10:12 min[a]/18:09 min[a]/28:08 min
Possible decision situations and options • Minimum 5, maximum 9 decision situations (unnecessary repetitions excluded) • Minimum 11 decision options in total (without repetitions—shortest walk-through) up to 18 decision options (longest walkthrough due to forced repetitions as result of bad decisions (unnecessary repetitions excluded))	
Basic design considerations 1. Repetitions are possible to support learning, 2. wrong decisions lead to learning scenarios, 3. use humor and reward good behavior, 4. use memes and realistic scenarios to attract the target group, covering possible real-world circumstances (closed IT-Department)	

[a] W/o time for decision-making

followed by students of industrial engineering (n = 25), students of business administration (n = 5), and 1 student of computer science. Since the purpose of the LO is to be reused in different courses, we analyze all fields of study as one group. The structure of the survey is depicted in Table 2 and will be described in the following. In order to ensure that our results are meaningful for educators who want to address different target groups, such as freshmen students as well as students in higher semesters, we collected data within a first-semester lecture and a seminar which is suggested for students of the fifth semester. The student's current semester of study is described by the following distribution: 1st-, 2nd-, and 3rd-semester students (n = 38), 5th- and 6th-semester students (n = 15), 7th-semester students and above (n = 7). All data has been collected within one week to reduce the risk of bias. **The sample size for the qualitative evaluation** is consistent with the pretest (n = 60). We introduced our survey as part of our research namely an "evaluation of a digital educational element for teaching at universities". Participation in the study was voluntary. To ensure that the results of the pre- and posttest can be linked, students were asked to create a unique but anonymous code (based on assembled letters) which is only used for this purpose.

Assessing the extent to which an educational design element is successful is essential and desirable design knowledge for educators and researchers, which we aim to derive by answering RQ1. Therefore, we evaluate the learning goal of this educational approach which is to raise ISA for the handling of unknown and potentially harmful USB sticks and reporting security incidents by students. We applied the

Table 2 Structure of the surveys

	Description	No. of items (w/o demographic items)
1st survey	HAIS-Q quant. pretest (n = 60)	9
2nd survey	HAIS-Q quant. posttest (n = 60)	9
	LOES-S qual. questions (n = 60)	2
	Control measure (n = 60)	4

HAIS-Q of Parsons et al. (2017) as a quantitative measure to determine the level of ISA (see Sect. 2) and whether the interactive video affects learning outcomes. For reproducibility and transparency, we point out that we use five points of the Likert scale, following the initial HAIS-Q developers (e.g., Parsons et al. 2017; McCormac et al. 2016), instead of applying a four points of Likert scale (e.g., like Cindana and Ruldeviyani 2018).

Beyond measuring learning outcomes, it is essential to know the design factors that influenced these learning outcomes. Thus, in order to answer RQ2, we evaluate the feedback of students. With this in mind, we include the two qualitative questions of the "Learning Object Evaluation Scale for Students"-questionnaire (LOES-S) of Kay and Knaack (2009) in our survey because these questions offer the opportunity for students to give qualitative feedback for a specific LO and provide design knowledge for further improvements—the applied questions are: *1. What, if anything, did you LIKE about the learning object? 2. What, if anything, did you NOT LIKE about the learning object?* To analyze all answers for our LO, we use the 3 applicable categories ('Learning', 'Engagement', 'Quality') of the coding schema provided by Kay and Knaack (2009) with the slight adaption of the subcategories to align it to the format of an interactive video. The applied subcategories are presented and discussed with regard to the results in Sect. 4.4. In addition to the two LOES-S items, we ask the students (as a control measure for our qualitative feedback), if they "would recommend this information security training to [their] fellow students" using a 10-point scale and further, if they "would participate again in an information security training that uses interactive video formats like this training". Both questions include an input field for explanations. The purpose of the control measure is further outlined in the following section.

4.2 Methodology for Evaluating Learning Outcomes and Qualitative Feedback

Our dataset includes a **pre- and posttest**, which is essential to determine whether the interactive video fulfills its purpose in reaching the learning goal (an increased level of ISA). To assess this and **answer RQ1**, we compare these tests and use the t-test for dependent samples. Initially, we assess the reliability of our measured HAIS-Q constructs, this means we calculate Cronbach's Alpha for the HAIS-Q focus area 'incident reporting' and one subarea from the focus area 'information handling', which is 'inserting removable media'. The internal consistency of the focus area 'incident reporting' is reliable for both, the pretest with $\boldsymbol{\alpha = 0.801}$ and the posttest with $\boldsymbol{\alpha = 0.712}$. However, Cronbach's alpha for the subarea 'inserting removable media' is insufficient. In consequence, we exclude this subarea from the analysis. To compare the pre- and posttest we apply the t-test of dependent samples and calculated the effect size using the method of Cohen's d (see next section). Given the robustness of the t-test for $n > 30$, we do not check for normal distribution. We checked the dataset for outliers but found none. Furthermore, we analyzed the pretest data, in particular the mean values of the constructs to see if there were differences in students' prior knowledge between lower (1–3) and higher (5–7) semester groups, but these differences were not significant.

The learning content was designed according to the HAIS-Q focus area 'incident reporting' and one subarea from the focus area 'information handling'. Therefore, we also use the corresponding HAIS-Q items of the focus area 'incident reporting' to measure learning outcomes, but without the items of 'information handling' (see Table 3). 'Incident reporting' consists of 3 subareas with 3 items each (one item per dimension: knowledge, attitude, behavior). In conclusion, we used 9 items in total with a 5-point Likert scale ranging from '1—strongly disagree' to '5—strongly agree' and recoded reversely scored items. The level of ISA is a result of mean values and to measure this, we (1) calculate the mean value of each subarea by summing up the mean values of each subarea item score (minimum 3–maximum 15 points), then, (2) we calculate the mean value for the (overall) subarea score (minimum 1–maximum 5 points) to perform the t-test and (3) discuss the scores from (1) and (2) as a measured representation of the level of ISA in Sect. 4.4. We are aware of literature that suggests applying weightings to the dimensions (knowledge, attitude, behavior) of the HAIS-Q focus areas (e.g., Cindana and Ruldeviyani (2018) or Firsty Arisya et al. (2020)). However, in order to increase transferability, we decided to weight all dimensions equally, which is also common practice (e.g., see Wahyudiwan et al. (2017) or Salem et al. (2021)). To determine whether the ISA score of an HAIS-Q subarea or HAIS-Q focus area is sufficient, average, or alarming and requires action (here: further educational interventions), we follow the current literature, e.g. Wahyudiwan et al. (2017) or Firsty Arisya et al. (2020), and use the following categorization (but without weighting): good awareness (80–100% of all possible points per subarea (= 12–15 points)), average awareness (60–79% of all points), poor awareness (< 60% of all points). In order to evaluate the **qualitative user feedback on the LO** and to derive **design factors to answer RQ2**, we first, analyze all provided qualitative statements for the LOES-S items, but also second, the control measure items. More details about the evaluation procedure are outlined in the previous Sect. 4.1. Here, we refer to this procedure and add information about how we derive findings. First, the posttest data set (n = 60), including the two qualitative LOES-S items, provide statements about positive and negative design factors that are categorized by applying our adopted coding framework from Kay and Knaack (2009). This means that statements are assigned to the framework (sub-) categories and numbered in cases where the meanings of provided statements are similar. Second, the same dataset contains students' responses to the four further items of the control measure, these are 2 quantitative items and 2 qualitative items. It is known that collecting qualitative data is likely to be influenced by interfering factors like social desirability (Crowne and Marlowe 1960). Thus, the quantitative items and qualitative items of the control measure are included as an indicator for social desirability and thus, provide indications regarding the reliability and validity of the findings (Crowne and Marlowe 1960) that are based on the LOES-S items. In other words, we assume that not every student would recommend our educational approach

Table 3 Reliability testing using Cronbach's alpha (9 items)

Sample	HAIS-Q constructs (Parsons et al. 2017)	Cronbach's α
HAIS-Q pretest (n = 60)	Focus area: incident reporting (9 items)	0.801 (satisfying)
HAIS-Q posttest (n = 60)	Focus area: incident reporting (9 items)	0.712 (satisfying)
HAIS-Q pretest (n = 60)	Focus area: information handling → subarea: inserting removable media (3 items)	0.299 (insufficient, excluded[a])
HAIS-Q posttest (n = 60)	Focus area: information handling → subarea: inserting removable media (3 items)	0.488 (insufficient, excluded[a])

[a] Because alpha is substantially lower than acceptable values such as $\alpha \leq 0.7$ (Taber 2018)

without restrictions. Thus, we would further assume a high likeliness that our findings are influenced by social desirability if the statements of respondents are contradictory or almost every student would fully "recommend this information security training to fellow students" and in case almost every student "would participate again in an information security training that uses interactive video formats like this training". More precisely, we state that our findings would be questionable if our approach is evaluated as "perfect". In consequence, we review the dataset for contradictory statements and outliers.

4.3 Results

The result of our t-test for dependent samples is calculated by the mean values of each subarea before and after treatment and indicates that our interactive video (see Table 4) **significantly** increases the level of ISA for the subarea 'Reporting suspicious behavior (RSB)' $t(59) = -2.616$, $p = 0.011$*, $d = 0.81$. In addition, the video **significantly** increases the level of ISA for the subarea 'Ignoring poor security behavior by col. (IPSBC)' $t(59) = -3.096$, $p = 0.003$**, $d = 0.99$, furthermore, it **significantly** increases the level of ISA for the subarea 'Reporting all incidents (RAI)' $t(59) = -2.109$, $p = 0.039$*, $d = 0.98$. Based on this data we can interpret, that the interactive video has a significant effect on increasing the level of ISA for all three subareas of the HAIS-Q focus area 'incident reporting' if used in a university lecture for bachelor students. After screening all qualitative statements, we found 59 statements (n = 60; one blank answer excluded) that refer to what they LIKE about the LO and 34 comments on what they did NOT LIKE. Here, it is noteworthy, that 6 students gave further positive feedback answering the "NOT LIKE" question and thus, these parts of the statements are reframed as "LIKE" statements. For instance, one student answered the "NOT LIKE" question by stating "Even the option to replay was good to find different outcomes of the Story" and thus, the statement is obviously positive instead of negative. Within the further analysis, we excluded individual indifferent and inaccurate answers like "all good", "nothing", "everything was perfect" or "not everything was good" as they cannot be categorized and are questionable regarding their information value.

To analyze the qualitative feedback statements we use the coding schema of Kay and Knaack (2009) including the three main categories "Learning", "Engagement" but also "Quality". However, we discarded the sub-category "help" because there is no statement which refers to it directly. In addition, the following categories offered no statements for the "NOT LIKE" item: 'Learning: beneficial visual feature'; 'Learning: occurred learning/teaching issue'; 'Engagement: using the artifact is fun/enjoyable/engaging/interesting'; 'Engagement: comparison to other methods of teaching'. The rigorous analysis revealed that there are statements that only show slight differences, e.g., "Learning content was not challenging/obvious solutions" sets a focus on challenging learning content in general, and "Learning content was too obvious to students with prior knowledge" adds information that this might only concern students with prior knowledge. With that in mind, we outline and discuss the key findings and declare the number of statements referring to it within the text or by the number within parentheses at the end of a finding, e.g., 'statement 1 (4)'.

First, we analyze the statements related to the "***Learning category***". For the sub-category "*challenging learning content*" 1 student liked the vivid and understandable learning content, 1 student liked that they learned something new (e.g., the location of the computer department) and 1 more student noted that the content is applicable and even 'beneficial' for students of other bachelor programs. Contrary, a considerable number of students stated that the learning content was not challenging or included obvious solutions (8) and thus, that it might be too obvious to students with prior knowledge (1). The next sub-category is "*beneficial visual feature*". Students mentioned positively that real-world video pictures support tangible awareness of real threats (2), decision paths support positive learning experiences and 'look and

Table 4 Results of comparing the HAIS-Q pre- and posttest (dependent t-test, Cohen's d)

Subareas of focus area: incident reporting	Level of ISA (mean values; n = 60)		t-test (df = 59; $*p < 0.05$; $**p < 0.01$)	
	Pre- versus posttest	SD/dif.	t; $p*/p**$	Cohen's d
Reporting suspicious behavior (RSB)	4.2778 (pretest)	0.80603/– 0.27222	– 2.616; **0.011***	**0.81**
	4.5500 (posttest)			
Ignoring poor security behavior by col. (IPSBC)	3.8667 (pretest)	0.98671/– 0.39444	– 3.096; **0.003****	**0.99**
	4.2611 (posttest)			
Reporting all incidents (RAI)	4.1778 (pretest)	0.97964/– 0.26667	– 2.109; **0.039***	**0.98**
	4.444 (posttest)			

Bold values denotes that these results are statistically significant feel' (2), they also liked the integration of learning scenarios, that are explained by the educator (2), and further, that decision screens enabled the reflection of own behavior (1). The last sub-category "*occurred learning/teaching issue*" provided only one statement, namely "no issues".

Second, we analyze the statements related to the "***Engagement category***". Regarding the sub-category "*using the artifact is fun/enjoyable/engaging/ interesting*", a considerably high number of students provided positive feedback, namely that the video is entertaining, interesting, and engaging, so it supports active learning (10), generally the video is enjoyable and exciting (2) and one student would like to watch more videos like this, further, students mentioned that the included decision paths increase curiosity (2) and makes the learning content engaging (2) in a way, that it motivates even "not attractive learning content" (1). In addition, statements related to the sub-category "*comparison to other methods of teaching*" revealed that the method is perceived as something new or refreshing (6), that fosters a better focus on learning content (e.g., compared to non-interactive videos) (3), furthermore, the first-person perspective makes it immersive (2), and the interactive method activates learning better than passive methods (1). However, related to the sub-category "*occurred issues with technology*", a minor number of students report problems with technology: The visual representation within the LMS (1) is not sufficient, the video stops in some cases after wrong decisions (1) and that decision options disappeared (1).

Third, we identify a high number of statements that refer to the "**Quality category**". For instance, regarding the sub-category "*interactive parts*": A high number of students liked the interactivity in general (12) and that different decisions within a story support immersive interactions (7) or that a variety of options are available, not just the right or wrong (3). Thus, some report that this supports learning the key statements (3). Positive feedback related to the sub-category "*animation*" includes the following: Realistic scenario recordings in general (4), first person-perspective (4), using time-lapse of real-world recordings (1), and real persons' actions made it look real (1). Nevertheless, students report negative aspects as well, such that the e-mail on the recorded screen was hardly readable (2), the time-lapse scene was a bit too long (1) and the video quality (resolution) should be improved (1). For the sub-category "*control while using the learning object*" four positive feedback statements are identified, to be specific, students liked to control the path of the story within the video through their own decisions, but one student criticizes that decision paths are not predictable before taking any action. Regarding the sub-category "*ease of use*", 2 students mentioned positively that the decision paths are traceable and realistic making them easy to understand, contrary to this, 2 students state a problem regarding the understanding of the decision path and option wording, and 1 student criticizes the pace of the storytelling in the video. Only three statements are related to the sub-category "*theme*": 3 statements emphasized the importance of the topic, 1 student liked the "useful content", remaining 1 student stating the theme was not complex enough. Statements that relate to the sub-category of "organization of the learning object" are: Students liked the creativity regarding the whole video (3), the gameful experience (2) real person actors within the video (2), using humor

(2), appropriate design (1), that content is designed to reflect the known real-world environment of the target group (1), the storyline (1), and the option to replay (1). However, 5 statements include that the story was predictable to some degree, non-professional actors show limited emotions and acting skills but also dialog quality looks staged (4), options that are obvious to the user are not presented, which interrupts the immersive gameplay (1), and that the video needs too much time (2). Statements related to the sub-category "*audio*" only include critique, namely the voice of the actors seem a bit robotic (1), the audio quality should be improved (1) and one student reports the ringtone of the smartphone used in the video as a negative aspect.

The results of analyzing the control measure items show that 28 students would recommend this ISA training to other students (9–10 points), and 12 students scored 8 points. Further, 34 students would participate again in an ISA training which is using interactive videos (9–10 points), and 10 students rated 8 points. Explanation of students that rated lower than 9 points are mostly similar, which means that decision options and solutions are too obvious, they do not recommend lectures in general, or feel very confident regarding their level of ISA. This indicates that a high number of students rate our approach positively, but some students do so with limitations. Thereby, the differentiated explanations confirm both the quantitative scoring and our findings to be consistent and so we assume our qualitative findings to be valid and reliable.

4.4 Discussion

In order to determine the level of ISA on basis of the results of the t-test, we calculate the ISA score by the summed-up mean values of the subareas, but also of the focus area, and assign them to the categorical levels of ISA (good, average, poor). Here, it is noteworthy that the ISA average level was 'good' before treatment for the *whole* focus area (summed up mean value of points: 12.23 points $\geq$ 82%). However, as 2 out of 3 subareas reached a level of 80%, the score of the sub-category 'Ignoring poor security behavior by colleagues' revealed a need for action as it was only average (11.6 points $\leq$ 78%). The ISA level *after treatment* increased to a considerably high level for the whole focus area (summed up mean value of points: 13.26 points $\geq$ 88%) and also for the previously lower rated subarea 'Ignoring poor security behavior by colleagues' (12.79 points $\geq$ 85%). So RQ1 can be answered with regard to the level of ISA and in combination with the significant results of the t-test. Both results indicate evidence that the interactive video strongly increased the level of ISA of students and thus, supports positive learning outcomes to a significant extent. In addition, RQ2 can be answered by outlining the qualitative findings. These indicate that an interactive narrative can be an important design factor for successful educational approaches since it supports active learning and engagement with the learning content, e.g., by fostering curiosity using choice-based interactions and the reflection of own decisions. Further, the statements indicate that for cybersecurity education, videos recorded in first-person perspective for a specific target group, and real-world recordings in general, foster immersive and credible learning content but also convey the importance of the topic realistically. Nevertheless, a high number of students reported that the approach is "refreshing/something new" and although this seems positive at first sight, it may also indicate that learning effects are also related to the novelty of interactive videos themselves and may differ if interactive videos would become ubiquitous. The results also contain criticisms that are important for further design iterations, e.g., that the learning content and solutions for decisions might be too limited and obvious (but can also be considered a low-barrier training format for students without prior knowledge). Hence, more complex but traceable decision options should be integrated. Thus, we consider differentiation for different key-user groups in the future. Additionally, the results indicate that the video should be further streamlined, including fastening the pace of the storytelling and shortening the video length. Although only mentioned in three statements, technical problems must be solved in the future to provide a positive learning experience for all students, e.g., the visual representation within the LMS or bugs while interacting within the decision process should be reviewed.

In summary, the quantitative and qualitative results strongly indicate that the interactive video achieved its aim, namely educating students and training ISA. Furthermore, the video improves the level of ISA and was enjoyable even for students with prior knowledge and this indicates that it can be applied as a refreshing measure.

5 Conclusion: Implications and Limitations

The design and the evaluation of our artifact provides meaningful design knowledge for practitioners and researchers. In response to RQ1, we state that our interactive educational video has a **strong significant effect on building ISA** for the reporting of security incidents. Furthermore, by analyzing the qualitative students' feedback and answering RQ2, we provide important novel design knowledge for effective security education in general and the development of design principles in future design cycles for effective interactive videos that rely on choice-based storytelling. Thus, for better transferability toward future design principles, we formulate the following recommendations for information security educators in accordance to Gregor et al. (2020) but note that for mature design principles further evidence is needed: Educators should implement a wide variety of meaningful decision options including different levels of challenge to support active learning and engagement with the content. In addition, learning videos should be designed using real-world recordings and varying storylines to foster curiosity, relatedness and interest, so that it creates value for the students. Further, using humor and implementing an interactive design in general is crucial for educational videos in the field of security education because students perceive such an approach to be refreshing, enjoyable but also engaging. Pitfalls that educators should avoid are, technical issues with accessing the content, including too few decision options within the video and providing too much video content in length.

Future research should focus on determining a range for an appropriate number of decision options and length of video content. However, there are also limitations: (a) We evaluated only one focus area of the HAIS-Q and thus, other areas should be included in future design iterations. Further, (b) using a within-subject design without a control group only reveals the effectiveness of the interactive video but provides no direct evidence whether it performs better than other ways of delivery. However, some qualitative statements indicate a better performance and therefore, we state that this is a promising point for future research.

References

Abawajy, J. (2014) 'User preference of cyber security awareness delivery methods', *Behaviour & Information Technology*, vol. 33, no. 3, pp. 237–248.

Almeida, C., Kalinowski, M. and Feijo, B. (2021) 'A Systematic Mapping of Negative Effects of Gamification in Education/Learning Systems', *2021 47th Euromicro Conference on Software Engineering and Advanced Applications (SEAA)*. Palermo, Italy, 01.–03.09.2021, IEEE, pp. 17–24.

Alyami, A., Sammon, D., Neville, K. and Mahony, C. (2022) 'The Critical Success Factors for Security Education, Training and Awareness (SETA) Programmes', *2022 Cyber Research Conference - Ireland (Cyber-RCI)*. Galway, Ireland, 25.04.2022, IEEE, pp. 1–12.

Baldwin, S. and Ching, Y.-H. (2017) 'Interactive Storytelling: Opportunities for Online Course Design', *TechTrends*, vol. 61, no. 2, pp. 179–186.

Beheshti, M., Taspolat, A., Kaya, O. S. and Sapanca, H. F. (2018) 'Characteristics of Instructional Videos', *World Journal on Educational Technology: Current Issues*, vol. 10, no. 1, pp. 61–69 [Online]. Available at https://eric.ed.gov/?id=ej1170366.

Brehmer, M. (2023) *Interaktives Lernvideo zur Bildung von Informationssicherheitsbewusstsein: ein zielgruppenspezifisches Training für Studierende* [Online], University of Augsburg. Available at https://www.digillab.uni-augsburg.de/kursarchiv/interaktives-lernvideo-zur-bildung-fuer-informationssicherheitsbewusstsein-ein-zielgruppenspezifisches-training-fuer-studierende/.

Brehmer, M. and Reinelt, R. (2023) 'Gamifying a Learning Management System: Narrative and Team Leaderboard in the Context of Effective Information Security Education', *Proceedings of the 56th Annual Hawaii International Conference on System Sciences*, 03.–06.01.2023.

Brehmer, M., Abbas, E. A. and Vaidyanathan, N. (2021) 'Towards Designing A Method To Create Sticky Information Security Training For SMEs: Identifying Design Factors', *29th European Conference on Information Systems*, 14.–16.06.2021 (ECIS).

Chen, C.-C., Huang, Ching Chih, Gribbins, M. and Swan Karen (2018) 'Gamify Online Courses with Tools Built into Your Learning Management System (LMS) to Enhance Self-Determined and Active Learning', *Online Learning*, vol. 22, no. 3.

Chouhan, R. (2021) 'Effective interactive video assignments and rewatch analytics for online flipped classrooms', *2021 IEEE 1st International Conference on Advanced Learning Technologies on Education & Research (ICALTER)*. Lima, Peru, 16.–18.12.2021, IEEE, pp. 1–4.

Cindana, A. and Ruldeviyani, Y. (2018) 'Measuring Information Security Awareness on Employee Using HAIS-Q: Case Study at XYZ Firm', *2018 International Conference on Advanced Computer Science and Information Systems (ICACSIS)*. Yogyakarta, Indonesia, 27.–28.10.2018, IEEE, pp. 289–294.

Croasdell, D., Elste, J. and Hill, A. (2018) 'Cyber Clinics: Re-imagining Cyber Security Awareness', *Hawaii International Conference on System Sciences 2018 (HICSS-51)* [Online]. Available at https://aisel.aisnet.org/hicss-51/ks/ks_security/8.

Crowne, D. P. and Marlowe, D. (1960) 'A new scale of social desirability independent of psychopathology', *Journal of Consulting Psychology*, vol. 24, pp. 349–354.

Csikszentmihalyi, M. (1990) *Flow: The psychology of optimal experience*, New York, Harper & Row.

D'Arcy, J., Herath, T. and Shoss, M. K. (2014) 'Understanding Employee Responses to Stressful Information Security Requirements A Coping Perspective', *Journal of Management Information Systems*, vol. 31, no. 2, pp. 285–318.

Deci, E. L. and Ryan, R. M. (2000) 'The "What" and "Why" of Goal Pursuits: Human Needs and the Self-Determination of Behavior', *Psychological Inquiry*, vol. 11, pp. 227–268.

Deterding, S., Dixon, D., Khaled, R. and Nacke, L. (2011) 'From game design elements to gamefulness', *Proceedings of the 15th International Academic MindTrek Conference on Envisioning Future Media Environments*. Tampere, Finland, 28.–30.09.2011. New York, USA, p. 9.

Dincelli, E. and Chengalur-Smith, I. (2020) 'Choose your own training adventure: designing a gamified SETA artefact for improving information security and privacy through interactive storytelling', *European Journal of Information Systems*, vol. 29, no. 6, pp. 669–687.

Fertig, T., Henkelmann, D. and Schütz, A. (2022) '360 Degrees of Security: Can VR Increase the Sustainability of ISA Trainings?', *Proceedings of the 55th Hawaii International Conference on System Sciences* (HICSS).

Firsty Arisya, K., Ruldeviyani, Y., Prakoso, R. and Lailatul Fadhilah, A. (2020) 'Measurement of Information Security Awareness Level: A Case Study of Mobile Banking (M-Banking) Users', *2020 Fifth International Conference on Informatics and Computing (ICIC)*. Gorontalo, Indonesia, 03.–04.11.2020, IEEE, pp. 1–5.

Grasse, K. M., Kreminski, M., Wardrip-Fruin, N., Mateas, M. and Melcer, E. F. (2022a) 'Using Self-Determination Theory to Explore Enjoyment of Educational Interactive Narrative Games: A Case Study of Academical', *Frontiers in Virtual Reality*, vol. 3.

Grasse, K. M., Melcer, E. F., Kreminski, M., Junius, N., Ryan, J. and Wardrip-Fruin, N. (2022b) 'Academical: A Choice-Based Interactive Storytelling Game for Enhancing Moral Reasoning, Knowledge, and Attitudes in Responsible Conduct of Research', in *Games and Narrative: Theory and Practice*, Springer, Cham, pp. 173–189.

Gregor, S., Kruse, L. and Seidel, S. (2020) 'Research Perspectives: The Anatomy of a Design Principle', *Journal of the Association for Information Systems*, vol. 21, pp. 1622–1652.

Hamari, J., Koivisto, J. and Sarsa, H. (2014) 'Does Gamification Work? – A Literature Review of Empirical Studies on Gamification', *2014 47th Hawaii International Conference on System Sciences*. Waikoloa, HI, 06.–09.01.2014, IEEE, pp. 3025–3034.

Hu, S., Hsu, C. and Zhou, Z. (2021) 'Security Education, Training, and Awareness Programs: Literature Review', *Journal of Computer Information Systems*, pp. 1–13.

Kay, R. H. and Knaack, L. (2009) 'Assessing learning, quality and engagement in learning objects: the Learning Object Evaluation Scale for Students (LOES-S)', *Educational Technology Research and Development*, vol. 57, no. 2, pp. 147–168.

Kirova, D. and Baumöl, U. (2018) 'Factors that Affect the Success of Security Education, Training, and Awareness Programs: A Literature Review', *Journal of Information Technology Theory and Application (JITTA)*, vol. 19, no. 4 [Online]. Available at https://aisel.aisnet.org/jitta/vol19/iss4/4/.

Knop, D. (2023) 'Ransomware: Daten von Uni Duisburg-Essen im Darknet, Uni Innsbruck attackiert', *heise online*, 17 January [Online]. Available at https://www.heise.de/news/Ransomware-Daten-von-Uni-Duisburg-Essen-im-Darknet-Uni-Innsbruck-attackiert-7461603.html (Accessed 23 February 2023).

Martin, A. (2023) 'Switzerland's largest university confirms 'serious cyberattack'', *The Record from Recorded Future News*, 3 February [Online]. Available at https://therecord.media/switzerlands-largest-university-confirms-serious-cyberattack/ (Accessed 23 February 2023).

McCormac, A., Calic, D., Parsons, K., Zwaans, T., Butavicius, M. and Pattinson, M. (2016) 'Test-retest reliability and internal consistency of the Human Aspects of Information Security Questionnaire (HAIS-Q)', in *ACIS 2016 Proceedings*.

Melcer, E. F., Grasse, K. M., Ryan, J., Junius, N., Kreminski, M., Squinkifer, D., Hill, B. and Wardrip-Fruin, N. (2020) 'Getting Academical: A Choice-Based Interactive Storytelling Game for Teaching Responsible Conduct of Research', *International Conference on the Foundations of Digital Games*. Bugibba Malta, 15.–18.09.2020. New York, NY, USA, ACM, pp. 1–12.

Murray, J. H. (2018) 'Research into Interactive Digital Narrative: A Kaleidoscopic View', in Rouse, R., Koenitz, H. and Haahr, M. (eds) *Interactive Storytelling: 11th International Conference on Interactive Digital Storytelling, ICIDS 2018, Dublin, Ireland, December 5–8, 2018, Proceedings*, Cham, Springer International Publishing, pp. 3–17.

Nguyen, T. A. and Pham, H. (2020) 'A Design Theory-Based Gamification Approach for Information Security Training', *2020 RIVF International Conference on Computing and Communication Technologies (RIVF)*. Ho Chi Minh City, Vietnam, 14.–15.10.2020, IEEE, pp. 1–4.

Parsons, K., McCormac, A., Butavicius, M., Pattinson, M. and Jerram, C. (2014) 'Determining employee awareness using the Human Aspects of Information Security Questionnaire (HAIS-Q)', *Computers & Security*, vol. 42, pp. 165–176.

Parsons, K., Calic, D., Pattinson, M., Butavicius, M., McCormac, A. and Zwaans, T. (2017) 'The Human Aspects of Information Security Questionnaire (HAIS-Q): Two further validation studies', *Computers & Security*, vol. 66, pp. 40–51.

Peffers, K., Tuunanen, T., Rothenberger, M. A. and Chatterjee, S. (2007) 'A Design Science Research Methodology for Information Systems Research', *Journal of Management Information Systems*, vol. 24, no. 3, pp. 45–77.

Rajadell, M. and Garriga-Garzón, F. (2017) 'Educational videos: After the why, the how', *Intangible Capital*, vol. 13, no. 5, p. 903.

Ralston, W. (2021) *The untold story of a cyberattack, a hospital and a dying woman* [Online] (SECURITY). Available at https://www.wired.co.uk/article/ransomware-hospital-death-germany (Accessed 15 May 2022).

Ryan, R. M. and Deci, E. L. (2000) 'Self-determination theory and the facilitation of intrinsic motivation, social development, and well-being', *American Psychologist*, vol. 55, no. 1, pp. 68–78.

Salem, Y., Moreb, M. and Rabayah, K. S. (2021) 'Evaluation of Information Security Awareness among Palestinian Learners', *2021 International Conference on Information Technology (ICIT)*. Amman, Jordan, 14.–15.07.2021, IEEE, pp. 21–26.

Shelton, C. C., Warren, A. E. and Archambault, L. M. (2016) 'Exploring the Use of Interactive Digital Storytelling Video: Promoting Student Engagement and Learning in a University Hybrid Course', *TechTrends*, vol. 60, no. 5, pp. 465–474.

Taber, K. S. (2018) 'The Use of Cronbach's Alpha When Developing and Reporting Research Instruments in Science Education', *Research in Science Education*, vol. 48, no. 6, pp. 1273–1296 [Online]. https://doi.org/10.1007/s11165-016-9602-2.

Tischer, M., Durumeric, Z., Foster, S., Duan, S., Mori, A., Bursztein, E. and Bailey, M. (2016) 'Users Really Do Plug in USB Drives They Find', *2016 IEEE Symposium on Security and Privacy (SP)*. San Jose, CA, 22.–26.05.2016, IEEE, pp. 306–319.

Tung, L. (2022) 'Ransomware warning: Cyber criminals are mailing out USB drives that install malware', *ZDNET*, 10 January [Online]. Available at https://www.zdnet.com/article/fbi-cybercriminals-are-mailing-out-usb-drives-that-will-install-ransomware/ (Accessed 23 February 2023).

Ulsamer, P., Schütz, A., Fertig, T. and Keller, L. (2021) 'Immersive Storytelling for Information Security Awareness Training in Virtual Reality', *Proceedings of the 54th Hawaii International Conference on System Sciences* (HICSS).

Ulven, J. B. and Wangen, G. (2021) 'A Systematic Review of Cybersecurity Risks in Higher Education', *Future Internet*, vol. 13, no. 2, p. 39.

Venable, J., Pries-Heje, J. and Baskerville, R. (2012) 'A Comprehensive Framework for Evaluation in Design Science Research', *Design Science Research in Information Systems. Advances in Theory and Practice*. Berlin, Heidelberg, Springer Berlin Heidelberg, pp. 423–438.

Wahyudiwan, D. D. H., Sucahyo, Y. G. and Gandhi, A. (2017) 'Information security awareness level measurement for employee: Case study at ministry of research, technology, and higher education', *2017 3rd International Conference on Science in Information Technology (ICSITech)*. Bandung, 25.–26.10.2017, IEEE, pp. 654–658.

Wang, F. (2022) 'College Students' experience of using online video and educational video', *2022 10th International Conference on Orange Technology (ICOT)*. Shanghai, China, 10.–11.11.2022, IEEE, pp. 1–4.

Wilson, M. and Hash, J. (2003) *Building an Information Technology Security Awareness and Training Program* [Online], NIST.

Yoo, C. W., Sanders, G. L. and Cerveny, R. P. (2018) 'Exploring the influence of flow and psychological ownership on security education, training and awareness effectiveness and security compliance', *Decision Support Systems*, vol. 108, pp. 107–118.

Using Hexad Archetypes to Motivate Students in a Chatbot-Enhanced Web-Based-Training

Ricarda Schlimbach, Jannika Behne, Tim Lange, and Susanne Robra-Bissantz

Abstract This study explores the challenge of maintaining motivation in further education for working students, who face the double burden of work and learning. To address this issue, we investigate the design and implementation of a pedagogical conversational agent (PCA) within a web-based training (WBT) platform. Drawing on literature, interviews with 11 experts, and a creative workshop with 14 working students, we use the Hexad user type framework to tailor the WBT to each user's motivational archetype. We prioritize design features for each of the six archetypes and instantiate these in a prototype. In a field experiment with 17 working students using the WBT prototype for exam preparation, we observe a significant increase in intrinsic and extrinsic motivation. This study contributes to the emerging field of PCA-enhanced digital learning, highlighting the potential of personalized motivation in persuasive dialogue systems.

Keywords Hexad archetypes · Pedagogical conversational agent · Motivation · Persuasive system · Higher education

1 Introduction

The outbreak of the COVID-19 pandemic in 2020 resulted in the closure of schools and the implementation of remote digital learning (Ngwacho 2023). While the digitization of education had been a slow and gradual process in previous years, the pandemic created a sense of urgency and accelerated the pace of change (Sakkir et al. 2021). Digital learning differs significantly from traditional classroom-based instruction in terms of the available teaching tools. Instead of relying solely on

R. Schlimbach (✉)
Hochschule Heilbronn, Fakultät MV, Schwäbisch Hall, Germany
e-mail: ricarda.schlimbach@hs-heilbronn.de

R. Schlimbach · J. Behne · T. Lange · S. Robra-Bissantz
TU Braunschweig, Lehrstuhl für Service-Informationssysteme, Braunschweig, Germany
e-mail: s.robra-bissantz@tu-braunschweig.de

D. Beverungen et al. (eds.), *Transforming the Digitally Sustainable Enterprise*, Lecture Notes in Information Systems and Organisation 76,
https://doi.org/10.1007/978-3-031-80125-9_26

the teacher to mediate learning content, digital components like pre-recorded web-based trainings (WBT) penetrate (further) education (Patel et al. 2019). However, it has become apparent, especially during the pandemic, that many learners struggle with self-motivation in digital learning environments (Ertan and Kocadere 2022), in particular when facing multiple loads like studying and working in parallel (Rinn et al. 2022; Sakkir et al. 2021). Motivation is a major success factor in (technology-enhanced) learning (Morisano et al. 2010), and adapting motivational variables to users of digital learning tools is one of the key pillars to leverage the potential of adaptive learning, although their implementation is still underrepresented (Plass and Pawar 2020; Schlimbach et al. 2022), especially in Pedagogical Conversational Agents (PCAs) as motivational, virtual learning facilitators (Schlimbach et al. 2022; Yin et al. 2021). However, PCAs as intelligent dialogue systems could be designed to react adaptively to students' motivational drivers according to the six archetypes on the hexad scale by Tondello et al. (2016). By embedding a PCA into a WBT aligned with the hexad framework, the resulting motivationally customized interaction to the user's hexad archetype appears promising to enhance engagement and motivation in the learning process. Its positive motivational impact has been proven successful in other contexts like gaming (Şenocak et al. 2021; Tondello et al. 2016). Nevertheless, education research barely touches upon this aspect in individualizing learning in (further) education (Steinherr and Reinelt 2022).

The present study investigates the design of a PCA that can adapt to the six hexad archetypes to foster motivation in digital learning environments. In addition to deriving design features tailored to each archetype by triangulating literature, expert interviews and a creative workshop, the goal of this paper is to instantiate these in the form of a prototype and measure its impact on intrinsic and extrinsic motivation in a field experiment with a class taking the WBT as exam preparation.

2 Research Background

User types originated in the video game industry (Bartle 1996), with models such as Bartle's player type framework and the BrainHex model identifying different player motivations (Busch et al. 2016). However, these approaches revealed to be not applicable to all types of players (Monterrat et al. 2015) and may not transfer to non-game contexts either (Steinherr and Reinelt 2022). Marczewski (2015) was the first to develop a standardized scale for player types based on human motivation with practical experiments. Drawing on the prior knowledge base, he introduced the hexad model, which provides a broader scope beyond gaming and suggests archetype-appropriate use of gamification in information systems. The hexad model takes into account users' motivational structures and preferences, incorporating established theories such as the Self-Determination Theory (Ryan and Deci 2000a), which defines three key intrinsic motivators: mastery, autonomy, and relatedness. Additionally, Marczewski (2015) considers Pink's (2011) drive theory, which introduces purpose as an additional motivator. The hexad model thus comprises six archetypes: *Player,*

Free Spirit, Achiever, Disruptor, Socializer, and *Philanthropist*, along with specific design recommendations for motivating each archetype (Marczewski 2015). Table 1 on the next page depicts each hexad user type and its main characteristics.

Tondello et al. (2016) further refined the model and validated it using a 24-point survey response scale, which helps to illustrate participants' preferences towards the six hexad archetypes. Today, the hexad model has undergone extensive empirical validation through various contexts (Berehil 2022). By applying it to educative contexts, it might create a more personalized and engaging experience for students, catering to their specific motivational preferences (Steinherr and Reinelt 2022).

The launch of ChatGPT and the penetration of PCAs in their role as naturally communicating dialogue systems to facilitate learning (Hobert and Meyer von Wolff 2019; Khosrawi-Rad et al. 2022) are disrupting education in its core, but are yet to be designed with more individualized features to learner's motivational drivers (Schlimbach et al. 2022; Yin et al. 2021). Embedding the hexad model into a PCA-enhanced WBT might thus be an effective approach to increase students' motivation and engagement empowered by a tool adaptive or adaptable to motivational archetypes (Plass and Pawar 2020; Schlimbach et al. 2022).

Table 1 Hexad user types

User type and motivation		Main characteristics and description	
Socializer	Relatedness	Strongly oriented towards others	Desire of being part of a group, want to interact with others and create social connections; values interaction itself
Philanthropist	Purpose		Are altruistic and willing to give without expecting a reward
Achiever	Mastery	Like to win, driven by progress, may be self-centered	Looking for overcoming challenging obstacles, completing every possible task, learning new skills, reaching 100%, the reward is seen in a feeling of mastery
Player	Extrinsic reward		Focusing on extrinsic rewards, which they gain through a variety of strategies
Free Spirit	Autonomy	Creative, value independence, tend to be self-centered	Looking for self-expression and act without external control, reward lies in finding one's way within the given boundaries
Disruptor	Change		Tend to disrupt either directly or through others to force negative or positive changes, like to test the boundaries and try to push further, reward lies in the triggering of change

Sources Diamond et al. (2015) and Steinherr and Reinelt (2022)

3 Research Design

In this work, we follow the Design Science Research Paradigm (DSR) to ensure a structured and scientifically grounded approach (Hevner 2007). Our aim is to create a digital artifact in co-creation with the target audience supported by expert interviews while evaluating its impact on motivation (Grönroos and Voima 2013; Ryan and Deci 2000b). That way, we generate knowledge about an existing problem and its practical solution (Hevner et al. 2004). We follow the five steps from *problem awareness* to *conclusion* as suggested by Kuechler and Vaishnavi (2012). Our focus lies on deriving hexad archetype-specific design features for learning in further education and their instantiation in a PCA-enhanced WBT to address the lack of motivational personalization (*problem awareness*). To tackle this issue, we aim to create a PCA embedded into a WBT unit that is tailored to the learner's motivational archetype (*suggestion*). We derive matching design features from literature grounding our scientific knowledge base, from interviews with 11 experts on hexad user types to decipher design recommendations, and from a workshop where the target audience (employed further education students) discusses what motivates them in IT-supported learning while proposing concrete features from their practical perspective. We then develop a Figma prototype complementing the current WBT (*development*) that embeds *rigor* from the literature and expert interviews while also ensuring *relevance* (Hevner 2007).

Regarding the **expert interviews** that lasted 45–60 min, we followed a semi-structured interview approach. We interviewed eleven German-speaking experts who had engaged with hexad types in literature and had also practically implemented them in project work or conceptual prototypes. We divided the interviewees into five groups, each focusing on two closely linked hexad archetypes in learning (Steinherr and Reinelt 2022), namely Free Spirits and Disruptors (FD), Achievers and Players (AP) and Socializers and Philanthropists (SP) to generate more detailed results. Each interviewee is attributed an ID, for example, "I1FD" represents interviewee 1 from the focus group on Free Spirits and Disruptors. We discussed practical design suggestions for motivational PCAs to support a WBT learning unit with the experts. We explored tangible situations such as motivating learners to initiate the WBT, assessing knowledge in a quiz, reviewing learning material, or collaborating with peers in the digital environment to be addressed by matching features. We transcribed and coded all interviews in terms of (de)- motivational aspects for each archetype and resulting design recommendations and features (Mayring 2020).

For the creative **workshop** on desired design features, we involved a class majoring in business management consisting of 18 students from OKS Braunschweig who use WBTs for exam preparation and have some prior experience with PCAs. The objective of guided group discussions was to generate an exchange of ideas on the motivational design of a PCA to be embedded into their WBT used in class. The students (aged 26 on average; working in parallel, diverse in gender and professional backgrounds) were divided into three hexad type groups pairing the same two archetypes as in the interviews. Each group discussion was guided by a moderator and lasted for 45 min, split into two phases. The first phase targeted the general design cues of motivational PCAs, while the second phase transferred these into design features specified for each archetype. To speed up quickly, we gave the student teams one minute to collect their own ideas before pairing up to then compiling them together in another two minutes. Finally, each team presented and evaluated their ideas in front of the whole group. In the second phase, each team ranked their brainstormed hexad-type-specific features in terms of their relevance to motivate in the given context.

We afterward designed a **Figma Prototype** that combines the findings from the studies and instantiates these with design features adaptable to each hexad type. Three months after the creative workshop, we presented the implemented artifact to the same class of further education students preparing for an exam on the WBT's learning unit on balance sheets to review our instantiation. In a within-subject design (comparing the original WBT with our prototypical enrichment) with 17 students, we measured a potential increase in extrinsic and intrinsic motivation (Amabile et al. 1994) after learning with the revised WBT *(evaluation)* to then deduct our final design recommendations (*conclusion*). We surveyed students' motivation decomposed to the scales for compilation, outward, enjoyment, and challenge on a 7-point Likert scale (1 = strongly disagree; …; 7 = strongly agree) as suggested by Amabile (1994). We integrated reversed labeled items into the survey to check participants' attention. Moreover, we gathered qualitative feedback on the PCA-enhanced WBT in an open discussion to collect more information on learners' requirements regarding the actual implementation (i.e., potential adaptivity of the hexad types; usage context, general feedback, and further ideas).

4 Results

4.1 Findings from Literature

In their 2022 published literature review on the use of hexad types in different domains, Steinherr and Reinhelt identified 26 scientific papers, but only three of those relate to the field of education. These cover gamified Information Systems to teach programming (Ardiana and Loekito 2020), physics (Amado and Roleda 2010) or scale the archetypes (Tondello et al. 2016), but do neither tackle PCAs in learning nor students in further education. Though, understanding the type and character of the learner is one of the most important factors influencing the success of educational programs in general, regardless of whether they are based on information systems or not (Ertan and Kocadere 2022; Huang 2012). Incorporating gamification elements that are tailored to hexad user types in information systems has been shown to increase user motivation and engagement, with varying effects based on the user's hexad type (Passalacqua et al. 2021). Moreover, existing literature offers design recommendations for gaming elements that effectively cater to the distinct hexad types. For instance, introducing progressive levels can motivate *achievers,* while allowing *players* to earn experience points or coins to foster their engagement (Ertan and Kocadere 2022). Offering certificates for achievers and allowing *free spirits* to explore and find hidden surprises on their own are also suggested (Câmara and Pinto de Lima 2021). For *disruptors*, creating closed groups and chats for exchanging ideas can be effective (Böckle and Kwaku 2019), while *socializers* are motivated by open social constructs such as online communities that foster social exchange. *Philanthropists*, on the other hand, become motivated by opportunities to give something to others or to share their knowledge with them (Passalacqua et al. 2021). Although the hexad user types and their associated gaming elements (Tondello et al. 2016) are established in a variety of use cases, they are only gradually penetrating the educational sector to promote student motivation and engagement.

4.2 Design Recommendations from the Expert Interviews

Expert interviews provided insights into the motivating core characteristics of the **Free Spirit and Disruptor**. According to interviewees I1FD, I2FD, and I3FD, the Free Spirit is characterized by decision-making freedom, autonomy, proactivity, and rejection of boundaries, with the additional trait of being a creative type who tests the system. In contrast, the Disruptor seeks to overcome the limits of a system, using innovative elements and striving for positive (and sometimes negative) change (I1FD, I4FD). To communicate with the Free Spirit, interviewees recommended a more open approach, with the Free Spirit leading the conversation and the PCA responding to their questions (I1FD, I3FD). For the Disruptor, interviewee I2FD suggested intensive communication with the PCA, as the PCA represents an innovative element in the learning context that motivates the Disruptor, and communication can also help the latter identify potential errors. The role of the PCA is to provide support when needed and freedom of choice.

According to the experts, the **Achiever and Player** hexad types, are driven by motivation through rewards and success as their core characteristics (I1AP). The Player, in particular, is mostly motivated by external factors such as competition (I4AP). To achieve better performance than their competitors, the PCA is recommended to offer appropriate rewards (I2AP, 14AP). I1AP also noted that the Player prefers to showcase their successes publicly, while they prefer to remain anonymous in case of failures. The Achiever, on the other hand, seeks to be the best for themselves and not necessarily to be recognized for accomplishments (I2AP, I4AP). For the Achiever, the rewards should always be linked to a real value. For example, achieving a specific performance in a web-based learning context could lead to a grade advantage in a written exam (I1AP, I2AP). In the event of a wrong answer during training, I3AP recommended not deducting points or imposing negative consequences for both archetypes to prevent demotivation. Instead, the PCA should provide additional information to help balance knowledge gaps. The interaction between the PCA and these two archetypes is mostly motivated by rewards and positive feedback.

For the **Philanthropist**, the interviewees primarily described intrinsic motivation through a higher sense of purpose and meaning, without expecting a reward in return. Translated to the learning context, the higher purpose could be, for example, passing on knowledge to other learners (I1SP, I3SP). Similarly, for the **Socializer**, increased intrinsic motivation was mentioned, particularly through interaction with other people and a sense of belonging (I2SP, I3SP). The interviewees extensively explained the function of a group chat as a central design element. This might be moderated by a PCA and should involve a maximum of four to six participants (I2SP) for productive exchange. In this context, it was discussed whether groups should be composed of people with the same or different levels of knowledge. While it was agreed that the Philanthropist prefers to be grouped with people of lower knowledge levels to share their experiences (I2SP), no clear preference was identified for a Socializer. The interviewees also suggested team competitions and jointly working on learning chapters within the group chat to strengthen team spirit (I2SP, I3SP). The role of the PCA in relation to the two hexad types was primarily described in the interviews as mediator. I3SP identified promoting discussions and facilitating idea exchange as the PCA's main task.

4.3 Design Features Proposed in the Workshop by the Target Group

We derived design features by ideating gamification elements based on the specific characteristics of the Hexad types, as outlined in Tondello et al. (2016). For instance, it characterizes the Free Spirit as motivated by autonomy and thus suggests avoiding predetermined content. *The Periodic Table of Gamification Elements* (Marczewski 2015) supports this notion, listing elements like 'Exploration', 'Easter Eggs', and 'Unlockables' for the Free Spirit. Applying these characteristics to the WBT, we aimed to offer Free Spirits the freedom of choice in various features while their creative side is engaged through avatar creation and storytelling, for example. Given that the motivating elements for the different hexad types in the Periodic Table and Tondello's paper (2016) are quite general, we linked features with the ideas collected during the workshop and refined them to be more specific for our particular application. Table 2 represents the final rankings from the creative workshop for each hexad user type pair, whereby features recommended for general implementation (G) are marked, as well as features consistent with the literature (book icon) or suggested by the experts (bubble icon). We suggest an option to deactivate the G features because it might otherwise demotivate certain archetypes. Disruptors get their own top5 ranking (1-D to 5-D), since they differed clearly from Free Spirits, so we decided against their compilation.

In line with the literature and the interviewed experts, students of the Free Spirit and Disruptor group suggested individual customization and feedback. The Players

Table 2 Proposed design features and their ranking

Rank	Free spirit and disruptor	Player and achiever	Socializer and philanthropist
1	Layout adaption (**G**)	Quiz duel	Interact in network
2	Avatar creation (**G**)	Comparison with peers	Share something with others (e.g., results, knowledge)
3	Story telling	Ranking	Build teams
4	Select difficulty level	Collect points	Get feedback (result summary) (**G**)
5	Unlock joker	Weekly or daily challenges	Collect trophies
6	1-D finding bugs in WBT	Links to additional material (podcasts, videos, help button) (**G**)	Interact with peers and PCA (**G**)
7	2-D feedback on the WBT (incl. star rating)	Level/study plan (connected to challenges and PCA) (**G**)	Collaborate with classmates (on learning materials and results)
8	3-d reward finding bugs	Medals	Illustration (**G**)
9	4-D ranking (**G**)		
10	5-D set time limit (**G**)		

and Achievers prioritized direct comparison with other learners and personal challenges, while the group for Socializers and Philanthropists valued exchange with other learners, in various forms such as networking, sharing knowledge, or forming team chats.

4.4 Instantiating the Prototype

We considered elements more strongly for the prototype if they were mentioned more frequently or extensively discussed in the interview and received a high ranking in the workshop. Additionally, we re-evaluated whether the functionality aligned with the motivational needs of the hexad types and the findings from the literature. We then weighed the expected cost–benefit ratio for the implementation and whether the feature should be implemented generically or specifically for a hexad type. Based on this evaluation, we made a selection of features to be implemented. Thereby, the idea for practical implementation is to initially identify the dominant hexad archetype of a student using the hexad user test from Tondello et al. (2016), and subsequently activate suitable features in the WBT.

According to our knowledge base, the most relevant feature for the **Free Spirit** is the selection of an avatar and the unlocking of additional attributes for it (I2FD, I3FD,

I4FD; Rank 2). Another relevant design element for stimulating decision-making is the PCA's question about a username (I1FD, I2FD). This feature was also included in the prototype for the other Hexad types, as the ranking comparison requires a greater set of participants. Furthermore, the PCA's question about an individual layout was mentioned multiple times by interview participants (I2FD, I3FD) and ranked as the most important feature in the workshop. Additionally, the PCA should allow the Free Spirit to freely choose the learning content (I1FD, I2FD, I3FD). Based on the literature (Diamond et al. 2015; Tondello et al. 2016) and interview results (I4FD), we embed an easter egg (here: finding snowflakes to initiate background effects) into the prototype for the Free Spirit to proactively explore the system. The PCA also hands over the choice to display a time limit at the beginning and a ranking after completing the training (I1FD, I2FD). To prevent a decrease of motivation after a wrong answer, the PCA offers whether to repeat the question or to proceed to the next question. Figure 1 depicts selected screenshots of the WBT to illustrate general features in blue and individual features for each hexad type in orange (cf.: https://shorturl.at/qILXY).

The knowledge base suggests that the most relevant feature for the **Disruptor** is the ability to induce changes in the system through the PCA. Therefore, the most important design element is the ability to provide feedback during training. This functionality was mentioned in the literature (Tondello et al. 2016) and suggested in the interviews (I2FD, I4FD), while also being ranked first in the workshop. In addition, at the end of the training, the PCA surveys a star rating and qualitative feedback, since it was considered relevant in all three strands (Rank 2; I2FD, I4FD). Subsequently, the PCA should provide feedback on the suggested improvements (I1FD, I4FD). If successfully implemented, according to the interviews (I3FD, I4FD) and the workshop (Rank 3), the Disruptor should receive a reward, such as a joker.

Fig. 1 Screenshots of the prototype

Features such as hiding or showing the time limit were considered less relevant in the workshop (Rank 5).

The highest-priority feature for the **Achievers and Players** was the ability to compete with other learners in the form of a quiz duel. Therefore, the PCA serves as a mediator matching students to compete over several rounds, whereby students try to correctly answer as many multiple-choice questions as possible within a given time frame. After each round, the WBT reveals the correct answers and the winner of the game. This functionality is best suited for the player type, as it allows them to earn points in competitions which is a powerful source of motivation following Tondello et al. (2016). We decided that this feature should be accessible to all learners for more cognitive engagement in learning (Chi and Wylie 2014). Daily or weekly challenges for earning bonus points motivate Players while climbing the rankings, and challenge achievers mastering new tasks. Besides, the PCA interacts proactively, is motivational and highlights progress made and what is needed to reach the next level. A reward system, mentioned multiple times by interview participants and also ranked second and third in the workshop is represented in a ranking list. We implemented it for all hexad types since this collaborative feature needs a strong network. However, settings for the anonymous display of user names and results are available to prevent demotivating effects (Ertan and Kocadere 2022). The ranking list is important for achievers to track their own learning progress (Tondello et al. 2016). To associate the earned points with a value, a reward system was chosen where learners can unlock additional avatars and, after successfully completing all chapters, unlock a special crown for their character. The player can pursue their extrinsic motivation in collecting rewards, while the achiever gets confirmed in competence. The interviews claimed that the acquired items should have value, or they may not be considered desirable. Therefore, we designed unlockable characters as rewards. Despite being mentioned multiple times, our prototype does not adapt to difficulty levels, as it resulted technically too complex.

The interviews, literature, and workshop findings have all demonstrated the importance of networking features for **Socializers and Philanthropists** (Rank 1). In the chapter overview, the WBT displays the number of other learners who are simultaneously active in each chapter and is prompted with a chat message to team up for an exchange. The display (in contrast to the PCA's prompt) is adopted for all archetypes to promote interaction. The prototype features a group chat function (I1SP, I2SP) for Socializers during training and after a quiz, and promotes knowledge exchange across the archetypes. In addition to the group chat function, Philanthropists can share knowledge through by commenting on the quiz questions through the PCA (Rank 2). The Socializer's ability to share results was suggested in both the interview and workshop (I1SP, I3SP) and aligns with motivational theories in the literature. However, it was ultimately omitted from the prototype due to the need for an interface with social media platforms, which would require considerable effort in the implementation process. Similarly, the implementation of a profile page was dismissed (I3SP) as the fellow learners know each other from class, making this element more suitable for larger groups. The concept of rewarding incorrect answers for Philanthropists was rejected (I1SP) as it would affect the evaluation system for all learners and its effectiveness in promoting learning success was dubious. Additionally, the introduction of achievements as a motivator for learning was declined in favor of a higher purpose to motivate Philanthropists (I1SP). This approach was considered more effective given that individuals in this category may already find learning intrinsically motivating.

5 Evaluation

We evaluated our instantiation with 17 students (28 years on average,) of the focus class in a discussion. 12 students (6 female, 6 male) fully completed both surveys to compare the motivational effect of the original WBT in comparison with our hexad-specific instantiation. All of them are regularly using WBTs and have prior experience to PCAs.

5.1 Quantitative Outcomes

To check the applicability of our dataset, we first calculated the reliability of each construct and eliminated items when necessary to exceed the Cronbach's alpha threshold value of 0.7 and push the corrected item scale correlation above 0.3, indicating sufficient reliability (Hair et al. 2014; Nunnally and Bernstein 1994). We also validated the constructs using confirmatory factor analysis (CFA) to exclude items with factor loadings < 0.5. After that, the conditions for average variance extracted (AVE) > 0,5 (Urbach and Ahlemann 2010), composite reliability (CR) > 0,8 (ibid.), KMO values > 0.5 (Kaiser and Rice 1974), explained variance > 50% (Backhaus et al. 1994), and factor loadings > 0.5 (Chin 1998) were met, except for the enjoyment scale (AVE < 0.35; CR < 0.7). Thus, the informative value of this construct is limited.

We then extracted the mean values (MV) and standard deviations (SD) and conducted paired univariate tests (Student's t or Wilcoxon W depending on whether the Shapiro–Wilk test indicates the normal distribution) to check whether the four measured constructs for compilation scale (CS), outward scale (OS), enjoyment scale (ES) and challenge scale (CH) differ significantly ($\alpha = 0.05$) between the original WBT and the one adapted to hexad user types (hexWBT). Table 3 summarizes the results.

The experiment's descriptive data reveal a positive trend on MVs for all four scales in favor of the hexWBT, which was thus rated more motivational than the original WBT. However, the paired univariate tests only show a significant difference for the constructs CH ($p < 0.002$) with a large positive effect ($r = 0.487$) of the motivational features and with a large effect size ($d = 0.836$) on CS ($p < 0.07$) as well. Following Amabile (1994) the added features thus positively influence both intrinsic and extrinsic motivation in learning with the WBT.

Table 3 Quantitative result overview

Factors		Dependent variable	Mean value		Std.	Dev.	df	Statistic	Cohen's d	Rank biserial corr.	*p*
F_1	F_2		F_1	F_2	s_1	s_2					
HexWBT versus WBT		Compensation scale	4.96	4.08	1.03	0.85	11	Student's t	0.836	–	**0.007**
		Outward scale	3.27	3.15	1.40	1.06	11	Student's t	0.112	–	0.353
		Enjoyment scale	5.22	4.92	0.90	1.08	11	Wilcoxon W	–	0.487	0.073
		Challenge scale	3.86	3.29	1.27	1.44	11	Wilcoxon W	–	0.697	**0.022**

Note Bold means: significant for $p <= 0.05$

5.2 *Qualitative Outcomes*

The workshop survey included 17 students, all of whom emphasized the strong motivational effect of the revised WBT. Participants appreciated its motivational elements, noting, "*learning together is more enjoyable*" and another suggesting they could "*learn on the fly*" with the new features because "*it motivates us to make progress collaboratively*".

Regarding the use of the *hexad user scale test* to determine individual hexad types for targeted motivation features, 12 out of 17 participants preferred this approach. However, some participants raised concerns that matching motivational features could depend on the task or the learner's mood besides the archetype, which is consistent with the dimensions for learning adaptivity (Plass and Pawar 2020). As such, they suggested the importance of adaptability in allowing learners to adjust motivational features themselves, with one participant advocating for the "*human in the loop*" approach (Li et al. 2017). Participants also suggested the need for more matching features for collaboration across different hexad types. Several students expressed appreciation that the revised WBT would not become monotonous by challenging them more on the content, and many could imagine using it more frequently. Overall, the survey confirmed the effectiveness of the revised WBT and highlighted the importance of matching motivational features to individual learning styles while still allowing for adaptability.

6 Discussion and Outlook

In our study triangulating expert interviews, literature, and insights from further education students on the intended motivational design of a PCA-supported WBT, we contribute to both research and practice in several ways.

Firstly, we have collected design features to create a motivating WBT that is tailored to the user's hexad type in learning. By triangulating derived design suggestions and instantiating them in a real WBT, we intend to support practitioners with high usability in practical usage. Our prioritized features overlap strongly with recommended hexad features from other contexts, particularly from the gaming industry.

Secondly, we enrich the underrepresented learning context for hexad types and contribute to the increasingly demanded individualization coupled with (e.g., gamified) motivation effects in education (Davies et al. 2021; Passalacqua et al. 2021; Schlimbach et al. 2022). In this regard, we were able to demonstrate statistically significant motivational effects on intrinsic and extrinsic levels in a learning unit on balance sheets mediated by our prototype. The significant differences in the Challenge (CH) and Compilation scales (CS) between both WBTs identical in learning content but manipulated towards hexad features indicate that the hexWBT motivated learners strongly (Amabile et al. 1994) to invest more effort, time, and energy in learning the accounting content (CS) and to take on the challenge of the tasks (CH). However, the Enjoyment (ES) and Outward scales (OS) did not show significant differences between the prototypes, which contradicts the probands' qualitative feedback that their enjoyment and feelings of recognition actually did increase while completing the learning tasks. This discrepancy might be statistically linked back to the low AVE and CR for ES and should thus be further investigated in a repeated study. OS might be blurred by the upcoming exam because students were already strongly extrinsically motivated to pass it with a good grade so that it was hard to further increase OS. Overall, coupled qualitative feedback and statistical results indicate that applying the hexad model with modified features for learning can enhance learners' motivation in WBT usage.

Thirdly, we have strongly incorporated requirements and gathered empowering feedback from further education students as our target group acted as co-creators (Grönroos and Voima 2013). In the course of this collaborative approach, some students raised concerns that the WBT may ignore the students' emotional state, the nature of the learning task, or other context parameters and thus make wrong decisions on the most appropriate hexad features in that specific situation. This requirement of contextualization is in line with recent literature (Şenocak et al. 2021; van der Zandt et al. 2021). Students thus express a preference for the adaptability of the tool with pre-assigned recommendations as a managerial implication. This contrasts with current research that emphasizes the adaptivity of digital tools over adaptability (Plass and Pawar 2020; Schlimbach et al. 2022).

Fourthly, we implicitly address the recent disruption of chatbots in the learning context, such as ChatGPT, since our initial contribution opens up a new research field on how the currently functional disruptive technology could be enriched with motivational and collaborative elements. As claimed by the students, the embedded PCA encourages collaboration among students across archetypes and fosters engagement as predicted by the motivational drivers of the self-determination theory (Ryan and Deci 2000a). These findings align with previous research indicating that incorporating team elements facilitates community building (Aldemir et al. 2018) and foster social relatedness by giving students a common goal (Sailer et al. 2017). Mechanisms for competition and collaboration need to be balanced to counteract the otherwise demotivating effects of competition (Ertan and Kocadere 2022). Despite their potential, personalized motivational features are still largely underrepresented in PCAs, since the adaptation of cognitive variables dominates (Schlimbach et al. 2022)—a gap that needs to be addressed.

In summary, our study has shown the potential of using hexad user types to personalize WBTs to increase motivation. However, limitations in our study include not measuring students' actual hexad archetypes, a limited sample size and the evaluation with a low-fidelity prototype. Future research could explore the impact of individual hexad design features on each archetype's motivation and learning outcomes in a more mature application (i.e., with AI-enabled activation of matching features), while also considering that most learners embody a combination of these archetypes. Overall, the potential for personalized, motivational learning tools through the application of the hexad model presents an exciting area for future research.

Acknowledgements We would like to thank the master students Charlotte Koopmann, Niels Meinhardt, Paula Philipp and Seyma Sapmaz for their valuable insights and constant support in this research project, as well as the students from Oskar Kämmer Schule Braunschweig for participating in this study. Our research is funded by the German Federal Ministry of Education and Research (BMBF); Grant # 21INVI06.

References

Aldemir, T., Celik, B., & Kaplan, G. (2018). A qualitative investigation of student perceptions of game elements in a gamified course. *Computers in Human Behavior, 78*, 235–254. https://doi.org/10.1016/j.chb.2017.10.001.

Amabile, T. M., Hill, K. G., Hennessey, B. A., & Tighe, E. M. (1994). The Work Preference Inventory: Assessing intrinsic and extrinsic motivational orientations. *Journal of Personality and Social Psychology, 66*, 950–967. https://doi.org/10.1037/0022-3514.66.5.950.

Amado, C. M., & Roleda, L. S. (2010). Game Element Preferences and Engagement of Different Hexad Player Types in a Gamified Physics Course. *Proceedings of the 2020 11th International Conference on E-Education, E-Business, E-Management, and E-Learning*, 261–267. https://doi.org/10.1145/3377571.3377610.

Ardiana, D., & Loekito, L. (2020). Gamification design to improve student motivation on learning object-oriented programming. *Journal of Physics: Conference Series, 1516*. https://doi.org/10.1088/1742-6596/1516/1/012041.

Backhaus, K., Erichson, B., Plinke, W., & Weiber, R. (1994). *Multivariate Analysemethoden Eine anwendungsorientierte Einführung*. Springer Verlag. https://doi.org/10.1007/978-3-662-12552-6.

Bartle, R. (1996). Hearts, clubs, diamonds, spades: Players who suit MUDs. *Journal of Multi-User Dungeons Research, 1*(1).

Berehil, M. (2022). Boosting Students Motivation Through Gamified Hybrid Learning Environments Bleurabbit Case Study. *Smart Innovation, Systems and Technologies, 237*, 561–576. Scopus. https://doi.org/10.1007/978-981-16-3637-0_40.

Böckle, M., & Kwaku, Y.-A. (2019). Designing at the Intersection of Gamification and Persuasive Technology to Incentivize Energy-Saving. *Digital Transformation for a Sustainable Society in the 21st Century: 18th IFIP WG 6.11 Conference on e-Business, e-Services, and e-Society, I3E 2019, Trondheim, Norway, September 18–20, 2019, Proceedings*, 316–328. https://doi.org/10.1007/978-3-030-29374-1_26.

Busch, M., Mattheiss, E., Orji, R., Fröhlich, P., Lankes, M., & Tscheligi, M. (2016). Player Type Models. *Proceedings of the 2016 CHI Conference Extended Abstracts on Human Factors in Computing Systems*. https://www.academia.edu/24953974/Player_Type_Models_Towards_Empirical_Validation.

Câmara, L., & Pinto de Lima, A. (2021). *Gamification of Mobile Applications as a Tool for Optimising the Experience of Museums. 2015*(SIST), 185–198.

Chi, M. T. H., & Wylie, R. (2014). The ICAP Framework: Linking Cognitive Engagement to Active Learning Outcomes. *Educational Psychologist, 49*(4), 219–243. https://doi.org/10.1080/00461520.2014.965823.

Chin, W. W. (1998). The partial least squares approach for structural equation modeling. In *Modern methods for business research*. (pp. 295–336). Lawrence Erlbaum Associates Publishers.

Davies, J. N., Verovko, M., Verovko, O., & Solomakha, I. (2021). *Personalization of e-learning process using AI-powered chatbot integration: Vol. 1265 AISC* (p. 216). Scopus. https://doi.org/10.1007/978-3-030-58124-4_20.

Diamond, L., Nacke, L., Tondello, G., Tscheligi, M., & Marczewski, A. (2015). *The HEXAD Gamification User Types Questionnaire: Background and Development Process*.

Ertan, K., & Kocadere, S. A. (2022). *Gamification Design to Increase Motivation in Online Learning Environments: Systematic Review*. 7(2), 151–159.

Grönroos, C., & Voima, P. (2013). Critical Service Logic: Making Sense of Value Creation and Co-Creation. *Journal of the Academy of Marketing Science, 41*, 133–150. https://doi.org/10.1007/s11747-012-0308-3.

Hair, J. F., Black, W. C., Babin, B. J., & Anderson, R. E. (2014). *Multivariate data analysis* (J. F. Hair, Ed.; 7. ed., Pearson new internat. ed). Pearson.

Hevner, A. R. (2007). A Three Cycle View of Design Science Research. *Scandinavian Journal of Information Systems, 19*, 7.

Hevner, A., R, A., March, S., T, S., Park, Park, J., Ram, & Sudha. (2004). Design Science in Information Systems Research. *Management Information Systems Quarterly, 28*, 75–106.

Hobert, S., & Meyer von Wolff, R. (2019). Say Hello to Your New Automated Tutor – A Structured Literature Review on Pedagogical Conversational Agents. *Wirtschaftsinformatik 2019 Proceedings*. https://aisel.aisnet.org/wi2019/track04/papers/2.

Huang, C.-M. (2012). Designing effective behaviors for educational embodied agents. *Proceedings of the 2012 ACM Annual Conference Extended Abstracts on Human Factors in Computing Systems Extended Abstracts - CHI EA'12*, 931. https://doi.org/10.1145/2212776.2212868.

Kaiser, H. F., & Rice, J. (1974). Little Jiffy, Mark Iv. *Educational and Psychological Measurement, 34*(1), 111–117. https://doi.org/10.1177/001316447403400115.

Khosrawi-Rad, B., Rinn, H., Schlimbach, R., Gebbing, P., Yang, X., Lattemann, C., Markgraf, D., & Robra-Bissantz, S. (2022, June 18). Conversational Agents in Education – A Systematic Literature Review. *ECIS 2022 Proceedings*. https://aisel.aisnet.org/ecis2022_rp/18.

Kuechler, W., & Vaishnavi, V. (2012). A Framework for Theory Development in Design Science Research: Multiple Perspectives. *J. Assoc. Inf. Syst.* https://doi.org/10.17705/1jais.00300.

Li, J., Miller, A. H., Chopra, S., Ranzato, M., & Weston, J. (2017). *Dialogue learning with human-in-the-loop*. 5th International Conference on Learning Representations, ICLR 2017 - Conference Track Proceedings. Scopus.

Marczewski, A. (2015). *Even Ninja Monkeys Like to Play* (Univorn Edition). Gamified UK. https://www.gamified.uk/even-ninja-monkeys-like-to-play/amp/.

Mayring, P. (2020). Qualitative Forschungsdesigns. In G. Mey & K. Mruck (Eds.), *Handbuch Qualitative Forschung in der Psychologie: Band 2: Designs und Verfahren* (pp. 3–17). Springer Fachmedien. https://doi.org/10.1007/978-3-658-26887-9_18.

Monterrat, B., Desmarais, M., Lavoué, E., & George, S. (2015). A Player Model for Adaptive Gamification in Learning Environments. *Proceedings of the 17th International Conference on Artificial Intelligence in Education.* (AIED 2015), Madrid, Spain. https://doi.org/10.1007/978-3-319-19773-9_30.

Morisano, D., Hirsh, J. B., Peterson, J. B., Pihl, R. O., & Shore, B. M. (2010). Setting, elaborating, and reflecting on personal goals improves academic performance. *Journal of Applied Psychology, 95*(2), 255.

Ngwacho, G. A. (2023). *Online Teaching Competencies for Efficacious Competency-Based Implementation in Higher Education* (online-teaching-competencies-for-efficacious-competency-based-implementation-in-higher-education). IGI Global. https://www.igi-global.com/gateway/chapter/www.igi-global.com/gateway/chapter/318580.

Nunnally, J., & Bernstein, I. (1994). *Psychometric Theory 3rd edition (MacGraw-Hill, New York).*

Passalacqua, M., Sylvain Senecal, P. D., Fredette, M., Nacke, L., Pellerin, R., & Leger, P.-M. (2021). Should Gamification be Personalized? A Self-deterministic Approach. *AIS Transactions on Human-Computer Interaction, 13*(3), 265–286. https://doi.org/10.17705/1thci.00150.

Patel, N. P., Parikh, D. R., Patel, D. A., & Patel, R. R. (2019). AI and Web-Based Human-Like Interactive University Chatbot (UNIBOT). *2019 3rd International Conference on Electronics, Communication and Aerospace Technology (ICECA)*, 148–150. https://doi.org/10.1109/ICECA.2019.8822176.

Pink, D. H. (2011). *Drive: The Surprising Truth About What Motivates Us* (Reprint edition). Riverhead Books.

Plass, J. L., & Pawar, S. (2020). Toward a taxonomy of adaptivity for learning. *Journal of Research on Technology in Education, 52*(3), 275–300. https://doi.org/10.1080/15391523.2020.1719943.

Rinn, H., Khosrawi-Rad, B., Schlimbach, R., Masurek, M., Robra-Bissantz, S., & Markgraf, D. (2022). *Needs of Students in Further Education - A Mixed Methods Study.*

Ryan, R. M., & Deci, E. L. (2000a). Self-determination theory and the facilitation of intrinsic motivation, social development, and well-being. *American Psychologist, 55*(1), 68–78. https://doi.org/10.1037/0003-066X.55.1.68.

Ryan, R. M., & Deci, E. L. (2000b). Intrinsic and Extrinsic Motivations: Classic Definition and New Directions. *Contemporary Educational Psychology, 25*, 54–67. https://doi.org/10.1006/ceps.1999.1020.

Sailer, M., Hense, J. U., Mayr, S. K., & Mandl, H. (2017). How gamification motivates: An experimental study of the effects of specific game design elements on psychological need satisfaction. *Computers in Human Behavior, 69*, 371–380. https://doi.org/10.1016/j.chb.2016.12.033.

Sakkir, G., Dollah, S., & Ahmad, J. (2021). E-Learning in COVID-19 Situation: Students' Perception. *EduLine: Journal of Education and Learning Innovation, 1*(1), 9–15. https://doi.org/10.35877/454RI.eduline378.

Schlimbach, R., Rinn, H., Markgraf, D., & Robra-Bissantz, S. (2022). A Literature Review on Pedagogical Conversational Agent Adaptation. *PACIS 2022 Proceedings*. https://aisel.aisnet.org/pacis2022/20.

Şenocak, D., Büyük, K., & Bozkurt, A. (2021). Examination of the Hexad User Types and their Relationships with Gender, Game Mode, and Gamification Experience in the Context of Open and Distance Learning. *Online Learning, 25*, 170–186. https://doi.org/10.24059/olj.v25i4.2276.

Steinherr, V. M., & Reinelt, R. (2022). *Using Hexad User Types to Identify Motivational Preferences among Learners.* AMCIS 2022 Proceedings.

Tondello, G. F., Wehbe, R. R., Diamond, L., Busch, M., Marczewski, A., & Nacke, L. E. (2016). The Gamification User Types Hexad Scale. *CHI PLAY'16: Proceedings of the 2016 Annual Symposium on Computer-Human Interaction in Play*, 229–243. https://doi.org/10.1145/2967934.2968082.

Urbach, N., & Ahlemann, F. (2010). Structural equation modeling in information systems research using partial least squares. *Journal of Information Technology Theory and Application (JITTA), 11*(2), 2.

van der Zandt, L., van der Stappen, E., & Van Turnhout, K. (2021). Towards Real-Life Adoption of Conversational Interfaces: Exploring the Challenges in Designing Chatbots That Live up to User Expectations. *Proceedings of the 34th British HCI Conference*, 306–311. https://doi.org/10.13140/RG.2.2.35102.25927/1.

Yin, J., Goh, T.-T., Yang, B., & Xiaobin, Y. (2021). Conversation Technology with Micro-Learning: The Impact of Chatbot-Based Learning on Students' Learning Motivation and Performance. *Journal of Educational Computing Research, 59*(1), 154–177. https://doi.org/10.1177/0735633120952067.

An Integrative Model of AI Competencies for Business Students and Where to Acquire Them

Muhammed-Fatih Kaya, Christopher Zirnig, Marah Blaurock, Felix Zechiel, and Mareike Schoop

Abstract Today, value is created by making use of technologies based on artificial intelligence (AI) in almost all parts of the value chain. Business students need to acquire AI competencies to unleash the full potential of AI in organisations. Therefore, institutions of higher education need to teach AI to business students. The present research aims to identify which AI-related competencies are relevant for business graduates and which courses exist to teach respective skills. To this end, we firstly provide a comprehensive overview of the AI competence demand in today's business world by means of a literature review and a qualitative study. Secondly, we conduct a quantitative study to analyse the curricula of leading universities and online platforms providing AI teaching. The results reveal an AI competence model for business students, an overview of current curriculum offers, and the gaps in current curricula.

Keywords Artificial intelligence · AI competencies · Higher education · AI curriculum · Business students

M.-F. Kaya (✉) · C. Zirnig · M. Blaurock · F. Zechiel · M. Schoop
University of Hohenheim, Stuttgart, Germany
e-mail: Muhammed-Fatih.Kaya@uni-hohenheim.de

C. Zirnig
e-mail: christopher.zirnig@uni-hohenheim.de

M. Blaurock
e-mail: m.blaurock@uni-hohenheim.de

F. Zechiel
e-mail: felix.zechiel@uni-hohenheim.de

M. Schoop
e-mail: Schoop@uni-hohenheim.de

D. Beverungen et al. (eds.), *Transforming the Digitally Sustainable Enterprise*, Lecture Notes in Information Systems and Organisation 76,
https://doi.org/10.1007/978-3-031-80125-9_27

1 Introduction

Economic development is increasingly geared towards the digitalisation of business processes to assert in the global competition for sales markets (Dörr et al. 2021; Kagermann 2015). Across industries, value is created more and more by making use of technologies based on artificial intelligence (AI) (Wamba-Taguimdje et al. 2020). The term AI is used as an umbrella term that encompasses a variety of different technologies which enable machines to mimic human intelligence. As a result, AI applications can nowadays perform tasks that used to require human intelligence. Utilising AI technologies in organisations promises efficiency gains and is crucial for staying competitive. However, to make profitable use of AI in today's techno-centric business world, organisations need employees with AI competencies (Åström et al. 2022). Ideally, employees have both the required technical knowledge and the necessary business skills. In reality, such employees do not always exist. Therefore, the missing skills should be acquired. In this paper, we focus on business students as well as on information systems students and industrial engineering students with business courses; all of them need to be able to integrate their domain knowledge with AI principles. Due to the business-related nature of these degree programmes, all of the above students are referred to as business students for the sake of simplicity. Graduates of these programmes need fundamental AI knowledge to understand AI-enriched business processes and to be able to transform current developments into business value in a value-adding way. In addition to technical expertise, knowledge is required of how to evaluate, operate and manage technical systems in organisational processes and working environments on a permanent basis. To perform such tasks, it is crucial for business students to have an opportunity to acquire such competencies (Chen 2022). However, as of now, there is no clear framework that integrates relevant AI competencies focusing on business students with courses that are offered at higher education institutions.

The aim of this research is twofold. Firstly, we analyse which AI competencies are relevant for business students to meet the requirements of today's business reality (i.e., demand analysis). Secondly, we provide an overview of the status quo of teaching AI competencies in higher education and identify gaps (i.e., market analysis). The following two research questions will thus be answered: (1) *What are relevant AI-related competencies for business students?* and (2) *To what extent do universities meet the current demand?*

Two studies were conducted to answer the research questions, namely (1) a literature review paired with a qualitative study and (2) a quantitative market analysis. The first study (1) represents the basis for our AI competencies model for business graduates. In contrast to existing competencies models, the AI competencies are specifically geared towards business students and aligned with the current demands in the workplace. The model offers a comprehensive overview of relevant AI competencies for business students and their interrelationships. In our second study (2), AI courses offered by the top-ranked universities in the Times Higher Education (THE) ranking, online learning platforms and selected universities are analysed and categorised to find out to what degree AI competencies are covered and what kind of competence types of AI knowledge are being taught. Considering different platforms provides important insight to the question whether certain competencies are more likely to be represented or underrepresented in certain outlets. Finally, we highlight possible gaps between supply and demand and suggest how to close these gaps.

2 Scientific Background

2.1 AI-Related Competencies and Competence Fields

The International Organization for Standardization defines competencies as "the ability to apply knowledge and skills to achieve intended results" (ISO 2015, p. 27). In addition to this broad definition, we follow Vuorikari et al. (2022, p. 3) in defining competencies as "a combination of knowledge, skills, and attitudes, in other words, they are composed of concepts and facts (i.e., knowledge), descriptions of skills (e.g., the ability to carry out processes), and attitudes (e.g., a disposition, a mindset to act)". Knowledge is developed through the assimilation of information in learning processes and represents "the body of facts, principles, theories and practices that is related to a field of work or study" (ibid.). Skills are described as "the ability to apply knowledge and use know-how to complete tasks and solve problems and can be clustered in cognitive (involving the use of logical, intuitive and creative thinking) or practical (involving manual dexterity and the use of methods, materials, tools and instruments) skills" (ibid.). Finally, attitude is essentially the motivator of continued competent performance and is affected by an individual's "values, aspirations and priorities" (ibid.).

We follow Ferrari (2012) in defining AI-related competencies as a combination of knowledge, skills and attitudes that are required when AI is used or is to be used in the future in companies to perform tasks and as part of their own business model or innovate business models. Additionally, we define competence fields as a combination of competencies in a specific application area. Therefore, synonyms could be competence dimension or competence area.

2.2 DigComp 2.2

The Digital Competence Framework for Citizens 2.2. (DigComp 2.2) is the central digital competence model in the European Union and facilitates a mutual understanding of digital competence, thus creating a framework for developing education programs for digital competences (Vuorikari et al. 2022). DigComp consists of five competence areas, namely information and data literacy, communication and collaboration, digital content creation, safety and problem solving. The five competence areas are composed of 21 competence areas highlighting knowledge, skills and attitudes required for AI (Vuorikari et al. 2022).

3 Methodology

To answer our research questions, we followed a comprehensive research agenda. First, to identify relevant AI-related competencies for business students (i.e., demand analysis), we conducted a literature review and qualitative study. Second, we leveraged a quantitative approach to map which educational opportunities are currently offered in the marked comparing offers from different universities and online platforms (i.e., market analysis).

3.1 Qualitative Study to Identify Demanded AI-Related Competencies

Through comparative discussion and differentiation of DigComp 2.2 from other competence models (i.e., Blumberg and Kauffeld 2021; Dörr et al. 2021; Franken et al. 2022; Teuber et al. 2022; Vuorikari et al. 2022) identified through a comprehensive literature review, we identify five AI-specific competence areas, which provide the basis for our qualitative study.

1. *Basic Knowledge and Skills*: General technological and mathematical competencies on a higher education level. This includes basic knowledge of machine learning functions and AI design, basic programming skills and data literacy.
2. *AI Innovation*: Entrepreneurship or business development competencies to leverage the opportunities of AI-based technologies.
3. *AI Transformation (strategic)*: Competencies that allow managers to transform organisations into data-centric organisations with *data-first* approaches to process development.
4. *AI Management (operational)*: In contrast to AI transformation, the competence "AI management" contains the development of management practices for AI applications in organisations (including internal processes such as data management).
5. *AI Implications*: Evaluation of AI-based products and services, but also processes and business models from different perspectives by considering perspectives of all relevant stakeholders:

    - *Ethical* (e.g., following ethical actions): ethical aspects of AI are often context-related (e.g., picture recognition vs. face recognition). Additionally, ethics will be decisive for AI market value.

- *Ecological* (e.g., greenhouse gas emissions, green IT).
- *Social* (e.g., working conditions, change of social behaviour, health management).

In a next step, we put the findings obtained through our literature review to the practical test. By conducting 14 qualitative, semi-structured interviews with expert practitioners, we increased our understanding of which competencies are in demand regarding the use and handling of AI systems in practice and where previous deficits regarding employees and their training are to be located. We defined the profile of fitting interviewees for our research aim as follows: Experts from practice who manage interdisciplinary AI projects and/or have an overview of required competencies in such teams. Alternatively, employees of organisations that sell AI products or business angels who invest in AI business models as they have a great overview of the AI knowledge status quo. We approached experts from industries that most commonly leverage AI technologies and/or are disrupted by AI technology (Dwivedi et al. 2021) and that are popular employers for business students; this was based on analysing alumni surveys. 14 practitioners from seven different industries and in different positions agreed to an interview. All interviewees work in business organisations, consulting firms or trade unions and hold various positions with in-depth insights into (1) digital transformation, particularly with a focus on AI and its use, and (2) the requirements regarding AI competencies for (new) employees. These include experts in IT departments, project management or data analytics. Most experts were male (13 male; 1 female). Interviews were conducted online via Zoom and lasted about 60 minutes on average. The interview guide was based on our research questions and contained main questions as well as follow-up questions (DiCicco-Bloom and Crabtree 2006). After the interviewer provided information about data anonymity, the interview started with warm-up questions (e.g., about interviewees' position in their company) (Holstein and Gubrium 2020). Then four questions were discussed to identify important AI-related competencies for business graduates (e.g., what are the biggest challenges in AI-based projects in interdisciplinary teams in which business graduates are represented or are led by them? Which competence gaps lead to problems?). In a last part, we presented the practitioners with our preliminarily identified AI-competencies (i.e., Technological Basics, AI Innovation, AI Transformation, AI Management, AI Implications) and asked them if they found them relevant in practice and if so to what extent. Finally, we asked participants if any aspect was missing in our model.

All interviews were transcribed related to a priori defined transcription rules before being analysed based on an inductive, thematic template analysis (King 2004) using MAXQDA. Our literature-based initial competencies served as a priori codes. We leveraged hierarchical coding by using the competencies as higher-order codes (e.g., AI Innovation) and underlying aspects as lower-order codes (e.g., "Evaluating market value of AI-business models"). This effort led to five initial higher-order categories; in the process of analysing the data, we also allowed to add codes to the initial template that did not fit the initial codes (ibid.) to further expand our competence model. After the first round of coding, the research team discussed their coding and adapted the template; any inconsistencies were resolved by consensus. Finally, all material was coded again by a different member of the research team (Rust and Cooil 1994).

3.2 Quantitative Study to Identify Educational Offers to Obtain AI-Related Competencies

To answer our second research question and to assess which educational opportunities are currently offered in the field of AI, we conducted a two-fold analysis. To gather a valid, representative, and complementary sample of courses, we first chose to include the curricula of the top 8 AI universities worldwide according to the Times Higher Education World University Rankings (in the following THE-ranking): Oxford University, California Institute of Technology, Harvard University, Stanford University, Technical University of Munich, Ludwig-Maximilians University Munich, Humboldt University Berlin, University of Tübingen. The THE ranking is particularly well-suited as a benchmark, as it is used and followed worldwide (Times-Higher-Education 2022). Moreover, with nearly one-third of criteria included in the evaluation, it has a strong focus on "teaching" in the evaluation of universities (Ross 2017). In addition, four selected German universities were considered to ensure the regional perspective regarding offered AI competencies and to derive actionable implications for the German higher education landscape (i.e., University of Bayreuth, University of Hohenheim, Karlsruhe Institute of Technology and Frankfurt University of Applied Sciences). The two-fold analysis enables the comparison between national and international offers. For the selection of online learning platforms whose online courses we analysed, we were guided by the largest and most widely used platforms namely edX, Udemy and Coursera (Cooke 2022).

To determine relevant AI-specific modules, a systematic search was conducted using the following search string: "AI" OR "Artificial Intelligence" OR "DL" OR "Deep Learning" OR "ML" OR "Machine Learning" OR "Data Science" OR "* Mining". This search string was applied to various module catalogues of various study programs. Furthermore, a list of associated institute homepages of universities was searched to derive further AI-relevant modules. To analyse the data of the university search, the module name, the corresponding module description, learning goals, the type of course (i.e., lecture, tutorial, seminar), the participating study programs and the intended degree were documented. In the case of the online platforms, the platform name, the learning objectives, the target group, a brief description of the specified course, the title of the course, the costs and further information about the required prior knowledge were recorded.

We analysed the results obtained in each search in detail and categorised the collected data. The categories were based on the results of our qualitative study which revealed four main competence fields that mark necessary AI-related competencies for business students (i.e., basic knowledge and skills with relation to AI, AI Innovation, AI Management & Transformation, AI Reflection).

4 Results

4.1 AI Competencies Model

The results presented in this chapter derive from combining the competence fields based on our literature review with the empirical data from the interviews (study 1). A visualisation of the resulting competence model is depicted in Fig. 1.

First, as a foundation, higher mathematics/statistics competencies are necessary for any kind of intervention in AI-related projects. Those consist of *basic knowledge and skills* of machine learning functions and AI design, as well as basic programming skills and data literacy.

Second, *AI Innovation* describes the identification, evaluation, and design of AI-based products, services, processes or business models within and outside of the organisation. As such managers understand what added value AI brings to the organisation and what problems it solves. Hence, use case identification is important. An interviewee brings up the following example: "*For example, cloud applications, what do they mean economically? The business side has to be evaluated*" (Interviewee 4).

Third, we define the competence field of *AI Transformation* as developing the data-centric organisational structures to leverage the potential of AI in a (data-driven) organisation. This includes defining roles and responsibilities as well as installing change management and provide digital infrastructures. As an interviewee explains:

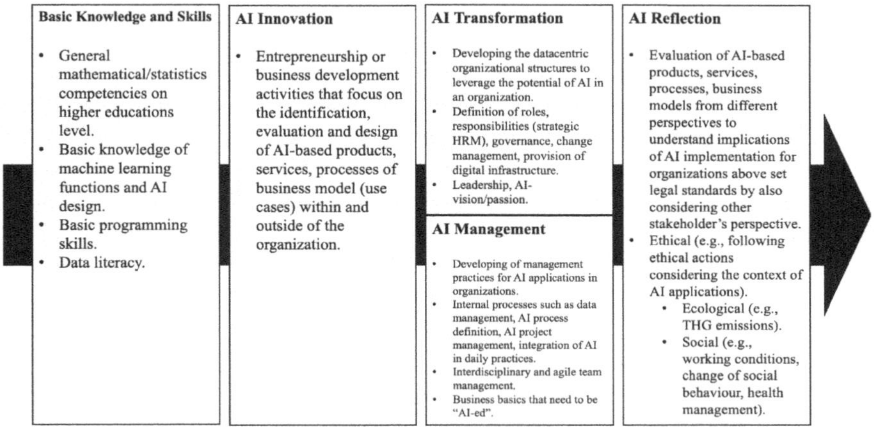

Fig. 1 AI competencies model

"*Transformation management is an absolute core requirement. Business model development is also part of it for me, being able to build the organisational structure behind it*" (Interviewee 4).

Hence, the competence field also includes leadership with AI vision and AI passion. If the organisation doesn't grow with its digital strategies, it cannot change successfully because the whole team has to be taken into account and responsibilities must be allocated in order to support the product development. This cannot be limited to a small section of the organisation or making single tasks easier, but entire processes across departments.

Next, *AI Management* is defined as developing management practices for AI applications in organisations, e.g., internal processes such as data management, AI process definition, AI project management, integration of AI into daily practice, interdisciplinary and agile team management. These competencies are needed when AI is already in use and operational activities need to be organized and managed. The competencies are based on standard business competencies but need to be "AI-ed" for AI-related projects. One interviewee explains the implication: "*With AI, a lot of disciplines have to work together. You have to have the ability for change processes, new thinking and innovation—in other words, creative technology, which probably also interests many people in economics*" (Interviewee 3).

AI-technologies need special, interdisciplinary expertise due to their complexity and also, they have the potential to change work environments completely (Kagermann 2015). Therefore, project management of AI projects requires a different set of competencies than non-AI-related projects. Management practices for AI applications need to be installed and with those internal processes such as data management, AI process definition and the integration of AI in daily practices needs managing. Also, more so than usual, interdisciplinary teams need to be formed and managed.

Finally, we define the competence *AI Reflection* as the knowledge, skills and abilities to evaluate AI-based products/services/processes/business models from different perspectives to understand implications of AI implementation for organisations above set legal standards also considering other stakeholder's perspectives. For example, ethical aspects are always context related. Image recognition and classifying a defect in semiconductor manufacturing, is straightforward in terms of ethics. However, face recognition on the street is more ethically complex. The two examples can consist of the same algorithm. Subsequently, ethics will decide over the market value of AI applications, as one interviewee puts it: "*If one designs a product in order to sell it, then there must be certain aspects considered: convenience, design, a certain elegance and so on. And in the future, when, for example, robots that move autonomously, AI controlled, then it absolutely needs to build in moral approaches and we do well to build in ethical stakes as well*" (Interviewee 7).

4.2 Existing AI Teaching Offers

75 relevant courses from the selected German universities, 154 relevant courses from top universities accroding to the THE-ranking and 130 relevant courses on online learning platforms were the result of our market analysis (study 2). As shown in Fig. 2, the courses are divided into four categories: Basic knowledge and skills, AI Innovation, AI Management and Transformation, and ethical, social and legal implications as part of AI Reflection.

The pie charts in Fig. 3 present the internal ratio of the four competence categories of the three course sources.

It shows that the competence group of Basic Knowledge and Skills represent the clear majority of competencies across all three sources, especially for the top universities from the world university ranking (with 64%) as well as for the online learning platforms (with 56%). They also take a primary role regarding the selected

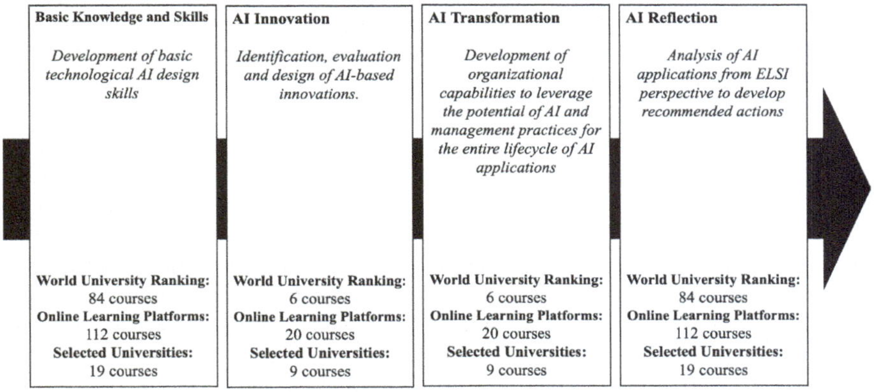

Fig. 2 Competence categories of relevant AI courses

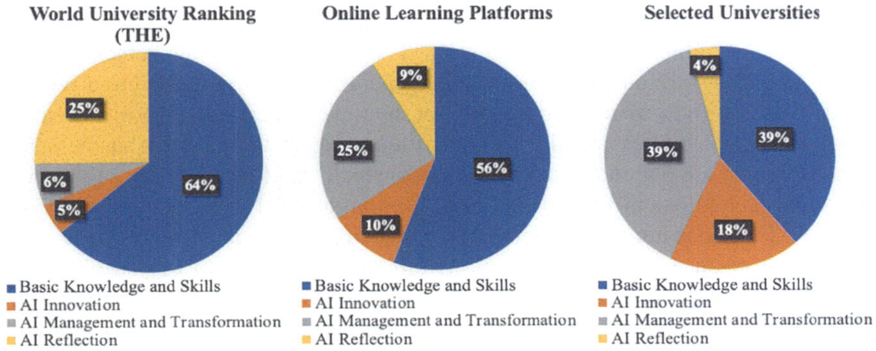

Fig. 3 Distribution of the relevant courses among the four competence categories

German universities (with 39%). Nevertheless, the share of competencies from AI Management and AI Transformation is just as big as the Basic Knowledge and Skills in the case of selected German universities. This shows that AI Management and AI Transformation topics might have a special importance at participating universities. A similar observation could be made for the online learning platforms. 25% of the competencies from considered online learning platforms could be assigned to the AI Management and Transformation category. This finding shows that online learning platforms also offer competencies on AI Management and Transformation in addition to a significant proportion of Basic Knowledge and Skills. A further focus on the competencies derived from the THE-ranking list shows a different picture. Here, competencies assigned to the AI Reflection category follow the Basic Knowledge and Skills with a share of 25%. However, the pie charts reflect that this is the only exception. AI Reflection competencies only appear in the minority by taking the participating universities and online learning platforms into consideration (see Fig. 3). Finally, the area of AI Innovation shows a relatively clear picture for the competencies derived from the THE ranking list and the online learning platforms. While competencies from AI Innovation are at least represented in the THE rankings (with only 5%), only 10% of the competencies can be assigned to this category in the online learning platforms.

5 Discussion

To answer our research questions, we conducted a qualitative and quantitative study. First, through a qualitative study paired with a literature review, we identify five overarching AI competence fields (i.e., basic AI knowledge and skills, AI Innovation, AI Management, AI Transformation, AI Reflection) which we organize in one, integrative framework (see Fig. 1). While we use DigComp 2.2 as a general basis for our model, our competence fields differ from DigComp 2.2 in specifically identifying AI competencies for business graduates and members of business organisations whereas DigComp 2.2 focuses on competencies for citizens. By analysing the qualitative data, we enriched our definitions with insights from the field. For example, practitioners made us aware of the importance of a clear vision and priority management of data driven/AI-based solutions throughout value generation. Managers need to drive AI-based initiative, show vision and passion for the topic, otherwise AI-projects easily are being neglected after a while. The practitioners argue that in daily business AI-initiatives often are put on top of regular tasks which, as of now, are smoothly done with older technological solutions. Employees might need to be convinced of the merit of AI-based solutions for their jobs and the importance needs to be made clear regularly to reach the full potential of AI-initiatives. This is not only true for the start of an AI initiative but also after implementation when input data and prediction models need to be maintained (Reim et al. 2020).

Moreover, our results reveal that practitioners mostly seem to look for candidates with a business background who bring basic AI competencies in all fields. Rather than having more in-depth experience in e.g., one particular programming language, practitioners seem to look for candidates who have a clear (basic) understanding of the mechanism of AI-based technology and the possibility of value creation using AI, what prerequisites are necessary and what implications AI implementation has for employees, customers, the organisation, and society at large. Hence, competencies such as AI Innovation, Transformation, and Reflection are important from a business point of view to design technologies in a sustainable way both ethically and economically.

Second, the results of the market analysis show a clear picture regarding the share of Basic Knowledge and Skills through all three educational sources. This current focus might be due to the fact that the technical implementation, feasibility and creation of a fundamental understanding are of great relevance for emerging fields of technology and represents a first precondition for being able to understand the subject area of AI at all. The acquisition of Basic Knowledge and Skills enables the expansion of the methodological learning box, especially regarding the processing of large data sets (Iafrate 2018). Universities as well as online learning platforms seem to see this trend of exponential data growth and try to educate students concerning the analysis possibilities. In this way, students can be attracted by broad technology and methodology teaching.

Our results also show that AI Reflection competencies are less represented among the participating universities and online learning platforms. In contrast, the top universities seem to be aware of the increasing relevance of ELSI competencies. This observation could be interpreted as a need for such competencies and indicate a new trend for online learning platforms and selected German universities.

Taking a closer look at the competencies AI Management and Transformation, we cannot identify a clear focus on these competencies of any of the three educational resources. While these competencies are underrepresented at the top universities, the online learning platforms and the selected German universities seem to have recognized an initial need. A similar finding can be observed for AI Innovations. Nevertheless, an inter-relational comparison suggests that especially AI Innovation and AI Management do not constitute the core construct of offerings in the case of the top universities. This could be since the fundamental understanding and application of AI may already represent significant hurdles for business students. Hence, fundamental resources might be required for this issue which could justify the current focus we find.

A fully fledged education for business students in the field of AI does not exist now. Thus, students as future and central decision-makers are only marginally prepared for new, complex questions and changed fields of activity surrounding the spread of AI. In particular, the starting position at universities regarding existing AI courses for business students is limited at the present time.

6 Limitations

We acknowledge some limitations of our work which open opportunities for future research. It should be noted that both studies are subject to a regional bias. The market analysis considers regional though internationally operating, companies and investigated universities in the market analysis represent only German universities. By including more institutions of higher education, this bias could be mitigated to a certain extent. Furthermore, it should be noted that the derived implications cannot be generalised for all types of degree programmes, since e.g., only those courses were taken into account in the market analysis which may be selected by business students. Another limitation is the assumption that AI-specific competencies can be taught exclusively through teaching. It might well be those certain parts of e.g., the AI Management competence area can mostly be acquired via working experience. This emphasises that establishments build on university competencies and expand them with additional knowledge. Existing competence models do help to divide existing competencies into competence groups. However, the practical feasibility shows that just the distinction between AI Management and AI Transformation does not always lead to a clear categorisation in both the demand and market analysis. The definition of further differentiation criteria is necessary here. On the other hand, the competence group on technological competencies enables simple categorisation decisions to be made. This category includes a broad set of methodological approaches. These should be differentiated especially for business students as they do not need to have internalized all types of technological variations. In summary, the fusion of both studies offers valuable insights for this research paper. However, no recommendations regarding the module content can be derived at the current stage as the categorisation was performed at the aggregation level of the competence fields. Further analytical milestones are conceivable within the scope of future research potentially by using descriptive content analysis methods that do not only screen the module descriptions but the whole lecture content.

7 Summary and Conclusion

Our research introduces an integrated AI competencies model for business graduates and provides an overview where to acquire such competencies in institutions of higher education. In terms of our first research question, i.e., what relevant AI-related competencies for business students are, we can state that AI-related management skills seem to be of great importance for companies in addition to the basic AI-related knowledge and skills. Equally, an understanding of transformation and innovation processes seems crucial. Finally, we identify a great need for reflective skills. For business graduates who want to manage AI projects in the future, it is necessary to learn to assess the economic, ethical, social, and ecological consequences and side effects of technology. The second research question which investigates to what extent universities meet the current demands of AI-related competencies shows that there is a shortage of non-technical seminars on AI at German universities. In contrast, our results reveal a greater offer of the THE-ranked universities and we conclude that the selected universities still need to make this development. The online platforms also have a strong offering of transformational, management and reflective content. The results of the demand and supply analysis combined reveal two main overarching implications.

First, both studies show that basic knowledge and skills are important, but the supply side seems to be overly focussed on this competence. This might be since without a basic understanding of AI technologies neither AI Innovations nor management or transformation can be investigated in detail. Another reason for the clear existence of courses in Basic Knowledge and Skills could be the generic application potential of AI technologies. Still, universities could consider focussing more on empowering business students to in depth reflection of AI technology and focus more on the AI Management and Transformation education. Since these competence fields represent a central perspective on elementary AI problems and are highly relevant for a holistic understanding of AI knowledge (Haefner et al. 2021). Our results emphasize this observation via the rising share of AI Innovation and AI Management with Transformation competencies in the offerings from online learning platforms and selected German universities. While Basic Knowledge and Skills are important, universities could consider collaborating with online suppliers and offering different online classes to students to acquire these necessary technological skills. For example, higher education organisations should consider licensing certain online suppliers and include them in their curricula.

Second, we identify a demand for or the derivation of ethical-social implications of AI technologies (i.e., AI Reflection). Indeed, the importance of critical reflections on AI use and evaluating the application potential of AI from a socio-ethical point of view is considered to be a highly relevant area of research. Consequently, in addition to pure feasibility studies of AI algorithms, the human-machine interaction and collaboration with AI systems is being investigated more and more (Shneiderman 2020; Wang et al. 2019). At the same time, we find a clear shortage of teaching in this particular competence field among the selected German universities and online platforms. Online suppliers might not teach AI Reflection related competencies well due to their business model. Asynchronous teaching does not foster in depth discussion between participants and tacit knowledge cannot be developed (Pappas n.d.). The top tier universities, however, seem to have already identified this trend.

In summary, to design relevant and more structured AI curricula at universities and higher education in general, our insights can be used to improve the weak points in the curricula. This can also succeed through cross-university teaching, for example, if economic, social science, and technical universities join forces.

References

Åström, J., Reim, W. & Parida, V. (2022), 'Value creation and value capture for AI business model innovation: a three-phase process framework'. *Review of Managerial Science* 1–23.

Blumberg, V. S. L. & Kauffeld, S. (2021), 'Kompetenzen und Wege der Kompetenzentwicklung in der Industrie 4.0'. *Gruppe. Interaktion. Organisation. Zeitschrift für Angewandte Organisationspsychologie (GIO)* **52**(2), 203–225.

Chen, L. (2022), 'Current and Future Artificial Intelligence (AI) Curriculum in Business School: A Text Mining Analysis'. *Journal of Information Systems Education* **33**(4), 416–426.

Cooke, C. (2022), https://upskillwise.com/online-learning-platforms/. Accessed: 08.12.22.

Dicicco-Bloom, B. & Crabtree, B. F. (2006), 'The qualitative research interview'. *Medical Education* **40**(4), 314–321.

Dörr, S. L., Schmidt-Huber, M. & Maier, G. W. (2021), 'Das LEaD-Kompetenzmodell–Wirksam Führen im Kontext der digitalen Transformation'. *Gruppe. Interaktion. Organisation. Zeitschrift für Angewandte Organisationspsychologie (GIO)* **52**(2), 325–339.

Dwivedi, Y. K., Hughes, L., Ismagilova, E., Aarts, G., Coombs, C., Crick, T., Duan, Y., Dwivedi, R., Edwards, J. & Eirug, A. (2021), 'Artificial Intelligence (AI): Multidisciplinary perspectives on emerging challenges, opportunities, and agenda for research, practice and policy'. *International Journal of Information Management* **57**, 101994.

Ferrari, A. (2012), 'Digital competence in practice: An analysis of frameworks'. *Sevilla: JRC IPTS* **10**, 82116.

Franken, S., Mauritz, N. & Prädikow, L. (2022), Kompetenzen für KI-Anwendungen: Theoretisches Modell und partizipative Erfassung und Vermittlung in Unternehmen, *in* 'Frühjahrskongress 2022: Technologie und Bildung in hybriden Arbeitswelten', GfA.

Haefner, N., Wincent, J., Parida, V. & Gassmann, O. (2021), 'Artificial intelligence and innovation management: A review, framework, and research agenda'. *Technological Forecasting and Social Change* **162**, 120392.

Holstein, J. A. & Gubrium, J. F. (2020), "Interviewing as a Form of Narrative Practice", *in 'Qualitative research'*, sage, pp. 69–86.

Iafrate, F. (2018), *Artificial intelligence and big data: The birth of a new intelligence.* John Wiley & Sons.

Iso 2015. Quality management systems-fundamentals and vocabulary. *In*: (ISO), I. O. F. S. (ed.) (*9000:2015*).

Kagermann, H. (2015), "Change through digitization—Value creation in the age of Industry 4.0", *in 'Management of permanent change'*, Springer, pp. 23–45.

King, N. (2004), '21—Using templates in the thematic analysis of text—'. *Essential guide to qualitative methods in organizational research* 256.

Pappas, C. (n.d.), https://elearningindustry.com/asynchronous-learning-advantages-and-disadvantages-in-corporate-training. Accessed: 08.12.22.

Reim, W., Åström, J. & Eriksson, O. (2020), 'Implementation of Artificial Intelligence (AI): A Roadmap for Business Model Innovation'. *AI* **1**(2), 180–191.

Ross, D. (2017), "Times Higher Education World University Rankings", *in 'Research Analytics: Boosting University Productivity and Competitiveness through Scientometrics'*, Auerbach Publications, pp. 137–146.

Rust, R. T. & Cooil, B. (1994), 'Reliability measures for qualitative data: Theory and implications'. *Journal of marketing research* **31**(1), 1–14.

Shneiderman, B. (2020), 'Human-centered artificial intelligence: Reliable, safe & trustworthy'. *International Journal of Human–Computer Interaction* **36**(6), 495–504.

Teuber, K., Dindarian, A. & Ekaterina, N. C.-V. N. (2022), "Künstliche Intelligenz und ihre Anforderungen an den Kompetenzerwerb", *in 'Kompetenzmodelle für den Digitalen Wandel – Orientierungshilfen und Anwendungsbeispiele'*, Springer, pp. 99–116.

Times-Higher-Education. (2022), https://www.timeshighereducation.com/world-university-rankings/2022. Accessed: 7.11.2022.

Vuorikari, R., Kluzer, S. & Punie, Y. (2022), *DigComp 2.2: The Digital Competence Framework for Citizens-With new examples of knowledge, skills and attitudes*. Publications Office of the European Union.

Wamba-Taguimdje, S.-L., Wamba, S. F., Kamdjoug, J. R. K. & Wanko, C. E. T. (2020), 'Influence of artificial intelligence (AI) on firm performance: the business value of AI-based transformation projects'. *Business Process Management Journal* **26**(7), 1893–1924.

Wang, D., Weisz, J. D., Muller, M., Ram, P., Geyer, W., Dugan, C., Tausczik, Y., Samulowitz, H. & Gray, A. (2019), 'Human-AI collaboration in data science: Exploring data scientists' perceptions of automated AI'. *Proceedings of the ACM on Human-Computer Interaction* **3**(CSCW), 1–24.

Designing Unlearning Support Systems: A Requirements Catalog

Marco Di Maria, David Walter, Thorsten Schoormann, and Ralf Knackstedt

Abstract As established routines and other forms of knowledge may prevent organizations to respond to changing situations, they need to learn how to break out of the old way of thinking and acting. While unlearning is among the most promising approaches to do so, there is only a limited understanding of the requirements for the effective design of unlearning support systems (USS). As part of a larger design research project, this research-in-progress paper reviews 41 articles on practical approaches for unlearning support and derives an initial catalog of 23 design requirements. Our work aims to guide designers in the implementation and operationalization of unlearning support.

Keywords Unlearning · Unlearning support · Design requirements · Digital transformation · Knowledge management

1 Introduction

Technological, economic, ecological, and social transformations exert pressure on organizations to continuously (re-)evaluate and change their processes, products, and business models (Hess et al. 2016; Schoormann et al. 2019). During a transformation, people have to learn, unlearn, and relearn dynamically to be able to adapt to the

M. Di Maria (✉) · D. Walter · R. Knackstedt
Information Systems, University of Hildesheim, Hildesheim, Germany
e-mail: marco.dimaria@uni-hildesheim.de

D. Walter
e-mail: walter002@uni-hildesheim.de

R. Knackstedt
e-mail: ralf.knackstedt@uni-hildesheim.de

T. Schoormann
Wirtschaftsinformatik—Data-Driven Enterprise, TU Braunschweig, Braunschweig, Germany
e-mail: thorsten.schoormann@tu-braunschweig.de

D. Beverungen et al. (eds.), *Transforming the Digitally Sustainable Enterprise*, Lecture Notes in Information Systems and Organisation 76,
https://doi.org/10.1007/978-3-031-80125-9_28

changing environment (Azmi 2008; Zhao et al. 2013). This is particularly true for knowledge-intensive industries, in which knowledge serves as a key resource that needs to be managed to build resilience, exploit opportunities in times of change, and harness innovation (March 1991; Becker 2008; Leal-Rodríguez et al. 2015). Sustainable knowledge management is therefore a vital prerequisite to responding to today's challenges. However, existing knowledge structures (Prahalad and Bettis 1986) prevent explorative turns (Raffaelli et al. 2019). Also, people tend to prefer the old way of doing things—the so-called *status quo bias*—demanding to break out of established routines and be open-minded about novel approaches to support acquiring and applying relevant knowledge. This is where *unlearning* comes into play. In contrast to accidental forgetting, unlearning refers to the purposeful forgetting (Holan and Phillips 2004), i.e. the conscious questioning of existing knowledge (e.g., Starbuck 1996) and the exploration of novel ways of thinking and acting (Grisold and Kaiser 2017). Unlearning has already been useful in various contexts (Becker 2018), such as sustainability (van Oers et al. 2023) and organizational change (Grisold and Kaiser 2017). Within these contexts, various approaches, including peer networks (McKeown 2012), reward systems (Becker et al. 2006), and feedback systems (Matsuo 2018) are employed to partly assist actors during unlearning.

While there are auspicious indications for the value of unlearning, existing solutions often neglect the holistic view, including activities and the entire unlearning process. As a consequence, there is a need for "*methods that can spur unlearning [and] knowledge structures that help organizations to challenge obsolete knowledge*" (Sharma and Lenka 2022, p. 1670). Further, guidance for developing and evaluating unlearning support (Rupčić 2017) is scarce, hindering designers from effectively implementing unlearning support (Lei et al. 1999). Against this backdrop, we ask: *What requirements need to be considered when designing unlearning support systems (USS)?*

To answer this question, we set out to derive design-relevant requirements for the broader class of unlearning support systems (USS), which we define as *any tangible or intangible artifact aimed at supporting unlearning in parts or as a whole.* To achieve this, we reviewed the literature on unlearning and created a requirements catalog. To the best of our knowledge, this is the first attempt to structure requirements for unlearning support in a holistic yet concise fashion as we streamline insights on unlearning support from multiple, heterogenous contexts and literature sources.

We think it is important to assist USS designers because of three main reasons: First, knowledge about requirements for unlearning is scattered across several disciplines (Sharma and Lenka 2019), which makes it difficult and time-consuming to gather and assess what design knowledge is useful and relevant for certain purposes. Second, designers face the challenge of proper contextualization and/or de-contextualization. They have to tailor the obtained knowledge to their specific needs, which leaves room for uncertainty and vagueness. Third, designers face diverse types of artifacts that support unlearning. For illustration, when the unlearning support artifact is immaterial (e.g., workshop), and the evidence for the effectiveness of unlearning appears weak, it is often difficult to understand the underlying design process and its key decisions.

As part of ongoing research, we provide an artifact in the form of a requirement catalog (Fellmann et al. 2015) following the tradition of evolutionary accumulation of design knowledge (vom Brocke et al. 2020). This way, we promote the design of more artifacts enabling unlearning, as well as pave the ground for further research efforts on using USS in practice to extend the knowledge on unlearning.

2 Research Approach

We applied a multi-method staged research approach to rigorously extract relevant requirements for unlearning (see Fig. 1). In **Stage 1**, we conducted an interdisciplinary systematic literature review (Webster and Watson 2002) on unlearning support. We further plan (**Stage 2**) to validate and refine our results through interviews with experts and practitioners, as well as (**Stage 3**) to analyze artifacts to extract knowledge captured in running systems (Chandra Kruse et al. 2019).

In this paper, we focus on **Stage 1** and thus conceptualize requirements based on a review of literature from sources within and beyond the IS discipline (Di Maria et al. 2023). Following our procedure (see Fig. 1, left), we first examined each paper to determine the extent to which it supplied practical, concrete insights for unlearning processes. Practical relevance was given if explicit insights were provided about an artifact (tangible, intangible) that helps to reduce the undesired influence of existing cognitive, behavioral, or social knowledge structures (Easterby-Smith and Lyles 2011). In doing so, we take into account the sociotechnical nature of design "*at the confluence of people, organizations, and technology*" (Hevner et al. 2004, p. 77). Two authors conducted the relevance check to reduce bias and ensure a sound methodological approach. As a result, we assembled a final sample of 41 papers.

This sample serves as the foundation for deriving design requirements. We choose design requirements due to two reasons. First, they offer "*sufficient degrees of freedom [...] to express a variety of forms and functions in the artifact*" (ibid., p. 86), so that designers can realize diverse types of artifacts (e.g., software applications, methods). Second, designers can adapt the design requirements to their specific needs, such as target audience (e.g., students, professionals) and context (e.g., education, business).

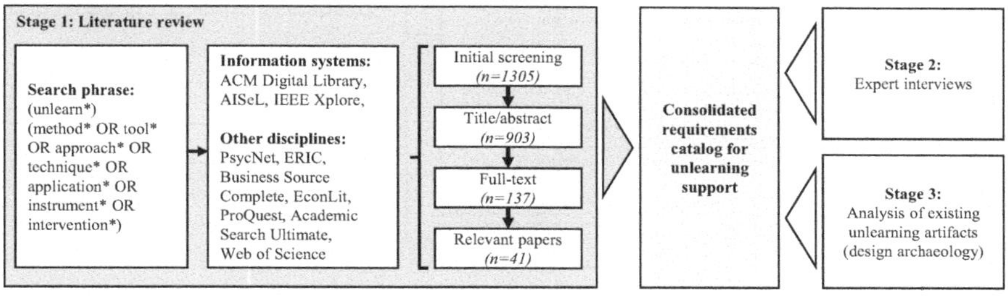

Fig. 1 Research approach (grey box = this paper; white boxes = future research)

3 Results: A Requirements Catalog for Unlearning Support

We condensed our set of rather isolated, single requirements into more abstract ones to obtain generalized design requirements for unlearning support (see Fig. 2) in the form of a catalog. We included only requirements in the final catalog that were supported by at least two of the examined contributions (i.e., paper from the sample) to arrive at a relevant yet parsimonious set allowing useful orientation for designers. Based on this coding, we conceptualized 17 activity-oriented (i.e., related to a specific unlearning activity) (see Fig. 3) and six general design requirements (see Fig. 4).

The **activity-oriented design requirements [R1.#–R7.#]** guide the implementation of USS along seven unlearning activities: (1) *Sense*, (2) *Prepare*, (3) *Destabilize*, (4) *Explore*, (5) *Discard*, (6) *Measure,* and (7) *Avoid*. We initially adopted categories (3), (4), and (5) from Fiol and O'Connor's (2017) three-step model for unlearning organizational routines (i.e., deduction). Additionally, we conceptualized activities (1), (2), (6), and (7) through open coding (i.e., induction).

Next, we explain each activity using references to support our conceptualization:

- ***Sense (1)*** pertains to **[R1.1]** identifying environmental cues emanating from sources such as customers or regulators, or **[R1.2]** stimuli from within the organization (e.g., rising costs, decreasing efficiency) that might act as potential triggers informing a subsequent unlearning process (see Fig. 2). Proactively, *[u]nlearning organisations don't wait for things to break before they fix them*" (Sherwood 2000, p. 34).
- ***Prepare (2)*** relates to **[R2.1]** the need to "*prepare actors for unlearning*" (Grisold et al. 2020, p. 605) to increase actors' acceptance. Using **[R2.2]** environmental signals, interventions are then **[R2.3]** tailored to specific goals in advance.
- ***Destabilize (3)*** includes triggering actors **[R3.1]** using positive or negative stimuli and **[R3.2]** rearranging of elements to initiate the unlearning process. Starbuck (1996, p. 730) sees them as "*[e]vents that violate expectations, both*

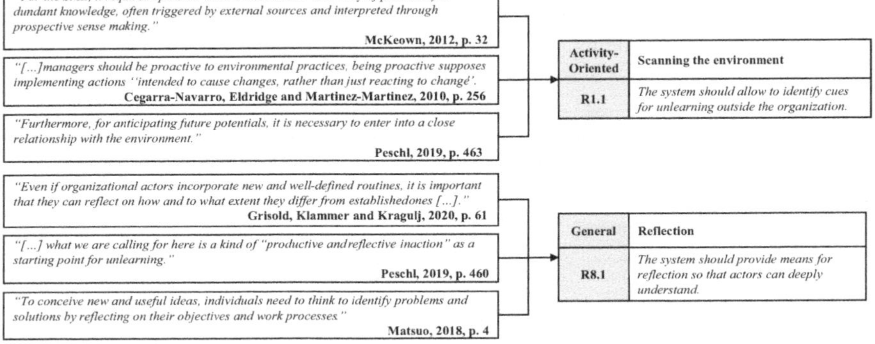

Fig. 2 Coding and generalization procedure

	Activity-Oriented	RID	Requirement Description: *The system should ...*	Count
R1	Sense	R1.1	*allow to identify cues for unlearning outside the organization.*	6
		R1.2	*allow to identify cues for unlearning inside the organization.*	3
R2	Prepare	R2.1	*prepare actors prior to unlearning intervention.*	5
		R2.2	*use relevant contextual information for planning the unlearning process.*	3
		R2.3	*assist in focusing unlearning activities towards a specific goal.*	7
R3	Destabilize	R3.1	*provide means for triggering actors with positive and negative signals.*	20
		R3.2	*enable rearrangement of human and non-human elements.*	8
R4	Explore	R4.1	*help actors identifying obsolete knowledge.*	12
		R4.2	*help actors understanding the value of old knowledge.*	13
		R4.3	*help actors understanding the value of new knowledge.*	11
		R4.4	*enable actors to experiment with new knowledge.*	19
		R4.5	*contrast benefits of new knowledge and disadvantages of old knowledge.*	7
R5	Discard	R5.1	*reduce influence of old knowledge.*	4
		R5.2	*reward application of new knowledge in organizational context.*	7
R6	Measure	R6	*provide means for measuring unlearning success.*	9
R7	Avoid	R7.1	*prevent actors from reverting to obsolete knowldge in the short term.*	7
		R7.2	*prevent actors from reapplying unlearned knowledge in the long term.*	4

Fig. 3 Catalog of activity-oriented design requirements for unlearning support

	General	RID	Requirement Description: *The system should ...*	Count
R8	Diversity	R8.1	*foster multiple perspectives to facilitate a holistic understanding.*	10
	Safe Environment	R8.2	*provide a safe and open environment for actors.*	14
	Feedback	R8.3	*provide means for feedback so that actors can improve iteratively.*	12
	Continuity	R8.4	*ensure a continuous and sustainble unlearning process.*	13
	Reflection	R8.5	*provide means for reflection so that actors can deeply understand.*	20
	Change Agents	R8.6	*include internal or external facilitators that support actors.*	10

Fig. 4 General design requirements for unlearning support

unpleasant disruptions and pleasant surprises, [that] can become opportunities for unlearning."

- ***Explore (4)*** refers to five activities aiming at using old and new knowledge. Actors need to **[R4.1]** identify obsolete knowledge (e.g., Cegarra-Navarro and Cepeda Carrión 2013), and **[R4.2]** to understand the value it had so far (Grisold et al. 2020). Then, actors need to **[R4.3]** comprehend the benefits of "*new habits, patterns and ways of doing*" (Cegarra-Navarro and Cepeda Carrión 2013, p. 87). This follows **[R4.4]** experimenting whereby "*[u]nlearning organisations make time for thinking, exploration, innovation.*" (Sherwood 2000, p. 34). Then, actors can **[R4.5]** contrast the value of old and new knowledge by doing a "*cost-benefit-analysis*" (Srithika & Bhattacharyya 2009, p. 69).
- ***Discard (5)*** applies to **[R5.1]** reducing the influence of old beliefs and behaviors while **[R5.2]** promotes the application of new knowledge. Peschl (2019, p. 465) captures that twofold idea well saying that "*unlearning is not only about letting go obsolete knowledge, but about being open toward future potentials*".
- ***Measure (6)*** covers **[R6]** activities of controlling the unlearning progress and ultimately the outcome of unlearning interventions. As Becker et al. (2006, p. 618) claim: "*It is also important to further understand the efficacy of different techniques used to ensure that reverting to past practice does not occur.*"
- ***Avoid (7)*** encompasses the prevention of actors reverting to obsolete knowledge (Morais-Storz and Nguyen 2017). This can be done **[R7.1]** in the short term, such as by using "*a 'fool-proof' mechanism*" (Srithika and Bhattacharyya 2009, p. 73). If measures are institutionalized by e.g., "*periodically reviewing obsolete beliefs and work routines*" (Matsuo 2018, p. 10), **[R7.2]** relapse in the long term can be achieved, i.e. "*maintenance*" (Nygren et al. 2017, p. 474).

The **general design requirements [R8.1–R8.6]** apply to all parts of the unlearning process. Thus, USS should **[R8.1]** incorporate multiple views (Clarke 1998) in the process offering actors **[R8.2]** an open and safe environment to feel emotionally safe. Further, USS should enable **[R8.3]** feedback between actors (Matsuo 2018) so that they can iteratively improve **[R8.4]** in a continuous process rather than a one-shot intervention. In doing so, time and space are granted for **[R8.5]** reflection at the start (Peschl 2019) or continuously (Almqvist et al. 2011). Each activity can be supported by **[R8.6]** change agents, e.g., external facilitators (McKeown 2012) or internal actors (Grisold et al. 2020).

In effect, the catalog provides a valuable resource for researchers and designers as a structured, systematic, and holistic overview of the requirements for the design of USS.

4 Conclusion and Outlook

In this study, we report on a design project aiming to guide how to build and evaluate a specific class of artifacts, namely Unlearning Support Systems (USS). To ensure transparency regarding the use of available knowledge (vom Brocke et al. 2020; Schoormann et al. 2023) as grounding for our research, we consolidated insights from a broad range of viewpoints and diverse disciplines that contribute to the emerging stream of unlearning support. Following our research approach, we (1) developed a requirements catalog for the design of USS. Moreover, during the analysis and clustering of the requirements collected from the literature, we (2) provided a preliminary extension to the unlearning process by adding four additional activities for sensing, preparing, measuring, and avoiding. This extension lays a more nuanced view on unlearning and poses a promising research direction. Overall, we complement the body of knowledge on unlearning by providing a useful reference for researchers and practice. In the future, we strive to understand how our requirements align with specific forms of unlearning, such as '*open-ended*' aiming for explorative innovation and '*goal-oriented*' seeking to replace the old (Grisold et al. 2020), as well as with different organizational levels (Felin et al. 2015).

Acknowledgements We thank the European Social Fund (ESF+) and the State of Lower Saxony (Nbank) for partly funding this research in the context of the research project "ProXHybrid" (ZAM 3-87002690).

References

Almqvist, R., Catasús, B. & Skoog, M. (2011), 'Towards the next generation of public management: A study of management control and communication in the Swedish Armed Forces', *International Journal of Public Sector Management* 24(2), 122–145. https://doi.org/10.1108/09513551111109035.

Azmi, F. T. (2008), 'Mapping the learn-unlearn-relearn model: Imperatives for strategic management', *European Business Review*. Bradford: Emerald Group Publishing Limited PP - Bradford, 20(3), pp. 240–259. https://doi.org/10.1108/09555340810871437.

Becker, K. (2008), 'Unlearning as a driver of sustainable change and innovation: three Australian case studies', *International Journal of Technology Management* 42(1/2), 89–106. https://doi.org/10.1504/IJTM.2008.018062.

Becker, K. (2018) 'Organizational Unlearning: Time to Expand Our Horizons?', *The Learning Organization* 25(3), 180–189.

Becker, K., Hyland, P. & Acutt, B. (2006), 'Considering unlearning in HRD practices: An Australian study', *Journal of European Industrial Training* 30(8), 608–621. https://doi.org/10.1108/03090590610712278.

Cegarra-Navarro, J. G. & Cepeda Carrión, G. (2013), 'Implementing telemedicine technologies through an unlearning context in a homecare setting', *Behaviour and Information Technology* 32(1), 80–90. https://doi.org/10.1080/0144929X.2011.586726.

Cegarra-Navarro, J.-G., Eldridge, S. & Martinez-Martinez, A. (2010), 'Managing environmental knowledge through unlearning in Spanish hospitality companies', *Journal of Environmental Psychology* 30(2), 249–257. https://doi.org/10.1016/j.jenvp.2009.11.009.

Chandra Kruse, L., Seidel, S. & vom Brocke, J. (2019), Design Archaeology: Generating Design Knowledge from Real-World Artifact Design, *in* 'Proceedings of the DESRIST', pp. 32–45. https://doi.org/10.1007/978-3-030-19504-5_3.

Clarke, M. (1998), 'Can specialists be general managers?: Developing paradoxical thinking in middle managers.', *Journal of Management Development* 17(3), 191–206. https://doi.org/10.1108/02621719810210730

Di Maria, M., Walter, D., Schoormann, T., & Knackstedt, R. (2023), Practical support for unlearning - A systematic review to organize the field, *in* 'Proceedings of the European Conference on Information Systems', AIS.

Easterby-Smith, M., & Lyles, M. A. (2011), 'In praise of organizational forgetting'. *Journal of Management Inquiry* 20(3), 311–316.

Felin, T., Foss, N. J., and Ployhart, R. E. (2015), 'The microfoundations movement in strategy and organization theory', *Academy of Management Annals* 9(1), 575–632.

Fellmann, M., Zarvic, N., Metzger, D. & Koschmider, A. (2015), Requirements Catalog for Business Process Modeling Recommender Systems, *in* 'Proceedings of the Wirtschaftsinformatik', pp. 393–407.

Fiol, C. M. & Connor, E. J. O. (2017), 'Unlearning established organizational routines – Part II', *The Learning Organization* 24(2), 82–92. https://doi.org/10.1108/TLO-09-2016-0063.

Grisold, T. & Kaiser, A. (2017), 'Leaving Behind What We are Not: Applying a Systems Thinking Perspective to Present Unlearning as an Enabler for Finding the Best Version of the Self', *Journal of Organisational Transformation and Social Change*. Taylor & Francis, 14(1), pp. 39–55. https://doi.org/10.1080/14779633.2017.1291145.

Grisold, T., Klammer, A. & Kragulj, F. (2020), 'Two forms of organizational unlearning: Insights from engaged scholarship research with change consultants', *Management Learning* 51(5), 598–619. https://doi.org/10.1177/1350507620916042.

Hess, T., Matt, C., Benlian, A. & Wiesböck, F. (2016), 'Options for formulating a digital transformation strategy', *MIS Quarterly Executive* 15(2), 123–139. https://doi.org/10.4324/9780429286797-7.

Hevner, A.R., March, S.T., Park, J. & Ram, S. (2004), 'Design Science in Information Systems Research', *MIS Quarterly* 28(1), 75–105.

Holan, P. M. D., & Phillips, N. (2004), 'Remembrance of things past? The dynamics of organizational forgetting', *Management Science* 50(11), 1603–1613.

Leal-Rodríguez, A.L., Eldridge, S., Roldán, J.L., Leal-Millán, A.G. & Ortega-Gutiérrez, J. (2015), 'Organizational unlearning, innovation outcomes, and performance: The moderating effect of firm size', *Journal of Business Research* 68(4), 803–809. https://doi.org/10.1016/J.JBUSRES.2014.11.032.

Lei, D., Slocum, J. W. & Pitts, R. A. (1999), 'Designing organizations for competitive advantage: The power of unlearning and learning', *Organizational Dynamics* 27(3), 24–38. https://doi.org/10.1016/S0090-2616(99)90019-0.

March, J. G. (1991), 'Exploration and Exploitation in Organizational Learning', *Organization Science* 2(1), 71–87.

Matsuo, M. (2018), 'Effects of team unlearning on employee creativity: The mediating effect of individual reflection', *Journal of Workplace Learning* 30(7), 531–544. https://doi.org/10.1108/JWL-03-2018-0045.

McKeown, I. (2012), 'Teaching Old Dogs New Tricks: Why Unlearning Matters in SMEs', *The International Journal of Entrepreneurship and Innovation* 13(1), 25–34. https://doi.org/10.5367/ijei.2012.0062.

Morais-Storz, M. & Nguyen, N. (2017), 'The role of unlearning in metamorphosis and strategic resilience', *Learning Organization* 24(2), 93–106. https://doi.org/10.1108/TLO-12-2016-0091.

Nygren, N. V., Jokinen, A. & Nikula, A. (2017), 'Unlearning in managing wicked biodiversity problems', *Landscape and Urban Planning* 167(2016), 473–482. https://doi.org/10.1016/j.landurbplan.2017.06.019.

Peschl, M. F. (2019), 'Unlearning towards an uncertain future: on the back end of future-driven unlearning', *Learning Organization* 26(5), 454–469. https://doi.org/10.1108/TLO-11-2018-0192.

Prahalad, C.K. & Bettis, R.A. (1986), The dominant logic: A new linkage between diversity and performance. *Strategic management journal* 7(6),485–501.

Raffaelli, R., Glynn, M. A. & Tushman, M. (2019), 'Frame flexibility: The role of cognitive and emotional framing in innovation adoption by incumbent firms', *Strategic Management Journal* 40(7), 1013–1039. https://doi.org/10.1002/smj.3011.

Rupčić, N. (2017), 'How to unlearn and change – that is the question!', *The Learning Organization* 24(2), 127–130. https://doi.org/10.1108/TLO-12-2016-0092.

Schoormann, T., Kutzner, K., Pape, S. & Knackstedt, R. (2019), 'Elevating social sustainability in business processes: A pattern-based approach', *in* 'Proceedings of the 40th International Conference on Information Systems', AIS.

Schoormann, T., Möller, F., & Chandra Kruse, L. (2023), The Beauty of Messiness: A Flexible Tool for Design Principle Projects, *in* 'Proceedings of the Hawaii International Conference on System Sciences', AIS, pp. 5146–5156.

Sharma, S. & Lenka, U. (2019), 'Value-added statement as a trigger to organizational unlearning', *Development and Learning in Organizations* 33(6), 22–25. https://doi.org/10.1108/DLO-02-2018-0021.

Sharma, S. & Lenka, U. (2022), *On the shoulders of giants: uncovering key themes of organizational unlearning research in mainstream management journals, Review of Managerial Science.* Springer Berlin Heidelberg. https://doi.org/10.1007/s11846-021-00492-7.

Sherwood, D. (2000), 'The Unlearning Organization', *Business Strategy Review*, 11(31–40).

Srithika, T. M. & Bhattacharyya, S. (2009) 'Facilitating organizational unlearning using appreciative inquiry as an intervention', *Vikalpa* 34(4), 67–77. https://doi.org/10.1177/0256090920090406.

Starbuck, W. H. (1996), 'Unlearning ineffective or obsolete technologies', *International Journal of Technology Management* 11(7), 725–737. https://doi.org/10.1504/IJTM.1996.025463.

van Oers, L., Feola, G., Runhaar, H. & Moors, E. (2023), 'Unlearning in sustainability transitions: Insight from two Dutch community-supported agriculture farms', *Environmental Innovation and Societal Transitions* 46. https://doi.org/10.1016/j.eist.2023.100693

vom Brocke, J., Winter, R., Hevner, A. and Maedche, A. (2020), 'Special Issue Editorial – Accumulation and Evolution of Design Knowledge in Design Science Research: A Journey Through Time and Space', *Journal of the Association for Information Systems* 21(3), 520–544. https://doi.org/10.17705/1jais.00611.

Webster, J. & Watson, R. T. (2002), 'Analyzing the past to prepare for the future: Writing a literature review', *MIS Quarterly* 26(2), xiii–xxiii.

Zhao, Y., Lu, Y. & Wang, X. (2013), 'Organizational unlearning and organizational relearning: A dynamic process of knowledge management', *Journal of Knowledge Management* 17(6), 902–912. https://doi.org/10.1108/JKM-06-2013-0242.

Understanding the Effectiveness of Interactive Elements in Video-Based Learning: An Experimental Study

Maximilian Raab, Julian Weidinger, Nico Hirschlein, Jan-Niklas Meckenstock, Lisa Thron, and Eric Felix Ulbricht

Abstract Video-based learning (VBL) depicts a key element of contemporary educational practice. While benefits have been identified in research and application, the lack of interactivity that can imply detrimental effects on the resulting learning performance in VBL should not be neglected. As a countermeasure, a plethora of interactive elements embedded in educational videos has emerged. By now, it remains unexplored how different interactive elements compare to one another regarding their effects on learning performance. To address this research gap, we conducted an experimental study in an undergraduate university course and investigated the respective effects of three interactive element types under similar conditions in a VBL environment. Our results offer indications that the specific addition of quizzes and annotations can imply significant improvements of learning performance, while navigation features possess no stimulation. Our work thereby provides educational practice and academia with new perspectives on interactive elements in VBL to improve their utilization.

Keywords Video-based learning · Interactive elements · Learning performance

---

M. Raab (✉) · J. Weidinger · N. Hirschlein · J.-N. Meckenstock · L. Thron · E. F. Ulbricht
University of Bamberg, Bamberg, Germany
e-mail: maximilian.raab@uni-bamberg.de

J. Weidinger
e-mail: julian.weidinger@uni-bamberg.de

N. Hirschlein
e-mail: nico.hirschlein@uni-bamberg.de

J.-N. Meckenstock
e-mail: jan-niklas.meckenstock@uni-bamberg.de

L. Thron
e-mail: lisa.thron@stud.uni-bamberg.de

E. F. Ulbricht
e-mail: eric-felix.ulbricht@stud.uni-bamberg.de

D. Beverungen et al. (eds.), *Transforming the Digitally Sustainable Enterprise*, Lecture Notes in Information Systems and Organisation 76,
https://doi.org/10.1007/978-3-031-80125-9_29

1 Introduction

The use of video technology in educational settings, from elementary schools (Palaigeorgiou et al. 2019) to higher education contexts (Albó et al. 2018), is a popular means to support learners in their learning processes. Video-recordings of lectures as a digital form of imparting knowledge have been long-standing elements of the toolbox for lecturers to convey teaching content (Yousef et al. 2014). The COVID-19 pandemic, however, has brought video-based learning (VBL) into the particular focus of teachers and scholars alike. As such, there was a radical shift towards the sole use of videos or recordings of lectures "since the teaching–learning process has to be online only" (Pal and Patra 2020, p. 1). Extant research has confirmed various benefits of VBL, including increased learner autonomy (Zainuddin and Perera 2018), improved motivation (Chen 2012), and learner satisfaction (Zhang et al. 2006).

Similarly, research reported potential downsides of VBL, such as a lack of human interaction (Chatti et al. 2016) and a rather passive learning experience, which may even lead to "insufficient viability of the learning effect" (Palaigeorgiou and Papadopoulou 2018, p. 1). Also, scholars reported detrimental effects on the student's learning performance (Dror 2008), mainly due to the lack of interactivity, which may also imply a reduced cognitive engagement with the video content (Palaigeorgiou and Papadopoulou 2018). As a countermeasure, a plethora of interactive element types has been developed, combined, and incorporated into educational videos. A common goal is to improve the effectiveness of VBL by increasing the student's engagement with the presented learning content, i.e., converting passive watchers into active learners.

While many studies focused on investigating a combination of various interactive elements, such as pointers, questions, and links, within educational videos (e.g., Delen et al. 2014; Palaigeorgiou and Papadopoulou 2018), few studies examined different interactive element types in isolation (Vural 2013). Consequently, research has reported how an educational video that incorporates combinations of interactive elements can promote students' learning performance in general. However, it is not yet fully understood how the addition of a specific element type in educational videos stimulates the student's learning performance in isolation. More importantly, it remains unexplored to which degree a distinct interactive element type impacts learning performance in VBL in comparison to other element types under similar conditions.

To understand how distinct types of interactive elements in educational videos can influence learning performance, we conducted a set of experiments in the context of higher education. The following research questions are addressed: *How effectively can distinct interactive element types in educational videos improve learning performance?* (**RQ1**) and *To which degree do distinct interactive element types impact learning performance when comparing each other's effects?* (**RQ2**). To address the RQs, the conducted study investigates the effect of three distinct interactive element types, namely quizzes, annotations, and navigation features, as interventions in VBL environments on resulting learning performances. During a set of experiments over a three-week period, each type of interactive element was tested in isolation and embedded in the educational videos for an elective information systems (IS) course. While the control group watched a standard video, the experiment group watched a video enhanced with interactive elements of the respective type.

We applied a *t*-test and ANOVA to compare the increase of knowledge gained, i.e., improvements in learning performance, in each week's control and experiment group. Our study contributes to and extends the current body of knowledge in the following ways: First, our results suggest that the addition of quizzes or annotations but not navigation features has a significant impact on learning performance. Second, we systematically compared the effects of three types of interactive elements in educational videos, thereby providing the first steps toward closing this research gap. More specifically, embedding either quizzes or annotations exerted, in contrast to navigation features, similar improvements of learning performance. Third, we derive avenues for future research, especially regarding the development of an interactive richness scale. Fourth, our results provide initial guidance for instructors on what different types of interactive elements positively affect VBL approaches.

2 Theoretical Background

2.1 Video-Based Learning and Interactive Videos

Using VBL to deliver educational content and foster knowledge gain is not entirely new (Yousef et al. 2014). With the COVID-19 pandemic forcing traditional lectures to shift to online settings, however, VBL experienced an attention boost. The widespread of online courses and video platforms made VBL an essential part of higher education (Weinert et al. 2021). In general, educational videos can either supplement traditional classroom work or constitute the primary content source in online environments (Sablić et al. 2020). The accompanying transition from teacher-centered classroom education to the more learner-centered setting in VBL holds the potential for significant benefits. Using auditory and visual cues, VBL can effectively engage learners and facilitate learning (Sablić et al. 2020). Amongst others, students can re-watch videos to better understand complex issues. They can easily access videos at any time, any place, from any device. Thus, VBL can provide a more self-directed and self-paced learning style and better meet students' individual learning needs (Brecht and Ogilby 2008).

Besides positive aspects, VBL may also come with drawbacks. They include a lack of human interaction, personal feedback, and assessment (Chatti et al. 2016). Thus, watching videos can become a passive activity (Chatti et al. 2016; Zhang et al. 2006). Students may get less engaged with lectures, reluctant to learn, and demotivated (Wachtler et al. 2016). To increase engagement, research suggests adding interactive elements in videos. The resulting *interactive videos* typically include dynamic information and interaction points overlaying the video that exceed standard interactions like play or pause buttons (Kolas 2015; Palaigeorgiou et al. 2019). Therefore, they may encourage engagement between students and the video content (Benkada and Moccozet 2017). Examples of interaction points include polls, quizzes, assessments, links for navigation or external resources, annotations by teachers or students, and tools to take notes and enable between-student interactions (Kleftodimos et al. 2020; Palaigeorgiou et al. 2019; Yürüm et al. 2022).

Several studies confirm the educational benefits of interactive videos. They can facilitate deeper learning, fostering the transfer from short-term to long-term memory (Cairncross and Mannion 2001). They may allow students to learn independently, maintaining their own pace (Palaigeorgiou et al. 2018; Schoeffmann et al. 2015). Embedded quizzes or tests can challenge students' understanding and provide personalized feedback (Priyakanth et al. 2021; Wachtler et al. 2016). Overall, interactive videos can provide a call for action, stimulate cognitive processes, and overcome the passiveness of non-interactive videos (Chen 2012; Wachtler et al. 2016). As positive side effects, interactive videos can raise enjoyment (Palaigeorgiou and Papadopoulou 2018), motivation (Barut Tugtekin and Dursun 2022; Weinert et al. 2021), satisfaction, and engagement (Wachtler et al. 2016; Zhang et al. 2006). Altogether, interactive videos can contribute to pleasant educational experiences with improved learning performance and better knowledge retention (Palaigeorgiou et al. 2019; Wachtler et al. 2016).

2.2 Related Work About Interactive Elements

Prior studies in the field of digital education and learning found that VBL improved learning performance compared to traditional classroom settings (e.g., Merkt et al. 2011). The degree of interactivity proved to be among the crucial factors (Zhang et al. 2006). Thus, different interactive element types have been developed and combined to analyze their effectiveness in VBL. The plethora of interactive elements includes 3D objects and interactive maps (Kolas 2015), quizzes (Vural 2013; Wachtler et al. 2016), the option for students to annotate a video with their comments (Mitrovic et al. 2017), colored arrows as hints (Althwaini and Mahmoud 2021), and several others.

Most studies examined combinations of interactive element types without considering their individual effects. Kleftodimos et al. (2020) analyzed links, games, puzzles, questions, and activity tables. Also, improved learning performance is reported when combining notetaking elements, supplemental resource links, and quizzes (Cattaneo et al. 2015; Delen et al. 2014). Similarly, interactive videos with added gamified elements can foster students' engagement (Weinert et al. 2021). Opposed to that, Yürüm et al. (2022) reported no significant impact when combining quizzes, annotations, and links. Beyond that, many studies only mention the platform used to develop interactive videos (e.g., H5P) instead of the element types studied

(Benkada and Moccozet 2017; Dieck-Assad et al. 2020; Ku et al. 2019; Priyakanth et al. 2021). Overall, most studies illustrate a positive effect through the addition of multiple element types within a video.

What usually remains unclear is the individual element type' share in the overall effect. In sum, research reported how a combination of interactive element types promotes learning performance. However, it remains mostly unexplored to which degree a distinct isolated type impacts learning performance. Additionally, the comparison of distinct interactive element types analyzed under similar conditions contributes to and extends the current body of knowledge. Our study aims to develop a more systematic understanding of how three distinct types of commonly used interactive elements affect learning performance and compare them to one another.

3 Research Model

Against this theoretical backdrop, we assume that interactive elements in VBL can increase learning performance. To quantify this abstract concept, we measure the additional knowledge gained through watching a video enhanced with a distinct interactive element type (Subhash and Cudney 2018). For additional insights, we take an explorative stance in comparing the different interactive element types to each other in their effects on improved learning performance. In our study, we chose three distinct element types: *quizzes*, *annotations*, and *navigation features*. First, these three are among the most widespread element types in commonly-used VBL systems (Palaigeorgiou et al. 2019). This ensured availability for implementation by the researchers and familiarity to the users. Second, literature indicates both the efficacy and the significantly different effects of all three element types, as the following paragraphs will describe.

Enhancing educational videos with quizzes (e.g., memorization or application questions) can strengthen the presented information. Quizzes are among the most utilized interactive element types in VBL (Palaigeorgiou and Papadopoulou 2018) and serve as a form of formative assessment (Zainuddin et al. 2020). Hence, quizzes can induce information recall (Palaigeorgiou et al. 2019; Vural 2013) by challenging the students' knowledge of previously displayed learning segments (Wachtler et al., 2016). In this vein, quizzes facilitate active learning by fostering interactivity via answering questions (Cook and Babon 2016). Also, embedded quizzes provide the possibility of reflection, specifically when not knowing the correct answer to a question. By providing meaningful and personalized feedback, quizzes guide students on what specific section of an educational video should be viewed again, which reflects the gap between the current and preferred learning outcomes (Nicol and Macfarlane-Dick 2006). In sum, quizzes in educational videos can increase learning performance by inducing information recall and reflection (e.g., Vural 2013; Weinert et al. 2021). Thus, we hypothesize:

H1: *Educational videos that embed quizzes have a greater positive effect on learning performance than non-interactive educational videos.*

Furthermore, interactivity in educational videos can be achieved using annotations and other signaling mechanisms to draw attention to critical information, thereby guiding students' attention when watching an educational video. Annotations aim to facilitate information processing and include visual hints, highlighting, images, and discussions (Seidel 2015). In this vein, annotations serve as an additional semantic layer of information (e.g., through summarizing concepts) that supports students in their learning process (Bruning 1983). Hence, annotations can strengthen students' understanding of the teaching content, which positively affects learning performance (Althwaini and Mahmoud 2021). Moreover, annotations can guide students' attention to specific areas or information within the video and provoke them to think about the presented issues. Thus, annotations can stimulate the student's attention and support them in selecting information while watching the educational video. In sum, annotations guide students to take a closer look at the teaching content, which is beneficial in increasing learning performance (Palaigeorgiou et al. 2019). Thus, we hypothesize:

H2: *Educational videos that embed annotations have a greater positive effect on learning performance than non-interactive educational videos.*

In addition, educational videos can embed hyperlinks to external resources or video segments and provide search or branching functions to explore the video on a non-linear path. Such navigation features provide opportunities to individually explore learning content. They include skipping already known content, repeating specific content, and jumping to specific video sections (Meixner 2014; Palaigeorgiou et al. 2018). They may stimulate metacognitive learning strategies, such as facilitating the cognitive flexibility of knowledge construction or monitoring the knowledge construction process itself (Spiro and Jehng 1990). Educational videos can provide personalized learning activities with individual pacing that have effects on the student's self-regulated learning abilities (Cattaneo et al. 2015). Hence, students deemed this an interactive and engaging activity that increases active studying of the content (Cuka and Bufasi 2022). As such, an active approach to viewing educational videos may serve as a key enabler in increasing learning performance (Palaigeorgiou et al. 2018). Thus, we hypothesize:

H3: *Educational videos that embed navigation features have a greater positive effect on learning performance than non-interactive educational videos.*

Besides analyzing each interactive element type in isolation, our study compares the effect of the different interactive element types with each other to answer the second RQ. As noted, the comparison of different element types, especially in their particular effects on learning performance, embodies a substantial research gap. Each type introduces a set of interactive elements that facilitates interactivity in a particular way. In this vein, quizzes (H1) may induce information recall and reflection, annotations (H2) shed light on critical information, and navigation features

(H3) allow for individual knowledge construction. Despite the theoretically known effects of the above-mentioned element types, there is still a nascent knowledge base on which interactive element type in educational videos has a greater influence on learning performance. As extant work often analyzed different types of interactive elements in combination, we cannot hypothesize which interactive element type can be more effective in increasing learning performance. Consequently, our study aims to explore these effects under similar conditions to gain initial indications to fill the above-mentioned research gap.

4 Empirical Study

We conducted three subsequent weekly experiments to test how different interactive element types affect learning performance. They involved second year IS bachelor students and were conducted over a three-week period in the Fall 2022/2023 semester. For each experiment week, we randomly divided students into two groups: one watched the standard video, the other watched the enhanced interactive video.

Materials. The course provided videos for each week's lecture content covering the fundamentals of systems theory (week 1), modeling approaches (week 2), and data modeling (week 3). The lecture content was the same for the control and experiment groups. Also, each video had the same standard play-pause-speed buttons, a table of contents, and a scrubbable timeline, constituting the control group's standard video. Each week's experiment group video incorporated interactive elements of one type based on H5P (https://h5p.com/), reflecting the hypotheses H1, H2, or H3. Thus, to induce information recall and reflection, week 1's video added versatile types of quizzes with feedback (H1). To draw the students' attention to critical information, week 2's video embedded additional annotations, such as highlighting, pictograms or pictures, and chat messages (H2). To provide options for individual knowledge construction, week 3's video embedded additional navigation features, such as links to external resources, internal links reflecting a keyword-search-like feature, and branching possibilities (H3). Exemplary implementations for each week are displayed in Fig. 1.

Procedure. The study participation was voluntary. To delineate our hypothesis tests and rule out learning effects, we used unique videos and weeks for each hypothesis. In week 1, half of the students enrolled in the course were randomly assigned either to the control or the experiment group. In week 2, each student was assigned to the opposite group to ensure that each student was assigned to both groups at least once. In week 3, students were assigned randomly to the groups again. Within a week, each student took a pre-test with 18 multiple-choice questions to assess the prior knowledge. Test scores can range from 0 to 18. Then, students watched the video. Next, they took a post-test with 18 similar but different multiple-choice questions. Two experts developed the pre-test and post-test questions that covered the concepts the respective video introduced. Each experiment was open for seven days and non-overlapping.

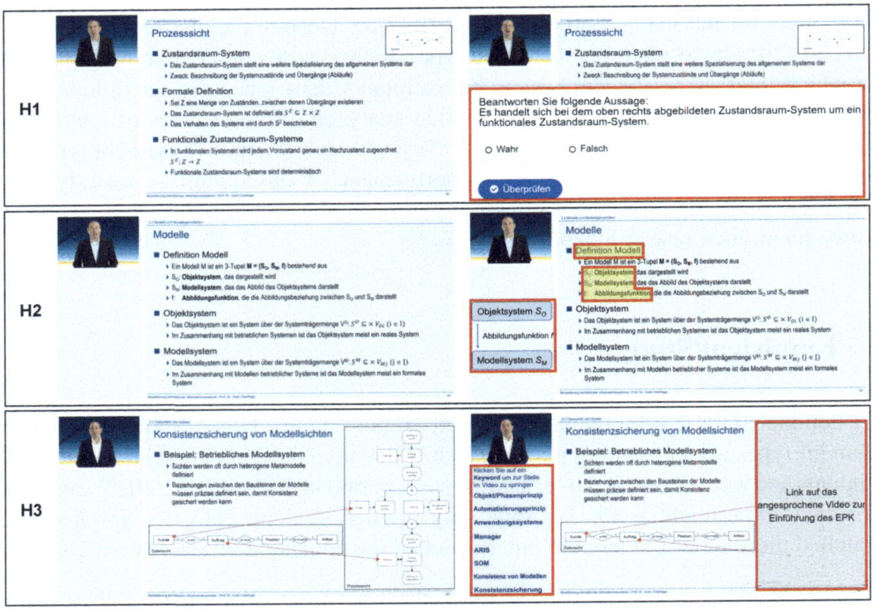

Fig. 1 Standard video slides (left), added interactive elements (right, marked red): quizzes (top, week 1, H1), annotations (middle, week 2, H2), navigation features (bottom, week 3, H3)

Data analysis. We excluded data sets when students took longer than 45 min (upper cut-off limit) to complete the post-test, assuming they rewatched the video or looked up solutions to score better post-test results. We also excluded data sets when students finished a test faster than the two experts who developed them, suggesting a lack of serious effort in answering the questions. To test our hypotheses, we compared the student's learning performance measured as the difference between the student's post-test and pre-test scores between the control and the experiment group (e.g., Subhash and Cudney 2018; Zhang et al. 2006). A significantly increased knowledge gain in the experiment group would indicate greater learning performance from the video with the interactive element type for each week. Thus, we applied a *t*-test to compare the increase of knowledge gained in each week's control and experiment groups.

5 Results

5.1 *Impact of Quizzes, Annotations, and Navigation Features on Knowledge Gain*

To analyze the impact of VBL with different types of interactive elements (either quizzes, annotations, or navigation) on students' knowledge gain, we accounted for whether a *t*-test is suitable. Both test assumptions for normality and homogeneous variances are met for pre-test scores, post-test scores, and knowledge gain. Before analyzing the interactive elements' impact on knowledge gain, we examined if the students in the control and experiment group have similar prior knowledge regarding each week's covered topic. To do so, this study used an independent samples *t*-test to compare the mean pre-test scores between the control and experiment group. Table 1 shows the results.

No significant difference between the mean pre-test scores of the groups can be reported. Thus, we conclude that the experiment and control groups have similar prior knowledge regarding each experiment week's covered topic. To analyze if each experiment week's added interactive element type significantly increases knowledge gain, i.e., exceeding the impact of standard educational videos with no additional interactive elements, we applied an independent samples *t*-test to compare the mean knowledge gain between the control and experiment group (see Table 2).

Regarding H1, the twelve students in the experiment group who watched an educational video with added quizzes (M = 6.17, SD = 3.79) compared to the eleven students in the control group who watched the standard video (M = 3.63, SD = 3.11) did achieve a significantly greater knowledge gain measured as the difference between the post-test score and pre-test score, $t(21) = 1.74$, $p = 0.047$ with an impact factor of 0.72, corresponding to a medium effect (Cohen 1988). Regarding H2, the 15 students in the experiment group who watched an educational video with added annotations (M = 7.07, SD = 3.13) compared to the twelve students in the control group who watched the standard video (M = 4.67, SD = 3.80) did achieve a significantly greater knowledge gain, $t(25) = 1.80$, $p = 0.042$ with a medium impact

Table 1 Independent samples *t*-test results for pre-test scores compared by group

	Group	N	M	SD	df	t
H1 (quiz)	Experiment	12	7.00	2.86	21	-1.66^{ns}
	Control	11	9.09	3.18		
H2 (annotation)	Experiment	15	7.26	2.49	25	-1.68^{ns}
	Control	12	9.00	2.86		
H3 (navigation)	Experiment	13	9.61	2.66	26	0.67^{ns}
	Control	15	8.93	2.74		

Note ^{ns} = non-significant, $^{*}p < 0.05$, $^{**}p < 0.01$, $^{***}p < 0.001$

Table 2 Independent samples *t*-test results for knowledge gain compared by group

	Group	N	M	SD	df	t	d
H1 (quiz)	Experiment	12	6.17	3.79	21	1.74*	0.72
	Control	11	3.63	3.11			
H2 (annotation)	Experiment	15	7.07	3.13	25	1.80*	0.69
	Control	12	4.67	3.80			
H3 (navigation)	Experiment	13	2.16	3.00	26	0.35^{ns}	0.13
	Control	15	1.74	3.33			

Note d = Cohen's d, ^{ns} = non-significant, $*p < 0.05$, $**p < 0.01$, $***p < 0.001$

factor of 0.69. Regarding H3, the 13 students in the experiment group who watched an educational video with additional navigation features (M = 2.16, SD = 3) compared to the 15 students in the control group who watched the standard video (M = 1.74, SD = 3.33) did achieve an almost identical knowledge gain, $t(26) = 0.35$, $p = 0.37$ with an almost non-existent impact factor of 0.13. Thus, we find support for H1 and H2 but must reject H3.

5.2 *Comparing the Interactive Element Types' Impact on Knowledge Gain*

To answer whether there is any significant difference in the students' knowledge gains regarding the different types of interactive elements, we applied an ANOVA analysis with each experiment group's knowledge gain as the dependent variable and the experiment week as the independent variable. The prerequisites for ANOVA, especially homoscedasticity, have been confirmed to avoid a Type I error. The ANOVA result in Table 3 shows a significant difference between each week's experiment group's knowledge gain ($F(2, 37) = 8.46$, $p < 0.001$). The Tukey HSD method was conducted as a post hoc test to further analyze significant differences between each element type's influence on knowledge gain. Table 3 shows that the knowledge gain was significantly higher when students watched an educational video with additional quizzes (H1) or a video with additional annotations (H2) when compared to a video with additional navigation features (H3). Thus, H1 and H2 outperformed H3, but no significant difference was found when comparing the knowledge gain of H1 and H2. Thus, these interactive elements have a similar positive impact on knowledge gain.

Table 3 Results of one-way ANOVA on knowledge gain (experiment group) and Tukey HSD

	N	M	SD	F	Tukey HSD		
H1 (quiz)	12	6.17	3.79	8.46***		H2	H3
H2 (annotation)	15	7.07	3.13		H1	– 0.9^{ns}	4.01*
H3 (navigation)	13	2.16	3.00		H2	–	4.91**

Note Experiment group only, ^{ns} = non-significant, *$p < 0.05$, **$p < 0.01$, ***$p < 0.001$

5.3 Robustness Tests

To test if the improved knowledge gain is subject to the week's taught lecture content, we analyzed the differences in knowledge gain regarding the control groups. There are no significant differences ($F(2, 37) = 2.56$, $p > 0.05$). Thus, the experiment group's greater knowledge gain should be influenced by the addition of interactive elements.

Instead of a cut-off limit of 45 min for completing the post-tests, we applied two different upper cut-off limits (35 min and 55 min) to verify the stability of our results, especially in light of the relatively small sample size. Applying the same *t*-tests and Tukey HSD, results remain consistent with the previously reported ones. The significance level dropped slightly from $p < 0.05$ to $p = 0.07$ only for H2 with the 55-min upper cut-off limit. Still, the impact on knowledge gain was significantly higher for H1 and H2 in comparison to H3, with no significant difference between H1 and H2 (Table 4).

Table 4 Independent samples *t*-test results for knowledge gain (left) and Tukey HSD (right)

		G	N	M	SD	df	t	d	Tukey HSD		
Upper cut-off 35 min	H1 (quiz)	Exp.	11	6.45	3.38	20	1.90*	0.81		H2	H3
		Con.	11	3.63	3.11						
	H2 (annotation)	Exp.	14	7.22	3.19	24	1.85*	0.73	H1	– 0.76 ns	4.30**
		Con.	12	4.67	3.80						
	H3 (navigation)	Exp.	13	2.16	3.00	26	0.35^{ns}	0.13	H2	–	5.06**
		Con.	15	1.74	3.33						
Upper cut-off 55 min	H1 (quiz)	Exp.	12	6.17	3.79	21	1.74*	0.72		H2	H3
		Con.	11	3.63	3.11						
	H2 (annotation)	Exp.	16	6.69	3.38	26	1.49^{a}	0.57	H1	– 0.52^{ns}	4.01*
		Con.	12	4.67	3.80						
	H3 (navigation)	Exp.	13	2.16	3.00	26	0.35^{ns}	0.13	H2	–	4.53**
		Con.	15	1.74	3.33						

Note Comparison of mean knowledge gain between groups, Exp. = Experiment, Con. = Control, d = Cohen's d, ^{ns} = non-significant, $^{a}p < 0.1$, *$p < 0.05$, **$p < 0.01$, ***$p < 0.001$

6 Discussion

6.1 Key Findings

The study results suggest that the isolated addition of quizzes (H1) or annotations (H2) in educational videos significantly increases students' knowledge gain when compared to a standard video with typical play-pause-speed buttons, a table of content, and a scrubbable timeline. Apparently, an educational video in higher education enhances learning performance on a higher scale if it gets enriched with interactive elements that can provide information recall and reflection (quizzes) or guide attention to critical information (annotations). This first observation aligns with extant research (Althwaini and Mahmoud 2021; Vural 2013). Going beyond that, our results emphasize that these interactive element types equally contribute to learning performance. As can be inferred from this observation, leveraging engagement while learning with educational videos may contribute to learning performance. What still needs approvement is the theoretical reasoning behind these effect mechanisms, leaving potential for future research.

In contrast, interactive elements concerning navigation features (H3) that foster individual knowledge construction seem not to result in a significant improvement in learning performance. Moreover, our results suggest that the other two interaction types have a greater influence on learning performance. Delving deeper into navigation features, those include elements like links that provide students with additional material that is not directly embedded in the educational video. As a consequence, studying such material requires an active cognitive engagement of students (Redmond et al. 2018). According to Kleftodimos et al. (2020), cognitive engagement requires visible benefits prior to executing an additional task, which may be one reason why we found no significant effect in our study. In addition, consuming additional learning material expects students to plan and control their learning process, which refers to the application of metacognitive learning strategies. The generation of effective metacognitive learning strategies represents a much more cognitively challenging task compared to answering a question in a quiz or being guided by additional annotations (e.g., Mitsea and Drigas 2019). This depicts a potential way to explain our results as quizzes and annotations might be used in a more straight-up fashion compared to navigation features, which leads to performance increases on shorter notice. To subsume, a future research avenue lies in investigating if and how particular navigation features in educational videos can enable improvements in learning performance.

6.2 Implications for Academia and Educational Practice

Our results have implications for academia and educational practice alike. However, they should be considered in relation to our research context, i.e., higher education videos that teach IS lecture content via presentations. Essentially, our study corroborates extant research regarding the potential of interactive elements to foster learning performance, analyzing their effects in isolation under similar conditions. In contrast to quizzes and annotations, we could not observe such an effect for navigation features. More importantly, we could not identify any study in the extant body of knowledge that systematically compared the effects of different interactive element types in educational videos. Accordingly, our study provides an initial step toward closing this literature gap. In this vein, our results suggest that quizzes and annotations can increase learning performance more effectively than navigation features.

The gained insights provide several avenues for future research. By now, our set of experiments compared three commonly used and easy-to-implement types of interactive elements, considering each type in isolation. As a further advancement, it might be a fruitful next step to compare different combinations of interactive element types in a systematic fashion. Navigation features that cannot increase learning performance on their own, might perhaps further increase the effectiveness of other interactive element types. This approach may point towards a rating of a variety of element combinations. Based on that, this might answer the question of whether increased interactivity richness, i.e., more interactivity in videos simultaneously with a broader variety of interactive elements, will always prove beneficial. There might also be a concise set of few element types that most effectively supports learning performance while keeping the implementation effort bearable.

Regarding implications for educational practice, we provide guidance about what interactive elements exist and how these can be integrated effectively into educational videos, aiming at converting passive watchers into active learners (Kolas 2015; Wachtler et al. 2016). Thereby, quizzes and annotations showed significant effects, whereas navigation features do not lead to significant performance increases. Thus, these results show that inducing recall through quizzes and drawing attention to critical information through annotations represent two effective possibilities to stimulate learning performance. For example, implementing short memorization questions or highlighting specific information can already lead to significant performance increases. Our observations suggest that interactive elements in educational videos should be implemented with clear motives in mind, ensuring that their predefined goals (e.g., increasing learning performance) can be suitably addressed.

7 Limitations and Concluding Remarks

Our findings are not without limitations. In conducting our study in the context of a specific IS course, we ensured similar conditions for the comparison of interactive element types. At the same time, this led to a relatively small sample size, which may limit the generalizability of our findings. Nonetheless, the results appear stable since typical test assumptions such as normality, homogeneity, and homoscedasticity have been confirmed before applying the statistical approaches. Robustness tests affirmed the validity of our findings, as the applied Tukey HSD indicates significant differences between the examined groups. As another limitation, the experiment design did not allow the collection of interaction data, i.e., in which way the students employed the embedded interactive elements. By collecting such data, we may better understand how students perceive and accept distinct interactive element types in VBL and investigate in what way they stimulate learning performance. Potential investigations may focus on the duration, intensity, and frequency of use of interactive elements in isolation. Consequently, further reasons for the ineffectiveness of navigation features (H3) could be uncovered.

Future research may investigate larger sample sizes to further increase the validity of our findings. To strengthen the generalizability, the impact of the interactive element types across different (non-IS) courses or subject areas may be examined. In addition, the analysis of further isolated interactive element types in VBL would contribute to our understanding of their particular effects on learning performance. Even though we studied several interactive element types resulting from our literature review, we leave a few elements out of scope, e.g., search functions, live discussions, and fully branched videos. Future research endeavors may employ further interactive element types and analyze their respective ways of stimulating student engagement. Beyond that, the effects of embedded interactive elements may be compared to subsequent interactions like external quizzes. As a further avenue, there is a need to explore further possible goal(s) of VBL. During our study, we focused on the concept of learning performance, measured in terms of gained knowledge through pre-tests and post-tests. Future research could examine other effects like satisfaction and attention, or, as a notable extension, the interrelationships between such effects. Even though we acknowledge that our findings imply limited generalizability, we think they provide a starting point for future endeavors while guiding practitioners toward a better application of interactive elements in higher education teaching contexts.

Acknowledgements This study has been funded by the "Innovation in der Hochschullehre" foundation as part of the "Digitale Kulturen der Lehre entwickeln (DiKuLe)" project.

References

Albó, L., Hernández-Leo, D. and Moreno Oliver, V. (2018). 'Smartphones or Laptops in the Collaborative Classroom? A Study of Video-Based Learning in Higher Education', *Behaviour & Information Technology* **38**(6), 637–649.

Althwaini, S. N. and Mahmoud, S. M. (2021). 'The Effect of the Number of Hints Accompanying Content in Interactive Videos on Achieving Some Learning Outcomes for Female Students in Hail Schools', *International Journal of Advanced and Applied Sciences* **8**(3), 120–129.

Barut Tugtekin, E. and Dursun, O. O. (2022). 'Effect of Animated and Interactive Video Variations on Learners' Motivation in Distance Education', *Education and Information Technologies* **27**, 3247–3276.

Benkada, C. and Moccozet, L. (2017). Enriched Interactive Videos for Teaching and Learning, *in* 'Proceedings of the 21st International Conference Information Visualisation', pp. 344–349.

Brecht, H. D. and Ogilby, S. M. (2008). 'Enabling a Comprehensive Teaching Strategy: Video Lectures', *Journal of Information Technology Education* **7**, 71–86.

Bruning, I. L. (1983). 'An Information Processing Approach to a Theory of Instruction', *Educational Technology Research and Development* **31**, 91–101.

Cairncross, S. and Mannion, M. (2001). 'Interactive Multimedia and Learning: Realizing the Benefits', *Innovations in Education and Teaching International* **38**(2), 156–164.

Cattaneo, A., Nguyen, A. T., Sauli, F. and Aprea, C. (2015). 'Scuolavisione: Teaching and Learning with Hypervideos in the Swiss Vocational System', *Journal of e-Learning and Knowledge Society* **11**(2), 27–47.

Chatti, M. A., Marinov, M., Sabov, O., Laksono, R., Sofyan, Z., Fahmy Yousef, A. M. and Schroeder, U. (2016). 'Video Annotation and Analytics in Coursemapper', *Smart Learning Environments* **3**(10), 1–21.

Chen, Y.-T. (2012). 'The Effect of Thematic Video-Based Instruction on Learning and Motivation in E-Learning', *International Journal of the Physical Sciences* **7**(6), 957 - 965.

Cohen, J. (1988). The Analysis of Variance, in Cohen, J. (Ed.) *Statistical Power Analysis for the Behavioral Sciences (2nd Ed.).* Lawrence Erlbaum Associates, pp. 274–287.

Cook, B. R. and Babon, A. (2016). 'Active Learning through Online Quizzes: Better Learning and Less (Busy) Work', *Journal of Geography in Higher Education* **41**(1), 24–38.

Cuka, K. and Bufasi, E. (2022). 'Hyper Video for Improving Students' Math Performance', *European Journal of Education and Pedagogy* **3**(5), 13–15.

Delen, E., Liew, J. and Willson, V. (2014). 'Effects of Interactivity and Instructional Scaffolding on Learning: Self-Regulation in Online Video-Based Environments', *Computers & Education* **78**, 312–320.

Dieck-Assad, G., Hinojosa-Olivares, J. M. and Colomer-Farrarnos, J. (2020). 'Study of the Effectiveness of Interactive Videos in Applied Electronics Courses', *International Journal on Interactive Design and Manufacturing* **14**, 983–1001.

Dror, I. E. (2008). 'Technology Enhanced Learning', *Pragmatics & Cognition* **16**(2), 215–223.

Kleftodimos, A., Lappas, G. and Evangelidis, G. (2020). 'Edutainment and Practice in Video-Based Learning: Enriching Educational Videos with Interactive Activities and Games', *International Journal of Entertainment Technology and Management* **1**(1), 5–33.

Kolas, L. (2015). Application of Interactive Videos in Education, *in* 'Proceedings of the International Conference on Information Technology Based Higher Education and Training', IEEE, pp. 1–6.

Ku, W.-P., Yang, K.-H. and Chang, W.-L. (2019). The Design and Evaluation of Interactive Video-Based Flipped Classroom on Mathematics Learning, *in* 'Proceedings of the 8th International Congress on Advanced Applied Informatics', IEEE, pp. 1041–1042.

Meixner, B. (2014). 'Annotated Interactive Non-Linear Video - Software Suite, Download and Cache Management', *Fakultät für Informatik und Mathematik.* Passau. Universität Passau, p. 410.

Merkt, M., Weigand, S., Heier, A. and Schwan, S. (2011). 'Learning with Videos Vs. Learning with Print: The Role of Interactive Features', *Learning and Instruction* **21**(6), 687–704.

Mitrovic, A., Dimitrova, V., Lau, L., Weerasinghe, A. and Mathews, M. (2017). Supporting Constructive Video-Based Learning: Requirements Elicitation from Exploratory Studies, in André, E., Baker, R., Hu, X., Rodrigo, M. and du Boulay, B. (Eds.) *Artificial Intelligence in Education*. Springer, pp. 224–237.

Mitsea, E. and Drigas, A. (2019). 'A Journey into the Metacognitive Learning Strategies', *International Journal of Online and Biomedical Engineering* **15**(14), 4–20.

Nicol, D. J. and Macfarlane-Dick, D. (2006). 'Formative Assessment and Self-Regulated Learning: A Model and Seven Principles of Good Feedback Practice', *Studies in Higher Education* **31**(2), 199–218.

Pal, D. and Patra, S. (2020). 'University Students' Perception of Video-Based Learning in Times of Covid-19: A Tam/Ttf Perspective', *International Journal of Human–Computer Interaction* **37**(10), 903–921.

Palaigeorgiou, G., Chloptsidou, I. and Lemonidis, C. (2018). Computational Estimation in the Classroom with Tablets, Interactive Selfie Video and Self-Regulated Learning, *in* 'Proceedings of the Interactive Mobile Communication Technologies and Learning', Springer, pp. 475–486.

Palaigeorgiou, G. and Papadopoulou, A. (2018). 'Promoting Self-Paced Learning in the Elementary Classroom with Interactive Video, an Online Course Platform and Tablets', *Education and Information Technologies* **24**, 805–823.

Palaigeorgiou, G., Papadopoulou, A. and Kazanidis, I. (2019). Interactive Video for Learning: A Review of Interaction Types, Commercial Platforms, and Design Guidelines, in Tsitouridou, M., A. Diniz, J. and Mikropoulos, T. (Eds.) *Technology and Innovation in Learning, Teaching and Education*. Springer, pp. 503–518.

Priyakanth, R., Abburi, R. and Praveena, M. (2021). 'Design and Impact of Interactive Video Content for the Improvement of Student Engagement and Learning', *Journal of Engineering Education Transformations* **34**, 518–523.

Redmond, P., Heffernan, A., Abawi, L., Brown, A. and Henderson, R. (2018). 'An Online Engagement Framework for Higher Education', *Online Learning* **22**(1), 183–204.

Sablić, M., Mirosavljević, A. and Škugor, A. (2020). 'Video-Based Learning (Vbl) - Past, Present and Future: An Overview of the Research Published from 2008 to 2019', *Technology, Knowledge and Learning* **26**(4), 1061–1077.

Schoeffmann, K., Hudelist, M. A. and Huber, J. (2015). 'Video Interaction Tools', *ACM Computing Surveys* **48**(1), 1–34.

Seidel, N. (2015). Interaction Design Patterns for Spatio-Temporal Annotations in Video Learning Environments, *in* 'Proceedings of the 20th European Conference on Pattern Languages of Programs', pp. 1–21.

Spiro, R. J. and Jehng, J.-C. (1990). Cognitive Flexibility and Hypertext: Theory and Technology for the Nonlinear and Multidimensional Traversal of Complex Subject Matter, *Cognition, Education, and Multimedia: Exploring Ideas in High Technology*. Lawrence Erlbaum Associates, Inc. Hillsdale, NJ, US, pp. 163–205.

Subhash, S. and Cudney, E. A. (2018). 'Gamified Learning in Higher Education: A Systematic Review of the Literature', *Computers in Human Behavior* **87**, 192–206.

Vural, Ö. F. (2013). 'The Impact of a Question-Embedded Video-Based Learning Tool on E-Learning', *Educational Sciences: Theory & Practice* **13**(2), 1315–1323

Wachtler, J., Hubmann, M., Zöhrer, H. and Ebner, M. (2016). 'An Analysis of the Use and Effect of Questions in Interactive Learning-Videos', *Smart Learning Environments* **3**(13), 1–16.

Weinert, T., Benner, D., Dickhaut, E., Janson, A., Schöbel, S. and Leimeister, J. M. (2021). 'Unterstützung Digitaler Bildungsprozesse Durch Interaktive Gamifizierte Lernvideos – Wie Innovative Lernvideos Motivation Und Lernerfolg Steigern Können', *HMD Praxis der Wirtschaftsinformatik* **58**(6), 1483–1503.

Yousef, A. M. F., Chatti, M. A. and Schroeder, U. (2014). 'The State of Video-Based Learning: A Review and Future Perspectives', *International Journal on Advances in Life Sciences* **6**(3), 122–135.

Yürüm, O. R., Yildirim, S. and Temizel, T. T. (2022). 'An Intervention Framework for Developing Interactive Video Lectures Based on Video Clickstream Behavior: A Quasi-Experimental Evaluation', *Interactive Learning Environments*, 1–22.

Zainuddin, Z. and Perera, C. J. (2018). 'Supporting Students' Self-Directed Learning in the Flipped Classroom through the Lms Tes Blendspace', *On the Horizon* **26**(4), 281–290.

Zainuddin, Z., Shujahat, M., Haruna, H. and Chu, S. K. W. (2020). 'The Role of Gamified E-Quizzes on Student Learning and Engagement: An Interactive Gamification Solution for a Formative Assessment System', *Computers & Education* **145**.

Zhang, D., Zhou, L., Briggs, R. O. and Nunamaker, J. F. (2006). 'Instructional Video in E-Learning: Assessing the Impact of Interactive Video on Learning Effectiveness', *Information & Management* **43**(1), 15–27.

Addressing Learners' Heterogeneity in Higher Education: An Explainable AI-Based Feedback Artifact for Digital Learning Environments

Felix Haag, Sebastian A. Günther, Konstantin Hopf, Philipp Handschuh, Maria Klose, and Thorsten Staake

Abstract Due to the advent of digital learning environments and the freedom they offer for learners, new challenges arise for students' self-regulated learning. To overcome these challenges, the provision of feedback has led to excellent results, such as less procrastination and improved academic performance. Yet, current feedback artifacts neglect learners' heterogeneity when it comes to prescriptive feedback that should meet personal characteristics and self-regulated learning skills. In this paper, we derive requirements from self-regulated learning theory for a feedback artifact that takes learners' heterogeneity into account. Based on these requirements, we design, instantiate, and evaluate an Explainable AI-based approach. The results demonstrate that our artifact is able to detect promising patterns in data on learners' behaviors and characteristics. Moreover, our evaluation suggests that learners perceive our feedback as valuable. Ultimately, our study informs Information Systems research in the design of future Explainable AI-based feedback artifacts that seek to address learners' heterogeneity.

Keywords Digital learning · Higher education · Feedback · Explainable artificial intelligence · Counterfactual explanations

---

F. Haag (✉) · S. A. Günther · K. Hopf · T. Staake
Information Systems and Energy Efficient Systems, University of Bamberg, Bamberg, Germany
e-mail: felix.haag@uni-bamberg.de

S. A. Günther
e-mail: sebastian.guenther@uni-bamberg.de

K. Hopf
e-mail: konstantin.hopf@uni-bamberg.de

T. Staake
e-mail: thorsten.staake@uni-bamberg.de

P. Handschuh · M. Klose
Leibniz Institute for Educational Trajectories, Bamberg, Germany
e-mail: philipp.handschuh@lifbi.de

M. Klose
e-mail: maria.klose@lifbi.de

D. Beverungen et al. (eds.), *Transforming the Digitally Sustainable Enterprise*, Lecture Notes in Information Systems and Organisation 76,
https://doi.org/10.1007/978-3-031-80125-9_30

1 Introduction

Many institutions in higher education have responded to the growing popularity of Massive Open Online Courses (MOOCs) by either complementary or fully adapting face-to-face courses to digital learning environments. While the shift towards digital learning environments provides several advantages to instructors and learners (e.g., flexibility in scheduling teaching and learning sessions), this freedom also comes along with challenges for learners. More specifically, there is evidence that students with poor self-regulated skills suffer especially from this shift, potentially resulting in lower academic performance, whereas those with strong skills can cope well with a more digital setting (Kizilcec et al. 2017).

To support learners in digital learning environments, a plethora of artifacts came into existence that harnesses the potential of digital data traces recording their learning activities (Ifenthaler and Yau 2020). Recent examples in Information Systems (IS) research include learner support in the form of gamification elements (Benner et al. 2022; Leung et al. 2022), digital companions (Kruse et al. 2023), chatbots (Gupta and Chen 2022), and peer information (Li et al. 2021). Feedback (i.e., the provision of prescriptive information) thereby resembles an inherent way to support learners and represents a core mechanism for many of such IS artifacts. In general, feedback studies document intriguing behavioral effects on reducing procrastination or improving learning outcomes (see, e.g., Gunther 2021; Theobald and Bellhauser 2022).

Yet, due to their design, many of the feedback artifacts only support a specific type of learner (i.e., regarding self-regulated skills and prior knowledge of a topic). For instance, feedback in the mid of the semester designed to increase learning engagement might produce behavior change for students with low structuring skills (i.e., metacognition), while being less helpful for students with higher skills. This conjecture might also explain why studies often find mixed effects among different types of learners (see, e.g., Li et al. 2021; Leung et al. 2022). What is currently missing in IS research are approaches for feedback provision that directly address different types of learners regarding their heterogeneity and provide personalized instructions of a prescriptive nature.

We argue that technological advances in Machine Learning (ML) and Explainable Artificial Intelligence (XAI) can empower students by addressing learners' heterogeneity regarding their personal characteristics and Self-regulated Learning (SRL) skills through personalized instructions. ML has the capability to capture promising patterns in learning activities, learners' characteristics, and the interplay of both (i.e., activities and characteristics) that may resemble successful factors for individual academic success (Arnold and Pistilli 2012; Nguyen et al. 2020). Recent ML algorithms are able to model real-world relationships but usually hide the patterns detected in data from their users. XAI aims to overcome this issue by translating these patterns into a human-interpretable form (Meske et al. 2020). A potentially suitable XAI approach that allows to derive instructions of prescriptive nature from ML models is Counterfactual Explanations (CEs) (Fernández-Loría et al. 2022; Molnar 2019). CEs are motivated by the phenomenon that humans tend to judge events by the potential reasons why a desired event did not occur (Miller 2019), e.g., "Why did I get a poor grade in the exam instead of an excellent one?". To provide answers to such questions from the perspective of a ML model, CEs derive explanations in the form of required changes for a desired model outcome (Mothilal et al. 2020). Such explanations might also hold for real-world problems, e.g., "If I had spent more time in the learning platform, I wouldn't have had a poor grade in the exam". Hence, CEs have the potential to guide students' learning in digital environments through context-specific instructions that build on the learned patterns of the respective ML model. Therefore, this paper seeks to answer the following Research Question (RQ): **RQ**: *How should an XAI-based artifact be developed that guides learning in digital environments through feedback provision while addressing learners' heterogeneity (e.g., regarding their characteristics and SRL skills)?*

To address this research question, we design, implement, and evaluate a user-centered feedback artifact that intends to leverage recent advances in ML and XAI to recognize learners' activities and characteristics and their interplay to derive meaningful feedback and therefore effective guidance during online learning. The overall goal of this study is to map the knowledge generated in SRL theory to an XAI-based artifact, which will contribute to the debate on providing effective learner support in digital environments (Gupta and Bostrom 2009). While our artifact opens a window to further research opportunities, we focus within this paper on the feasibility of such an approach.

Our paper is structured as follows: In the subsequent section, we outline the foundations of SRL theory to understand students' learning activities and introduce ML and XAI as concepts for learner guidance. Building on this background, we derive issues from phenomena documented in the literature that emerge for the design of such an artifact addressing learner heterogeneity. Relying on these issues, we synthesize requirements for the design of our artifact and use them to test our implementation. We finally highlight and discuss principles for future IS that implement XAI-based feedback to address subject heterogeneity in digital learning environments.

2 Background

2.1 Self-regulated Learning (SRL) Theory

Higher education poses many challenges to the learning processes of students. In contrast to secondary education, individuals have to rely more on their own self-regulated learning capabilities (i.e., the skill to plan, monitor and evaluate one's work and to control one's motivation and emotion) (Vosniadou 2020). Indeed, there is a stream of research under the notion of SRL that tries to understand which antecedents shape individuals' learning processes (see, e.g., Crede and Phillips 2011; Pintrich 2004;

Wild and Schiefele 1994). Within the SRL framework, individuals differ with respect to cognitive, metacognitive, and resource management skills (Panadero 2017), which are fundamentally related to their context-specific choice of self-learning strategies. For instance, students with a higher level of time management skills tend to plan their learning better (e.g., by making and executing plans), while weaker skills could be related to self-regulation issues (e.g., procrastination). Therefore, to effectively guide students' SRL implies acknowledging these differences in students and also keeping students' motivation for learning high, as motivation is seen as a fundamental basis for SRL to take place (Pintrich 1999).

It is important to note that literature also provides a process-oriented view of how learners engage in SRL. More specifically, literature commonly distinguishes between several cyclical phases of SRL. For instance, Zimmerman and Moylan (2009) classify SRL activities into three consecutive phases: the forethought phase, the performance phase, and the self-reflection phase. In the forethought phase, learners plan tasks and set their learning goals, which also involves analyzing the value of the tasks at hand as well as assessing self-motivation beliefs (e.g., regarding their self-efficacy or outcome expectation in addressing a specific task) (Zimmerman and Moylan 2009). Subsequently, in the performance phase, learners execute different learning strategies (e.g., elaborate and repeat contents), as well as observe themselves to stay cognitively engaged and motivated (Panadero 2017). Finally, in the self-reflection phase, learners judge the progress towards their goals and make, based on the progress, attributions to their selves. For instance, in meeting or not meeting the learning goals of the forethought phase, learners might evaluate the suitability of the chosen learning strategies or reflect on themselves (e.g., eliciting positive or negative emotions associated with learning) (Zimmerman and Moylan 2009).

2.2 ML and XAI for Learner Guidance

Recent advances in the field of ML—one of the core technologies of Artificial Intelligence (AI)—have opened up new avenues for addressing the challenges of higher education learning in digital learning environments (Ouyang et al. 2022). Given that ML algorithms are capable of capturing complex patterns in large amounts of data (e.g., Berente et al. 2019), they could provide learners and instructors with additional insights. Examples include the early detection of students at-risk of failing an exam (Baneres et al. 2019) or the recommendation of courses (Bousbahi and Chorfi 2015).

Although the high predictive power of modern ML approaches is beneficial for application fields such as learning, models often come along with a lack of transparency and thus hide the patterns they detect in data from their users, leaving their potential to assist humans through the exposure of captured patterns untapped (Meske et al. 2020). The field of research that aims to improve the transparency of complex ML models is referred to as XAI (Barredo Arrieta et al. 2020).

A recent approach in XAI are CE methods that provide data-driven explanations on "what-if" questions (i.e., if a learner did a specific set of quizzes and videos, a model would estimate a better grade) (Fernández-Loría et al. 2022; Molnar 2019). CEs methods search for causal changes in features to shift a prediction to a desired output (Mothilal et al. 2020), thus allowing—on the premise that the model reflects real-world relationships (Štrumbelj et al. 2009)—for guidance involving the derivation of personalized instructions. Hence, CEs may be beneficial for higher education learning in three ways: First, by using CEs to demonstrate individually how to achieve a desired learning outcome (i.e., achieve more exam points). Second, as ML uses data on past learning behavior that has led to high and low learning success, the approach could suggest weaker students learning strategies from strong students. Exposing the behaviors of strong learners to potentially struggling learners has already been found to be effective in prior SRL studies (Davis et al. 2017). Third, by providing guidance on an individual level that is to some degree automated, it does not require much involvement of instructors.

3 Research Approach and Artifact Requirements

The research approach of our study is inspired by the principles of design science research (Hevner et al. 2004; Peffers et al. 2007). We thereby strive to tackle the challenge that current digital learning feedback artifacts do not account sufficiently for learners' heterogeneity (i.e., our problem specification). Following a nomothetic genre of design science inquiry (Baskerville et al. 2015), we identify issues from established knowledge (i.e., SRL and XAI literature) resulting from natural challenges in digital learning environments for the design of an XAI-based feedback artifact addressing learners' heterogeneity. Relying on these issues, we derive Meta-Requirements (MRs), implement the artifact, and evaluate it against measurable criteria. We finally outline design knowledge from artifact development and evaluation in the form of Design Principles (DPs) to address the general problem class at hand (i.e., effectively guide learners within the scope of digital learning environments). Given the limited scope of this paper, we briefly summarize the issues and related MRs below and outline the derived DPs inspired by Gregor et al. (2020) in Sect. 6.

We divide the MRs into functional (i.e., what the artifact must be able to do) and non-functional (i.e., properties of the artifact that need to be measurable) requirements according to Sommerville (2011), where we inherently consider the functional requirements for development and evaluate the non-functional ones against the artifact (Fig. 1). In summary, we identified seven issues from literature. I1 to I6—derived from the cyclical phase model of self-regulatory feedback by Zimmerman and Moylan (2009)—aim to account for potential sources of heterogeneity in SRL. From these six issues, we derived four MRs. The first requirement (**MR1**), the provision of personalized feedback, should support students in specifying learning outcomes by informing them about the potential benefits of responding to feedback and allowing students to set specific task goals (I1) in accordance with their time management (I3). Moreover, the feedback should help them to metacognitively monitor their learning

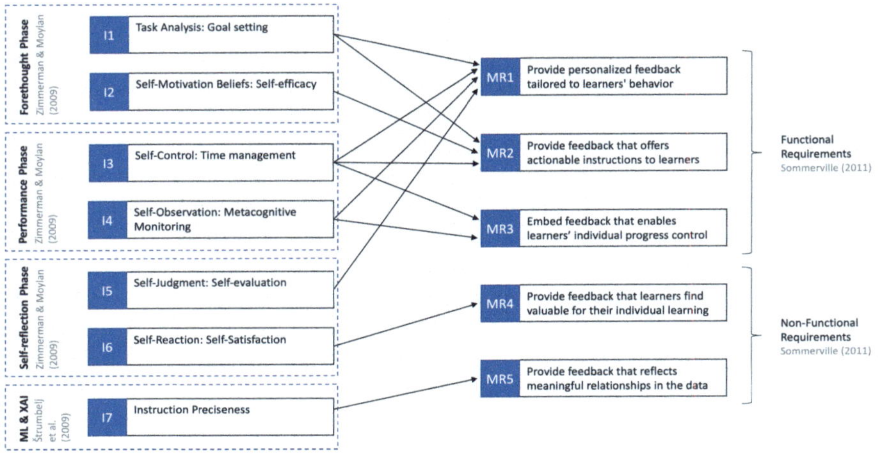

Fig. 1 Issues (I1–I7) from SRL and XAI literature and MRs of the feedback artifact

processes (I4), as well as to compare their progress to an evaluative standard (e.g., self-goals) (I5). Second, the artifact should meet the **MR2**, namely the provision of feedback in the form of actionable instructions to learners. Such instructions should stimulate goal setting (I1) and associated time management processes (I3), as well as lead to feelings of self-efficacy in case the tasks are perceived as manageable (I2). As the third requirement (**MR3**), the feedback of the artifact shall be embedded into a course overview page to enable learners' progress control. With the help of such progress control, learners who have deficits in time management (I3) and metacognitive monitoring (I4) can be supported, as the feedback might enable them to track their learning processes. Fourth, the artifact should provide feedback that learners find valuable for their individual learning (**MR4**), consequently be perceived as useful and be accepted by the learner (Strijbos et al. 2010). Valuable feedback is important for learners' self-satisfaction (I6), as learners prefer learning activities that previously led to satisfaction (compared to Bandura 2001). We evaluate this non-functional requirement within a user-based evaluation. The fifth requirement (**MR5**) stems from the XAI literature and refers to the precision of the instructions provided by the artifact (I7). More specifically, Štrumbelj et al. (2009) argue that the better the model recognizes domain concepts, the higher the quality of a data-driven explanation, and vice versa. The recognition of domain concepts, approximated through predictive performance, is therefore a prerequisite for the meaningful reflection of relationships in real-world data, and thus an essential non-functional system requirement for instruction quality.

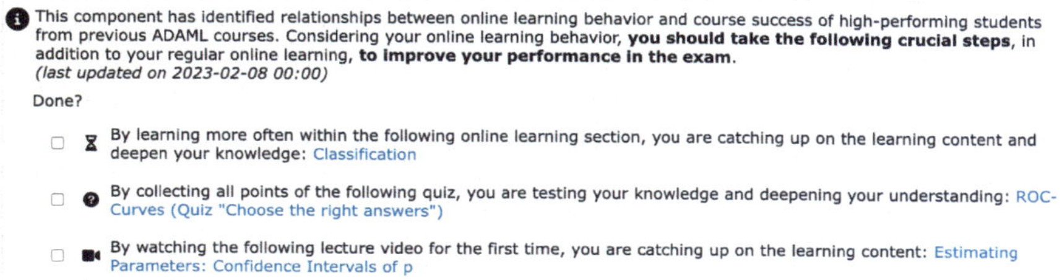

Fig. 2 Exemplary component output for learners generated by the artifact

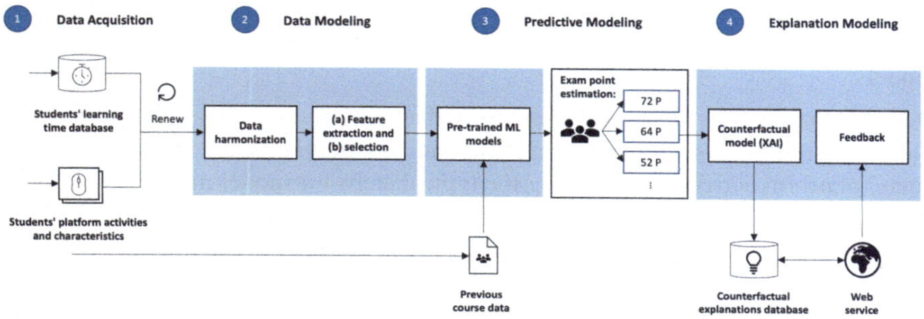

Fig. 3 Quantitative modeling of the artifact

4 Artifact Description

Our artifact is embedded into a digital learning environment and displays instructional feedback in the form of a component. The development builds on the aforementioned requirements and is designed to address learners' heterogeneity. Figure 2 illustrates an exemplary output of the component, displaying feedback to learners. The component consists of three elements and addresses MR1-MR3 (i.e., functional requirements): First, the introductory text, which refers to MR1 by pointing to the personalization of feedback and its tailoring to one's past online learning behavior. In doing so, the component explains that the additional implementation of instructions can lead to increased exam performance. Second, the three actionable instructions addressing MR2. We limit the instructions to three items because we argue that more instructions might lead to reactance in learners due to the considerable increase in additional workload. Third, check boxes learners can mark as "Done" to enable progress control, which addresses MR3.

The quantitative modeling of our artifact to obtain feedback comprises four steps (Fig. 3). These steps serve, on the one hand, for initially instantiating pre-trained ML models, and on the other, for generating feedback for an ongoing course. The paragraphs below describe each step in detail.

Data Acquisition. For data acquisition, our artifact collects behavioral data from an Open edX[1] online learning platform hosted by our university. On Open edX, students can access instructional videos, slides, and quizzes. The artifact considers extensive data on students' behavior and characteristics through built-in plugins in three ways. First, through the integration of the JavaScript library TimeMe.js[2] into the learning environment to more precisely record the *students' learning time* and save these data in an operational database. Second, by logging text files that record *students' platform activities and characteristics* in the form of user events on the edX environment (e.g., file downloads and videos watched etc.) and answers obtained from a built-in survey. Third, through the consideration of *previous course data* of prior semesters on students' learning time, platform activities, characteristics, and achieved exam points (i.e., the target variable) for a supervised training of the ML models.

Data Modeling. The functionality of our artifact initially performs *data harmonization* by merging the student learning time data and the log data containing the students' platform activities. Following the typical steps for model instantiation (Kühl et al. 2021), the resulting data set passes two successive preparation steps: *Feature extraction* (a) to obtain processable and meaningful features (i.e., predictor variables) that the artifact can feed into the ML algorithms. We list all features the artifact considers and mark features of type purely "predictive" with a "P" and all "actionable" features that we consider as part of our feedback artifact with "A" (Table 1). The rationale behind predictive-only features is that some may be misleading (e.g., video pauses) for feedback or hardly alterable but seem common for academic performance prediction (e.g., gender) due to their impact on students' learning (Hellas et al. 2018; Schoemer et al. 2021; Yukselturk and Bulut 2009). Finally, the artifact organizes the data set in an expanding window to ensure time-related predictive models and to consider only content and learner behavior that is relevant up to a certain point in time (e.g., for weekly granularity and feedback updates: Starting in the first semester week and gradually expanding the data set up to the final week). Moreover, we applied automatic *feature selection* (b) to capture the most important features and eliminate irrelevant ones. In doing so, our artifact includes a mutual information regression module (Kraskov et al. 2004; Ross 2014) that can cope with numerical and categorical features while maintaining interpretability.

Predictive Modeling. For the provision of feedback, we instantiate ML models to learn the relationship between learner behavior and characteristics, and course success. Our artifact predicts exam points achieved instead of the grade to avoid unnecessary dependent variable transformations and excludes exam retakers, and students with zero exam points from the target variable not to bias the ML models. We embed four well-recognized ML algorithms for predicting students' exam points that stem from different categories of ML algorithms (e.g., Migueis et al. 2018). We choose Extreme Gradient Boosting (XGBoost), CatBoost, Random Forest, and

[1] https://openedx.org/de/.

[2] https://github.com/jasonzissman/TimeMe.js/.

Table 1 Variables used for prediction and actionable feedback

Group	Variable	Description	Data type[a]	Type[b]
Video	VideoViews.Total	Total number of video views	Int	A
	ViewsTotal.Complete	Total number of completely viewed videos	Int	A
	ViewsPerVideo{ID}	Indicates (unique) whether a specific video has already been watched	Int	A
	ViewsPerVideo{ID}. Complete	Indicates (unique) whether a video has already been watched completely	Int	A
	VideoPauses.Total	Total number of pauses while watching videos	Int	P
	VideoPlaybackSpeed.Total	Average speed with which the videos are played	Dbl	P
	VideoTranscriptHidden.Total	Total number of times a student hides the video transcript	Int	P
Quiz	QuizzesTaken.Total	Total number of quizzes taken	Int	A
	QuizTakenPerQuiz.{ID}	Indicates (unique) whether a specific quiz has already been taken	Int	A
	CorrectPerQuiz.{ID}	Total number of times a student achieved the maximum points of a specific quiz	Int	A
	CorrectRatioPerQuiz.{ID}	Ratio between the mean achieved points and the maximum points of a specific quiz	Dbl	P
File download	AssetDownload.{ID}	Indicates (unique) how often the slides of a specific tutorial/lecture have been downloaded	Int	A
Platform activity	Time.Total	Total time spent on the learning platform (incl. sum, SD, max)	Dbl	A
	HoursDuringDay.Total	Total time spent on the learning platform during the day (6:00 a.m.–8:00 p.m.)	Dbl	P
	HoursDuringNight.Total	Total time spent on the platform during night	Dbl	P
	TimePerSection.{ID}	Total time spent per learning section	Dbl	A
	Requests.Total	Total number of HTTP request on the learning platform (incl. sum, SD, max)	Int/Dbl	P
	RequestsPerSection.{ID}	Total number of HTTP request per learning section	Int	P
	Sessions.Total	Total number of learning sessions (i.e., logins) on the learning platform (incl. sum, SD, max)	Int/Dbl	A
	SessionsPerSection.{ID}	Total number of learning sessions (i.e., logins) on the platform per learning section	Int	A
	BonusExerciseDone.{ID}	Indicates whether students have submitted a specific bonus assignment in the course to achieve extra points in the exam	Cat	P
Student characteristics	StudyProgram	Indicates the program (e.g., Information Systems) in which the student is enrolled	Cat	P
	Gender	Gender of the student (female, male, diverse)	Cat	P

[a] *Int* integer; *Dbl* double; *Cat* categorical
[b] *A* actionable; *P* predictive

Support Vector Regression as estimators. The models are trained separately for each period within the expanding window. To reduce sampling bias, the artifact applies a stratified 80/20 train-test split according to students' exam points. Building on the training data set, we integrate the previously instantiated feature selection to build feature configurations using a percentage proportion p of the total features with $p \in \{20, 40, 60, 80, 100\}$ (i.e., $p\%$ of features with the highest score). Our artifact then trains models for each feature configuration and performs parameter tuning using a grid search applying a 5-fold cross-validation. The artifact automatically picks the model with the lowest prediction error on the test set according to the Root Mean Square Error (RMSE) to choose the best ML model for each period in time. Finally, our artifact fits *pre-trained models* on the whole data set (i.e., the entire previous course data, e.g., for a specific week) as the basis for generating CEs.

Explanation Modeling. To derive feedback for students, we rely on the XAI method Diverse Counterfactual Explanations (DiCE) introduced by Mothilal et al. (2020). The method seeks to propose diverse CEs (i.e., offer multiple explanations for behavioral change to increase exam points), which is desirable for real-world scenarios (Kusner et al. 2017). Given that our feedback is limited to three instructions, we employ the XAI method Shapley Additive Explanations (SHAP) (Lundberg et al. 2020; Lundberg and Lee 2017) for changes that affect more than three features. The *counterfactual model* stores the instructions for each student in an *CEs database*. Finally, the *feedback* component (Fig. 2) displays instructions to learners by accessing the CEs database through a *web service*. We list the translation of CEs to actionable feedback in the Appendix (see Table 3).

5 Artifact Evaluation

Given the inherent fulfillment of functional requirements due to a corresponding development, we focus on the non-functional requirements for evaluation. Thereby, we follow the chronological order of the development process, starting with the evaluation of MR5 regarding the reflection of meaningful relationships followed by the evaluation of MR4. For artifact evaluation, we considered two distinct courses to obtain a more holistic picture across course levels: First, we employed feedback in a bachelor's IT Project Management course in the summer semester of 2022, and second, in a master's course on Data Analytics in the winter semester 2022/2023 from course week 7 on, respectively. As the artifact evolved between both iterations as part of the design cycle process, we had not yet included a feature selection method in the bachelor's course. Thus, we focus exemplarily on the master's course for MR5 and report the perceived value of feedback for both courses within the evaluation of MR4, as the wording of the feedback instructions remained consistent.

MR5 Evaluation. To assess the artifact's capability to reflect meaningful relationships, we considered data from three prior runs of the data analytics course summing up to $N = 118$ learners (Table 2). We combined the data from all three course runs

Table 2 Overview of past data from three runs of the data analytics course

	Winter 2019/2020	Winter 2020/2021	Winter 2021/2022
Students (all course weeks)	46	39	33
Exam points mean (SD)	44.67 (24.40)	54.92 (20.60)	57.00 (17.43)
Learning time events	14,753	23,196	15,309
Platform activity events	284,334	196,037	159,080

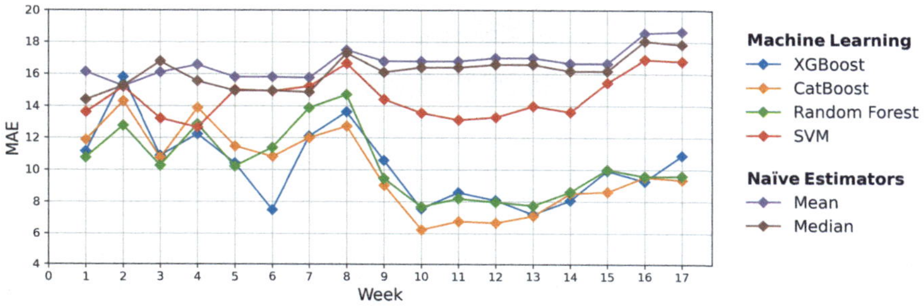

Fig. 4 Predictive performance of the pre-trained ML models (MAE)

and configured the artifact to account for weekly periods for training and evaluation of the ML models. Within the course, students can score 0–90 points in the exam.

Following Štrumbelj et al. (2009), we use predictive performance as a proxy metric and thereby leverage three well-established regression error measures: The Mean Absolute Error (MAE), Mean Absolute Percentage Error (MAPE), and RMSE (see Hastie et al. 2009 for details on the measures). Overall, we observe a decreasing error with increasing weekly data for all ML estimators on the test sets from week 9, which remains fairly constant for the following weeks (Fig. 4). More specifically, we find the following error metric means (SDs) across all weeks and models the artifact relies up on: MAE = 9.38 (2.18), MAPE = 23.98 (6.09), and RMSE = 11.90 (2.64). To justify the usefulness of the ML approach, we additionally compare the residuals of the selected ML models with the naïve estimators (predicting with the respective Mean and Median of the train set), indicating the best performance for the mid (week 9) and end of the semester (week 17). To this end, we perform paired one-sided two-sample t-tests on the residuals of the test set (CatBoost vs. Median). The test results reveal a statistically significant decrease in the residuals of the ML models for the course week 9 ($t(21) = -2.55$, $p = 0.009$, $d = 0.54$) and 17 ($t(23) = -3.28$, $p = 0.002$, $d = 0.67$). Thus, we conclude that the ML approach is reasonable and assume that the artifact has the capability to model meaningful patterns of students' learning in the data.

MR4 Evaluation. We conducted online surveys in both courses (i.e., IT Project Management in summer 2022 and Data Analytics in winter 2022/2023) approxi-

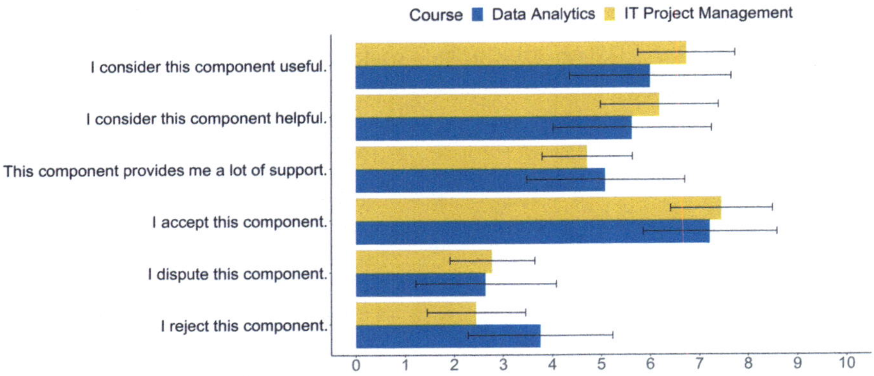

Fig. 5 User-based evaluation results (items range from 1-fully disagree to 10-fully agree)

mately two weeks before the exam to assess the subjective value of our feedback artifact for students' learning after feedback had been exposed to a group of learners during the semester. To increase participation in the surveys, we incentivized the students with the opportunity to win an energy efficiency device worth approximately 60€. In summary, $N = 36$ learners responded to our surveys for which we used the sub-scales "usefulness" and "acceptance" of the scale "perceived adequacy of feedback" (Strijbos et al. 2010). Given that we have so far only exposed feedback to a subset of course participants, we collected responses on the sub-scales from 15 students, where 8 took the IT Project Management and 7 the Data Analytics course. Figure 5 displays the mean (SE) for both courses and each item. The results of our evaluation demonstrate that feedback recipients perceive the component similarly in both courses. On average, learners accept the component, perceive it as useful and helpful, and hardly reject or dispute it. However, we observe a high SE in the sub-scales due to the small sample size. We also find that 45.83% of the students that received feedback and participated in the final exam interacted with the component (i.e., through clicks on check boxes or instruction hyperlinks).

Based on our results, we assume that all artifact requirements (MR1-MR5) are fulfilled. Despite the encouraging results, the small sample size calls for further runs to refine the artifact as part of the design cycle process.

6 Discussion

To answer our RQ, we synthesize two DPs of the category "Design principles about an artifact" (Gregor et al. 2020) for the design of future XAI-based feedback artifacts to address learners' heterogeneity. First, we find that it is a key DP to *divide features associated with learners into predictive and actionable features to assure that learners can actually implement the displayed feedback instructions* (**DP1**). While the ML models consider every extracted feature to predict our dependent variable, the nature of our XAI-based feedback required us to curate the associated CEs outputs. Specifically, we divide the features into those that are predictive-only (i.e., hardly alterable characteristics such as study program or features that may be inappropriate) and those that are also actionable (i.e., from which the counterfactual method should obtain guiding instructions to stimulate, e.g., the repetition of specific videos). The purely predictive features thereby serve to represent learner heterogeneity properly by considering learners' activities that are potentially not suited for instructional feedback (e.g., "increase video playback speed" as the output from CEs) and rather immutable characteristics of learners. Second, from the artifact development and evaluation, we find that it is a key DP to *model learner-specific factors to assure that learners receive meaningful feedback instructions* (**DP2**). In contrast to a more technical application of ML for predictive analytics or XAI methods explaining why a model generates a particular output (e.g., for model inspection), XAI-based feedback that creates feedback addressing learners' heterogeneity requires embracing a socio-technical perspective. Thus, the design of such an artifact should not fully rely on correlations in the data, but also consider insights from validated theoretical models of human behavior. Our XAI-based feedback is inspired by SRL theory in the form that many of our ML features should stimulate and guide cognitive learning strategies (e.g., watch a specific video to repeat its content) and all phases of the SRL process (e.g., progress control in the performance phase). This may also hold for XAI-based feedback within other domains such as resource conservation (Wastensteiner et al. 2021), where theory from environmental psychology and human-computer interaction can guide the design of such artifacts.

7 Conclusion and Future Work

In this paper, we presented a novel feedback artifact that addresses learners' heterogeneity using XAI and CEs. The first evaluation highlights the feasibility of such an artifact and raises further questions on the effects of our feedback component. We anticipate that our feedback will have a positive impact on learners' online learning time, exam-taking behavior, and exam performance. In addition, we aim to investigate in future studies which type of learner benefits most from our feedback regarding academic success. In doing so, we plan to overcome the limitations of the first artifact iterations (e.g., small sample size). By shedding light on this form of feedback, our work will add to the understanding of how to effectively support students in digital learning environments, an area that has recently received much attention in the IS discipline.

Acknowledgements This work was funded in part by "Stiftung Innovation in der Hochschullehre" within the project "Digitale Kulturen der Lehre entwickeln (DiKuLe)".

Appendix: Feedback Instructions

Table 3 Translation of actionable variables to feedback instructions

Actionable variable	Feedback (initial instruction)	Feedback (repeated instruction)
VideoViews.Total	By watching lecture videos for the first time, you are catching up on the learning content	By watching more lecture videos, you are catching up on the learning content and deepen your understanding
ViewsTotal.Complete	By watching lecture videos for the first time completely, you are catching up on the learning content	By watching more lecture videos completely, you are catching up on the learning content and deepen your understanding
ViewsPerVideo{ID}	By watching the following lecture video for the first time, you are catching up on the learning content: {Video Name}	You already know the learning content of the following lecture video. Watch this lecture video again to deepen your understanding: {Video Name}
ViewsPerVideo{ID}.Complete	You are still missing parts of a lecture video. Watch the following lecture video for catching up on the missing parts: {Video Name}	You already know the learning content of the following lecture video. Watch this lecture video again completely to deepen your understanding: {Video Name}
QuizzesTaken.Total	By taking quizzes for the first time, you are testing your knowledge on the learning content	By taking more quizzes, you are testing and monitoring your knowledge on the learning content
QuizTakenPerQuiz.{ID}	By taking the following quiz for the first time, you are testing your knowledge: {Quiz Name}	You have already tested your knowledge with the following quiz. Try the quiz again for monitoring your knowledge: {Quiz Name}
CorrectPerQuiz.{ID}	By collecting all points of the following quiz, you are testing your knowledge and deepening your understanding: {Quiz Name}	You have already tested your knowledge with the following quiz. Try to solve the quiz again correctly for monitoring your knowledge: {Quiz Name}
AssetDownload.{ID}	By downloading and working through the following slides, you are catching up on the learning content: {File Name}	You have already downloaded these slides. Open and work through them again to deepen your understanding: {File Name}
Time.Total	You have already spent valuable learning time on the edX platform. By further increasing your online learning time, you are catching up on the learning content and deepen your knowledge	
TimePerSection.{ID}	You have already spent valuable learning time on the edX platform. By spending more online learning time in the following learning section, you are catching up on the learning content and deepen your knowledge: {Section Name}	
Sessions.Total	By learning more often within the edX platform, you are catching up on the learning content and deepen your knowledge	
SessionsPerSection.{ID}	By learning more often within the following online learning section, you are catching up on the learning content and deepen your knowledge: {Section Name}	

References

Arnold, K. E. & Pistilli, M. D. (2012), Course signals at Purdue: using learning analytics to increase student success, *in* 'Proceedings of the 2nd International Conference on Learning Analytics and Knowledge', LAK'12, Association for Computing Machinery, New York, NY, USA, pp. 267–270.

Bandura, A. (2001), 'Social cognitive theory: An agentic perspective', *Annual Review of Psychology* **52**(1), 1–26. tex.eprint: https://doi.org/10.1146/annurev.psych.52.1.1.

Baneres, D., Rodriguez, M. E. & Serra, M. (2019), 'An Early Feedback Prediction System for Learners At-Risk Within a First-Year Higher Education Course', *IEEE Transactions on Learning Technologies* **12**(2), 249–263.

Barredo Arrieta, A., Díaz-Rodríguez, N., Del Ser, J., Bennetot, A., Tabik, S., Barbado, A., Garcia, S., Gil-Lopez, S., Molina, D., Benjamins, R., Chatila, R. & Herrera, F. (2020), 'Explainable Artificial Intelligence (XAI): Concepts, taxonomies, opportunities and challenges toward responsible AI', *Information Fusion* **58**, 82–115.

Baskerville, R. L., Kaul, M. & Storey, V. C. (2015), 'Genres of Inquiry in Design-Science Research: Justification and Evaluation of Knowledge Production', *MIS Quarterly* **39**(3), 541–564. Publisher: Management Information Systems Research Center, University of Minnesota.

Benner, D., Schöbel, S. & Süess, C. (2022), Towards Gamified Conversational Agents for Self-Regulated Learning in Digital Education, *in* 'ICIS 2022 Proceedings', Copenhagen, Denmark.

Berente, N., Seidel, S. & Safadi, H. (2019), 'Research Commentary-Data-Driven Computationally Intensive Theory Development', *Information Systems Research* **30**(1), 50–64.

Bousbahi, F. & Chorfi, H. (2015), 'MOOC-Rec: A Case Based Recommender System for MOOCs', *Procedia - Social and Behavioral Sciences* **195**, 1813–1822.

Credé, M. & Phillips, L. A. (2011), 'A meta-analytic review of the motivated strategies for learning questionnaire', *Learning and Individual Differences* **21**(4), 337–346.

Davis, D., Jivet, I., Kizilcec, R. F., Chen, G., Hauff, C. & Houben, G.-J. (2017), Follow the successful crowd: Raising mooc completion rates through social comparison at scale, *in* 'Proceedings of the 7th International Learning Analytics & Knowledge Conference', ACM Press, Vancouver, BC, Canada, pp. 454–463.

Fernández-Loría, C., Provost, F. & Han, X. (2022), 'Explaining data-driven decisions made by AI systems: The counterfactual approach', *MIS Quarterly* **46**(3), 1635–1660.

Gregor, S., Chandra Kruse, L. & Seidel, S. (2020), 'Research Perspectives: The Anatomy of a Design Principle', *Journal of the Association for Information Systems* **21**, 1622–1652.

Günther, S. A.(2021), The impact of social norms on students' online learning behavior: Insights from two randomized controlled trials, *in* 'LAK21: 11th International Conference on Learning Analytics & Knowledge', ACM, Irvine, CA, USA, pp. 12–21.

Gupta, S. & Bostrom, R. (2009), 'Technology-Mediated Learning: A Comprehensive Theoretical Model', *Journal of the Association for Information Systems* **10**, 686–714.

Gupta, S. & Chen, Y. (2022), 'Supporting inclusive learning using chatbots? A chatbot-led interview study', *Journal of Information Systems Education* **33**(1), 98–108.

Hastie, T., Tibshirani, R. & Friedman, J. (2009) , *The Elements of Statistical Learning*, Springer Series in Statistics, Springer New York.

Hellas, A., Ihantola, P., Petersen, A., Ajanovski, V. V., Gutica, M., Hynninen, T., Knutas, A., Leinonen, J., Messom, C. & Liao, S. N. (2018), Predicting academic performance: a systematic literature review, *in* 'Proceedings Companion of the 23rd Annual ACM Conference on Innovation and Technology in Computer Science Education', Larnaca, Cyprus, pp. 175–199.

Hevner, March, Park & Ram (2004), 'Design Science in Information Systems Research', *MIS Quarterly* **28**(1), 75.

Ifenthaler, D. & Yau, J. Y.-K. (2020), 'Utilising learning analytics to support study success in higher education: a systematic review', *Educational Technology Research and Development* **68**(4), 1961–1990.

Kizilcec, R. F., Pérez-Sanagustín, M. & Maldonado, J. J. (2017), 'Self-regulated learning strategies predict learner behavior and goal attainment in Massive Open Online Courses', *Computers & Education* **104**, 18–33.

Kraskov, A., Stögbauer, H. & Grassberger, P. (2004), 'Estimating mutual information', *Physical Review E* **69**(6), 066138.

Kruse, L. C., Bergener, K., Conboy, K., Lundström, J. E., Maedche, A., Sarker, S., Seeber, I., Stein, A. & Tømte, C. E. (2023), 'Understanding the digital companions of our future generation', *Communications of the Association for Information Systems* **52**(1), 22.

Kusner, M. J., Loftus, J., Russell, C. & Silva, R. (2017), Counterfactual fairness, *in* 'Advances in Neural Information Processing Systems', Vol. 30, Curran Associates, Inc.

Kühl, N., Hirt, R., Baier, L., Schmitz, B. & Satzger, G. (2021), 'How to Conduct Rigorous Supervised Machine Learning in Information Systems Research: The Supervised Machine Learning Report Card', *Communications of the Association for Information Systems* **48**(1), 589–615.

Leung, A. C. M., Santhanam, R., Kwok, R. C.-W. & Yue, W. T. (2022), 'Could gamification designs enhance online learning through personalization? lessons from a field experiment', *Information Systems Research*.

Li, Z., Wang, G. & Wang, H. (2021) , 'Peer effects in competitive environments: Field experiments on information provision and interventions', *MIS Quarterly* **45**(1), 163–191.

Lundberg, S. M., Erion, G., Chen, H., DeGrave, A., Prutkin, J. M., Nair, B., Katz, R., Himmelfarb, J., Bansal, N. & Lee, S.-I. (2020), 'From local explanations to global understanding with explainable AI for trees', *Nature Machine Intelligence* **2**(1), 56–67.

Lundberg, S. M. & Lee, S.-I. (2017), A unified approach to interpreting model predictions, *in* 'Advances in neural information processing systems', Vol. 30, Curran Associates, Inc.

Meske, C., Bunde, E., Schneider, J. & Gersch, M. (2020) , 'Explainable Artificial Intelligence: Objectives, Stakeholders, and Future Research Opportunities', *Information Systems Management* pp. 1–11.

Miguéis, V., Freitas, A., Garcia, P. J. & Silva, A. (2018), 'Early segmentation of students according to their academic performance: A predictive modelling approach', *Decision Support Systems* **115**, 36–51.

Miller, T. (2019), 'Explanation in artificial intelligence: Insights from the social sciences', *Artificial Intelligence* **267**, 1–38.

Molnar, C. (2019), *Interpretable machine learning - A Guide for Making Black Box Models Explainable*.

Mothilal, R. K., Sharma, A. & Tan, C. (2020), Explaining machine learning classifiers through diverse counterfactual explanations, *in* 'Proceedings of the 2020 Conference on Fairness, Accountability, and Transparency', ACM, Barcelona Spain, pp. 607–617.

Nguyen, A., Gardner, L. & Sheridan, D. (2020) , 'Data Analytics in Higher Education: An Integrated View', *Journal of Information Systems Education* **31**(1), 61–71.

Ouyang, F., Zheng, L. & Jiao, P. (2022), 'Artificial intelligence in online higher education: A systematic review of empirical research from 2011 to 2020', *Education and Information Technologies* **27**(6), 7893–7925.

Panadero, E. (2017), 'A review of self-regulated learning: Six models and four directions for research', *Frontiers in Psychology* **8**.

Peffers, K., Tuunanen, T., Rothenberger, M. A. & Chatterjee, S. (2007), 'A Design Science Research Methodology for Information Systems Research', *Journal of Management Information Systems* **24**(3), 45–77.

Pintrich, P. R. (1999), 'The role of motivation in promoting and sustaining self-regulated learning', *International Journal of Educational Research* **31**(6), 459–470.

Pintrich, P. R. (2004), 'A conceptual framework for assessing motivation and self-regulated learning in college students', *Educational Psychology Review* **16**(4), 385–407.

Ross, B. C. (2014), 'Mutual Information between Discrete and Continuous Data Sets', *PLoS ONE* **9**(2), e87357.

Schoemer, D., Laumer, S., Wilbers, K., Wolbring, T., Weigert, J. & Treischl, E. (2021), Data-driven Student Advisory and Potential Direct Discrimination: A Literature Review on Machine Learning for Predicting Students' Academic Success, *in* 'AMCIS 2021 Proceedings', Montreal, Canada.

Sommerville, I. (2011), *Software engineering*, 9th ed edn, Pearson, Boston. OCLC: ocn462909026.

Strijbos, J.-W., Narciss, S. & Dünnebier, K. (2010), 'Peer feedback content and sender's competence level in academic writing revision tasks: Are they critical for feedback perceptions and efficiency?', *Learning and instruction* **20**(4), 291–303. Publisher: Elsevier.

Štrumbelj, E., Kononenko, I. & Šikonja, M. R. (2009), 'Explaining instance classifications with interactions of subsets of feature values', *Data & Knowledge Engineering* **68**(10), 886–904. Publisher: Elsevier.

Theobald, M. & Bellhäuser, H. (2022), 'How am i going and where to next? elaborated online feedback improves university students' self-regulated learning and performance', *The Internet and Higher Education* **55**, 100872.

Vosniadou, S. (2020), 'Bridging secondary and higher education. the importance of self-regulated learning', *European Review* **28**(S1), S94–S103.

Wastensteiner, J., Weiss, T., Haag, F. & Hopf, K. (2021), Explainable AI for Tailored Electricity Consumption Feedback - an Experimental Evaluation of Visualizations, *in* 'ECIS 2021 Research Papers', 29, Marrakech, Morocco.

Wild, K.-P. & Schiefele, U. (1994), 'Lernstrategien im studium: Ergebnisse zur faktorenstruktur und reliabilität eines neuen fragebogens', *Zeitschrift für Differentielle und Diagnostische Psychologie* **15**(4), 185–200.

Yukselturk, E. & Bulut, S. (2009), 'Gender differences in self-regulated online learning environment', *Journal of Educational Technology & Society* **12**(3), 12–22. Publisher: JSTOR.

Zimmerman, B. J. & Moylan, A. R. (2009), Self-regulation: Where metacognition and motivation intersect, *in* 'Handbook of metacognition in education', Routledge, pp. 311–328.

Digital Health and Wellbeing

Design and Development of Virtual Patients for Healthcare Education: State of the Art and Research

Carolin Gellner, Anne-Katrin Witte, and Till J. Winkler

Abstract The digital transformation of healthcare and the COVID-19 pandemic have accelerated research and deployment of virtual patients (VP), that is, interactive computer simulations used in healthcare education to train students on clinical processes. To help researchers and practitioners understand the state of the art in VP development, we conducted a systematic literature review of 48 papers. Our analysis focused on educational level, medical specialty, competencies, technologies, technical format, and operating systems and tools. We found that VPs are primarily used in the medical field and student education as interactive patient scenarios based on multimedia system technology. VP authoring systems were identified as the primary tool for developing primary clinical reasoning skills. Based on our findings, we suggest implications for medical education research and practice.

Keywords Virtual patient · Literature review · Simulation · Technology

1 Introduction

The aim of digital transformation in healthcare is to improve the health and well-being of patients by promoting quality of care and patient autonomy (Bratan et al. 2022). To meet the evolving needs of patients and society, modern healthcare systems require high-quality medical education and training. Traditional tools like lectures and books

C. Gellner · A.-K. Witte · T. J. Winkler (✉)
FernUniversität in Hagen, Hagen, Germany
e-mail: till.winkler@fernuni-hagen.de

C. Gellner
e-mail: carolin.gellner@fernuni-hagen.de

A.-K. Witte
e-mail: a.witte@tu-berlin.de

T. J. Winkler
Department of Digitalization, Copenhagen Business School, Frederiksberg, Denmark

D. Beverungen et al. (eds.), *Transforming the Digitally Sustainable Enterprise*, Lecture Notes in Information Systems and Organisation 76,
https://doi.org/10.1007/978-3-031-80125-9_31

are no longer sufficient to address challenges such as medical errors and the rapidly expanding knowledge base. More efficient learning methods, such as case-based and patient-centered learning, are deemed necessary (Berman et al. 2016).

In recent years, virtual patients (VPs) have gained significant attention as a means to train the diagnostic skills of physicians and address the challenges in medical education (Ellaway and Davies 2011; Kononowicz et al. 2019). VPs are "*[…] interactive computer simulations of real-life clinical scenarios for health professions training, education, or assessment.*" (Kononowicz et al. 2019). Since the onset of the COVID-19 pandemic, VP research has gained even more importance due to the temporary closure of universities to maintain social distancing, which has deprived medical students of access to clinical departments. This has highlighted the need for clinical training methods that do not require bedside didactic activities (Furlan et al. 2021).

Current research suggests that VPs can be at least as effective as traditional training in improving skills such as clinical reasoning and procedural knowledge (Kononowicz et al. 2019). Previous literature reviews have primarily focused on VPs evaluation results, for instance, the effectiveness in developing clinical skills (Kononowicz et al. 2019), or specific in clinical reasoning (Plackett et al. 2022) and communication (Kelly et al. 2022; Lee et al. 2020), or specific domains such as pharmacy (Gharib et al. 2023; Richardson et al. 2020) and psychology (Chaby et al. 2022). Authors have called for further exploring the development of VPs to support the medical curriculum and increase the use and impact of digital technology in medical education and training (Frangoudes et al. 2021; Martini and Datt 2022). However, to date, there is limited research that provides an overview of the state of the art in VP development. Having such an overview would be crucial for VP developers to learn how to effectively develop VPs as a simulation-based learning method for healthcare education. Accordingly, our research question is as follows: *What design and development technologies have been used in VP research and for what healthcare fields and educational areas?*.

This literature review aims to provide an overview of the state of the art and the state of research on VP design and development, including technologies, healthcare fields, and educational areas in VP research. The study includes insights into educational level, medical field or coverage, learning outcomes competencies, technologies, technical format, and operating systems and tools for VP development. In addition, our review identified seven categories of operating systems and tools for VP development. Among these, we found that VPs are primarily developed as interactive patient scenarios for clinical reasoning training in medical student education based on web-based multimedia systems implemented using specific VP authoring systems.

To this end, the paper gives a brief background on VPs, and explains the methodological approach, followed by the results of the literature review and a discussion of the findings, and concludes with implications and a summary of the main points.

2 Background on Virtual Patients

The current literature describes VPs as flexible and easily accessible simulation-based learning technologies that provide a technology-enabled and multimedia opportunity to practice clinical, problem-solving, and decision-making skills in real-life situations without putting patients at risk (Sahu et al. 2019; Frangoudes et al. 2021). Such simulations support the pedagogical approaches of active, problem-based, situated, and gamified learning (Sahu et al. 2019). The simulations can be effectively integrated into the medical education process by coordinating with other learning activities and assessments, and by eliminating some lectures and textbook assignments to free up space in the course (Berman et al. 2016). Previous studies on VPs have been used for cases in internal medicine and critical care, but also for cases in psychiatric or psychosocial nature, radiology, dermatology, cardiology, and surgery (Kononowicz et al. 2019).

VPs used in different ways in healthcare education and training, which are shown and described in Table 1. According to Kononowicz et al. (2015), the VPs differ in terms of competencies (e.g., clinical reasoning, patient communication skills, procedural and basic clinical skills) and technologies (e.g., multimedia system, conversational character, virtual world), whereby the predominant class is the interactive patient scenario followed by high-fidelity software simulations, and virtual standardised patients. Less frequently used forms are VP games, case presentations, human standardized patients, and high fidelity manikins (Kononowicz et al. 2015).

The creation of VPs can be performed manually using standard web and multimedia tools or with dedicated authoring systems that offer specific VP functionalities, such as CASUS, CAMPUS classic, and OpenLabyrinth (Huwendiek et al. 2009). Kononowicz et al. (2019) identified CASUS, Web-SP, Virtual People Factory, Laerdal vSim, and Laerdal MicroSim as the most often used VP systems as well as some other, but less rarely used, systems, such as DecisionSim/VpSim and CAMPUS Card. In addition, e-learning authoring tools (e.g. Articulate Storyline), learning management systems (e.g., Moodle) or game authoring tools were used sporadically, and sometimes no special systems were used at all (Kononowicz et al. 2019).

Huwendiek et al. (2009) proposed a taxonomy for developing VPs, consisting of four categories: general (e.g., title and description), educational (e.g., objectives and outcomes), instructional design (e.g., interactivity), and technical (e.g., format). As the categories *general* and *instructional design* would not have provided useful insights into the research question, because our study did not aim to gain insights into instructional design or information such as title or identifier of a VP, we focus on categories *educational* and *technical,* which are briefly explained in Table 2.

Table 1 VP classes, competencies and technologies according to Kononowicz et al. (2015)

VP class	Competency	Technology	Description
Case presentation	Knowledge	Multimedia system	Interactive multimedia case presentations of a patient for knowledge teaching
Interactive patient scenario	Clinical reasoning	Multimedia system	Interactive multimedia presentation of a patient case for mainly clinical reasoning skills training
VP game	Clinical reasoning, team training	Virtual world	Virtual world to simulate high risk scenarios for clinical reasoning or team training
High-fidelity software simulation	Procedures or basic skills	Dynamic simulation or mixed reality	Real-time simulation of physiology for procedures or basic skills training (e.g. surgical). Can include mixed reality technologies
Human standardized patient	Patient communication	Multimedia system	Multimedia system with video-recorded patient actors for teaching patient communication skills
High fidelity manikins	Procedural and basic skills, team training	Manikin and part-task trainer	Anatomically realistic manikins for complex procedural and basic clinical skills or team training (e.g. endoscopy)
Virtual standardised patient	Patient communication	Conversational character	Virtual representation of a human using artificial intelligence and natural language processing technologies to train communication skills in form of conversational characters

Table 2 Selected factors of VP taxonomy according to Huwendiek et al. (2009)

Category	Factor	Brief description
Educational	Level	Target group (e.g. undergraduate students, graduated professionals)
	Coverage	Topic areas (esp. medical field, e.g. internal medicine)
	Objectives and outcomes	Objectives/outcomes of the VP (e.g. clinical reasoning skills)
Technical	Format	Technical format used for user end (e.g. web)
	Operation system	Tool or system used for VP creation (e.g. CASUS system)

3 Literature Review Method

The literature review uses a rather (qualitative) systematic approach according to Paré et al. (2015) and review characteristics according to taxonomy by Cooper (1988). Accordingly, the presented study review has a narrow focus on design and development practices and applications in VPs, and a comprehensive search strategy is employed to gather relevant data. The collected data is integrated using a narrative synthesis method into the concept matrix. The aim is to present a neutral and exhaustive coverage of the literature with selective citation. The results are presented conceptually, catering to both scholars and practitioners in the field of information and learning systems/healthcare education. Table 3 highlights in grey the review's key characteristics.

The literature search and selection followed the guidelines by Webster and Watson (2002). A preliminary search for the systematic search was conducted to identify suitable databases, search terms, inclusion criteria and time frame. The systematic search used the databases PubMed, IEEE Xplore, and ACM Digital Library to cover medical and technical fields with the search string 'virtual patient' in abstract or title. The search term was chosen in accordance with Kononowicz et al. (2015) and in order to keep the focus on the definition of virtual patients, as other terms (e.g. simulation or digital patient) led to many inappropriate results without focus on healthcare education. Accordingly, no synonyms were used as the term is widely used in research articles and provided sufficient hits (Kononowicz et al. 2019, 2015). However, the AISeLibrary database was not included since it did not yield any suitable hits on the term for the chosen period. The search results were limited to academic journals and conference proceedings from January 2020 to January 2023 in order to capture the most important recent developments in the field of VPs, which is reflected in the large increase in the number of research articles for this period compared to previous years, as the preliminary search showed. In the process, the first author screened and analyzed the retrieved papers and regularly discussed the analysis with the other authors. We evaluated every paper against pre-determined inclusion criteria:.

Table 3 Literature review characteristics according to Cooper (1988)

<table>
<tr><th>Characteristic</th><th colspan="6">Categories</th></tr>
<tr><td>Focus</td><td>Research outcomes</td><td colspan="2">Research methods</td><td colspan="2">Theories</td><td>Practices/ applications</td></tr>
<tr><td>Goal</td><td colspan="2">Integration</td><td colspan="2">Criticism</td><td colspan="2">Central issues</td></tr>
<tr><td>Organisation</td><td colspan="2">Historical</td><td colspan="2">Conceptual</td><td colspan="2">Methodological</td></tr>
<tr><td>Perspective</td><td colspan="3">Neutral representation</td><td colspan="3">Espousal of position</td></tr>
<tr><td>Audience</td><td>Specialised scholars</td><td colspan="2">General scholars</td><td colspan="2">Practitioners/politicians</td><td>General public</td></tr>
<tr><td>Coverage</td><td>Exhaustive</td><td colspan="2">Exhaustive and selective</td><td colspan="2">Representative</td><td>Central/ pivotal</td></tr>
</table>

Reference		Educational							Technical								
				Objective / Competency					Format / Technology					Format (add.)			
Autor(s)	Year	Level	Coverage	Knowledge	Clinical Reasoning	Team Training	Procedural & Basic Skills	Patient Communication	Multimedia System	Virtual World	Dynamic Simulation or Mixed Realitiy	Manikin and part task trainer	Conversational Character	Web	Mobile	Desktop	Operating System(s)
Example et al	2022	medical students	internal medicine		x			(x)	x					x			OpenLabyrith

Fig. 1 Concept matrix template incl. example

- *Type*: Peer-reviewed journal or conference paper.
- *Access*: As full text available for the authors.
- *Language*: Written in English.
- *Context*: Research in healthcare education.
- *Topic*: Research on VP according to the meanings of Kononowicz et al. (2015).
- *Data*: Contains information on educational level, coverage, competence or objective, technology, technical format and operating system according to the concept matrix.

The synthesis was carried out using a concept matrix (Webster and Watson 2002), which is a combination of the VP technologies and competences according to (Kononowicz et al. 2015) and the selected *educational* (level, coverage, objective) and *technical* factors (format and operating system) according to (Huwendiek et al. 2009) described in the background section. The *objectives* were grouped into the VP *competencies* and *format* into the VP *technologies*. Figure 1 shows the concept matrix including an example. In the course of the synthesis, subgroups were formed for the results in the columns *level*, *coverage* and *operating system(s)*. These additional classifications are described in detail in the results section.

4 Results

The initial search results (n = 419) were refined by removing duplicates and non-English papers. The remaining 335 papers were screened for context (n = 138) and VP topic (n = 103) based on abstract and title. The remaining papers were checked for full text access (n = 81), and screened for data (n = 51). Three papers were supplementary excluded because they described VPs already included in the set. Ultimately, **48** eligible papers were identified through the search and selection process (see Fig. 2).

Accordingly, these 48 papers were analyzed for synthesis, spanning from 2020 to January 2023. The distribution of publications by year was as follows: 18 papers in 2020, 11 papers in 2021, 18 papers in 2022, and one paper in January 2023. The papers were published across 34 journals or conference proceedings, primarily in medical and health-related fields. The top journals were BMC Medical Education,

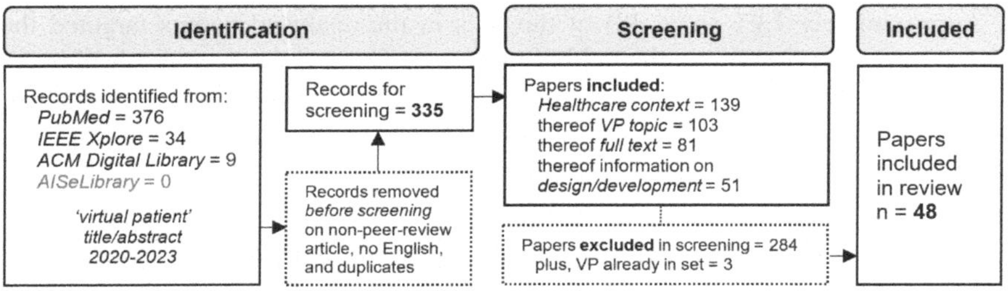

Fig. 2 Search and selection process

with five papers, followed by JMIR Medical Education, Journal of Medical Internet Research, and International Journal of Environmental Research and Public Health, with three papers each. The results of the synthesis and data aggregation of these papers are presented below.

4.1 Virtual Patient Application Areas in Healthcare Education

The concept matrix results were analyzed to answer the research question based on the healthcare education application areas, which represented the *coverage* and *educational level*. The classification into two educational levels, *education* and *training*, was derived from the target group described in the papers. The *education* level referred to basic education for students or trainees, while the *training* level referred to continuing education and training for healthcare professionals. The *coverage* areas were classified based on the medical specialties or diseases targeted by the VPs. Table 4 presents the results, which are described below.

The VPs described in the analyzed papers were focused on six *coverage* fields: medicine, dentistry, nursing, midwifery, pharmacy, and logopedics. Medicine accounted for the largest proportion of VPs at approximately 69% (n = 36), while the other five fields were less represented with 1–5 VPs each.

Table 4 Frequency of VP coverage and educational level

Coverage level	Medicine	Dentistry	Nursing	Midwifery	Pharmacy	Logopedics	Total
Education	25	3	4	2	3	1	38
Training	11	1	1		1		14
Total	36	4	5	2	4	1	

Approximately 73% (n = 38) of the VPs in the analysed papers targeted the *education level*, primarily in the field of medicine. The *training level* for healthcare professionals was the focus of 14 VP papers, with 11 belonging to the field of medicine.

4.2 Design and Development Technologies in Virtual Patients

We conducted a cross-analysis of the competencies and technologies synthesized in this work using the approach outlined in in Kononowicz et al. (2015) to replicate the VP classification based on more recent papers. During synthesis, we discovered that 14 VPs targeted multiple competencies, with only the predominant competency counted for the total, and additional secondary competencies integrated into the table as (+*x*). Conversely, 34 VPs targeted only one competency. We also cross-analyzed the technologies based on the technical *format* and *operating system*, deriving tool groups after synthesis for operating system. Totals were not shown in the table for the respective technology, as several operating systems or formats were mentioned in some VPs. The results are presented in Table 5.

The majority of the analyzed VPs (25 out of 48) had *clinical reasoning* as their primary competence, e.g. McNamara et al. (2022), Furlan et al. (2021) and Kiesewetter et al. (2020), while it was a secondary competence in two other VPs. *Patient communication* was the second most common learning objective, appearing in 11 VPs, e.g. Campillos-Llanos et al. (2021) and Miles et al. (2021), and was an additional competence in six others. *Procedural and basis skills* was the primary competence in seven VPs and secondary in one. *Knowledge* was the primary objective in five VPs and a secondary objective in six others. *Team training* was not the primary competence in any VP, but as a secondary in two.

According to the technologies, the majority (n = 28) were developed using a *multimedia system* technology, e.g. (Schnieders et al. 2022; Jacklin et al. 2021; Lucero et al. 2020), followed by *dynamic simulation or mixed reality* technology (n = 10), e.g. Lem et al. (2022) and Lerner et al. (2020). *Conversational character* was used in six VPs, e.g. Co et al. (2022) and Suárez et al. (2022), while *virtual world* technology was employed in three VPs, e.g. Antoniou et al. (2020). The technology of *manikin and part task trainer* was not utilized.

Based on the cross-analysis of competence and technology, the *interactive patient scenario* VP class was the most represented with 19 VPs, e.g. (Fuoad et al. 2022; Mardani et al. 2020; Kikuchi et al. 2022). Seven VPs belonged to the *high-fidelity software simulation* class, e.g. (Lerner et al. 2020; Chua et al. 2022), five each to *human standardized patient*, e.g. (Rothlind et al. 2021), and *virtual standardized patient*, e.g. (Dupuy et al. 2021). In addition, four VPs corresponded to *case presentation*, two to *VP game* and none to *high-fidelity manikin*. No concrete VP class resulted for six VPs.

Table 5 Frequency of design and development technologies in VPs

Technology	Multimedia system	Virtual world	Dynamic simulation or mixed reality	Manikin and part task trainer	Conversational character	Total
Competency	*28*	*3*	*10*	*0*	*6*	
Knowledge	**4** (+3) *Case presentation*		1 (+3)			*5 (+6)*
Clinical reasoning	**19** *Interactive patient scenario*	**2** *VP game*	2 (+1)		1 (+1)	*25 (+2)*
Team training			(+2)			*(+2)*
Procedural and basis skills	(+1)		**7** *High-fidelity software simulation*			*7 (+1)*
Patient communication	**5** (+4) *Human standardised patient*	1	(+1)		**5** (+1) *Virtual standardised patient*	*11 (+6)*
Format						
Web	**26**	3	4		3	*36*
Desktop	2	1	4		1	*8*
Mobile	2	1	2		3	*8*
Operating system						
VP	**16**		1		2	*19*
eLearning	**6**					*6*
AI	1				4	*5*
VR or gaming		2	**10**		1	*13*
Programming	5					*5*
Graphics, motion, video	5	1				*6*
Communication			1		1	*2*

Most of the VPs (75%) were developed in web *format*, while approximately 17% (n = 8) were implemented as either a desktop or mobile application. Some VPs were available in multiple formats. Therefore, the total number of formats for a technology does not correspond to the number of formats based on the competency in Table 5.

Finally, the results for *operating system* in the concept matrix were inductively classified into seven tool groups after synthesis including *VP authoring*, *E-Learning authoring*, *AI*, *VR or Gaming*, *Programming*, *Graphics*, *Motion*, *Video*, and *Communication*. Table 6 shows an overview of these groups including tools mentioned in the papers and which are described below in more detail.

The first group *VP authoring* covers free or commercial applications that exist specifically for the implementation of VPs or simulations in a medical educational context, and that provide functionality and templates for VP authors (Huwendiek et al. 2009). The tools were developed by universities or other educational institutions or by companies. According to Table 5, 19 VPs were implemented with such VP authoring systems in the papers analysed (e.g. Iguacel et al. 2022; Rothlind et al. 2021; Kotwal et al. 2021; Rouleau et al. 2020; Rakofsky et al. 2020; Newsome et al. 2020), with 12 different systems mentioned. The majority of the tools were used to develop a VP *multimedia system* such as e.g. the German CASUS and English MedicActiV, Interactive Case System (VIC), vpSim, and OpenLabyrinth. In addition, the Virtual People Factory 2.0 and the USC Standard Patient were used to develop *conversational character* and the tool Body Interact™ for *dynamic simulation or mixed reality*.

The second group *E-Learning authoring* covers authoring systems for the development of general e-learning applications, without a specific focus on VPs. As shown in Table 5, six VPs (Fuoad et al. 2022; Ganji et al. 2022; Kikuchi et al. 2022; McNamara et al. 2022; Schnieders et al. 2022; Mardani et al. 2020) were implemented

Table 6 Operating systems and tools for VP design and development

Group	Operating systems and tools
VP authoring	CASUS (INSTRUCT gGmbH 2022), MedicActiV (SimforHealth 2019), DecisionSim™ (Kynectiv Inc 2023a, b), Virtual Interactive Case System (VIC) (University Health Network 2013), BSAsim (Stockholms Universitet 2019), Aquifer® (Aquifer Inc 2023a, b), Medscape MedSims Patient Simulations (WebMD LLC 2023), SIMmersion™ (SIMmersion™ 2023), vpSim (University of Pittsburgh 2019), and OpenLabyrinth (University of Calgary 2022), Virtual People Factory 2.0 (University of Florida n.d.) and USC Standard Patient, Body Interact™ (Take The Wind 2023)
E-learning authoring	Articulate Rise 360 and Articulate Storyline (Articulate Global LLC 2023a, b), iSpring Suite (iSpring Nordics Oy 2023), Moodle (Moodle Pty Ltd 2023), NAVID (Tehran University of Medical Sciences 2023)
AI	Dialogflow (Google Ireland Limited 2023), Natural Language Toolkit for Python (NLTK Project 2023)
VR or gaming	Microsoft HoloLens VR platform, TweenityVR, Meta Quest 2 platform, HTC Vive platform and HTC Vive Pro headsets and controllers, Unity Games Technologies, Autodesk Maya, Adobe Mixamo, Body Interact™
Programming	HTML, CSS, JavaScript, Java, Python
Graphics, motion, video	Autodesk Maya, Adobe Creative Cloud (After Effects, Photoshop, Audition, Premiere Pro), Draw.io, Crazy Talk Animator, Camtasia Studio
Communication	Telegram Instant Messenger, Zoom

with such e-learning authoring systems in the papers analysed, with a total of five different systems mentioned. All of the tools were used to develop *multimedia system* including the following tools such as e.g. Articulate Rise 360, and iSpring Suite, or learning management systems such as Moodle and NAVID.

The third group, *AI*, includes tools for developing conversational Artificial Intelligence (AI) solutions, for example in the form of conversational characters with natural language processing (NLP). According to Table 5, AI-tools were used rather less, with five VPs implemented (Co et al. 2022; Suárez et al. 2022; Campillos-Llanos et al. 2021; Miles et al. 2021; Furlan et al. 2021). Four of them were used to develop a VP *conversational character* technology and one for a *multimedia system*. The papers mentioned two tools, Dialogflow and the Natural Language Toolkit for Python.

The fourth group, *VR or Gaming*, includes operating systems and tools specifically for game and virtual reality development. These systems were mentioned in 13 VPs, most of which were for *dynamic simulations and mixed reality* using tools such as e.g. Microsoft HoloLens VR, Unity Games Technologies, and Adobe Mixamo.

The fifth group, *Programming*, covers the manual development of VPs using classical programming languages such as HTML or Java. According to Table 5, manual programming was used rather less, with five VPs implemented (Jacklin et al. 2021; Richardson et al. 2021; Setrakian et al. 2020; Thompson et al. 2020; Furlan et al. 2021), all of which were used to develop a VP *multimedia system* technology.

The sixth group, *Graphics, Motion, Video*, includes applications specifically for graphics, motion and video design. These applications were mentioned in six VPs (e.g. (Thompson et al. 2020; Bahrami et al. 2021)), with most using for *multimedia systems*. Tools such as Adobe Creative Cloud, or Camtasia Studio were used.

The last group, *Communication*, includes tools for written or verbal communication such as instant messenger and videophone systems. According to Table 5, two VPs used communication tools (Suárez et al. 2022; Chua et al. 2022) where Telegram Instant Messenger and Zoom were named.

5 Discussion

To address the research question of the design and development technologies used in VP research and their application in healthcare fields and educational areas, this study conducted a literature review to identify the state of the art. Based on these findings, implications for practice and research are provided to promote the integration of more effective learning methods in healthcare education. Finally, the limitations of the study are discussed.

5.1 Design and Development in Virtual Patients

Between 2020 and January 2023, VPs were mainly developed and utilized for medical education of students and trainees, with less emphasis on training medical professionals. The scope of application was primarily focused on medicine, with sporadic use in other areas, such as nursing or pharmacy. This is consistent with Kononowicz et al.'s (2019) findings that VPs were mostly used in the field of medicine with undergraduate students. Our literature review indicates that VPs were primarily employed for training clinical reasoning skills, followed by patient communication and procedural and basic skills. VP research placed less emphasis on team training and medical knowledge acquisition. These findings are similar to Kononowicz et al.'s (2015) research, where most VPs were designed for clinical reasoning, with about half as many for patient communication and procedural and basic skills.

According to the literature review findings, VPs were primarily utilized in the development of multimedia systems technology. The second most common use was for dynamic simulations or mixed reality technologies, followed by conversational character technology as the third most frequent technology. The use of virtual world technology and VPs in the form of manikins were less prevalent. These results also follows the findings of Kononowicz et al. (2015), and also showed the Interactive Patient Scenario class as the most used, followed by High-Fidelity Software Simulation class as well as Human Standardised Patient and Virtual Standardised Patient, and Case Presentations and VP Game as least used according to Kononowicz et al. (2015).

Furthermore, VPs were predominantly developed and designed for web using VP authoring or simulation operating systems, with a focus on multimedia applications. The second most common operating systems used for VP development were those for virtual reality and gaming, primarily for dynamic simulations or mixed reality technologies. Some VP multimedia systems were created using e-learning authoring systems, graphics, motion, and video tools, and manual programming with classical programming languages. Artificially intelligent technology was utilized in the implementation of conversational characters. Communication tools were infrequently incorporated. The results go in the direction of the results by Kononowicz et al. (2019) and showed also a primary use of specific VP authoring systems, of which a few coincided with our research, but many of the systems mentioned did not appear in the papers in our research and other systems were mentioned at the same time.

In summary, the state of the art and research on design and development of VPs in healthcare education have remained largely unchanged for many years. VPs are still predominantly created as Interactive Patient Scenarios to train clinical reasoning skills, using VP authoring systems, e.g. such as CASUS, MedicActiV, DecisionSim or Virtual Interactive Case System (VIC) as web multimedia systems.

However, unlike Kononowicz et al. (2015) and Kononowicz et al. (2019), this paper offers a combination of both, providing a differentiated analysis of the tools, systems and technical formats used for each VP class, in order to show researchers and practitioners the state of the art of the tools that can be used for VP design and development, depending on the VP class and the targeted competencies. In addition, this study provides a grouped overview of the identified VP tools and systems, including those not mentioned in previous contributions.

5.2 Implications for Research and Practice

The study conducted supports Kononowicz et al.'s (2019) suggestion to increase the use and exploration of VPs (VPs) in healthcare professions beyond medicine. The study also indicates a lack of representation of VPs in areas such as nursing and pharmacy, and underutilization of VPs for continuing education and training of healthcare professionals. Therefore, it is recommended that researchers and practitioners focus on developing and studying VPs for these fields.

Traditionally, VPs have been created to train clinical reasoning. However, to enhance healthcare professionals' competencies, there is a need to focus on other areas such as patient communication, team training, and medical knowledge. Additionally, VPs are typically designed as simple multimedia applications, and thus, it is proposed that researchers and practitioners shift their focus to more interactive formats such as conversational agents or virtual worlds, like serious games.

Although there is a substantial body of literature on VPs, there is still limited or ambiguous information on the approaches and technologies used in designing and developing VPs. Most papers only briefly describe the design of VPs without technical details and focus mainly on its evaluation. Therefore, it is suggested that researchers provide a detailed description of their contributions from a design and development perspective or employ design science approaches to enhance the quality of research.

5.3 Limitations

The following limitations merit consideration. First, the search was limited to only three scientific databases and a narrow time frame. Expanding the search to additional databases and a broader time period may have resulted in more publications and potentially different outcomes. Second, the search was restricted to the use of "virtual patient" as the search term. Including other search terms related to simulations and digital patient-oriented learning methods in medical education could have resulted in additional suitable papers for synthesis. Third, while we carried out a systematic procedure, subjective bias may have influenced the selection and synthesis process due to ambiguous descriptions in some papers. This could have led to the exclusion of suitable findings or discrepancies in the classification of information in the concept matrix.

6 Conclusions

VPs have gained popularity as an effective way to train physicians' diagnostic skills in medical education and training. To provide practitioners and researchers with a comprehensive understanding of the current state of the art in VP development, we conducted a systematic literature review of 48 recent papers from a range of outlets. The analysis revealed that VPs are predominantly utilized in the medical field and student education as interactive patient scenarios based on multimedia system technology, with VP authoring systems being the primary tool for developing primary clinical reasoning skills. Based on these findings, researchers and practitioners should focus on developing and investigating underrepresented interactive VP technology approaches, competences, and educational areas. This literature review offers a comprehensive analysis of the latest research on designing and developing VPs in healthcare and educational domains. We are hopeful to assist researchers and practitioners in creating effective VPs as a digital, simulation-based learning method for healthcare education that meets the needs of patients and society in today's digitally transformed healthcare system.

Acknowledgements This paper was produced as part of the research project "Digital competences of the medical profession for prescribing health apps [Digitale Kompetenzen der Ärzteschaft zur Verschreibung von Gesundheits-Apps]" and the associated research focus "Work-Education-Digitisation [Arbeit-Bildung-Digitalisierung]" of the FernUniversität in Hagen, founded by the German Ministry of Culture and Science of Nordrhein-Westfalen.

References

Antoniou, P. E., Arfaras, G., Pandria, N., Athanasiou, A., Ntakakis, G., Babatsikos, E., Nigdelis, V., & Bamidis, P. (2020). Biosensor Real-Time Affective Analytics in Virtual and Mixed Reality Medical Education Serious Games: Cohort Study. *JMIR Serious Games*, *8*(3), e17823. https://doi.org/10.2196/17823.

Aquifer Inc. (2023). *Aquifer: Your trusted source for clinical learning*. https://aquifer.org.

Articulate Global LLC. (2023a). *Articulate Rise 360*. https://articulate.com/360/rise.

Articulate Global LLC. (2023b). *Articulate Storyline 360*. https://articulate.com/360/storyline.

Bahrami, M., Hadadgar, A., & Fuladvandi, M. (2021). Designing Virtual Patients for Education of Nursing Students in Cancer Course. *Iranian Journal of Nursing and Midwifery Research*, *26*(2), 133–136. https://doi.org/10.4103/ijnmr.IJNMR_327_20.

Berman, N. B., Durning, S. J., Fischer, M. R., Huwendiek, S., & Triola, M. M. (2016). The Role for Virtual Patients in the Future of Medical Education. *Academic Medicine: Journal of the Association of American Medical Colleges*, *91*(9), 1217–1222. https://doi.org/10.1097/ACM.0000000000001146.

Bratan, T., Schneider, D., Heyen, N. B., Pullmann, L., Friedewald, M., Kuhlmann, D., Brkic, N., & Hüsing, B. (2022). *E-Health in Deutschland: Entwicklungsperspektiven und internationaler Vergleich [E-health in Germany: development perspectives and international comparison]: Studien zum deutschen Innovations system* (12-2022). Berlin. http://hdl.handle.net/10419/251366.

Campillos-Llanos, L., Thomas, C., Bilinski, É., Neuraz, A., Rosset, S., & Zweigenbaum, P. (2021). Lessons Learned from the Usability Evaluation of a Simulated Patient Dialogue System. *Journal of Medical Systems*, *45*(7), 69. https://doi.org/10.1007/s10916-021-01737-4.

Chaby, L., Benamara, A., Pino, M., Prigent, E., Ravenet, B., Martin, J.-C., Vanderstichel, H., Becerril-Ortega, R., Rigaud, A.-S., & Chetouani, M. (2022). Embodied Virtual Patients as a Simulation-Based Framework for Training Clinician-Patient Communication Skills: An Overview of Their Use in Psychiatric and Geriatric Care. *Frontiers in Virtual Reality*, *3*. https://doi.org/10.3389/frvir.2022.827312

Chua, W. L., Ooi, S. L., Chan, G. W. H., Lau, T. C., & Liaw, S. Y. (2022). The Effect of a Sepsis Interprofessional Education Using Virtual Patient Telesimulation on Sepsis Team Care in Clinical Practice: Mixed Methods Study. *Journal of Medical Internet Research*, *24*(4), e35058. https://doi.org/10.2196/35058.

Co, M., John Yuen, T. H., & Cheung, H. H. (2022). Using clinical history taking chatbot mobile app for clinical bedside teachings - A prospective case control study. *Heliyon*, *8*(6), e09751. https://doi.org/10.1016/j.heliyon.2022.e09751.

Cooper, H. M. (1988). Organizing knowledge syntheses: A taxonomy of literature reviews. *Knowledge in Society*, *1*(1), 104–126. https://doi.org/10.1007/BF03177550.

Dupuy, L., Sevin, E. de, Cassoudesalle, H., Ballot, O., Dehail, P., Aouizerate, B., Cuny, E., Micoulaud-Franchi, J.-A., & Philip, P. (2021). Guidelines for the design of a virtual patient for psychiatric interview training. *Journal on Multimodal User Interfaces*, *15*(2), 99–107. https://doi.org/10.1007/s12193-020-00338-8.

Ellaway, R. H., & Davies, D. (2011). Design for learning: Deconstructing virtual patient activities. *Medical Teacher*, *33*(4), 303–310. https://doi.org/10.3109/0142159X.2011.550969.

Frangoudes, F., Hadjiaros, M., Schiza, E. C., Matsangidou, M., Tsivitanidou, O., & Neokleous, K. (2021). An Overview of the Use of Chatbots in Medical and Healthcare Education. In P. Zaphiris & A. Ioannou (Eds.), *Lecture Notes in Computer Science. Learning and Collaboration Technologies: Games and Virtual Environments for Learning* (Vol. 12785, pp. 170–184). Springer International Publishing. https://doi.org/10.1007/978-3-030-77943-6_11.

Fuoad, S. A., El-Sayed, W., & Marei, H. (2022). Effect of different teaching/learning approaches using virtual patients on student's situational interest and cognitive load: A comparative study. *BMC Medical Education*, *22*(1), 763. https://doi.org/10.1186/s12909-022-03831-8.

Furlan, R., Gatti, M., Menè, R., Shiffer, D., Marchiori, C., Giaj Levra, A., Saturnino, V., Brunetta, E., & Dipaola, F. (2021). A Natural Language Processing-Based Virtual Patient Simulator and Intelligent Tutoring System for the Clinical Diagnostic Process: Simulator Development and Case Study. *JMIR Medical Informatics*, *9*(4), e24073. https://doi.org/10.2196/24073.

Ganji, J., Shirvani, M. A., Motahari-Tabari, N., & Tayebi, T. (2022). Design, implementation and evaluation of a virtual clinical training protocol for midwifery internship in a gynecology course during COVID-19 pandemic: A semi-experimental study. *Nurse Education Today*, *111*, 105293. https://doi.org/10.1016/j.nedt.2022.105293.

Gharib, A. M., Bindoff, I. K., Peterson, G. M., & Salahudeen, M. S. (2023). Computer-Based Simulators in Pharmacy Practice Education: A Systematic Narrative Review. *Pharmacy (Basel, Switzerland)*, *11*(1). https://doi.org/10.3390/pharmacy11010008.

Google Ireland Limited. (2023). *Dialogflow*. https://cloud.google.com/dialogflow.

Huwendiek, S., Leng, B. A. de, Zary, N., Fischer, M. R., Ruiz, J. G., & Ellaway, R. (2009). Towards a typology of virtual patients. *Medical Teacher*, *31*(8), 743–748. https://doi.org/10.1080/01421590903124708.

Iguacel, I., Abecia, B., Bernal, J. L., & Martínez-Jarreta, B. (2022). Changing Attitudes towards Occupational Medicine with Blended Learning Methods Is Possible among Medical Students in Spain: A Longitudinal Study. *International Journal of Environmental Research and Public Health*, *19*(2). https://doi.org/10.3390/ijerph19020878.

INSTRUCT gGmbH. (2022). *CASUS*. https://vhb.casus.net/.

iSpring Nordics Oy. (2023). *iSpring Suite 11: Mit iSpring Suite Kurse entwerfen wie ein Profi*. https://www.ispringlearn.de/ispring-suite.

Jacklin, S., Maskrey, N., & Chapman, S. (2021). Shared Decision-Making With a Virtual Patient in Medical Education: Mixed Methods Evaluation Study. *JMIR Medical Education*, *7*(2), e22745. https://doi.org/10.2196/22745.

Kelly, S., Smyth, E., Murphy, P., & Pawlikowska, T. (2022). A scoping review: Virtual patients for communication skills in medical undergraduates. *BMC Medical Education*, *22*(1). https://doi.org/10.1186/s12909-022-03474-9.

Kiesewetter, J., Sailer, M., Jung, V. M., Schönberger, R., Bauer, E., Zottmann, J. M., Hege, I., Zimmermann, H., Fischer, F., & Fischer, M. R. (2020). Learning clinical reasoning: How virtual patient case format and prior knowledge interact. *BMC Medical Education*, *20*(1), 73. https://doi.org/10.1186/s12909-020-1987-y.

Kikuchi, J. Y., Le Neveu, M., Arnold, S., Offnick, A., Muñiz, K. S., Pandya, P., Feroz, R., Long, J. B., Ledebur, L. R., Patterson, D., & Chen, C. C. G. (2022). Creation and Implementation of Virtual Urogynecology Patient Cases for Medical Student Education. *MedEdPORTAL: The Journal of Teaching and Learning Resources*, *18*, 11259. https://doi.org/10.15766/mep_2374-8265.11259.

Kononowicz, A. A., Woodham, L. A., Edelbring, S., Stathakarou, N., Davies, D., Saxena, N., Car, L. T., Carlstedt-Duke, J., Car, J., & Zary, N. (2019). Virtual patient simulations in health professions education: Systematic review and meta-analysis by the digital health education collaboration. *Journal of Medical Internet Research*, *21*(7). https://doi.org/10.2196/14676.

Kononowicz, A. A., Zary, N., Edelbring, S., Corral, J., & Hege, I. (2015). Virtual patients - What are we talking about? A framework to classify the meanings of the term in healthcare education. *BMC Medical Education*, *15*(1). https://doi.org/10.1186/s12909-015-0296-3.

Kotwal, S., Fanai, M., Fu, W., Wang, Z., Bery, A. K., Omron, R., Tevzadze, N., Gold, D., Garibaldi, B. T., Wright, S. M., & Newman-Toker, D. E. (2021). Real-world virtual patient simulation to improve diagnostic performance through deliberate practice: A prospective quasi-experimental study. *Diagnosis (Berlin, Germany)*, *8*(4), 489–496. https://doi.org/10.1515/dx-2020-0127.

Kynectiv Inc. (2023). *DECISIONSIM: Technology*. https://app.decisionsim.com.

Lee, J., Kim, H., Kim, K. H., Jung, D., Jowsey, T., & Webster, C. S. (2020). Effective virtual patient simulators for medical communication training: A systematic review. *Medical Education*, *54*(9), 786–795. https://doi.org/10.1111/medu.14152.

Lem, W. G., Kohyama-Koganeya, A., Saito, T., & Oyama, H. (2022). Effect of a Virtual Reality Contact-Based Educational Intervention on the Public Stigma of Depression: Randomized Controlled Pilot Study. *JMIR Formative Research*, *6*(5), e28072. https://doi.org/10.2196/28072.

Lerner, D., Mohr, S., Schild, J., Göring, M., & Luiz, T. (2020). An Immersive Multi-User Virtual Reality for Emergency Simulation Training: Usability Study. *JMIR Serious Games*, *8*(3), e18822. https://doi.org/10.2196/18822.

Lucero, K. S., Spyropoulos, J., Blevins, D., Warters, M., Norton, A., & Cohen, J. (2020). Virtual Patient Simulation in Continuing Education: Improving the Use of Guideline-Directed Care in Venous Thromboembolism Treatment. *Journal of European CME*, *9*(1), 1836865. https://doi.org/10.1080/21614083.2020.1836865.

Mardani, M., Cheraghian, S., Naeeni, S. K., & Zarifsanaiey, N. (2020). Effectiveness of virtual patients in teaching clinical decision-making skills to dental students. *Journal of Dental Education*, *84*(5), 615–623. https://doi.org/10.1002/jdd.12045.

Martini, N., & Datt, A. (2022). Virtual patients in clinical decision making – A design-based research approach. *Pharmacy Education*, *22*(1), 129–141. https://doi.org/10.46542/pe.2022.221.129141.

McNamara, L., Scott, K., Boyd, R. N., Farmer, E., Webb, A., Bosanquet, M., Nguyen, K., & Novak, I. (2022). Can web-based implementation interventions improve physician early diagnosis of cerebral palsy? Protocol for a 3-arm parallel superiority randomised controlled trial and cost-consequence analysis comparing adaptive and non-adaptive virtual patient instructional designs with control to evaluate effectiveness on physician behaviour, diagnostic skills and patient outcomes. *BMJ Open*, *12*(11), e063558. https://doi.org/10.1136/bmjopen-2022-063558.

Miles, A., Hayden, S., Carnell, S., Halan, S., & Lok, B. (2021). What do speech pathology students gain from virtual patient interviewing? A WHO International Classification of Functioning

Disability and Health (ICF) analysis. *BMJ Simulation and Technology Enhanced Learning, 7*(4), 239–245. https://doi.org/10.1136/bmjstel-2020-000616.
Moodle Pty Ltd. (2023). *Willkommen in der Moodle-Community*. https://moodle.org/.
Newsome, J. S., Wallace-Gay, T. D., & Shoair, O. A. (2020). Virtual Versus Paper-based Cases in Reinforcing the Collect and Assess Elements of the Pharmacists' Patient Care Process. *American Journal of Pharmaceutical Education, 84*(7), ajpe7806. https://doi.org/10.5688/ajpe7806.
NLTK Project. (2023). *Natural Language Toolkit (NLTK)*. https://www.nltk.org/.
Paré, G., Trudel, M.-C., Jaana, M., & Kitsiou, S. (2015). Synthesizing information systems knowledge: A typology of literature reviews. *Information & Management, 52*(2), 183–199. https://doi.org/10.1016/j.im.2014.08.008.
Plackett, R., Kassianos, A. P., Mylan, S., Kambouri, M., Raine, R., & Sheringham, J. (2022). The effectiveness of using virtual patient educational tools to improve medical students' clinical reasoning skills: A systematic review. *BMC Medical Education, 22*(1), 365. https://doi.org/10.1186/s12909-022-03410-x.
Rakofsky, J. J., Talbot, T. B., & Dunlop, B. W. (2020). A Virtual Standardized Patient-Based Assessment Tool to Evaluate Psychiatric Residents' Psychopharmacology Proficiency. *Academic Psychiatry: The Journal of the American Association of Directors of Psychiatric Residency Training and the Association for Academic Psychiatry, 44*(6), 693–700. https://doi.org/10.1007/s40596-020-01286-x.
Richardson, C. L., Chapman, S., & White, S. (2021). Establishing the acceptability and usability of an animated virtual patient simulation. *Exploratory Research in Clinical and Social Pharmacy, 4*, 100069. https://doi.org/10.1016/j.rcsop.2021.100069.
Richardson, C. L., White, S., & Chapman, S. (2020). Virtual patient technology to educate pharmacists and pharmacy students on patient communication: A systematic review. *BMJ Simulation and Technology Enhanced Learning, 6*(6), 332–338. https://doi.org/10.1136/bmjstel-2019-000514.
Rothlind, E., Fors, U., Salminen, H., Wändell, P., & Ekblad, S. (2021). Virtual patients reflecting the clinical reality of primary care - a useful tool to improve cultural competence. *BMC Medical Education, 21*(1), 270. https://doi.org/10.1186/s12909-021-02701-z.
Rouleau, G., Pelletier, J., Côté, J., Gagnon, M.-P., Martel-Laferrière, V., Lévesque, R., & Fontaine, G. (2020). Codeveloping a Virtual Patient Simulation to Foster Nurses' Relational Skills Consistent With Motivational Interviewing: A Situation of Antiretroviral Therapy Nonadherence. *Journal of Medical Internet Research, 22*(7), e18225. https://doi.org/10.2196/18225.
Sahu, P. K., Chattu, V. K., Rewatkar, A., & Sakhamuri, S. (2019). Best practices to impart clinical skills during preclinical years of medical curriculum. *Journal of Education and Health Promotion, 8*, 57. https://doi.org/10.4103/jehp.jehp_354_18.
Schnieders, E., Röhr, F., Mbewe, M., Shanzi, A., Berner-Rodoreda, A., Barteit, S., Louis, V. R., Andreadis, P., Syakantu, G., & Neuhann, F. (2022). Real-life Evaluation of an Interactive Versus Noninteractive e-Learning Module on Chronic Obstructive Pulmonary Disease for Medical Licentiate Students in Zambia: Web-Based, Mixed Methods Randomized Controlled Trial. *JMIR Medical Education, 8*(1), e34751. https://doi.org/10.2196/34751.
Setrakian, J., Gauthier, G., Bergeron, L., Chamberland, M., & St-Onge, C. (2020). Comparison of Assessment by a Virtual Patient and by Clinician-Educators of Medical Students' History-Taking Skills: Exploratory Descriptive Study. *JMIR Medical Education, 6*(1), e14428. https://doi.org/10.2196/14428.
SimforHealth. (2019). *MedicActiV: Virtual simulators for medical education*. https://www.medicactiv.com/en.
SIMmersion™. (2023). *SIMmersion Immersive Simulations: Realistic People. Real Change. AI powered virtual role-players with memory and emotions*. https://www.simmersion.com/.
Stockholms Universitet. (2019). *BSAsim: Välkommen till BSAsim!* https://bsa.dsv.su.se/bsasim.
Suárez, A., Adanero, A., Díaz-Flores García, V., Freire, Y., & Algar, J. (2022). Using a Virtual Patient via an Artificial Intelligence Chatbot to Develop Dental Students' Diagnostic Skills.

International Journal of Environmental Research and Public Health, 19(14). https://doi.org/10.3390/ijerph19148735.

Take The Wind. (2023). *Body Interact™: Learn with virtual patients, save real lives.* https://bodyinteract.com.

Tehran University of Medical Sciences. (2023). *What is NAVID? Learning Management System used in Tehran University of Medical Sciences.* https://tumsnavid.vums.ac.ir/.

Thompson, J., White, S, & Chapman, S (2020). Virtual patients as a tool for training pre-registration pharmacists and increasing their preparedness to practice: A qualitative study. *PloS One, 15*(8), e0238226. https://doi.org/10.1371/journal.pone.0238226.

University Health Network. (2013). *Virtual Interactive Case System.* https://pie.med.utoronto.ca/VIC.

University of Calgary. (2022). *OpenLabyrinth.* https://openlabyrinth.ca.

University of Florida. (n.d.). *Virtual People Factory 2.0.* Retrieved March 5, 2023, from http://virtualpeoplefactory.com.

University of Pittsburgh. (2019). *vpSim.* http://vpsim.pitt.edu.

WebMD LLC. (2023). *Medscape MedSims® Patient Simulations.* https://www.medscape.org/simulation.

Webster, J., & Watson, R. T. (2002). Analyzing the Past to Prepare for the Future: Writing a Literature Review. *MIS Quarterly, 26*(2), xiii–xxiii.

Building Habits in the Digital Age: Incorporating Psychological Needs and Knowledge from Practitioners to Inform the Design of Digital Therapeutics

Jeannette Stark, Thure Weimann, Felix Reinsch, Maren Kählig, Emily Hickmann, Carola Gisske, and Peggy Richter

Abstract Interventions for noncommunicable diseases (NCDs) often require changing behaviors. In this regard, habitual behaviors (i.e., habits) are positively evaluated to foster behavioral changes. Forming habits is challenging but can be supported digitally. This paper reviews the requirements of forming habits and investigates how these requirements are implemented in habit apps. Based on the results, design principles are discussed for digital therapeutics. In contrast to conventional apps, digital therapeutics have a medical purpose and can be prescribed for the time it needs for a habit to form. The results reveal that conventional apps try to bind the user and ignore the state where the habit needs to be strengthened by decreasing technology use. In this regard, digital therapeutics reveal potential in supporting the formation of habits to prevent and treat NCDs.

J. Stark · T. Weimann · F. Reinsch · M. Kählig · E. Hickmann (✉) · C. Gisske · P. Richter
Research Group Digital Health, Technische Universität Dresden, Dresden, Germany
e-mail: emily.hickmann@tu-dresden.de

J. Stark
e-mail: jeannette.stark@tu-dresden.de

T. Weimann
e-mail: thure.weimann@tu-dresden.de

F. Reinsch
e-mail: felix.reinsch@mailbox.tu-dresden.de

M. Kählig
e-mail: maren.kaehlig@tu-dresden.de

C. Gisske
e-mail: carola.gisske@tu-dresden.de

P. Richter
e-mail: peggy.richter@tu-dresden.de

D. Beverungen et al. (eds.), *Transforming the Digitally Sustainable Enterprise*, Lecture Notes in Information Systems and Organisation 76,
https://doi.org/10.1007/978-3-031-80125-9_32

Keywords Behavioral change · Digital therapeutics · Habits · Habit apps · Noncommunicable diseases

1 Introduction

Noncommunicable diseases (NCDs), such as diabetes, obesity, and cardiovascular diseases, are the most significant cause of death, accounting for 74% of all deaths worldwide (WHO 2020, 2023). Many of the deaths are lifestyle-related. For example, more than 20% of worldwide deaths are associated with dietary factors (e.g., high in sugar-sweetened beverages) increasing metabolic risks (e.g., high body-mass-index; Afshin et al. 2019). After the onset of chronic disease, therapy programs focus on limiting disease progression and positively influencing the disease trajectory by taking appropriate treatment steps. Thereby, it is crucial for the treatment success that the care plan is adhered to and lifestyle behaviors associated with the pathogenesis are changed (Aboumatar et al. 2022). The digital transformation in healthcare opens potential to support these behavioral changes with so-called "Digital Therapeutics" (DTx).

DTx are software applications that, in contrast to conventional apps, treat, manage or prevent a concrete disease or disorder (DTx Alliance 2022) and that are designed for patients as end consumers (i.e., patient-facing; Sim 2019). From a broad IS perspective, DTx can be considered as instances of "virtual coaches" that promote health behavior change toward a certain goal (Fürstenau et al. 2023; Weimann et al. 2022). Recently, health insurance companies have begun reimbursing DTx, with Germany taking a pioneering role through the introduction of the "DiGA" (Gerke et al. 2020). While DTx holds potential for stimulating and maintaining health behavior changes, long-term evidence remains elusive (Beleigoli et al. 2019; Craig et al. 2021). In this regard, prior research indicates that conventional interventions focus on intentional psychological processes required to adopt new behaviors yet fall short in aiding the transition of these behaviors into automated, subconscious habits that seamlessly integrate into daily routines (Lakka et al. 2022; Vogelsang et al. 2022).

A habit is an automatically executed behavior in a specific context due to its consistent and repeated occurrence within that context (Lally and Gardner 2013). In contrast to overwhelming goals such as walking 10,000 steps per day, habits are manageable and seamlessly blend into daily routines. Habits are implemented by repeatedly performing a behavior in a context so that a cognitive link between behavior and context is created (Neal et al. 2006). For example, seeing a fruit basket (context) may foster healthy fruit intake (behavior). When the behavior is repeated in the same context, the cognitive link strengthens, leading to a strong, automatically executed habit (Gardner 2015). Information Systems (IS) in general, and DTx in particular, can be vital in forming habits by providing the necessary support for sustained adherence (Weimann and Stark 2022). While habit formation mechanisms have become increasingly popular in conventional "lifestyle-optimization" apps for the general healthy population, their use in professional medical care is still in its infants (Lakka et al. 2022; Stawarz et al. 2015). This paper aims to harness the potential of IS and DTx in successfully forming habits that tackle NCDs (Rippe 2018). In doing so, we follow the design science paradigm (Hevner et al. 2004; Peffers et al. 2007) to explore how habits can be formed. We contribute to the body of design literature for DTx by proposing design principles (DPs) for habit-based DTx and hence answer the following research question: *Which design principles could enhance the formation (i.e., implementation and strengthening) of habits within DTx?*

By following the design science procedure outlined in (Peffers et al. 2007) we conducted a literature review on literature in psychology and human-computer interaction (HCI) to determine meta-requirements (MRs) for implementing and strengthening habits (Sect. 2). Additionally, we examined habit apps employing a content analysis to learn from conventional habit apps and hence add to the MR (Sect. 3). Sect. 4 proposes the design principles, discusses limitations and future research.

2 Requirements for Implementing and Strengthening Habits

This section aims to provide a background on prior research in psychology and human-computer interaction (HCI) related to habit formation and its digital support to extrapolate MRs for effective app design. Previous research defines habits as a memory-based tendency to automatically respond to a specific cue acquired through the repetition of the behavior in stable contexts (Verplanken and Wood 2006, Verplanken et al. 2018; Wood and Neal 2007, 2009).

The first part of this definition characterizes habits as automatic behavior in response to a particular context. For example, the context of seeing a fruit basket in the kitchen may prompt the behavior of fruit intake. Once the link between the context and the behavior becomes strong, through constant repetition, the behavior is likely to be executed automatically (Gardner 2015). Although it is not inevitable, it now requires effort to resist and act in a way that is counter to the habit (Wood and Neal 2009).

The second part of the above definition describes the process of how habits form. Prior psychology research details the habit formation process into four stages (Lally and Gardner 2013; Fig. 1): In the first stage, a decision to take action is made. Typically, an intention is formulated for the new habit that serves as a foundation for its implementation. During the second stage, the intention transitions into action, enabling an initial assessment of the habit's advantages and disadvantages. This assessment informs the subsequent decision to maintain or abandon the habit. To solidify the habit, the behavior is repeatedly performed in the same context in stage three (Lally et al. 2010). In this stage, the focus shifts from defining and testing the habit to strengthening it. In the fourth stage, the new action is repeated in a fashion that is conducive to the development of automaticity, including creating

Fig. 1 Stages to habit formation according to (Lally et al. 2010, 2013)

salient cues, reducing behavioral complexity, and avoiding extrinsic rewards that have the potential to hinder the habit-formation process (Lally and Gardner 2013). In the following, we describe (i) the individual stages of habit formation and (ii) discuss digital strategies that have the potential to support these stages.

2.1 First Stage: Decision to Take Action and Formulation of an Implementation Intention

In the first stage, a decision is made to take action (Lally and Gardner 2013). To support decision-making for a potential habit, a typical strategy is information provision (Webb et al. 2010; Nilsen et al. 2012) aimed at providing data that can alter users' decisional balance (Pinder et al. 2018). Typically, information is related to statistics on positive or negative health outcomes. Information provision has demonstrated a (small) impact on behavior change, as shown in a meta-analysis (Anker et al. 2016).

MR1: Information should be provided to enable informed habit selection

After choosing a habit, an implementation intention for this habit needs to be formulated to create a first mental association between the behavior and the context (Lally and Gardner 2013). For example, an implementation intention might involve associating the context "**if** *I am on the bus for work*" with the behavior "**then** *I will get off one stop earlier and walk*".

MR2: The process of formulating an implementation intention should be supported to effectively link the context to the behavior

To help remember the habit in a later stage, it is essential to feasibly describe context-specific cues. Typical contexts include physical settings (kitchen), time (9 a.m.), people (alone), prior behavior (getting up), internal state (being stressed), and combinations thereof (Ji and Wood 2007). To facilitate remembering the habit, the context-specific cue should include all aspects as necessary to distinguish the context (Stawarz et al. 2020).

MR3: A detailed contextual specification should enable remembering the habit

2.2 Second Stage: The Intention to Act Is Translated into Behavior

After deciding on a habit and formulating its implementation intention, it must be translated into a behavior (Lally and Gardner 2013). The user can integrate this habit into their daily routine to assess the experience of executing it and determine if any modifications are required in the selected context (Stawarz et al. 2020). In this stage, digital strategies encourage repeated behavior, providing sufficient time to determine whether to sustain or abandon the habit and adjust and enhance the implementation intention (Stawarz et al. 2015). Furthermore, repeatedly executing the behavior in the context helps foster the mental association between the behavior and the contextual cues (Wood and 2007; Lally et al. 2010). In this stage, prior HCI literature highlights strategies to provide trigger events that serve as cues and help maintain repetition (Stawarz et al. 2014). Such digital strategies include visual cues or reminders on the smartphone's home screen. Typically, just-in-time reminders (Stawarz et al. 2015) are used when the system predicts that the user may be at risk of developing bad habits or is missing opportunities to execute good habits (Nahum-Shani et al. 2018; Pinder et al. 2018).

MR4: Trigger events should be used as cues to maintain repetition

2.3 Third Stage: Repeating the Behavior Consistently in Response to the Context

After deciding to implement a habit and optimizing the implementation intention, the habit must be strengthened (Lally and Gardner 2013). This strengthening occurs when the behavior, prompted by a specific context, is consistently and repeatedly performed (Verplanken and Aarts 1999; Wood and Neal 2009; Lally and Gardner 2013), allowing to strengthen the mental association established in the implementation intention. Once the habit is strengthened, the cognitive effort required to act decreases, and the habit becomes second nature (Lally et al. 2011). Alternatives (*staying on the bus*) become less accessible (Danner et al. 2007, 2008). Hereby, the repetition strategy of the previous stage should be phased out and abandoned at the end of this stage. In this stage, the use of reminders as trigger events is criticized as they might only maintain the habit at a superficial level (Stawarz et al. 2015). One argument is that the behavior is likely to be abandoned once the technology fosters it is not used anymore (Pinder et al. 2018). To strengthen the habit, reminding should not be used as a trigger event sent at the moment of habit execution. Instead, it should reinforce the implementation intention (Stawarz et al. 2015). In this regard, notifications are sent, for example, in the morning (e.g., when I take the bus to work later, I will remember to get off a station earlier and walk) (Stawarz et al. 2015). This kind of reminder encourages the user to recall the behavior later when the context arises. The following two MRs on habit formation can be derived from this.

MR5: Reminders should be used to reinforce the implementation intention instead rather than solely functioning as trigger events

MR6: Reminders should phase out so that users do not become reliant on notifications

Nowadays, users receive many reminders and visual cues (Pielot et al. 2018). Therefore, solely using reminders and visual cues may be insufficient to prompt the repetition of habits or reinforce the implementation intention. Other digital strategies are consequently also needed for a complementary application with reminders. Overall, supporting the individual's internal self-regulatory processes plays a key role in stages two and three (Lally and Gardner 2013). According to Bandura's social-cognitive theory, self-regulation is a process consisting of three subfunctions: Self-monitoring, self-judgment, and the resulting self-reactions (Bandura 1991). Particularly self-monitoring support is a common ingredient of behavior change interventions and is considered in tandem with feedback (Michie et al. 2013). With regard to the stages of habit formation, self-monitoring is applicable across the second and third stages. In contrast, feedback is most applicable in the third stage when the actual behavior is executed (Lally and Gardner 2013). Self-monitoring captures information about behavior and often reveals previously unknown information to the user (e.g., visualize the number of steps during a day; Thaler and Sunstein 2009). According to Bandura (1991), feedback can stimulate self-regulation by providing information about "how one is doing" when monitoring alone is insufficient to get evidence of the individual progress. Obtaining feedback by being praised for executing the behavior (e.g., in the evening, when checking for habit adherence) can associate the behavior with a positive feeling and, with that, reinforce the behavior. Furthermore, praise can also be used to reinforce the implementation intention by repeating it, such as "*Congratulation, you have done your 7-minute workout after brushing your teeth this morning! Well done.*". To promote self-regulation, recent IS literature also discusses the concept of gamification, i.e., the application of game characteristics to non-game contexts (Deterding et al. 2011a, b; Deterding et al. 2011a, b). For example, to promote an individual's self-judgment and "intervention stickiness", apps include levels of difficulty or specific challenges (Hervas et al. 2017).

MR7: Facilitating self-regulation processes in the form of self-observation, self-assessment, and self-reactions should make an important contribution to translating the intention into the targeted behavior, but also to maintaining repetition (stage 2) and maintaining repetition and reinforcing the behavior (stage 3).

2.4 Fourth Stage: Reaching Automaticity and Abandoning Technology

In the fourth stage, the new habit is repeated in a fashion conducive to the development of automaticity (Lally and Gardner 2013). This stage includes creating salient cues for the activity, emphasizing consistency, reducing behavioral complexity, and avoiding extrinsic rewards that have the potential to hinder the habit-formation process (Lally and Gardner 2013). Hence, digital strategies used in the previous stages must be reduced and finally abandoned (Stawarz et al. 2014). This doesn't mean that the technology should not be used anymore, but that gamification, praise, and reminding should be avoided for the particular habit, which now reaches a higher level of automaticity. Instead, the technology may still be used to introduce new habits and to have an overview of the overall habits that have been implemented and strengthened. Such an overview may help the user to review their lifestyle annually or biannually and adjust accordingly, e.g., by altering existing ones. Furthermore, strong habits can serve as contextual cues for new habits. Using strong habits as a contextual cue for newer ones has been extensively discussed in the self-help literature as habit stacking (e.g., Clear 2018). In this regard, a new habit is added to another, serving as a contextual cue for the new one.

MR8: The habit that is about to gain automaticity should not be reinforced by technology anymore

MR9: Strong habits should be used for habit stacking

3 Content Analysis of Habit Apps

3.1 Design

To add knowledge of conventional habit apps to the requirements of section 2, this paper employs a content analysis according to Krippendorff (2018). To determine the sample, we used an API-based approach analog to (Catozzi et al. 2020; Richter et al. 2021) to investigate apps available on the Apple App Store for iOS devices. We refrained from including the Google Play Store as this platform does not support the API-based approach. To create an API query, the following components needed to be addressed: the basic search layer, the URL-encoded search term, the ISO country code (DE), the media entity (software), and the number of results (50) per search term. The following search terms were used: *Habit, Habit Tracking, Habit Tracker, Pattern Tracker, Pattern Tracking, Streak Tracker, and Streak Tracking.* Applying the search term resulted in a total of 320 apps. After removing duplicates, 149 apps remained. Furthermore, 29 apps that exhibited an app score of zero were excluded. Subsequently, one author manually reviewed the remaining apps towards their ability to form habits and their applicability for various purposes. Apps that were serving a specific purpose (e.g., weight loss, increased fitness) and those that were used to limit device functionality were not included in the investigation. Sixty-four apps were marked as suitable, of which three needed to be excluded due to technical problems and four due to a paid version only. Ultimately, 57 apps were identified and selected for examination.

Subsequently, we used the meta-requirements summarized in section 2 to approach the first set of categories to analyze the apps. In this stage, 20 apps were evaluated by downloading and trying the app to assess all features the application has to offer. Each app was assessed by at least two authors. In total, five authors engaged in evaluating the apps. This approach helped to discuss the evaluation results and to determine further categories. The remaining apps were evaluated after agreeing on a final set of categories and clarifying the evaluation procedures. Any uncertainties encountered during the evaluation process were discussed to ensure consistency.

3.2 Results

The analyzed apps were assessed based on their adherence to the MRs, with the degree of fulfillment being classified into three distinct levels: Full compliance, partial compliance, and non-compliance with the MRs. When considering the provision of information (**MR1**), we observed that only 28% (16) of the 57 apps partially adhere to this requirement. An approach commonly used to partially adhere to this MR was categorizing habits into goals to facilitate information (e.g., HabitMinder 2022). **MR2** addresses the formulation of an implementation intention, linking the context to the behavior. This can be incorporated into apps by allowing users to describe the behavior and associate it with a specific place, time, or another behavior as a contextual reference. Only 19% (11) of the 57 apps partially fulfill this requirement. For example, Focus Habits Streaks Progress (2023) employ a question-based approach to guide users in formulating their implementation intention, while Success Coach—Life Planner (2023) additionally provides a diary to reflect on the context's appropriateness.

Within **MR3**, we examined the capability of integrating multiple contexts for habit implementation. Out of 57 apps, 72% (41) offer the option to incorporate two contexts, while only seven apps provide the ability to add even more contexts. The most advanced apps in this regard also use location as context (Habit—Daily Tracker 2023) and even allow for incorporating Apple Health data into the habit implementation phase (Awesome Habits 2023). **MR4** emphasizes providing trigger events, such as reminders, to facilitate habit repetition. For most apps, 96% (55 out of 57) enable users to set up reminders for specific dates and times for each habit. Notably, apps like (Daily Habits —Habit Tracker 2021) go even further by allowing users to personalize their reminder texts. **MR5** examines whether reminders are employed to reinforce the implementation intention rather than being solely used as trigger events. However, after evaluating the 57 apps, no indications of this particular approach were found.

MR6 introduces the concept of gradually reducing reminders in order to foster habit strength. This aspect was only partially found in a single app (Better Habits of Health 2021). This app implements a living progress action score, which indicates the completion of a habit. Once a desired score is achieved, users can either conclude the habit technologically or restart it if necessary. In **MR7**, additional digital strategies aimed at promoting habit repetition and reinforcement were examined. Self-monitoring, for instance, was facilitated through various tools such as visual progress bars, experience points, and picture elements. These self-monitoring tools were employed by a significant majority of the apps (53 out of 57; 93%). Furthermore, gamification elements were found in 88% (50) of the apps. An example of gamification can be seen in Flora (2023) where figurative elements, like a growing plant, are utilized to enhance user engagement. In terms of positive reinforcement, praise is used by 61% (35 out of 57) of the apps. One example is Rabit (2022), which offers users motivational messages containing famous quotes as positive reinforcement.

MR8 aims to minimize extrinsic stimuli for habit execution so that the habit can strengthen. However, during the content analysis, no instance of phasing out extrinsic stimuli (0 of 57) without requiring any action from the user were observed. It seems that the apps did not proactively incorporate mechanisms to gradually reduce stimuli. **MR9** centers around leveraging strong habits as a contextual framework for introducing new habits. The goal is to create a synergistic relationship between habits, where existing habits provide support for the development of new ones. Out of the 57 apps, only 18% (10 apps) were found to meet this MR. Notably, best practice apps like (North Star 2022) strive to induce routines or milestones to facilitate the integration of new habits. However, none of the apps use already-formed habits to stack new habits.

During the first phase of the content analysis, additional categories were identified that did not directly align with the MRs. One such category is **flexible habit management**, which facilitates habit implementation. It was found that 81% (46 out of 57) apps offered this feature. In this context, flexibility was considered present when users could define parameters such as time and frequency per week. Notably, Awesome Habits (2023) provides a skipping function for habits, allowing users more flexibility in their habit routines. In terms of **avoiding information overload**, gradually introducing a variety of habits was a helpful approach to habit implementation. However, it was observed that 89% (51 out of 57) of the apps display all habits at once without aiming to avoid information overload. Partial fulfillment was given when targets were displayed on a daily basis. Another way to prevent information overload was introduced by *The* Fabulous (2023), who avoids overload by introducing habits step by step as a journey. Related to MR7, the content analysis revealed the utilization of **social interaction** as a means to reinforce habits. Among the apps, 23% (13 out of 57) allow users to include their social contacts. Furthermore, 37% (21 out of 57) of the apps enable users to share their habit successes with friends, fostering a sense of accountability and support. Additionally, a habit community feature was found in

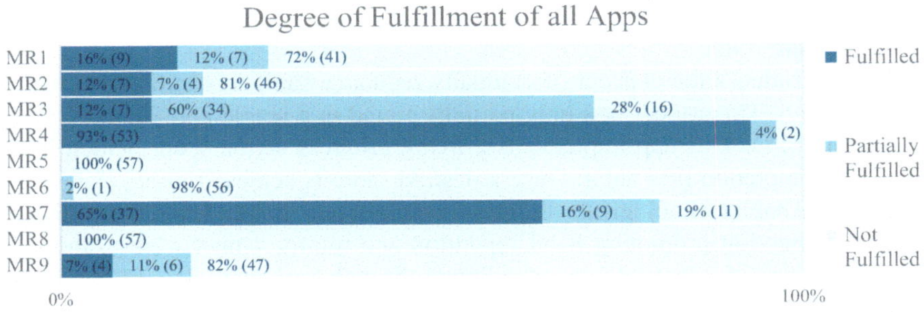

Fig. 2 Overview of the content analysis results in regard to the meta-requirements (MR)

26% (15 out of 57) of the apps, allowing users to engage with a community of like-minded individuals. Noteworthy apps such as (Habitify, 2022) and (Coach.me, 2019) incorporate these social interaction functionalities. Additionally, 56% (32 out of 57) of the apps allow users to set a **habit focus**. Partial compliance in this aspect was observed when apps provided the ability to mark habits with colors or group them. Approximately 32% (18 out of 57) of the apps offer grouping proposals. Another possibility to categorize habits is by distinguishing them into build and quit habits, which is implemented by 30% (17 out of 57) of the apps. To improve **usability**, the three categories of personalizing i) behavior, ii) context, and iii) the general app appearance were found. Personalization of behavior is implemented by six apps through initial short questions about the users' personal goals or preferences. Context personalization is possible with 61% (35 out of 57) of the apps. Only 54% (31 out of 57) of the apps allow contextualized time and date, and 7% (4 out of 57) contextualize additional content (Grow, 2023). The general appearance of the app can be personalized, for example, by different color schemes or language settings. 61% (35 out of 57) of the apps offer at least one or several options (e.g., Today 2022). Figure 2 provides an overview of the results of the content analysis.

4 Discussion

This work summarizes prior research to form (i.e., implement and strengthen) habits. In accordance with a previous review of HCI research by Stawarz et al. (2015), our study has identified apps with the potential to support stages 1 and 2 of the habit formation process. However, none of the identified applications meet the requirements for strengthening habits at stages 3 and 4. Considering the proliferation of habit-forming apps since 2015 and the coverage of related topics in the self-help literature (e.g., Clear 2018; Wood 2019), we suspect the lack of technical support for habit strengthening is likely due to a lack of incentive. In fact, many habit apps follow a commercial interest, requiring the user to adopt the app continually (Krell et al. 2009). In contrast, forming habits, at some point, requires phasing out and abandoning technology (Stawarz et al. 2015; Pinder et al. 2018). Due to this contradiction, we also suspect that conventional habit apps may not be appropriate tools to implement and strengthen habits. With the rise of DTx, there is, however, a market that may allow filling this gap. To facilitate the design of DTx that have the potential to support implementing and strengthening habits, we now summarize design principles based on the MR and the insight we gained from using the conventional apps. These design principles are outlined in Table 1.

Stage 1—Decision to act: Some apps investigated in the content analysis provided information on potentially beneficial habits to support the decision-making process on which habits to implement (Pinder et al. 2018; **DP1**). Beyond listing habits, some apps also categorized these habits into goals or journeys (**DP 4**). HabitMinder (2022) categorized habits into goals, while The Fabulous (2023) used journeys to reduce overload. When embarking on a journey (e.g., *mental fitness*), information for the next habit unlocks stepwise. In this regard, information overload by having too much information is reduced, and the user is guided to try out a new habit related to the selected journey one after another. Once the decision for a habit has been taken, an implementation intention must be formulated (**DP2**). Such a formulation was

Table 1 Design principles for DTx; Stage 1—Decision to act, Stage 2—Intention to act is translated into behavior, Stage 3—Behavior is repeatedly performed in the same context, Stage 4—Habit is performed automatically; Origin MR-meta-requirement; CA-content analysis.

Design Principles for Habit-based DTx	Stages	Origin
DP1: Information should be provided to enable informed habitat selection.	1	MR1
DP2: The process of formulating an implementation intention should be supported to effectively link the context to the behavior.	1	MR2
DP3: A detailed contextual specification should enable remembering the habit.	1	MR3
DP4: Information overload should be avoided (e.g., by implementing a (habit-) journey or clear habit focus).	1	CA
DP5: Build (e.g., exercise in the morning) and quit habits (reduce coffee) should be distinguished.	1	CA
DP6: Flexible habit management should be allowed.	2–4	CA
DP7: Trigger events should be used as cues to maintain repetition.	2	MR4
DP8: Personalization should be enabled or offered at all stages.	1–4	CA
DP9: Comparison and feedback should be offered.	2-3	MR7, CA
DP10: Reminders should be used to reinforce the implementation intention rather than solely functioning as trigger events.	2-3	MR5
DP11: Reminders should phase out so that users do not become reliant on notifications (tapered reminding).	3	MR6
DP12: The habit that is about to gain automaticity should no longer be reinforced by technology.	4	MR8
DP13: Habit stacking options should be implemented by using strong habits.	4	MR9, CA

possible in some apps (19%, 11 out of 57). However, hardly any app guided the user to link the behavior with the context in an implementation intention (Gollwitzer and Sheeran 2006; Lally and Gardner 2013). For a precise specification of context (**DP3**) within the implementation intention, most apps allowed to specify time and date (72%, 41 out of 57), but only 11% (6 out of 57) of the apps included location (e.g., kitchen or bedroom as for example in Habio 2023). No app allowed to select prior habits (**DP 13**), or internal states (being stressed) as context. Combinations of contexts were supported partially in (Habio, 2023). The context may also vary for build or quit habits, so distinguishing these types of habits is important (**DP5**). Furthermore, this stage potentially benefits from personalizing the decision-making process of which habit to implement (**DP8**). In this regard, we found five apps that used questionnaires to narrow the selection of possible habits.

Stage 2—Intention to act is translated into behavior: Once the habit is selected and an implementation intention is formulated, it needs to be translated into daily life. In this stage, digital support can provide trigger elements (**DP7**). Most apps use reminders via email or smartphone screen to trigger the habit. This stage may also profit from flexible habit management (**DP6**). Some apps allow to detail habits as being due based on intervals or timeframes per day, week, or month or to skip habits in case of holidays or illness (e.g., Awesome Habits 2023). Furthermore, personalization may increase repetition in this stage by presenting users with customized reminders and notifications (**DP8**). Repetition may also be increased by providing comparison mechanisms (**DP9**). To effectively support self-regulatory processes, apps could provide mechanisms to enable a comparison with the user himself (self-comparison), other users (social-comparison), between groups (collective comparison), and/or to defined standard norms (Bandura 1991). Comparing the current behavioral performance or behavioral outcomes with these referential values also forms the foundation for providing dedicated feedback to the user via the app (Kramer and Kowatsch 2017). A special type of evaluative feedback is praise (positive feedback), which may be accompanied by (virtual) rewards such as trophies (Michie et al. 2013; Lehto and Oinas-Kukkonen 2015). For addressing this DP, some of the analyzed apps leverage gamification design features such as leaderboards or social sharing (Habitify 2022) to stimulate a social comparison, but also badges or experience points (Daylio 2023) based on defined target norms. Particularly social comparison is a promising approach in the treatment of behavior-modifiable diseases (e.g., obesity or diabetes) where different strategies, such as upward, downward, or lateral comparison and comparison to other individuals or a group as a whole, underscore the need for personalization (see **DP8;** Arigo et al. 2021; Zhu et al. 2021).

Stage 3—Repeating the behavior consistently in response to the context: In this stage, one strategy is to foster repetition as described in stage 2 (e.g., through **DP9**). Beyond fostering repetition, this stage also aims to reinforce the implementation intention (**DP10**). In this regard, reminders (**DP10**) and gamification (**DP9**) should be used to repeat the implementation intention so that the association between context and behavior can strengthen (Stawarz et al. 2015). To further allow the habit to strengthen, reminders as trigger elements should be phased out (**DP11**). Personalization in this stage may focus on finding an individual timeline to phase out reminders, e.g., by prompting notifications when the behavior hasn't been executed frequently and phasing out after the users have found their way back to the habit (**DP8**).

Stage 4—Reaching automaticity and abandoning technology: To strengthen the habit, digital support must be abandoned so that the habit can integrate into daily life without relying on technology (**DP12**). However, technology may still help to implement and strengthen new habits. In this regard, the new habit may be stacked with a habit that is already strong (**DP13**).

This work has methodical limitations. For example, we focus on habit apps and not on to-do apps. While some to-do apps, such as (Todoist 2023), also allow the implementation of habits, TickTick (2023) explicitly focuses on implementing habits. We included these two apps as they have also been found using our search terms. However, we did not search for to-do apps. Furthermore, we excluded habits we could not test without paying for a subscription. When required, we entered a subscription and then canceled the subscription before payments became due. Based on this decision, we only had a few days to explore the apps. A thorough investigation until the habits finally become strong may help investigate and ultimately weigh design principles. Furthermore, we excluded apps that only followed a specific focus (e.g., sleep, meditation) as we aimed to examine the mechanisms to implement and strengthen habits in general. Nonetheless, investigating apps with a specific focus may help formulate design principles that focus on quit habits. The paper also has thematical limitations. Firstly, the paper focuses on habit apps and their implementation in supporting behavior change for NCDs. While this focus allows for in-depth analysis, it may limit the generalizability of the findings to other types of interventions. Furthermore, concerning DP 12, it is worth critically reflecting on the usage of apps in general to reinforce habits. The content analysis reveals that apps foster reliance on technology to encourage continued usage. It would be valuable to compare the effectiveness of habit formation with and without technology, such as using handwritten habit scorecards (Clear 2018). This comparison would shed light on the role of technology in habit formation. This work is embedded in a broader project. After initially diving into the design of an effective habit app in Weimann et al. (2022), our goal is to bolster the development of habit-based DTx by a) offering effective DPs and b) establishing an open, AI-supported habit repository to aid in treating and preventing NCDs. This repository would be beneficial in particular to enhance stage 1 of the habit formation process.

5 Conclusion

This paper summarizes meta-requirements to implement and strengthen habits and executes a content analysis using conventional habit apps. Based on the requirements and insights from the content analysis, we formulated design principles for habit-based DTx. So far, conventional apps support mainly the first two stages of forming habits and hence help to decide on a habit (stage 1) and translate it into behavior (stage 2). However, for a habit to become strong, the behavior must be repeated consistently in response to the context without being triggered. Ultimately technology must be abandoned (Stage 3-4). So far, these two stages are rarely focused on by conventional apps. However, since DTx can be prescribed for the time, it needs for a habit to strengthen, these apps may contribute to forming habitual behavior that is directed toward long-term NCD prevention and treatment. From a theoretical perspective, the derived MRs and DPs provide a framework of the main "ingredients" of habit-based DTx and may facilitate deeper investigation of single aspects. On the practitioner side, our research could provide system developers and UX experts with a starting point for the conceptualization of novel habit-based DTx that may improve the self-management of NCDs.

References

Aboumatar, H., Pitts, S., Sharma, R., Das, A., Smith, B.M., Day, J., Holzhauer, K., Yang, S., Bass, E.B. & Bennett, W.L. (2022), 'Patient engagement strategies for adults with chronic conditions: an evidence map', *Systematic Reviews*, **11**(1), p. 39. Available at: https://doi.org/10.1186/s13643-021-01873-5.

Afshin, A., Sur, P.J., Fay, K.A. et al. (2019), 'Health effects of dietary risks in 195 countries, 1990–2017: a systematic analysis for the Global Burden of Disease Study 2017', *The Lancet*, **393**(10184), pp. 1958–1972. Available at: https://doi.org/10.1016/S0140-6736(19)30041-8.

Anker, A.E., Feeley, T.H., McCracken, B. & Lagoe, C.A. (2016), 'Measuring the effectiveness of mass-mediated health campaigns through meta-analysis', *Journal of health communication*, **21**(4), pp. 439–456.

Arigo, D., Roberts, S.R. & Butryn, M.L. (2021), 'Social comparisons between group members during behavioural weight loss treatment: comparison direction, scale, and associations with weight loss maintenance', *Psychology & Health*, pp. 1–16. Available at: https://doi.org/10.1080/08870446.2021.1967953.

Awesome Habits (2023), *Awesome Habits*. Available at: https://www.awesome-habits.com/ (Accessed: 3 March 2023).

Bandura, A. (1991), 'Social cognitive theory of self-regulation', *Organizational Behavior and Human Decision Processes*, **50**(2), pp. 248–287. Available at: https://doi.org/10.1016/0749-5978(91)90022-L.

Beleigoli, A.M., Andrade, A.Q., Cançado, A.G., Paulo, M.N., Diniz, M.D.F.H. & Ribeiro, A.L. (2019), 'Web-Based Digital Health Interventions for Weight Loss and Lifestyle Habit Changes in Overweight and Obese Adults: Systematic Review and Meta-Analysis', *Journal of Medical Internet Research*, **21**(1), p. e298. Available at: https://doi.org/10.2196/jmir.9609.

Better Habits of Health (2021), *App Store*. Available at: https://apps.apple.com/de/app/better-habits-of-health/id954911327 (Accessed: 8 March 2023).

Catozzi, D., Gualano, M.R., Voglino, G., Corradi, A., Bert, F. & Siliquini, R. (2020), 'Mobile Apps for Vaccination: an in-depth scan of Apple App Store', *European Journal of Public Health*, **30**(Supplement_5), p. ckaa165.1034. Available at: https://doi.org/10.1093/eurpub/ckaa165.1034.

Clear, J. (2018), *Atomic Habits*. Random House.

Coach.me (2019), *App Store*. Available at: https://apps.apple.com/de/app/coach-me-goals-habits/id530911645 (Accessed: 8 March 2023).

Daily Habits - Habit Tracker (2021), *App Store*. Available at: https://apps.apple.com/de/app/daily-habits-habit-tracker/id1133119692 (Accessed: 8 March 2023).

Danner, U.N., Aarts, H. & de Vries, N.K. (2007), 'Habit formation and multiple means to goal attainment: Repeated retrieval of target means causes inhibited access to competitors', *Personality and Social Psychology Bulletin*, **33**(10), pp. 1367–1379.

Danner, U.N., Aarts, H. & de Vries, N.K. (2008), 'Habit vs. intention in the prediction of future behaviour: The role of frequency, context stability and mental accessibility of past behaviour', *British Journal of Social Psychology*, **47**(2), pp. 245–265.

Daylio (2023), *App Store*. Available at: https://apps.apple.com/de/app/daylio-tagebuch-gewohnheiten/id1194023242 (Accessed: 8 March 2023).

Deterding, S., Khaled, R., Nacke, L.E. & Dixon, D. (2011), 'Gamification: Toward a definition', in *CHI 2011 gamification workshop proceedings*. ACM Vancouver, BC, Canada, p. 15.

Deterding, S., Sicart, M., Nacke, L., O'Hara, K. & Dixon, D. (2011), 'Gamification. using game-design elements in non-gaming contexts', in *CHI'11 extended abstracts on human factors in computing systems*, pp. 2425–2428.

DTx Alliance (2022), *Digital Therapeutics Alliance, Digital Therapeutics Alliance*. Available at: https://dtxalliance.org/ (Accessed: 27 December 2022).

Flora (2023), *App Store*. Available at: https://apps.apple.com/de/app/flora-green-focus/id1225155794 (Accessed: 8 March 2023).

Focus Habits. Streaks Progress. (2023),. Available at: https://apps.apple.com/de/app/focus-habits-streaks-progress/id1071663315?uo=4 (Accessed: 8 March 2023).

Fürstenau, D., Gersch, M. and Schreiter, S. (2023) 'Digital Therapeutics (DTx)', *Business & Information Systems Engineering*. Available at: https://doi.org/10.1007/s12599-023-00804-z.

Gardner, B. (2015), 'A review and analysis of the use of 'habit'in understanding, predicting and influencing health-related behaviour', *Health psychology review*, **9**(3), pp. 277–295.

Gerke, S., Stern, A.D. & Minssen, T. (2020), 'Germany's digital health reforms in the COVID-19 era: lessons and opportunities for other countries', *npj Digital Medicine*, **3**(1), p. 94. Available at: https://doi.org/10.1038/s41746-020-0306-7.

Gollwitzer, P.M. & Sheeran, P. (2006), 'Implementation intentions and goal achievement: A meta-analysis of effects and processes', *Advances in experimental social psychology*, **38**, pp. 69–119.

Grow: Automatic Habit Tracker (2023), *App Store*. Available at: https://apps.apple.com/de/app/grow-automatic-habit-tracker/id1560604814 (Accessed: 8 March 2023).

Habio (2023), *Habio - your habit assistant*. Available at: https://habio.app (Accessed: 3 March 2023).

Habit — Daily Tracker (2023),. Available at: https://apps.apple.com/de/app/habit-daily-tracker/id1445651730 (Accessed: 8 March 2023).

Habitify (2022), *Habitify, App Store*. Available at: https://apps.apple.com/de/app/habitify-to-do-liste/id1111447047 (Accessed: 8 March 2023).

HabitMinder (2022), *App Store*. Available at: https://apps.apple.com/de/app/habitminder/id1253577148 (Accessed: 8 March 2023).

Hervas, R., Ruiz-Carrasco, D., Mondejar, T. & Bravo, J. (2017), 'Gamification mechanics for behavioral change: a systematic review and proposed taxonomy', in *Proceedings of the 11th EAI International Conference on Pervasive Computing Technologies for Healthcare. PervasiveHealth '17: 11th EAI International Conference on Pervasive Computing Technologies for Healthcare*, Barcelona Spain: ACM, pp. 395–404. Available at: https://doi.org/10.1145/3154862.3154939.

Hevner, A.R., March, S.T., Park, J. & Ram, S. (2004), 'Design science in information systems research', *Management information systems quarterly*, **28**(1), pp. 75–106.

Ji, M.F. & Wood, W. (2007), 'Purchase and consumption habits: Not necessarily what you intend', *Journal of Consumer Psychology*, **17**(4), pp. 261–276.

Kramer, J.-N. & Kowatsch, T. (2017), 'Using Feedback to Promote Physical Activity: The Role of the Feedback Sign', *Journal of Medical Internet Research*, **19**(6), p. e192. Available at: https://doi.org/10.2196/jmir.7012.

Krell, K., Matook, S. & Rohde, F. (2009), The effect of regulatory pressure on information system adoption success: An institutional theory perspective. In: *Proceedings of the 17th European Conference on Information Systems (ECIS).*

Krippendorff, K. (2018), *Content analysis: An introduction to its methodology*. Sage publications.

Lakka, T.A., Aittola, K., Järvelä-Reijonen, E., Tilles-Tirkkonen, T., Männikkö, R., Lintu, N., Karhunen, L., Kolehmainen, M., Harjumaa, M., Mattila, E., Järvenpää, R., Ermes, M., Mikkonen, S., Martikainen, J., Poutanen, K., Schwab, U., Absetz, P., Lindström, J. & Pihlajamäki, J. (2022), 'Real-world effectiveness of digital and group-based lifestyle interventions as compared with usual care to reduce type 2 diabetes risk – A stop diabetes pragmatic randomised trial', *The Lancet Regional Health - Europe*, p. 100527. Available at: https://doi.org/10.1016/j.lanepe.2022.100527.

Lally, P. & Gardner, B. (2013), 'Promoting habit formation', *Health psychology review*, **7**(sup1), pp. S137–S158.

Lally, P., Van Jaarsveld, C.H., Potts, H.W. & Wardle, J. (2010), 'How are habits formed: Modelling habit formation in the real world', *European journal of social psychology*, **40**(6), pp. 998–1009.

Lally, P., Wardle, J. & Gardner, B. (2011), 'Experiences of habit formation: a qualitative study', *Psychology, health & medicine*, **16**(4), pp. 484–489.

Lehto, T. & Oinas-Kukkonen, H. (2015), 'Examining the persuasive potential of web-based health behavior change support systems', *AIS Transactions on Human-Computer Interaction*, **7**(3), pp. 126–140.

Michie, S., Richardson, M., Johnston, M., Abraham, C., Francis, J., Hardeman, W., Eccles, M.P., Cane, J. & Wood, C.E. (2013), 'The Behavior Change Technique Taxonomy (v1) of 93 Hierarchically Clustered Techniques: Building an International Consensus for the Reporting of Behavior Change Interventions', *Annals of Behavioral Medicine*, **46**(1), pp. 81–95. Available at: https://doi.org/10.1007/s12160-013-9486-6.

Nahum-Shani, I., Smith, S.N., Spring, B.J., Collins, L.M., Witkiewitz, K., Tewari, A. & Murphy, S.A. (2018), 'Just-in-time adaptive interventions (JITAIs) in mobile health: key components and design principles for ongoing health behavior support', *Annals of Behavioral Medicine*, **52**(6), pp. 446–462.

Neal, D.T., Wood, W. & Quinn, J.M. (2006), 'Habits—A repeat performance', *Current directions in psychological science*, **15**(4), pp. 198–202.

Nilsen, P., Roback, K., Broström, A. & Ellström, P.-E. (2012), 'Creatures of habit: accounting for the role of habit in implementation research on clinical behaviour change', *Implementation Science*, **7**(1), pp. 1–6.

North Star (2022), *App Store*. Available at: https://apps.apple.com/de/app/north-star-your-goals/id1480448999 (Accessed: 8 March 2023).

Peffers, K., Tuunanen, T., Rothenberger, M.A. & Chatterjee, S. (2007), 'A Design Science Research Methodology for Information Systems Research.', *Journal of Management Information Systems*, **24**(3), pp. 45–77. Available at: Article.

Pielot, M., Vradi, A. & Park, S. (2018), 'Dismissed! a detailed exploration of how mobile phone users handle push notifications', in *Proceedings of the 20th International Conference on Human-Computer Interaction with Mobile Devices and Services*. New York, NY, USA: Association for Computing Machinery (MobileHCI '18), pp. 1–11. Available at: https://doi.org/10.1145/3229434.3229445.

Pinder, C., Vermeulen, J., Cowan, B.R. & Beale, R. (2018), 'Digital behaviour change interventions to break and form habits', *ACM Transactions on Computer-Human Interaction (TOCHI)*, **25**(3), pp. 1–66.

Rabit (2022), *App Store*. Available at: https://apps.apple.com/de/app/rabit-a-simple-habit-tracker/id1512605216 (Accessed: 8 March 2023).

Richter, J.G., Chehab, G., Kiltz, U., Becker, A., von Jan, U., Albrecht, U.-V., Schneider, M. & Specker, C. (2021), 'Identifikation rheumatologischer Gesundheits-Apps im Apple App Store mit der Methode der „semiautomatischen retrospektiven App Store-Analyse"', *Zeitschrift für*

Rheumatologie, **80**(10), pp. 943–952. Available at: https://doi.org/10.1007/s00393-021-01099-9.

Rippe, J.M. (2018), 'Lifestyle Medicine: The Health Promoting Power of Daily Habits and Practices', *American Journal of Lifestyle Medicine*, **12**(6), pp. 499–512. Available at: https://doi.org/10.1177/1559827618785554.

Sim, I. (2019), 'Mobile Devices and Health', *New England Journal of Medicine*, **381**(10), pp. 956–968. Available at: https://doi.org/10.1056/NEJMra1806949.

Stawarz, K., Cox, A.L. & Blandford, A. (2014), 'Don't forget your pill! Designing effective medication reminder apps that support users' daily routines', in *Proceedings of the SIGCHI Conference on Human Factors in Computing Systems*, pp. 2269–2278.

Stawarz, K., Cox, A.L. & Blandford, A. (2015), 'Beyond self-tracking and reminders: designing smartphone apps that support habit formation', in *Proceedings of the 33rd annual ACM conference on human factors in computing systems*, pp. 2653–2662.

Stawarz, K., Gardner, B., Cox, A. & Blandford, A. (2020), 'What influences the selection of contextual cues when starting a new routine behaviour? An exploratory study', *BMC Psychology*, **8**(1), p. 29. Available at: https://doi.org/10.1186/s40359-020-0394-9.

Success Coach - Life Planner (2023),. Available at: https://apps.apple.com/de/app/success-coach-life-planner/id586970083 (Accessed: 8 March 2023).

Thaler, R.H. & Sunstein, C.R. (2009), *Nudge: Improving decisions about health, wealth, and happiness*. Penguin.

The Fabulous (2023), Available at: https://www.thefabulous.co/ (Accessed: 6 January 2023).

Thomas Craig, K.J., Morgan, L.C., Chen, C.-H., Michie, S., Fusco, N., Snowdon, J.L., Scheufele, E., Gagliardi, T. & Sill, S. (2021), 'Systematic review of context-aware digital behavior change interventions to improve health', *Translational Behavioral Medicine*, **11**(5), pp. 1037–1048. Available at: https://doi.org/10.1093/tbm/ibaa099.

TickTick (2023), *TickTick*, *TickTick*. Available at: https://ticktick.com (Accessed: 6 March 2023).

Today (2022), *App Store*. Available at: https://apps.apple.com/de/app/today-gewohnheits-tracker/id1055295863 (Accessed: 8 March 2023).

Todoist (2023), *Todoist*. Available at: https://tost.com/de/ (Accessed: 6 March 2023).

Verplanken, B. & Aarts, H. (1999), 'Habit, attitude, and planned behaviour: is habit an empty construct or an interesting case of goal-directed automaticity?', *European review of social psychology*, **10**(1), pp. 101–134.

Verplanken, B. & Wood, W. (2006), 'Interventions to break and create consumer habits', *Journal of public policy & marketing*, **25**(1), pp. 90–103.

Verplanken, Bas, Verplanken, B., & Ryan (2018), *Psychology of habit*. Springer.

Vogelsang, A., Hinrichs, C., Fleig, L. & Pfeffer, I. (2022), 'Study protocol for the description and evaluation of the "Habit Coach" - a longitudinal multicenter mHealth intervention for healthy habit formation in health care professionals', *BMC Public Health*, **22**(1), p. 1672. Available at: https://doi.org/10.1186/s12889-022-13986-0.

Webb, T., Joseph, J., Yardley, L. & Michie, S. (2010), 'Using the internet to promote health behavior change: a systematic review and meta-analysis of the impact of theoretical basis, use of behavior change techniques, and mode of delivery on efficacy', *Journal of medical Internet research*, **12**(1), p. e1376.

Weimann, T.G., Schlieter, H. and Brendel, A.B. (2022) 'Virtual Coaches: Background, Theories, and Future Research Directions', *Business & Information Systems Engineering*, **64**(4), pp. 515–528.

Weimann, T. and Stark, J. (2022), "Supporting habit formation for long-term weight loss maintenance with a Virtual Coach – A Research Model. In: *Proceedings of the Wirtschaftsinformatik Conference 2022*

WHO (2020), *The top 10 causes of death. Fact Sheet., The top 10 causes of death*. Available at: https://www.who.int/news-room/fact-sheets/detail/the-top-10-causes-of-death (Accessed: 10 August 2021).

WHO (2023), *Non communicable diseases*. Available at: https://www.who.int/news-room/fact-sheets/detail/noncommunicable-diseases (Accessed: 16 February 2023).

Wood, W. & Neal, D.T. (2007), 'A new look at habits and the habit-goal interface.', *Psychological review*, **114**(4), p. 843.

Wood, W. & Neal, D.T. (2009), 'The habitual consumer', *Journal of Consumer Psychology*, **19**(4), pp. 579–592.

Wood, W. (2019), *Good habits, bad habits: The science of making positive changes that stick*. Pan Macmillan.

Zhu, J., Dallal, D.H., Gray, R.C., Villareale, J., Ontañón, S., Forman, E.M. & Arigo, D. (2021), 'Personalization Paradox in Behavior Change Apps: Lessons from a Social Comparison-Based Personalized App for Physical Activity', *Proceedings of the ACM on Human-Computer Interaction*, **5**(CSCW1), pp. 1–21. Available at: https://doi.org/10.1145/3449190.

Digital Follow-Up After Surgery—A Randomized Controlled Trial and Its Effects on Patients' Adherence and Doctor-Patient Relationship

Kirsten Hannah Seerig, Nikola Finze, Cui Yang, and Heiko Gewald

Abstract The increasing digitalization of healthcare fosters the use of digital applications for patient treatment, especially regarding rehabilitation and aftercare. This study focuses on patients' adherence to aftercare via a mobile health application and the role of the altered doctor-patient relationship. In a randomized controlled trial at a German university hospital, digital follow-up after surgery is compared to conventional outpatient aftercare. Qualitative interviews with medical personnel and patients in the intervention and the control group will be conducted after one year of implementation to investigate if digital aftercare could replace outpatient follow-up. Preliminary findings indicate the benefits of digital follow-up, like immediate contact with medical staff and higher patient involvement. Doctor-patient communication remains crucial even in the digital space.

Keywords Post-operative follow-up · Digital aftercare · mHealth · Patients' adherence · Doctor-patient relationship

---

Disclosure Cui Yang supervises the randomized controlled trial at the University Hospital of Mannheim. The authors declare that they do not have any potential conflict of interest or any financial funding to disclose. German Clinical Trials Register number: DRKS00027520. Ethics vote number: #2021–695-MA.

K. H. Seerig (✉) · N. Finze · H. Gewald
Neu-Ulm University of Applied Sciences, Wileystraße 1, 89231 Neu-Ulm, Germany
e-mail: Kirsten.Seerig@hnu.de

N. Finze
e-mail: Nikola.Finze@hnu.de

H. Gewald
e-mail: Heiko.Gewald@hnu.de

C. Yang
Department of Surgery, Medical Faculty Mannheim, University Medicine Mannheim, University of Heidelberg, Theodor-Kutzer-Ufer 1-3, 68167 Mannheim, Germany
e-mail: Cui.Yang@umm.de

D. Beverungen et al. (eds.), *Transforming the Digitally Sustainable Enterprise*, Lecture Notes in Information Systems and Organisation 76,
https://doi.org/10.1007/978-3-031-80125-9_33

1 Introduction

Demographic change poses major challenges to healthcare. On the one hand, the United Nations (UN) predicts that by 2050, the number of people aged 65 years or older will surpass the population aged 15–24 years (UN, 2019). Older adults are more frequently experiencing multimorbidity than younger people, which is associated with higher healthcare service utilization (WHO, 2015). On the other hand, the World Health Organization (WHO) estimates a shortfall of approximately 18 million healthcare workers by 2030 (WHO, 2016). These challenges are further exacerbated by the financial unsustainability of many healthcare systems (Meskó et al., 2017) following the COVID-19 pandemic, globally pushing the infrastructures of healthcare systems to their limits and calling for a reduction in personnel-intensive face-to-face consultations (Baumgart, 2020). The increasing utilization of telemedicine is posed to ease the aforementioned challenges (Gjellebæk et al., 2020). At the onset of the pandemic, 58% of all countries used telemedicine as a substitute for face-to-face consultations (Negreiro, 2021).

Following the definition of the WHO, telemedicine or digital health is the remote delivery of healthcare services using digital tools (WHO, 2022). Information and communication technologies are used to enhance public health reporting and improve disease surveillance, monitoring, treatment, diagnosis, and prevention (WHO & ITU, 2012). Technology makes data available equally to patients and caregivers, leading to collaborative decision-making and a substantial change within the doctor-patient relationship (Meskó et al., 2017). Rehabilitation and aftercare are emerging fields of interest for digital health applications (Baniasadi et al., 2020; Patel & Thind, 2020; van der Meij et al., 2018; Williams et al., 2018). Patients' adherence and attrition rates from aftercare are concerning due to long travel distances or inconvenient clinic appointments (Arnaert et al., 2020; Yang et al., 2022). Digital health technologies, especially mobile Health (mHealth) applications, can counteract these barriers and foster patients' self-management (Ghose et al., 2022; Rodriguez-Villa & Torous, 2019).

This study aims to implement a smartphone-based follow-up after surgery at a German university hospital, applying a randomized controlled trial (RCT) to compare a digitally followed-up patient group with a conventionally followed-up control group. The primary outcomes of this RCT indicate a high level of patient satisfaction, particularly regarding ease of use and direct contact with medical staff. A systematic review of mHealth applications for post-operative aftercare conducted by Patel and Thind (2020) reveals that most digital aftercare applications are used for 2–4 weeks, and long-term follow-up tends to be the exception. While many studies investigate the usability of digital health applications and user satisfaction (Maramba et al., 2019; Patel & Thind, 2020), further research is needed on patients' adherence to digital aftercare as well as activation and engagement (Arnaert et al., 2020; Su et al., 2019). Since the doctor-patient relationship is most critical for patients' adherence, it should also be investigated how it is affected by digitalization (Laugesen et al., 2015; Zhang et al., 2020). This study addresses these problems by adopting a longitudinal study design, considering a one-year utilization phase, and examining the following research questions:

(1) *Which factors influence patients' adherence to digital aftercare?*
(2) *How is the doctor-patient relationship affected in digital aftercare?*

The paper is structured as follows. First, the current state of research is outlined within a brief overview of related work, and our methodology and the study design are described. Subsequently, the preliminary results from the pilot study and the interviews conducted prior to the study are presented. The paper concludes with an outlook on further steps to substantiate our expected results.

2 Related Work

2.1 Patients' Adherence

Patients' adherence to the physician's recommended treatment is essential for successful recovery (Laugesen et al., 2015; Planel-Ratna & Juwaheer, 2021; Zhang et al., 2020). Within this section, the *Health Belief Model (HBM)* is introduced as a theoretical foundation along with supplementary aspects to explain patients' adherence in general. Based on the HBM, *barriers* and *benefits* regarding the use of mHealth applications for digital aftercare and patients' adherence to using these applications are illustrated.

The HBM developed by Rosenstock is an expectancy-value model designed to explain health behavior. It focuses on *threat perception*, *behavioral evaluation*, and *perceived benefits* and *barriers* to behaving accordingly (Rosenstock, 1974). Later, *health motivation* and *self-efficacy* were also recognized as important factors in explaining health behavior (Abraham & Sheeran, 2015; Umaki et al., 2012). Using the HBM in combination with additional factors, we can discuss why patients may or may not adopt a certain health behavior, in this case, whether or not they adhere to a recommended treatment. Additional factors from former studies impacting patients' adherence include patient activation, patients' attitudes and knowledge, physicians' competence, and the doctor-patient relationship as a primary determinant (Laugesen et al., 2015; Zhang et al., 2020). Since particular interest is placed on the doctor-patient relationship within our study, it is described in more detail in Sect. 2.2.

The most frequently reported *barriers* to adherence in digital aftercare are technical issues, poor usability, a loss of motivation due to redundant questions, and a lack of personalized care (Arnaert et al., 2020; Yang et al., 2022). These barriers were also reported in the qualitative interviews conducted within our pilot study.

In contrast, high usability is a *benefit* for the use of mHealth applications and patients' adherence. In case of high usability, digital health applications used in post-operative settings can facilitate earlier discharge, better tracing of potential complications, reduction of in-person follow-ups, improved accessibility, and user well-being, as well as enhanced doctor-patient communication (Maramba et al., 2019; Patel & Thind, 2020). In addition, mHealth applications and the inherent sovereignty over one's health can improve patient empowerment, patient satisfaction, and engagement in recovery. Within our pilot study, participants were mostly satisfied with the application's usability. Apart from usability, further perceived *benefits* regarding the use of post-operative mHealth applications include cost and time savings due to the reduction of travel times and avoidable waiting times at the hospital, no loss of working hours, as well as the flexibility to organize aftercare according to one's timetable and the enhanced responsibility for the own state of health (Arnaert et al., 2020; Williams et al., 2018; Yang et al., 2022). In addition to ease of use, the elimination of on-site visits to the hospital and associated time savings were also reported as benefits within our pilot study. Overall, patients with strong internal motivation or belief in the benefits of the mHealth application are more likely to adhere to its usage (Scott et al., 2017).

2.2 Doctor-Patient Relationship

Laugesen et al. (2015) identify doctor-patient communication as the most significant factor influencing patients' adherence and mention a potential change in the relationship through digital technologies. Traditionally, the doctor-patient relationship was characterized as paternalistic, with the physician holding authority over information and making the necessary treatment decisions in the patient's interest (Kaba & Sooriakumaran, 2007; Potter & McKinlay, 2005). Through digital health applications, patients gain better access to health information, changing the doctor-patient relationship from an information asymmetry to a more collaborative relationship at the eye level (Laugesen et al., 2015; Meskó et al., 2017).

Digital technologies enable patients to monitor their health status remotely, shifting the point of care from the doctor's office to the patient (Meskó et al., 2017). Consequently, patients become more active in medical decision-making, and care becomes more patient-centered. Equally, for physicians, this new relationship also poses the challenge of their authority being questioned. Apart from technical opportunities, the doctor-patient relationship is also influenced by the severity of the disease, and patients tend to adopt a more passive role in decisions requiring medical expertise or regarding severe illnesses (Lo & Parham, 2010).

3 Research Methods

RCTs are widely used in medically oriented Information Systems research (Dick et al., 2017) and focus on examining the effects of health-related interventions (Gabriele et al., 2011; Kelley et al., 2011). Our study compares post-operative digital aftercare via a mHealth application to conventional outpatient aftercare to investigate if it could be an effective alternative. The RCT is conducted at a German university hospital within the scope of bariatric surgery and will run for one year. Obesity and its related comorbidities and associated early mortality are rising globally (Arnaert et al., 2020; Sniehotta et al., 2019; Yang et al., 2022). Bariatric surgery is often the only effective and lasting treatment for severe obesity and its related conditions (Arnaert et al., 2020; Bradley et al., 2016; Mingrone et al., 2018; Yang et al., 2022). Consistent follow-up is essential to sustain treatment success and avoid post-operative complications (Sniehotta et al., 2019). Prior to our study, a pilot study with 26 participants was carried out to investigate their satisfaction with the digital aftercare application. To assess participants' satisfaction, the System Usability Scale (SUS) was used as a quantitative metric, and qualitative telephone interviews were carried out (see chapter 4). Additionally, a qualitative interview with a clinical study coordinator at the university hospital was conducted to obtain an initial impression of the experiences with digital aftercare on behalf of the medical professionals. The pilot study's findings and interview insights provide the basis for our further research.

Within our research, we will conduct qualitative, semi-structured interviews with medical personnel and patients who partook in the RCT for one year. Participants will be interviewed concerning their contentment with the digital follow-up, their respective expectations regarding doctor-patient communication, and their perceived self-efficacy. An interview guideline will be developed to address all aspects relevant to answering the research questions. In this context, satisfaction with the digital application, self-efficacy, and doctor-patient communication will be central elements, as these are cited in the literature as important influencing factors on patients' adherence and the doctor-patient relationship. All interviews will be anonymized and verbatim transcribed, coded, and analyzed using the software MAXQDA. An inductive qualitative content analysis will be performed to extract relevant research subjects from the interviews (Mayring & Fenzl, 2022). Additionally, the messages sent via the mHealth application will be evaluated in terms of content, response time, and prevailing communication style and tone to investigate doctor-patient communication. In this context, responses will be independently evaluated and coded (positive, negative, neutral) by two reviewers. Consideration is also given to including the Patient-Doctor Relationship Questionnaire (PDRQ-9) as an additional quantitative measure for assessing the doctor-patient relationship (Van der Feltz-Cornelis et al., 2004). Participants' responses to the Bariatric Quality of Life Questionnaire (BQL) throughout the study will also be considered. Quantitative methods, such as the BQL index, are included to capture a comprehensive picture of the effectiveness of the digital follow-up.

The patients are enrolled in the study during their first follow-up visit to the hospital after bariatric surgery. Patients are randomly assigned to the intervention or control group. For the intervention group, digital follow-up is provided by a mHealth application, whereas the control group is followed up every three months in presence. One year after surgery, both groups will undergo a final face-to-face visit. The RCT was initiated in July 2022, and 140 patients are currently enrolled. Prospectively, the trial should be a multicentre one and include further study sites. Based on the pre-study, a sample size calculation was performed, and a targeted sample size of 410 participants determined for all sites. The targeted sample size for the university hospital, which already runs the study and is considered within this paper, amounts to 205 participants. Inclusion criteria are an undergone primary bariatric surgery, the legal age of majority, possession of a smartphone with internet access, and written informed consent. Exclusion criteria are a re-do surgery, serious early complications until the first personal follow-up visit, language barriers, or the inability to attend the final face-to-face visit at the end of the trial. The qualitative interviews will be conducted once at the end of each follow-up. The results of the PDRQ-9 and the SUS will also be collected once at the end of the study.

4 Preliminary Findings

Within the pilot study, patients were predominantly satisfied with digital follow-up. Three groups (satisfied, neutral, and dissatisfied) were formed based on the results of the SUS, and telephone interviews were conducted with two randomly selected participants from each group. The majority of interview participants (I) positively emphasized the ease of use of the mHealth application and the chat function, including direct contact with medical personnel and timely replies: *"For instance, I write in the app and get an answer to my problems relatively quickly. That was really good." (I 10)*. Other positive aspects were good support and the introduction to the application by the hospital personnel, the receipt of reminders, and the perceived benefit of eliminating trips to the hospital.

Technical problems were mentioned as the main barriers to using the application. In some cases, questionnaires had to be sent several times, or error messages were displayed: "*So, sometimes we sent it back three times." (I 1)*. Partly, questionnaires were difficult to understand or formulated too generally, highlighting the need for better questionnaire phrasing, and personal contact was missed in the digital space.

As suggestions for improvement, the interview participants named greater provision of health information, integration of medication plans, more possibilities for exchanging medical data and interaction, and comment functions within the questionnaires. The latter idea is already implemented in the current study by means of free-text fields.

The interview with the clinical coordinator (C) underscores the importance of patients' adherence to treatment success and the vital role of doctor-patient communication. According to the clinical coordinator, particular attention should be paid to patients' adherence: *"I think rather the [adherence] would be important for me. It is a well-known problem that [adherence] is worse among patients. (…) That means they tend to lose weight if they are [adherent]. If they are not [adherent], they tend less." (C)* The interviewee expressed hope that patients' adherence might increase with constant reminders in the mHealth application, also addressing the idea of health motivation and perceived barriers and benefits. Furthermore, the clinical coordinator emphasized better accessibility and a lower threshold for patients to contact the medical staff within digital aftercare. In the digital space, doctor-patient communication is shifting from the physician's dominant role to eye-level communication. This change has the advantage that patients are more relaxed and provide more information. One drawback, however, is that patients are sometimes less respectful in their communication. According to the clinical coordinator, the benefits outweigh the disadvantages. While the interviewee believes that face-to-face contact may only be needed if problems arise, for some patients, contact through the mHealth application is not sufficient: "*(…) but there are actually a few patients who dropped out of the study because they feel they do not have enough personal contact through the app." (C)* This quote demonstrates the essential role of the doctor-patient relationship in patients' adherence.

5 Limitations and Next Steps

In our study, based on our preliminary results from the pilot study and the interviews, we will pay special attention to patients' adherence and the influence of the doctor-patient relationship on digital aftercare. As a next step, we will set up semi-structured interview guidelines to continue the data collection beyond the pilot study and systematically analyze the interview data. We expect our results to serve as a solid foundation for future digital aftercare as a new and improved method of outpatient follow-up. The predominantly qualitative design of our data collection enquires mostly participants' subjective evaluations. Through the complementary use of quantitative measures, we aim to counteract this limitation and provide broad insights into digital aftercare.

References

United Nations, Department of Economic and Social Affairs, Population Division (UN) (2019). World Population Prospects 2019: Highlights (ST/ESA/SER.A/423).

Abraham, C., & Sheeran, P. (2015). The health belief model. In M. Conner & P. Norman (Eds.), *Predicting and changing health behaviour. Research and Practice with Social Cognition Models* (3 ed., pp. 30–69). Open University Press.

Arnaert, A., Girard, A., Craciunas, S., Shang, Z., Ahmad, H., Debe, Z., & Demyttenaere, S. (2020). Patients' experiences of telenursing follow-up care after bariatric surgery. *Journal of Clinical Nursing*, 1-10. https://doi.org/10.1111/jocn.15955

Baniasadi, T., Ghazisaeedi, M., Hassaniazad, M., Niakan Kalhori, S. R., Shahi, M., & Esmaeili, M. (2020). Surgical Patients Follow-Up by Smartphone-Based Applications: A Systematic Literature Review. In G. Schreier, D. Hayn, & A. Eggerth (Eds.), *dHealth 2020 – Biomedical Informatics for Health and Care. Proceedings of the 14th Health Informatics Meets Digital Health Conference* (Vol. 271, pp. 85–92). IOS Press. https://doi.org/10.3233/SHTI200079

Baumgart, D. C. (2020). Digital advantage in the COVID-19 response: perspective from Canada's largest integrated digitalized healthcare system. *NPJ Digit Med*, *3*. https://doi.org/10.1038/s41746-020-00326-y

Bradley, L. E., Sarwer, D. B., Forman, E. M., Kerrigan, S. G., Butryn, M. L., & Herbert, J. D. (2016). A Survey of Bariatric Surgery Patients' Interest in Post-operative Interventions. *OBES SURG*, *26*(2), 332-338. https://doi.org/10.1007/s11695-015-1765-9

Dick, S., O'Connor, Y., & Heavin, C. (2017). RANDOMISED CONTROLLED TRIALS AS A METHOD OF EVALUATING MOBILE HEALTH INTERVENTIONS. Proceedings of the 25th European Conference on Information Systems (ECIS), Guimarães, Portugal.

Gabriele, J. M., Carpenter, B. D., Tate, D. F., & Fisher, E. B. (2011). Directive and nondirective e-coach support for weight loss in overweight adults. *Ann Behav Med*, *41*(2), 252-263. https://doi.org/10.1007/s12160-010-9240-2

Ghose, A., Guo, X., Li, B., & Dang, Y. (2022). Empowering Patients Using Smart Mobile Health Platforms: Evidence of a Randomized Field Experiment. *MIS Quarterly*, *46*(1), 151–192. https://doi.org/10.25300/misq/2022/16201

Gjellebæk, C., Svensson, A., Bjørkquist, C., Fladeby, N., & Grundén, K. (2020). Management challenges for future digitalization of healthcare services. *Futures*, *124*. https://doi.org/10.1016/j.futures.2020.102636

Kaba, R., & Sooriakumaran, P. (2007). The evolution of the doctor-patient relationship. *Int J Surg*, *5*(1), 57-65. https://doi.org/10.1016/j.ijsu.2006.01.005

Kelley, H., Chiasson, M., Downey, A., & Pacaud, D. (2011). The Clinical Impact of eHealth on the Self-Management of Diabetes: A Double Adoption Perspective. *Journal of the Association for Information Systems*, *12*(3), 208-234.

Laugesen, J., Hassanein, K., & Yuan, Y. (2015). The Impact of Internet Health Information on Patient Compliance: A Research Model and an Empirical Study. *J Med Internet Res*, *17*(6). https://doi.org/10.2196/jmir.4333

Lo, B., & Parham, L. (2010). The impact of web 2.0 on the doctor-patient relationship. *J Law Med Ethics*, *38*(1), 17–26. https://doi.org/10.1111/j.1748-720X.2010.00462.x

Maramba, I., Chatterjee, A., & Newman, C. (2019). Methods of usability testing in the development of eHealth applications: A scoping review. *International Journal of Medical Informatics*, *126*, 95-104. https://doi.org/10.1016/j.ijmedinf.2019.03.018

Mayring, P., & Fenzl, T. (2022). Qualitative Inhaltsanalyse. In N. Baur & J. Blasius (Eds.), *Handbuch Methoden der empirischen Sozialforschung* (3 ed., pp. 691–706). Springer VS. https://doi.org/10.1007/978-3-658-37985-8_43

Meskó, B., Drobni, Z., Bényei, E., Gergely, B., & Győrffy, Z. (2017). Digital health is a cultural transformation of traditional healthcare. *mHealth*, *3*. https://doi.org/10.21037/mhealth.2017.08.07

Mingrone, G., Bornstein, S., & Le Roux, C. W. (2018). Optimisation of follow-up after metabolic surgery. *Lancet Diabetes Endocrinol*, *6*(6), 487-499. https://doi.org/10.1016/S2213-8587(17)30434-5

Negreiro, M. (2021). *The rise of digital health technologies during the pandemic.*

Patel, B., & Thind, A. (2020). Usability of Mobile Health Apps for Post-operative Care: Systematic Review. *JMIR Perioper Med*, *3*(2). https://doi.org/10.2196/19099

Planel-Ratna, C., & Juwaheer, T. D. (2021). Assessing the Impact of Digitalization and Technology on Patient Compliance in Healthcare Services. *HighTech and Innovation Journal*, *2*(3), 216–223. https://doi.org/10.28991/hij-2021-02-03-06

Potter, S. J., & McKinlay, J. B. (2005). From a relationship to encounter: an examination of longitudinal and lateral dimensions in the doctor-patient relationship. *Soc Sci Med*, *61*(2), 465-479. https://doi.org/10.1016/j.socscimed.2004.11.067

Rodriguez-Villa, E., & Torous, J. (2019). Regulating digital health technologies with transparency: the case for dynamic and multi-stakeholder evaluation. *BMC Med*, *17*(1). https://doi.org/10.1186/s12916-019-1447-x

Rosenstock, I. M. (1974). Historical Origins of the Health Belief Model. *Health Education Monographs*, *2*(4), 328–335. https://doi.org/10.1177/109019817400200403

Scott, A. R., Alore, E. A., Naik, A. D., Berger, D. H., & Suliburk, J. W. (2017). Mixed-Methods Analysis of Factors Impacting Use of a Post-operative mHealth App. *JMIR Mhealth Uhealth*, *5*(2). https://doi.org/10.2196/mhealth.6728

Sniehotta, F. F., Evans, E. H., Sainsbury, K., Adamson, A., Batterham, A., Becker, F., Brown, H., Dombrowski, S. U., Jackson, D., Howell, D., Ladha, K., McColl, E., Olivier, P., Rothman, A. J., Steel, A., Vale, L., Vieira, R., White, M., Wright, P., & Arau' jo-Soares, V. (2019). Behavioural intervention for weight loss maintenance versus standard weight advice in adults with obesity: A randomised controlled trial in the UK (NULevel Trial). *PLoS Med*, *16*(5). https://doi.org/10.1371/journal.pmed.1002793

Su, D., Michaud, T. L., Estabrooks, P., Schwab, R. J., Eiland, L. A., Hansen, G., DeVany, M., Zhang, D., Li, Y., Pagán, J. A., & Siahpush, M. (2019). Diabetes Management Through Remote Patient Monitoring: The Importance of Patient Activation and Engagement with the Technology. *Telemed J E Health*, *25*(10), 952-959. https://doi.org/10.1089/tmj.2018.0205

Umaki, T. M., Umaki, M. R., & Cobb, C. M. (2012). The psychology of patient compliance: a focused review of the literature. *J Periodontol*, *83*(4), 395-400. https://doi.org/10.1902/jop.2011.110344

Van der Feltz-Cornelis, C. M., Van Oppen, P., Van Marwijk, H. W., De Beurs, E., & Van Dyck, R. (2004). A patient-doctor relationship questionnaire (PDRQ-9) in primary care: development and psychometric evaluation. *Gen Hosp Psychiatry*, *26*(2), 115-120. https://doi.org/10.1016/j.genhosppsych.2003.08.010

van der Meij, E., Anema, J. R., Leclercq, W. K. G., Bongers, M. Y., Consten, E. C. J., Schraffordt Koops, S. E., van de Ven, P. M., Terwee, C. B., van Dongen, J. M., Schaafsma, F. G., Meijerink, W. J. H. J., Bonjer, H. J., & Huirne, J. A. F. (2018). Personalised perioperative care by e-health after intermediate-grade abdominal surgery: a multicentre, single-blind, randomised, placebo-controlled trial. *The Lancet*, *392*(10141), 51–59. https://doi.org/10.1016/S0140-6736(18)31113-9

World Health Organization & International Telecommunication Union (WHO & ITU) (2012). National eHealth strategy toolkit. https://apps.who.int/iris/handle/10665/75211 Accessed: 21.06.2023

Williams, A. M., Bhatti, U. F., Alam, H. B., & Nikolian, V. C. (2018). The role of telemedicine in post-operative care. *mHealth*, *4*(11). https://doi.org/10.21037/mhealth.2018.04.03

World Health Organization (WHO) (2015). World report on ageing and health. https://apps.who.int/iris/handle/10665/186463. Accessed: 21.06.2023

World Health Organization (WHO) (2016). Working for health and growth: Investing in the health workforce. https://www.who.int/publications/i/item/9789241511308. Accessed: 21.06.2023

World Health Organization (WHO) (2022). Consolidated telemedicine implementation guide. https://www.who.int/publications/i/item/9789240059184. Accessed: 21.06.2023

Yang, C., Kessler, M., Taebi, N., Moorthy, P., Reissfelder, C., Otto, M., & Vassilev, G. (2022). Smartphone application-based follow-up care of patients after bariatric surgery: A mixed-method study of usability. *Digital Health*, *8*, 1-8. https://doi.org/10.1177/20552076221129072

Zhang, X., Zhang, R., & Lu, X. (2020). Exploring the Effects of Patient Activation in Online Health Communities on Patient Compliance. *Telemed J E Health*, *26*(11), 1373-1382. https://doi.org/10.1089/tmj.2019.0258

IT-Related Time Poverty: Identifying Antecedents and Consequences of a Lack of Time Related to IT Use

Manfred Schoch and Christoph Weinert

Abstract Time poverty is the subjective perception of inadequate freely disposable time, which results in negative consequences for individuals. Although information systems (IS) research knows that information technology (IT) use change time perception, research is incomplete in explaining IT-related antecedents and consequences of time poverty. Because time is a scarce resource, individuals, organizations, and society have a responsibility to manage time to protect individuals from adverse consequences. We conduct a structured literature review to identify indications of how IT use influences time poverty and its adverse consequences. We identified 16 papers, which we analyzed with respect to different components of IT use and possible consequences of time poverty. Based on the data, we develop an overview of the antecedents and consequences of IT-related time poverty and a research agenda. We contribute to the research by introducing IT-related time poverty as a new IS construct and providing an in-depth research agenda.

Keywords Time poverty · Sustainable development goals · IT use · Digital responsibility

1 Introduction

Statistics show that 80% of employed Americans report that they "never had enough time" (Whillans 2019). When individuals have insufficient freely disposable time, they are time-poor (Irani and Vemireddy 2021). Thus, time poverty is defined as one's

M. Schoch (✉)
University of Hohenheim, Stuttgart, Germany
e-mail: manfred.schoch@fim-rc.de

Branch Business and Information Systems Engineering of the Fraunhofer FIT, Bayreuth, Germany

C. Weinert
University of Bamberg, Bamberg, Germany
e-mail: christoph.weinert@uni-bamberg.de

D. Beverungen et al. (eds.), *Transforming the Digitally Sustainable Enterprise*, Lecture Notes in Information Systems and Organisation 76,
https://doi.org/10.1007/978-3-031-80125-9_34

subjective perception of an inadequate amount of freely disposable time (Vickery 1977; Zheng et al. 2022). Psychology literature reveals multiple antecedents of time poverty that may be embedded in society, organizations, or individual psychology (Giurge et al. 2020). For example, work has become more complex and knowledge-intensive, which requires more time. Time is a scarce resource, and if the freely disposable time is limited, individuals tend to suffer from health issues and low well-being (Urakawa et al. 2020; Zheng et al. 2022). Previous research has shown that 70% of time-poor individuals experienced fatigue and half of them felt exhausted (Giurge et al. 2020). This is, for example, because when individuals feel time-poor, they begin to sacrifice time normally spent for basic psychological needs, such as sleep or physical activity.

Although we know that information technology (IT) use changes time perception (Ivaturi and Chua 2021) and psychological research demonstrates initial evidence for IT-related antecedents, such as the always-on mentality (Giurge et al. 2020), information systems (IS) research pays little attention to the issue of time poverty. IT usage time for work and leisure averages nearly seven hours per day and has increased by 50 min per day over the past decade (Howarth 2023). Individuals also report spending more time on social networking platforms "than they should" (Ravindran et al. 2014). In addition, complex IS, IT interruptions, or computer failures tie up time by forcing users to deal with them to use IT effectively.

As time is a scarce resource, individuals, organizations, and society have a responsibility to manage time to prevent individuals from feeling time-poor and suffering from health problems and low well-being. Increased use of IT may be an accelerator of time poverty because IT makes it easier to spend time and changes the perception of time (Ivaturi and Chua 2021). On the other hand, IT may also be a cure for time poverty by helping us switch between multiple time-consuming tasks or automate them altogether. Thus, it is essential to understand the IT-related antecedents and consequences of time poverty, to understand how IT use contributes to the share of freely disposable time, and then to empower IT users to manage their time effectively to avoid adverse consequences. The importance of understanding IT-related time poverty is also evident in the seventeen Sustainable Development Goals (SDGs) (Nilsson et al. 2016). More concretely, the first goal is to reduce poverty in all forms, which includes time poverty. IS research is committed to addressing these global sustainability challenges (Ospina-Forero et al. 2022; Watson et al. 2021) and increasing digital responsibility (Mihale-Wilson et al. 2022). Consequently, addressing time poverty is of great importance for IS research. Thus, we directly address the issue by identifying the IS-related antecedents and consequences of time poverty in this paper and aim to answer the following research question:

What are IT-related antecedents and consequences of time poverty?

To answer this research question, we build upon psychological research to conceptualize IT-related time poverty. Based on a review of IS literature, we identify IT-related antecedents and consequences of time poverty. The results are summarized in a conceptual overview which we use to develop a research agenda for future research. Our findings contribute to the literature by focusing on time poverty from an IS perspective and suggesting ways to address digital responsibility. We identify IT-related antecedents and consequences and reveal fruitful avenues for future research by demonstrating how to investigate the topic of IT-related time poverty.

2 Theoretical Background on Time Poverty

According to the United Nations (UN) the fundamental understanding of poverty is the *"denial of choices and opportunities, a violation of human dignity [..]"* (Gordon 2005). From a research perspective, we understand poverty as having critically low levels of resources (Williams et al. 2016). However, poverty has different forms (Michel and Tanner 2021). Among others, individuals can also be time-poor.

The literature demonstrates that time is a complex concept that can be multiply conceptualized (Ivaturi and Chua 2021). By adopting a clock time vision, time is understood as a scarce resource that can be lost, spent, or wasted (Saunders et al. 2004).

Research builds upon this clock time vision by separating the 24 h of a day into four kinds of time (Charmes 2022; Irani and Vemireddy 2021). *Necessary time* (1) refers to basic physiological needs. This time is needed to satisfy basic needs such as sleep, food intake, health, and hygiene. *Contracted time* (2) refers to paid work, including any work that involves receiving payment for the activities or spending money on, for example, education (including travel to and from work or education and waiting times). *Committed time* (3) refers to the time we must spend on all activities we have previously committed to and that are unrelated to livelihood activities (the sum of 1 and 2) (Arora 2015). This time is spent on household care, care work, or leisure. For example, buying a horse ties up time because we must feed it, keep it clean, and possibly ride it. The time needed for those activities every day is then constrained in such a way that we cannot dispose this time freely. *Free time* (4) is the time that can be freely allocated. The amount of free time is calculated by removing all three other kinds of time from the 24 h of a day. The remaining amount of time is freely disposable for each individual. It can be spent on leisure, rest, or other activities.

Time poverty occurs when individuals perceive that they do not have a sufficient amount of free time. Time-poor individuals think they have inadequate time for rest, leisure, or other activities they would like to do (Irani and Vemireddy 2021). Time poverty is defined as one's subjective perceptions of the amount of inadequate freely disposable time (Vickery 1977; Zheng et al. 2022). When individuals perceive that they do not have enough time to allocate freely, they are time-poor.

Time poverty research discusses additional time-related constructs which have a conceptual overlap with time poverty but are different and might interact with time poverty. Time pressure is the perception of scarce time for performing any type of activity (Zheng et al. 2022). This time pressure can be perceived for all kinds of time. For example, looking at the contracted time, individuals may feel they do not have enough time to accomplish all their work tasks. Time urgency (or scarcity) refers to the perception that the resource of time is limited, accelerating the pace of action.

It includes the perception of limited time and the behavior of individuals to manage time actively (Zheng et al. 2022). Despite the differences, initial indications show that time pressure, urgency, and poverty are intertwined such that time pressure at work can lead to over hours, which can lead to the sacrifice of free time. On the contrary, time-poor individuals feel pressured to complete tasks quickly to protect the small amount of freely disposable time, leading to time urgency and additional time pressure. While time pressure and time urgency are often discussed in relation to work demands (and thus contracted time), they equally apply to committed time or even necessary time.

Time poverty has been examined in relation to income poverty (Chatzitheochari and Arber 2012; Williams et al. 2016). Some papers focus on time poverty by developing a measurement scale for the construct (Whillans and West 2022). Most of the research on time poverty focuses on individual characteristics (e.g., gender, age) and household care (e.g., parenting), and work care factors (e.g., unemployment) (Chatzitheochari and Arber 2012; Kalenkoski et al. 2011; Nackerdien and Yu 2022; Vermeire et al. 2023). The aim of this research stream is to analyze which individual, household, and work factors increase the likelihood of time poverty. Regarding the consequences, the literature has focused on behaviors such as healthy diets, physiological activity, or health problems such as low well-being, stress, and fatigue (Qi and Dong 2018; Whillans and West 2022; Williams et al. 2016). It is remarkable that time poverty has been studied in countries where income poverty is also high, such as China, Ghana, India and Pakistan (Chatzitheochari and Arber 2012; Nackerdien and Yu 2022; Qi and Dong 2018).

3 Methodology

To answer our research question and to gain an understanding of how IT use contributes to time poverty, we conducted a literature review. Because literature in the area is scarce, we use a Grounded Theory approach (Wolfswinkel et al. 2013). The aim of this approach is to *"reach a thorough and theoretically relevant analysis of a topic"* (p. 1) and *"to point to well-rooted and fruitful new links between variables"* (p.2). The suggested five-stage processes involve coding the identified literature and allow researchers to achieve depth and breadth of analysis.

Following the five stages, we make several methodological decisions. First, we focus on literature in the field of IS because we aim to assess the state of the art and to derive implications for this field of research. We verified the lack of existing IS research on time poverty by broadly searching for time poverty (in AIS Electronic Library, which contains all leading conferences, AIS Senior Scholar Basket of Eight, and further unstructured search). Second, to adequately scope our contribution, we limit our search to the AIS Senior Scholar Basket of Eight. We did so because we found that time poverty was a new concept in IS research and that other time-related constructs had to be considered to develop a theory on IT-related time poverty. With

Table 1 Five-stage grounded-theory method (based on Wolfswinkel et al. 2013)

Stages	Task	Details for this paper
Define	Sources	AIS senior scholar basket of eight
	In-/exclusion criteria	Papers from the last ten years that discuss or investigate the following constructs
	Search terms	"Time poverty" OR "time scarcity" OR "time pressure" OR "time stress" OR "time urgency" OR "time famine"
Search	Search	Total sample: 63
Select	Refine sample	After screening: 31 After full-text analysis: 16
Analyze	Coding	Open coding, axial coding
Present	Structure content	See below

this focus, we limit the scope of this broader search while ensuring to capture high-quality contributions. Because we perform an in-depth Grounded Theory analysis that requires manual coding of the papers, we limit our search to the past ten years (2013–2023). The vast majority of the papers on the subject originate from the 2000s with an increase in volume. Further, the relevance of the papers within our time frame drastically declines over time. Thus, there are certainly more contributions beyond these outlets and this time frame, but we consider them a good starting point for our analysis. It must also be mentioned that we looked for seminal work on time poverty and IS beyond our search results to ensure that we did not miss any papers doing conceptual work on the subject.

We selected our **search terms** following conceptual work on time poverty (Williams et al. 2016) and included constructs that relate to time poverty. Our search for these terms in the entire text body resulted in 63 papers. We screened the papers for relevance and excluded papers that did not discuss any of the constructs (e.g., because the terms only appear in the references). Next, the author coded the sections of the papers that discussed aspects of time. We discussed the resulting open codes, aggregated them where necessary, grouped them into categories (axial coding), and discussed relationships. Table 1 describes the five-stage process and summarizes our decisions.

4 Results

Our literature review resulted in 16 relevant papers in the context of IT-related time poverty. An overview of how these papers contribute to our understanding of IT-related time poverty is provided in Table 1.

Time poverty relates to time urgency and time pressure. Most of the identified papers relate to time pressure; only a few papers explicitly mention time urgency, time poverty, or critically low levels of time. Yet, several identified relationships can be mapped to IT-related time poverty. Our results emphasize that the phenomenon is fairly new and not extensively studied.

In our study, we aim to investigate the role of IT use on time poverty. We suggest that the emergence of IT-related time poverty necessitates an interaction (or a lack thereof) between the individual that experiences time poverty and the IT use of the individual. IT use is *"a user's employment of an [IT] system to perform a task"* (Burton-Jones and Gallivan 2007, p. 659). A rich conceptualization proposes that the elements *user, IT system,* and *task* are relevant for a complete understanding of *IT use* (Burton-Jones and Straub 2006). User refers to the individual using an IT system, including its personality and characteristics. IT system encompasses the technology that is used to perform a task. Task is the function being performed with the help of the IT system. We believe that all parts of a rich conceptualization of IT use may influence time perception and, thus, IT-related time poverty. Therefore, we analyze the literature aiming to identify IT-related antecedents of time poverty from all parts of IT use as well as its IT-related consequences. We provide an overview of our findings in Fig. 1.

First, we demonstrate the identified IT-related antecedents of time poverty structured according to user, IT systems, task, and IT use (Burton-Jones and Gallivan 2007) (Table 2).

User characteristics that lead to a lack of time and in turn to IT-related time poverty use are discussed. Poverty has long been discussed as a social problem that

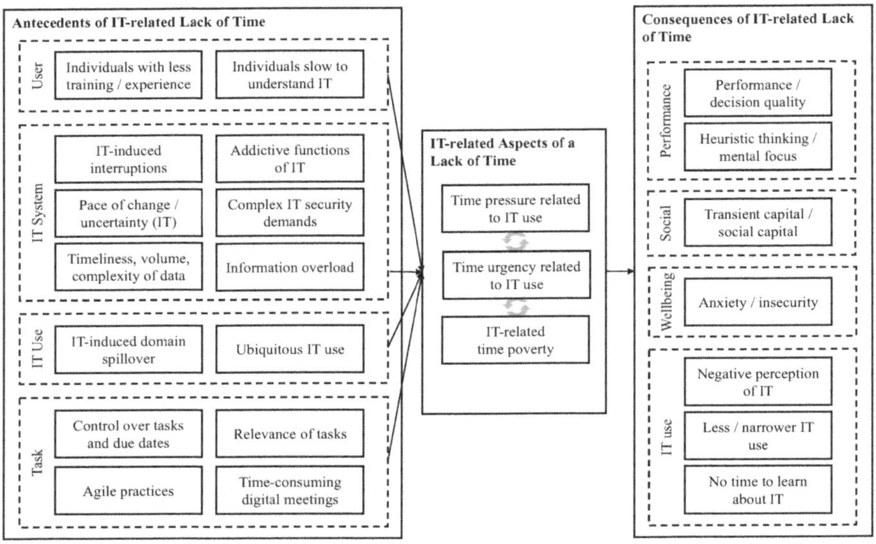

Fig. 1 Overview of factors studied in relation to an IT-related lack of time

Table 2 Descriptive summary of IT-related antecedents and consequences of time poverty

#	Author	Year	Descriptive Summary
1	Arnott and Gao	2022	Information overload increases time pressure, which impairs decision-making & increases biases
2	Benlian	2022	Agile work practices cause time pressure, which may be positive or negative; high IT mindfulness helps handle it
3	Cram et al	2022	Time pressure prohibits that gig workers deal with algorithmic transparency & well-being
4	Liang and Xue	2022	Time pressure impairs decision-making, narrows breadth of IT use and increases negative perception of IT
5	Yazdanmehr et al	2022	Complex IT security demands require time and effort; particularly problematic for low self-efficacy employees without help
6	Ghasemaghaei and Turel	2021	Complex and timely data requires time and cognitive effort to process, may cause stress & reduces knowledge sharing (time pressure)
7	Ivaturi and Chua	2021	Ubiquitous technology creates ubichronic perception of time, separates work into smaller chunks, stretches it throughout the day & blurs boundaries (time urgency)
8	Riemenschneider and Armstrong	2021	Time pressure is part of IT professionals' identity, influenced by pace of technology change, uncertainty, and job task pace
9	Benlian	2020	IT has positive and negative influences related to time pressure; Spillover effects between private and work life
10	Bouayad et al	2020	Time pressure may impair decision-making and the use of recommender systems in healthcare; there may be a habituation to time pressure
11	Tams et al	2020	IT-induced interruptions create spillover effects between private and work domains
12	Venkatesh et al	2020	Citizens of poor/rural areas need time to understand and use healthcare IT
13	vom Brocke et al	2020	IT can impose time pressure through urgency cues, and addictive features may cause individuals to spend more time
14	Phang et al	2019	IT changes the time sequencing of work and family life to be more fluid and flexible (time urgency)

(continued)

Table 2 (continued)

#	Author	Year	Descriptive Summary
15	Addas and Pinsonneault	2018a	Email load and IT-induced interruptions may increase perception of time loss and time pressure
16	Addas and Pinsonneault	2018b	IT-induced interruptions increase time pressure and have ripple effects on coworkers

originates from inequalities between individuals (Gordon 2005). While much work on time poverty centers around gender inequality, the literature on IT-related time poverty does not. Yet, in a study on healthcare IT adoption of rural Indians, Venkatesh et al. (2020) state that individuals under investigation are slow to understand IT and need additional time to adopt IT. Further, individuals with less experience and training in IT are said to experience more time pressure (Bouayad et al. 2020).

Demands that relate to the **IT systems** may relate to time poverty. Multiple studies deal with demands related to IT-induced interruptions (Addas and Pinsonneault 2018a, 2018b). Such interruptions are said to impair workflows and have high cognitive costs, which reduce efficiency and thus may draw out contracted time. Similarly, a growing number of emails, and other sources of communication are drivers of information overload (Addas and Pinsonneault 2018a). Information overload may increase the perception of time pressure (Arnott and Goa 2022). Another aspect is our growing dependence on timely data sets to fulfill work demands that may require immediate attention and are increasingly complex and large (Ghasemaghaei and Turel 2021). Such data sets take time to process and reduce cognitive resources for other activities. Further, the pace of change and uncertainty regarding new IT is a driver for the perception of many IT professionals that they do not have enough time to meet their work demands (Riemenschneider and Armstrong 2021). The growing dependency on IT at the workplace and beyond have also increased the need for IT-security measures that impose complex IT security demands on individuals (Yazdanmehr et al. 2022). Such demands require substantial time and may create the perception of overload and may cause anxiety. This is particularly true for individuals with low self-efficacy (Yazdanmehr et al. 2022). Lastly, modern IT often includes addictive functionality that increases the amount of time spent on the internet beyond initially planned levels—this is particularly true for individuals with low self-efficacy. This may cause individuals to lose social contact and thus social capital—at least in the physical world. Modern IT—particularly in the private domain—often includes addictive functionality that increase the amount of time spent on the internet beyond initially planned levels (vom Brocke et al. 2020). This is may cause individuals to lose social contact and, thus, social capital.

We identify aspects of the **tasks** that may increase the probability of a lack of time and in turn IT-related time poverty. For instance, agile practices that are present in many IT-related jobs are said to have the potential to increase time pressure and the perception of a lack of time (Benlian 2022; Riemenschneider and Armstrong

2021). This may be due to suddenly assigned urgent projects or little influence over due dates (Riemenschneider and Armstrong 2021). Not only is agility often used in IT projects, but IT systems are often a critical factor in agile project management. Further, frequent time-consuming (digital) meetings shift attention away from tasks that are perceived as more meaningful and can increase the perception of time pressure (Benlian 2022). In addition, research suggests that the relevance of tasks plays an important role in the perception of time in a way that less relevant tasks that are time-consuming are considered particularly costly (Ghasemaghaei and Turel 2021).

We identify **IT use** demands that may influence IT-related time poverty. The presence of IT-induced interruptions during non-work are mentioned as a source of spillover effects that directly affect available free time (Benlian 2020; Tams et al. 2020). We consider this a demand associated with IT use because individuals can turn off notifications or devices to counteract such interruptions if social norms allow it. An interesting contribution regards ubiquitous IT use. The authors conceptualize that ubiquitous IT use may change our perception of time to what they call ubichronic time. Ubichronic time is a discontinuous view of time that allows individuals to work in short blocks of time that are spread across the workday and contain shorter tasks (Ivaturi and Chua 2021). Such an approach to IT use and to work stretches the workday, blurs boundaries, and biases individuals towards working longer (Ivaturi and Chua 2021).

Second, we identify several indications of the **consequences of IT-related time poverty**. Many studies that focus on time pressure clearly relate it to a decrease in performance or decision quality that are often associated with heuristic thinking or a lack of mental focus due to limited cognitive capacity (e.g., Arnott and Gao 2022; Liang and Xue 2022; Riemenschneider and Armstrong 2021). While time pressure does not necessarily need to translate to time poverty, it is easy to see that a lack of performance may be compensated by longer work hours to maintain a successful social status or social capital at work. In a similar vein, research proposes that transient capital is impaired through a lack of time. In contrast to social capital, transient capital is a property of an individual and refers to the sum of positive and negative (social) encounters over time (Ivaturi and Chua 2021). Further, IT-related time poverty may directly relate to the well-being and health of individuals. For example, users embedded in a ubiquitous IT environment may sacrifice sleep to gain personal time—a clear symptom of time scarcity or time poverty—which has detrimental consequences that may include burnout (Ivaturi and Chua 2021). Further, direct effects of time pressure on anxiety (Liang and Xue 2022), insecurity (Benlian 2022), or stress-related strains (Yazdanmehr et al. 2022) may occur. Lastly, IT-related time poverty also may have consequences that relate to IT use. Research has identified that time pressure may result in less IT use and amplification of negative perception of IT (Liang and Xue 2022).

Further and related to the aforementioned limited cognitive capacity, users tend to focus on a narrower set of IT when under time pressure and revert to those features that have previously proven to be useful (Liang and Xue 2022). This narrow focus may also inhibit users from learning about IT, which has been investigated in relation to algorithmic transparency (Cram et al. 2022). Further, users under time pressure may be reluctant to use knowledge sharing tools, particularly regarding complex knowledge (Ghasemaghaei and Turel 2021).

5 IT-Related Time Poverty—A Research Agenda

From the analysis of the literature, we develop next a research agenda to demonstrate fruitful avenues for future investigations of IT-related time poverty (see Table 3). These potential areas of research are relevant because time is a limited resource, and investigating these questions may help us understand what role IT plays in the development of IT-related time poverty and how to design and use IT to mitigate its adverse effects.

User characteristics and their effects on IT-related time poverty: The literature on time poverty focuses on social inequality issues, such as gender differences, or the role of time poverty in countries that have high-income poverty (e.g., Chatzitheochari and Arber 2012; Kalenkoski et al. 2011; Nackerdien and Yu 2022; Vermeire et al. 2023). In contrast, IS literature that deals with a lack of time often discusses time pressure in relation to work demands and, thus, contracted time. In light of increased digital responsibility and the social implications of IS (Mihale-Wilson et al. 2022), future work should investigate IT-related time poverty from a diversity perspective.

Table 3 Possible areas of inquiry for all areas

Area		Possible areas of inquiry
Antecedents of IT-related time poverty	User	• How do diversity aspects, such as gender, influence IT-related time poverty?
	IT system	• What role does the design of IT systems play in IT-related time poverty?
	Task	• What role do different forms of digital work (e.g., gig work) play in the emergence of IT-related time poverty?
	IT use	• How does IT use in the private domain affect IT-related time poverty?
Aspects of IT-related time poverty		• What exactly is the reciprocal relationship between time pressure and time urgency with IT-related poverty? • What potential positive relationship exist between IT use and IT-related time poverty and what are moderators for the relationship?
Consequences of IT-related time poverty		• What role does circularity, e.g., of IT use (both an antecedent and an outcome), play in IT-related time poverty? • What is the digital responsibility of individuals, organizations, and society to address IT-related time poverty? • How can we design modern IT systems and new digital workplaces to counteract IT-related time poverty?

IT system and their effects on IT-related time poverty: The design of IT artifacts plays an important role in IS research. Consequently, conceptual work at the overlap of IS and well-being has identified it as an important aspect to improve IT use and mitigate its consequences (Tarafdar et al. 2019). Early contributions at the overlap of time and IS design have indicated that the IS design can indeed influence the sense of time, which may, for example, stimulate user engagement (Rapp 2022). The role of the design of IS systems in counteracting time poverty warrants further research.

Tasks and their effects on IT-related time poverty: Tasks and task design are essential to understanding IT use. The literature indicates that not only do tasks affect our perception of time (Ghasemaghaei and Turel 2021) but also that we might have to rethink work arrangements to suit ubiquitous IT use and modern ways of working (Ivaturi and Chua 2021). Future work should investigate what role different forms of digital work (e.g., gig work) play in the perception of IT-related time poverty and how work tasks (and potentially private tasks) may be shaped to reduce it.

IT use and its effects on IT-related time poverty: Our literature review reveals that the majority of IS contributions on the role of time are from the realm of work-related IT use. However, limited insights exist on how IT use in the private domain may affect IT-related time poverty. Yet, committed time and necessary time are equally important for understanding time poverty. For example, it would be interesting to investigate whether IT use in the private domain may have positive effects on IT-related time poverty. Further, ubiquitous IT use may increase flexibility and thus positively influence the efficient allocation of time under certain conditions (Ivaturi and Chua 2021).

Aspects of IT-related time poverty: While research from psychology indicates that there is a relationship between time pressure, time urgency, and time poverty (Zheng et al. 2022), our understanding of how they interplay and under which circumstances time pressure may have an increased chance to lead to time poverty, is not well understood. This is particularly relevant because previous IS research has primarily focused on the construct of time pressure related to IT use. Future work should shed light on the relationship between time pressure related to IT use and IT-related time poverty.

Most papers identified in our literature review discuss a lack of time due to IT use from a negative point of view and discuss how IT use can lead to time pressure or how time pressure may have negative consequences regarding IT use. While this is understandable and has greatly enriched our understanding of the phenomenon, it seems obvious that there may also be positive aspects of IS use in this relationship. Two contributions have highlighted this duality against the backdrop of spillover effects and agile work (Benlian 2020, 2022). Yet, little research has investigated the bright and dark side of IS use in relation to IT-related time poverty.

Consequences of IT-related time poverty: Our literature review provides different consequences which may relate to IT-related time poverty. Many of them match research on general time poverty. One aspect of the outcomes is particularly striking: IT use is both an antecedent and a consequence of IT-related time poverty, indicating potential circularity. Research from the realm of IS coping has similarly indicated such a relationship (Salo et al. 2020). Future work should investigate this circularity, for example, to identify perpetuating effects. Further, future research should focus on how the consequences of IT-related time poverty can be counteracted on different levels (such as individuals, organizations, and society). Several contributions hint at possibilities, such as seeking external resources for individuals, providing better training (for organizations), or designing better technologies (IT providers). Yet, the aspect of digital responsibility in relation to IT-related time poverty and where which responsibilities lie, are not well understood. In particular, previous literature indicates that we need more sophisticated designs of IT systems and novel ways of structuring work itself to accompany human-centered ubiquitous IT use, and the possibilities of flexible work to harness IT as a means to reduce IT-related time poverty (Ivaturi and Chua 2021).

6 Discussion, Contributions, and Limitations

IS research pays little attention to the scarce resource of time and knows little about how IT use is related to time poverty, which is understood as the perception of low levels of freely disposable time. However, IT use ties up time, and time-poor individuals suffer from health problems and low well-being. Therefore, this paper aims to identify IT-related antecedents and consequences of time poverty. We increase our understanding of the relationship between IT use and time poverty by analyzing and summarizing relevant IS literature. We derive antecedents and consequences of IT-related time poverty from the literature. Based on the data, we develop a research agenda that highlights several areas for further research. In doing so, we make several research contributions.

First, we examine time poverty from an IS perspective. On the one hand, previous literature on time poverty has mainly focused on antecedents related to society, organizations, public administration, or individuals (Giurge et al. 2020). Yet, the role of IT has largely been overlooked. On the other hand, IS research has shown that time perception is heavily influenced by IT use (Ivaturi and Chua 2021), but has neglected the issue of time poverty. We contribute to the literature by investigating how IT use is related to time poverty and provide a valuable starting point for future in-depth exploration of IT-related time poverty.

Second, we contribute to the current body of knowledge by addressing a first-order effect of IT use on one of the SDGs. Previous research has shown that IT use has a positive impact on SDGs. For example, smart grid technology reduces greenhouse gas emissions (Watson et al. 2021). We contribute to the body of research (Ospina-Forero et al. 2022; Watson et al. 2021) by identifying IT-related antecedents and consequences to holistically understand IT-related time poverty, enabling researchers and practitioners to counteract IT-related time poverty.

Third, previous IS literature shows that IT use changes the perception of time (Ivaturi and Chua 2021). However, only a few IS papers focus on the scarce resource of time (Ivaturi and Chua 2021; Venkatesh et al. 2020). Thus, IS literature has largely overlooked the phenomenon of IT-related time poverty. Nonetheless, our literature review shows that IS research is beginning to suggest aspects of IT use that may influence the perception of freely disposable time—which touches on the subject of IT-related time poverty. We contribute to existing research in the field (Ivaturi and Chua 2021; Venkatesh et al. 2020) by reviewing IS literature and identifying IT-related antecedents and consequences of IT-related time poverty. Based on this analysis, we develop a research agenda that identifies several valuable areas for future research. The research agenda distinguishes between different areas of antecedents related to IT use, such as users, IT systems, IT use itself, and tasks (Burton-Jones and Straub 2006). Further, we discuss the consequences of IT-related time poverty and ways to mitigate them. For each, we provide specific areas of inquiry. In summary, prior to this study, time poverty received little to no attention within the IS discipline. Now, we provide a clear overview of the IT-related antecedents and consequences of IT-related time poverty and guide future research to explore this phenomenon in depth.

The issue of time poverty is highly relevant to individuals, organizations, and society. In the modern world, IT use is often considered ubiquitous (Ivaturi and Chua 2021), and it comes with both positive and negative consequences and implications (Benlian 2020). Regarding IT-related time poverty, these consequences are often ethical and social in nature. Thus, researchers and practitioners alike have an obligation to understand the role of IT use in this phenomenon and contribute to mitigating its various adverse effects on individuals, organizations, and society. For individuals, it is important to understand how IT use consumes their time, especially how it reduces their freely disposable time—particularly important in light of increased autonomy and flexibility at the workplace. Our paper identifies how IT use relates to IT-related time poverty so that individuals can develop countermeasures to time poverty. Reduced time poverty can increase resilience to stressors and free up mental resources necessary to make more prudent decisions. For organizations, the scarce resource of time is becoming increasingly critical. For example, the majority of a representative sample of Americans would sacrifice money to have more time (Whillans and Dunn 2019). Work is becoming more complex and time fragmented, so understanding the drivers and consequences of time poverty enables organizations to manage the impact of IT use on their workforce's time contingency. For society, it is essential to understand how IT use influences time poverty, as the time spent using IT increases every year (Howarth, 2023).

Certainly, our paper is not without limitations which allow for future work. First, while we made sure to capture all contributions that directly relate to IT-related time poverty, our broader literature review is limited to the top IS journals and the last ten years. Even though we find show that literature on the subject is new, as all relevant contributions have emerged over the last five years, we cannot rule out that there are other relevant contributions. While we consider this sufficient for or our goal of introducing the concept of IT-related time poverty in this conference paper, future work should take a larger corpus into account. We further recognize that additional and more nuanced conceptual work on IT-related time poverty is necessary.

7 Conclusion

This paper focuses on time poverty—the perception of having only a small amount of freely disposable time—and identifies possible antecedents and consequences of IT-related time poverty. We conducted a structured literature review to examine how IT use affects time poverty and its negative consequences. We identified 16 relevant articles that were analyzed in terms of the various components of IT use and the potential consequences of time poverty. Based on the data, we provide an overview and a research agenda on the antecedents and consequences of IT-related time poverty. We contribute to the research by introducing IT-related time poverty as a new IS construct and by providing a detailed research agenda.

References

Addas, S., and Pinsonneault, A. 2018a. "E-mail interruptions and individual performance: Is there a silver lining?" *MIS Quarterly* (42:2), 381-A20 (https://doi.org/10.25300/MISQ/2018/13157).

Addas, S., and Pinsonneault, A. 2018b. "Theorizing the Multilevel a of Interruptions and the Role of Communication Technology," *Journal of the Association for Information Systems* (19:11), pp. 1097-1129 (https://doi.org/10.17705/1jais.00521).

Arnott, D., and Gao, S. 2022. "Behavioral economics in information systems research: Critical analysis and research strategies," *J Inf technol* (37:1), pp. 80-117 (https://doi.org/10.1177/02683962211016000).

Arora, D. 2015. "Gender Differences in Time-Poverty in Rural Mozambique," *Review of Social Economy* (73:2), pp. 196-221 (https://doi.org/10.1080/00346764.2015.1035909).

Benlian, A. 2020. "A Daily Field Investigation of Technology-Driven Stress Spillovers from Work to Home," *MIS Quarterly* (44:3), pp. 1259-1300 (https://doi.org/10.25300/MISQ/2020/14911).

Benlian, A. 2022. "Sprint Zeal or Sprint Fatigue? The Benefits and Burdens of Agile ISD Practices Use for Developer Well-Being," *Information Systems Research* (33:2), pp. 557-578 (https://doi.org/10.1287/isre.2021.1069).

Bouayad, L., Padmanabhan, B., and Chari, K. 2020. "Can Recommender Systems Reduce Health-care Costs? The Role of Time Pressure and Cost Transparency in Prescription Choice," *MIS Q* (44:4), pp. 1859-1903 (https://doi.org/10.25300/MISQ/2020/14435/).

Burton-Jones, A., and Gallivan, M. J. 2007. "Toward a Deeper Understanding of System Usage in Organizations: A Multilevel Perspective," *MIS Quarterly* (31:4), pp. 657-679 (https://doi.org/10.2307/25148815).

Burton-Jones, A., and Straub, D. W. 2006. "Reconceptualizing System Usage: An Approach and Empirical Test: An Approach and Empirical Test," *Information Systems Research* (17:3), pp. 228-246 (https://doi.org/10.1287/isre.1060.0096).

Charmes, J. 2022. "Variety and change of patterns in the gender balance between unpaid care-work, paid work and free time across the world and over time: A measure of wellbeing?" *Wellbeing, Space and Society* (3), p. 100081 (https://doi.org/10.1016/j.wss.2022.100081).

Chatzitheochari, S., and Arber, S. 2012. "Class, gender and time poverty: a time-use analysis of British workers' free time resources," *The British journal of sociology* (63:3), pp. 451-471 (https://doi.org/10.1111/j.1468-4446.2012.01419.x).

Cram, W. A., Wiener, M., Tarafdar, M., and Benlian, A. 2022. "Examining the Impact of Algorithmic Control on Uber Drivers' Technostress," *J. Manage. Inf. Syst* (39:2), pp. 426-453 (https://doi.org/10.1080/07421222.2022.2063556).

Ghasemaghaei, M., and Turel, O. 2021. "Possible negative effects of big data on decision quality in firms: The role of knowledge hiding behaviours," *Information Systems Journal* (31:2), pp. 268-293 (https://doi.org/10.1111/isj.12310).
Giurge, L. M., Whillans, A. V., and West, C. 2020. "Why time poverty matters for individuals, organisations and nations," *Nature human behaviour* (4:10), pp. 993-1003 (https://doi.org/10.1038/s41562-020-0920-z).
Gordon, D. 2005. *Indicators of Poverty & Hunger*. https://www.un.org/esa/socdev/unyin/documents/ydiDavidGordon_poverty.pdf. Accessed 7 March 2023.
Howarth, J. 2023. *Alarming Average Screen Time Statistics (2023)*. https://explodingtopics.com/blog/screen-time-stats. Accessed 28 February 2023.
Irani, L., and Vemireddy, V. 2021. "Getting the measurement right! quantifying time poverty and multitasking from childcare among mothers with children across different age groups in rural north India," *Asian Population Studies* (17:1), pp. 94-116 (https://doi.org/10.1080/17441730.2020.1778854).
Ivaturi, K., and Chua, C. 2021. "Rethinking time: ubichronic time and its impact on work," *Eur J Inf Syst*, pp. 1–16 https://doi.org/10.1080/0960085X.2021.1966326.
Kalenkoski, C. M., Hamrick, K. S., and Andrews, M. 2011. "Time Poverty Thresholds and Rates for the US Population," *Social Indicators Research* (104:1), pp. 129-155 (https://doi.org/10.1007/s11205-010-9732-2).
Liang, H., and Xue, Y. 2022. "Save Face or Save Life: Physicians' Dilemma in Using Clinical Decision Support Systems," *Information Systems Research* (33:2), pp. 737-758 (https://doi.org/10.1287/isre.2021.1082).
Michel, J., and Tanner, M. 2021. "Poverty Is Not Poverty: The Reality on the Ground Including the Rural-Urban Divide and How We Can Turn the Tide on NCDs," in *Lifestyle and Epidemiology - Poverty and Cardiovascular Diseases a Double Burden in African Populations [Working Title]*, IntechOpen.
Mihale-Wilson, C., Hinz, O., van der Aalst, W., and Weinhardt, C. 2022. "Corporate Digital Responsibility," *Business & Information Systems Engineering* (64:2), pp. 127-132 (https://doi.org/10.1007/s12599-022-00746-y).
Nackerdien, F., and Yu, D. 2022. "Defining and measuring time poverty in South Africa," *Development Southern Africa*, pp. 1–20 https://doi.org/10.1080/0376835x.2022.2028606.
Nilsson, M., Griggs, D., and Visbeck, M. 2016. "Policy: Map the interactions between Sustainable Development Goals," *Nature* (534:7607), pp. 320-322 (https://doi.org/10.1038/534320a).
Ospina-Forero, L., Castañeda, G., and Guerrero, O. A. 2022. "Estimating networks of sustainable development goals," *Information & Management* (59:5), p. 103342 https://doi.org/10.1016/j.im.2020.103342.
Phang, C. W., Luo, X., and Fang, Z. 2019. "Mobile Time-Based Targeting: Matching Product-Value Appeal to Time of Day," *J. Manage. Inf. Syst* (36:2), pp. 513-545 (https://doi.org/10.1080/07421222.2019.1598696).
Qi, L., and Dong, X. 2018. "Gender, Low-Paid Status, and Time Poverty in Urban China," *Feminist Economics* (24:2), pp. 171-193 (https://doi.org/10.1080/13545701.2017.1404621).
Rapp, A. 2022. "Time, engagement and video games: How game design elements shape the temporalities of play in massively multiplayer online role-playing games," *Information Systems Journal* (32:1), pp. 5-32 (https://doi.org/10.1111/isj.12328).
Ravindran, T., Yeow Kuan, A. C., and Hoe Lian, D. G. 2014. "Antecedents and effects of social network fatigue," *Journal of the Association for Information Science and Technology* (65:11), pp. 2306-2320 (https://doi.org/10.1002/asi.23122).
Riemenschneider, C., and Armstrong, D. 2021. "The Development of the Perceived Distinctiveness Antecedent of Information Systems Professional Identity," *MIS Q* (45:3), pp. 1149-1186 (https://doi.org/10.25300/MISQ/2021/14626).
Salo, M., Makkonen, M., and Hekkala, R. 2020. "The interplay of IT users' coping strategies: Uncovering momentary emotional load, routes, and sequences," *MIS Quarterly* (44:3), pp. 1143-1175 (https://doi.org/10.25300/MISQ/2020/15610).

Saunders, C., Craig Van Slyke, and Vogel, D. R. 2004. "My Time or Yours? Managing Time Visions in Global Virtual Teams," *Academy of Management Executive* (18:1), pp. 19-31.

Tams, S., Ahuja, M., Thatcher, J., and Grover, V. 2020. "Worker stress in the age of mobile technology: The combined effects of perceived interruption overload and worker control," *The Journal of Strategic Information Systems* (29:1), p. 101595 https://doi.org/10.1016/j.jsis.2020.101595.

Urakawa, K., Wang, W., and Alam, M. 2020. "Empirical Analysis of Time Poverty and Health-Related Activities in Japan," *Journal of Family and Economic Issues* (41:3), pp. 520-529 (https://doi.org/10.1007/s10834-020-09671-2).

Venkatesh, V., Sykes, T. A., and Zhang, X. 2020. "ICT for Development in Rural India: A Longitudinal Study of Women's Health Outcomes," *MIS Q* (44:2), pp. 605-629 (https://doi.org/10.25300/MISQ/2020/12342).

Vermeire, J., Crucke, S., Mutesi, J., and Vinck, A. 2023. "Tackling climate change under time-poverty: Cooperatives as temporal pacers," *Sustainable Development* (31:1), pp. 253-264 (https://doi.org/10.1002/sd.2387).

Vickery, C. 1977. "The time-poor: A new look at poverty," *Journal of Human Resources* (12:1), pp. 27-48.

vom Brocke, J., Hevner, A., Léger, P. M., Walla, P., and Riedl, R. 2020. "Advancing a NeuroIS research agenda with four areas of societal contributions," *Eur J Inf Syst* (29:1), pp. 9-24 (https://doi.org/10.1080/0960085X.2019.1708218).

Watson, R. T., Elliot, S., Corbett, J., Farkas, D., Feizabadi, A., Gupta, A., Iyer, L., Sen, S., Sharda, R., Shin, N., Thapa, D., and Webster, J. 2021. "How the AIS can Improve its Contributions to the UN's Sustainability Development Goals: Towards A Framework for Scaling Collaborations and Evaluating Impact," *Communications of the Association for Information Systems* (48:1), pp. 476-502 (https://doi.org/10.17705/1CAIS.04841).

Whillans, A. 2019. "Time for happiness: Why the pursuit of money isn't bringing you joy – and what will. Harvard Business Review.," *Harvard Business Review*.

Whillans, A., and West, C. 2022. "Alleviating time poverty among the working poor: a pre-registered longitudinal field experiment," *Scientific reports* (12:1), p. 719 (https://doi.org/10.1038/s41598-021-04352-y).

Whillans, A. V., and Dunn, E. W. 2019. "Valuing time over money is associated with greater social connection," *Journal of Social and Personal Relationships* (36:8), pp. 2549-2565 (https://doi.org/10.1177/0265407518791322).

Williams, J. R., Masuda, Y. J., and Tallis, H. 2016. "A Measure Whose Time has Come: Formalizing Time Poverty," *Social Indicators Research* (128:1), pp. 265-283 (https://doi.org/10.1007/s11205-015-1029-z).

Wolfswinkel, J. F., Furtmueller, E., and Wilderom, C. P. M. 2013. "Using grounded theory as a method for rigorously reviewing literature," *Eur J Inf Syst* (22:1), pp. 45-55 (https://doi.org/10.1057/ejis.2011.51).

Yazdanmehr, A., Li, Y., and Wang, J. 2022. "Employee responses to information security related stress: Coping and violation intention," *Information Systems Journal* (https://doi.org/10.1111/isj.12417).

Zheng, X., Zhang, Q., Li, X., and Wu, B. 2022. "Being busy, feeling poor: The scale development and validation of perceived time poverty," *International Journal of Selection and Assessment* (30:4), pp. 596-613 (https://doi.org/10.1111/ijsa.12395).

Patient Centricity in IS Healthcare—A Framework Proposing Enablement, Empowerment, and Engagement of Patients as Individual IS Users

Jan Maschewski and Kristina Lemmer

Abstract The core of medicine and care is assisting patients with their health-related problems achieving the best results possible. Yet, recent Information Systems (IS) literature describes patient centered IS healthcare as "supporting assistants with IS". In need of the patient in the center of the digital transformation process in healthcare, we focus our study on examining the IS scientific community's contribution to digital healthcare regarding patients in the digital transformation process. We conducted an explorative, systematic but selective review of journal articles published in the best Senior Scholar Journals of the Association of Information Systems. Our results reveal a) a framework for digital health research in IS indicating underrepresented research directions, and b) three propositions on patient centricity in IS healthcare focusing on patient enablement, empowerment, and engagement as central streams.

Keywords Digital healthcare · Patient-centricity · Literature review · Framework

1 Introduction

The healthcare sector is facing tremendous challenges: an ageing population, an increase in diagnosed diseases and multimorbidity put enormous pressure on the providers of healthcare (Hickmann et al., 2022; OECD, 2021). Consequently, hopes are high for advancements in Information Systems (IS) to help increase efficiency and capacity while improving therapy results at the same time (Hibbard and Greene, 2013; Shortell et al., 2017). In the past, initiatives to increase efficiency and capacity through IS mostly focused on healthcare professionals (Currie and Guah, 2007;

J. Maschewski (✉) · K. Lemmer
Institute of Information Systems, Leuphana University Lüneburg, Lüneburg, Germany
e-mail: jan.maschewski@leuphana.de

K. Lemmer
e-mail: kristina.lemmer@leuphana.de

D. Beverungen et al. (eds.), *Transforming the Digitally Sustainable Enterprise*, Lecture Notes in Information Systems and Organisation 76,
https://doi.org/10.1007/978-3-031-80125-9_35

Klecun et al., 2019). This is due to the professional side's lower diversity and smaller number of individuals while accessibility was higher which fueled hopes for fast and effective progress (Currie and Guah, 2007; Klecun et al., 2019).

More recently however, the patient's role in successful health intervention received more attention (Hibbard and Greene, 2013; Hickmann et al., 2022; Shortell et al., 2017). There might be several reasons for this recalibration in focus, e.g., more efficient potentials for improving therapeutic outcomes or overall greater availability and usage of digital products by the population (Hibbard and Greene, 2013; Hickmann et al., 2022; Shortell et al., 2017). However, the increased interest leads us to examine the IS scientific community's contribution to digital healthcare regarding patients in the digital transformation process.

This study is structured as follows. In the second section, we give a short background of IS in healthcare practice and science. Sect. 3 describes the research design of this study. In Sect. 4, findings of our research are presented. Sect. 5 conceptualizes a framework for IS healthcare resulting in three propositions regarding patient centricity in IS healthcare. Sect. 6 discusses implications of our research and outlines possible next steps to deepen the understanding in this field.

2 Background

The provision of healthcare is a complex field which requires multiple experts to effectively cooperate for the well-being of the patient (Gianchandani, 2011; Goh et al., 2011; Malm-Nicolaisen et al., 2023). Accordingly, the healthcare sector relies extensively on IS to organize the process and precision of care provision (Aanestad et al., 2017; Goh et al., 2011; Yaraghi et al., 2015). In the last 20 years a great deal of effort was invested by researchers, politicians, information technology (IT) and healthcare professionals to digitally transform and better integrate the existing support systems of the sector (Klecun et al., 2019; Mergel et al., 2019; Yaraghi et al., 2015). It seems, however, that the patient—focal point of healthcare—got neglected in process (Bombard et al., 2018; Klecun, 2016). As the primary users of these information systems are professionals it is only plausible for the IS discipline to focus its efforts on topics like successful implementation of new supporting systems or data exchange between applications and professional actors (Klecun et al., 2019; Yaraghi et al., 2015).

Reflecting the high effect of patient engagement for therapeutic success and the advancing digital transformation of the greater population's daily lives, it is worthwhile to reconsider this focus (Bombard et al., 2018; Hibbard and Greene, 2013; Shortell et al., 2017). After all, healthcare is about helping the patient and therapy outcome heavily relies on the patient's active participation during the screening, treatment, and recovery processes (Hibbard and Greene, 2013; Shortell et al., 2017). Given the improvements achieved in IS in general (e.g., Internet of Thing and digital platforms) and the field of professional healthcare IS in particular (e.g., electronic health records and information exchange), new opportunities for integrating the patient more closely into the healthcare process seem attainable, valuable, and desirable (Bombard et al., 2018; Hickmann et al., 2022). Utilizing these opportunities is even more important as IT enables patients to better inform, monitor and optimize themselves leading them to demand a more active role in healthcare (Dadgar and Joshi, 2018; Ghose et al., 2021; Karazivan et al., 2015). This process got further accelerated by the COVID -pandemic, which raised awareness for the potentials of digital health applications at the patient's side (Budd et al., 2020; Peek et al., 2020).

Looking at industries like mobility and hospitality offers an outlook at the potential that lays in integrating services and making them more accessible for customers. Mobility might be a prime example, where the integration of multiple services from independent providers (e.g., public transport, ride-sharing, and bike-rentals) creates an overall better experience for the user (Stopka et al., 2018). Another example for a meta-platform can be found in comparison portals, e.g., for hotel bookings or insurances (Abbas et al., 2022). Of course, IS integration brings additional challenges for practitioners and researchers in any sector it is coming to (Aanestad et al., 2017; Hanseth and Bygstad, 2015; Maruping and Matook, 2020).

Given the beforementioned neglection of the patient as a primary stakeholder in IS research in combination with the changing (self-)conception of the patient in healthcare, we ask as research question (RQ):

RQ: Which Patient-Centric Research Streams (e.g., Based on Stakeholder, Technical Applications and Organizational Themes) Can Be Identified in IS Healthcare Literature?

3 Method

In our explorative systematic literature review, we applied the framework for reviewing literature as proposed by vom Brocke et al. (2009) consisting of 5 phases: (I) definition of review and scope, (II) conceptualization of topic, (III) literature search, (IV) literature analysis and synthesis and (V) research agenda. To define the focus for our review (phase I) we relied on Cooper's taxonomy for literature reviewing (Cooper, 1988) and additional suggestions by vom Brocke et al. (2015). Following these frameworks, we focus this review on research outcomes with special emphasis on its object of analysis and aim at a neutral representation of the central issues covered by existing IS literature. This review is conducted with an audience of general scholars in mind. We started our search with publications in the premier IS journals as proposed by the Association for Information Systems College of Senior Scholars (2023) and went forward and backward for central publications. Tables 1 and 2 present the scope of our review.

Table 1 Taxonomy of literature review (following vom Brocke et al. (2009) and Cooper (1988)) aligned to our research

Focus	Goal	Organisation	Perspective	Audience	Coverage
Research outcomes	Integration	Historical	Neutral representation	Specialised scholars	Exhaustive
Research methods	Criticism	Conceptual		General scholars	Exhaustive and selective
Theories	Central issues	Methodological	Espousal of position	Practioners/ politicians	Representative
Applications				General public	Central/pivotal

Table 2 Search scope of literature review (following vom Brocke et al. (2015)) aligned for our research

Process	Sources	Coverage	Techniques
Sequential	Citation indexing services	Comprehensive	Keyword search
Iterative	Bibliographic databases	Representative	Backward search
	Publications	Seminal works	Forward search

In a subsequent step (phase II) we conceptualized our topic. Starting from our main interest—namely identifying patient-centric research streams in digital health IS research—we used patient-centric as our first search term in IS databases. The term patient-centric is a healthcare adapted variation of customer-centric, which describes the configuration of a business in such a way that it focusses on a customer's needs and establishes a mutually satisfactory relationship (Hickmann et al., 2022; Lamberti, 2013). As a result, we came across a variety of terms that describe the focus on patients. For example, patient-centered/patient-centred was a term more frequently used in the 2000s in the UK as politics initiated reforms in the healthcare sector to serve the citizens more efficiently and more suited towards their needs (Currie and Guah, 2007; McGrath et al., 2008; Klecun, 2016). Hence, following previous literature (Boell and Cecez-Kecmanovic, 2015; vom Brocke et al., 2015) to get a broad picture of the field and not overlook important publications, we included a variety of terms describing a focus on the patient for our further analysis (i.e., *patient-centric*, *patient-centered*, *patient-centred*, *patient-focus*, *patient-side* and *patient-led*). As we were particularly interested in the ways IS helps patients in an overarching manner, linking multiple health-related services, we included the terms *platform* and *guide* in our search. *Platforms* bring two or more groups of stakeholders together and enable interactions among them (Fürstenau et al., 2020; Hagiu and Wright, 2015), describing our research interest. Acknowledging digital healthcare as a complex field, stakeholders need orientation and help in using corresponding information technology (Ghose et al., 2021; Gianchandani, 2011; Karazivan et al., 2015). Thus, we included *guide* as an additional keyword. We used both terms *health* and *healthcare* to limit our search to publications from the domain of interest. To further specify the search, we included *digital* in the search string of our literature search, yielding us the following search string: *digital AND (health OR healthcare) AND (platform OR guide) AND (patient-centric OR patient-centered OR patient-centred OR patient-focus OR patient-side OR patient-led).*

In phase III, literature search, we used the identified combination of terms for our actual literature search. As recommended by previous literature (Boell and Cecez-Kecmanovic, 2015; vom Brocke et al., 2009; Webster and Watson, 2002), we focused our review on high quality articles and included only journals, that were considered the best in Information Systems research by the Association for Information Systems' College of Senior Scholars (2023) (i.e., the European Journal of Information Systems, Information Systems Journal, Information Systems Research, Journal of AIS, Journal of Information Technology, Journal of MIS, Journal of Strategic Information Systems, MIS Quarterly). We relied on the publishers' databases and entered the keywords according to the before mentioned logic, searching all field for the longest available timespan until 2022. Table 3 shows the structure and results of our review.

After we conducted the literature search, we analyzed and synthesized our literature (phase IV) as recommended by Webster and Watson (2002). We found 544 articles matching our search criteria, 110 of which were found relevant for our review. The filtering process included title and abstract screening of the search results on the publishers' archives according to our research subject (i.e. focus on social/behavioral analyzes (as opposed to technical or coding-centered articles) while also excluding

Table 3 Analyzed journals

Journal	Database	Coverage	Hits	Reviewed
Decision Support Systems	Science Direct	1985–2022	57	12
European Journal of Information Systems	Taylor & Francis Online	1991–2022	59	12
Information and Management	Science Direct	1977–2022	41	15
Information and Organization	Science Direct	2001–2022	29	7
Information Systems Journal	Wiley Online Library	1991–2022	58	11
Information Systems Research	Informs PubsOnLine	1990–2022	94	19
Journal of AIS	AIS eLibrary	2000–2022	46	8
Journal of Information Technology	SAGE journals	1986–2022	42	6
Journal of MIS	Taylor & Francis Online	1984–2022	40	8
Journal of Strategic Information Systems	Science Direct	1991–2022	18	2
MIS Quartely	AIS eLibrary	1977–2022	60	10
			Σ544	Σ110

research removed from the information system itself e.g., business models, financial performance analyzes or vendor strategies). Following our research questions, we analyzed the eligible papers and structured them in according to their stakeholders, type of technical applications used to assist their stakeholders, and emerging organizational themes.

The ultimate (phase V) purpose of a literature review is to present a research agenda for future analyses (vom Brocke et al., 2009; Webster and Watson, 2002; Sect. 5).

4 Findings

While analyzing and synthesizing the literature, we identified four groups of stakeholders represented in IS research, that are comparable to prior analysis (Klecun et al., 2019) and narrowed them down to our conceptualization from phase II: healthcare professionals (including physicians, nurses, care takers and other professions taking care of patients' health), patients (people with acute, chronic and/or age related health conditions), IT professionals (providers of IT-services spanning all phases from planning and project to implementation and operation) as well as politicians as decision makers with extensive influence on national healthcare sectors. Additionally, just like this literature review, some articles investigate the role of researchers or give advice for future research directions, so we included researchers as an additional stakeholder for IS research. While recording our findings in a matrix according to Webster and Watson (2002), it became apparent that some research articles addressed not one but multiple stakeholders. This underlines the central and connecting role of information systems and was reflected by us in capturing multiple stakeholders for one article. Table 4 shows the coverage of stakeholders within the reviewed literature.

In line with previous research (Currie and Guah, 2007; Klecun et al., 2019), we found that healthcare professionals are the main stakeholders of interest in the IS research dealing with patient-centric healthcare. Patients are represented in IS research, but more in the role of a passive application partner on whom technology is used, instead of an active user of technology for whom it is designed (e.g. Ghose et al. (2021) or Jiang and Cameron (2020)). The patient in IS literature is present due to the role of healthcare serving patients in need. However, if patients are the

Table 4 Stakeholders in patient-centric research streams on digital healthcare

Stakeholders	No. of articles
Healthcare professionals [HP]	59
Patients [PAT]	44
IT professionals [IT]	25
Politicians [POL]	13
Researchers [R]	8

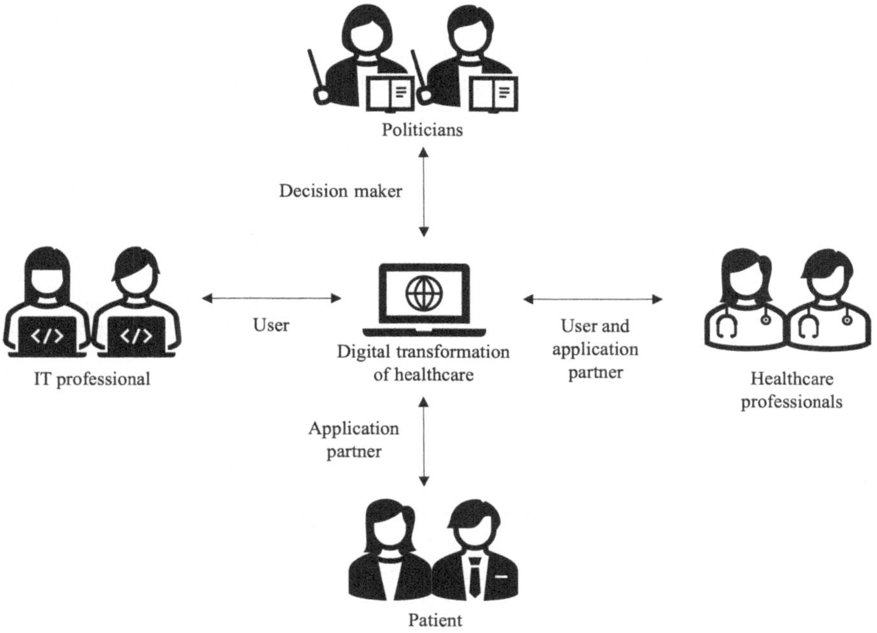

Fig. 1 Overview of identified stakeholders and their role in patient-centric research streams on digital healthcare

primary stakeholder of the technical application used, this application frequently is detached from professional healthcare and more often is an online community or self-help service. Figure 1 gives an overview of the stakeholders and their dominant role in IS-healthcare.

Similarly, to stakeholders, we found a set of technical applications that are commonly investigated in healthcare related IS research. Some of our categories have clear demarcations and have been defined before, while other emerged during our review. We summarized one major category, which has been extensively researched under the term Electronic Health Records (EHR), which the ISO (2005) defines as a "*repository of information regarding the health status of a subject of care, in computer processable form, stored and transmitted securely and accessible by multiple authorized users, having a standardized or commonly agreed logical information model that is independent of EHR systems and whose primary purpose is the support of continuing, efficient and quality integrated health care*". Under this category we also subsumed the related concepts of electronic patient record (EPR) and electronic health information (EHI) systems including patient health history, prescriptions, medical examination results and its digital transmission between healthcare professionals (Health Information Exchange (HIE)). Another important IS application in healthcare is the software used by the organization (e.g., hospital or practice) itself. Applications in this category often include tools for communicating between professionals as well as basic communication from professionals to patients (e.g., appointment scheduling or secure channels for teleconsultations). Additionally, specialized healthcare applications dealing with one narrow use case are more extensively covered by IS researchers (e.g., diabetes tracking, stroke aftercare, ALS). For patient-facing applications, two categories where commonly present in IS literature. The first application can be described as online communities for patients with certain medical conditions, often in the form of self-help groups (e.g., Hur et al. (2019) or Kordzadeh and Warren (2017)). The second category includes different applications offering health or treatment related information to patients like Q&A-portals (e.g., Chen et al. (2019) or Khurana et al. (2019)). Corresponding Information Architecture (IA) for providing the technical applications described before is another major subject of research. Table 5 shows technical applications in IS. Again, some articles covered multiple types of technical applications.

In line with our expectations after our initial conceptualization (phase II) we found that EHR and hospital / practice software are the two most investigated types of technical applications while information architecture was covered less extensive. Specialized health applications were a common research interest as well. For the patient-facing services we only found two types to be relevant in IS literature: 1) online communities (especially for patients and their relatives) to exchange experiences and give moral support and 2) the search for medical and health related information and suggestions on disease treatments.

Whilst reviewing the identified literature in phase IV, we recognized multiple themes, many of the articles shared. While inductively forming the themes and iterating with the reviewed body of literature as suggested by grounded theory (Gioia and Pitre, 1990) we sharpened the emerging organizational themes inspired by the Technology-Organization-Environment (TOE) Framework (Tornatzky and Fleischer, 1990). Accordingly, we assign one of our themes to each article whenever possible, yielding the results shown in Table 6.

The most common organizational theme is Electronic Health Records and Information Exchange, which is corresponding to its presence within the researched technical applications and references its broad use in organizational and inter-organizational settings. The patient-facing applications "Online Community" and "Search for health/treatment information" showed extensive overlaps and were combined to the organizational theme "Online community and information seeking".

Table 5 Technical applications in patient-centric research streams on digital healthcare

Technical applications	No of articles
Hospital/practice software [HPS]	33
Electronic health record and information exchange [EHR]	28
Specialized health application [SHA]	25
Online community [OC]	17
Search for health/treatment information [SMI]	18
Information architecture [IA]	7

Table 6 Common organizational themes identified in patient-centric research streams on digital healthcare

Organizational themes	No. of articles
Electronic health records and information exchange [EHR]	20
Online community and information seeking [OCIS]	22
Adoption and implementation of professional side IT [AIPIT]	27
Use of wearables, sensors, and telemedicine [WST]	21

Decoupled from previously described categories, two common themes in IS research on digital healthcare are a) the "Adoption and implementation of professional-side IT systems" presenting results from research about implementation projects of information systems aimed at healthcare professional (e.g., Goh et al. (2011) or Novak et al. (2012)) and b) the "Use of wearables, sensors, and telemedicine" for adding new data streams to treatments and detaching the provision of care from physical presence (e.g,. Chatterjee et al. (2018) or Thompson et al (2020)).

5 Conceptualizing Patient-Centricity in IS Healthcare

In summary, current IS healthcare literature can be structured in the dimension's stakeholders, technical applications, and organizational themes. In terms of stakeholders, healthcare professionals are the group of stakeholders most investigated. Furthermore, we noticed, more than 20 years of research deal with technical applications, corresponding processes, and institutional logics. Hence, there is a dominance of literature covering the adoption and implementation of IS for the professional side of healthcare as well as electronic health records and information exchange. The patient, however, as an individual and user of IS, got increased attention due to the emergence of wearables, sensors, and telemedicine application (Table 7). As professional side IS is getting more mature considering the development of platform services and advancing internet availability, the trend towards a more prominent role of patients in IS is likely to continue.

Based on our results, indicating underrepresented research directions for digital health research in IS (framework, Table 7) we make three propositions as an agenda for future research: First, based on recent research, we found that patients only play a passive role as application partner in the use of IS for healthcare (e.g., Dadgar and Joshi (2018) or Klecun et al. (2019)). Understanding the emergence of customer IS, e.g., wearables, sensors, and telemedicine, the role of patients is developing more and more from a passive application partner towards an active user of IS healthcare. Based on our findings, we propose Proposition 1:

Proposition 1 *Patient enablement is significant to enhance the usage of IS healthcare.*

Table 7 Framework for patient-centric research streams on digital healthcare in IS [No. of articles in parentheses] (underrepresented research directions highlighted)

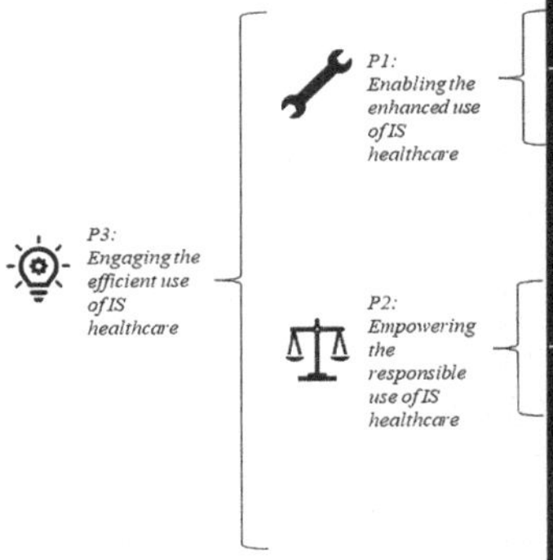

Stakeholders	Healthcare Professionals [59]	Patients [44]	IT-Professionals [25]
	Politicians [13]	Researchers [8]	
Technical Applications	Hospital / Practice Software [33]	Electronic Health Record & Information Exchange [28]	Specialized health application [25]
	Online Community [17]	Search for medical / health information [18]	Information Architecture [7]
Organizational Themes	Electronic Health Records & Information Exchange [20]	Online community & information seeking [22]	
	Adoption & implementation of professional side IT [27]	Use of wearables, sensors, and telemedicine [21]	

Proposition 1 describes patient enablement, as part of enhancing the usage of IS healthcare. As an important antecedent for enhancing the usage, digital competences on how to use IS healthcare is needed. Thus, health literacy, the competences on how patients can use IS healthcare technologies are important. Additional to patient enablement, we found in previous research, that patient enablement leads to empowerment of patients while using IS healthcare (Hickmann et al., 2022). Empowerment thereby describes "an enabling process or an outcome of a process involving a shift in the balance of power" (Cerezo et al., 2016). Especially using IS healthcare patients have the possibility to not only use given power by e.g., healthcare or IT professionals but instead take power and design their own information process using IS healthcare. Thus, we propose:

Proposition 2 *Patient empowerment will allow patients to interact with their own IS healthcare information transparently and responsibly.*

Based on the idea of patients actively taking the power in the process of using IS healthcare, patients are not only able to make decisions about their own IS healthcare information further they are able to interact with stakeholders in the process efficiently through technology. Based on Proposition 2, we align with Hickmann et al. (2022), and propose that patient empowerment will lead to patient engagement supporting the interaction and decision-making process with stakeholders and further technical applications on an organizational level.

Proposition 3 *Patient engagement will lead patients to interact with stakeholders and technical applications efficiently especially regarding emerging organizational themes such as the use of wearables, sensors, and telemedicine.*

6 Discussion

Initial, this study identifies research streams in IS healthcare literature on patient centricity. Analyzing IS healthcare literature based on patient centricity shows emerging types of stakeholders, technology applications and organizational themes evolving. Developing a framework structuring current literature gives rise to conceptualizing patient centricity in IS healthcare literature. Aligned to our framework for patient-centric research streams on digital healthcare in IS, this study identifies three propositions showing how patient centricity can evolve in future research. Primary, patient enablement focuses on enhancing the use of IS healthcare and the competencies needed (1st proposition) for being empowered to use IS healthcare in their daily lives (2nd proposition). Following, patients will start to engage with different groups of stakeholders also connected to the IS healthcare infrastructure enabling new organizational themes to develop in the next years (3rd proposition).

With this literature review we make multiple contributions for both, theory, and practice. First for theory, we structure existing knowledge about digital health in IS publications. Inspired by the TOE-Framework (Technical, Organizational and Environmental-Framework), which focuses on the adoption of new technology, we found three categories for structuring IS healthcare literature adapting the perspective of patient-centricity (Kuan and Chau, 2001). In detail, we found the following categories stakeholders, technical applications, and organizational themes by which the current IS-healthcare literature can be structured. Stakeholders are inspired by the users' perspective on IS in healthcare and the environmental dimension of the TOE framework, as they have the possibility to influence emerging topics from societies point of view. Technical applications refer to the technology dimension of the TOE-framework defining technological trends in IS-healthcare literature. Organizational themes refer to the organizational dimension of the TOE framework, identifying organizational opportunities by adapting a patient-centric perspective in IS-healthcare services. Also, researchers might be interested in investigating how artificial intelligence affects those developments (Schaefer et al., 2021).

Second, by applying our framework and analyzing the existing body of IS research on digital health, we show the predominance of scientific interest in healthcare professionals and respective technical applications over other stakeholders and types of IS artifacts. Also, we show a high interest in two organizational themes that revolve around healthcare professionals. Future research may investigate what patient-facing service might be possible to offer, desired by users and how to design corresponding artifacts. Additionally, an even higher integration among professional care providers represents an opportunity to contribute to the IS body of knowledge.

Third, we provide the following research agenda: Understanding the role of patients and IT-professionals in the digital transformation of the healthcare sector has the potential to encourage enablement, empowerment, and engagement of patients. An especially promising way to do so is by studying these stakeholders in conjunction with information architecture and / or the use of wearables, sensors, and telemedicine. Also, investigating possible interdependencies between the identified stakeholders seems worthwhile. By providing this research agenda, we support avoiding the emergence of blank spots in IS literature and foster development of suitable IS artifacts, thereby fulfilling a literature reviews ultimate purpose (vom Brocke et al., 2009).

From our research some implications for practice emerge. First, drawing more attention on patients in IS research on digital health seems advisable given the dominance of articles dealing with healthcare professionals in the field. This is especially the case when considering the great potential for achieving better therapeutic results (Hibbard and Greene, 2013; Hickmann et al., 2022; Shortell et al., 2017) and opportunities for a better orchestration of existing services or introduction of new services for the patient (e.g., meta-platforms (Abbas et al., 2022; Fürstenau et al., 2020; Maruping and Matook, 2020)). We also call for practitioners to explore these possibilities and develop corresponding artifacts and techniques for the greater good. We see opportunities to do so among others in services that integrate existing applications and make the patient journeys more seamless ("*one-stop-shop-solution*") or developing design processes that focus artifact design on usability and attractiveness for patients.

7 Limitations and Outlook

As with all literature reviews conducted, our study contains several methodological limitations based on the structural decisions of the literature review process. For example, one limitation of our work is the body of knowledge used. While large, it only stems from the eight most respected journals of the IS community. Extending the considered outlets offers potential for sharpening the view on the topic and extend our understanding of the digital health discipline. Particularly promising for this endeavor is the inclusion of journals recommended by the AIS Special Interest Group on Digital Health as well as proceedings of the top conferences on IS. Top outlets from the field of medicine and medical and health informatics also bear the potential to broaden our understanding of the scientific community's engagement in digital healthcare research. By integrating additional literature, it is possible that new and relevant stakeholders, applications, or themes will emerge. As the body of knowledge is ever expanding, we welcome those additions to our framework just as much as we recommend revisiting the framework at a later point in time to keep it up to date.

Overall, providing patients with good and affordable healthcare will remain an ongoing challenge. Turning more attention towards the patients both in science and practice, holds great opportunities to cope with these challenges. With the development of our framework for digital health research in IS, which we presented in this article, we shed a light on challenges, opportunities, and ways ahead. We would like to encourage researcher and developers to design more relevant technical applications in emerging organizational themes such as the use of wearables, sensors, and telemedicine. We like to invite to especially focus on the IT infrastructure from the users' point of view, namely the patient and IT professionals. For example, IT professionals could focus via methods of service design on the needs of patients using IS healthcare. This method would support the design of IS healthcare based on the users' needs, putting patients in the center of attention.

Acknowledgements This work was supported by the Federal Ministry of Health within the project DIGITALIS for the digital transformation of the public health department in the county of Lueneburg (Project-ID: NI-P512MP10212). We thank the anonymous reviewers and our colleagues and friends for their constructive feedback on our manuscript.

References

Aanestad, M., Grisot, M., Hanseth, O., Vassilakopoulou, P., 2017. Information Infrastructures for eHealth, in: Aanestad, M., Grisot, M., Hanseth, O., Vassilakopoulou, P. (Eds.), Information Infrastructures within European Health Care, Health Informatics. Springer International Publishing, Cham, pp. 11–23. https://doi.org/10.1007/978-3-319-51020-0_2

Abbas, A., Ofe, H., Zuiderwijk-van Eijk, A., de Reuver, Mark, 2022. Research Data - Toward Business Models for a Meta Platform: Exploring Value Creation in the Case of Data Marketplaces. https://doi.org/10.4121/21103867

Association for Information Systems' College of Senior Scholars, 2023. Senior Scholars' List of Premier Journals [WWW Document]. URL https://aisnet.org/page/SeniorScholarListofPremierJournals

Boell, S.K., Cecez-Kecmanovic, D., 2015. On being 'Systematic' in Literature Reviews in IS. Journal of Information Technology 30, 161–173. https://doi.org/10.1057/jit.2014.26

Bombard, Y., Baker, G.R., Orlando, E., Fancott, C., Bhatia, P., Casalino, S., Onate, K., Denis, J.-L., Pomey, M.-P., 2018. Engaging patients to improve quality of care: a systematic review. Implementation Sci 13, 98. https://doi.org/10.1186/s13012-018-0784-z

vom Brocke, J., Simons, A., Niehaves, B., Reimer, K., Plattfaut, R., Cleven, A., 2009. RECONSTRUCTING THE GIANT: ON THE IMPORTANCE OF RIGOUR IN DOCUMENTING THE LITERATURE SEARCH PROCESS, in: ECIS 2009 Proceedings. Presented at the ECIS 2009, p. 14.

vom Brocke, J., Simons, A., Riemer, K., Niehaves, B., Plattfaut, R., Cleven, A., 2015. Standing on the Shoulders of Giants: Challenges and Recommendations of Literature Search in Information Systems Research. CAIS 37. https://doi.org/10.17705/1CAIS.03709

Budd, J., Miller, B.S., Manning, E.M., Lampos, V., Zhuang, M., Edelstein, M., Rees, G., Emery, V.C., Stevens, M.M., Keegan, N., Short, M.J., Pillay, D., Manley, E., Cox, I.J., Heymann, D., Johnson, A.M., McKendry, R.A., 2020. Digital technologies in the public-health response to COVID-19. Nat Med 26, 1183–1192. https://doi.org/10.1038/s41591-020-1011-4

Cerezo, P.G., Juvé-Udina, M.-E., Delgado-Hito, P., 2016. Concepts and measures of patient empowerment: a comprehensive review. Rev. esc. enferm. USP 50, 667–674. https://doi.org/10.1590/S0080-623420160000500018

Chatterjee, S., Byun, J., Dutta, K., Pedersen, R.U., Pottathil, A., Xie, H. (Qi), 2018. Designing an Internet-of-Things (IoT) and sensor-based in-home monitoring system for assisting diabetes patients: iterative learning from two case studies. European Journal of Information Systems 27, 670–685. https://doi.org/10.1080/0960085X.2018.1485619

Chen, L., Baird, A., Straub, D., 2019. Fostering Participant Health Knowledge and Attitudes: An Econometric Study of a Chronic Disease-Focused Online Health Community. Journal of Management Information Systems 36, 194–229. https://doi.org/10.1080/07421222.2018.1550547

Cooper, H.M., 1988. Organizing knowledge syntheses: A taxonomy of literature reviews. Knowledge in Society 1, 104–126. https://doi.org/10.1007/BF03177550
Currie, W.L., Guah, M.W., 2007. Conflicting Institutional Logics: A National Programme for IT in the Organisational Field of Healthcare. Journal of Information Technology 22, 235–247. https://doi.org/10.1057/palgrave.jit.2000102
Dadgar, M., Joshi, K.D., 2018. The Role of Information and Communication Technology in Self-Management of Chronic Diseases: An Empirical Investigation through Value Sensitive Design. JAIS 86–112. https://doi.org/10.17705/1jais.00485
Fürstenau, D., Auschra, C., Klein, S., 2020. A Configuration Approach to Multi-Sided Platforms in Healthcare: An ALS Platform Case 18.
Ghose, A., Guo, X., Li, B., Dang, Y., 2021. Empowering Patients Using Smart Mobile Health Platforms: Evidence From A Randomized Field Experiment. https://doi.org/10.48550/ARXIV.2102.05506
Gianchandani, E.P., 2011. Toward Smarter Health and Well-Being: An Implicit Role for Networking and Information Technology. Journal of Information Technology 26, 120–128. https://doi.org/10.1057/jit.2011.5
Gioia, D.A., Pitre, E., 1990. Multiparadigm Perspectives on Theory Building.
Goh, J.M., Gao, G. (Gordon), Agarwal, R., 2011. Evolving Work Routines: Adaptive Routinization of Information Technology in Healthcare. Information Systems Research 22, 565–585. https://doi.org/10.1287/isre.1110.0365
Hagiu, A., Wright, J., 2015. Multi-sided platforms. International Journal of Industrial Organization 43, 162–174. https://doi.org/10.1016/j.ijindorg.2015.03.003
Hibbard, J.H., Greene, J., 2013. What The Evidence Shows About Patient Activation: Better Health Outcomes And Care Experiences; Fewer Data On Costs. Health Affairs 32, 207–214. https://doi.org/10.1377/hlthaff.2012.1061
Hickmann, E., Richter, P., Schlieter, H., 2022. All together now – patient engagement, patient empowerment, and associated terms in personal healthcare. BMC Health Serv Res 22, 1116. https://doi.org/10.1186/s12913-022-08501-5
Hur, I., Cousins, K.C., Stahl, B.C., 2019. A critical perspective of engagement in online health communities. European Journal of Information Systems 28, 523–548. https://doi.org/10.1080/0960085X.2019.1620477
Jiang, J., Cameron, A.-F., 2020. IT-Enabled Self-Monitoring for Chronic Disease Self-Management: An Interdisciplinary Review. MISQ 44, 451–508. https://doi.org/10.25300/MISQ/2020/15108
Karazivan, P., Dumez, V., Flora, L., Pomey, M.-P., Del Grande, C., Ghadiri, D.P., Fernandez, N., Jouet, E., Las Vergnas, O., Lebel, P., 2015. The Patient-as-Partner Approach in Health Care: A Conceptual Framework for a Necessary Transition. Academic Medicine 90, 437–441. https://doi.org/10.1097/ACM.0000000000000603
Khurana, S., Qiu, L., Kumar, S., 2019. When a Doctor Knows, It Shows: An Empirical Analysis of Doctors' Responses in a Q&A Forum of an Online Healthcare Portal. Information Systems Research 30, 872–891. https://doi.org/10.1287/isre.2019.0836
Klecun, E., 2016. Transforming healthcare: policy discourses of IT and patient-centred care. European Journal of Information Systems 25, 64–76. https://doi.org/10.1057/ejis.2014.40
Klecun, E., Zhou, Y., Kankanhalli, A., Wee, Y.H., Hibberd, R., 2019. The dynamics of institutional pressures and stakeholder behavior in national electronic health record implementations: A tale of two countries. Journal of Information Technology 34, 292–332. https://doi.org/10.1177/0268396218822478
Kordzadeh, N., Warren, J., 2017. Communicating Personal Health Information in Virtual Health Communities: An Integration of Privacy Calculus Model and Affective Commitment. JAIS 18, 45–81. https://doi.org/10.17705/1jais.00446
Kuan, K.K.Y., Chau, P.Y.K., 2001. A perception-based model for EDI adoption in small businesses using a technology–organization–environment framework. Information & Management 38, 507–521. https://doi.org/10.1016/S0378-7206(01)00073-8

Lamberti, L., 2013. Customer centricity: the construct and the operational antecedents. Journal of Strategic Marketing 21, 588–612. https://doi.org/10.1080/0965254X.2013.817476

Malm-Nicolaisen, K., Pedersen, R., Fagerlund, A.J., 2023. Exploring the Emergence of Open Platforms in Healthcare: Design Considerations and Experiences from an Initial Case in Norwegian Primary Care. Presented at the 56th Hawaii International Conference on System Sciences, Maui. https://hdl.handle.net/10125/102976

Maruping, L.M., Matook, S., 2020. The evolution of software development orchestration: current state and an agenda for future research. European Journal of Information Systems 29, 443–457. https://doi.org/10.1080/0960085X.2020.1831834

McGrath, K., Hendy, J., Klecun, E., Young, T., 2008. The Vision and Reality of 'Connecting For Health': Tensions, Opportunities, and Policy Implications of the UK National Programme. CAIS 23. https://doi.org/10.17705/1CAIS.02333

Mergel, I., Edelmann, N., Haug, N., 2019. Defining digital transformation: Results from expert interviews. Government Information Quarterly 36, 101385. https://doi.org/10.1016/j.giq.2019.06.002

Novak, L., Brooks, J., Gadd, C., Anders, S., Lorenzi, N., 2012. Mediating the intersections of organizational routines during the introduction of a health IT system. European Journal of Information Systems 21, 552–569. https://doi.org/10.1057/ejis.2012.2

OECD, 2021. Health at a Glance 2021: OECD Indicators, Health at a Glance. OECD. https://doi.org/10.1787/ae3016b9-en

Peek, N., Sujan, M., Scott, P., 2020. Digital health and care in pandemic times: impact of COVID-19. BMJ Health Care Inform 27, e100166. https://doi.org/10.1136/bmjhci-2020-100166

Schaefer, C., Lemmer, K., Kret, S.K., Ylinen, M., Mikalef, P., Niehaves, B., 2021. Truth or Dare? – How can we Influence the Adoption of Artificial Intelligence in Municipalities? Presented at the 54th Hawaii International Conference on System Sciences, Hawaii.

Shortell, S.M., Poon, B.Y., Ramsay, P.P., Rodriguez, H.P., Ivey, S.L., Huber, T., Rich, J., Summerfelt, T., 2017. A Multilevel Analysis of Patient Engagement and Patient-Reported Outcomes in Primary Care Practices of Accountable Care Organizations. J GEN INTERN MED 32, 640–647. https://doi.org/10.1007/s11606-016-3980-z

Stopka, U., Pessier, R., Günther, C., 2018. Mobility as a Service (MaaS) Based on Intermodal Electronic Platforms in Public Transport, in: Kurosu, M. (Ed.), Human-Computer Interaction. Interaction in Context, Lecture Notes in Computer Science. Springer International Publishing, Cham, pp. 419–439. https://doi.org/10.1007/978-3-319-91244-8_34

Technical Committee: ISO/TC 215 Health informatics, 2005. ISO/TR 20514:2005. Health informatics — Electronic health record — Definition, scope and context.

Thompson, S., Whitaker, J., Kohli, R., Jones, C., 2020. Chronic Disease Management: How IT and Analytics Create Healthcare Value Through the Temporal Displacement of Care. MISQ 44, 227–256. https://doi.org/10.25300/MISQ/2020/15085

Tornatzky, L.G., Fleischer, M., 1990. The processes of technological innovation, Issues in organization and management series. Lexington Books, Lexington, Mass.

Webster, J., Watson, R.T., 2002. ANALYZING THE PAST TO PREPARE FOR THE FUTURE: WRITING A LITERATURE REVIEW. MIS Quarterly Vol. 26, 11.

Yaraghi, N., Du, A.Y., Sharman, R., Gopal, R.D., Ramesh, R., 2015. Health Information Exchange as a Multisided Platform: Adoption, Usage, and Practice Involvement in Service Co-Production. Information Systems Research 26, 1–18. https://doi.org/10.1287/isre.2014.0547

Interoperability Maturity Model: Orchestrator Tool for Platform Ecosystems

Lars Stegemann

Abstract The orchestration of platform ecosystems is becoming increasingly complex due to the growing number of players, complementary services and technological innovations. Interoperability is an important prerequisite for convincing customer journeys as well as functional and quality-assured data exchange and offers increasing potential for automation, especially with the help of machine learning or artificial intelligence. The interoperability maturity model developed in this study can be used as a conceptual framework to measure the interoperability of current and future platform ecosystem components and complements. The model, developed as an artifact of design science research, was evaluated using an iterative approach with orchestrators of health data platforms and their ecosystem. The results suggest that it can contribute to achieving and sustaining integrated value chains with multiple actors and diverse technologies, and can be used to assess the interoperability of care chains (e.g., care scenarios such as diabetes or cardiac insufficiency) and guide future interoperability considerations.

Keywords Maturity model · Interoperability · Design science research · Health care platform ecosystem

1 Introduction

Several countries have implemented electronic health records (EHRs), which can serve as a central data hub to make current data silos accessible to exchange and reuse the data for health care, innovative health services, as well as research, using a platform approach (Kohli and Tan, 2016; Hermes et al., 2020; Reza et al., 2020). The goal is to make transactions more efficient and cost-effective, while improving the quality of care through the availability of information (e.g., Kohli and Tan, 2016; Hermes et al., 2020). Indeed, the challenge for platform owners and orchestrators in healthcare

L. Stegemann (✉)
Department of Information Systems, Freie Universität, Berlin, Germany
e-mail: lars.stegemann@fu-berlin.de

D. Beverungen et al. (eds.), *Transforming the Digitally Sustainable Enterprise*, Lecture Notes in Information Systems and Organisation 76,
https://doi.org/10.1007/978-3-031-80125-9_36

is to make data available throughout the patient journey and to the many stakeholders involved (Hermes et al., 2020). To achieve frictionless data flows, interoperability through transmission standards is essential. Both in the design and construction phase of the platform's architecture, as well as in the design of the ecosystem's outbound interfaces and standards for the integration of complementary services (Ghazawneh and Henfridsson, 2013; Fürstenau et al., 2019; Gawer and Cusumano, 2014). *Interoperability* refers to "the ability of two or more systems or components to exchange information and to use the information that has been exchanged" (IEEE, 2002, p. 42). Interoperability issues can be considered at various levels, including technical, structural, syntactic, semantic, and pragmatic (e.g., Hodapp and Hanelt, 2022; Oemig and Snelick, 2016). As the level/degree of interoperability increases, the potential for automation also increases (Oemig and Snelick, 2016). This is particularly important for data-driven services such as health apps, as well as digital therapeutics (DTx; Fürstenau et al., 2023; Patel and Butte, 2020), a minimum degree of interoperability is necessary (Gregory et al., 2021), especially with self-learning algorithms such as artificial intelligence (AI; e.g., Lehne et al., 2019).

The primary purpose of *DTx* is to support and coordinate medical interventions through (different types of) digital applications which can be tailored to the individual conditions and needs of patients to support hybrid care scenarios (Fürstenau et al., 2023). Data are being created, and many data, such as from EHRs, are needed for data-driven services, such as AI. In order to assess whether the data quality meets the desired goals of the platform ecosystem, i.e., the functionality of the service can be guaranteed, determining the quality of the exchanged data is an important indicator for the integration of potential complementary services. Hodapp and Hanelt's (2022) call for research addresses the issue of making interoperability measurable. There are few maturity models (MM) in the literature for making interoperability measurable (e.g. MEASURE Evaluation, 2017). In the platform literature there are links to interoperability such as tools or frameworks in the area of platform construction (Baldwin and Woodard, 2009; Fürstenau et al., 2019), management of openness (Parker and van Alstyne, 2018), and boundary resources (Ghazawneh and Henfridsson, 2013) or MM for evaluating the platforms technology (Deale et al., 2019), but not with a focus on evaluating data flows and their quality (interoperability), which is very relevant for certain services, especially in health care (e.g. Lehne et al., 2019). This leads to the following research question:

How Should a Maturity Model Be Designed to Support Orchestrators of Platform Ecosystems in Evaluating the Interoperability of Service Offerings?

To answer this question, the study followed a Design Science Research (DSR) to design a tool for platform ecosystem orchestrators to assess the nature of the data provided and exchanged to ensure the frictionless transfer of data and information, which also guarantees the quality of service of complementary service providers.

The subsequent sections of this study are organized as follows: Sect. 2 provides an overview of the concepts used. Sect. 3 explains the methodological approach and the data used to develop the MM, which is evaluated and demonstrated in Sect. 4. Finally, Sect. 5 discusses the results and their implications for future research.

2 Related Work

2.1 Digital Platform Ecosystems

Hein et al. (2019) define *digital platform ecosystem* as follows: "digital platform ecosystem comprises a platform owner that implements governance mechanisms to facilitate value creating mechanisms on a digital platform between the platform owner and an ecosystem of autonomous complements and consumers". In highly regulated environments such as health care, especially in Germany, the architecture and core of the technical design as well as the infrastructure is largely specified (e.g., Stegemann and Gersch, 2021), and the role of platform providers is primarily to orchestrate transactions of care pathways via own and third-party services in the in the ecosystem, with less free governance than in other markets.

Cooperation with partners/complementors (e.g., manufacturers of DTx) should increase the added value of the platform and generate direct as well as indirect network effects (e.g., Eisenmann et al., 2008; Gregory et al., 2021). Depending on the strategy of both the platform and the partner, collaborations vary in the depth of integration into the platform ecosystem, from loosely coupled application offerings in the ecosystem to tightly coupled ones (Hein et al., 2019) that are deeply integrated into the platform (e.g., as a white-label service). Integration of complementary services from partners requires a certain openness of the platform (Parker et al., 2017; Eisenmann et al., 2008) and different requirements for interoperability depending on the level of integration as well as the technology used (Ondrus et al., 2015). The health care sector is inherently complex due to its numerous sectors and diverse stakeholders (Hanseth and Bygstad, 2015). As a result, healthcare platforms face challenges in achieving interoperability while orchestrating the complexities arising from disparate technological systems, varying levels of integration, and the provision of complementary services (e.g., Ozalp et al., 2022). This complexity is further amplified by the emergence of DTx (Patel and Butte, 2020) and the integration of health devices such as wearable devices, sensors, and vital signs trackers (Witte et al., 2020). The integration and interoperability of these technologies within healthcare platforms poses significant challenges, requiring careful coordination and standardization efforts to ensure seamless data exchange and effective functioning of the ecosystem.

2.2 Overview of Maturity Models for Interoperability

MMs have been developed for more than five decades (Carvalho et al., 2019) and have been defined by Pöppelbuss and Röglinger (2011) as "[based on the assumption of predictable patterns of evolution and change, maturity models usually include a sequence of levels (or stages) that together form an anticipated, desired, or logical path from an initial state to maturity". MMs are commonly used to assess a current state, to derive and prioritize actions for improvement, and to monitor progress (Iversen et al., 1999). In research on informatics as well as information systems (IS), MMs are common tools to objectively evaluate complex technical conditions in order to derive decisions (e.g., Pereira and Serrano, 2020). MMs are used in various areas of application in research on IS (Becker et al., 2009), there are models for assessing business processes (Röglinger et al., 2012; Rosemann and Bruin, 2005; Scott, 2007), the digitalization of a health care system (Lee et al., 2022), digitalization at hospitals (HIMSS Analytics, 2017; DigitalRadar, 2023) and digitalization of public health agencies (Eymann et al., 2023). However, those models are usually designed for a particular use case or purpose. Depending on how applicable existing models are, they have to be adapted, or else a new model has to be created, at least according to the approach of Becker et al. (2009).

The literature contains several examples of MMs for interoperability. The first significant attempts to measure interoperability targeted levels of system interoperability—for example, C4ISR in 1988 (Campos et al., 2013)—and established a foundation on which later models were developed. Subsequent models, by contrast, focused more on a specific purpose or use case, including from the perspectives of enterprises (Campos et al., 2013; van Velsen et al., 2016), organizations (Clark and Jones, 1999), and government bodies (Gottschalk, 2009). Recent discussions about interoperability have shown that, along with a rather technical view, other dimensions are relevant when considering interoperability, including from the process perspective (e.g., Hodapp and Hanelt, 2022; European Commission, 2017), a regulatory or legal perspective (e.g., European Commission, 2017), and the perspective of the individual following an user-centric approach and the outcomes—for instance, for customer journeys, value in use, and learning and adaptation loops of service systems and/or data flows (e.g., Gohar et al., 2021; Sayeed et al., 2020). With the considerations afforded by an MM for interoperability, potential participants can use the model for orientation and to realize collaboration (Campos et al., 2013).

3 Method

3.1 Research Design

Following Design Science Research (DSR) as an overarching research paradigm (e.g., Hevner et al., 2004; March and Smith, 1995; Nunamaker et al., 1990), the MM for interoperability was developed to answer the research question. The MM developed can be understood as an IT artifact which solves the problem of making the orchestrator's interoperability criterion measurable and assessable (e.g., for selecting complements to their platform ecosystem). The research design, shown in Fig. 1, is inspired by Berger et al. (2020) and follows the DSR approach according to Hevner et al. (2004). The core development of the artifact is adapted from Becker et al.'s (2009) eight steps for designing an MM and complemented by additional iterative and structured evaluation (Eval) steps by Sonnenberg and vom Brocke (2012), all to meet the criteria for quality and rigor in IT artifacts. Step 1 of Becker et al.'s (2009) MM design approach includes understanding and defining the problem, the requirements and field observations are part of the *Problem Space* (see Sect. 3.2). In Step 2, knowledge of existing MMs for interoperability and relevant dimensions characterizing interoperability in the literature are examined in the *Solution & Knowledge Space* (see Sect. 3.3). In Step 3, the design strategy is represented according to the DSR approach in this section (see Sect. 3.1). The iteratively developed of the MM is defined in Step 4 and *ex ante* evaluated in Step 5 (see Sect. 3.4). The demonstration and *ex post* evaluation occur in Steps 6 and 7 (see Sect. 4), while Step 8 entails publishing the approach, which claims to be a generalized approach and template for assessing interoperability for a specific use case or scenario according to individual weighted scores, as in follow-up publications (see outlook in Sect. 5).

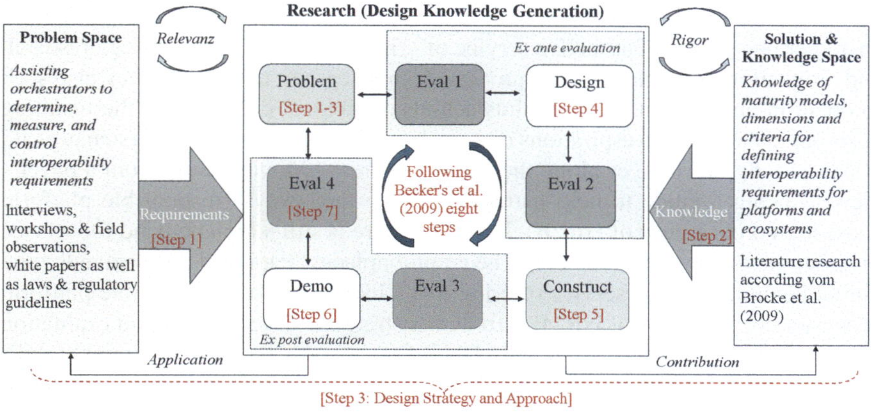

Fig. 1 Research design, adapted from Hevner et al. (2004) and Sonnenberg and vom Brocke (2012) with embedded steps of the procedure model for MM according to Becker et al. (2009)

3.2 Problem Space

The empirical data for the study was collected from 2021 to 2023 and included the documented field notes and results of a series of six workshops funded by the German Federal Ministry of Health from November 2021 to April 2022 and two additional workshops in December 2022 and February 2023. A total of 23 semi-structured interviews were conducted (Miles et al., 2014) in the development and evaluation process of the artifact, 12 interviews with platform ecosystem orchestrators from five health insurance companies (HICs; i.e., which includes approximately 40% of all insured people in Germany), four digital health experts, two of whom focus on interoperability, two interviews with patient representatives, three interviews with DTx manufacturers, and two interviews with digital health regulators in Germany. The field notes and interview transcripts were qualitatively analyzed (Miles et al., 2014) and partially coded within a software to handle the requirements and feedbacks in the evaluation phases of the artifact development, details are presented in the Sect. 3.4.

The MM was developed for platform ecosystem orchestrators of statutory HICs in Germany. Statutory HICs in Germany are required to provide each insured person an EHR that can be accessed by physicians and therapists. The insurant can access the EHR through an app provided by the HICs. In addition to the EHR functionality, most insurers offer a complementary set of services to differentiate themselves from the competition. In 2023, the EHR is projected to have a small number of users (BMG, 2023); however, insurers are aware that the number of users can be increased, especially through value-added and complementary innovative digital services in the platform ecosystem. In general, the EHR already contains data that can be used for additional services: "It is fundamentally important to make the data usable for other applications and services" (responsible platform ecosystem orchestrator of HIC A; this and the following quotes were translated from German). HICs want to be trusted digital healthcare providers and orchestrate the necessary services to achieve customer perception of attractive service offerings for healthy people (e.g., research and prevention), especially in the process from disease to treatment. They also seek to do so in an efficient way and thus achieve individual control over the resulting costs per insurant. Both aspirations require the orchestration of DTx (Fürstenau et al., 2023) and digital services along the patient journey. "Moving away from a payer's view to being a guide to help patients navigate their way" (responsible platform ecosystem orchestrator of HIC B). However, there is still a high demand for service integration, which users consider to be commonplace: "Patients have demands for a digital health insurance service offering that's like Amazon" (responsible platform ecosystem orchestrator of HIC B). To demonstrate the development and evaluation of the artifact, two indication areas and their Disease Management Programs (DMP) were considered: cardiac insufficiency and diabetes. For both indications, different applications and devices (e.g., sensors, wearable devices, and closed-loop injection pumps) are available on the market. The scenarios and patient pathways are examined in the context of the two DMPs, so that the artifact can better provide objective help in selecting partners and complements for evaluating solutions from an interoperability perspective.

3.3 Solution Space and Knowledge Space

To gain an overview of existing models for interoperability, a systematic literature review was conducted following vom Brocke et al. (2009) to expand the knowledge space for the design process. The review sought an overview of the dimensions of interoperability for the artifact. Because there are few models of interoperability and because some of the MMs mentioned above are not state-of-the-art due to subsequent technological progress and/or do not emphasize platforms. Therefore, the review also looked for frameworks for addressing and characterizing dimensions of interoperability in general. The results were found using the following search string:

```
"interoperab*" NEAR/2 (framework OR maturit* OR model) in Title
```

The search was executed in three databases: EBSCOhost (i.e., in Academic Search Ultimate, Business Source Premier, and EconLit), Web of Science, and AISEL (in all repositories in the database). The search query returned 263 results in EBSCOhost, 186 in Web of Science, and 87 in AISEL, for a total of 536 hits. The results were iteratively filtered in the search process. First, the articles had to be in English or German, peer-reviewed, and not duplicated in the result set, which left 349 articles. Second, the articles needed to relate to a conceptualization of interoperability, which left 59 articles. Third, the articles had to provide a generalized conceptualization of interoperability in order to derive criteria and dimensions for the model, leaving 16 articles. Fourth, using a forward and backward search, five additional relevant articles were found for the result set, bringing the total to 21 articles. In the analysis phase described by vom Brocke et al. (2009), the articles were examined more closely and classified. Four of the 21 articles had very strong relations to the same models or frameworks and were therefore eliminated due to strong redundancy. Based on the 17 remaining articles, 164 dimensions and views were identified, all redundancies were eliminated, and the remaining 89 dimensions were iteratively condensed into seven dimensions that all characterize interoperability. The dimensions were part of the artifact and its design process and were therefore iteratively condensed and validated in the evaluation cycles. The condensed dimension in relation to the corresponding articles is shown in Table 1, while the definitions of the dimensions are described in Sect. 4.1.

Table 1 Concept matrix of the condensed dimensions from the literature

Author(s) and kind of contribution (i.e., F or M)		Dimensions						
		Individual	Care Process	Legal & Governance	Organizational & Business	Application & Service	Data & Information	Technical
Berre et al., (2007) [ATHENA]	F		X		X	X	X	
Bastiaansen et al., (2020)	F	X		X	X		X	X
Benson and Grieve, (2016)	F	X		x	X		X	X
Campos et al., (2013)	M	x	X				X	x
Clark and Jones, (1999)	M		X		X	x		X
eHealth Network, (2015) [EIF]	F		X	X	X	X	X	X
European Commission, (2017) [REIF]	F	X	X	X	X	x	X	X
Guédria et al., (2015) [NEHTA]	M		X	x	X	X	X	X
Gottschalk, (2009)	M	x	X		X		X	X

(continued)

Table 1 (continued)

Author(s) and kind of contribution (i.e., F or M)		Dimensions						
		Individual	Care Process	Legal & Governance	Organizational & Business	Application & Service	Data & Information	Technical
Hodapp and Hanelt, (2022)	F	X		X	X	X	X	X
Legner and Wende, (2006)	F		X		X	x	X	X
MEASURE Evaluation, (2017)	M	X		x	X		X	X
Ndlovu et al., (2021)	F	x					x	X
Panetto, (2007)	M				X		X	X
Peristeras et al., (2009)	F		X				X	X
Sullivan, (2017) [GCIMM]	M	X	X	X	X		X	X
van Velsen et al., (2016)	M		X					X

Legend X = fully applicable, x = partly applicable, F = Interoperability Framework, M = Interoperability Maturity Model

3.4 Design and Evaluation Process

Figure 1 shows the iteratively development approach of the MM, starting with the first phase *problem and requirements analysis* **(Problem & Eval 1)**. The implications were gathered from three of the funded workshops conducted in 2021–2022 on the topic of interoperability of DTx with, among others, digital health experts, DTx manufacturers, physicians and patient representatives. In addition, the workshop findings were refined through interviews with suitable workshop participants; two patient representatives, two manufacturers of DTx, two orchestrators of the digital platform ecosystem of HIC, two representatives of standardization organizations and regulators to study the problem space. Inspired by the implications and collected requirements of the first phase, a first prototype of the artifact was designed in the second phase of the *interim evaluation* **(Design & Eval 2)** and evaluated through four interviews: two with responsible orchestrators of the digital ecosystem of public health insurers, one with a representative of the German authority for digital health regulation, and one with a manufacturer of DTx. As a result of the feedback, the artifact was significantly revised e.g., by expanding the dimensions of interoperability from the original five to seven, as described in Sects. 3.3 and 4.1. Feedback on this topic included "Legal requirements also need to be considered" (platform orchestrator of HIC C) and "Data use and reuse can help in contracting with health insurance companies" (representative of digital health regulation in Germany). In the third phase, *refactoring* **(Construct & Eval 3)**, additional requirements for the revision were collected in interviews with five orchestrators of the digital platform ecosystem of HIC conducted in 2021–2022 and two digital health experts, as well as field notes, implications of the workshop series, and recent developments in health care digitization. At the end of the revision process, the model approach was presented for discussion in two workshops with IS researchers and health experts, with the result of simplifying the model and clarifying the definitions of the dimensions and the five levels (see Sect. 4.1 and 4.2). In the final evaluation phase **(Demo & Eval 4)**, the MM was evaluated based on two scenarios (i.e., diabetes and cardiac insufficiency; see Sect. 4.3) using iterative steps after each interview conducted from January to March 2023, with four responsible orchestrators of the digital platform ecosystem of three HIC and two health experts in interoperability.

4 Maturity Model of Interoperability

4.1 Dimensions of the Interoperability Framework

Table 2 shows the elaborated and evaluated dimensions with their related subdimensions from the literature based on the concept matrix (see Table 1), descriptions, and guiding questions. First, the *Technical* dimension captures the ability to transfer data via communication formats or protocols, within an infrastructure or with another system (e.g., Benson and Grieve, 2016). The *Data & Information* dimension, by contrast, captures the nature of the exchanged data in terms of syntactic structure (e.g., per standards such as HL7 and FHIR) as well as semantic nature in view of reference or information models and coding based on terminologies such as LOINC or SNOMED CT. Next, the *Application & Service* dimension considers interoperability in terms of whether and how the exchanged data can be processed in order to guarantee functionality, which requires latencies, availability, and findability (e.g., European Commission 2017). Meanwhile, the *Organizational & Business* dimension describes to what extent necessary data are available to perform a service or action based on the data (e.g., according to contracts or process instructions) and includes pragmatic interoperability standards (e.g., medical guidelines), which partly overlaps with the process view according to Gottschalk (2009). The *Legal & Governance* dimension captures general conditions and requirements for interoperability that are recommended or mandatory specified by standard development organizations for instance (Sullivan, 2017).

The dimension of the *Care Process* considers data exchange as a process—for instance, as a care path along which actors participate beginning with data exchange and can aggregate the data in a generative way. However, alternative views understand interoperability and the correctness of data entry and coding from a human perspective (e.g., Campos et al., 2013), an aspect not considered in this MM. Early interoperability MMs indeed examined interoperability from the perspective of single point-to-point data exchange. Last, the *Individual* dimension considers self-determination of the exchange of data as well as the flexibility or even possibility of data transmission (e.g., European Commission, 2017; Bastiaansen et al., 2020).

4.2 Level of Interoperability Maturity

The literature contains many examples of a gradation of maturity in five levels that date back to early models in the field of interoperability (e.g., Clark and Jones, 1999; Gottschalk, 2009). From the literature and empirical data collected in this study, including field observations and interviews, the five levels shown in Fig. 2, were derived, developed, and evaluated as described in Sect. 3.2 and 3.4. The gradation of interoperability in the area of platform solutions starts at *Level 1* and is characterized by a fragmented and unstructured data exchange. *Level 2* represents the typical industry as well as regulatory and legal minimum requirements for interoperability, which are exceeded in *Level 3*, were the data offer a higher potential for automation due to the semantic nature. *Level 4* represents international interoperability with a high degree of automation, "the goal should be to operate across national borders" (platform orchestrator of HIC D), while *Level 5* stands for the possibility of flexible cross-domain data exchange. According to one interviewee, "Levels 1–3 are currently the reality; Levels 4–5 are the future" (digital health and interoperability expert I). The five levels provide gradations of a current state and offer an outlook for future development.

Table 2 Guiding questions and definition of the dimensions of interoperability

Dimension	Subdimension	Definition	Core question
Individual	Data sovereignty, digital empowerment, user-centricity	Enables sovereign handling of shared and exchanged data from an individual's perspective	Can users exchange and share data in a self-determined manner?
Care process	Patient's journey, data accessibility, process	Interoperability considerations from a patient journey perspective, sections of a care scenario and stakeholders, as well as different applications	Will the assessment be conducted from a care scenario or process perspective?
Legal and regulatory	Laws, regulations	Aspects of legal as well as regulatory compliance of interoperability	Are regulatory and legal requirements considered and adhered to?
Organizational and business	Policies, guidelines, pragmatic and procedural standards, contracts, agreements	Organizationally and inter-organizationally compliant actions based on the exchanged data/information according to instructions	Does the data exchanged support and comply with the relevant agreements, contracts, and guidelines?
Application and service	Software, latencies data representation, availability, findability	Exchange of data and/or information without loss and its processing and comprehension in a timely manner	Are the required data and information findable, accessible, and reliable?
Data and information	Reusability, metadata knowledge, sematic & syntactic standards, data or information models or profiles	Nature of the data and/or information in terms of syntactic and semantic standards and data and/or information models	How are the data structured and coded?
Technical	Architecture, infrastructure, network protocols	Aspects of the required infrastructure as well as system architecture for data exchange	Is the compatibility with the necessary infrastructure given?

4.3 Demonstration and Adaption of the Artifact

The maturity model can be demonstrated from the perspective of an HIC that orchestrates the service offerings of its platform ecosystem in order to support care paths digitally. The assessment always depends on the use case and may require adjustments to the model—for instance, adapting the dimensions to the five levels and weighting in scoring, "Depending on the core user and use-case, dimensions are weighted differently e.g., that data is made usable in the care process" (platform orchestrator of HIC E). In the following, the use of the MM is outlined with an example in the diabetes DMP. In the first step, the choice of the use case for the

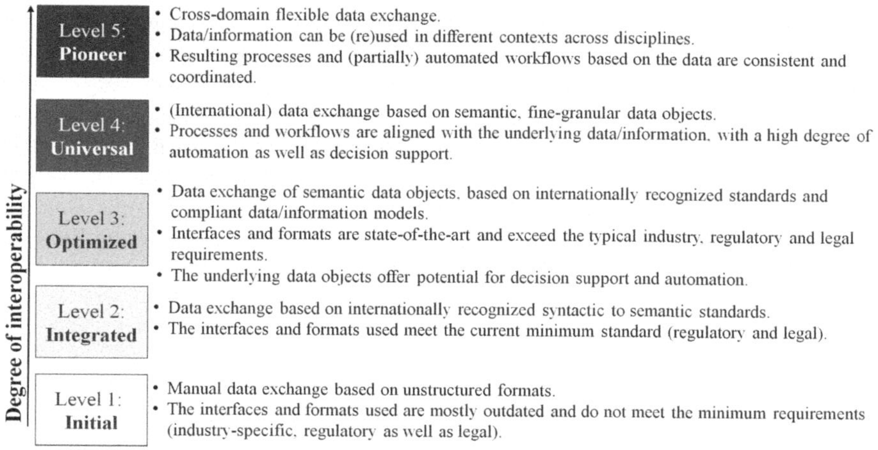

Fig. 2 Level of interoperability maturity

platform's vision is made. The health insurer wants to implement a frictionless care pathway, with a high degree of integrated care processes between the players involved in the DMP. In the second step, the target interoperability level for the use case is defined (see Fig. 2), and the necessary properties related to the use case are adapted in the model (e.g., by adding dimensions and specific questions for the evaluation). In step 3, potential applications are evaluated using the adapted MM (e.g., use-case specific the dimensions and levels in a matrix). For that purpose, an a DTx, consisting of an App with the associated devices and sensors (e.g., diabetes meters) is evaluated. In the following, the assessment along the 7 dimensions and the classification in the 5 levels are described, with a short justification for the classification in the respective level and what was missing for the next level. In the *Individual* dimension, the application reaches Level 3 out of the 5 levels, because the data are encapsulated in the application and access to the data is restricted via the portal. The transfer of data from and to other systems (e.g., other manufacturer) is not supported. Considering the *Care Process* dimension, Level 3 is reached, because the data along the care path are fragmented, and not all health data can be included in the digital path for the DMP. Considering the *Legal & Governance* dimension, the DTx is a certified medical product in Germany that complies with all regulations and laws (e.g., data protection), meaning that it reaches Level 4. As for the *Organizational & Business* dimension, the product is based on medical guidelines and is a digital component of DMPs and thus achieves Level 3 on that count (automated processes and cross-domain scenarios are not yet considered). Regarding the *Application & Service* dimension, the patient can give the physician access to the data but not for the software of the physician's practice that would allow its use with existing data. As such, the product reaches Level 2 in that dimension. Regarding the *Data & Information* dimension, the data can be exported and structured to be machine-readable (e.g., using HL7 FHIR R4) as well as unstructured for human reading as a PDF, but only manually and cannot be processed by third-party applications. Thus, it also reaches Level 2 in that dimension. On the T*echnical* dimension, the application works only with components, devices, and sensors from the same manufacturer, which keeps it at Level 1 in that regard. On average across all dimensions (without separate weighting) the diabetes application achieved an interoperability score (Level) of 2.6 and did not yet reach the estimated interoperability Level of 3 for the insurance platform ecosystem. Suggestions for improvement are therefore to better integrate the Technical as well as the *Data & Information* dimensions in the process—for instance, by connecting to the EHR as a central data hub.

5 Discussion

The interoperability MM, with its seven dimensions and five levels of interoperability maturity, was created based on a systematic literature review and empirical field observations in discussions about digital health and in several workshops and interviews following an iterative evaluation approach using two indication areas, one of which (i.e., diabetes) was outlined for an application (see Sect. 4.3). In this study, two use cases, both consisting of an application and a medical device (sensor), were evaluated to assess the data flow from the sensor along a typical patient journey. However, the MM provide a framework that needs to be adapted depending on the use case, including the weighting of the dimensions as well as the transfer of the five levels and the meaning of the dimensions based on the use case.

The **practical implications** of the study relate to addressing the challenges discussed for orchestrators, such as the complexity of orchestrating integrated and interoperable care scenarios. To ensure data flow in the care scenarios, the Interoperability MM can help define requirements and evaluate both proprietary and potential third-party platform ecosystem components (e.g., data, sensors, and devices).

The **research implications** of the study: firstly, the literature does not yet contain an interoperability MM for platforms. This study contributes to closing that gap by discussing interoperability challenges from a platform perspective and evaluating them in the development of the interoperability MM. The MM can be part of a toolkit in the platform development process (e.g., Fürstenau et al., 2019), for example, to evaluate the component from an interoperability perspective along care chains i.e., the patient journey. Second, another key implication is that in an increasingly connected, data-driven world, interoperability is an important criterion that will be assessed in multiple dimensions to realize integrated and interoperable service offerings along care chains—for example, using orchestration components and complements in care scenarios for insurants. Thirdly, beyond that, the interoperability MM responds to Hodapp and Hanelt's (2022) call for research geared toward making interoperability measurable.

As for the study's **limitations**, aside from general doubts in the literature regarding the broad generalization of artifacts (e.g., Beck et al., 2013), the interoperability MM revealed that a suitable compromise has to be found between general validity and the necessary concretization for specific use cases. The MM seems to address important points of interoperability with the five levels and seven dimensions through core questions. However, use case specific adaptations may still be necessary.

Outlook. Levels 4 and 5 of the MM imply scenarios for potential developments of interoperability and thus offer opportunities for future research on the orchestration of platform ecosystems—for example, increasing the merging of data sources internationally, including the European Commission's (2023) "My Health at EU", as well as across domains scenarios, including into smart health and smart living. Those scenarios become conceivable in the context of data spaces (e.g., Beverungen et al., 2022) as well as legislative initiatives (e.g., European health data space). The scope of orchestration becomes much more extensive due to the multiple actors in a data space and offers potential for use as part of an orchestrator's tool box.

References

Baldwin, C. Y. and Woodard, C. J. (2009) 'The Architecture of Platforms: A Unified View', in Gawer, A. (ed) *Platforms, Markets and Innovation,* Edward Elgar Publishing.

Bastiaansen, H., Dalmolen, S., Kollenstart, M. and van Engers T.M. (2020) 'User-Centric Network-Model for Data Control with Interoperable Legal Data Sharing Artefacts', *PACIS 2020 Proceedings*.

Beck, R., Weber, S. and Gregory, R. W. (2013) 'Theory-generating design science research', *Information Systems Frontiers*, vol. 15, no. 4, pp. 637–651.

Becker, J., Knackstedt, R. and Pöppelbuß, J. (2009) 'Developing Maturity Models for IT Management', *Business & Information Systems Engineering*, vol. 1, no. 3, pp. 213–222.

Benson, T. and Grieve, G. (eds) (2016) *Principles of Health Interoperability*, Cham (CH), Springer Publishing.

Berger, S., Bitzer, M., Häckel, B. and Voit, C. (2020) 'Approaching Digital Transformation - Development of a multi-dimensional Maturity Model', *European Conference on Information Systems (ECIS)*.

Berre, A.-J., Elvesæter, B., Figay, N., Guglielmina, C., Johnsen, S. G., Karlsen, D., Knothe, T. and Lippe, S. (2007) 'The ATHENA Interoperability Framework', in Gonçalves, R. J., Müller, J. P., Mertins, K. and Zelm, M. (eds) *Enterprise Interoperability II,* London, Springer London, pp. 569–580.

BMG (2023) *Gemeinsam Digital: Digitalisierungsstrategie für das Gesundheitswesen und die Pflege* [Online], Bundesministerium für Gesundheit. Available at https://www.bundesgesundheitsministerium.de/fileadmin/Dateien/3_Downloads/D/Digitalisierungsstrategie/BMG_Broschuere_Digitalisierungsstrategie_bf.pdf (Accessed 9 March 2023).

Campos, C., Chalmeta, R., Grangel, R. and Poler, R. (2013) 'Maturity Model for Interoperability Potential Measurement', *Information Systems Management*, vol. 30, no. 3, pp. 218–234.

Carvalho, J. V., Rocha, Á., Vasconcelos, J. and Abreu, A. (2019) 'A health data analytics maturity model for hospitals information systems', *International Journal of Information Management*, vol. 46, pp. 278–285.

Clark, T. and Jones, R. (1999) 'Organisational Interoperability Maturity Model for C2', *Computer Science* [Online]. Available at https://www.semanticscholar.org/paper/Organisational-Interoperability-Maturity-Model-for-Clark/cafb145a69ba790bd3f9fd634fab5a7e865af0e0

Deale, N., Herman, H., Grobbelaar, S. and Edlmann, F. R. P. (2019) 'Towards a maturity model for technology platforms in the South African healthcare context', *2019 IEEE International Conference on Engineering*, pp. 1–10.

DigitalRadar (2023) *Digitale Reife messen* [Online], Konsortium DigitalRadar. Available at https://www.digitalradar-krankenhaus.de/.

eHealth Network (2015) *Refined eHealth European Interoperability Framework* [Online]. Available at https://ec.europa.eu/research/participants/documents/downloadPublic?documentIds=080166e5b56dffdc&appId=PPGMS (Accessed 4 November 2022).

Eisenmann, T. R., Parker, G. and van Alstyne, M. W. (2008) 'Opening Platforms: How, When and Why?', *SSRN Electronic Journal*.

European Commission (2017) *New European Interoperability Framework: Promoting seamless services and data flows for European public administartions* [Online], Luxembourg:, Publications Office of the European Union. Available at https://doi.org/10.2799/78681.

HIMSS Analytics (2017) *Electronic Medical Record Adoption Model* [Online]. Available at http://www.himss.eu/healthcare-providers/emram

Eymann, T., Fürstenau, D., Gersch, M., Kauffmann, A. L., Neubauer, M., Schick, D., Schlömer, N., Schulte-Althoff, M., Stark, J. and Welczeck, L. von (2023) 'Das Reifegradmodell für den Öffentlichen Gesundheitsdienst – Ein Instrument zur Erfassung und Verbesserung des digitalen Reifegrades von deutschen Gesundheitsämtern', *Bundesgesundheitsblatt, Gesundheitsforschung, Gesundheitsschutz*, vol. 66, no. 2, pp. 136–142.

Fürstenau, D., Auschra, C., Klein, S. and Gersch, M. (2019) 'A process perspective on platform design and management: evidence from a digital platform in health care', *Electronic Markets*, vol. 29, pp. 581–596.

Fürstenau, D., Gersch, M. and Schreiter, S. (2023) 'Digital Therapeutics (DTx)', *Business & Information Systems Engineering*.

Gawer, A. and Cusumano, M. A. (2014) 'Industry Platforms and Ecosystem Innovation', *Journal of Product Innovation Management*, vol. 31, no. 3, pp. 417–433.

Ghazawneh, A. and Henfridsson, O. (2013) 'Balancing platform control and external contribution in third-party development: the boundary resources model', *Information Systems Journal*, vol. 23, no. 2, pp. 173–192.

Gohar, A., AbdelGaber, S. and Salah, M. (2021) 'A proposed patient-centric healthcare framework for better Semantic interoperability using Blockchain', *International Journal of Computer Science and Information Security*, vol. 19, no. 11.

Gottschalk, P. (2009) 'Maturity levels for interoperability in digital government', *Government Information Quarterly*, vol. 26, no. 1, pp. 75–81.

Gregory, R. W., Henfridsson, O., Kaganer, E. and Kyriakou, H. (2021) 'The Role of Artificial Intelligence and Data Network Effects for Creating User Value', *Academy of Management Review*, vol. 46, no. 3, pp. 534–551.

Guédria, W., Naudet, Y. and Chen, D. (2015) 'Maturity model for enterprise interoperability', *Enterprise Information Systems*, vol. 9, no. 1, pp. 1–28.

Hanseth, O. and Bygstad, B. (2015) 'Flexible generification: ICT standardization strategies and service innovation in health care', *European Journal of Information Systems*, vol. 24, no. 6, pp. 645–663.

Hein, A., Schreieck, M., Riasanow, T., Setzke, D. S., Wiesche, M., Böhm, M. and Krcmar, H. (2019) 'Digital platform ecosystems', *Electronic Markets*, vol. 43, no. 1.

Hermes, S., Riasanow, T., Clemons, E. K., Böhm, M. and Krcmar, H. (2020) 'The digital transformation of the healthcare industry: exploring the rise of emerging platform ecosystems and their influence on the role of patients', *Business Research*, vol. 13, no. 3, pp. 1033–1069.

Hevner, A. R., March, S. T., Park, J. and Ram, S. (2004) 'Design Science in Information Systems Research', *MIS QUARTERLY*, Vol. 28, no. 1, pp. 75–105.

Hodapp, D. and Hanelt, A. (2022) 'Interoperability in the era of digital innovation: An information systems research agenda', *Journal of Information Technology*, vol. 37, no. 4.

IEEE (2002) *Interoperability: Terminology of Software Engineering, Standard Glossary of Software Engineering Terminology*, Piscataway, NJ, IEEE.

Iversen, J., Nielsen, P. A. and Norbjerg, J. (1999) 'Situated assessment of problems in software development', *ACM SIGMIS Database: the DATABASE for Advances in Information Systems*, vol. 30, no. 2, pp. 66–81.

Kohli, R. and Tan, S. S.-L. (2016) 'Electronic Health Records: How Can IS Researchers Contribute to Transforming Healthcare?', *MIS Quarterly*, vol. 40, no. 3, pp. 553–573.

Lee, E. L., Barrett, M., Price, K. and Oborn, E. (2022) 'Developing your digital maturity for competitive advantage: From models to practices in enabling digital transformation', *Cambridge Judge Business School*.

Legner, C. and Wende, K. (2006) 'Towards an Excellence Framework for Business Interoperability', *BLED Proceedings*.

Lehne, M., Sass, J., Essenwanger, A., Schepers, J. and Thun, S. (2019) 'Why digital medicine depends on interoperability', *NPJ digital medicine*, vol. 2, no. 79.

March, S. T. and Smith, G. F. (1995) 'Design and natural science research on information technology', *Decision Support Systems*, vol. 15, no. 4, pp. 251–266.

MEASURE Evaluation (2017) *Health Information Systems Interoperability Maturity Toolkit* [Online]. Available at https://www.measureevaluation.org/resources/tools/health-information-systems-interoperability-toolkit.

Miles, M. B., Huberman, A. M. and Saldaña, J. (2014) *Qualitative data analysis: A methods sourcebook*, 3rd edn, Los Angeles, Calif., Sage.

Ndlovu, K., Mars, M. and Scott, R. E. (2021) 'Interoperability frameworks linking mHealth applications to electronic record systems', *BMC health services research*, vol. 21, no. 1, pp. 1–10 [Online]. https://doi.org/10.1186/s12913-021-06473-6.

Nunamaker, J. F., Chen, M. and Purdin, T. D. (1990) 'Systems Development in Information Systems Research', *Journal of Management Information Systems*, vol. 7, no. 3, pp. 89–106.

Oemig, F. and Snelick, R. (eds) (2016) *Healthcare Interoperability Standards Compliance Handbook*, Cham (CH), Springer International Publishing.

Ondrus, J., Gannamaneni, A. and Lyytinen, K. (2015) 'The Impact of Openness on the Market Potential of Multi-Sided Platforms: A Case Study of Mobile Payment Platforms', *Journal of Information Technology*, vol. 30, no. 3, pp. 260–275.

Ozalp, H., Ozcan, P., Dinckol, D., Zachariadis, M. and Gawer, A. (2022) '"Digital Colonization" of Highly Regulated Industries: An Analysis of Big Tech Platforms' Entry into Health Care and Education', *California Management Review*, vol. 64, no. 4, pp. 78–107.

Panetto, H. (2007) 'Towards a classification framework for interoperability of enterprise applications', *International Journal of Computer Integrated Manufacturing*, vol. 20, no. 8, pp. 727–740 [Online]. https://doi.org/10.1080/09511920600996419.

Parker, G. and van Alstyne, M. (2018) 'Innovation, Openness, and Platform Control', *Management Science*, vol. 64, no. 7, pp. 3015–3032.

Parker, G., van Alstyne, M. W. and Jiang, X. (2017) 'Platform Ecosystems: How Developers Invert the Firm', *MIS QUARTERLY*, Vol. 41, no. 1, pp. 255–266.

Patel, N. A. and Butte, A. J. (2020) 'Characteristics and challenges of the clinical pipeline of digital therapeutics', *NPJ digital medicine*, vol. 3, no. 1, p. 159.

Pereira, R. and Serrano, J. (2020) 'A review of methods used on IT maturity models development: A systematic literature review and a critical analysis', *Journal of Information Technology*, vol. 35, no. 2, pp. 161–178.

Peristeras, V., Tarabanis, K. and Goudos, S. K. (2009) 'Model-driven eGovernment interoperability: A review of the state of the art', *Computer Standards & Interfaces*, vol. 31, no. 4, pp. 613–628 [Online]. https://doi.org/10.1016/j.csi.2008.09.034.

Pöppelbuss, J. and Röglinger, M. (2011) 'What makes a useful maturity model? A framework of general design principles for maturity models and its demonstration in business process management', *European Conference on Information Systems (ECIS)*.

Reza, F., Prieto, J. T. and Julien, S. P. (2020) 'Electronic Health Records: Origination, Adoption, and Progression', in Magnuson, J. A. and Dixon, B. E. (eds) *Public Health Informatics and Information Systems,* Cham, Springer International Publishing, pp. 183–201.

Röglinger, M., Pöppelbuß, J. and Becker, J. (2012) 'Maturity models in business process management', *Business Process Management Journal*, vol. 18, no. 2, pp. 328–346.

Rosemann, M. and Bruin, T. de (2005) 'Towards a Business Process Managment Maturity Model', *ECIS 2005 Proceedings.*

Sayeed, R., Gottlieb, D. and Mandl, K. D. (2020) 'SMART Markers: collecting patient-generated health data as a standardized property of health information technology', *NPJ digital medicine*, vol. 3, p. 9.

Scott, J. E. (2007) 'Mobility, Business Process Management, Software Sourcing, and Maturity Model Trends: Propositions for the IS Organization of the Future', *Information Systems Management*, vol. 24, no. 2, pp. 139–145.

Sonnenberg, C. and vom Brocke, J. (2012) 'Evaluations in the Science of the Artificial – Reconsidering the Build-Evaluate Pattern in Design Science Research', vol. 7286, pp. 381–397.

Stegemann, L. and Gersch, M. (2021) 'The Emergence and Dynamics of Electronic Health Records – A Longitudinal Case Analysis of Multi-Sided Platforms from an Interoperability Perspective', *Proceedings of the 54th Hawaii International Conference on System Sciences*, pp. 6183–6192.

Sullivan, L. (2017) *Government of Canada Interoperability Maturity Model* [Online]. Available at https://open.canada.ca/ckan/en/dataset/922cf2be-bedc-5ed6-b26a-c27b79685915 (Accessed 30 November 2022).

van Velsen, L., Hermens, H. and d'Hollosy, W. O.-N. (2016) 'A maturity model for interoperability in eHealth', *2016 IEEE 18th International Conference on e-Health Networking, Applications and Services (Healthcom).* Munich, Germany, 14.09.2016 - 16.09.2016, IEEE, pp. 1–6.

vom Brocke, J., Simons, A., Niehaves, B., Reimer, K., Plattfaut, R. and Cleven, A. (2009) 'Reconstructing the Giant: On the Importance of Rigour in Documenting the Literature Search Process', in Newell, S. (ed) *Information systems in a globalising world: Challenges, ethics and practices; ECIS 2009, 17th European Conference on Information Systems, 8 - 10 June 2009, Verona, Italy,* Verona, pp. 2206–2217.

Witte, A., Fürstenau, D. and Zarnekow, R. (2020) 'Digital Health Ecosystems for Sensor Technology Integration - A Qualitative Study on the Paradox of Data Openness', *41st International Conference on Information Systems (ICIS) 2020 At: Hyderabad, India.*

The manufacturer's authorised representative in the EU is Springer Nature Customer Service Centre GmbH, Europaplatz 3, 69115 Heidelberg, Germany. If you have any concerns regarding our products, please contact ProductSafety@springernature.com

Printed and bound by CPI Group (UK) Ltd, Croydon, CR0 4YY
01/10/2026
02225957-0017